Mastering TypeScript 3
Third Edition

Build enterprise-ready, industrial-strength web applications
using TypeScript 3 and modern frameworks

Nathan Rozentals

BIRMINGHAM - MUMBAI

Mastering TypeScript 3
Third Edition

Commissioning Editor: Pavan Ramchandani
Acquisition Editor: Shahnish Khan
Content Development Editor: Digvijay Bagul
Technical Editor: Ashi Singh
Copy Editor: Safis Editing
Project Coordinator: Ulhas Kambali
Proofreader: Safis Editing
Indexer: Pratik Shirodkar
Graphics: Tom Scaria
Production Coordinator: Aparna Bhagat

First edition: April 2015
Second edition: February 2017
Third edition: February 2019

Production reference: 1270219

Published by Packt Publishing Ltd.
Livery Place
35 Livery Street
Birmingham
B3 2PB, UK.

ISBN 978-1-78953-670-6

www.packtpub.com

`mapt.io`

Mapt is an online digital library that gives you full access to over 5,000 books and videos, as well as industry leading tools to help you plan your personal development and advance your career. For more information, please visit our website.

Why subscribe?

- Spend less time learning and more time coding with practical eBooks and Videos from over 4,000 industry professionals

- Improve your learning with Skill Plans built especially for you

- Get a free eBook or video every month

- Mapt is fully searchable

- Copy and paste, print, and bookmark content

Packt.com

Did you know that Packt offers eBook versions of every book published, with PDF and ePub files available? You can upgrade to the eBook version at `www.packt.com` and as a print book customer, you are entitled to a discount on the eBook copy. Get in touch with us at `customercare@packtpub.com` for more details.

At `www.packt.com`, you can also read a collection of free technical articles, sign up for a range of free newsletters, and receive exclusive discounts and offers on Packt books and eBooks.

Contributors

About the author

Nathan Rozentals has been building commercial software for over 30 years. Like many programmers at that time, he helped save the world in the year 2000.

He has worked with and tried to master many object-oriented languages, starting with plain old C, moving to C++, Java, and then C#. In TypeScript, he found a language in which he could bring all of the object-oriented design patterns and principles he had learned over the years to JavaScript.

When he is not programming, he is thinking about programming. To stop thinking about programming, he goes windsurfing, plays soccer, or simply watches the professionals play soccer. They are so much better at it than he is.

I would like to thank my partner, Kathy, for being there for me through thick and thin, and for teaching me what love means. To Ayron and Dayna, I think about you guys each and every day, and am so proud of each of you. To Matt, just keep being you.

To everyone at Vix, thanks for making work so enjoyable. What we are doing is not easy, but that makes it worthwhile. I have never met so many highly talented people concentrated in a single place.

About the reviewers

Gaurav Aroraa has an MPhil in computer science. He is an MVP, a life-time member of the Computer Society of India (CSI), an advisory member of IndiaMentor, certified as a scrum trainer/coach, XEN for Information Technology Infrastructure Library-Foundation (ITIL-F) and APMG for Projects In Controlled Environments-F (PRINCE-F) and Projects In Controlled Environments-P (PRINCE-P). Gaurav is an open source developer, and the founder of Ovatic Systems. Recently, Gaurav was awarded *Icon of the year – excellence in Mentoring Technology Startups* for 2018-19 by Radio City – A Jagran Initiative for his extraordinary work during his 20-year career in the industry in the field of technology mentoring. You can tweet Gaurav on his Twitter handle, @g_arora.

Ruchitha Sahabandu is a software engineer, technical trainer, and mentor with more than 14 years of experience in designing and developing business applications and embedded systems built on JavaScript frameworks, JEE, Oracle, and C/C++ technologies. He has worked on many challenging projects run on Agile and TDD, SDLC methodologies in areas such as Automatic Fare Collection (AFC), resource planning and scheduling (MRP), Supply Chain Management (SCM), and production floor automation for customers around the globe.

He graduated from the University of Colombo, Sri Lanka, in Computer Science in 2006. He is currently based in Perth, Australia, and is working full-time alongside with Nathan Rozentals developing a next-generation AFC product.

Packt is searching for authors like you

If you're interested in becoming an author for Packt, please visit authors.packtpub.com and apply today. We have worked with thousands of developers and tech professionals, just like you, to help them share their insight with the global tech community. You can make a general application, apply for a specific hot topic that we are recruiting an author for, or submit your own idea.

Table of Contents

Preface

The TypeScript language and compiler has been a huge success story since its release in late 2012. It quickly carved out a solid footprint in the JavaScript development community, and continues to go from strength to strength. Many large-scale JavaScript projects, including projects by Adobe, Mozilla, and Asana, have made the decision to switch their code base from JavaScript to TypeScript. In 2014, the Microsoft and Google teams announced that Angular 2.0 would be developed using TypeScript, thereby merging Google's AtScript language and Microsoft's TypeScript languages into one.

This large-scale industry adoption of TypeScript shows the value of the language, the flexibility of the compiler, and the productivity gains that can be realized with its rich development toolset. On top of this industry support, the ECMAScript 6 and ECMAScript 7 standards are getting closer and closer to publication, and TypeScript provides a way to use features of these standards in our applications today.

Writing TypeScript applications has been made even more appealing with the large collection of declaration files that have been built by the TypeScript community. These declaration files seamlessly integrate a large range of existing JavaScript frameworks into the TypeScript development environment, bringing with it increased productivity, early error detection, and advanced IntelliSense features.

The JavaScript language is not confined to web browsers, however. We can now write server-side JavaScript, drive mobile phone applications using JavaScript, and even control micro devices designed for the Internet of Things with JavaScript. All of these JavaScript targets are therefore accessible to a developer writing TypeScript, because TypeScript generates JavaScript.

Who this book is for

This book is a guide to the TypeScript language that starts with basic concepts, and then builds on this knowledge to introduce more advanced language features and frameworks. No prior knowledge of JavaScript is required, although some prior programming skill is assumed. If you are aiming to learn TypeScript, this book will give you all of the necessary knowledge and skills to tackle any TypeScript project. If you are already an experienced JavaScript or TypeScript developer, then this book will take your skills to the next level. You will learn how to use TypeScript with a multitude of modern frameworks, and choose the best framework for your project requirements. You will investigate techniques for test-driven development, explore industry standard design patterns, and learn how to put together a full production-ready TypeScript application.

What this book covers

Chapter 1, *TypeScript Tools and Framework Options*, sets the scene for beginning TypeScript development. It discusses the benefits of using TypeScript as a language and compiler, and then works through setting up a complete development environment using a number of popular IDEs.

Chapter 2, *Types, Variables, and Function Techniques*, introduces the reader to the TypeScript language, starting with basic types and type annotations, and then moves on to discuss variables, functions, and advanced language features.

Chapter 3, *Interfaces, Classes, and Inheritance*, builds on the work from the previous chapter, and introduces the object-oriented concepts and capabilities of interfaces, classes, and inheritance. It then shows these concepts at work through the Factory Design Pattern.

Chapter 4, *Decorators, Generics, and Asynchronous Features*, discusses the more advanced language features of decorators and generics, before working through the concepts of asynchronous programming. It shows how the TypeScript language supports these asynchronous features through promises and the use of `async await` constructs.

Chapter 5, *Declaration Files and Strict Compiler Options*, walks the reader through building a declaration file for an existing body of JavaScript code, and then lists some of the most common syntax used when writing declaration files, as a cheat sheet. It then discusses the strict compiler settings that are available for the compiler—where they should be used, and what benefits they bring.

Chapter 6, *Third-Party Libraries*, shows the reader how to use declaration files from the DefinitelyTyped repository within the development environment. It then moves on to show how to write TypeScript code that is compatible with three popular JavaScript frameworks—Backbone, AngularJS (version 1), and ExtJS.

Chapter 7, *TypeScript Compatible Frameworks*, takes a look at popular frameworks that have full TypeScript language integration. It explores the MVC paradigm, and then compares how this design pattern is implemented in Backbone, Aurelia, Angular 2, and React. A sample program that uses form-based input is implemented in each of these frameworks.

Chapter 8, *Test-Driven Development*, starts with a discussion on what test-driven development is, and then guides the reader through the process of creating various types of unit tests. Using the Jasmine library, it shows how to use data-driven tests, and how to test asynchronous logic. The chapter finishes with a discussion on test runners, test reporting, and using continuous integration build servers.

Chapter 9, *Testing TypeScript Compatible Frameworks*, shows how to test the sample application built with each of the TypeScript compatible frameworks. It breaks down the testing strategy into Model tests, View tests, and Controller tests, and shows the differences between the testing strategies of these frameworks.

Chapter 10, *Modularization*, explores what modules are, how they can be used, and the two types of module generation that the TypeScript compiler supports: CommonJS and AMD. It then shows how modules can be used with module loaders, including Require and SystemJS. This chapter then takes an in-depth look at using modules within Node in order to build a sample Express application. Finally, it discusses the use of modules in a serverless environment using AWS Lambda functions.

Chapter 11, *Object-Oriented Programming*, discusses the concepts of object-oriented programming, and then shows how to arrange application components to conform to object-oriented principles. It then takes an in-depth look at implementing object-oriented best practices by showing how the State and Mediator design patterns can be used to manage complex UI interactions.

Chapter 12, *Dependency Injection*, discusses the concepts of service location and dependency injection, and how they can be used to solve common application design problems. It then shows how to implement a simple dependency injection framework using decorators.

Chapter 13, *Building Applications*, explores the fundamental building blocks of web application development, showing how to integrate an Express server and an Angular site. It then explores the all important authorization mechanisms that any site must have in place, with an in-depth discussion of JWT tokens. Finally, this chapter shows how to integrate social medial logins, such as Google or Facebook, into a site.

Chapter 14, *Let's Get Our Hands Dirty*, builds a single-page application using Angular and Express by combining all of the concepts and components built throughout the book into a single application. These concepts include test-driven development, the State and Mediator pattern, designing and using Express REST endpoints, object-oriented design principles, and modularization. This chapter also explores common techniques when using observables to handle most types of REST API interaction.

To get the most out of this book

You will need the TypeScript compiler and an editor of some sort. The TypeScript compiler is available on Windows, MacOS, and Linux as a Node plugin. Chapter 1, *TypeScript Tools and Framework Options*, describes the setup of a development environment.

Download the example code files

You can download the example code files for this book from your account at www.packt.com. If you purchased this book elsewhere, you can visit www.packt.com/support and register to have the files emailed directly to you.

You can download the code files by following these steps:

1. Log in or register at www.packt.com.
2. Select the **SUPPORT** tab.
3. Click on **Code Downloads & Errata**.
4. Enter the name of the book in the **Search** box and follow the onscreen instructions.

Once the file is downloaded, please make sure that you unzip or extract the folder using the latest version of:

- WinRAR/7-Zip for Windows
- Zipeg/iZip/UnRarX for Mac
- 7-Zip/PeaZip for Linux

The code bundle for the book is also hosted on GitHub at `https://github.com/PacktPublishing/Mastering-TypeScript-3`. In case there's an update to the code, it will be updated on the existing GitHub repository.

We also have other code bundles from our rich catalog of books and videos available at `https://github.com/PacktPublishing/`. Check them out!

Download the color images

We also provide a PDF file that has color images of the screenshots/diagrams used in this book. You can download it here: `http://www.packtpub.com/sites/default/files/downloads/9781789536706_ColorImages.pdf`.

Conventions used

There are a number of text conventions used throughout this book.

`CodeInText`: Indicates code words in text, database table names, folder names, filenames, file extensions, pathnames, dummy URLs, user input, and Twitter handles. Here is an example: "This `gruntfile.js` is necessary to set up all of the Grunt tasks."

A block of code is set as follows:

```
test = this is a string
test = 1
test = function (a, b) {
 return a + b;
}
```

When we wish to draw your attention to a particular part of a code block, the relevant lines or items are set in bold:

```
declare function describe(
    description: string,
    specDefinitions: () => void
): void;
```

Any command-line input or output is written as follows:

```
npm install -g typescript
```

Bold: Indicates a new term, an important word, or words that you see on screen. For example, words in menus or dialog boxes appear in the text like this. Here is an example: "Select **System info** from the **Administration** panel."

 Warnings or important notes appear like this.

 Tips and tricks appear like this.

Get in touch

Feedback from our readers is always welcome.

General feedback: If you have questions about any aspect of this book, mention the book title in the subject of your message and email us at customercare@packtpub.com.

Errata: Although we have taken every care to ensure the accuracy of our content, mistakes do happen. If you have found a mistake in this book, we would be grateful if you would report this to us. Please visit www.packt.com/submit-errata, selecting your book, clicking on the Errata Submission Form link, and entering the details.

Piracy: If you come across any illegal copies of our works in any form on the internet, we would be grateful if you would provide us with the location address or website name. Please contact us at copyright@packt.com with a link to the material.

If you are interested in becoming an author: If there is a topic that you have expertise in, and you are interested in either writing or contributing to a book, please visit authors.packtpub.com.

Reviews

Please leave a review. Once you have read and used this book, why not leave a review on the site that you purchased it from? Potential readers can then see and use your unbiased opinion to make purchase decisions, we at Packt can understand what you think about our products, and our authors can see your feedback on their book. Thank you!

For more information about Packt, please visit `packt.com`.

1
TypeScript Tools and Framework Options

JavaScript is a truly ubiquitous language—the more you look, the more JavaScript you find running in the most unlikely of places. Just about every website that you visit in the modern world is using JavaScript to make the site more responsive, more readable, or more attractive to use. Even traditional desktop applications are moving online. Where we once needed to download and install a program to generate a diagram, or write a document, we can now do all of this on the web, from within the confines of our humble browser.

This is the power of JavaScript. It enables us to rethink the way we use the web. But it also enables us to rethink the way we use web technologies. Node, for example, allows JavaScript to run server-side, rendering entire large-scale websites, complete with session handling, load balancing, and database interaction. This shift in thinking regarding web technologies, however, is only the beginning.

Apache Cordova is a fully-fledged web server that runs as a native mobile phone application. This means that we can build a mobile phone application using HTML, CSS, and JavaScript, and then interact with the phone's accelerometer, geolocation services, or file storage. With Cordova, therefore, JavaScript and web technologies have moved into the realm of native mobile phone applications.

Likewise, projects such as *Kinoma* are using JavaScript to drive devices for the **Internet Of Things (IoT)**, running on tiny microprocessors embedded in all sorts of devices. **Espruino** is a microcontroller chip purposefully designed to run JavaScript. So, JavaScript can now control microprocessors on embedded devices.

Desktop applications can also be written in JavaScript, and interact with the filesystem using projects such as *Electron*. This allows a write-once, run on any operating system approach, out of the box. In fact, two of the most popular source code editors, Atom and Visual Studio Code, have been built using *Electron*.

Learning JavaScript, therefore, means that you have the ability to build websites, mobile phone applications, desktop applications, and IoT applications to run on embedded devices.

The JavaScript language is not a difficult language to learn, but it does present challenges when writing large, complex programs, particularly in a team working on a single project. One of the main challenges is that JavaScript is an interpreted language—and therefore has no compilation step. To check that all written code has no minor mistakes means that you have to run it in an interpreter. It has also been traditionally difficult to implement object-oriented principles natively in the language, and it takes great care and discipline to build good, maintainable, and understandable JavaScript. For programmers that are moving from other strongly typed, object-oriented languages, such as Java, C#, or C++, JavaScript can seem like a completely foreign environment, especially when targeting earlier versions of JavaScript.

TypeScript bridges this gap. It is a strongly typed, object-oriented language that uses a compiler to generate JavaScript. The compiler will identify errors within the code base even before it is run in an interpreter. TypeScript also allows you to use well-known, object-oriented techniques and design patterns to build JavaScript applications. Bear in mind that the generated JavaScript is just JavaScript, and so will run wherever JavaScript can run—in the browser, on the server, on a mobile device, on the desktop, or even in an embedded device.

This chapter is divided into two main sections. The first section is a quick overview of some of the benefits of using TypeScript, while the second section deals with setting up a TypeScript development environment.

If you are an experienced TypeScript programmer, and already have a development environment set up, then you might want to skip this chapter. If you have never worked with TypeScript before, and have picked up this book because you want to understand what TypeScript can do, then read on.

We will cover the following topics in this chapter:

- The benefits of TypeScript:
    - Compilation
    - Strong typing
    - Integration with popular JavaScript libraries
    - Encapsulation
    - Public and private accessors

- Setting up a development environment:
  - Node-based compilation
  - Visual Studio Code
  - Visual Studio 2017
  - WebStorm
  - Other editors and Grunt

What is TypeScript?

TypeScript is a programming language designed by *Anders Hejlsberg*, the founder of the C# language. It is the result of an assessment of the JavaScript language, and what could be done to help developers when writing JavaScript. TypeScript includes a compiler which will transform code written in TypeScript into JavaScript. It's beauty is really in its simplicity. We can take existing JavaScript, add a few TypeScript keywords here and there, and transform our code into a strongly-typed, object-oriented, syntax-checked code base. By adding a compile step, we can validate that we have written sound JavaScript that is going to behave as we intended it to.

TypeScript generates JavaScript—it's as simple as that. This means that wherever JavaScript can be used, TypeScript can be used to generate the same JavaScript, but with added compile-time validations to ensure that it does not break certain rules. Having these extra validations before we even run the JavaScript is an immense time-saver, particularly where development teams are large, or where the resulting JavaScript is published as a library.

TypeScript also includes a Language Service, which can be used by tools such as code editors to help us understand how we should use JavaScript functions and libraries. These editors can then automatically provide a programmer with code suggestions and hints on how to use these libraries.

The TypeScript language, it's compiler, and associated tools helps JavaScript developers to be more productive, find bugs quicker, and help each other understand how their code should be used. It allows us to use tried and tested object-oriented concepts and Design patterns in our JavaScript code in a very simple and easy to understand manner. Let's try to understand how it does this.

JavaScript and the ECMAScript Standard

JavaScript as a language has been around for a long time. Originally designed as a language to support HTML within a single web browser, it inspired multiple clones of the language, each with its own implementations. Eventually, a global standard was introduced, allowing websites to support multiple browsers. The language defined in this standard is called **ECMAScript**.

Each JavaScript interpreter must deliver functions and features that conform to the ECMAScript standard. The ECMAScript standard that was published in 1999 was officially called **ECMA-262, 3rd edition**, but became known simply as **ECMAScript 3**. This version of JavaScript became widely adopted and formed the basis for the explosive popularity and growth of the internet as we know it.

With the popularity of the language, and the increase in usage outside of a web browser, the ECMAScript standard has been revised and updated a number of times. Unfortunately, the time it takes between proposing new language features and the ratification of a new standard to cover them can be rather lengthy. Even when a new version of the standard is published, web browsers only adopt these standards over time, and may also implement parts of the standard before others.

Before choosing which standard to adopt, therefore, it is important to understand which browsers, or more accurately, which runtime engine will need to be supported. To support these decisions, there are a number of reference sites that list support in what is known as a compatibility table.

Currently, there are three main versions of ECMAScript to choose from: ES3, ES5 and the newly ratified ES6. ES3 has been around for a long time, and pretty much any web browser will support it. ES5 is supported by most modern web browsers. ES6 is the latest version of the standard, and by far the biggest update to the language thus far. It introduces classes into the language for the first time, making object-oriented programming easier to implement.

The TypeScript compiler has a parameter that can switch between different versions of the ECMAScript standard. TypeScript currently supports ES3, ES5, and ES6. When the compiler runs over your TypeScript, it will generate compile errors if the code you are attempting to compile is not valid for that standard. The team at Microsoft has committed to follow the ECMAScript standards in any new versions of the TypeScript compiler, so, as and when new editions are adopted, the TypeScript language and compiler will follow suit.

The benefits of TypeScript

To give you a flavor of the benefits of TypeScript, let's take a very quick look at some of the things that TypeScript brings to the table:

- Compilation
- Strong typing
- Type definitions for popular JavaScript libraries
- Encapsulation
- Public and private accessors

Compiling

One of the most-loved features of JavaScript is the lack of a compilation step. Simply change your code, refresh your browser, and the interpreter will take care of the rest. There is no need to wait for a while until the compiler is finished in order to run your code.

While this may be seen as a benefit, there are many reasons why you would want to introduce a compilation step. A compiler can find silly mistakes, such as missing braces or missing commas. It can also find other more obscure errors, such as using a single quote (') where a double quote (") should have been used. Every JavaScript developer will tell horror stories of hours spent trying to find bugs in their code, only to find that they have missed a stray closing brace } , or a simple comma , .

Introducing a compilation step into your workflow really starts to shine when managing a large code base. There is an old adage that states that we should fail early and fail loudly, and a compiler will shout very loudly at the earliest possible stage when errors are found. This means that any check-in of source code will be free from bugs that the compiler has identified.

When making changes to a large code base, we also need to ensure that we are not breaking any existing functionality. In a large team, this often means using the branching and merging features of a source code repository. Running a compilation step before, during, and after merges from one branch to another gives us further confidence that we have not made any mistakes, or that the automatic merge process has not made any mistakes either.

If a development team is using a continuous integration process, the **continuous integration** (CI) server can be responsible for building and deploying an entire site, and then running a suite of unit and integration tests on the newly checked-in code. We can save hours of build time and hours of testing time by ensuring that there are no syntax errors in the code, before we embark on deploying and running tests.

Lastly, as mentioned before, the TypeScript compiler can be configured to output ES3, ES5, or ES6 JavaScript. This means that we can target different runtime versions from the same code base.

Strong typing

JavaScript is not strongly typed. It is a language that is very dynamic, as it allows objects to change their properties and behavior on the fly. As an example of this, consider the following code:

```
var test = "this is a string";
console.log('test=' + test);

test = 1;
console.log('test=' + test);

test = function (a, b) {
    return a + b;
}
console.log('test=' + test);
```

On the first line of this code snippet, a variable named `test` is declared, and assigned a string value. To ensure that this is the case, we have logged the value to the console. We then assign a numeric value to the `test` variable, and again log its value to the console. Note, however the final snippet of code. We are assigning a function that takes two parameters to the `test` variable. If we run this code, we will get the following results:

```
test = this is a string
test = 1
test = function (a, b) {
    return a + b;
}
```

Here, we can clearly see the changes we are making to the `test` variable. It changes from a string value to a numeric value, and then becomes a function.

Changing the type of a variable at runtime can be a very dangerous thing to do, and can cause untold problems. This is why traditional object-oriented languages enforce strict typing. In other words, they do not allow the nature of a variable to change once declared.

While all of the preceding code is valid JavaScript – and could be justified – it is quite easy to see how this could cause runtime errors during execution. Imagine that you were responsible for writing a library function to add two numbers, and then another developer inadvertently reassigned your function to subtract these numbers instead.

These sorts of errors may be easy to spot in a few lines of code, but it becomes increasingly difficult to find and fix these as your code base and development team expands.

TypeScript's syntactic sugar

TypeScript introduces a very simple syntax to check the type of an object at compile time. This syntax has been referred to as syntactic sugar, or more formally, type annotations. Consider the following version of our original JavaScript code, but written in TypeScript:

```
var test: string = "this is a string";
test = 1;
test = function(a, b) { return a + b; }
```

Note that on the first line of this code snippet, we have introduced a colon : and a `string` keyword between our variable and its assignment. This type annotation syntax means that we are setting the type of our variable to be of type `string`, and that any code that does not adhere to these rules will generate a compile error. Running the preceding code through the TypeScript compiler will generate two errors:

```
hello.ts(3,1): error TS2322: Type 'number' is not assignable to type
'string'.
hello.ts(4,1): error TS2322: Type '(a: any, b: any) => any' is not
assignable to type 'string'.
```

The first error is fairly obvious. We have specified that the variable `test` is a `string`, and therefore attempting to assign a number to it will generate a compile error. The second error is similar to the first, and is in essence saying that we cannot assign a function to a string.

In this way, the TypeScript compiler introduces strong, or static typing to our JavaScript code, giving us all of the benefits of a strongly typed language. TypeScript is therefore described as a superset of JavaScript. We will explore this in more detail in `Chapter 2`, *Types, Variables, and Function Techniques*.

Type definitions for popular JavaScript libraries

As we have seen, TypeScript has the ability to annotate JavaScript, and bring strong typing to the JavaScript development experience. But how do we strongly type existing JavaScript libraries? The answer is surprisingly simple: by creating a definition file. TypeScript uses files with a `.d.ts` extension as a sort of header file, similar to languages such as C++, in order to superimpose strong typing on existing JavaScript libraries. These definition files hold information that describes each available function and or variables, along with their associated type annotations.

Let's have a quick look at what a definition would look like. As an example, consider a function from the popular Jasmine unit testing framework called `describe`:

```
var describe = function(description, specDefinitions) {
  return jasmine.getEnv().describe(description, specDefinitions);
};
```

Note that this `describe` function has two parameters – `description` and `specDefinitions`. But JavaScript does not tell us what sort of variables these are. We would need to have a look at the Jasmine documentation to figure out how to call this function: If we head over to `http://jasmine.GitHub.io/2.0/introduction.html`, we will see an example of how to use this function:

```
describe("A suite", function () {
    it("contains spec with an expectation", function () {
        expect(true).toBe(true);
    });
});
```

From the documentation, then, we can easily see that the first parameter is a `string`, and the second parameter is a `function`. But there is nothing in JavaScript that forces us to conform to this API. As mentioned before, we could easily call this function with two numbers, or inadvertently switch the parameters around, sending a function first, and a string second. We will obviously start getting runtime errors if we do this, but TypeScript, using a definition file, can generate compile-time errors before we even attempt to run this code.

Let's have a look at a piece of the `jasmine.d.ts` definition file:

```
declare function describe(
    description: string,
    specDefinitions: () => void
): void;
```

This is the TypeScript definition for the `describe` function. Firstly, `declare function describe` tells us that we can use a function called `describe`, but that the implementation of this function will be provided at runtime.

Clearly, the `description` parameter is strongly typed to be a `string`, and the `specDefinitions` parameter is strongly typed to be a `function` that returns `void`. TypeScript uses the double braces `()` syntax to declare functions, and the arrow syntax to show the return type of the function. Hence, `() => void` is a function that does not return anything. Finally, the describe function itself will return `void`.

Imagine that our code were to try and pass in a function as the first parameter, and a string as the second parameter (clearly breaking the definition of this function), as shown in the following example:

```
describe(() => { /* function body */}, "description");
```

In this instance, TypeScript will generate the following error:

```
hello.ts(11,11): error TS2345: Argument of type '() => void' is not
assignable to parameter of type 'string'.
```

This error is telling us that we are attempting to call the describe function with invalid parameters. We will look at definition files in more detail in later chapters, but this example clearly shows that TypeScript will generate errors if we attempt to use external JavaScript libraries incorrectly.

DefinitelyTyped

Soon after TypeScript was released, *Boris Yankov* started a GitHub repository to house definition files, called DefinitelyTyped (http://definitelytyped.org). This repository has now become the first port of call for integrating external libraries into TypeScript, and it currently holds definitions for over 1,600 JavaScript Libraries. The growth of this site, and the rate at which type definitions have been generated for many JavaScript libraries, shows the popularity of TypeScript.

Encapsulation

One of the fundamental principles of object-oriented programming is encapsulation, the ability to define data, as well as a set of functions that can operate on that data, into a single component. Most programming languages have the concept of a class for this purpose—providing a way to define a template for data and related functions.

Let's first take a look at a simple TypeScript class definition:

```
class MyClass {
    add(x, y) {
        return x + y;
    }
}

var classInstance = new MyClass();
var result = classInstance.add(1,2);
console.log(`add(1,2) returns ${result}`);
```

This code is pretty simple to read and understand. We have created a class, named MyClass, with a simple add function. To use this class, we simply create an instance of it, and call the add function with two arguments.

JavaScript, prior to ES6, does not have a class statement, but instead uses functions to reproduce the functionality of classes. Encapsulation through classes is accomplished by either using the prototype pattern, or by using the closure pattern. Understanding prototypes and the closure pattern, and using them correctly, is considered a fundamental skill when writing enterprise-scale JavaScript.

A closure is essentially a function that refers to independent variables. This means that variables defined within a closure function remember the environment in which they were created. This provides JavaScript with a way to define local variables, and provide encapsulation. Writing the MyClass definition in the preceding code, using a closure in JavaScript, would look something like this:

```
var MyClass = (function () {
    // the self-invoking function is the
    // environment that will be remembered
    // by the closure
    function MyClass() {
        // MyClass is the inner function,
        // the closure
    }
    MyClass.prototype.add = function (x, y) {
        return x + y;
    };
    return MyClass;
})();
var classInstance = new MyClass();
var result = classInstance.add(1, 2);
console.log("add(1,2) returns " + result);
```

We start with a variable called MyClass, and assign it to a function that is executed immediately – note the }) (); syntax near the bottom of the closure definition. This syntax is a common way to write JavaScript in order to avoid leaking variables into the global namespace. We then define a new function named MyClass, and return this new function to the outer calling function. We then use the prototype keyword to inject a new function into the MyClass definition. This function is named add and takes two parameters, returning their sum.

The last few lines of the previous code snippet show how to use this closure in JavaScript. Create an instance of the closure type, and then execute the add function. Running this code will log **add(1,2) returns 3** to the console, as expected.

Looking at the JavaScript code versus the TypeScript code, we can easily see how simple the TypeScript looks compared to the equivalent JavaScript. Remember how we mentioned that JavaScript programmers can easily misplace a brace {, or a bracket (? Have a look at the last line in the closure definition: }) (); Getting one of these brackets or braces wrong can take hours of debugging to find.

TypeScript classes generate closures

The JavaScript as shown previously is actually the output of the TypeScript class definition. So, TypeScript actually generates closures for you.

 Adding the concept of classes to the JavaScript language has been talked about for years, and is currently a part of the **ECMAScript 6th Edition**. Microsoft has committed to follow the ECMAScript standard in the TypeScript compiler, as and when these standards are published.

Public and private accessors

A further object-oriented principle that is used in encapsulation is the concept of data hiding—that is, the ability to have public and private variables. Private variables are meant to be hidden to the user of a particular class—as these variables should only be used by the class itself. Inadvertently exposing these variables can easily cause runtime errors.

Unfortunately, JavaScript does not have a native way of declaring variables private. While this functionality can be emulated using closures, a lot of JavaScript programmers simply use the underscore character (_) to denote a private variable. At runtime though, if you know the name of a private variable, you can easily assign a value to it. Consider the following JavaScript code:

```javascript
var MyClass = (function() {
    function MyClass() {
        this._count = 0;
    }
    MyClass.prototype.countUp = function() {
        this._count ++;
    }
    MyClass.prototype.getCountUp = function() {
        return this._count;
    }
    return MyClass;
}());

var test = new MyClass();
```

```
test._count = 17;
console.log("countUp : " + test.getCountUp());
```

The `MyClass` variable is actually a closure, with a `constructor` function, a `countUp` function, and a `getCountUp` function. The `_count` variable is supposed to be a private member variable that is used only within the scope of the closure. Using the underscore naming convention gives the user of this class some indication that the variable is private, but JavaScript will still allow you to manipulate the `_count` variable. Take a look at the second last line of the code snippet. We are explicitly setting the value of `_count` to 17, which is allowed by JavaScript, but not desired by the original creator of the class. The output of this code would be **countUp : 17**.

TypeScript, however, introduces the `public` and `private` keywords that can be used on class member variables. Trying to access a class member variable that has been marked as `private` will generate a compile time error. As an example of this, the previous JavaScript code can be written in TypeScript as follows:

```
class CountClass {
    private _count: number;
    constructor() {
        this._count = 0;
    }
    countUp() {
        this._count ++;
    }
    getCount() {
        return this._count;
    }
}

var countInstance = new CountClass() ;
countInstance._count = 17;
```

Here, on the second line of our code snippet, we have declared a `private` member variable named `_count`. Again, we have a constructor, a `countUp` function, and a `getCount` function. If we compile this file, the compiler will generate an error:

```
hello.ts(39,15): error TS2341: Property '_count' is private and only
accessible within class 'CountClass'.
```

This error is generated because we are trying to access the private variable, `_count`, in the last line of the code.

The TypeScript compiler is therefore helping us to adhere to public and private accessors by generating a compile error when we inadvertently break this rule.

Remember, though, that these accessors are a compile-time feature only, and will not affect the generated JavaScript. You will need to bear this in mind if you are writing JavaScript libraries that will be consumed by third parties. Note that, by default, the TypeScript compiler will still generate the JavaScript output file, even if there are compile errors. This option can be modified, however, to force the TypeScript compiler not to generate JavaScript if there are compilation errors.

TypeScript IDEs

The purpose of this section of the chapter is to get you up and running with a TypeScript environment so that you can edit, compile, run, and debug your TypeScript code. TypeScript has been released as an open source project, and includes both a Windows variant, as well as a Node variant. This means that the compiler will run on Windows, Linux, macOS, and any other operating system that supports Node. On Windows environments, we can either install Visual Studio, which will register `tsc.exe` (TypeScript compiler) in our `c:\Program Files` directory, or we can use Node. On Linux and macOS environments, we will need to use Node.

In this section, we will be looking at the following IDEs:

- Node-based compilation
- Visual Studio Code
- Visual Studio 2017
- WebStorm
- Using Grunt

Node-based compilation

The simplest and leanest TypeScript development environment consists of a simple text editor, and a Node-based TypeScript compiler. Head over to the Node website (`https://nodejs.org/`) and follow the instructions to install Node on your operating system of choice.

Once Node is installed, TypeScript can be installed by simply typing the following:

```
npm install -g typescript
```

This command invokes the Node Package Manager (npm) to install TypeScript as a global module (the -g option), which will make it available no matter what directory we are currently in. Once TypeScript has been installed, we can display the current version of the compiler by typing the following:

```
tsc -v
```

At the time of writing, the TypeScript compiler is at version 3.3.3, and therefore the output of this command is as follows:

```
Version 3.3.3
```

Let's now create a TypeScript file named hello.ts with the following content:

```
console.log('hello TypeScript');
```

From the command line, we can use TypeScript to compile this file into a JavaScript file by issuing the following command:

```
tsc hello.ts
```

Once the TypeScript compiler has completed, it will have generated a hello.js file in the current directory. We can run this file using Node by typing the following:

```
node hello.js
```

This will output the following to the console:

```
hello TypeScript
```

Creating a tsconfig.json file

The TypeScript compiler uses a tsconfig.json file at the root of the project directory to specify any global TypeScript project settings and compiler options. This means that instead of compiling our TypeScript files one by one (by specifying each file on the command line), we can simply type tsc from the project root directory, and TypeScript will recursively find and compile all TypeScript files within the root directory and all sub-directories. The tsconfig.json file that TypeScript needs in order to do this can be created from the command line by simply typing the following:

```
tsc --init
```

The result of this command is a basic `tsconfig.json` file as follows:

```
{
    "compilerOptions": {
        "target": "es5",
        "module": "commonjs",
        "strict": true,
        "esModuleInterop": true
    }
}
```

This is a simple JSON format file, with a single JSON property named `compilerOptions`, which specifies compile options for the project. The `target` property indicates the preferred JavaScript output to generate, and can be either `es3`, `es5`, `es6`, `ES2016`, `ES2017`, or `ESNext`. The option named `strict` is a flag to turn on all strict type-checking options. We will explore the meaning of these options in `Chapter 5`, *Declaration Files and Strict Compilation Options*. The `esModuleInterop` option has to do with the generation of modules, which we will also discuss in `Chapter 10`, *Modularization*.

 TypeScript allows for multiple `tsconfig.json` files within a directory structure. This allows different sub directories to use different compiler options.

With our `tsconfig.json` file in place, we can compile our application by simply typing the following:

```
tsc
```

This command will invoke the TypeScript compiler, using the `tsconfig.json` file that we have created, and generate a `hello.js` JavaScript file. In fact, any TypeScript source file that has a file extension of `.ts` will generate a JavaScript file with an extension of `.js`.

We have successfully created a simple Node-based TypeScript development environment, with a simple text editor and access to the command line.

Localized messages

When invoking the TypeScript compiler through the command line, we can also specify that any messages should be displayed in a specific language. This is accomplished via the `--locale` command-line option, as follows:

```
tsc --locale pl
```

Here, we are compiling our source code as per usual, but the message output will be in Polish, as follows:

```
error TS2322: Typu „number" nie można przypisać do typu „string"
```

As at the time of writing, the possible values that can be used for the `--locale` compile option are as follows:

```
en English US
cs Czech
de German
es Spanish
fr French
it Italian
ja Japanese
ko Korean
pl Polish
ru Russian
tr Turkish
```

There is no corresponding `tsconfig.json` option for the `--locale` command-line option, so this will need to be included whenever running `tsc` from the command line.

When building TypeScript applications, all of the frameworks and supporting tools you will need come with a command-line interface. It is not unusual to see a developer running multiple command-line windows, one for automatic code compilation, one for running a web server, and another to run unit tests, as and when the code base changes. If you are developing on Windows, then take a look at the excellent command-line emulator named cmder (http://cmder.net/). It supports multiple tabs, split screens, and includes a Linux emulator with out-of-the-box git support.

If you are looking for a good TypeScript source code editor, then you simply must consider Visual Studio Code (VSCode). Using a Node-based command-line environment and VSCode is all you will need to build any TypeScript project on any operating system. If you are familiar with Microsoft Visual Studio, or Webstorm, and like a fully integrated development environment, then these two IDEs may be best suited.

Visual Studio Code

Visual Studio Code (**VSCode**) is a lightweight development environment produced by Microsoft that runs on Windows, Linux, and macOS. It includes development features such as syntax highlighting, bracket matching, Intellisense, and also has support for many different languages. These languages include TypeScript, JavaScript, JSON, HTML, CSS, C#, C++, Java, and many more, making it ideal for TypeScript development targeting either web pages or Node. Its main focus is Node development with TypeScript, and ASP.NET Core development with C#. It also has strong Git support out of the box, and was even built using TypeScript and Electron.

Installing VSCode

VSCode can be installed on Windows by simply downloading and running the installer. On Linux systems, VSCode is provided as either a `.deb` package, an `.rpm` package, or a binary `tar` file. In macOS, download the `.zip` file, unzip it, and then copy the `Visual Studio Code.app` file to your applications folder.

Exploring VSCode

Create a new directory to hold your source code, and fire up VSCode. This can be done by navigating to the directory, and executing `code .` from the command line. On Windows systems, fire up VSCode, and then Select **File** | **Open folder** from the menu bar. Hit *Ctrl+N* to create a new file, and type the following:

```
console.log("hello vscode");
```

Note that there is no syntax highlighting at this stage, as VSCode does not know what type of file it is working with. Hit *Ctrl+S* to save the file, and name it `hello.ts`. Now that VSCode understands that this is a TypeScript file, you will have full Intellisense and syntax highlighting available.

Creating a tasks.json file

VSCode uses a special `tasks.json` file in order to run commonly used tasks that you may need in your development life cycle. Obviously, one of the most common tasks you will need to run is the compilation step, otherwise known as the build step. The keyboard shortcut to build a project in VSCode is *Ctrl+Shift+B*.

In order to run a build step with *Ctrl+Shift+B*, we will need to create a `tasks.json` file, and configure it correctly to run the `tsc` command to build our project. If you do not already have a `tsconfig.json` file for your project, then go ahead and create one from the command line by typing the following:

```
tsc --init
```

Once we have a `tsconfig.json` file for our project, we can configure the default build task. In VSCode, hit *Ctrl+Shift+B*. This will bring up an option to select a build task to run. Select the **tsc : build - tsconfig.json** option. This will execute the `tsc` compilation step for your project, and show the results in the built-in terminal.

Unfortunately, if we hit *Ctrl+Shift+B* again, we will be prompted to select a build task once more. This means that, although we have configured a build task, we have not specified what task should be run by default when we hit the build shortcut. There are two ways that we can specify this default build task. The first is by selecting the menu option **Tasks | Configure Default build task**. This will bring up an option where we can select the **tsc : build - tsconfig.json** task as our default. Choosing this option will open the `tasks.json` file in the `.vscode` directory in the editor.

The second way to specify the default build task is through the command pallet. VSCode has many commands that can be configured through the command pallet, and each one can be tied to a specific shortcut key. Selecting the menu option **View | Command Pallet**, or the shortcut key *Ctrl+Shift+P*, will bring up a list of available commands. This list can be filtered by simply typing a keyword. If we start typing the word `task`, the list is automatically filtered to only show commands that contain the word "task". We can then select the **Tasks : configure default build task** to open the `tasks.json` file in the editor.

Note that there are many available commands that can be selected via the **View | Command Pallet** menu option, or by hitting the shortcut key, *Ctrl+Shift+P*. Take a few minutes to scroll through the list of commands to see how configurable VSCode actually is.

Whether we have navigated to the configure default build tasks via the menu option, or from the command pallet, VSCode will open our `tasks.json` file in the editor, as follows:

```
{
    // See https://go.microsoft.com/fwlink/?LinkId=733558
    // for the documentation about the tasks.json format
    "version": "2.0.0",
    "tasks": [
        {
            "type": "typescript",
            "tsconfig": "tsconfig.json",
            "problemMatcher": [
```

```
            "$tsc"
        ],
        "group": {
            "kind": "build",
            "isDefault": true
        }
    }
    ]
}
```

This `tasks.json` file has a `version` property and a `tasks` property. The `tasks` property is an array of tasks that have a number of sub-properties. VSCode has automatically created a task for us that will compile our project, and specified via the `group.isDefault` property that this is the default build task.

Note that ,when editing this file, VSCode will automatically show us what properties are available depending on which part of the file we are modifying, as follows:

Here, we can see that VSCode is showing us that the available configuration properties for a task include `identifier`, `isBackground`, `label`, and others.

A handy property to keep in mind is the `label` property, which we can use to specify an easy-to-remember name for our task. Let's add this `label` property, and set its value to `Run tsc build`. Now, whenever we see this build task in a list of options, it will be displayed as `Run tsc build`, which helps us to remember which task is which.

Building the project

Our sample project can now be built by hitting *Ctrl+Shift+B*. Note that, in the base directory of our project, we now have a `hello.js` and a `hello.js.map` file as the result of the compilation step.

Creating a launch.json file

VSCode includes an integrated debugger that can be used to debug TypeScript projects. If we switch to the **Debugger** panel, or simply hit *F5* to start debugging, VSCode will ask us to select a debugging environment. For the time being, select the **Node.js** option, which will create a `launch.json` file in the `.vscode` directory, and again open it for editing. Find the option named `program`, and modify it to read `"${workspaceFolder}/hello.js"`. Hit *F5* again, and VSCode will launch `hello.js` as a Node program and output the results to the debugging window:

```
node --debug-brk=34146 --nolazy hello.js
debugger listening on port 34146
hello vscode
```

Setting breakpoints

Using breakpoints and debugging at this stage will only work on the generated `.js` JavaScript files. We will need to make a change to the `tsconfig.json` file to enable debugging directly in our TypeScript files. Edit the `tsconfig.json` file, and add a property with the name `sourceMaps` and the property value `true`. This instructs the compiler to output a source map file (named `.map`) for each TypeScript file we are compiling. Once we rebuild the project, these map files will appear in our source code tree. Now, we can set breakpoints directly in our `.ts` files for use by the VSCode debugger:

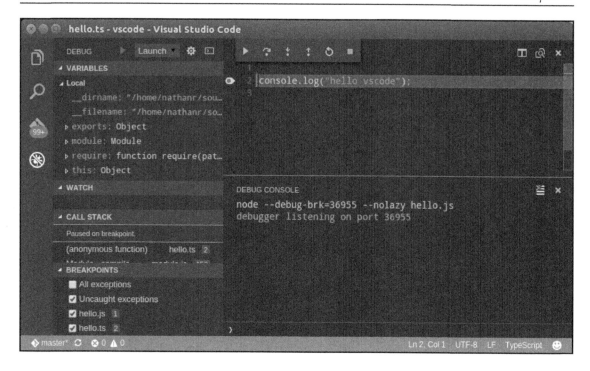

Debugging web pages

Debugging TypeScript, which is running within a web page in VSCode, requires a little more setup. VSCode uses the Chrome debugger to attach to a running web page. To enable debugging web pages, we will firstly need to add a Debug configuration to our `launch.json` file. Luckily, VSCode has a toolbar command for this, and will generate a launch configuration for us. Select the **Debug | Add Configuration** menu option, and then select the **Chrome Attach** option. This will modify our `launch.json` file as follows:

```
"configurations": [
    {
        "type": "chrome",
        "request": "attach",
        "name": "Attach to Chrome",
        "port": 9222,
        "webRoot": "${workspaceFolder}"
    },
    {
        "type": "node",
        ...
    }
]
```

This launch option is named `Attach to Chrome`, and will attach to a running instance of Chrome using the debug port `9222`. Save the `launch.json` file, and create an HTML page named `index.html` at the root directory of the project, as follows:

```html
<html>
    <head>
    <script src="helloweb.js"></script>
    </head>
    <body>
        hello vscode
        <div id="content"></div>
    </body>
</html>
```

This is a very simple page that loads the `helloweb.js` file, and displays the text, `hello vscode`. Our `helloweb.ts` file is as follows:

```typescript
window.onload = () => {
    console.log("hello vscode");
};
```

This TypeScript code simply waits for the web page to load, and then logs `hello vscode` to the console.

The next step is to fire up Chrome using the debug port option. On Linux systems, this is done from the command prompt, as follows:

```
google-chrome --remote-debugging-port=9222
```

Note that you will need to ensure that there are no other instances of Chrome running in order to use it as a debugger with VSCode.

Next, load the `index.html` file in the browser by using *Ctrl+O*, and selecting the file to load. You should see the HTML file rendering the `hello vscode` text.

Now, we can go back to VSCode, click on the debugging icon, and select the **Attach Chrome** option in the **launcher** dropdown. Hit *F5*, and the VSCode debugger should now be attached to the running instance of Chrome. We will then need to refresh the page in Chrome in order to start debugging:

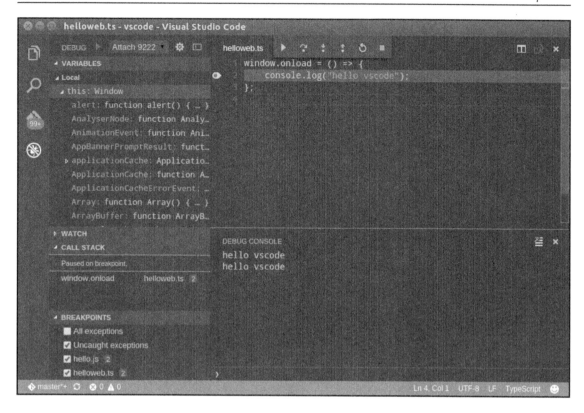

With a slight tweak to our `launch.json`, we can combine these manual steps into a single launcher, as follows:

```
{
    "name": "Launch chrome",
    "type": "chrome",
    "request" : "launch",
    "url" : "file:/// ... insert full path here ... /index.html",
    "runtimeArgs": [
        "--new-window",
        "--remote-debugging-port=9222"
    ],
    "sourceMaps": true
}
```

In this launch configuration, we have changed the `request` property from `attach` to `launch`, which will launch a new instance of Chrome, and automatically navigate to the file path specified in the `url` property. The `runtimeArgs` property also now specifies the remote debugging port of `9222`. With this launcher in place, we can simply hit *F5* to launch Chrome, with the correct URL and debugging options for the debugging of HTML applications.

Microsoft Visual Studio

Let's now look at Microsoft Visual Studio. This is Microsoft's primary IDE, and comes in a variety of pricing combinations. At the time of writing, Microsoft's latest version is Visual Studio 2017. Microsoft has an Azure-based licensing model, starting at around $45 per month, all the way up to a professional license with an MSDN subscription at around $1,199. The good news is that Microsoft also has a Community edition, which can be used in non-enterprise environments for both free and non-paid products. The TypeScript compiler is included in all of these editions.

Visual Studio can be downloaded as either a web installer or an `.iso` CD image. Note that the web installer will require an internet connection during installation, as it downloads the required packages during the installation step. Visual Studio will also require Internet Explorer 10 or later, but will prompt you during installation if you have not upgraded as yet. If you are using the `.iso` installer, just bear in mind that you may be required to download and install additional operating system patches if you have not updated your system in a while.

Creating a Visual Studio project

Once Visual Studio 2017 is installed, fire it up and create a new project (**File** | **New Project**). There are many different options available for new project templates, depending on your choice of language. Under the **Templates** section on the left-hand side, you will see an **Other Languages** option, and under this, a **TypeScript** option. The project templates that are available are slightly different in Visual Studio 2017 than they were in Visual Studio 2015, and are geared toward Node development. Visual Studio 2015 included a template named **Html Application with TypeScript**, which will create a very simple, single-page web application for you. Unfortunately, this option has been removed in Visual Studio 2017:

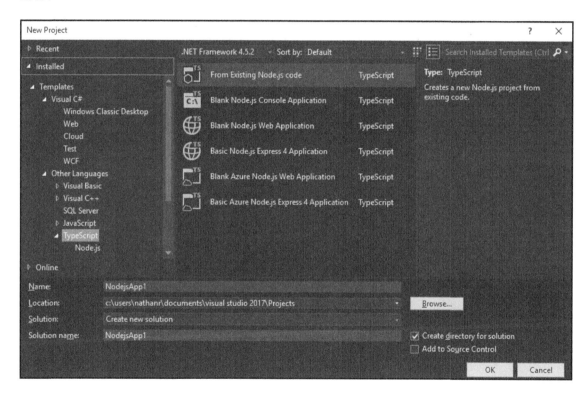

To create a simple TypeScript web application in Visual Studio 2017, we will need to create a blank web application first, and then we can add TypeScript files to this project as required. From our **Templates** dialog, select the **Visual C#** template option, and then select the **Web** option. This will give us a project template named **ASP.NET Web Application**. Select a **Name** and a **Location** for the new project, and then click on **Ok,** as demonstrated in the following screenshot:

Once we have selected the basic information for our new project, Visual Studio will generate a second dialog box asking what sort of ASP.NET project we would like to generate. Select the **Empty** template, and click on **Ok**:

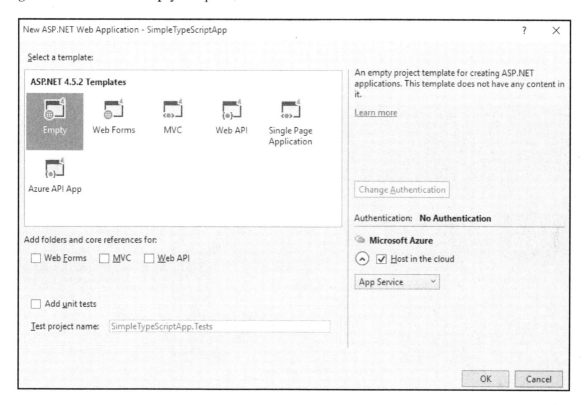

Visual Studio 2017 will then pop up another dialog named **Create App Service**, which provides options for creating a host in Azure for your new web application. We will not be publishing our application to Azure, so we can click on **Skip** at this stage.

Default project settings

Once a new Empty ASP.NET web application has been created, we can start adding files to the project by right-clicking on the project itself, and selecting **Add** then **New Item**. There are two files that we are going to add to the project, namely, an `index.html` file, and an `app.ts` TypeScript file. For each of these files, select the corresponding Visual Studio template, as follows:

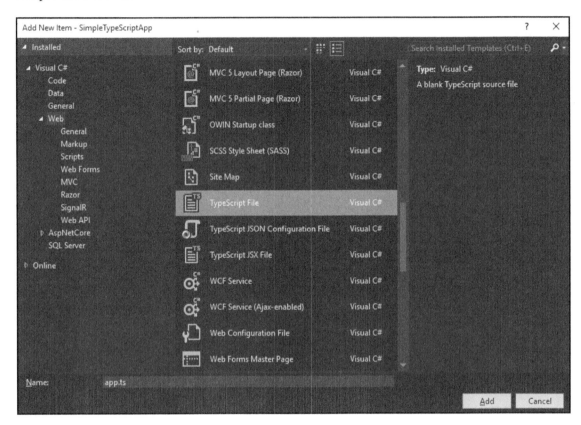

We can now open up the `app.ts` file and start typing the following code:

```
class MyClass {
    public render(divId: string, text: string) {
        var el: HTMLElement = document.getElementById(divId);
        el.innerText = text;
    }
}

window.onload = () => {
    var myClass = new MyClass();
    myClass.render("content", "Hello World");
};
```

Here, we have created a class named `MyClass`, that has a single `render` function. This function takes two parameters, named `divId` and `text`. The function finds an HTML DOM element that matches the `divId` argument, and then sets the `innerText` property to the value of the `text` argument. We then define a function to be called when the browser calls `window.onload`. This function creates a new instance of the `MyClass` class, and calls the `render` function.

Do not be alarmed if this syntax and code is a little confusing. We will be covering all of the language elements and syntax in later chapters. The point of this exercise is simply to use Visual Studio as a development environment for editing TypeScript code.

You will notice that Visual Studio has very powerful Intellisense options, and will suggest code, function names, or variable names as and when you are typing your code. If they are not automatically appearing, then hitting *Ctrl+spacebar* will bring up the Intellisense options for the code you are currently typing.

With our `app.ts` file in place, we can compile it by hitting *Ctrl+Shift+B*, or *F6*, or by selecting the **Build** option from the toolbar. If there are any errors in the TypesScript code that we are compiling, Visual Studio will automatically pop up an **Error List** panel, showing current compilation errors. Double-clicking on any one of these errors will bring up the file in the editor panel, and automatically move the cursor to the offending code.

The generated `app.js` file is not included in the Solution Explorer in Visual Studio. Only the `app.ts` TypeScript file is included. This is by design. If you wish to see the generated JavaScript file, simply click on the **Show All Files** button in the Solution Explorer toolbar.

To include our TypeScript file in the HTML page, we will need to edit the index.html file, and add a `<script>` tag to load app.js, as follows:

```
<!DOCTYPE html>
<html>
<head>
    <meta charset="utf-8" />
    <title></title>
    <script src="app.js"></script>
</head>
<body>
    <div id="content"></div>
</body>
</html>
```

Here, we have added the `<script>` tag to load our app.js file, and have also created a `<div>` element with the id of content. This is the DOM element that our code will modify the innerHtml property of. We can now hit *F5* to run our application:

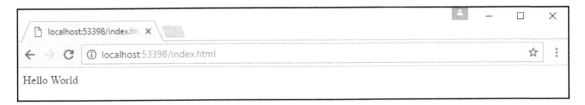

Debugging in Visual Studio

One of the best features of Visual Studio is that it is truly an integrated environment. Debugging TypeScript in Visual Studio is exactly the same as debugging C# or any other language in Visual Studio, and includes the usual **Immediate**, **Locals**, **Watch**, and **Call stack** windows.

To debug TypeScript in Visual Studio, simply put a breakpoint on the line you wish to break on in your TypeScript file (move your mouse into the breakpoint area next to the source code line, and click). In the following screenshot, we have placed a breakpoint within the window.onload function. To start debugging, simply hit *F5*:

```
class MyClass {
    public render(divId: string, text: string) {
        var el: HTMLElement = document.getElementById(divId);
        el.innerText = text;
    }
}

window.onload = () => {
    var myClass = new MyClass();
    myClass.render("content", "Hello World");
};
```

When the source code line is highlighted in yellow, simply hover your mouse over any of the variables in your source, or use the **Immediate**, **Watch**, **Locals**, or **Call stack** windows.

Note that Visual Studio only supports debugging in **Internet Explorer 11**. If you have multiple browsers installed on your machine (including Microsoft Edge), make sure that you select **Internet Explorer** in your **Debug** toolbar, as shown in the following screenshot:

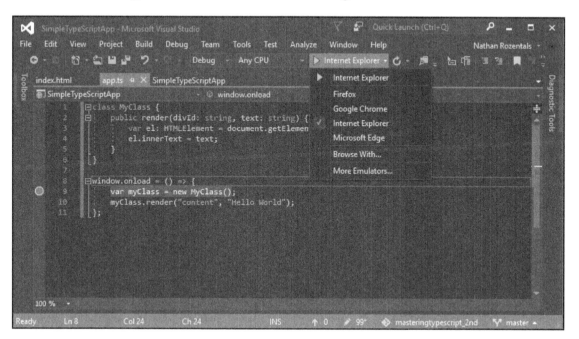

WebStorm

WebStorm is a popular IDE by JetBrains (`http://www.jetbrains.com/webstorm/`), and will run on Windows, macOS, and Linux. Prices range from $59 per year for a single developer to $129 per year for a commercial license. JetBrains also offers a 30-day trial version.

WebStorm has a couple of great features, including live edit, code refactoring suggestions, and Intellisense. Live edit, in particular, allows you to keep a browser open that will automatically update based on changes to CSS, HTML, and JavaScript as you type it. Code suggestions, which are also available with another popular JetBrains product, ReSharper, will highlight code that you have written and suggest better ways of implementing it. WebStorm also has a large number of project templates, which are seamlessly integrated into the IDE, automatically downloading and including the relevant JavaScript or CSS files in your project.

On Windows systems, setting up WebStorm is as simple as downloading the package from the website, and running the installer. On Linux systems, Webstorm is provided as a tar ball. Once unpacked, install WebStorm by running the `webstorm.sh` script in the `bin` directory. Note that on Linux systems, a running version of Java must be installed before setup will continue.

Creating a WebStorm project

To create a WebStorm project, fire up WebStorm, and hit **File** | **New Project**. Select a template from the left-hand menu, and fill in the configuration options in the right-hand panel. Depending on which template is chosen for the project, the configuration options will change. For this project, we will select the **Twitter Bootstrap** template, which only requires a location and a bootstrap version:

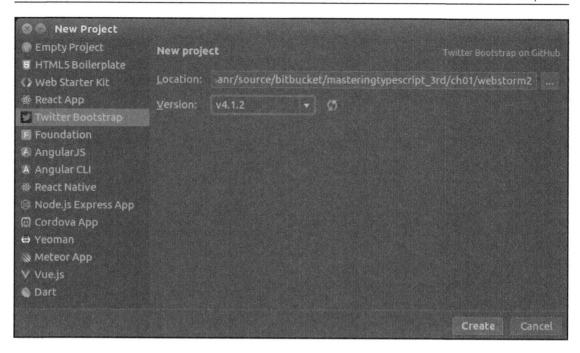

Default files

Once a project template has been selected, WebStorm will create a default project directory tree, and download the required files in order for us to start using this template. For a Bootstrap project, note that Webstorm has conveniently created a css and js directory, and downloaded and included the relevant CSS and JavaScript files automatically. Note that the project template has not created an index.html file for us, nor has it created any TypeScript files. So let's create an index.html file.

Simply click on **File** | **New** and select **HTML** file, enter index as a name, and click **OK**.

Next, let's create a TypeScript file in a similar manner. Select **File | New**, and then TypeScript file. We will call this file app (or app.ts), in order to mirror the Visual Studio project that we created earlier. As we click inside the new app.ts file, WebStorm will pop up a message at the top of the file, with a suggestion reading **Compile TypeScript to JavaScript?**, with three options – **OK**, **No**, and **Configure**, as shown in the following screenshot:

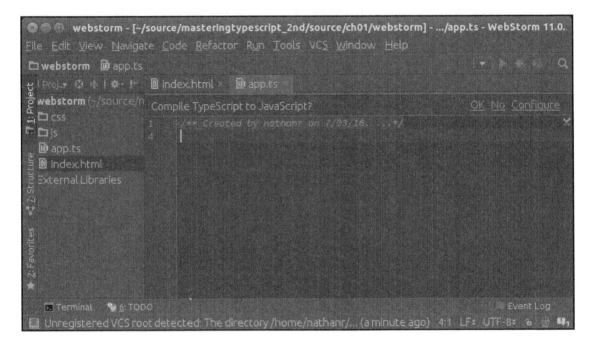

Clicking on **Configure** will bring up the **Settings** panel for TypeScript. There are a number of options on this panel, but, for the time being, we can simply accept the defaults, and click **Ok**.

Building a simple HTML application

Now that we have configured WebStorm to compile our Typescript files, let's create a simple TypeScript class and use it to modify the `innerText` property of an HTML `div`. While you are typing, you will notice WebStorm's autocompletion or Intellisense feature helping you with available keywords, parameters, and naming conventions, among others. This is one of the most powerful features of WebStorm, and is similar to the enhanced Intellisense seen in Visual Studio. To see a list of TypeScript compilation errors, we can open the TypeScript output window by navigating to **View** | **Tool Windows** | **TypeScript**. As we type code into this file, WebStorm will automatically compile our file (without needing to save it), and report any errors in the TypeScript tool window. Go ahead and type the following TypeScript code, during which you will get a good feeling of WebStorm's available autocompletion, and the error-reporting capabilities:

```
class MyClass {
    public render(divId: string, text: string) {
        var el: HTMLElement | null = document.getElementById(divId);
        if (el) {
            el.innerText = text;
        }
    }
}

window.onload = () => {
    var myClass = new MyClass();
    myClass.render("content", "Hello World");
}
```

This code is similar to the sample we used for Visual Studio 2017.

If you have any errors in your TypeScript file, these will automatically show up in the output window, giving you instant feedback while you type.

With this TypeScript file created, we can now include it in our `index.html` file and try some debugging.

Open the `index.html` file, and add a `script` tag to include the `app.js` JavaScript file, along with a `div` with an `id` of `content`. Just as we saw with TypeScript editing, you will find that WebStorm has powerful Intellisense features when editing HTML as well:

```
<!DOCTYPE html>
<html>
<head lang="en">
    <meta charset="UTF-8">
    <title></title>
    <script src="app.js"></script>
```

```
</head>
<body>
    <div id="content"></div>
</body>
</html>
```

Again, this HTML is the same as we used earlier in the Visual Studio example.

Running the web page in Chrome

When viewing or editing HTML files in WebStorm, you will notice a small set of browser icons popping up in the top-right corner of the editing window. Clicking on any one of the icons will launch your current HTML page using the selected browser:

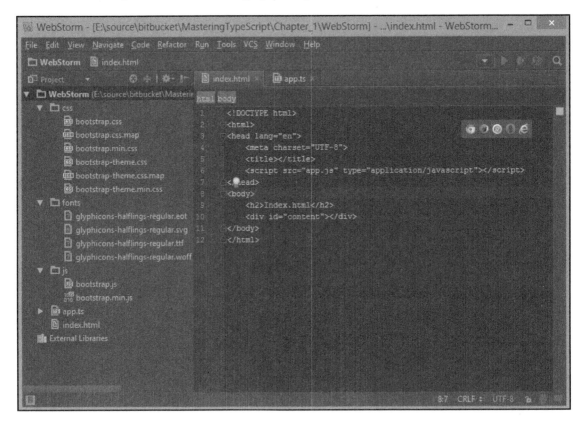

To debug our web application in WebStorm, we will need to set up a debug configuration for the `index.html` file. Click on **Run | Debug**, and then edit configurations. Click on the plus (**+**) button, select the **JavaScript debug** option on the left, and give this configuration a name. Note that WebStorm has already identified that `index.html` is the default page, but this can easily be modified. Next, click on **Debug** at the bottom of the screen, as shown in the following screenshot:

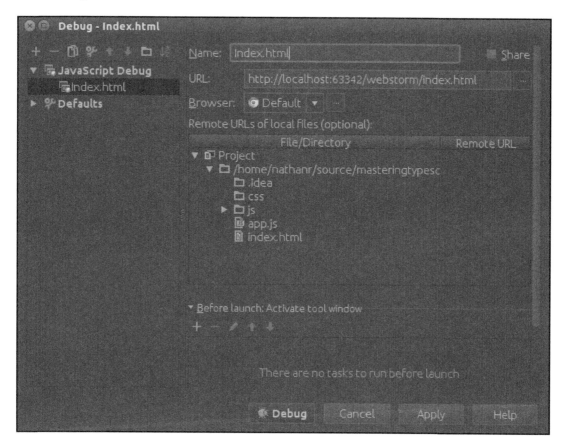

WebStorm uses a Chrome plugin to enable debugging in Chrome and will prompt you the first time you start debugging to download and enable the `JetBrains IDE Support` Chrome plugin. With this plugin enabled, WebStorm has a very powerful set of tools to inspect JavaScript code, add watchers, view the console, and many more, right inside the IDE, as demonstrated in the following screenshot:

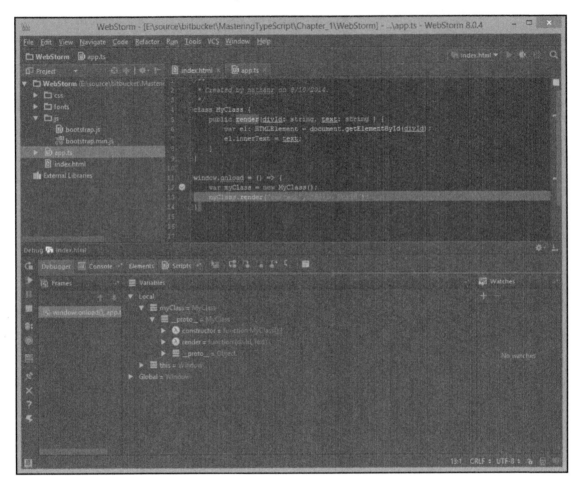

Other editors

There are a number of editors that include support for TypeScript, such as Atom, Brackets, and even the age-old Vim editor. Each of these editors have varying levels of TypeScript support, including syntax highlighting and Intellisense. Using these editors represents a bare-bones TypeScript development environment, relying on the command line to automate build tasks. They do not have built-in debugging tools, and therefore do not qualify as an **Integrated Development Environment** (**IDE**) *per se*, but can easily be used to build TypeScript applications. The basic workflow using these editors would be as follows:

1. Create and modify files using the editor
2. Invoke the TypeScript compiler from the command line
3. Run or debug applications using existing debuggers

Using --watch and Grunt

In a bare-bones environment, any change to a TypeScript file means that we need to reissue the tsc command from the command line every time we wish to compile our project. Obviously, it is going to be very tedious to have to switch to the command prompt and manually compile our project every time we have made a change. Fortunately, the TypeScript compiler provides the --watch option that will run a background task to monitor files for changes, and automatically recompile them when a change is detected. From the command line, we can run the following:

```
tsc --watch
```

Here, we have invoked the TypeScript compiler with the --watch option, which will then start the compilation step in watch mode. As and when we modify .ts files in our project directory, the compilation step will re-execute, and report any errors found.

If we have a more complicated build process that compiles our project, for example, and then needs to uglify the resulting JavaScript, we can use an automated task runner such as Grunt or Gulp. As an example of this process, let's replicate the --watch option by using Grunt to automatically invoke the tsc compiler when a file is saved. Gulp is a very similar task runner to Grunt, and, in certain circumstances, can perform steps faster than Grunt. Grunt, however, has a simpler syntax for configuration, and so we will use it in this section to introduce the concept of automated task runners.

Grunt runs in a Node environment, and therefore needs to be installed as an npm dependency of our project. To install Grunt, we will first need to create a packages.json file in the base directory of the project that will list all of the npm package dependencies that we may need. To create this packages.json file, open up a command prompt, navigate to the base directory of your project, and then simply type the following:

```
npm init
```

Then follow the prompts. You can pretty much leave all of the options as their defaults, and always go back to edit the packages.json file that is created from this step, should you need to tweak any changes.

Now that we have a packages.json file created, we can install Grunt. Grunt has two components that need to be installed independently. Firstly, we need to install the Grunt command-line interface that allows us to run Grunt from the command line. This can be accomplished as follows:

```
npm install -g grunt-cli
```

The second component is to install the Grunt files within our project directory:

```
npm install grunt --save-dev
```

The --save-dev option will install a local version of Grunt in the project directory. This is done so that multiple projects on your machine can use different versions of Grunt. We will also need the grunt-exec package, as well as the grunt-contrib-watch package installed for the project. These can be installed with the following commands:

```
npm install grunt-exec --save-dev
npm install grunt-contrib-watch --save-dev
```

Lastly, we will need a GruntFile.js. Using an editor, create a new file, save it as GruntFile.js, and enter the following JavaScript. Note that we are creating a JavaScript file here, not a TypeScript file. You can find a copy of this file in the sample source code that accompanies this chapter:

```
module.exports = function (grunt) {
    grunt.loadNpmTasks('grunt-contrib-watch');
    grunt.loadNpmTasks('grunt-exec');
    grunt.initConfig( {
        pkg: grunt.file.readJSON('package.json'),
        watch : {
            files : ['**/*.ts'],
            tasks : ['exec:run_tsc']
        },
        exec: {
```

```
            run_tsc: { cmd : 'tsc'}
        }
    });
    grunt.registerTask('default', ['watch']);
};
```

This `GruntFile.js` contains a simple function to initialize the Grunt environment, and specify the commands to run. The first two lines of the function are loading `grunt-contrib-watch` and `grunt-exec` as `npm` tasks. We then call `initConfig` to configure the tasks to run. This configuration section has a `pkg` property, a `watch` property, and an `exec` property. The `pkg` property is used to load the `package.json` file that we created earlier as part of the `npm init` step.

The `watch` property has two sub-properties. The `files` property specifies a matching algorithm for Grunt to identify which files to watch for. In this case, it is set to find any `.ts` files within our entire source tree. The `tasks` array specifies that we should kick off the `exec:run_tsc` command once a file has changed. Finally, we call `grunt.registerTask`, specifying that the default task is to watch for file changes.

We can now run `grunt` from the command line, as follows:

```
grunt
```

As can be seen from the command line output, Grunt is running the `watch` task, and is waiting for changes to any `.ts` files, as follows:

```
Running "watch" task
Waiting...
```

Open up any TypeScript file, make a small change (add a space or something), and then hit *Ctrl+S* to save the file. Now, check back on the output from the Grunt command line. You should see something like the following:

```
>> File "hellogrunt.ts" changed.
Running "exec:run_tsc" (exec) task
Done, without errors.
Completed in 1.866s at Fri Jul 20 2018 22:22:52 GMT+0800 (AWST) -
Waiting...
```

This command line output is confirmation that the Grunt watch task has identified that the `hellogrunt.ts` file has changed, run the `exec:run_tsc` task, and is waiting for the next file to change. We should now also see a `hellogrunt.js` file in the same directory as our Typescript file.

Summary

In this chapter, we have had a quick look at what TypeScript is and what benefits it can bring to the JavaScript development experience. We also looked at setting up a development environment using some popular IDEs, and had a look at what a bare-bones development environment would look like. Now that we have a development environment set up, we can start looking at the TypeScript language itself in a bit more detail. In the next chapter, we will discuss the basic types that are available within TypeScript, and then discuss the various ways that these types can be used with variables or functions.

Types, Variables, and Function Techniques

2

TypeScript introduces strong typing to JavaScript through a simple syntax, referred to by *Anders Hejlsberg* as syntactic sugar. This sugar is what assigns a type to a variable. This strong typing syntax, which is officially called type annotation, is used wherever a variable is used. In other words, we can use type annotation in a variable declaration, a function parameter, or to describe the return type of a function itself.

As we discussed in `Chapter 1`, *TypeScript – Tools and Framework Options*, there are many benefits to enforcing types in a development language. These include better error checking, the ability for an IDE to provide more intelligent code suggestions, and the ability to introduce object-oriented techniques into the coding experience.

The TypeScript language uses several basic types, such as number and boolean, and also uses a few common rules to identify the type of a variable. Understanding these rules and applying them to your code is a fundamental skill when writing TypeScript code.

Along with these basic rules, the TypeScript compiler also adopts ES6 syntax to allow for more advanced object manipulation. This chapter introduces these basic types, the rules that the compiler uses for type checking, and then explores advanced object manipulation.

We will cover the following topics in this chapter:

- Basic types and type syntax—strings, numbers, and booleans
- Inferred typing and duck typing
- Template strings
- Arrays, and using `for...in` and `for...of`
- The `any` type and explicit casting
- Enums

- The `const` and `let` keywords
- Definite assignment and dotted property types
- Functions and anonymous functions
- Function parameters
- Function callbacks, function signatures, and function overrides
- Try catch
- Advanced types, including union types, type guards, and type aliases
- The `never` and `unknown` types
- Object rest and spread
- Tuples
- Bigint

 If you already have experience with TypeScript and have a good understanding of the language, then you can have a quick read through the entire chapter. Otherwise, you can skip on to the later parts of the chapter, where more advanced types, such as `never`, are explored.

Basic types

JavaScript, by nature, is described as a dynamically typed language. This means that any particular variable can hold a number of data types, including numbers, strings, arrays, objects, and functions. The type of a variable in JavaScript is determined by assignment. This means that when we assign a value to a variable, the JavaScript runtime interpreter determines the type of that variable.

However, the JavaScript runtime can also reassign the type of a variable depending on how it is being used, or on how it is interacting with other variables. It may assign a number to a string, for example, in certain cases.

Let's take a look at an example of this dynamic typing in JavaScript and what errors it can introduce. Then, we will explore the strong typing that TypeScript uses and its basic type system.

JavaScript typing

As we saw in `Chapter 1`, *TypeScript - Tools and Framework Options*, JavaScript objects and variables can be changed or reassigned on the fly. As an example of this, consider the following JavaScript code:

```
function doCalculation(a,b,c) {
    return (a * b) + c;
}
var result = doCalculation(2,3,1);
console.log('doCalculation():' + result);
```

Here, we have a `doCalculation` function that is computing the product of the arguments a and b, and then adding the value of c. We are then calling the `doCalculation` function with the arguments 2, 3, and 1, and logging the result to the console. The output of this sample would be as follows:

doCalculation():7

This is the expected result as *2 * 3 = 6*, and *6 + 1 = 7*. Now, let's take a look at what happens if we inadvertently call the function with strings instead of numbers:

```
result = doCalculation("2","3","1");
console.log('doCalculation():' + result);
```

The output of this code sample is as follows:

doCalculation():61

The result of 61 is very different from our expected result of 7. So what is going on here?

If we take a closer look at the code in the `doCalculation` function, we start to understand what JavaScript is doing with our variables and their types.

The product of two numbers, that is, *(a * b)*, returns a numeric value; so JavaScript is automatically converting the 2 and 3 values to numbers in order to compute the product and is correctly computing the 6 value. This is a particular rule that JavaScript applies when it needs to convert strings to numbers, and comes into play when the result of a calculation should be a number. The addition symbol, (+), however, can be used with numbers as well as strings. Because the argument c is a string, JavaScript is converting the 6 value into a string in order to add two strings. This results in the 6 string being added to the 1 string, which results in the 61 value.

This code snippet is an example of how JavaScript can modify the type of a variable based on how it is used. This means that to effectively work with JavaScript, we need to be aware of this sort of type conversion, and understand when and where this conversion could take place. Obviously, these sorts of automatic type conversions can cause unwanted behavior in our code.

TypeScript typing

TypeScript, on the other hand, is a strongly typed language. Once you have declared a variable to be of a certain type, you cannot change it. As an example, if you declare a variable to be of type `string`, then you can only assign `string` values to it, and any instance of this variable can only treat it as though it has a type of `string`. This helps to ensure that code that we write will behave as expected. When we know immediately that the value of a variable will always be a `string`, we will know which of these conversion rules JavaScript will use.

JavaScript programmers have always relied heavily on documentation to understand how to call functions, and the order and type of the correct function parameters. But what if we could take all of this documentation and include it within the IDE?

Then, as we write our code, our compiler could point out to us—automatically—that we were using variables or functions in a JavaScript library in the wrong way. Surely this would make us more efficient, more productive programmers, and allow us to generate better code with fewer errors?

TypeScript does exactly that. It introduces a very simple syntax to define the type of a variable in order to ensure that we are using it in the correct manner. If we break any of these rules, the TypeScript compiler will automatically generate errors, pointing us to the lines of code that are in error.

This is how TypeScript got its name. It is JavaScript with strong typing, hence TypeScript. Let's take a look at this very simple language syntax that enables the Type in TypeScript.

Type syntax

The TypeScript syntax for declaring the type of a variable is to include a colon (:) after the variable name, and then indicate its type. As an example of this, let's rewrite our problematic doCalculation function to only accept numbers. Consider the following TypeScript code:

```
function doCalculation(
    a : number,
    b : number,
    c : number) {
    return ( a * b ) + c;
}

var result = doCalculation(3,2,1);
console.log("doCalculation():" + result);
```

Here, we have specified that the doCalculation function needs to be invoked with three numbers. This means that the properties a, b, and c must be of type number in order to call this function. If we now attempt to call this function with strings, as we did with the JavaScript sample, as follows:

```
var result = doCalculation("1", "2", "3");
console.log("doCalculation():"" + result);
```

The TypeScript compiler will generate the following error:

error TS2345: Argument of type '"1"' is not assignable to parameter of type 'number'.

This error message clearly tells us that we cannot pass a string into our function, where a numeric value is expected.

To further illustrate this point, consider the following TypeScript code:

```
var myString : string;
var myNumber : number;
var myBoolean : boolean;
myString = "1";
myNumber = 1;
myBoolean = true;
```

Here, we are telling the compiler that the `myString` variable is of type `string`, even before the variable itself has been used. Similarly, the `myNumber` variable is of type `number`, and the `myBoolean` variable is of type `boolean`. TypeScript has introduced the `string`, `number`, and `boolean` keywords for each of these basic JavaScript types.

If we then attempt to assign a value to a variable that is not of the same type, the TypeScript compiler will generate a compile-time error. Given the variables declared in the preceding code, consider the following TypeScript code:

```
myString = myNumber;
myBoolean = myString;
myNumber = myBoolean;
```

This is what happens after our attempt to mix these basic types:

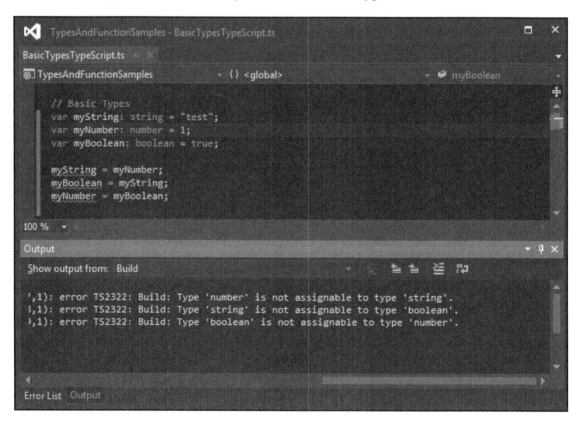

The TypeScript compiler has now started generating compile errors because it has detected that we are attempting to mix these basic types:

- The first error is generated because we cannot assign a number value to a variable of type string
- Similarly, the second compile error indicates that we cannot assign a string value to a variable of type boolean
- And the third error is generated because we cannot assign a boolean value to a variable of type number

The strong typing syntax that the TypeScript language introduces means that we need to ensure that the types on the left-hand side of an assignment operator (=) are the same as the types on the right-hand side of the assignment operator.

To fix the preceding TypeScript code and remove the compile errors, we would need to do something similar to the following:

```
myString = myNumber.toString();
myBoolean = (myString === "test");
if (myBoolean) {
    myNumber = 1;
}
```

Here, our first line of code has been changed to call the .toString() function on the myNumber variable (which is of type number), in order to return a value that is of type string. This line of code, then, does not generate a compile error because both sides of the equal sign (or assignment operator) are strings.

Our second line of code has also been changed, so that the right-hand side of the assignment operator returns the result of a Boolean comparison, myString === "test", which will return a value of type boolean. The compiler will, therefore, allow this code because both sides of the assignment resolve to a value of type boolean.

The last line of our code snippet has been changed to only assign the value 1 (which is of the type number) to the myNumber variable if the value of the myBoolean variable is true.

This is the feature that *Anders Hejlsberg* describes as syntactic sugar. In other words, with a little sugar on top of comparable JavaScript code, TypeScript has enabled our code to transform into a strongly typed language. Whenever you break these strong typing rules, the compiler will generate errors for the offending code.

Inferred typing

TypeScript also uses a technique called inferred typing to determine the nature of a variable. This means that even if we do not specify the type, the compiler will check where the variable has first been used, and then use this type for the remainder of the code block. As an example of this, consider the following TypeScript code:

```
var inferredString = "this is a string"";
var inferredNumber = 1;
inferredString = inferredNumber;
```

We start by declaring a variable named `inferredString` and assign a string value to it. TypeScript identifies that this variable has been assigned a value of type `string` and will infer that the `inferredString` variable is of type `string`. Any further usage of this variable, therefore, will need to treat it as a `string` type. Our second variable, `inferredNumber`, has a number assigned to it. Again, TypeScript is inferring the type of this variable to be of type `number`.

If we then attempt to assign the `inferredString` variable (of type `string`) to the `inferredNumber` variable (of type `number`) in the last line of code, TypeScript will generate a familiar error message:

```
error TS2322: Type 'number' is not assignable to type 'string'
```

This error is generated because of TypeScript's inferred typing rules.

Duck typing

TypeScript also uses a method called duck typing for more complex variable types. Duck typing suggests that if it looks like a duck, and walks like a duck, then it probably is a duck. In other words, two variables are considered equal if they have the same properties and methods, as they can be exchanged for one another, but will still provide the same behavior. Consider the following TypeScript code:

```
var complexType = { name: "myName", id: 1 };
complexType = { id: 2, name: "anotherName" };
```

We start with a variable named `complexType` that has been assigned a simple JavaScript object with a `name` and `id` property. On our second line of code, we are reassigning the value of this `complexType` variable to another object that also has an `id` and a `name` property. The compiler will use duck typing in this instance to figure out whether this assignment is valid. In other words, if an object has the same set of properties as another object, then they are considered to be of the same type.

To further illustrate this point, let's see how the compiler reacts if we attempt to assign an object to our `complexType` variable that does not conform to this duck typing:

```
var complexType = { name: "myName", id: 1 };
complexType = { id: 2 };
```

Here, the first line of this code snippet defines our `complexType` variable and assigns to it an object that contains both an `id` and `name` property. From this point on, TypeScript will use this inferred type for the `complexType` variable. On our second line of code, we are attempting to reassign the `complexType` variable to a value that only has an `id` property and not the `name` property. This line of code will generate the following compilation error:

```
error TS2322: Type '{ id: number; }' is not assignable to type '{ name:
string; id: number; }'.

Property 'name' is missing in type '{ id: number; }'.
```

The error message is pretty self-explanatory. In this instance, TypeScript is using duck typing to ensure type safety. As the `complexType` variable has both an `id` and a `name` property, any object that is assigned to it must also have both an `id` and a `name` property.

Note that the following code will also generate an error message:

```
var complexType = { name: "myName", id: 1 };
complexType = { name : "extraproperty", id : 2, extraProp: true };
```

The error generated here is as follows:

```
error TS2322: Type '{ name: string; id: number;
extraProp: boolean; }' is not assignable to type '{ name: string; id:
number; }'.

Object literal may only specify known properties, and 'extraProp' does not
exist in type '{ name: string; id: number; }'.
```

As can be seen in this error message, the `complexType` variable does not have an `extraProp` property, and therefore the assignment fails.

Inferred typing and duck typing are powerful features of the TypeScript language, bringing strong typing to variables that are made up of many properties, all without the need to use explicit typing.

Template strings

Before we continue with our discussion on types, let's explore a simple method for logging the value of any variable to the console. It is worth noting that TypeScript allows for ES6 template string syntax, which is a convenient syntax for injecting values into strings. Consider the following code:

```
var myVariable = "test";
console.log("myVariable=" + myVariable);
```

Here, we are simply assigning a value to a variable, and then logging the result to the console. Note that the `console.log` function uses a little bit of formatting to make the message readable, by concatenating the strings with the `"string" + variable` syntax. Let's now take a look at the equivalent TypeScript code that uses the ES6 template string syntax:

```
var myVariable = "test";
console.log(`myVariable=${myVariable}`);
```

Here, on the second line of this code snippet, we are logging some information to the console, and are using the template string syntax. There are two important things to note here. Firstly, we have switched the string definition from a double quote (") to a backtick (`). Using a backtick signals to the TypeScript compiler that it should look for template values within the string enclosed by the backticks, and replace them with actual values. Secondly, we have used a special `${ ... }` syntax within the string to denote a template. TypeScript will inject the value of any variable that is currently in scope into the string for us. This is a convenient method of dealing with string formatting.

The TypeScript compiler will parse this ES6 style of string templates, and generate JavaScript code that uses standard string concatenation. In this way, ES6 string template syntax can be used no matter what JavaScript version is being targeted.

In the remainder of this chapter, we will use this string template syntax whenever we log values to the console.

Another handy way of using this template string syntax is when we need to log an entire complex object, including all of its properties, to the console. Consider the following code:

```
var complexObject = {
    id: 2,
    name: 'testObject'
}

console.log(`complexObject = ${JSON.stringify(complexObject)}`);
```

Here, we define an object named `complexObject` that has an `id` and a `name` property. We are then using template string syntax to log the value of this object to the console. But in this example, we are calling the `JSON.stringify` function, and passing in the `complexObject` variable as a parameter. This means that anything within the `${ ... }` is not limited to simple types, but can be valid TypeScript. The output of this code is as follows:

```
complexObject = {"id":2,"name":"testObject"}
```

Here, we can see that the result of calling the `JSON.stringify` function is a string representation of the entire object, which we are logging to the console.

Arrays

Besides the basic JavaScript types of `string`, `number`, and `boolean`, TypeScript also has two other basic data types that we will now take a closer look at—arrays and enums. Let's look at the syntax for defining arrays.

An array is simply marked with the `[]` notation, similar to JavaScript, and each array can be strongly typed to hold values of a specific type, as seen in the following code:

```
var arrayOfNumbers: number [] = [1,2,3];
arrayOfNumbers = [3,4,5,6,7,8,9];
console.log(`arrayOfNumbers: ${arrayOfNumbers}`);
arrayOfNumbers = ["1", "2", "3"];
```

Here, we start by defining an array named `arrayOfNumbers`, and further specifying that each element of this array must be of type `number`. We then reassign this array to hold some different numerical values. Interestingly enough, we are able to assign any number of elements to an array, as long as each element is of the correct type. We then use a simple template string to print the value of the array to the console.

The last line of this snippet, however, will generate the following error message:

```
error TS2322: Type 'string[]' is not assignable to type 'number[]'.
```

This error message is warning us that the variable `arrayOfNumbers` is strongly typed to only accept values of the type `number`. As our code is trying to assign an array of strings to this array of numbers, an error is generated. The output of this code snippet is as follows:

```
arrayOfNumbers: 3,4,5,6,7,8,9
```

for...in and for...of

When working with arrays, it is common practice to loop through array items in order to perform a task. This is generally accomplished within a `for` loop by manipulating an array index, as shown in the following code:

```
var arrayOfStrings : string[] = ["first", "second", "third"];

for( var i = 0; i < arrayOfStrings.length; i++ ) {
    console.log(`arrayOfStrings[${i}] = ${arrayOfStrings[i]}`);
}
```

Here, we have an array named `arrayOfStrings`, and a standard `for` loop that is using the variable `i` as an index into our array. We access the array item using the syntax `arrayOfStrings[i]`. The output of this code is as follows:

```
arrayOfStrings[0] = first
arrayOfStrings[1] = second
arrayOfStrings[2] = third
```

TypeScript can also use the ES6 `for...in` syntax to simplify looping through arrays. Here is an example of the previous `for` loop expressed using this new syntax:

```
for( var itemKey in arrayOfStrings) {
    var itemValue = arrayOfStrings[itemKey];
    console.log(`arrayOfStrings[${itemKey}] = ${itemValue}`);
}
```

Here, we have simplified the `for` loop by using the `itemKey in arrayOfStrings` syntax. Note that the value of the variable `itemKey` will iterate through the keys of the array, and not the array elements themselves. Within the `for` loop, we are first de-referencing the array to extract the array value for this `itemKey`, and then logging both the `itemKey` and the `itemValue` to the console. The output of this code is as follows:

```
arrayOfStrings[0] = first
arrayOfStrings[1] = second
arrayOfStrings[2] = third
```

If we do not necessarily need to know the keys of the array and are simply interested in the values held within the array, we can further simplify looping through arrays using the `for...of` syntax. Consider the following code:

```
for( var arrayItem of arrayOfStrings ) {
    console.log(`arrayItem = ${arrayItem} `);
}
```

Here, we are using the `for...of` syntax to iterate over each value of the `arrayOfStrings` array. Each time that the `for` loop is executed, the `arrayItem` variable will hold the next element in the array. The output of this code is as follows:

```
arrayItem = first
arrayItem = second
arrayItem = third
```

The any type

All this type checking is well and good, but JavaScript does not have strong typing, and allows variables to be mixed and matched. Consider the following code snippet that is actually valid JavaScript code:

```
var item1 = { id: 1, name: "item 1" };
item1 = { id: 2 };
```

Here, we assign an object with an `id` property and a `name` property to the variable `item1`. We then reassign this variable to an object that has an `id` property but not a `name` property. Unfortunately, as we have seen previously, this is not valid TypeScript code, and will generate the following error:

```
error TS2322: Type 'string[]' is not assignable to type 'number[]'.
```

TypeScript introduces the `any` type for such occasions. Specifying that an object has a type of `any`, in essence, relaxes the compiler's strict type checking. The following code shows how to use the `any` type:

```
var item1 : any = { id: 1, name: "item 1" };
item1 = { id: 2 };
```

Note how our first line of code has changed. We specify the type of the `item1` variable to be of type : `any`. This special TypeScript keyword then allows a variable to follow JavaScript's loosely defined type rules, so that anything can be assigned to anything. Without the type specifier of : `any`, the second line of code would normally generate an error.

Explicit casting

As with any strongly typed language, there comes a time where you need to explicitly specify the type of an object. This concept will be expanded upon more thoroughly in the next chapter, but it is worthwhile making a quick note of explicit casting here. An object can be cast to the type of another by using the < > syntax.

 This is not a cast in the strictest sense of the word; it is more of an assertion that is used at compile time by the TypeScript compiler. Any explicit casting that you use will be compiled away in the resultant JavaScript and will not affect the code at runtime.

Let's rewrite our previous sample, and use explicit casting, as follows:

```
var item1 = <any>{ id: 1, name: "item 1" };
item1 = { id: 2 };
```

Here, we have now replaced the : any type specifier on the left-hand side of the assignment with an explicit cast of <any> on the right-hand side. This tells the compiler to explicitly treat the { id: 1, name: "item 1" } object on the right-hand side of the assignment operator as a type of any. In essence, this syntax is equivalent to our earlier examples and specifies the type of the item1 variable to be of type any (due to TypeScript's inferred typing rules). This then allows us to assign an object with only the { id: 2 } property to the variable item1 on the second line of code. This technique of using the < > syntax on the right-hand side of an assignment is called explicit casting.

While the any type is a necessary feature of the TypeScript language and is used for backward compatibility with JavaScript, its usage should really be limited as much as possible. As we have seen with untyped JavaScript, over-use of the any type will quickly lead to coding errors that will be difficult to find. Rather than using the any type, try to figure out the correct type of the object you are using, and then use this type instead.

We use an acronym within our programming teams—**Simply Find an Interface for the Any Type (S.F.I.A.T)**, pronounced as sweat. While this may sound silly, it brings home the point that the any type should always be replaced with an interface, so simply find it. An interface is a way of defining custom types in TypeScript, which we will cover in the next chapter. Just remember that by actively trying to define what an object's type should be, we are building strongly typed code, and therefore, protecting ourselves from future coding errors and bugs.

In short, avoid the any type at any cost.

Enums

Enums are a special type that has been borrowed from other languages such as C#, C++, and Java, and provides a solution to the problem of special numbers. An enum associates a human-readable name for a specific number. Consider the following code:

```
enum DoorState {
    Open,
    Closed,
    Ajar
}
```

Here, we have defined an enum called DoorState to represent the state of a door. Valid values for this door state are Open, Closed, or Ajar. Under the hood (in the generated JavaScript), TypeScript will assign a numeric value to each of these human-readable enum values. In this example, the enum value DoorState.Open will equate to a numeric value of 0. Likewise, the enum value DoorState.Closed will equate to the numeric value of 1, and the enum value DoorState.Ajar will equate to 2. Let's take a quick look at how we would use these enum values:

```
var openDoor = DoorState.Open;
console.log(`openDoor is: ${openDoor}`);
```

Here, the first line of this snippet creates a variable named openDoor, and sets its value to DoorState.Open. The second line simply logs the value of the openDoor variable to the console. The output of this would be as follows:

openDoor is: 0

This clearly shows that the TypeScript compiler has substituted the enum value of DoorState.Open with the numeric value 0.

Now, let's use this enum in a slightly different way:

```
var closedDoor = DoorState["Closed"];
console.log(`closedDoor is : ${closedDoor}`);
```

This code snippet uses a string value of "Closed" to look up the enum type, and assigns the resulting enum value to the closedDoor variable. The output of this code would be as follows:

closedDoor is : 1

This sample clearly shows that the `enum` value of `DoorState.Closed` is the same as the `enum` value of `DoorState["Closed"]`, because both variants resolve to the numeric value of `1`.

Enums are a handy way of defining an easily remembered, human-readable name to a special number. Using human-readable enums, instead of just scattering various special numbers around in our code, makes the intent of the code clearer. Using an application-wide value named `DoorState.Open` or `DoorState.Closed` is far simpler than remembering to set a value to `0` for `Open`, `1` for `Closed`, and `3` for `Ajar`. As well as making our code more readable, and more maintainable, using enums also protects our code base whenever these special numeric values change, because they are all defined in one place.

One last note on enums is that we can set the numeric value manually, if needs be, as follows:

```
enum DoorState {
    Open = 3,
    Closed = 7,
    Ajar = 10
}
```

Here, we have overridden the default values of the `enum` to set `DoorState.Open` to 3, `DoorState.Closed` to 7, and `DoorState.Ajar` to 10.

Const enums

A slight variant of the `enum` type is the `const` enum, which simply adds the keyword `const` before the `enum` definition, as follows:

```
const enum DoorStateConst {
    Open,
    Closed,
    Ajar
}
var constDoorOpen = DoorStateConst.Open;
console.log(`constDoorOpen is : ${constDoorOpen}`);
```

`const` enums have been introduced largely for performance reasons. Let's take a quick look at the JavaScript that is generated from this `DoorStateConst` enum:

```
var constDoorOpen = 0 /* Open */;
```

Note how the compiler has simply resolved the `DoorStateConst.Open` enum to its internal value of `0`, and removed the `const enum` definition entirely.

String enums

A further variant of the enum type is what is known as a string enum, where the numeric values are replaced by strings, as follows:

```
enum DoorStateString {
    Open = "open",
    Closed = "closed",
    Ajar = "ajar"
}

var openDoorString = DoorStateString.Open;
console.log(`openDoorString = ${openDoorString}`);
```

Here, we have an enum named `DoorStateString`, where each of the enum values are now of type `string`. The output of this code snipped would be as follows:

openDoorString = open

As expected, the TypeScript compiler is resolving the enum value of `DoorStateString.Open` to the string `"open"`.

Enum implementation

When TypeScript generates the JavaScript for enums, it uses the closure and **Immediately Invoked Function (IIF)** patterns to define a JavaScript object with the correct properties that can be used as an enum. Let's take a look at this implementation. Given our `DoorState` enum, which is defined as follows:

```
enum DoorState {
    Open,
    Closed,
    Ajar
}
```

We know that we can reference the `DoorState.Open` value, which will be represented as a numeric value of 0, `Closed` as 1, and `Ajar` as 2. But what happens if we reference an enum using an array-type syntax, as follows:

```
var ajarDoor = DoorState[2];
console.log(`ajarDoor is : ${ajarDoor}`);
```

Here, we assign the variable `ajarDoor` to an enum value based on the second index value of the `DoorState` enum. The output of this code, though, is surprising:

ajarDoor is : Ajar

You may have been expecting the output to simply be 2, but here we are getting the `Ajar` string, which is a string representation of our original enum value. This is actually a neat little trick allowing us to access a string representation instead of a simple number. The reason that this is possible is down to the JavaScript that has been generated by the TypeScript compiler. Let's take a look, then, at the closure that the TypeScript compiler has generated:

```
var DoorState;
(function (DoorState) {
    DoorState[DoorState["Open"] = 0] = "Open";
    DoorState[DoorState["Closed"] = 1] = "Closed";
    DoorState[DoorState["Ajar"] = 2] = "Ajar";
})(DoorState || (DoorState = {}));
```

This strange looking syntax is building an object that has a specific internal structure. It is this internal structure that allows us to use this enum in the various ways that we have seen. If we interrogate this structure while debugging our JavaScript, we will see that the internal structure of the `DoorState` object is as follows:

```
DoorState
{...}
    [prototype]: {...}
    [0]: "Open"
    [1]: "Closed"
    [2]: "Ajar"
    [prototype]: []
    Ajar: 2
    Closed: 1
    Open: 0
```

The `DoorState` object has a property called `"0"`, which has a string value of `"Open"`. Unfortunately, in JavaScript, the number `0` is not a valid property name, so we cannot access this property by simply using `DoorState.0`. Instead, we must access this property using either `DoorState[0]` or `DoorState["0"]`. Accessing the value of this property will return the string value of `"Open"`. Note that the `DoorState` object also has a property named `Open`, which is set to the numeric value `0`. The word `Open` is a valid property name in JavaScript, so we can access this property using `DoorState["Open"]`, or simply `DoorState.Open`, which equates to the same JavaScript property.

> Note that the internal structure of string enums does not have number-based properties, so we cannot use the `enum[propertyIndex]` syntax when using string enums.

Const values

The TypeScript language also allows us to define a variable as a constant, by using the `const` keyword. If a variable has been marked as `const`, then its value can only be set when the variable is defined, and cannot be modified afterward. Consider the following code:

```
const constValue = "test";
constValue = "updated";
```

Here, we have defined a variable named `constValue`, and indicated that it cannot be changed by using the `const` keyword. Attempting to compile this code will result in the following compile error:

```
error TS2450: Left-hand side of assignment expression cannot be a constant
or a read-only property.
```

This error is, in fact, generated for the second line of code, where we are attempting to modify the value of the `constValue` variable to the string `"updated"`.

The let keyword

Variables in JavaScript are defined by using the `var` keyword. Unfortunately, the JavaScript runtime is very lenient on where these definitions occur, and will allow a variable to be used before it has been defined. If the JavaScript runtime comes across a variable that has not been previously defined, or given a value, then the value for this variable will be `undefined`. Consider the following code:

```
console.log(`anyValue = ${anyValue}`);
var anyValue = 2;
console.log(`anyValue = ${anyValue}`);
```

Here, we start by logging the value of a variable named `anyValue` to the console. Note, however, that the `anyValue` variable is only defined on the second line of this code snippet. In other words, we can use a variable in JavaScript before it is defined. The output of this code is as follows:

```
anyValue = undefined
anyValue = 2
```

The semantics of using the `var` keyword presents us with a small problem. Using the `var` keyword does not check to see whether the variable itself has been defined before we actually use it. This could obviously lead to unwanted behavior, since the value of an undefined or unallocated variable is always `undefined`.

TypeScript introduces the `let` keyword that can be used in the place of the `var` keyword when defining variables. One of the advantages of using the `let` keyword is that we cannot use a variable name before it has been defined. Consider the following code:

```
console.log(`letValue = ${lValue}`);
let lValue = 2;
```

Here, we are attempting to log the value of the variable `lValue` to the console, even before it has been defined, similar to how we were using the `anyValue` variable earlier. However, when using the `let` keyword instead of the `var` keyword, this code will generate an error, as follows:

```
error TS2448: Block-scoped variable 'lValue'' used before its declaration.
```

To fix this code, then, we need to define our `lValue` variable before it is first used, as follows:

```
let lValue = 2;
console.log(`lValue = ${lValue}`);
```

This code will compile correctly, and output the following to the console:

```
lValue = 2
```

Another side effect of using the `let` keyword is that variables defined with `let` are block-scoped. This means that their value and definition are limited to the block of code that they reside in. As an example of this, consider the following code:

```
let lValue = 2;
console.log(`lValue = ${lValue}`);

if (lValue == 2) {
    let lValue = 2001;
    console.log(`block scoped lValue : ${lValue} `);
}
console.log(`lValue = ${lValue}`);
```

Here, we define the `lValue` variable on the first line using the `let` keyword, and assign a value of 2 to it. We then log the value of `lValue` to the console. On the first line within the `if` statement, note how we are redefining a variable named `lValue` to hold the value 2001. We are then logging the value of `lValue` to the console (within the `if` statement block). The last line of this code snippet again logs the value of the `lValue` variable to the console, but this time, `lValue` is outside of the `if` statement block-scope. The output of this code is as follows:

```
lValue = 2
block scoped lValue : 2001
lValue = 2
```

What these results demonstrate is that `let` variables are confined to the scope in which they are defined. In other words, the `let lValue = 2001;` statement defines a new variable that will only be visible inside the `if` statement block of code. As it is a new variable, it will also not influence the value of the `lValue` variable that is outside of its scope. This is why the value of `lValue` is 2 both before and after the `if` statement block, and 2001 within it.

The `let` statement, therefore, provides us with a safer way of declaring variables and limiting their validity to the current scope.

 The TypeScript compiler will automatically generate errors for variables that have been used before they have been defined if we use the `--strictNullChecks` option in our `tsconfig.json` file. We will explore these compiler options in more detail in `Chapter 5`, *Declaration Files and Strict Compiler Options*.

Definite assignment

There are occasions, however, where we would like to declare a variable using the `let` keyword and use it, before TypeScript thinks that it has been defined. Consider the following code:

```
let globalString: string;

setGlobalString();

console.log(`globalString : ${globalString}`);

function setGlobalString() {
    globalString = "this has been set";
}
```

Here, we have declared a variable named `globalString`. We then call a function named `setGlobalString`, which sets the value of the `globalString` variable. So, according to the logic of this code, the `globalString` variable is not `undefined`, and should contain a value at this stage. The next line of code logs the value of `globalString` to the console.

Unfortunately, the TypeScript compiler does not, and cannot, follow our execution path in order to validate whether a particular variable has been used before it has a value. As far as the compiler is concerned, we have declared the `globalString` variable, but have not assigned a value to it before it is used in the `console.log`. Compiling this code will produce the following error:

error TS2454: Variable 'globalString' is used before being assigned.

To cater for this scenario, we can use an assignment assertion syntax, which is to append an exclamation mark (`!`) after the variable that has already been assigned. There are two places that we can do this in order to allow our code to compile.

The first is in the declaration of the variable, as follows:

```
let globalString!: string;
```

Here, we have appended an exclamation mark to the declaration of the `globalString` variable. This tells the compiler that we are asserting that the variable has been assigned, and that it should not generate an error if it thinks that it has been used before being assigned.

The second place we can do an assignment assertion is where the variable is actually used, so we could modify our `console.log` function as follows:

```
console.log(`globalString : ${globalString!}`);
```

Here, we are using an assignment assertion where the `globalString` variable is being used by appending an exclamation mark to the variable.

 While we do have the ability to break standard TypeScript rules by using assignment assertions, the more important question is: why ? Why do we need to structure our code in this way? Why are we using a global variable in the first place? Why not use other object-oriented techniques to avoid this scenario? We will cover object orientation in the next chapter, and see how we can use inheritance and interfaces to find a more robust way of tackling these issues.

Dotted property types

When working with JavaScript objects, it is fairly common to define them with property names that are strings, as can be seen in the following code:

```
let normalObject = {
    id : 1,
    name : "test"
}

let stringObject = {
    "testProperty": 1,
    "anotherProperty": "this is a string"
}
```

Here, we have defined an object named `normalObject` that has an id and a name property. We can access these properties by referencing `normalObject.id`, or `normalObject.name`, as we have seen many times before. Note, however, the minor change in the definition of the `stringObject` object. Here, each property name is enclosed in double quotes (""), making it a string property. We can reference these string properties in two ways:

```
let testProperty = stringObject.testProperty;
console.log(`testPropertyValue = ${testProperty}`);

let testStringProperty = stringObject["testProperty"];
console.log(`"testPropertyValue" = ${testStringProperty}`);
```

Here, we are using both the `stringObject.testProperty` syntax, as well as the `stringObject["testProperty"]` syntax to access the `testProperty` property. To TypeScript, these are one and the same, as the output of this code snippet shows:

```
testPropertyValue = 1
"testPropertyValue" = 1
```

Numeric separators

TypeScript also includes support for the ECMAScript standard to allow an underscore separator (_) when defining large numbers. Consider the following code:

```
let oneMillion = 1_000_000;
console.log(`oneMillion = ${oneMillion}`);
```

Here, we have defined a numeric variable named `oneMillion` with the value of 1 million. Note the use of the _ character to allow for a more human-readable representation of this large number. When TypeScript emits the equivalent JavaScript, it will convert this human readable number to a decimal equivalent, so the output of this code will be as follows:

```
oneMillion = 1000000;
```

These numeric separators can also be used on other numbers, such as hexadecimal values, as follows:

```
let limeGreenColor = 0x00_FF_00;
console.log(`limeGreenColor = ${limeGreenColor}`);
```

Here, we have defined a numeric value called `limeGreenColor`, and assigned the hexadecimal value of `00FF00` to it. Note again, that the separators make this number more human readable, and that the emitted JavaScript will contain the decimal equivalent, which means the output of this code would be as follows:

```
limeGreenColor = 65280
```

Functions

So far, we have explored how to add type annotations to variables and objects. However, this simple syntax can also be used with functions in order to introduce type safety whenever a function is used. Let's now examine the type annotation syntax as it applies to functions, and explore these rules in more detail.

Function return types

Using the very simple syntactic sugar that TypeScript uses, we can easily define the type of a variable that a function should return. In other words, when we call a function, and it returns a value, what type should the return value be treated as?

Consider the following TypeScript code:

```
function addNumbers(a: number, b: number) : string {
    return a + b;
}
var addResult = addNumbers(2,3);
console.log(`addNumbers returned : ${addResult}`);
```

Here, we have added a :number type to both of the parameters of the addNumbers function (a and b), and we have also added a :string type just after the ( ) braces in the function definition. Placing a type annotation after the function definition means that we are defining the return type of the entire function. In our example, then, the return type of the addNumbers function must be of type string.

Unfortunately, this code will generate an error message as follows:

error TS2322: Type 'number' is not assignable to type 'string'

This error message is indicating that the return type of the addNumbers function must be a string. Taking a closer look at the code, we will note that the offending code is, in fact, return a + b. Since a and b are numbers, we are returning the result of adding two numbers, which is of type number. To fix this code, then, we need to ensure that the function returns a string, as follows:

```
function addNumbers(a: number, b: number) : string  {
    return (a + b).toString();
}
```

This code will now compile correctly, and will output the following:

addNumbers returned : 5

Anonymous functions

The JavaScript language also has the concept of anonymous functions. These are functions that are defined on the fly and don't specify a function name. Consider the following JavaScript code:

```
var addVar = function(a,b) {
    return a + b;
}

var addVarResult = addVar(2,3);
console.log("addVarResult:"" + addVarResult);
```

Here, we define a function that has no name and adds two values. Because the function does not have a name, it is known as an anonymous function. This anonymous function is then assigned to a variable named `addVar`. The `addVar` variable can then be invoked as a function with two parameters, and the return value will be the result of executing the anonymous function. The output of this code will be as follows:

addVarResult:5

Let's now rewrite the preceding anonymous JavaScript function in TypeScript, as follows:

```
var addFunction = function(a:number, b:number) : number {
    return a + b;
}
var addFunctionResult = addFunction(2,3);
console.log(`addFunctionResult : ${addFunctionResult}`);
```

Here, we see that TypeScript allows anonymous functions in the same way that JavaScript does, but also allows standard type annotations. The output of this TypeScript code is as follows:

addFunctionResult : 5

Optional parameters

When we call a JavaScript function that is expecting parameters, and we do not supply these parameters, then the value of the parameter within the function will be `undefined`. As an example of this, consider the following JavaScript code:

```
var concatStrings = function(a,b,c) {
    return a + b + c;
}
var concatAbc = concatStrings("a", "b", "c");
```

```
console.log("concatAbc :" + concatAbc);

var concatAb = concatStrings("a", "b");
console.log("concatAb :" + concatAb);
```

The output of this code is as follows:

concatAbc :abc
concatAb :abundefined

Here, we have defined a function called `concatStrings` that takes three parameters, a, b, and c, and simply returns the sum of these values. We are then calling this function with three arguments, and assigning the result to the variable `concatAbc`. As can be seen from the output, this returns the string `"abc"` as expected. If, however, we only supply two arguments, as seen with the usage of the `concatAb` variable, the function returns the string `"abundefined"`. In JavaScript, if we call a function and do not supply a parameter, then the missing parameter will be `undefined`, which in this case is the parameter c.

TypeScript introduces the question mark ? syntax to indicate optional parameters. This allows us to mimic JavaScript calling syntax, where we can call the same function with some missing arguments. As an example of this, consider the following TypeScript code:

```
function concatStrings( a: string, b: string, c?: string) {
    return a + b + c;
}
var concat3strings = concatStrings("a", "b", "c");
console.log(`concat3strings : ${concat3strings}`);
var concat2strings = concatStrings("a", "b");
console.log(`concat2strings : ${concat2strings}`);
var concat1string = concatStrings("a");
```

Here, we have a strongly typed version of the original `concatStrings` JavaScript function that we were using previously. Note the addition of the ? character in the syntax for the third parameter: `c?: string`. This indicates that the third parameter is optional, and therefore, all of the preceding code will compile cleanly, except for the last line. The last line will generate an error:

error TS2554: Expected 2-3 arguments, but got 1

This error is generated because we are attempting to call the concatStrings function with only a single parameter. Our function definition, though, requires at least two parameters, with only the third parameter being optional.

> Any optional parameters must be the last parameters defined in the function definition. You can have as many optional parameters as you want, as long as non-optional parameters precede the optional parameters.

Default parameters

A subtle variant of the optional parameter syntax allows us to specify the default value of a parameter, if it is not supplied. Let's modify our preceding function definition to use an optional parameter with a default value, as follows:

```
function concatStringsDefault(
   a: string,
   b: string,
   c: string = "c") {
      return a + b + c;
}
var defaultConcat = concatStringsDefault("a", "b");
console.log(`defaultConcat : ${defaultConcat}`);
```

This function definition has now dropped the ? optional parameter syntax, but instead has assigned a value of "c" to the last parameter, c:string = "c". By using default parameters, if we do not supply a value for the parameter named c, the concatStringsDefault function will substitute the default value of "c" instead. The argument c, therefore, will not be undefined. The output of this code will therefore be as follows:

defaultConcat : abc

> Note that using a default parameter value will automatically make the parameter that has a default value optional.

Rest parameters

The JavaScript language also allows a function to be called with a variable number of arguments. To illustrate this point, we can make use of a quirk of the JavaScript language. Every JavaScript function has access to a special variable, named arguments, that can be used to retrieve all arguments that have been passed into the function. As an example of this, consider the following JavaScript code:

```javascript
function testArguments() {
    if (arguments.length > 0) {
        for (var i = 0; i < arguments.length; i++ ) {
            console.log("argument[" + i + "] = " + arguments[i]);
        }
    }
}
testArguments(1,2,3);
testArguments("firstArg");
```

Here, we have defined a function, named testArguments, which does not have any named parameters. Note, though, that we can use the special variable, named arguments, to test whether the function was called with any arguments. In our sample, we simply loop through the arguments array, and log the value of each argument to the console, by using an array index, arguments[i]. The output of this code is as follows:

```
argument[0] = 1
argument[1] = 2
argument[2] = 3
argument[0] = firstArg
```

In order to express the equivalent function definition in TypeScript, we will need to use a syntax that is known as rest parameter syntax. Rest parameters use the TypeScript syntax of three dots (. . .) in the function declaration to express a variable number of function parameters. Here is the equivalent testArguments function, expressed in TypeScript:

```typescript
function testArguments(... argArray: number []) {
    if (argArray.length > 0) {
        for (var i = 0; i < argArray.length; i++) {
            console.log(`argArray[${i}] = ${argArray[i]}`);
            // use JavaScript arguments variable
            console.log(`arguments[${i}] = ${arguments[i]}`)
        }
    }
}

testArguments(9);
testArguments(1,2,3);
```

Note the use of the ...argArray: number[] syntax for our testArguments function parameter. This syntax is telling the TypeScript compiler that the function can accept any number of arguments, as long as each argument is a number. We can therefore call this function as seen in the last two lines of the preceding code with any number of numeric values. There are also two console.log statements in this for loop. The first uses argArray[i], which is referencing the rest parameter name, and the second uses the standard JavaScript arguments variable, arguments[i], which is still available for use in TypeScript.

The output of this code is as follows:

```
argArray[0] = 9
arguments[0] = 9
argArray[0] = 1
arguments[0] = 1
argArray[1] = 2
arguments[1] = 2
argArray[2] = 3
arguments[2] = 3
```

> The subtle difference between using argArray and arguments is the inferred type of the argument. Since we have explicitly specified that argArray is of type number, TypeScript will treat any item of the argArray array as a number. However, the internal arguments array does not have an inferred type, and so will be treated as type any.

We can also combine normal parameters along with rest parameters in a function definition, as long as the rest parameters are the last to be defined in the parameter list, as follows:

```
function testNormalAndRestArguments(
    arg1: string,
    arg2, number,
    ...argArray: number[]
) {
}
```

Here, we have two normal parameters named arg1 and arg2, and then an argArray rest parameter. Mistakenly placing the rest parameter at the beginning of the parameter list will generate a compile error.

Function callbacks

One of the most powerful features of JavaScript and, in fact, the technology that Node was built on, is the concept of callback functions. A `callback` function is a function that is passed into another function, and is then generally invoked inside the function. This is how asynchronous programming is achieved. By supplying a `callback` function, we are saying to the function we are calling, go and do what you need to do, and then when you are finished, call this function. Just as we can pass a value into a function, we can also pass a function into a function.

This is best illustrated by taking a look at some sample JavaScript code:

```
var callbackFunction = function(text) {
    console.log('inside callbackFunction ' + text);
}

function doSomethingWithACallback( initialText, callback ) {
    console.log('inside doSomethingWithCallback ' + initialText);
    callback(initialText);
}

doSomethingWithACallback('myText'', callbackFunction);
```

Here, we start with a variable named `callbackFunction` that is a function that takes a single parameter. This `callbackFunction` simply logs the `text` argument to the console. We then define a function named `doSomethingWithACallback` that takes two parameters, `initialText` and `callback`. The first line of this function simply logs `"inside doSomethingWithACallback"` to the console. The second line of the `doSomethingWithACallback` is the interesting bit. It assumes that the `callback` argument is in fact a `function`, and invokes it, passing in the `initialText` variable. If we run this code, we will get two messages logged to the console, as follows:

```
inside doSomethingWithCallback myText
inside callbackFunction myText
```

This output clearly shows that we enter into the `doSomethingWithACallback` function, log a message to the console, and then invoke the `callbackFunction`.

But what happens if we make a mistake, and do not pass a function as a callback when we should? There is nothing in the preceding code that signals to us that the second parameter of `doSomethingWithACallback` must be a function. If we inadvertently called the `doSomethingWithACallback` function with two strings, as shown in the following code snippet:

```
doSomethingWithACallback('myText', 'anotherText');
```

We would get a JavaScript runtime error:

TypeError: callback is not a function

Defensive-minded JavaScript programmers, however, would first check whether the `callback` parameter was in fact a function before invoking it, as follows:

```
function doSomethingWithACallback( initialText, callback ) {
    console.log('inside doSomethingWithCallback ' + initialText);
    if (typeof callback === "function") {
      callback(initialText);
    } else {
        console.log(initialText + ' is not a function !!')
    }
}
doSomethingWithACallback('myText'', ''anotherText'');
```

Note the third line of this code snippet, where we check the nature of the `callback` variable before invoking it. If it is not a function, we then log a message to the console. The output of the code snippet would be as follows:

inside doSomethingWithCallback myText
anotherText is not a function !!

JavaScript programmers, therefore, need to be careful when working with callbacks. Firstly, they need to code around the invalid use of callback functions, and secondly, they need to document and understand which parameters are, in fact, callbacks.

What if we could document our JavaScript callback functions in our code, and then warn users when they are not passing a function when one is expected? The type annotations for callback functions will do this for us, and generate compile errors when we break these rules. Let's take a look at how this is accomplished in TypeScript.

Function signatures

The TypeScript syntactic sugar that enforces strong typing on normal variables can also be used with callback functions. In order to do this, TypeScript introduces a new syntax, named the fat arrow syntax, `() =>`. When the fat arrow syntax is used, it means that one of the parameters to a function needs to be another function. Let's take a closer look at what this means. We will rewrite our previous JavaScript callback sample in TypeScript, as follows:

```
function callbackFunction(text: string) {
    console.log(`inside callbackFunction ${text}`);
}
```

We start with the initial callback function, which takes a single text parameter, and logs a message to the console when this function is called. We can then define the `doSomethingWithACallback` function, as follows:

```
function doSomethingWithACallback(
        initialText: string,
        callback : (initialText: string) => void
    ) {
    console.log(`inside doSomethingWithCallback ${initialText}`);
    callback(initialText);
}
```

Here, we have defined our `doSomethingWithACallback` function with two parameters. The first parameter is `initialText`, and is of type `string`. The second parameter is named `callback`, and now uses the fat arrow syntax to indicate that this parameter must be a function. Let's take a look at this syntax in a little more detail:

```
callback: (initialText: string) => void
```

The `callback` argument used here is typed (by the : syntax) to be a function, by using the fat arrow syntax, `() =>`. Additionally, this function takes a parameter named `initialText` that is of type `string`. To the right of the fat arrow syntax, we can see a new TypeScript basic type, called `void`. `void` is a keyword that is used to denote that a function does not return a value.

So, the `doSomethingWithACallback` function will only accept, as its second argument, a function that takes a single string parameter and returns `void`.

We can then use this function as follows:

```
doSomethingWithACallback("myText"", callbackFunction);
```

This code snippet is the same as was used in our JavaScript sample earlier. TypeScript will check the type of the `callbackFunction` parameter that was passed in, and ensure that it is, in fact, a function that accepts a single string as an argument, and does not return anything. If we try to invoke this `doSomethingWithACallback` incorrectly, say with two strings, as follows:

```
doSomethingWithACallback("myText", "this is not a function");
```

The compiler will generate the following message:

```
error TS2345: Argument of type '"this is not a function"' is not assignable
to parameter of type '(initialText: string) => void'.
```

This error message is clearly stating that the second argument, which is `"this is not a function"`, is not a function of the type `(initialText: string) => void`, as expected.

Given this function signature for the `callback` parameter, the following code would also generate compile time errors:

```
function callbackFunctionWithNumber(arg1: number) {
    console.log(`inside callbackFunctionWithNumber ${arg1}`)
}
doSomethingWithACallback("myText"", callbackFunctionWithNumber);
```

Here, we are defining a function named `callBackFunctionWithNumber`, that takes a number as its only parameter. When we attempt to compile this code, we will get an error message indicating that the `callback` parameter, which is now our `callBackFunctionWithNumber` function, also does not have the correct function signature, as follows:

```
error TS2345: Argument of type '(arg1: number) => void' is not assignable
to parameter of type '(initialText: string) => void'.
```

This error message is clearly stating that a parameter of type `(initialText: string) => void` is expected, but an argument of type `(arg1: number) => void` was used instead.

In function signatures, the parameter name (`arg1` or `initialText`) does not need to be the same. Only the number of parameters, their types, and the return type of the function need to be the same.

This is a very powerful feature of TypeScript – defining in code what the signatures of functions should be, and warning users when they do not call a function with the correct parameters. Defining types for functions also allows the IDE we are working in to offer Intellisense features that will notify us of the correct usage of a particular function as and when we are using it.

As we saw in our introduction to TypeScript, this can also be significant when we are working with third-party libraries. Instead of needing to keep a copy of the documentation handy when working with a library, we can use Intellisense features in a more powerful way. However, before we are able to use third-party functions, classes, or objects in TypeScript, we need to define what their function signatures are. These function definitions are put into a special type of TypeScript file, called a declaration file, and saved with a `.d.ts` extension. We will take an in-depth look at declaration files in `Chapter 5`, *Declaration Files and Strict Compiler Options*.

Function overrides

As JavaScript is a dynamic language, we can often call the same function with different argument types. Consider the following JavaScript code:

```
function add(x,y) {
    return x + y;
}

console.log('add(1,1)=' + add(1,1));
console.log('add("1","1")=' + add("1","1"));
```

Here, we are defining a simple add function that returns the sum of its two parameters, x and y. We are then simply logging the result of the add function with different types – two numbers and two strings. If we run the preceding code, we will see the following output:

```
add(1,1)=2
add("1","1")=11
```

In order to reproduce this ability to call the same function with different types, TypeScript introduces a specific syntax, called function overrides. If we were to replicate the preceding code in TypeScript, we would need to use this function override syntax, as follows:

```
function add(a: string, b: string) : string;
function add(a: number, b: number) : number;
function add(a: any, b: any): any {
    return a + b;
}

console.log(`add(1,1)= ${add(1,1)}`);
console.log(`add("1","1")= ${add("1","1")}`);
```

Here, we specify a function override signature for the add function that accepts two strings and returns a string. We then specify a second function override that uses the same function name but uses numbers as parameters. These two function overrides are then followed by the actual body of the function. The last two lines of this snippet are calling the add function, firstly with two numbers, and then with two strings. The output of this code is as follows:

```
add(1,1)= 2
add("1","1")= 11
```

There are three points of interest here. Firstly, none of the function signatures on the first two lines of the snippet actually have a function body. Secondly, the final function definition uses the type specifier of any and eventually includes the function body. To override functions in this way, we must follow this convention, and the final function signature (that includes the body of the function) must use the any type specifier, as anything else will generate compile-time errors.

The last point to note is that even though the final function body uses the type of any, this signature is essentially hidden by using this convention. We are actually limiting the add function to only accept either two strings, or two numbers. If we call the function with two boolean values, as follows:

```
console.log(`add(true,false)= ${add(true,false)}`);
```

TypeScript would generate compile errors:

```
error TS2345: Argument of type 'true' is not assignable to parameter of
type 'number'.
```

Try catch

TypeScript allows for for the use of `try... catch` blocks in the same way that JavaScript does. Consider the following code:

```
try {
    console.log(`1. attempting to parse JSON`);
    JSON.parse(`abcd=234`);
} catch (error) {
    console.log(`2. try catch error : ${error}`);
} finally {
    console.log(`3. finally`);
}
```

Here, within the `try` block, we are logging a message to the console, and then attempting to call a function that may or may not throw an error. The `JSON.parse` function will throw an error if it is unable to parse the input string as valid JSON. In this code block, we are deliberately causing an error by using an invalid JSON string. If an error is thrown, the `catch` block will execute, and then the `finally` block will execute, irrespective of whether an error was thrown. The output of this code snippet would be as follows:

```
1. attempting to parse JSON
2. try catch error : SyntaxError: Unexpected token a in JSON at position 0
3. finally
```

This output is as expected, and is logging the messages to the console in order.

We can also omit the error parameter from the `catch` block if we are not interested in what error has been thrown, as follows:

```
try {
    console.log(`1. attempting to parse JSON`);
    JSON.parse(`abcd=234`);
} catch {
    console.log(`2. caught`);
} finally {
    console.log(`3. finally`);
}
```

The output of this code would be as follows:

```
1. attempting to parse JSON
2. caught
3. finally
```

Advanced types

TypeScript also has some advanced language features that can be used when working with basic types and objects. These features allow us to mix and match types a little more, as well as to create new types that are combinations of other types. In this section of the chapter, we will take a quick look at these advanced type features, including the following:

- Union types
- Type guards
- Type aliases
- Null and undefined
- Never and unknown
- Object rest and spread
- Tuples
- BigInt

Union types

TypeScript allows us to express a type as the combination of two or more other types. These types are known as union types, and their declaration uses the pipe symbol (|) to list all of the types that will make up the new type. Consider the following TypeScript code:

```
var unionType : string | number;

unionType = 1;
console.log(`unionType : ${unionType}`);

unionType = "test";
console.log(`unionType : ${unionType}`);
```

Here, we have defined a variable named `unionType`, which uses the union type syntax to denote that it can hold either a `string` or a `number`. We are then assigning a number to this variable, and logging its value to the console. We then assign a string to this variable, and again log its value to the console. This code snippet will output the following:

```
unionType : 1
unionType : test
```

Using union types may seem a little strange at first. After all, why would a simple variable need to hold both a number and a string? Surely this is breaking our strong typing rules in some way. The benefits of union types, however, can be seen when using functions, or when calling REST endpoints that may return different response structures.

Type guards

When working with union types, the compiler will still apply its strong typing rules to ensure type safety. As an example of this, consider the following code:

```
function addWithUnion(
    arg1 : string | number,
    arg2 : string | number
) {
    return arg1 + arg2;
}
```

Here, we are defining a function named addWithUnion, which accepts two parameters, and returns their sum. The arg1 and arg2 arguments are union types, and can therefore be either a string or a number. Compiling this code, however, will generate the following error:

error TS2365: Operator '+' cannot be applied to types 'string | number' and 'string | number'.

What the compiler is telling us here is that within the body of the function, where it attempts to add arg1 to arg2, it cannot tell what type arg1 is at the point of trying to use it. Is it a string, or is it a number?

This is where type guards come in. A type guard is an expression that performs a check on our type, and then guarantees that type within its scope. Consider the following code:

```
function addWithTypeGuard(
    arg1 : string | number,
    arg2 : string | number
    ) : string | number
    {
    if( typeof arg1 ==="string") {
        // arg1 is treated as string within this code
        console.log('first argument is a string');
        return arg1 + arg2;
    }
    if (typeof arg1 === "number" && typeof arg2 === "number") {
        // arg1 and arg2 are treated as numbers within this code
        console.log('both arguments are numbers');
```

```
            return arg1 + arg2;
        }
        console.log('default return');
        return arg1.toString() + arg2.toString();
    }
```

Here, we have a function named `addWithTypeGuard` that takes two arguments, and is using our union type syntax to indicate that `arg1` and `arg2` can either be a `string` or a `number`.

Within the body of the code, we have two `if` statements. The first `if` statement checks to see whether the type of `arg1` is a string. If it is a string, then the type of `arg1` is treated as a string within the body of the `if` statement. The second `if` statement checks to see whether both `arg1` and `arg2` are of type `number`. Within the body of this second `if` statement, both `arg1` and `arg2` are treated as numbers. These two `if` statements are our type guards.

Note that our final return statement is calling the `toString` function on `arg1` and `arg2`. All basic JavaScript types have a `toString` function by default, so we are, in effect, treating both arguments as strings, and returning the result. Let's take a look at what happens when we call this function with different combinations of types:

```
console.log(`addWithTypeGuard(1,2)= ${addWithTypeGuard(1,2)}`) ;
```

Here, we are calling the function with two numbers, and receive the following output:

```
both arguments are numbers
addWithTypeGuard(1,2)= 3
```

This shows that the code has satisfied our second `if` statement. If we call the function with two strings, as follows:

```
console.log(`addWithTypeGuard("1","2")= ${addWithTypeGuard("1","2")}`) ;
```

We can see here that the first `if` statement is being satisfied:

```
first argument is a string
addWithTypeGuard("1","2")= 12
```

Lastly, when we call the function with a number and a string, as follows:

```
console.log(`addWithTypeGuard(1,"2") =
    ${addWithTypeGuard(1,"2""")}`) ;
```

In this case, both of our type guard statements return `false`, and so our default return code is being hit:

```
default return
addWithTypeGuard(1,"2")= 12
```

Type guards, therefore, allow you to check the type of a variable within your code, and then guarantee that the variable is of the type you expect within your block of code.

Type aliases

Sometimes, when using union types, it can be difficult to remember what types are allowed. To cater for this, TypeScript introduces the concept of a type alias, where we can create a special named type for a type union. A type alias is, therefore, a convenient naming convention for union types. Type aliases can be used wherever normal types are used, and are denoted by using the `type` keyword. We can, therefore, simplify the use of union types in our code as follows:

```
type StringOrNumber = string | number;

function addWithAlias(
    arg1 : StringOrNumber,
    arg2 : StringOrNumber
) {
    return arg1.toString() + arg2.toString();
}
```

Here, we have defined a type alias, named `StringOrNumber`, which is a union type that can be either a string or a number. We are then using this type alias in our function signature to allow both `arg1` and `arg2` to be either a string or a number.

Interestingly, type aliases can also be used for function signatures, as follows:

```
type CallbackWithString = (string) => void;

function usingCallbackWithString( callback: CallbackWithString) {
    callback("this is a string");
}
```

Here, we have defined a type alias, named `CallbackWithString`, which is a function that takes a single `string` parameter and returns a `void`. Our `usingCallbackWithString` function accepts this type alias (which is a function signature) as its `callback` argument type.

When we need to use union types frequently within our code, type aliases provide an easier and more intuitive way of declaring named union types.

Null and undefined

In JavaScript, if a variable has been declared, but not assigned a value, then querying its value will return undefined. JavaScript also includes the keyword null, in order to distinguish between cases where a variable is known, but has no value (null), and where it has not been defined in the current scope (undefined). Consider the following JavaScript code:

```
function testUndef(test) {
    console.log('test parameter :' + test);
}

testUndef();
testUndef(null);
```

Here, we have defined a function named testUndef, that takes a single argument named test. Within this function, we are simply logging the value to the console. We then call it in two different ways.

The first call to the testUndef function does not have any arguments. This is, in effect, calling the function without knowing, or without caring, what arguments it needs. Remember that arguments to JavaScript functions are optional. In this case, the value of the test argument within the testUndef function will be undefined, and the output will be as follows:

```
test parameter :undefined
```

The second call to the testUndef function passes null as the first argument. This is basically saying that we are aware that the function needs an argument, but we choose to call it without a value. The output of this function call will be as follows:

```
test parameter :null
```

TypeScript has included two keywords that we can use in these cases, named `null` and `undefined`. Let's rewrite this function in TypeScript, as follows:

```
function testUndef(test : null | number) {
    console.log('test parameter :' + test);
}
```

Here, we have defined the `testUndef` function to allow for the function to be called with either a `number` value, or a `null` value. If we try to call this function in TypeScript without any arguments, as we did in JavaScript:

```
testUndef();
```

TypeScript will generate an error:

error TS2554: Expected 1 arguments, but got 0.

Clearly, the TypeScript compiler is ensuring that we call the `testUndef` function with either a `number`, or `null`. It will not allow us to call it without any arguments.

This ability to specify that a function can be called with a `null` value allows us to ensure that the correct use of our function is known at compile time.

Similarly, we can define an object to allow `undefined` values, as follows:

```
let x : number | undefined;

x = 1;
x = undefined;
x = null;
```

Here, we have defined a variable named x, that is allowed to hold either a `number`, or `undefined`. We then attempt to assign the values `1`, `undefined`, and `null` to this variable. Compiling this code will result in the following TypeScript error:

error TS2322: Type 'null' is not assignable to type 'number | undefined'.

The TypeScript compiler, therefore, is protecting our code to ensure that the variable x can only hold either a `number` or `undefined`, while not allowing it to hold a `null` value.

Null operands

TypeScript will also check for null or undefined values when we use basic operands, such as addition, multiplication, less than, modulus, and power of. This can best be seen by using a simple example, as follows:

```
function testNullOperands(arg1: number, arg2: number | null | undefined) {
    let a = arg1 + arg2;
    let b = arg1 * arg2;
    let c = arg1 < arg2;
}
```

Here, we have defined a function named `testNullOperands` that takes two arguments, `arg1` and `arg2`, which can either be `number`, `null`, or `undefined`. Attempting to compile this code will result in a number of errors, as follows:

```
(92,20): error TS2533: Object is possibly 'null' or 'undefined'
(93,20): error TS2533: Object is possibly 'null' or 'undefined'
(94,20): error TS2533: Object is possibly 'null' or 'undefined'
```

TypeScript has generated an error for all three of our attempted computations. This is a very powerful extra source of type checking, and the key to these errors is that the argument `arg2` may be a valid `number`, or it may be `null` or `undefined`. The addition operator (+) will not allow us to attempt adding `null` to a number, nor will it allow us to add `undefined` to a number, hence the first error. The multiplication operator (*) and the less than operator (<) have the same constraints, which are generating the second and third errors.

TypeScript will detect where we are using operands, and ensure that both sides of the operands are valid numbers.

Never

TypeScript introduces a type in order to indicate instances where something should never occur. A typical example of this is where a function will always throw an error, and as such will never return a value. Consider the following code:

```
function alwaysThrows() {
    throw "this will always throw";
    return -1;
}
```

Here, we have defined a simple function named `alwaysThrows`. The first line of this function throws an error, and as such, the second line of this function will never be executed. This is valid TypeScript, but does indicate that there is a flaw in our logic, as the return statement will never be executed. We can guard against this by using the return type of `never` in our function definition as follows:

```
function alwaysThrows(): never {
    throw "this will always throw";
    return -1;
}
```

Here, we have used the `never` keyword to indicate that this function will never return a value. The compiler will now generate an error, as follows:

```
error TS2322: Type '-1' is not assignable to type 'never'
```

The error message is clearly stating that the function, which should return `never`, is trying to return the value −1. We have clearly stated the end effect of our function, which is that it will never return anything, and the compiler is helping us to enforce this.

A much more practical use of the `never` keyword is to trap flaws in our code logic that we know should never occur. As an example of this, consider the following code:

```
enum TestNeverEnum {
    FIRST,
    SECOND
}

function getEnumValue(value: TestNeverEnum): string {
    switch (value) {
        case TestNeverEnum.FIRST: return "First case";
    }
    let returnValue: never = value;
}
```

Here, we have defined an enum named `TestNeverEnum` that has two values, `FIRST` and `SECOND`. We then define a function named `getEnumValue` that is designed to return a `string` based on the enum value passed in. After the `switch` statement, we define a value named `returnValue`, of type `never`, and assign the incoming `value` argument to it. This code will generate a compile error as follows:

```
error TS2322: Type 'TestNeverEnum.SECOND' is not assignable to type 'never'
```

What is happening here is that our `switch` statement is not handling the case of `TestNeverEnum.SECOND`. This logic flaw means that the flow of code will actually drop down to the `let returnValue : never = value` line. As we have used `never` as a type here, the compiler is generating the error. This code needs to be fixed as follows:

```
function getEnumValue(value: TestNeverEnum): string {
    switch (value) {
        case TestNeverEnum.FIRST: return "First case";
        case TestNeverEnum.SECOND: return "Second case";
    }
    let returnValue: never = value;
}
```

Here, we have added a `case` statement for the `TestNeverEnum.SECOND` value, and therefore, the last line of code will never be executed.

Using `never` as a type in this instance helps us to guard against logic flaws in our code. In large and long-lived projects, this can occur quite often. Enums, in particular, are constantly getting added to as project requirements grow. By using `never` in these instances, we can trap logic errors where we have modified an enum, but have not added the correct switch cases correctly.

Unknown

In a similar vein to `never`, TypeScript 3 introduces a type named `unknown`. The `unknown` type can be seen as a type-safe equivalent of the type `any`. In other words, before we use a variable that has been marked as `unknown`, we must explicitly cast it to a known type. Let's explore the similarities between `unknown` and `any`, as follows:

```
let unknownType: unknown = "an unknown string";
console.log(`unknownType : ${unknownType}`);

unknownType = 1;
console.log(`unknownType : ${unknownType}`);
```

Here, we have defined a variable named `unknownType`, and assigned a `string` value to it. We then log its value to the console. Note that we have also explicitly typed this variable to be of type `unknown`.

We then assign a numeric value of 1 to the `unknownType` variable, and again log its value to the console. The type behavior of this variable is the same as `any`, in that we can reassign its type on the fly. The output of this code is as follows:

```
unknownType : an unknown string
unknownType : 1
```

As we can see from the output, the value of the `unknownType` variable has changed from a `string` to a `number`, similar to the `any` type.

If, however, we attempt to assign the `unknownType` variable to a known type, we start to see the difference between `any` and `unknown`, as follows:

```
let numberType: number;
numberType = unknownType;
```

Here, we have a variable named `numberType`, which is of type `number`, and we are attempting to assign the value of `unknownType` to it. This will generate the following error:

```
error TS2322: Type 'unknown' is not assignable to type 'number'
```

To fix this error, we will need to explicitly cast the `unknownType` variable to a `number` type as follows:

```
numberType = <number>unknownType;
```

Note the explicit cast on the right-hand side of the assignment operator, `<number>unknownType`. This code compiles without error.

Again, the `unknown` type is seen as a type-safe version of the `any` type, as we are forced to explicitly cast from an unknown type to a known type before we make use of a variable.

Object rest and spread

When working with basic JavaScript objects, we often need to copy the properties of one object to another, or do some mixing and matching of properties from various objects. Similar to the way that we defined a function as having a variable number of arguments, we can use this same syntax on standard objects. This technique is called **object rest and spread**. Consider the following TypeScript code:

```
let firstObj = { id: 1, name: "firstObj" };

let secondObj = { ...firstObj };
console.log(`secondObj : ${JSON.stringify(secondObj)}`);
```

Here, we start by defining a simple JavaScript object named `firstObj`, that has an `id` and a `name` property. We then use the new ES7 syntax to copy all of the properties of `firstObj` into another object called `secondObj`, by using the rest syntax, which is three dots preceding the variable `{ ...firstObj }`. To test that this has indeed copied all properties, we then log the value of the `secondObj` variable to the console. The output of this code is as follows:

```
secondObj : {"id":1,"name":"firstObj"}
```

Here, we can see that the values of the `id` and `name` properties have been copied from `firstObj` into `secondObj`, using the rest ES7 syntax.

We can also use this syntax to combine multiple objects together. This is known as object spread, as follows:

```
let nameObj = { name: "nameObj" };
let idObj = { id: 2 };

let obj3 = { ...nameObj, ...idObj };
console.log(`obj3 : ${JSON.stringify(obj3)}`);
```

Here, we have an object named `nameObj`, which defines a single property named `name`. We then define a second object named `idObj` that defines a single property named `id`. We then create `obj3`, out of `nameObj` and `idObj`, by using the rest syntax `{ ...nameObj, ...idObj }`. This syntax means that we intend to copy all properties from `nameObj`, and all properties from `idObj` into a new object named `obj3`. The result of this code is as follows:

```
obj3 : {"name":"nameObj","id":2}
```

This shows us that both objects' properties have been merged into a single object, using object spread.

Spread precedence

When using object spread, properties will be copied incrementally. In other words, if two objects both have a property with the same name, then the object property that was specified last will take precedence. As an example of this, consider the following code:

```
let objPrec1 = { id: 1, name: "object prec 1" };
let objPrec2 = { id: 1001, description: "object prec 2 descripton" }

let obj4 = { ...objPrec1, ...objPrec2 };
console.log(`obj4 : ${JSON.stringify(obj4)}`);
```

Here, we have defined two objects named `objPrec1` and `objPrec2`. Note that both have an `id` property, but `objPrec1` has a `name` property, and `objPrec2` has a `description` property. As we have already seen, the rest and spread syntax will combine the properties of both objects, but what does it do with the `id` property? Should it be `1` or `1001`? The rest and spread syntax will use the last defined property value. This can be seen by running this code, and checking the `obj4` object, as follows:

```
obj4 : {"id":1001,"name":"object prec 1","description":"object prec 2
descripton"}
```

Here, we can see that `obj4` has taken the value of `1001` for the `id` property, as expected.

Rest and spread with arrays

Interestingly enough, the rest and spread syntax can also be used with arrays. Consider the following code:

```
let firstArray = [1, 2, 3, 4, 5];
console.log(`firstArray=${firstArray}`);

firstArray = [...firstArray, 6, 7, 8];
console.log(`firstArray=${firstArray}`);
```

Here, we have defined an array name `firstArray` that has five elements, which are the numbers `1` through `5`. We are then logging this array to the console. Note the next line of this code snippet, where we are using the rest syntax to append the values `6`, `7`, and `8` to the existing array. We are then logging the `firstArray` array to the console. The output of this code is as follows:

```
firstArray=1,2,3,4,5
firstArray=1,2,3,4,5,6,7,8
```

As we can see, the values `6`, `7`, and `8` have been appended to the original array, all through using the rest and spread syntax in a slightly novel form. Note that this syntax can be used with arrays of any type, and can also be used as a substitute for array elements. Consider the following code:

```
let secondArray = [
    { id: 1, name: "name1" },
    { id: 2, name: "name2" }
]
console.log(`secondArray : ${JSON.stringify(secondArray)}`);

secondArray = [
```

```
      { id: -1, name: "name-1" },
      ...secondArray,
      { id: 3, name: "name3" },
];
console.log(`secondArray : ${JSON.stringify(secondArray)}`);
```

Here, we start with an array named secondArray that contains an array of complex types, where each type has an id and a name property, which we then log to the console.

Note, however, the third line of this code snippet. We are using the rest and spread syntax to redefine the elements that are in the array. This array now contains an element with an id property of -1, then all elements of the original array (using the rest . . . syntax), and then an element with an id property of 3. The output of this code snippet is as follows:

```
secondArray : [{"id":1,"name":"name1"},{"id":2,"name":"name2"}]
secondArray :
[{"id":-1,"name":"name-1"},{"id":1,"name":"name1"},{"id":2,"name":"name2"},
{"id":3,"name":"name3"}]
```

As can be seen from the output, the secondArray array started out with only two elements, and then, by using the rest and spread syntax, we have inserted an element at the beginning of the array, and an element at the end of the array.

Tuples

Tuples are a method of defining a type that has a finite number of unnamed properties. Each property has an associated type. When using a tuple, each one of these properties must be provided. This can be best explained in an example, as follows:

```
let tupleType: [string, boolean];
tupleType = ["test", false];
tupleType = ["test"];
```

Here, we have defined a variable named tupleType, whose type is defined as an array of types, the first of which is a string, and the second of which is a boolean. We then assign a value to the variable tupleType, and are using an array syntax to set the first property to the string "test", and the second property to the boolean value false. Note that on the last line of this snippet, we are attempting to assign a value to the tupleType variable that only has a string property. This last line will generate an error as follows:

```
error TS2322: Type '[string]' is not assignable to type '[string, boolean]'
```

What this error is showing us is that to use a tuple, each of the tuple's properties must be set, and that it is seen by the compiler as a type with two properties.

Tuples are generally used when we need to temporarily associate two normally unrelated properties.

Tuple destructuring

As tuples use the array syntax, they can be destructured, or disassembled, in two ways. The first is by means of simple array syntax as follows:

```
console.log(`tupleType[0] : ${tupleType[0]}`);
console.log(`tupleType[1] : ${tupleType[1]}`);
```

Here, we are simply logging each property of the `tupleType` variable to the console by referencing its index within the array, that is, `tupleType[0]` and `typleType[1]`. The output of this code would be as follows:

```
tupleType[0] : test
tupleType[1] : false
```

So we have now created a tuple with a string and boolean value, and destructured it with array syntax. Note that because we are using array syntax, we are able to interrogate the third property of this tuple as follows:

```
console.log(`tupleType[2] : ${tupleType[2]}`);
```

As our tuple does not have a third property, `typleType[2]` will be undefined, as can be seen in the output of this line of code:

```
tupleType[2] : undefined
```

This is obviously not ideal.

A better way of destructuring a tuple is to use the array syntax to create a matching tuple on the left-hand side of the assignment, as follows:

```
let [t1, t2] = tupleType;
console.log(`t1: ${t1}`);
console.log(`t2: ${t2}`);
```

Here, we are defining an array of two elements, named `t1` and `t2`, and assigning the value of the tuple to this array. We then log both `t1` and `t2` to the console. The output of this code is as follows:

```
t1: test
t2: false
```

This method of destructuring a tuple is preferred for a simple reason. We cannot define an array of elements that exceeds the number of properties in a tuple. Hence, the following code would not work:

```
let [et1, et2, et3] = tupleType;
```

Here, we are attempting to destructure our two-property tuple into a three-property tuple. The compiler, in this case, will generate the following error:

```
error TS2493: Tuple type '[string, boolean]' with length '2' cannot be
assigned to tuple with length '3'
```

Optional tuple elements

Similar to function signatures, we can also have optional tuple elements. This is achieved by using the `?` symbol within a tuple definition, as follows:

```
let optionalTuple: [string, boolean?];
optionalTuple = ["test2", true];
console.log(`optionalTuple : ${optionalTuple}`);
optionalTuple = ["test"];
console.log(`optionalTuple : ${optionalTuple}`);
```

Here, we have a defined variable named `optionalTuple` that has a mandatory `string` property, and an optional `boolean` property. We then assign a value of `["test2", true]` to it, and log it to the console. We are then assigning a value of `["test"]` to the same tuple, and log the value to the console. As the second property of the `optionalTuple` is, in fact, optional, this code will compile cleanly, and produce the following results, as expected:

```
optionalTuple : test2,true
optionalTuple : test
```

Tuples and rest syntax

Tuples can also use rest syntax, both in function definitions and in object rest and spread. As an example of using tuples and rest in a function definition, consider the following code:

```
function useTupleAsRest(...args: [number, string, boolean]) {
    let [arg1, arg2, arg3] = args;
    console.log(`arg1: ${arg1}`);
    console.log(`arg2: ${arg2}`);
    console.log(`arg3: ${arg3}`);
}

useTupleAsRest(1, "stringValue", false);
```

Here, we have defined a function named `useTupleAsRest`, which is using rest syntax, but also defining the `args` parameter as a tuple. This allows us to destructure the tuple into three variables named `arg1`, `arg2`, and `arg3` on the first line of this function. We then log all three values to the console. When we call this function, we must provide three values that match the tuple types. The output of this code is as follows:

arg1: 1
arg2: stringValue
arg3: false

Note that because the rest parameter is now a tuple, we will get compile errors if we attempt to call this function with anything other than a `number`, `string`, or `boolean` combination.

The second manner in which we can use rest syntax with tuples is in their definition. Consider the following code:

```
type RestTupleType = [number, ...string[]];
let restTuple: RestTupleType = [1, "string1", "string2", "string3"];
```

Here, we have defined a type named `RestTupleType`, which is a tuple with the first property of a number, and then a variable number of strings (using rest syntax). We are then creating a variable named `restTuple` with the number 1, and the strings `"string1"`, `"string2"`, and `"string3"` as properties.

Bigint

Proposals to the ECMAScript standard have recently included support for handling really large numbers. Most programming languages already natively support 64 bit numbers, but JavaScript has lagged behind in this respect, and currently only supports numbers that are at 53 bit precision. The reasons for this particular constraint are quite detailed, and boil down to the internal representation that JavaScript uses to store numbers in memory. Any number representation in memory needs to take into account both the sign, either positive or negative, and the precision of a number, or in other words the number of decimal places. In JavaScript, the largest number that can be used when using 53 bit precision is $9,007,199,254,740,991$, which, in layman's terms, is:

Nine quadrillion, seven trillion, one hundred ninety nine billion, two hundred fifty four million, seven hundred forty thousand, nine hundred ninety one. This is a really, really, really, large number.

While we may not need to work with nine quadrillion possible different values in our code, these types of numbers do come up in certain circumstances. We only need to look at modern cryptography routines to find examples. If your application is working with a bank, for instance, the bank may generate some sort of numeric token that is encrypted with an advanced cryptography routine, in order to represent the unique transaction ID for a particular payment. The larger this number is, the more difficult it is to decrypt, and the more secure the system. Obtaining a 64 bit number as a unique ID is therefore quite feasible.

Let's take a look at the limits of the current `number` type in JavaScript, with the following code:

```
console.log(`Number.MAX_SAFE_INTEGER : ${Number.MAX_SAFE_INTEGER}`);

let highest53bitNumber = 9_007_199_254_740_991;

for (let i = 0; i < 10; i++) {
 console.log(`${i} : ${highest53bitNumber + i}`);
}
```

Here, we start by logging the value of the constant named `Number.MAX_SAFE_INTEGER` to the console. This constant will return a number that is the maximum value of an integer that JavaScript supports. We then define a variable named `highest53bitNumber` and set it to this maximum value. The code then executes a simple `for` loop that adds the numbers 0 through 9 to this number, and logs the results to the console. The output of this code is as follows:

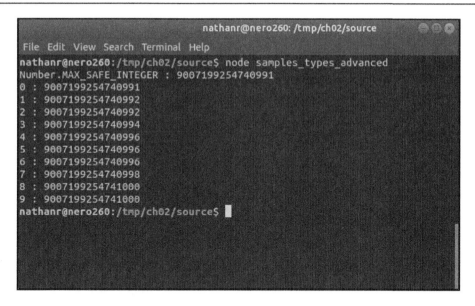

Here, we can see some pretty strange results. Adding the value 2 to the variable `highest53bitNumber`, or adding the value 1, surprisingly produce the same result. Adding the value 4 or 5 or 6 also produces the same result. What we are seeing here are the results of attempting to perform simple arithmetic on numbers that are beyond the `Number.MAX_SAFE_INTEGER` limit supported in JavaScript. As JavaScript does not support numbers beyond this limit, the results are indeterminate.

The latest versions of the ECMAScript standard have implemented a new basic type named `bigint` in order to handle these sorts of really large numbers. Let's take a look at the same loop we discussed in our previous code snippet using `bigint` as follows:

```
console.log(`using bigint :`);

let bigIntNumber: bigint = 9_007_199_254_740_991n;

for (let i = 0; i < 10; i++) {
  console.log(`${i} : ${bigIntNumber + BigInt(i)}`);
}
```

Here, we have defined a variable named `bigIntNumber`, and specified that it is of the `bigint` type. The `bigint` type is an addition to the basic types of `string`, `number`, and `boolean`, and is treated in the same way. This means that we cannot assign a `number` type to a `bigint` type in the same what that we cannot assign a `string` type to a `number` type. Note the definition of the value for this `bigint`. We have appended the letter `n` to the numeric value in order for the compiler to recognize that we are defining a `bigint` value.

Our loop is similar to the previous code snippet in that it is looping through the values 0 to 9, and adding this value to our `bigIntNumber` variable, and then logging the results to the console. Note, however that we need to create a `bigint` value from the variable `i`, which is actually of type `number`. This is accomplished by calling the `BigInt` static function, and passing our number type in as an argument. In other words, `BigInt(i)` is converting the variable `i`, which is of type `number`, to a type of `bigint`. Running this code now produces the following results:

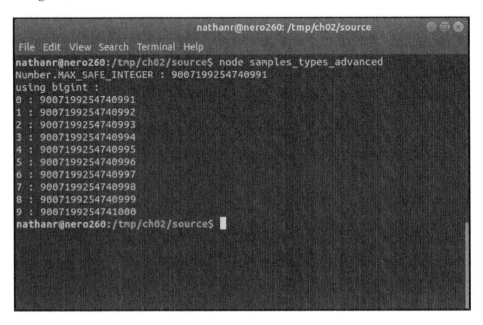

Here, we can see that using the new native `bigint` type, we are able to perform arithmetic calculations on numbers that are higher than the allowed 53 bit precision.

The implementation of `bigint` has not been back-ported by the TypeScript compiler to either ES5 or ES3, or anything below Esnext. This means that we must target `esnext` in our `tsconfig.json` file in order to successfully compile code that uses the `bigint` type. A further word of caution on this matter is that only two JavaScript runtime engines have implemented support for the `bigint` type as at the time of writing, so it really is bleeding-edge. You will need to run either the latest version of Chrome or Node version 11 and upward in order to use the `bigint` type.

Summary

In this chapter, we took a look at TypeScript's basic types, variables, and function techniques. We saw how TypeScript introduces syntactic sugar on top of normal JavaScript code to ensure strongly typed variables and function signatures. We also saw how TypeScript uses duck typing and explicit casting, and then discussed TypeScript functions, function signatures, and overrides. We completed the chapter with a discussion on advanced type techniques, including type guards, object rest and spread, tuples, and `bigint`.

In the next chapter, we will build on this knowledge and see how TypeScript extends these strongly typed rules into object-oriented concepts, such as interfaces, classes, and inheritance.

3
Interfaces, Classes, and Inheritance

We have already seen how TypeScript uses basic types, inferred types, function signatures and tuples to bring a strongly typed development experience to JavaScript. This strongly typed paradigm also includes object-oriented features that are similar to other languages, such as interfaces, classes, and inheritance. Where TypeScript has always had language constructs for interfaces and classes, these object-oriented features have only recently been ratified with the ECMAScript six standard. This means that, in order to use these object-oriented features in JavaScript, our target environment must support the ES6 standard. TypeScript, however, will take care of generating ES3 or ES5-compatible JavaScript. This means that, no matter what JavaScript runtime we are targeting, we are able to use all of the goodness of object-oriented TypeScript to design and build our applications. In this chapter, we will look at these object-oriented concepts, how they are used in TypeScript, and what benefits they bring to the JavaScript development experience.

This chapter is broken up into two main sections. The first section of this chapter is intended for readers who are using TypeScript for the first time, and covers interfaces, classes, and inheritance from the ground up. The second section of this chapter builds on this knowledge, and shows how to create and use classes, interfaces, and inheritance by building a sample **Factory Design pattern**.

If you have experience with TypeScript, are actively using interfaces and classes, and understand inheritance, then by all means skim through this chapter. You may be more interested in some of the keywords that TypeScript provides to compare the structure of classes, such as weak types, the `instanceof` operator, or the `in` operator. The later sections of the chapter discuss the Factory Design Pattern, and abstract classes.

This chapter will cover the following topics:

- Interfaces
- Weak types
- The `in` operator
- Classes
- Class constructors
- Class modifiers
- Static functions and properties
- Inheritance
- Abstract classes
- JavaScript closures
- `Instanceof` and type guards
- The Factory Design Pattern

Interfaces

An interface provides us with a mechanism to define what properties and methods an object must implement, and is, therefore, a way of defining a custom type. We have already explored the TypeScript syntax for strongly typing a variable to one of the basic types, such as a string or number. Using this syntax, we can also strongly type a variable to be of a custom type, or more correctly, an interface type. This means that the variable must have the same properties as described in the interface. If an object adheres to an interface, it is said that the object implements the interface. Interfaces are defined by using the `interface` keyword.

To illustrate the concept of interfaces, consider the following code:

```
interface IComplexType {
    id: number;
    name: string;
}
```

We start with an interface named `IComplexType` that has an `id` and a `name` property. The `id` property is strongly typed to be of type `number`, and the `name` property is of type `string`. This interface definition can then be applied to a variable, as follows:

```
let complexType : IComplexType;
complexType = { id: 1, name : "test" };
```

Here, we have defined a variable named `complexType`, and strongly typed it to be of type `IComplexType`. We are then creating an object instance, and assigning values to the object's properties. Note that the `IComplexType` interface defines both an `id` and a `name` property, and as such both must be present. If we attempt to create an instance of the object without both of these properties, as follows:

```
let incompleteType : IComplexType;
incompleteType = { id : 1};
```

TypeScript will generate the following error:

```
error TS2322: Type '{ id: number; }' is not assignable to type
'IComplexType'.
Property 'name' is missing in type '{ id: number; }'.
```

Optional properties

Interface definitions may also include optional properties, similar to the way that functions may have optional properties. Consider the following interface definition:

```
interface IOptionalProp {
    id: number;
    name?: string;
}
```

Here, we have defined an interface named `IOptionalProp`, which has an `id` property of type number, and an optional property called `name` that is of type `string`. Note how the syntax for optional properties is similar to what we have seen for optional parameters in function definitions. In other words, the `?` character after the `name` property is used to specify that this property is optional. We can therefore use this interface definition, as follows:

```
let idOnly : IOptionalProp = { id: 1 };
let idAndName : IOptionalProp = { id: 2, name : "idAndName" };

idAndName = idOnly;
```

Here, we have two variables, both of which are implementing the `IOptionalProp` interface. The first variable, named `idOnly`, is just specifying the `id` property. This is valid TypeScript, as we have marked the `name` property of the `IOptionalProp` interface as optional. The second variable is named `idAndName`, and is specifying both the `id` and `name` properties. Note the last line of this code snippet. Because both variables are implementing the `IOptionalProp` interface, we are able to assign them to each other. Without using an interface definition that has optional properties, this code would normally have caused an error.

If you are using an editor that has support for TypeScript, you should start to see some autocomplete or IntelliSense options popping up as you work with interfaces. This is because your editor is using TypeScript's language service to automatically pick up what type you are working with, and what properties and functions are available, as follows:

```
hello_ch03.ts - ch03 - Visual Studio Code

● hello_ch03.ts

20  // Optional properties
21  // ======================
22  interface IOptionalProp {
23      id: number;
24      name?: string;
25  }
26
27  var idOnly : IOptionalProp = { id: 1 };
28  var idAndName : IOptionalProp = { id: 2, name : "idAndName" };
29
30  idAndName = idOnly;
31
32  idOnly.
33           id
34           name  (property) IOptionalProp.name: string
35
36
37
38
39
40

master*              1    0              Ln 32, Col 8   UTF-8   LF   TypeScript
```

Here, we can see that the VSCode editor is using IntelliSense to automatically show us what properties are available on the idOnly variable. As it is defined as implementing the IOptionalProp interface, it has two available properties, which are shown by the editor.

Interface compilation

Interfaces are a compile-time language feature of TypeScript, and the compiler does not generate any JavaScript code from interfaces that you include in your TypeScript projects. Interfaces are only used by the compiler for type checking during the compilation step.

 In this book, we will be sticking to a simple naming convention for interfaces, which is to prefix the interface name with the letter I. Using this naming scheme helps when dealing with large projects where code is spread across multiple files. Seeing anything prefixed with I in your code helps you distinguish it as an interface immediately. You can, however, use any naming standard for your interfaces.

Weak types

When an interface contains only optional properties, it is considered a weak type. In other words, if we create an object that implements a weak type interface, can we really say that the object implements the interface? Let's consider some code to find out, as follows:

```
interface IWeakType {
    id?: number,
    name?: string
}

let weakTypeNoOverlap: IWeakType;
weakTypeNoOverlap = { description: "my description" };
```

Here, we have defined an interface named IWeakType that contains two properties, named id and name. As both of these properties are optional, this interface is considered to be a weak type. We then define a variable named weakTypeNoOverlap, and specify this object to be of type IWeakType. On the last line of this code, we assign a value to this variable that has a description property. Note that there is no overlap between the properties we have assigned to the variable and the interface that it is supposed to be implementing.

In this case, the TypeScript compiler will generate the following error:

```
error TS2322: Type '{ description: string; }' is not assignable to type
'IWeakType'.
Object literal may only specify known properties, and 'description' does
not exist in type 'IWeakType'.
```

Here, we can see that the compiler is detecting that the `weakTypeNoOverlap` variable must implement the `IWeakType` interface, or at least some part of it. As there is no overlap between the properties of the `IWeakType` interface and the variable assignment, the assignment will generate an error.

Type inference with the in operator

TypeScript also allows us to test an object for the presence of a property using the `in` operator. Imagine that we have the following interfaces:

```
interface IHasIdAndNameProperty {
    id: number;
    name: string;
}

interface IHasDescAndValueProperty {
    description: string;
    value: number;
}
```

Here, we have an interface named `IHasIdAndNameProperty` that defines an `id` and a `name` property. We also have an interface named `IHasDescAndValueProperty` that defines a `description` and `value` property. We can then write a function that can work with both interfaces, as follows:

```
function printNameOrDescription(
    value: IHasIdAndNameProperty
        | IHasDescAndValueProperty) {
    if ('id' in value) {
        console.log(`found id ! | name : ${value.name}`);
    }
    if ('value' in value) {
        console.log(`found value ! : description :
            ${value.description}`);
    }
}
```

Here, we have a function named `printNameOrDescription` that has a single argument named `value`. The type of the `value` argument is a union of the `IHasIdAndNameProperty` interface and the `IHasDescAndValueProperty` interface. Note that there is no overlap in properties between the two interfaces, so how do we tell which interface was passed in? In this case, we are using a type guard that is using the `in` operator:

```
if ('id' in value)
```

Our first type guard is testing the argument that is being passed in, and checking for the presence of a property named `id`. If this is true, then we know that the type that was passed in was of the `IHasIdAndNameProperty` type, and can therefore print the value of the `name` property to the console. Similarly, the second type guard is testing for the presence of the `value` property:

```
if ('value' in value)
```

If the `value` property is found, then we know that the nature of the `value` argument is of the `IHasDescAndNameProperty` type, and can log the value of the `description` property to the console.

Hence, TypeScript allows us to generate type guards for interfaces using the `in` operator, to test whether an interface has a particular property.

Classes

A class is a definition of an object, what data it holds, and what operations it can perform. Classes and interfaces form a cornerstone of the principles of object-oriented programming. Let's take a look at a simple class definition:

```
class SimpleClass {
    id: number;
    print() : void {
        console.log(`SimpleClass.print() called`);
    }
}
```

Here, we have used the `class` keyword to define a class named `SimpleClass`, and we have defined this class to have a property named `id`, and a `print` function. The `id` property has been defined as type `number`. The `print` function simply logs a message to the console. Note that all we have done here is to define what data this class can hold, and what it can do. If we attempt to compile this code, however, we will generate an error, as follows:

```
error TS2564: Property 'id' has no initializer and is not definitely
assigned in the constructor
```

What this error is indicating is that the `id` property, without being explicitly set, can in effect, still be `undefined`. If we attempt to use the `id` property, and it has not been set to a numeric value, then we might get a surprise if it is `undefined`. There are a number of ways to handle this error, but, for the time being, we can simply make the `id` property a type union, as follows:

```
id: number | undefined;
```

By adding the type union here, we are therefore making a conscious decision that we are going to allow the `id` property to possibly be `undefined`. This is an example of how the TypeScript compiler can pick up errors within our code that we may not have thought of initially.

In order to use this class definition, we need to create an instance of this class, which can be done as follows:

```
let mySimpleClass = new SimpleClass();
mySimpleClass.print();
```

Here, we define a variable named `mySimpleClass` to hold an instance of the `SimpleClass` class, and we then create this class using the `new` keyword. Once an instance of this class has been created, we can then call the `print` function on our class instance. The output of this code would be as follows:

```
SimpleClass.print() called
```

Class properties

A class is the definition of an object, and as such, includes the data that it can hold, in the form of class properties. These properties can be accessed by users of this class, if we so wish, or can be marked as not accessible. Regardless of what their accessibility rules are, code within the class will need to access these class properties. In order to access the properties of a class from within the class itself, we need to use the `this` keyword. As an example, let's update our `SimpleClass` definition, and print out the value of the `id` property within the `print` function, as follows:

```
class SimpleClass {
    id: number | undefined;
    print() : void {
        console.log(`SimpleClass has id : ${this.id}`);
    }
}
```

Here, we have modified the `print` function to reference the `id` property of the class instance within the template string, `${this.id}`. Whenever we are inside a class instance, we must use the `this` keyword in order to access any property or function available on the class definition. The `this` keyword, therefore, indicates to the compiler that we are referencing a class property, or class function.

Once we have created an instance of the class, we can set the `id` property, and then call the updated `print` function, as follows:

```
let mySimpleClass = new SimpleClass();
mySimpleClass.id = 1001;
mySimpleClass.print();
```

The output of this code will be as follows:

```
SimpleClass has id : 1001
```

Here, we have set the `id` property of the `mySimpleClass` variable, and have seen how the `print` function can access the `id` property from within the definition of the class itself in order to print the value to the console.

Implementing interfaces

Before we continue exploring classes, let's take a look at the relationship between classes and interfaces. A class is a definition of an object, including its properties and functions. An interface is the definition of a custom type, also including its properties and functions. The only real difference is that classes must implement functions and properties, whereas interfaces only describe them. This allows us to use interfaces to describe some common behavior of a group of classes, and then write code that will work with any one of these classes. Consider the following class definitions:

```
class ClassA {
    print() { console.log('ClassA.print()') };
}

class ClassB {
    print() { console.log(`ClassB.print()`)};
}
```

Here we have class definitions for two classes, `ClassA` and `ClassB`. Both of these classes just have a `print` function. Suppose that we wanted to write some code that did not really care what type of class we used, all it cared about was whether the class had a `print` function. Instead of writing a complex class that needed to deal with instances of both `ClassA` and `ClassB`, we can easily create an interface describing the behavior we need, as follows:

```
interface IPrint {
    print() : void;
}

function printClass( a : IPrint ) {
    a.print();
}
```

Here, we have created an interface named `IPrint` to describe the attributes of an object that we need within the `printClass` function. This interface has a single function named `print`. Therefore, any variable that is passed in as an argument to the `printClass` function must itself have a function named `print`.

We can now modify our class definitions to ensure that they can both be used by the `printClass` function, as follows:

```
class ClassA implements IPrint {
    print() { console.log('ClassA.print()') };
}

class ClassB implements IPrint {
    print() { console.log(`ClassB.print()`)};
}
```

Our class definitions now use the `implements` keyword to implement the `IPrint` interface. This allows us to use both classes within the `printClass` function, as follows:

```
let classA = new ClassA();
let classB = new ClassB();

printClass(classA);
printClass(classB);
```

Here, we are creating instances of `ClassA` and `ClassB`, and then calling the same `printClass` function with both instances. Because the `printClass` function is written to accept any object that implements the `IPrint` interface, it will work correctly with both class types.

Interfaces, therefore, are a way of describing class behavior. Interfaces can also be seen as a type of contract that classes must implement, if they are expected to provide certain behaviors.

Class constructors

Classes can accept parameters during their initial construction. This allows us to combine the creation of a class and the setting of its parameters into a single line of code. Consider the following class definition:

```
class ClassWithConstructor {
    id: number;
    name: string;
    constructor(_id: number, _name: string) {
        this.id = _id;
        this.name = _name;
    }
}
```

Here, we have defined a class named `ClassWithConstructor` that has two properties, an id property of type `number`, and a name property of type `string`. It also has a `constructor` function that accepts two parameters. The constructor function is assigning the value of the `_id` argument to the class property of id, and the value of the `_name` argument to the class property, name. Note that, because we are initializing both the id and name properties within the class constructor, we know that any class created will have set a value for these properties. We therefore do not need to use the `unspecified` type in this instance.

We can then construct an instance of this class as follows:

```
var classWithConstructor = new ClassWithConstructor(1, "name");

console.log(`classWithConstructor =
    ${JSON.stringify(classWithConstructor)}`);
```

The first line of this code creates an instance of the `ClassWithConstructor` class, using the constructor function. We are then simply logging a JSON version of this class to the console. The output of this code is as follows:

```
classWithConstructor = {"id":1,"name":"name"}
```

Class functions

All functions within a class adhere to the syntax and rules that we covered in the previous chapter on functions. As a refresher of these rules, all class functions can:

- Be strongly typed
- Use the `any` keyword to relax strong typing
- Have `Optional` parameters
- Have `Default` parameters
- Use argument arrays, or the rest parameter syntax
- Allow function callbacks and specify the function callback signature
- Allow function overloads

As an example of each of these rules, let's examine a class that has a number of different function signatures, and we will then discuss each one in detail, as follows:

```
class ComplexType implements IComplexType {
    id: number;
    name: string;
    constructor(idArg: number, nameArg: string);
    constructor(idArg: string, nameArg: string);
    constructor(idArg: any, nameArg: any) {
        this.id = idArg;
        this.name = nameArg;
    }
    print(): string {
        return "id:" + this.id + " name:" + this.name;
    }
    usingTheAnyKeyword(arg1: any): any {
        this.id = arg1;
    }
    usingOptionalParameters(optionalArg1?: number) {
        if (optionalArg1) {
            this.id = optionalArg1;
        }
    }
    usingDefaultParameters(defaultArg1: number = 0) {
        this.id = defaultArg1;
    }
    usingRestSyntax(...argArray: number []) {
        if (argArray.length > 0) {
            this.id = argArray[0];
        }
    }
    usingFunctionCallbacks( callback: (id: number) => string ) {
        callback(this.id);
    }

}
```

The first thing to note is the `constructor` function. Our class definition is using function overriding for the `constructor` function, allowing the class to be constructed using either a `number` and a `string`, or two strings. The following code shows how we would use each of these constructor definitions:

```
let ct_1 = new ComplexType(1, "ct_1");
let ct_2 = new ComplexType("abc", "ct_2");
let ct_3 = new ComplexType(true, "test");
```

The ct_1 variable uses the number, string variant of the constructor function, and the ct_2 variable uses the string, string variant. The ct_3 variable will generate a compile error, as we are not allowing a constructor to use a boolean, boolean variant. You may argue, however, that the last constructor function specifies an any, any variant and this should allow for our boolean, boolean usage. Just remember that constructor overloads follow the same rules as function overloads that we discussed in Chapter 2, *Types, Variables, and Function Techniques,* so this is not allowed.

We must be careful when using constructor overrides, however. Let's take a closer look at what happens when we call the string, string variant of the constructor:

```
let ct_2 = new ComplexType("abc", "ct_2");
ct_2.print();
```

Within the constructor function, we are assigning the value of the idArg argument to the id property on the class, as follows:

```
class ComplexType implements IComplexType {
    id: number;
    name: string;
    constructor(idArg: number, nameArg: string);
    constructor(idArg: string, nameArg: string);
    constructor(idArg: any, nameArg: any) {
        this.id = idArg;
        // careful - assigning a string to a number type
        this.name = nameArg;
    }
```

Even though we have defined the id property of the class to be of type number, when we call the constructor function with a string (because we have a constructor override), then the id property will actually be abc, which is clearly not a number type. TypeScript will not generate an error in this case, and will not automatically try to convert the value "abc" to a number. In cases where this type of functionality is required, we would need to use type guards to ensure type safety, as follows:

```
constructor(idArg: any, nameArg: any) {
    if (typeof idArg === "number") {
        this.id = idArg;
    }

    this.name = nameArg;
}
```

Here, we have introduced a type guard to ensure that the id property (which is of type number) is only assigned if the idArg parameter is, in fact, a number.

Let's now take a look at the rest of the function definitions that we have defined for the class, starting with the usingTheAnyKeyword function:

```
ct_1.usingTheAnyKeyword(true);
ct_1.usingTheAnyKeyword({ id: 1, name: "string"});
```

The first call in this sample is using a boolean value to call the usingTheAnyKeyword function, and the second is using an arbitrary object. Both of these function calls are valid, as the arg1 parameter is defined with the any type.

Next, there is the usingOptionalParameters function:

```
ct_1.usingOptionalParameters(1);
ct_1.usingOptionalParameters();
```

Here, we are calling the usingOptionalParameters function firstly with a single argument, and then without any arguments. Again, these calls are valid, since the optionalArg1 argument is marked as optional.

And now for the usingDefaultParameters function:

```
ct_1.usingDefaultParameters(2);
ct_1.usingDefaultParameters();
```

Both of these calls to the usingDefaultParameters function are valid. The first call will override the default value of 0, and the second call—without an argument—will use the default value of 0.

Next up is the usingRestSyntax function:

```
ct_1.usingRestSyntax(1,2,3);
ct_2.usingRestSyntax(1,2,3,4,5);
```

Our rest function, usingRestSyntax, can be called with any number of arguments, as we are using the rest parameter syntax to hold these arguments in an array. Both of these calls are valid.

Finally, let's look at the usingFunctionCallbacks function:

```
function myCallbackFunction(id: number): string {
    return id.toString();
}
ct_1.usingFunctionCallbacks(myCallbackFunction);
```

Here, we have defined a function named `myCallbackFunction`, which matches the callback signature required by the `usingFunctionCallbacks` function. This allows us to pass in `myCallbackFunction` as a parameter to the `usingFunctionCallbacks` function.

Note that, if you face any difficulty understanding these various function signatures, then please review the relevant sections in `Chapter 2`, *Types, Variables, and Function Techniques*, relating to functions, where each of these concepts is explained in detail.

Interface function definitions

Interfaces, like classes, follow the same rules when dealing with functions. To update our `IComplexType` interface definition to match the `ComplexType` class definition, we need to write a function definition for each of the new functions, as follows:

```
interface IComplexType {
    id: number;
    name: string;
    print(): string;
    usingTheAnyKeyword(arg1: any): any;
    usingOptionalParameters(optionalArg1?: number) : void;
    usingDefaultParameters(defaultArg1?: number) : void;
    usingRestSyntax(...argArray: number []) : void;
    usingFunctionCallbacks(callback: (id: number) => string);
}
```

This interface definition includes the `id` and `name` properties and a `print` function. We then have a function signature for the `usingTheAnyKeyword` function. It looks surprisingly like our actual class function, but does not have a function body. The `usingOptionalParameters` function definition shows how to use an optional parameter within an interface.

The interface definition for the `usingDefaultParameters` function, however, is slightly different to our class definition. Remember that an interface defines the shape of our class or object, and therefore cannot contain variables or values. We have therefore defined the `defaultArg1` parameter as optional, and left the assignment of the default value up to the class implementation itself. The definition of the `usingRestSyntax` function contains the rest parameter syntax, and the definition of the `usingFunctionCallbacks` function shows how to define a callback function signature. They are pretty much identical to the class function signatures.

The only thing missing from this interface is the signature for the `constructor` function. Interfaces cannot include signatures for a constructor function.

Let's take a look at why this causes errors in our compilation step. Suppose we were to include a definition for the `constructor` function in the `IComplexType` interface:

```
interface IComplexType {
    constructor(arg1: any, arg2: any);
}
```

The TypeScript compiler would then generate the following error:

```
error TS2420: Class 'ComplexType' incorrectly implements interface
'IComplexType'.
Types of property 'constructor' are incompatible.
```

This error shows us that, when we use a `constructor` function, the return type of the constructor is implicitly typed by the TypeScript compiler. Therefore, the return type of the `IComplexType` constructor would be `IComplexType`, and the return type of the `ComplexType` constructor would be `ComplexType`. Even though the `ComplexType` function implements the `IComplexType` interface, they are actually two different types. Therefore, the `constructor` signatures will always be incompatible, and are not allowed in interface definitions.

Class modifiers

As we discussed briefly in the opening chapter, TypeScript introduces the `public` and `private` access modifiers to mark class variables and functions as either `public` or `private`. Additionally, we can also use the `protected` access modifier, which we will discuss a little later.

A public class property can be accessed by any calling code. Consider the following code:

```
class ClassWithPublicProperty {
    public id: number | undefined;
}

let publicAccess = new ClassWithPublicProperty();
publicAccess.id = 10;
```

Here, we have defined a class named `ClassWithPublicProperty` that has a single property named `id`. We then create an instance of this class, named `publicAccess`, and assign the value of `10` to the `id` property of this instance. Let's now explore how marking a property `private` will affect access to this property, as follows:

```
class ClassWithPrivateProperty {
    private id: number;
```

```
        constructor(_id : number) {
            this.id = _id;
        }
    }

    let privateAccess = new ClassWithPrivateProperty(10);
    privateAccess.id = 20;
```

Here, we have defined a class named ClassWithPrivateProperty that has a single property named id, and which has now been marked as private. This class also has a constructor function that takes a single argument, named _id, and assigns the value of this argument to the id property. Note that we are using the this.id syntax in this assignment.

We then create an instance of this class, named privateAccess, and then attempt to assign the value 20 to the private id property. This code, however, will generate the following error:

```
    error TS2341: Property 'id' is private and only accessible within class
    'ClassWithPrivateProperty'.
```

As we can see from the error message, TypeScript will not allow assignment to the id property of this class outside the class itself, as we have marked it as private. Note that we are able to assign a value to the id property from within the class, as we have done in the constructor function.

 Class functions are public by default. Not specifying an access modifier of private for either properties or functions will cause their access level to default to public. Classes can also mark functions and properties as protected, but we will cover this keyword a little later when we discuss inheritance.

Constructor access modifiers

TypeScript also introduces a shorthand version of the constructor function, allowing you to specify parameters with access modifiers directly in the constructor. Consider the following code:

```
    class classWithAutomaticProperties {
        constructor(public id: number, private name: string){
        }
    }
```

```
let myAutoClass =
    new classWithAutomaticProperties(1, "className");
console.log(`myAutoClass id: ${myAutoClass.id}`);
console.log(`myAutoClass.name: ${myAutoClass.name}`);
```

This code snippet defines a class named `ClassWithAutomaticProperties`. The `constructor` function uses two arguments—an `id` of type `number`, and a `name` of type `string`. Note, however, the access modifiers of `public` for `id` and `private` for `name`, defined directly in the `constructor` function. This shorthand automatically creates a public `id` property on the `ClassWithAutomaticProperties` class, as well as a private `name` property.

 This shorthand syntax is only available within the `constructor` function.

We then create a variable named `myAutoClass` and assign a new instance of the `ClassWithAutomaticProperties` class to it. Once this class is instantiated, it automatically has two properties: an `id` property of type `number`, which is `public`, and a `name` property of type `string`, which is `private`. Compiling the previous code, however, will produce a TypeScript compile error:

```
Property 'name' is private and only accessible within class
'classWithAutomaticProperties'.
```

This error is telling us that the automatic property `name` is declared as `private`, and it is therefore unavailable to code outside the class itself.

 While this shorthand technique of creating automatic member variables is available, it can make the code more difficult to read. In the author's opinion, it is generally better to use the more verbose class definitions that do not use this shorthand technique. By not using this technique, and instead listing all of the properties at the top of the class, it becomes immediately visible to someone reading the code what variables this class uses, and whether they are `public` or `private`. Using the constructor's automatic property syntax hides these parameters somewhat, forcing developers to sometimes reread the code to understand it. Whichever syntax you choose, however, try to make it a coding standard, and use the same syntax throughout your code base.

Readonly properties

In addition to the `public`, `private`, and `protected` access modifiers, we can also mark a class property as `readonly`. This means that, once the value of the property has been set, it is not able to be modified, either by the class itself, or by any users of the class. There is only one place where a `readonly` property can be set, and this is within the constructor function itself. Consider the following code:

```
class ClassWithReadOnly {
    readonly name: string;
    constructor(_name : string) {
        this.name = _name;
    }
    setReadOnly(_name: string) {
        // generates a compile error
        this.name = _name;
    }
}
```

Here, we have defined a class named `ClassWithReadOnly` that has a `name` property of the `string` type that has been marked with the `readonly` keyword. The `constructor` function is setting this value. We have then defined a second function named `setReadOnly`, where we are attempting to set this `readonly` property. This code will generate the following error:

```
error TS2540: Cannot assign to 'name' because it is a constant or a read-
only property.
```

This error message is telling us that the only place where a `readonly` property can be set is in the `constructor` function.

Class property accessors

ECMAScript 5 introduces the concept of property accessors. An accessor is simply a function that is called when a user of our class either sets a property, or retrieves a property. This means that we can detect when users of our class are either getting or setting a property, and can be used as a trigger mechanism for other logic. To use accessors, we create a pair of `get` and `set` functions (with the same function name) in order to access an internal property. This concept is best understood with some code samples, as follows:

```
class ClassWithAccessors {
    private _id : number | undefined;
    get id() {
```

```
            console.log(`inside get id()`);
            return <number>this._id;
    }
    set id(value:number) {
            console.log(`inside set id()`);
            this._id = value;
    }
  }
```

This class has a private _id property and two functions, both called id. The first of these functions is prefixed by the get keyword. This get function is called when a user of our class retrieves, or reads, the property. In our sample, the get function logs a debug message to the console, and then simply returns the value of the internal _id property.

The second of these functions is prefixed with the set keyword and accepts a value parameter. This set function will be called when a user of our class assigns a value, or sets the property. In our sample, we simply log a message to the console, and then set the internal _id property. Note that the internal _id property is private, and as such cannot be accessed outside of the class itself.

We can now use this class, as follows:

```
var classWithAccessors = new ClassWithAccessors();
classWithAccessors.id = 2;
console.log(`id property is set to ${classWithAccessors.id}`);
```

Here, we have created an instance of this class, and named it classWithAccessors. Note how we are not using the two separate functions named get and set. We are simply using them as a single id property. When we assign a value to this property, the ECMAScript 5 runtime will call the set id(value) function, and when we retrieve this property, the runtime will call the get id() function. The output of this code is as follows:

```
inside set id()
inside get id()
id property is set to 2
```

Using getter and setter functions allows us to hook in to class properties, and execute code when these class properties are accessed.

> This feature is only available when using ECMAScript 5 and above. Be aware that some browsers do not support ECMAScript 5 (such as Internet Explorer 8), and will cause JavaScript runtime errors when attempting to use class accessors.

Static functions

Static functions are functions that can be called on a class without having to create an instance of the class first. These functions are almost global in their nature, and must be called by prefixing the function name with the class name. Consider the following class definition:

```
class StaticClass {
    static printTwo() {
        console.log(`2`);
    }
}

StaticClass.printTwo();
```

This class definition includes a single function, named `printTwo`, which is marked as `static`. As we can see from the last line of the code, we can call this function without needing to create a new instance of the `StaticClass` class. We can just call the function directly, as long as we prefix it with the class name.

Static properties

Similar to static functions, classes can also have static properties. If a property of a class is marked as `static`, then each instance of this class will have the same value for the property. In other words, all instances of the same class will share the static property. Consider the following code:

```
class StaticProperty {
    static count = 0;
    updateCount() {
        StaticProperty.count ++;
    }
}
```

This class definition uses the `static` keyword on the class property `count`. It has a single function named `updateCount`, which increments the static `count` property. Note the syntax within the `updateCount` function. Normally, we would use the `this` keyword to access properties of a class.

Here, however, we need to reference the full name of the property, including the class name, that is, `StaticProperty.count` to access this property, and is similar to what we have seen for static functions. We can then use this class, as follows:

```
let firstInstance = new StaticProperty();

console.log(`StaticProperty.count = ${StaticProperty.count}`);
firstInstance.updateCount();
console.log(`StaticProperty.count = ${StaticProperty.count}`);

let secondInstance = new StaticProperty();
secondInstance.updateCount();
console.log(`StaticProperty.count = ${StaticProperty.count}`);
```

This code snippet starts with a new instance of the `StaticProperty` class named `firstInstance`. We are then logging the value of `StaticProperty.count` to the console. We then call the `updateCount` function on this instance of the class, and again log the value of `StaticProperty.count` to the console. We then create another instance of this class, named `secondInstance`, call the `updateCount` function, and log the value of `StaticProperty.count` to the console. This code snippet will output the following:

```
StaticProperty.count = 0
StaticProperty.count = 1
StaticProperty.count = 2
```

What this output shows us is that the static property named `StaticCount.count` is indeed shared between two instances of the same class, that is, `firstInstance` and `secondInstance`. It starts out as `0`, and is incremented when `firstInstance.updateCount` is called. When we create a second instance of the class, it also retains its original value of `1` for this class instance. When `secondInstance` updates this count, it will then also be updated for `firstInstance`.

Namespaces

When working with large projects, and particularly when working with external libraries, there may come a time when two classes or interfaces share the same name. This will obviously cause compilation errors. TypeScript uses the concept of namespaces to cater for these situations.

Let's take a look at the syntax used for namespaces, as follows:

```
namespace FirstNameSpace {
    class NotExported {
    }
    export class NameSpaceClass {
        id: number | undefined;
    }
}
```

Here, we are defining a namespace using the `namespace` keyword, and have called this namespace `FirstNameSpace`. A namespace declaration is similar to a class declaration, in that it is scoped by the opening and closing braces, that is, `{` starts the namespace, and `}` closes the namespace. This namespace has two classes defined within it. These classes are named `NotExported`, and `NameSpaceClass`.

When using namespaces, a class definition will not be visible outside of the namespace, unless we specifically allow this using the `export` keyword. To create classes that are defined within a namespace, we must reference the class using the full namespace name. Let's take a look at how we would create instances of these classes:

```
let firstNameSpace = new FirstNameSpace.NameSpaceClass();
let notExported = new FirstNameSpace.NotExported();
```

Here, we are creating an instance of `NameSpaceClass`, and an instance of the `NotExported` class. Note how we need to use the full namespace name in order to correctly reference these classes, that is, `new FirstNameSpace.NameSpaceClass()`. As the `NotExported` class has not used the `export` keyword, the last line of this code will generate the following error:

```
error TS2339: Property 'NotExported' does not exist on type 'typeof
FirstNameSpace'.
```

We can now introduce a second namespace, as follows:

```
namespace SecondNameSpace {
    export class NameSpaceClass {
        name: string | undefined;
    }
}

let secondNameSpace = new SecondNameSpace.NameSpaceClass();
```

This namespace also exports a class that is named `NameSpaceClass`. On the last line of this code snippet, we are again creating an instance of this class using the full namespace name, that is, `new SecondNameSpace.NameSpaceClass();`. Using the same class name in this instance will not cause compilation errors, as each class (prefixed by the namespace name) is seen by the compiler as a separate class name.

Inheritance

Inheritance is another paradigm that is one of the cornerstones of object-oriented programming. Inheritance means that an object uses another object as its base type, thereby inheriting all of the base object's characteristics, including all properties and functions. Both interfaces and classes can use inheritance. An interface or class that is inherited from is known as the base interface or base class, and the interface or class that does the inheritance is known as the derived interface or derived class. TypeScript implements inheritance using the `extends` keyword.

Interface inheritance

As an example of interface inheritance, consider the following TypeScript code:

```
interface IBase {
    id: number | undefined;
}

interface IDerivedFromBase extends IBase {
    name: string | undefined;
}

class InterfaceInheritanceClass implements IDerivedFromBase {
    id: number | undefined;
    name: string | undefined;
}
```

We start with an interface called `IBase`, which defines an `id` property, of type `number` or `undefined`. Our second interface definition, `IDerivedFromBase`, extends (or inherits) from `IBase`, and therefore automatically includes the `id` property. The `IDerivedFromBase` interface then defines a `name` property, of type `string` or `undefined`. As the `IDerivedFromBase` interface inherits from `IBase`, it therefore actually has two properties—`id` and `name`. We then have a class definition, named `InterfaceInheritanceClass`, that implements this `IDerivedFromBase` interface. This class must, therefore, define both an `id` and a `name` property in order to successfully implement all of the properties of the `IDerivedFromBase` interface. Although we have only shown properties in this example, the same rules apply for functions.

Class inheritance

Classes can also use inheritance in the same manner as interfaces. Using our definitions of the `IBase` and `IDerivedFromBase` interfaces, the following code shows an example of class inheritance:

```
class BaseClass implements IBase {
    id: number | undefined;
}

class DerivedFromBaseClass
    extends BaseClass
    implements IDerivedFromBase {
        name: string | undefined;
    }
```

The first class, named `BaseClass`, implements the `IBase` interface, and as such, is only required to define a property of `id`, of type `number` or `undefined`. The second class, `DerivedFromBaseClass`, inherits from the `BaseClass` class (using the `extends` keyword), but also implements the `IDerivedFromBase` interface. As `BaseClass` already defines the `id` property required in the `IDerivedFromBase` interface, the only other property that the `DerivedFromBaseClass` class needs to implement is the `name` property. Therefore, we only need to include the definition of the `name` property in the `DerivedFromBaseClass` class.

TypeScript does not support the concept of multiple inheritance. Multiple inheritance means that a single class can be derived from multiple base classes. TypeScript only supports single inheritance and, therefore, any class can only have a single base class. A class can, however, implement multiple interfaces, as follows:

```
interface IFirstInterface {
    id : number | undefined;
}
interface ISecondInterface {
    name: string | undefined;
}
class MultipleInterfaces
    implements IFirstInterface, ISecondInterface {
    id: number | undefined;
    name: string | undefined;
}
```

Here, we have defined two interfaces named `IFirstInterface` and `ISecondInterface`. We then have a class named `MultipleInterfaces` that implements both `IFirstInterface` and `ISecondInterface`. This means that the `MultipleInterfaces` class must implement an `id` property to satisfy the `IFirstInterface` interface, and it must implement a `name` property to satisfy the `ISecondInterface` interface.

The super keyword

When using inheritance, both a base class and a derived class may have the same function name. This is most often seen with class constructors. If a base class has a defined constructor, then the derived class may need to call through to the base class constructor and pass through some arguments. This technique is called **constructor overriding**. In other words, the constructor of a derived class overrides, or supersedes, the constructor of the base class. TypeScript includes the super keyword to enable calling a base class's function with the same name. Consider the following classes:

```
class BaseClassWithConstructor {
    private id: number;
    constructor(_id: number) {
        this.id = _id;
    }
}

class DerivedClassWithConstructor
    extends BaseClassWithConstructor {
        private name: string;
        constructor(_id: number, _name: string) {
```

```
            super(_id);
            this.name = _name;
        }
    }
```

Here, we define a class named `BaseClassWithConstructor` that holds a private `id` property. This class has a `constructor` function that requires an `_id` argument. Our second class, named `DerivedClassWithConstructor`, extends (or inherits from) the `BaseClassWithConstructor` class. The constructor of `DerivedClassWithConstructor` takes an `_id` argument and a `_name` argument. However, it needs to pass the incoming `_id` argument through to the base class. This is where the `super` call comes in. The `super` keyword calls the function in the base class that has the same name as the function in the derived class. The first line of the `constructor` function for `DerivedClassWithConstructor` shows the call using the `super` keyword, passing the `id` argument it received through to the base class constructor.

Function overriding

The constructor of a class is, however, just a function. In the same way that we can use the `super` keyword in a constructor, we can also use the `super` keyword when a base class and its derived class use the same function name. This technique is called **function overriding**. In other words, the derived class has a function name that is the same name as that of a base class function, and it overrides this function definition. Consider the following code:

```
class BaseClassWithFunction {
    public id : number | undefined;
    getProperties() : string {
        return `id: ${this.id}`;
    }
}

class DerivedClassWithFunction
    extends BaseClassWithFunction {
        public name: string | undefined;
        getProperties() : string {
            return `${super.getProperties()}`
            + ` , name: ${this.name}`;
        }
    }
```

Here, we have defined a class named `BaseClassWithFunction` that has a public `id` property, and a function named `getProperties`, which just returns a `string` representation of the properties of the class. Our `DerivedClassWithFunction` class, however, also includes a function called `getProperties`. This function is a function override of the `getProperties` base class function. In order to call through to the base class function, we need to use the `super` keyword, as shown in the call to `super.getProperties`.

Let's take a look at how we would use these classes:

```
var derivedClassWithFunction = new DerivedClassWithFunction();
derivedClassWithFunction.id = 1;
derivedClassWithFunction.name = "derivedName";
console.log(derivedClassWithFunction.getProperties());
```

This code creates a variable named `derivedClassWithFunction`, which is an instance of the `DerivedClassWithFunction` class. It then sets both the `id` and `name` properties, and then logs the result of calling the `getProperties` function to the console. This code snippet will result in the following:

```
id: 1 , name: derivedName
```

The results show that the `getProperties` function of the `derivedClassWithFunction` variable will call through to the base class `getProperties` function, as expected.

Protected class members

When using inheritance, it is sometimes logical to mark certain functions and properties as accessible only within the class itself, or accessible to any class that is derived from it. Using the `private` keyword, however, will not work in this instance, as a private class member is hidden even from derived classes. TypeScript introduces the `protected` keyword for these situations. Consider the following two classes:

```
class ClassUsingProtected {
    protected id : number | undefined;
    public getId() {
        return this.id;
    }
}

class DerivedFromProtected
    extends ClassUsingProtected  {
    constructor() {
```

```
        super();
        this.id = 0;
    }
}
```

We start with a class named `ClassUsingProtected` that has an `id` property that is marked as `protected`, and a public function named `getId`. Our next `DerivedFromProtected` class, inherits from `ClassUsingProtected`, and has a single `constructor` function. Note that within this `constructor` function, we are calling `this.id = 0`, in order to set the protected `id` property to 0. Again, a derived class has access to `protected` member variables. Now, let's try to access this `id` property outside of the class, as follows:

```
var derivedFromProtected = new DerivedFromProtected();
derivedFromProtected.id = 1;
console.log(`getId returns: ${derivedFromProtected.getId()}`);
```

Here, we create an instance of the `DerivedFromProtected` class, and attempt to assign a value to its protected `id` property. The compiler will generate the following error message:

error TS2445: Property 'id' is protected and only accessible within class 'ClassUsingProtected' and its subclasses.

So, this `id` property is acting like a private property outside of the class `ClassUsingProtected`, but still allows access to it within the class, and any class derived from it.

Abstract classes

Another fundamental principle of object-oriented design is the concept of abstract classes. An abstract class is a definition of a class that cannot be instantiated. In other words, it is a class that is designed to be derived from. The abstract classes, sometimes referred to as abstract base classes, are often used to provide a set of basic functionality or properties that are shared among a group of similar classes. They are similar to interfaces in that they cannot be instantiated, but they can have function implementations, which interfaces cannot.

Abstract classes are a technique that allows for code reuse among groups of similar objects. Consider the following two classes:

```
class Employee {
    public id: number | undefined;
    public name: string | undefined;
    printDetails() {
        console.log(`id: ${this.id}`
            + `, name ${this.name}`);
    }
}

class Manager {
    public id: number | undefined;
    public name: string | undefined;
    public Employees: Employee[] | undefined;
    printDetails() {
        console.log(`id: ${this.id} `
            + `, name ${this.name}, `
            + ` employeeCount ${this.Employees.length}`);
    }
}
```

We start with a class named `Employee` that has an `id` and `name` property, as well as a function called `printDetails`. The next class is named `Manager`, and is very similar to the `Employee` class. It also has an `id` and `name` property, but it also has an extra property named `Employees` that is a list of employees that this manager oversees. There is a lot of code that is common to these two classes. Both have an `id` and `name` property, and both have a `printDetails` function. Using an abstract base class for both of these classes overcomes this problem with common properties and code. Let's rewrite these two classes, and introduce the concept of an abstract base class, as follows:

```
abstract class AbstractEmployee {
    public id: number | undefined;
    public name: string | undefined;
    abstract getDetails(): string;
    public printDetails() {
        console.log(this.getDetails());
    }
}

class NewEmployee extends AbstractEmployee {
    getDetails(): string {
        return `id : ${this.id}, name : ${this.name}`;
    }
}
```

```
class NewManager extends NewEmployee {
    public Employees: NewEmployee[] | undefined;
    getDetails() : string {
        return super.getDetails()
            + `, employeeCount ${this.Employees.length}`;
    }
}
```

Here, we have defined an abstract class named AbstractEmployee that includes an id and name property, which is common to both managers and employees. We then define what is known as an abstract function named getDetails. Using an abstract function means that any class that derives from this abstract class must implement this function. We then define a printDetails function to log details of this AbstractEmployee class to the console. Note how we are calling the abstract function getDetails from within the abstract class. This means that our code in the printDetails function will call the actual implementation of the function in the derived class.

Our second class, named NewEmployee, extends the AbstractEmployee class. As such, it must implement the getDetails function that has been marked as abstract in the base class. This getDetails function returns a string representation of the id and name properties of the NewEmployee class.

Next, we have a class named NewManager that derives from NewEmployee. This NewManager class, therefore, also has an id and name property, but has an extra property named Employees. Because this class already derives from NewEmployee, it does not necessarily need to define the getDetails function again. It could simply use the version of the getDetails function that the NewEmployee class provides. Note, however, that we have actually defined this getDetails function within the NewManager class. This function calls the base class getDetails function, through the super keyword, and then adds some extra information about its Employees property. Let's take a look at what happens when we create and use these classes, as follows:

```
var employee = new NewEmployee();
employee.id = 1;
employee.name = "Employee Name";

employee.printDetails();
```

Here, we have created an instance of the `NewEmployee` class, named `employee`, set its `id` and `name` properties, and called the `printDetails` function from the abstract class. Recall that the abstract class will then call the implementation of the `getDetails` function that we provided in the `NewEmployee` class, and therefore output the following to the console:

```
id: 1, name : Employee Name
```

Now, let's use our `NewManager` class in a similar way:

```
var manager = new NewManager();
manager.id = 2;
manager.name = "Manager Name";
manager.Employees = [];

manager.printDetails();
```

Here, we have created an instance of the `NewManager` class, named `manager`, and set its `id` and `name` properties as before. Because this class also has an array of `Employees`, we are setting the `Employees` property to a blank array. Note what happens, however, when we call the abstract class `printDetails` function on the last line. The output will be as follows:

```
id: 2, name : Manager Name, employeeCount 0
```

The abstract class implementation of the `printDetails` function calls the `getDetails` function of the derived class. Because the `NewManager` class also defines a `getDetails` function, the abstract class will call this function on the `NewManager` instance. The `getDetails` function on the `NewManager` instance then calls through to the base class implementation, that is, the `NewEmployee` instance of the `getDetails` function, as seen in the code `super.getDetails()`. It then appends some information regarding its employee count.

Using abstract classes and inheritance allows us to write our code in a cleaner and more reusable way. Abstraction, inheritance, polymorphism, and encapsulation are the foundations of good object-oriented design principles. As we have seen, the TypeScript language gives us the ability to incorporate each of these principles to help write good, clean JavaScript code.

JavaScript closures

Before we continue with this chapter, let's take a quick look at how TypeScript implements classes in the generated ES3 or ES5 JavaScript through a technique called closures. As we mentioned in Chapter 1, *TypeScript – Tools and Framework Options*, a closure is a function that refers to independent variables. These variables essentially remember the environment in which they were created. Consider the following JavaScript code:

```
function TestClosure(value) {
    this._value = value;
    function printValue() {
        console.log(this._value);
    }
    return printValue;
}

var myClosure = TestClosure(12);
myClosure;
```

Here, we have a function named `TestClosure` that takes a single parameter, named `value`. The body of the function first assigns the `value` argument to an internal property named `this._value`, and then defines an inner function named `printValue`. The `printValue` function simply logs the value of `this._value` to the console. The interesting bit is the last line in the `TestClosure` function—we are returning the `printValue` function.

Now, take a look at the last two lines of the code snippet. We create a variable named `myClosure` and assign to it the result of calling the `TestClosure` function. Note that because we are returning the `printValue` function from inside the `TestClosure` function, this essentially also makes the `myClosure` variable a function. When we execute this function on the last line of the snippet, it will execute the inner `printValue` function, but remember the initial value of `12` that was used when creating the `myClosure` variable. The output of the last line of the code will log the value of `12` to the console.

This is the essential nature of closures. A closure is a special kind of JavaScript object that combines a function with the initial environment in which it was created. In our preceding sample, since we stored whatever was passed in through the `value` argument into a local variable named `this._value`, JavaScript remembers the environment in which the closure was created. In other words, whatever was assigned to the `this._value` property at the time of creation will be remembered, and can be reused later.

With this in mind, let's take a look at the JavaScript that is generated by the TypeScript compiler for the `BaseClassWithConstructor` class we were just working with:

```
var BaseClassWithConstructor = (function () {
    function BaseClassWithConstructor(_id) {
        this.id = _id;
    }
    return BaseClassWithConstructor;
})();
```

Our closure starts with `function () {` on the first line, and ends with `}` on the last line. This closure first defines a function to be used as a constructor: `BaseClassWithConstructor(_id)`.

This closure is surrounded by an opening bracket, `(`, on the first line, and a closing bracket, `)`, on the last line—defining what is known as a JavaScript function expression. This function expression is then immediately executed by the last two braces, `();`. This technique of immediately executing a function is known as an **Immediately Invoked Function Expression (IIFE)**. Our preceding IIFE is then assigned to a variable named `BaseClassWithConstructor`, making it a first-class JavaScript object, and one that can be created with the `new` keyword. This is how TypeScript implements classes in JavaScript.

The implementation of the underlying JavaScript code that TypeScript uses for class definitions is actually a well-known JavaScript pattern known as the **module** pattern. The good news is that an in-depth knowledge of closures, how to write them, and how to use the module pattern for defining classes will all be taken care of by the TypeScript compiler, allowing us to focus on object-oriented principles without having to write JavaScript closures using this sort of boilerplate code.

instanceof

TypeScript also allows us to check whether an object has been created from a specific class using the `instanceof` keyword. To illustrate this, consider the following set of classes:

```
class A {
}

class BfromA extends A {
}

class CfromA extends A {
}

class DfromC extends CfromA {
}
```

Here, we have defined four classes, starting with a simple class named A. We then define two classes derived from A, called `BfromA` and `CfromA`. The final class definition is for a class named `DfromC`, which is derived from class `CfromA`. Let's now use the `instanceof` keyword to find out what the compiler thinks of this inheritance structure, as follows:

```
function checkInstanceOf(value: A | BfromA | CfromA | DfromC) {
    console.log(`checking instanceof :`)
    if (value instanceof A) {
        console.log(`found instanceof A`);
    }
    if (value instanceof BfromA) {
        console.log(`found instanceof BfromA`);
    }
    if (value instanceof CfromA) {
        console.log(`found instanceof CFromA`);
    }
    if (value instanceof DfromC) {
        console.log(`found instanceof DfromC`);
    }
}
```

Here, we have created a function named `checkInstanceOf` that has a single parameter, which can be any one of our four class types. Once we are inside the function, we log a message to the console indicating that we are starting to check the input argument. We then have four `if` statements, each of which is checking to see whether the type of the value argument matches any one of our four class types.

Let's use this function as follows:

```
checkInstanceOf(new A());
checkInstanceOf(new BfromA());
checkInstanceOf(new CfromA());
checkInstanceOf(new DfromC());
```

Here, we are calling the `checkInstanceOf` function with an instance of each of our four classes. The output of this code is as follows:

```
nathanr@nero16: ~/source/temp

checking instanceof :
found instanceof A
checking instanceof :
found instanceof A
found instanceof BfromA
checking instanceof :
found instanceof A
found instanceof CFromA
checking instanceof :
found instanceof A
found instanceof CFromA
found instanceof DfromC
```

Here, we can see that, if we call this function with a class of type A, our code is detecting this correctly, since `if (value instanceof A)` is returning `true`. Interestingly, when we send an instance of the `BfromA` class, we can see that both the `instanceof A` and the `instanceof BfromA` statements are returning `true`. This means that the compiler is correctly detecting that the `BfromA` class has been derived from A. The same logic applies to the class `CfromA`. Observe how the `DfromC` class will cause three of the `instanceof` operators to return `true`. Our code is detecting that `DfromC` is derived from `CfromA`, and that because `CfromA` derives from A, `DfromC` is also an instance of type A.

Using interfaces, classes, and inheritance – the Factory Design Pattern

To illustrate how we can use interfaces and classes in a large TypeScript project, we will take a quick look at a very well-known object-oriented design pattern—the Factory Design pattern.

Business requirements

As an example, let's assume that our business analyst gives us the following requirements:

1. You are required to categorize people, given their date of birth, into three different age groups—Infants, Children, and Adults.
2. Indicate with a `true` or `false` flag whether they are of a legal age to sign a contract.
3. A person is deemed to be an infant if they are less than two years old.
4. Infants cannot sign contracts.
5. A person is deemed to be a child if they are less than 18 years old.
6. Children cannot sign contracts either.
7. A person is deemed to be an adult if they are more than 18 years of age.
8. Only adults can sign contracts.
9. For reporting purposes, each type of person must be able to print their details. This should include the following:
   - Date of birth
   - Category of person
   - Whether they can sign contracts or not

What the Factory Design Pattern does

The Factory Design Pattern uses a Factory class to return an instance of one of several possible classes based on the information provided to it.

The essence of this pattern is to place the decision-making logic for what type of class to create in a separate class named the Factory class. The Factory class will then return one of several classes that are all subtle variations of each other, which will do slightly different things based on their specialty. As we do not know what type of class the Factory pattern will return, we need a way to work with any variation of the different types of class returned. This sounds like the perfect scenario for an interface.

To implement our required business functionality, we will create an `Infant` class, a `Child` class, and an `Adult` class. The `Infant` and `Child` classes will return `false` when asked whether they can sign contracts, and the `Adult` class will return `true`.

The IPerson interface

According to our requirements, the class instance that is returned by the Factory must be able to do two things—print the category of the person in the required format, and tell us whether they can sign contracts. Let's start by defining an enum and an interface to satisfy this requirement:

```
enum PersonCategory {
    Infant,
    Child,
    Adult,
    Undefined
}

interface IPerson {
    Category: PersonCategory;
    canSignContracts(): boolean;
    printDetails();
}
```

We start with an enum to hold the valid values for a `PersonCategory`, that is, `Infant`, `Child`, `Adult`, or `Undefined`. The `Undefined` enum value is used to indicate that we have not categorized the `Person` as yet. We then define an interface named `IPerson` that holds all of the functionality that is common to each type of person. This includes their `Category`, a function named `canSignContracts` that returns either `true` or `false`, and a function to print out their details, named `printDetails`.

The Person class

To simplify our code, we will create an abstract base class to hold all code that is common to infants, children, and adults. Again, abstract classes can never be instantiated, and, as such, are designed to be derived from. We will call this class `Person`, as follows:

```
abstract class Person implements IPerson {
    Category: PersonCategory;
    private DateOfBirth: Date;

    constructor(dateOfBirth: Date) {
        this.DateOfBirth = dateOfBirth;
        this.Category = PersonCategory.Undefined;
    }
    abstract canSignContracts(): boolean
    printDetails() : void {
        console.log(`Person : `);
        console.log(`Date of Birth : `
            + `${this.DateOfBirth.toDateString()}`);
        console.log(`Category       : `
            + `${PersonCategory[this.Category]}`);
        console.log(`Can sign       : `
            + `${this.canSignContracts()}`);
    }
}
```

This abstract `Person` class implements the `IPerson` interface, and as such, will need three things: a `Category` property, a `canSignContracts` function, and a `printDetails` function. In order to print the person's date of birth, we also need a `DateOfBirth` property, which we will set in our constructor function.

There are a couple of interesting things to note about this `Person` class. Firstly, the `DateOfBirth` property has been declared `private`. This means that the only class that has access to the `DateOfBirth` property is the `Person` class itself. Our requirements do not mention using the date of birth outside of the printing function, so there is no need to access or modify the date of birth once it has been set.

Secondly, the `canSignContracts` function has been marked as `abstract`. This means that any class that derives from this class is forced to implement the `canSignContracts` function, which is exactly what we wanted.

Thirdly, the `printDetails` function has been fully implemented in this abstract class. This means that a single `print` function is automatically available for any class that derives from `Person`.

Specialist classes

Now for the three types of specialist classes, all derived from the `Person` base class:

```
class Infant extends Person  {
    constructor(dateOfBirth: Date) {
        super(dateOfBirth);
        this.Category = PersonCategory.Infant;
    }
    canSignContracts(): boolean { return false; }
}

class Child extends Person  {
    constructor(dateOfBirth: Date) {
        super(dateOfBirth);
        this.Category = PersonCategory.Child;
    }
    canSignContracts(): boolean { return false; }
}

class Adult extends Person  {
    constructor(dateOfBirth: Date) {
        super(dateOfBirth);
        this.Category = PersonCategory.Adult;
    }
    canSignContracts(): boolean { return true; }
}
```

Each of these classes uses inheritance to extend the `Person` class. As the `DateOfBirth` property has been declared as `private`, and is therefore only visible to the `Person` class itself, we must pass it down to the `Person` class in each of our constructors. Each constructor also sets the `Category` property based on the class type. Finally, each class implements the abstract function `canSignContracts`.

One of the benefits of using inheritance in this way is that the definitions of the actual classes become very simple. In essence, our classes are only doing two things—setting the `Category` property correctly, and defining whether or not they can sign contracts.

The Factory class

Let's now move on to the Factory class itself. This class has a single, well-defined responsibility: given a date of birth, figure out whether it is less than two years ago, less than 18 years ago, or more than 18 years ago. Based on these decisions, return an instance of either an Infant, Child, or Adult class, as follows:

```
class PersonFactory {
    getPerson(dateOfBirth: Date) : IPerson {
        let dateNow = new Date(); // defaults to now.
        let currentMonth = dateNow.getMonth() + 1;
        let currentDate = dateNow.getDate();

        let dateTwoYearsAgo = new Date(
            dateNow.getFullYear() - 2,
            currentMonth, currentDate);

        let date18YearsAgo = new Date(
            dateNow.getFullYear() - 18,
            currentMonth, currentDate);
        if (dateOfBirth >= dateTwoYearsAgo) {
            return new Infant(dateOfBirth);
        }
        if (dateOfBirth >= date18YearsAgo) {
            return new Child(dateOfBirth);
        }
        return new Adult(dateOfBirth);
    }
}
```

The PersonFactory class has only one function, getPerson, which returns an object of type IPerson. The function creates a variable named dateNow, which is set to the current date. We then find the current month and date from the dateNow variable. Note that the JavaScript function, getMonth, returns 0 – 11, and not 1 – 12, so we correct this by adding 1. This dateNow variable is then used to calculate two more variables, dateTwoYearsAgo and date18YearsAgo. The decision logic then takes over, comparing the incoming dateOfBirth variable against these dates, and returns a new instance of either a new Infant, Child, or Adult class.

Using the Factory class

To illustrate how simple it becomes to use this `PersonFactory` class, consider the following code:

```
let factory = new PersonFactory();
let p1 = factory.getPerson(new Date(2017, 0, 20));
p1.printDetails();
let p2 = factory.getPerson(new Date(2010, 0, 20));
p2.printDetails();
let p3 = factory.getPerson(new Date(1969, 0, 20));
p3.printDetails();
```

We start with the creation of a variable, `personFactory`, to hold a new instance of the `PersonFactory` class. We then create three variables, named p1, p2, and p3, by calling the `getPerson` function of the `PersonFactory`, passing in three different dates to the same function. The output of this code is as follows:

We have satisfied our business requirements and implemented a very common design pattern at the same time. If we look back at our code, we can see that we have a few well-defined and simple classes. Our `Infant`, `Child`, and `Adult` classes are only concerned with logic relating to their classification, and whether they can sign contracts. Our `Person` abstract base class is only concerned with logic related to the `IPerson` interface, and `PersonFactory` is only concerned with the logic surrounding the date of birth. This sample illustrates how object-oriented design patterns and the object-oriented features of the TypeScript language can help with writing good, extensible, and maintainable code.

Summary

In this chapter, we explored the object-oriented concepts of interfaces, classes, and inheritance. We discussed both interface inheritance and class inheritance, and used our knowledge of interfaces, classes, and inheritance to create a Factory Design Pattern implementation in TypeScript. In the next chapter, we will look at advanced language features, including generics, decorators, and asynchronous function techniques.

4
Decorators, Generics, and Asynchronous Features

Above and beyond the concepts of classes, interfaces, and inheritance, the TypeScript language introduces a number of advanced language features in order to aid the development of robust object-oriented code. These features include decorators, generics, promises, and the use of the `async` and `await` keywords when working with asynchronous functions. Decorators allow for the injection and querying of metadata when working with class definitions, as well as the ability to programmatically attach to the act of defining a class. Generics provide a technique for writing routines where the exact type of an object used is not known until runtime. Promises provide the ability to write asynchronous code in a fluent manner, and `async await` functions will pause execution until an asynchronous function has completed.

When writing large-scale JavaScript applications, these language features become part of the programmers' toolbox and allow for the application of many design patterns within JavaScript code.

This chapter is broken into three parts. The first part covers decorators, the second part covers generics, and the third part deals with asynchronous programming techniques using promises and `async await`. In earlier versions of TypeScript, promises and `async await` could only be used in ECMAScript 6 and above, but this functionality has now been extended to include ECMAScript 3 targets.

We will cover the following topics in this chapter:

- Decorator syntax
- Decorator factories
- Class, method, and parameter decorators
- Decorator metadata
- Generic syntax
- Using and constraining the type of `T`

- Generic interfaces
- Promises and promise syntax
- Using promises
- `async` and `await`
- Handling `await` errors

Decorators

Decorators in TypeScript provide a way of programmatically tapping into the process of defining a class. Remember that a class definition describes the shape of a class. In other words, a class definition describes what properties a class has, and what methods it defines. It is only when a class is instantiated, that is, an instance of the class is created, that these properties and methods become available.

Decorators, however, allow us to inject code into the actual definition of a class. Decorators can be used on class definitions, class properties, class functions, and even method parameters. The concept of decorators exists in other programming languages, and are called attributes in C#, or annotations in Java.

In this section, we will explore what decorators are, how they are defined, and how they can be used. We will look at class, property, function, and method decorators.

Decorators are an experimental feature of the TypeScript compiler, and have been proposed as part of the ECMAScript 7 standard. TypeScript, however, allows for the use of decorators in ES3 and above. In order to use decorators, a new compile option needs to be added to the `tsconfig.json` file in the root of your project directory. This option is named `experimentalDecorators`, and needs to be set to `true`, as follows:

```
{
    "compilerOptions": {
        "target": "es5",
        "module": "commonjs",
        "lib": [
            "es2015",
            "dom",
        ],
        "strict": true,
        "esModuleInterop": true,
        "experimentalDecorators": true,
        "emitDecoratorMetadata": true,
    }
}
```

Here, we have specified that the compile options will be using es5 as a target platform, and that we are using the experimentalDecorators and emitDecoratorMetadata options as well. Note that we have also included a lib property, and specified es2015 and dom as library files that the compiler will use. We will experiment with these compiler options in the next chapter.

Decorator syntax

A decorator is simply a function that is called with a specific set of parameters. These parameters are automatically populated by the JavaScript runtime, and contain information about the class to which the decorator has been applied. The number of parameters and the types of these parameters determine where a decorator can be applied. To illustrate the syntax used for decorators, let's define a simple class decorator, as follows:

```
function simpleDecorator(constructor : Function) {
    console.log('simpleDecorator called.');
}
```

Here, we have defined a function named simpleDecorator that takes a single parameter, named constructor of type Function. This simpleDecorator function logs a message to the console indicating that it has been called. This function is our decorator definition. In order to use it, we will need to apply it to a class definition, as follows:

```
@simpleDecorator
class ClassWithSimpleDecorator {
}
```

Here, we have applied the decorator to the class definition of ClassWithSimpleDecorator by using the "at" symbol (@), followed by the decorator name. Running this simple decorator code will produce the following output:

simpleDecorator called.

Note, however, that we have not created an instance of the class as yet. We have simply specified the class definition, added a decorator to it, and our decorator function has automatically been called. This indicates to us that the decorators are applied when a class is being defined, and not when it is being instantiated. As a further example of this, consider the following code:

```
let instance_1 = new ClassWithSimpleDecorator();
let instance_2 = new ClassWithSimpleDecorator();

console.log(`instance_1 : ${JSON.stringify(instance_1)}`);
console.log(`instance_2 : ${JSON.stringify(instance_2)}`);
```

Here, we have created two instances of the `ClassWithSimpleDecorator` class, named `instance_1` and `instance_2`. We are then simply logging a message to the console. The output of this code snippet is as follows:

```
simpleDecorator called.
instance_1 : {}
instance_2 : {}
```

What this output shows us is that the decorator function has only been called once, no matter how many instances of the same class have been created or used. Decorators are only invoked as the class is being defined.

Multiple decorators

Multiple decorators can be applied one after another to the same target. As an example of this, consider the following code:

```
function secondDecorator(constructor : Function) {
    console.log('secondDecorator called.')
}

@simpleDecorator
@secondDecorator
class ClassWithMultipleDecorators {
}
```

Here, we have created another decorator named `secondDecorator`, which also simply logs a message to the console. We are then applying both the `simpleDecorator` (from our earlier code snippet) and the `secondDecorator` decorators to the class definition of the class named `ClassWithMultipleDecorators`. The output of this code is as follows:

```
secondDecorator called.
simpleDecorator called.
```

The output of this code shows us an interesting point about decorators. They are called in reverse order of their definition.

Decorators are evaluated in the order they appear in the code, but are then called in reverse order.

Decorator factories

In order to allow for decorators to accept parameters, we need to use what is known as a **decorator factory**. A decorator factory is simply a wrapper function that returns the decorator function itself. As an example of this, consider the following code:

```
function decoratorFactory(name: string) {
    return function (constructor : Function ) {
        console.log(`decorator function called with : ${name}`);
    }
}
```

Here, we have defined a function named decoratorFactory that accepts a single argument, named name, of type string. This function simply returns an anonymous decorator function that takes a single argument named constructor of type Function. The anonymous function (our decorator function) logs the value of the name parameter to the console.

Note here how we have wrapped the decorator function within the decoratorFactory function. This wrapping of a decorator function is what produces a decorator factory. As long as the wrapping function returns a decorator function, this is a valid decorator factory.

We can now use our decorator factory, as follows:

```
@decoratorFactory('testName')
class ClassWithDecoratorFactory {
}
```

Note how we can now pass a parameter to the decorator factory, as shown in the usage of @decoratorFactory('testName'). The output of this code is as follows:

decorator function called with : testName

There are a few things to note regarding decorator factories. Firstly, the decorator function itself will still be called by the JavaScript runtime with automatically populated parameters. Secondly, the decorator factory must return a function definition. Lastly, the parameters defined for the decorator factory can be used within the decorator function itself, as it is in the same scope as the decorator function.

Class decorator parameters

The examples we have seen so far are all class decorators. Remember that a decorator function will automatically be called by the JavaScript runtime when the class is declared. Our decorator functions up until this point have all been defined to accept a single parameter named `constructor`, which is of type `Function`. The JavaScript runtime will populate this `constructor` parameter automatically for us. Let's delve into this parameter in a little more detail.

Class decorators will be invoked with the `constructor` function of the class that has been decorated. As an example of this, consider the following code:

```
function classConstructorDec(constructor: Function) {
    console.log(`constructor : ${constructor}`);
}

@classConstructorDec
class ClassWithConstructor {
}
```

Here, we start with a decorator function named `classConstructorDec` that accepts a single argument named `constructor` of type `Function`. The first line of this function then simply prints out the value of the `constructor` argument. We are then applying this decorator to a class named `ClassWithConstructor`. The output of this code is as follows:

```
constructor : function ClassWithConstructor() {
    }
```

This output therefore shows us that our decorator function is being called with the full definition of the `constructor` function of the class that it is decorating.

Let's then update this decorator, as follows:

```
function classConstructorDec(constructor: Function) {
    console.log(`constructor : ${constructor}`);
    console.log(`constructor.name : ${(<any>constructor).name}`);
    constructor.prototype.testProperty = "testProperty_value";
}
```

Here, we have updated our `classConstructorDec` decorator with two new lines of code. The first new line prints the `name` property of the `constructor` function to the console. Note how we have had to cast the `constructor` parameter to a type of `any` in order to successfully access the `name` property. This is necessary, as the `name` property of a function is only available from ECMAScript 6, and is only partially available in earlier browsers.

The last line of this decorator function is actually modifying the class prototype, and adding a property named `testProperty` (with the value `testProperty_value`) to the class definition itself. This is an example of how decorators can be used to modify a class definition. We can then access this class property, as follows:

```
let classConstrInstance = new ClassWithConstructor();
console.log(`classConstrInstance.testProperty : `
    + `${(<any>classConstrInstance).testProperty}`);
```

Here, we are creating an instance of the `ClassWithConstructor` class, named `classConstrInstance`. We are then logging the value of the `testProperty` property of this class to the console. Note how we need to cast the type of `classConstrInstance` variable to `any` in order to access the `testProperty` property. This is because we have not defined the `testProperty` property on the class definition itself, but are injecting this property through the decorator. The output of this code would be as follows:

```
constructor : function ClassWithConstructor() {
    }
constructor.name : ClassWithConstructor
classConstrInstance.testProperty : testProperty_value
```

This output shows us that we can use the `name` property of the class constructor to find the name of the class itself. We can also inject a class property, named `testProperty`, into the class definition. As can be seen by the output, the value of this `testProperty` property is `testProperty_value`, which is being set within the decorator function.

Property decorators

Property decorators are decorator functions that can be used on class properties. A property decorator is called with two parameters—the class prototype itself, and the property name. As an example of this, consider the following code:

```
function propertyDec(target: any, propertyKey : string) {
    console.log(`target : ${target}`);
    console.log(`target.constructor : ${target.constructor}`);
    console.log(`class name : `
```

```
                + `${target.constructor.name}`);
        console.log(`propertyKey : ${propertyKey}`);
    }

    class ClassWithPropertyDec {
        @propertyDec
        name: string;
    }
```

Here, we have defined a property decorator named `propertyDec` that accepts two parameters—`target` and `propertyKey`. The `target` parameter is of type `any`, and the `propertyKey` parameter is of type `string`. Within this decorator, we are logging some values to the console. The first value we log to the console is the `target` argument itself. The second value logged to the console is the `constructor` property of the `target` object. The third value logged to the console is the name of the constructor function, and the fourth value is the `propertyKey` argument itself.

We are then defining a class named `ClassWithPropertyDec` that is now using this property decorator on the property named `name`. As in the case of class decorators, the syntax used to decorate a property is simply `@propertyDec` before the property to be decorated.

The output of this code is as follows:

```
target : [object Object]
target.constructor : function ClassWithPropertyDec() {
    }
target.constructor.name : ClassWithPropertyDec
propertyKey : name
```

Here, we can see the output of our various `console.log` calls. The `target` argument resolves to `[object Object]`, which simply indicates that it is an object prototype. The `constructor` property of the `target` argument resolves to a function named `ClassWithPropertyDec`, which is, in fact, our class constructor. The `name` property of this `constructor` function gives us the name of the class itself, and the `propertyKey` argument is the name of the property itself.

Property decorators, therefore, give us the ability to check whether a particular property has been declared on a class instance.

Static property decorators

Property decorators can also be applied to static class properties. There is no difference in calling syntax in our code—they are the same as normal property decorators. However, the actual arguments that are passed in at runtime are slightly different. Given our earlier definition of the property decorator `propertyDec`, consider what happens when this decorator is applied to a static class property, as follows:

```
class StaticClassWithPropertyDec {
    @propertyDec
    static name: string;
}
```

The output of the various `console.log` functions in our decorator is as follows:

```
target : function StaticClassWithPropertyDec() {
    }
target.constructor : function Function() { [native code] }
target.constructor.name : Function
propertyKey : name
```

Note here that the `target` argument (as printed in the first line of output) is not a class prototype (as seen before), but an actual `constructor` function. The definition of this `target.constructor` is then simply a function, named `Function`. The `propertyKey` remains the same, that is, `name`.

This means that we need to be a little careful about what is being passed in as the first argument to our property decorator. When the class property being decorated is marked as `static`, then the target argument will be the class constructor itself. When the class property is not static, the target argument will be the class prototype.

Let's modify our property decorator to correctly identify the name of the class in both of these cases, as follows:

```
function propertyDec(target: any, propertyKey : string) {
    if(typeof(target) === 'function') {
        console.log(`class name : ${target.name}`);
    } else {
        console.log(`class name : ${target.constructor.name}`);
    }
    console.log(`propertyKey : ${propertyKey}`);
}
```

Here, we start by checking the nature of the `target` argument. If the `typeof(target)` call returns `function`, then we know that the target argument is the class constructor, and can then identify the class name through `target.name`. If the `typeof(target)` call does not return `function`, then we know that the `target` argument is an object prototype, and that you need to identify the class name through the `target.constructor.name` property. The output of this code is as follows:

```
class name : ClassWithPropertyDec
propertyKey : name
class name : StaticClassWithPropertyDec
propertyKey : name
```

Our property decorator is correctly identifying the name of the class, whether it is used on a normal class property, or a static class property.

Method decorators

Method decorators are decorators that can be applied to a method on a class. Method decorators are invoked by the JavaScript runtime with three parameters. Remember that class decorators have only a single parameter (the class prototype) and property decorators have two parameters (the class prototype and the property name). Method decorators have three parameters. The class prototype, the method name, and (optionally) a method descriptor. The third parameter, the method descriptor is only populated if compiling for ES5 and above.

Let's take a look at a method decorator, as follows:

```
function methodDec (
    target: any,
    methodName: string,
    descriptor?: PropertyDescriptor)
{
    console.log(`target: ${target}`);
    console.log(`methodName : ${methodName}`);
    console.log(`target[methodName] : ${target[methodName]}`);
}
```

Here, we have defined a method decorator named `methodDec` that accepts our three parameters, `target`, `methodName`, and `descriptor`. Note that the `descriptor` property has been marked as optional. The first two lines inside the decorator simply log the values of `target` and `methodName` to the console. Note, however, the last line of this decorator. Here, we are logging the value of `target[methodName]` to the console. This will log the actual function definition to the console.

Now we can use this method decorator on a class, as follows:

```
class ClassWithMethodDec {
    @methodDec
    print(output: string) {
        console.log(`ClassWithMethodDec.print`
            + `(${output}) called.`);
    }
}
```

Here, we have defined a class named `ClassWithMethodDec`. This class has a single `print` function that accepts a single parameter named `output` of type `string`. Our `print` function is just logging a message to the console, including the value of the `output` argument. The `print` function has been decorated with the `methodDec` decorator. The output of this code is as follows:

```
target: [object Object]
methodName : print
target[methodName] : function (output) {
        console.log("ClassWithMethodDec.print(" + output + ") called.");
    }
```

As we can see by this output, the value of the `target` argument is the class prototype. The value of the `methodName` argument is, in fact, `print`. The output of the `target[methodName]` call is the actual definition of the `print` function.

Using method decorators

Since we have the definition of a function available to us within a method decorator, we could use the decorator to modify the functionality of a specific function. Suppose that we wanted to create an audit trail of some sort, and log a message to the console every time a method was called. This is the perfect scenario for method decorators.

Consider the following method decorator:

```
function auditLogDec(target: any,
    methodName: string,
    descriptor?: PropertyDescriptor) {

    let originalFunction = target[methodName];

    let auditFunction = function (this: any) {
        console.log(`auditLogDec : overide of `
            + ` ${methodName} called`);
        for (let i = 0; i < arguments.length; i++) {
```

```
                    console.log(`arg : ${i} = ${arguments[i]}`);
            }
            originalFunction.apply(this, arguments);
        }

        target[methodName] = auditFunction;
        return target;
    }
```

Here, we have defined a method decorator named `auditLogDec`. Within this decorator, we are creating a variable named `originalFunction` to hold the definition of the method that we are decorating, as `target[methodName]` will return the function definition itself. We then create a new function named `auditFunction`, with a single parameter named `this` of type `any`. The use of the parameter `this` in this instance is designed to work around one of the strict compiler rules named `noImplicitThis`. We will discuss these compiler rules in the next chapter.

The first line of the `auditFunction` function logs a message to the console indicating that the function has indeed been called. We are then iterating through the special JavaScript variable named `arguments` to log a list of the arguments to the console. Note, however, the last line of the `auditFunction` function. We are using the JavaScript `apply` function to call the original function, passing in the `this` parameter, and the `arguments` parameter.

After defining the `auditFunction` function, we then assign it to the original class function through the use of `target[methodName]`. In essence, we have replaced the original function with our new `auditFunction`, and, within the `auditFunction`, have invoked the original function through the `apply` method.

To show this in action, consider the following class declaration:

```
class ClassWithAuditDec {
    @auditLogDec
    print(arg1: string, arg2: string) {
        console.log(`ClassWithMethodDec.print`
            + `(${arg1}, ${arg2}) called.`);
    }
}

let auditClass = new ClassWithAuditDec();
auditClass.print("test1", "test2");
```

Here, we are creating a class named `ClassWithAuditDec`, and decorating the `print` function with our `auditLogDec` method decorator. The `print` function has two arguments, and simply writes a message to the console showing that this function has been called with two arguments. The last two lines of this code snippet are an example of how this class would be used, and will produce the following output:

```
auditLogDec : overide of  print called
arg : 0 = test1
arg : 1 = test2
ClassWithMethodDec.print(test1, test2) called.
```

As can be seen in this output, our decorator audit function is being called before the actual implementation of the `print` function on the class. It is also able to log the values of each argument to the console, and has then invoked the original function correctly. Using decorators in this way is a powerful method of injecting extra functionality non-intrusively into a class declaration. Any class we create can easily include the auditing functionality simply by decorating the relevant class methods.

Parameter decorators

The final type of decorator that we will cover are parameter decorators. Parameter decorators are used to decorate the parameters of a particular method. As an example, consider the following code:

```
function parameterDec(
    target: any,
    methodName : string,
    parameterIndex: number)
{
    console.log(`target: ${target}`);
    console.log(`methodName : ${methodName}`);
    console.log(`parameterIndex : ${parameterIndex}`);
}
```

Here, we have defined a function named `parameterDec`, with three arguments. The `target` argument will contain the class prototype, as we have seen before. The `methodName` argument will contain the name of the method that contains the parameter, and the `parameterIndex` argument will contain the index of the parameter. We can use this parameter decorator function, as follows:

```
class ClassWithParamDec {
    print(@parameterDec  value: string) {
    }
}
```

Here, we have a class named `ClassWithParamDec`, that contains a single `print` function. This `print` function has a single argument named `value`, which is of type `string`. We have decorated this `value` parameter with the `parameterDec` decorator. Note that the syntax for using a parameter decorator (`@parameterDec`) is the same as any other decorator. The output of this code is as follows:

```
target: [object Object]
methodName : print
parameterIndex : 0
```

Note that we are not given any information about the parameter that we are decorating. We are not told what type it is, or even what its name is. Parameter decorators, therefore, can only really be used to establish that a parameter has been declared on a method.

Decorator metadata

The TypeScript compiler also includes experimental support for something called decorator metadata. Decorator metadata is metadata that is generated on class definitions in order to supplement the information that is passed into decorators. This option is called `emitDecoratorMetadata`, and can be added to the `tsconfig.json` file, as follows:

```
{
    "compilerOptions": {
        // other options
        "experimentalDecorators": true
        ,"emitDecoratorMetadata": true
    }
}
```

With this compile option in place, the TypeScript compiler will generate extra information relating to our class definitions. To see the results of this compile option, we will need to take a closer look at the generated JavaScript. Consider the following parameter decorator and class definition:

```
function metadataParameterDec(target: any,
    methodName : string,
    parameterIndex: number) {
}

class ClassWithMetaData {
    print(
        @metadataParameterDec
        id: number,
        name: string) : number {
```

```
        return 1000;
    }
}
```

Here, we have a standard parameter decorator named `metadataParameterDec`, and a class definition named `ClassWithMetaData`. We are decorating the first parameter of the `print` function. If we are not using the `emitDecoratorMetadata` compile option, or if this option is set to `false`, our generated JavaScript would be defined as follows:

```
var ClassWithMetaData = (function () {
    function ClassWithMetaData() {
    }
    ClassWithMetaData.prototype.print = function (id, name) {
    };
    __decorate([
        __param(0, metadataParameterDec)
    ], ClassWithMetaData.prototype, "print");
    return ClassWithMetaData;
}());
```

This generated JavaScript defines a standard JavaScript closure for our `ClassWithMetaData` class. The code that we are interested in is near the bottom of the closure, where the TypeScript compiler has injected a method named __decorate. We will not concern ourselves with the full functionality of this __decorate method, other than to note that it contains information about the `print` function, and indicates that it is named `print`, and that it has a single parameter at index 0.

When the `emitDecoratorMetadata` option is set to `true`, the generated JavaScript will contain some extra information about this `print` function, as follows:

```
var ClassWithMetaData = (function () {
    function ClassWithMetaData() {
    }
    ClassWithMetaData.prototype.print = function (id, name) {
    };
    __decorate([
        __param(0, metadataParameterDec),
        __metadata('design:type', Function),
        __metadata('design:paramtypes', [Number, String]),
        __metadata('design:returntype', Number)
    ], ClassWithMetaData.prototype, "print");
    return ClassWithMetaData;
}());
```

Note how the __decorate function now includes extra calls to a function named __metadata, which is called three times. The first call uses a special metadata key of 'design:type', the second uses the metadata key 'design:paramtypes', and the third call uses the metadata key 'design:returntype'. These three function calls to the __metadata function are, in fact, registering extra information about the print function itself. The 'design:type' key is used to register the fact that the print function is of type Function. The 'design:paramtypes' key is used to register the fact that the print function has two parameters—the first a Number, and the second a String. The 'design:returntype' key is used to register the return type of the print function which, in our case, is a number.

Using decorator metadata

In order to use this extra information within a decorator, we will need to use a third-party library named reflect-metadata. We will discuss how to use third-party libraries in detail in future chapters, but for the time being, this library can be included in our project by typing the following from the command line:

```
npm install reflect-metadata --save-dev
```

Once this has been installed, we will need to reference it in our TypeScript file by including the following line at the top of the file:

```
import 'reflect-metadata';
```

Before we attempt to compile any code that is using the reflect-metadata library, we will need to install the declaration file for this library, as follows:

```
npm install @types/reflect-metadata --save-dev
```

We will discuss declaration files in detail in the next chapter.

We can now start to use this class metadata by calling the Reflect.getMetadata function within our decorator. Consider the following update to our earlier parameter decorator:

```
function metadataParameterDec(target: any,
    methodName : string,
    parameterIndex: number) {

    let designType = Reflect.getMetadata(
        "design:type", target, methodName);
    console.log(`designType: ${designType}`)
    let designParamTypes = Reflect.getMetadata(
        "design:paramtypes", target, methodName);
```

```
    console.log(`paramtypes : ${designParamTypes}`);
    let designReturnType = Reflect.getMetadata(
        "design:returntype", target, methodName);
    console.log(`returntypes : ${designReturnType}`);
}
```

Here, we have updated our parameter decorator, with three calls to the `Reflect.getMetadata` function. The first is using the `'design:type'` metadata key. This is the same metadata key that we saw earlier in the generated JavaScript, where the compiler generated calls to the `__metadata` function. We are then logging the result to the console. We then repeat this process for the `'design:paramtypes'` and `'design:returntype'` metadata keys. The output of this code is as follows:

```
designType: function Function() { [native code] }
paramtypes : function Number() { [native code] },function String() {
[native code] }
returntypes : function Number() { [native code] }
```

We can see from this output, then, that the nature of the `print` function (as recorded by the `'design:type'` metadata key) is a `Function`. We can also see that information returned by the `'design:paramtypes'` key is an array that includes a `Number` and a `String`. This array, therefore, indicates that the function has two parameters, the first of type `Number`, and the second of type `String`. Finally, our return type for this function is a `Number`.

Metadata that is generated automatically by the TypeScript compiler, and that can be read and interrogated at runtime, can be extremely useful. In other languages, such as C#, this type of metadata information is called **reflection**, and is a fundamental principle when writing frameworks for dependency injection, or for generating code analysis tools.

Generics

Generics are a way of writing code that will deal with any type of object, but still maintain the object type integrity. So far, we have used interfaces, classes, and TypeScript's basic types to ensure strongly typed (and less error-prone) code in our samples. But what happens if a block of code needs to work with any type of object?

As an example, suppose we wanted to write some code that could iterate over an array of objects and return a concatenation of their values. So, given a list of numbers, say [1,2,3], it should return the string 1,2,3. Or, given a list of strings, say [first,second,third], return the string first,second,third. We could write some code that accepted values of type any, but this might introduce bugs in our code—remember S.F.I.A.T.? We want to ensure that all elements of the array are of the same type. This is where generics come in to play.

Generic syntax

As an example of TypeScript generic syntax, let's write a class called Concatenator that will concatenate the values in an array. We will need to ensure that each element of the array is of the same type. This class should be able to handle arrays of strings, arrays of numbers, and, in fact, arrays of any type. In order to do this, we need to rely on functionality that is common to each of these types. As all JavaScript objects have a toString function (which is called whenever a string is needed by the runtime), we can use this toString function to create a generic class that outputs all values held within an array.

A generic implementation of this Concatenator class is as follows:

```
class Concatenator< T > {
    concatenateArray(inputArray: Array< T >): string {
        let returnString = "";

        for (let i = 0; i < inputArray.length; i++) {
            if (i > 0)
                returnString += ",";
            returnString += inputArray[i].toString();
        }
        return returnString;
    }
}
```

The first thing we notice is the syntax of the class declaration, Concatenator < T >. This < T > syntax is the syntax used to indicate a generic type, and the name used for this generic type in the rest of our code is T. The concatenateArray function also uses this generic type syntax, Array < T >. This indicates that the inputArray argument must be an array of the type that was originally used to construct an instance of this class.

Instantiating generic classes

To use an instance of this generic class, we need to construct the class and tell the compiler via the < > syntax what the actual type of T is. We can use any type for the type of T in this generic syntax, including base types, classes, or even interfaces. Let's create a few versions of this class, as follows:

```
var stringConcat = new Concatenator<string>();
var numberConcat = new Concatenator<number>();
```

Notice the syntax that we have used to instantiate the Concatenator class. On the first line of this sample, we create an instance of the Concatenator generic class, and specify that it should substitute the generic type, T, with the type string in every place where T is being used within the code. Similarly, the second line of this sample creates an instance of the Concatenator class, and specifies that type number should be used wherever the code encounters the generic type T.

If we use this simple substitution principle, then, for the stringConcat instance (which uses strings), the inputArray argument must be of type Array<string>. Similarly, the numberConcat instance of this generic class uses numbers, and so the inputArray argument must be an array of numbers. To test this theory, let's generate an array of strings and an array of numbers, and see what the compiler says if we try to break this rule:

```
var stringArray: string[] = ["first", "second", "third"];
var numberArray: number[] = [1, 2, 3];
var stringResult =
    stringConcat.concatenateArray(stringArray);
var numberResult =
    numberConcat.concatenateArray(numberArray);
var stringResult2 =
    stringConcat.concatenateArray(numberArray);
var numberResult2 =
    numberConcat.concatenateArray(stringArray);
```

Our first two lines define our stringArray and numberArray variables to hold the relevant arrays. We then pass in the stringArray variable to the stringConcat function—no problems there. On our next line, we pass the numberArray to the numberConcat—still okay.

Our problems, however, start when we attempt to pass an array of numbers to the `stringConcat` instance, which has been configured to only use strings. Again, if we attempt to pass an array of strings to the `numberConcat` instance, which has been configured to allow only numbers, TypeScript will generate errors as follows:

```
error TS2345: Argument of type 'number[]' is not assignable to parameter of
type 'string[]'.
Type 'number' is not assignable to type 'string'.
error TS2345: Argument of type 'string[]' is not assignable to parameter of
type 'number[]'.
Type 'string' is not assignable to type 'number'.
```

Clearly, we are attempting to pass an array of numbers where we should have used strings, and vice versa. Again, the compiler warns us that we are not using the code correctly, and forces us to resolve these issues before continuing.

 These constraints on generics are a compile-time-only feature of TypeScript. If we look at the generated JavaScript, we will not see any reams of code that have to jump through hoops to ensure that these rules are carried through into the resultant JavaScript. All of these type constraints and generic syntax are actually compiled away. In the case of generics, the generated JavaScript is actually a very simplified version of our code, with no type in sight.

Using the type T

When we use generics, it is important to note that all of the code within the definition of a generic class or a generic function must respect the properties of T as if it were any type of object. Let's take a closer look at the implementation of the `concatenateArray` function in this light:

```
class Concatenator< T > {
    concatenateArray(inputArray: Array< T >): string {
        let returnString = "";

        for (let i = 0; i < inputArray.length; i++) {
            if (i > 0)
                returnString += ",";
            returnString += inputArray[i].toString();
        }
        return returnString;
    }
}
```

The concatenateArray function strongly types the inputArray argument so that it should be of type Array < T >. This means that any code that uses the inputArray argument can use only those functions and properties that are common to all arrays, no matter what type the array holds. We have used inputArray in two places.

Firstly, within the declaration of the for loop, note where we have used the inputArray.length property. All arrays have a length property to indicate how many items the array has, so using inputArray.length will work on any array, no matter what type of object the array holds. Secondly, on the last line of the for loop, we referenced an object within the array when we used the inputArray[i] syntax.

This reference actually returns us a single object of type T. Remember that whenever we use T in our code, we must use only those functions and properties that are common to any object of type T. Luckily for us, we are only using the toString function, and all JavaScript objects, no matter what type they are, have a valid toString function. So this generic code block will compile cleanly.

Let's test this type T theory by creating a class of our own to pass into the Concatenator class:

```
class MyClass {
    private _name: string;
    constructor(arg1: number) {
        this._name = arg1 + "_MyClass";
    }
}
```

Here, we have a simple class definition, named MyClass, that has a constructor function accepting a number. This constructor function sets an internal variable name _name to the value of the arg1 argument.

Let's now create an array of MyClass instances, as follows:

```
let myArray: MyClass[] = [
    new MyClass(1),
    new MyClass(2),
    new MyClass(3)];
```

We can now create an instance of our generic Concatenator class, as follows:

```
let myArrayConcatentator = new Concatenator<MyClass>();
let myArrayResult =
    myArrayConcatentator.concatenateArray(myArray);
console.log(myArrayResult);
```

We start with an instance of the `Concatenator` class, specifying that this generic instance will only work with objects that are of type `MyClass`. We then call the `concatenateArray` function and store the result in a variable named `myArrayResult`. Finally, we print the result on the console. Running this code will produce the following output:

```
[object Object],[object Object],[object Object]
```

Not quite what we were expecting. This output is due to the fact that the string representation of an object—that is, not one of the basic JavaScript types—resolves to `[object type]`. Any custom object that you write needs to override the `toString` function to provide human-readable output. We can fix this code quite easily by providing an override of the `toString` function within our class, as follows:

```
class MyClass {
    private _name: string;
    constructor(arg1: number) {
        this._name = arg1 + "_MyClass";
    }
    toString(): string {
        return this._name;
    }
}
```

Here, we replaced the default `toString` function that all JavaScript objects inherit with our own implementation. Within this function, we simply returned the value of the `_name` private variable. Running this sample now produces the expected result:

```
1_MyClass,2_MyClass,3_MyClass
```

Constraining the type of T

When using generics, it is often desirable to constrain the type of `T` to be only a specific type, or subset of types. In these cases, we don't want our generic code to be available for any type of object; we only want it to be available for a specific subset of objects. TypeScript uses inheritance to accomplish this with generics.

As an example, let's define an interface for a football team, as follows:

```
enum ClubHomeCountry {
    England,
    Germany
}

interface IFootballClub {
```

```
getName() : string | undefined;
getHomeCountry(): ClubHomeCountry | undefined;
}
```

Here, we have defined an enum named `ClubHomeCountry` to indicate where the home country is for a football club. Our `IFootballClub` interface then defines two methods that any `FootballClub` class must implement—a `getName` function to return the name of the football club, and a `getHomeCountry` function to return the `ClubHomeCountry` enum value.

We will now define an abstract base class to implement this interface, as follows:

```
abstract class FootballClub implements IFootballClub {
    protected _name: string | undefined;
    protected _homeCountry: ClubHomeCountry | undefined;
    getName() { return this._name };
    getHomeCountry() { return this._homeCountry };
}
```

This abstract class, named `FootballClub`, implements the `IFootballClub` interface, by defining a `getName` and `getHomeCountry` function, which returns the values held in the protected variables named _name and _homeCountry, respectively. As this is an abstract class, we will need to derive from it to create concrete classes, as follows:

```
class Liverpool extends FootballClub {
    constructor() {
        super();
        this._name = "Liverpool F.C.";
        this._homeCountry = ClubHomeCountry.England;
    }
}

class BorussiaDortmund extends FootballClub {
    constructor() {
        super();
        this._name = "Borussia Dortmund";
        this._homeCountry = ClubHomeCountry.Germany;
    }
}
```

Here, we have defined two classes, named `Liverpool` and `BorussiaDortmund`, that derive from our abstract base class `FootballClub`. Both classes have a single constructor that sets the internal _name and _homeCountry properties.

We can now create a generic class that will work with any class implementing the
IFootballClub interface, as follows:

```
class FootballClubPrinter< T extends IFootballClub >
    implements IFootballClubPrinter< T > {
    print(arg : T) {
        console.log(` ${arg.getName()} is ` +
            `${this.IsEnglishTeam(arg)}` +
            ` an English football team.`
        );
    }
    IsEnglishTeam(arg : T) : string {
        if ( arg.getHomeCountry() == ClubHomeCountry.England )
            return "";
        else
            return "NOT"
    }
}
```

Here, we have defined a class named FootballClubPrinter that uses the generic syntax.
Note that the T generic type is now deriving from the IFootballClub interface, as
indicated by the extends keyword in < T extends IFootballClub >. Using
inheritance when defining a generic class constrains the type of class that can be used by
this generic code. In other words, any usage of the type T within the generic code will
substitute the interface IFooballClub instead. This means that the generic code will only
allow functions or properties that are defined in the IFootballClub interface to be used
wherever T is used.

These constraints can be seen within the print function, as well as within the
IsEnglishTeam function. In the print function, the argument arg is of type T, and
therefore, we are able to use arg.getName, which has been defined in the IFootballClub
interface. In the print function, we are also calling the IsEnglishTeam function, and
passing the argument arg to it. The IsEnglishTeam function is using the
getHomeCountry function that is also defined in the IFootballClub interface.

To illustrate how this generic FootballClubPrinter class can be used, consider the
following code:

```
let clubInfo = new FootballClubPrinter();
clubInfo.print(new Liverpool());
clubInfo.print(new BorussiaDortmund());
```

Here, we are creating an instance of the `FootballClubPrinter` class named `clubInfo`. Note how we do not need to specify the type (as we did with our earlier class `Concatenator`) when creating an instance of the class.

We are then calling the `print` function of the `clubInfo` generic class, passing in a new instance of the `Liverpool` class, and then passing in an instance of the `BorussiaDortmund` class. The output of this code is as follows:

```
Liverpool F.C. is an English football team.
Borussia Dortmund is NOT an English football team.
```

In summary, then, we can constrain the type of `T` that is used in generic syntax to a specific type by deriving the type `T` from another type using the `extends` syntax. In other words, if `T` extends a type, then the generic code can assume that `T` is of that type.

Generic interfaces

We can also use interfaces with the generic type syntax. If we were to create an interface for our `FootballClubPrinter` generic class, the interface definition would be as follows:

```
interface IFootballClubPrinter < T extends IFootballClub > {
    print(arg : T);
    IsEnglishTeam(arg : T);
}
```

This interface looks identical to our class definition, with the only difference being that the `print` and the `IsEnglishTeam` functions do not have an implementation. We have kept the generic type syntax using `< T >`, and further specified that the type `T` must implement the `IFootballClub` interface. To use this interface with the `FootballClubPrinter` class, we can modify the class definition, as follows:

```
class FootballClubPrinter< T extends IFootballClub >
    implements IFootballClubPrinter< T > {

}
```

This syntax seems pretty straightforward. As we have seen before, we use the `implements` keyword following the class definition, and then use the interface name. Note, however, that we pass the type `T` into the interface definition of `IFootballClubPrinter` as a generic type `IFootballClubPrinter<T>`. This satisfies the `IFootballClubPrinter` generic interface definition.

An interface that defines our generic classes further protects our code from being modified inadvertently. As an example of this, suppose that we tried to redefine the class definition of `FootballClubPrinter` so that `T` is not constrained to be of type `IFootballClub`:

```
class FootballClubPrinter< T  >
    implements IFootballClubPrinter< T > {

}
```

Here, we have removed the constraint on the type `T` for the `FootballClubPrinter` class. TypeScript will automatically generate an error:

error TS2344: Type 'T' does not satisfy the constraint 'IFootballClub'.

This error points us to our erroneous class definition; the type `T`, as used in the code (`FootballClubPrinter<T>`), must use a type `T` that extends from `IFootballClub` in order to correctly implement the `IFootballClubPrinter` interface.

Creating new objects within generics

From time to time, generic classes may need to create an object of the type that is passed in as the generic type `T`. Consider the following code:

```
class FirstClass {
    id: number | undefined;
}

class SecondClass {
    name: string | undefined;
}

class GenericCreator< T > {
    create(): T {
        return new T();
    }
}

var creator1 = new GenericCreator<FirstClass>();
var firstClass: FirstClass = creator1.create();

var creator2 = new GenericCreator<SecondClass>();
var secondClass : SecondClass = creator2.create();
```

Here, we have two class definitions, FirstClass and SecondClass. FirstClass just has a public id property, and SecondClass has a public name property. We then have a generic class that accepts a type T and has a single function, named create. This create function attempts to create a new instance of the type T.

The last four lines of the sample show us how we would like to use this generic class. The creator1 variable creates a new instance of the GenericCreator class using the correct syntax for creating variables of the type FirstClass. The creator2 variable is a new instance of the GenericCreator class, but this time is using SecondClass. Unfortunately, the preceding code will generate a TypeScript compile error:

```
error TS2304: Cannot find name 'T'.
```

According to the TypeScript documentation, in order to enable a generic class to create objects of type T, we need to refer to type T by its constructor function. We also need to pass in the class definition as an argument. The create function will need to be rewritten, as follows:

```
class GenericCreator< T > {
    create(arg1: { new(): T }) : T {
        return new arg1();
    }
}
```

Let's break this create function down into its component parts. First, we pass an argument, named arg1. This argument is then defined to be of the type { new(): T }. This is the little trick that allows us to refer to T by its constructor function. We are defining a new anonymous type that overloads the new() function and returns a type T. This means that the arg1 argument is a function that is strongly typed to have a single constructor that returns a type T. The implementation of this function simply returns a new instance of the arg1 variable. Using this syntax removes the compile error that we encountered before.

This change, however, means that we must pass the class definition to the create function, as follows:

```
var creator1 = new GenericCreator<FirstClass>();
var firstClass: FirstClass = creator1.create(FirstClass);

var creator2 = new GenericCreator<SecondClass>();
var secondClass : SecondClass = creator2.create(SecondClass);
```

Note the change in usage of the `create` function. We are now required to pass in the class definition for our type of `T`—`create(FirstClass)` and `create(SecondClass)` as our first argument. Try running this code to see what happens. The generic class will, in fact, create new objects of the types `FirstClass` and `SecondClass`, as we expected.

Advanced types with generics

The TypeScript compiler already gives us a large toolbox in order to define custom types, inherit types from each other, and use generic syntax to describe how our code is expecting to use these types. By combining these language features, we can start to describe some seriously advanced type definitions, including types based on other types, or types based on some or all of the properties of another type. By using some new TypeScript keywords, and applying some well-known language features, we can also start to query a type for its properties, check to see whether a type has certain properties, or completely modify a type by adding or removing properties as we see fit. Welcome to the mind-bending world of conditional types, inferred types, mapped types and more, or as the author describes it, simply "theoretical type mathematics". Be warned that the syntax of advanced types and generics can seem complicated at first, but, if we apply some simple rules, it eventually becomes understandable.

Remember that although types help us to describe our code, and also help us to harden our code, they do not affect the JavaScript that is generated. Simply describing a type is a theoretical exercise, and much of the advanced type mathematics that we will learn still only generate a type. We will still need to put these types to use in order to realize their benefit in a practical way.

Conditional types

One of the features of the TypeScript language includes a simple, streamlined version of an `if then else` statement, which uses the question mark (?) symbol to define the `if` statement, and the colon symbol (:) to define the `then` and `else` path. These are called `conditional statements`. The format of the conditional statement is as follows:

```
(conditional statement) ? (true value) : (false value);
```

We start with a conditional statement followed by a ? symbol. We then define the `true` value and the `false` value separated by the : symbol. As an example of this, consider the following code:

```
let trueValue = true;
let printValue = trueValue === true ? "true" : "false";

console.log(`printValue is : ${printValue}`);
```

Here, we have defined a variable named `trueValue`, and set it to `true`. Our conditional statement then sets the value of the `printValue` variable to the string `true` or `false`, based on the conditional check `if trueValue === true`. In other words, if `trueValue === true`, then use the string value of `true`, otherwise use the value after the colon symbol (`:`), which is the string value of `false`.

Conditional statements can also be used with types, using the same syntax, and the resultant types are called conditional types. Consider the following type definition:

```
type numberOrString<T> = T extends number ? number : string;
```

Here, we have defined a new type named `numberOrString` that is using generic syntax to indicate that it can only be used when given a type of `T`. If the type of `T` extends `number`, then the resultant `numberOrString` will be of type `number`. If the type of `T` does not extend `number`, then the resultant type will be of type `string`.

We can then use this conditional type in a function, as follows:

```
function isNumberOrString<T>(input: numberOrString<T>) {
    console.log(`numberOrString : ${input}`);
}
```

Here, we have a function named `isNumberOrString` that uses generic syntax, and therefore requires us to call this function with a type named `T`. The only parameter for this function is named `input`, and uses our conditional type named `numberOrString<T>`. What this means is that depending on the type of `T` that we invoke this function with, the input parameter may change from a `number` to a `string`. In other words, the parameter input is conditional on the type `T`. Let's try to call this function as follows:

```
isNumberOrString<number>(1);
isNumberOrString<number>("test");
```

Here, we start by calling the `isNumberOrString` function, specifying that the type of T is a number, and passing in an argument of 1. We then call the same function, with the same type of T, with an argument of `"test"`. Compiling this code will generate the following error:

```
error TS2345: Argument of type '"test"' is not assignable to parameter of
type 'number'.
```

So what is happening here ? We are calling the `isNumberOrString` function, passing in a type of number for the generic type T, and then passing in an argument of type string. Our conditional type `numberOrString<T>` is the key here. Looking back at the definition of this conditional type, we know that if the type of T is a number, then this will resolve to type number. If the type of T is not a number, then this will resolve to type string. So when we call the function `isNumberOrString`, and specify that the type of T is a number, the parameter input changes its type to a string. This means that to fix our compile error, we need to call this function as follows:

```
isNumberOrString<string>("test");
```

Here, the type of T is of type string, and therefore, the input parameter has changed its type to be of type string, so that we can call this function with an input argument of type string.

Let's now try a more complex example. We have the following types, named a, ab, and abc:

```
interface a {
    a: number;
}
interface ab {
    a: number;
    b: string;
}
interface abc {
    a: number;
    b: string;
    c: boolean;
}
```

Here, we have three types. Type `a` has a single property, named `a`, type `ab` has two properties, named `a` and `b`, and type `abc` has three properties, named `a`, `b`, and `c`. We can now create a conditional type, as follows:

```
type abc_ab_a<T> = T extends abc ? [number, string, boolean] :
    T extends ab ? [number, string] :
    T extends a ? [number]
    : never;
```

Here, we have defined a conditional type named `abc_ab_a`. If the type of `T` extends `abc`, (in other words, if it has an `a`, `b`, and `c` property) then return a tuple of `[number, string, boolean]`. If the type of `T` does not extend `abc`, we check whether it extends `ab`; in other words, does it have an `a` and `b` property ? If it does, then return a tuple of `[number, string]`. If the type of `T` does not extend `ab`, we then check whether it extends `a`, and return a tuple of `[number]`. If the type of `T` does not extend `abc`, `ab`, or `a`, then return `never`.

We can then write a function that uses this conditional type, as follows:

```
function getKeyAbc<T>(key: abc_ab_a<T>): string {
    let [...args] = key;
    let keyString = ":";
    for (let arg of args) {
        keyString += `${arg}:`
    }
    return keyString;
}
```

Our function is named `getKeyAbc`, and uses generic syntax to indicate that it must be called with a type named `T`. This function has a single argument named `key` that uses our conditional type `abc_ab_a`. Remember that our conditional type will return a tuple, so `key` is actually a tuple that could have three, two, or one elements. The body of this function is using a spread tuple to extract the values of the argument `key`, and concatenate them into a string. We can use this function as follows:

```
let key10 = getKeyAbc<a>([1]);
console.log(`key10 : ${key10}`);

let key20 = getKeyAbc<ab>([1, "test"]);
console.log(`key20 : ${key20}`);

let key30 = getKeyAbc<abc>([1, "test2", true]);
console.log(`key30 : ${key30}`);
```

Here, we start with a variable named `key10` that is calling our `getKeyAbc` function with a type of a. Note that because we are using the type a, the conditional type `abc_ab_a` will return a tuple of type `[number]`, so the `input` parameter to the `getKeyAbc` function must be a tuple of type `[number]`. We then print the value of the returned string to the console. The variable `key20` is calling the `getKeyAbc` function with a type of ab, and therefore must provide an `input` argument of type `[number, string]`. The variable `key30` is using the type abc, and therefore must provide an `input` argument of type `[number, string, boolean]`. The output of this code is as follows:

```
key10 : :1:
key20 : :1:test:
key30 : :1:test2:true:
```

All well and good. Let's now attempt to break the rules a little bit, as follows:

```
let keyNever = getKeyAbc<string>([1]);
```

Here, we are passing in a `string` as the type of T for our `getKeyAbc` function. This code will generate the following compile error:

```
error TS2345: Argument of type '"test"' is not assignable to parameter of
type 'never'.
```

The cause of this error is that we have used a type of `string` for the type of T. Looking back at our conditional type `abc_ab_a`, a `string` does not extend either a, ab, or abc, and therefore the conditional type is returning a type of `never`. This guarantees that the `getKeyAbc` function must be used with only one of the three allowed types.

If we have a mismatch in the type of T and the input parameter, as follows:

```
let keyABCWrong = getKeyAbc<abc>([1, "test"]);
```

The compiler will generate the following message:

```
error TS2345: Argument of type '[number, string]' is not assignable to
parameter of type '[number, string, boolean]'.
Property '2' is missing in type '[number, string]'
```

Here, we have specified that the type of T is of the type abc, and, therefore, the input parameter must be a tuple of type `[number, string, boolean]`.

Distributed conditional types

When defining a conditional type, we can also use distributive syntax to return one of a number of types. As an example of this, consider the following function definition:

```
function compareTwoValues(
    input : string | number | Date,
    compareTo : string | number | Date ) {
}
```

Here, we have defined a function named `compareTwoValues` that has two parameters, `input` and `compareTo`. Both the `input` and the `compareTo` parameters can accept either a `string` or a `number` or a `Date` type. But what if we wanted to apply the following rules:

- If the `input` parameter is of type `Date`, then only allow the `compareTo` parameter to be of type `Date`
- If the `input` parameter is of type `number`, then allow the `compareTo` parameter to be of type `number` or `Date`
- If the `input` parameter is of type `string`, then allow the `compareTo` parameter to be either type `number`, `Date` or `string`

Implementing this logic is where distributed conditional types come in handy, as follows:

```
type dateOrNumberOrString<T> =
    T extends Date ? Date :
    T extends number ? Date | number :
    T extends string ? Date | number | string : never;
```

Here, we have a conditional type named `dateOrNumberOrString`. The first condition states that if `T` is of type `Date`, then return a type of `Date`. The second condition states that if `T` is of type `number`, then return a type of `Date` or `number`, and the final condition states that if `T` is of type `string`, then return a type of `Date` or `number` or `string`. If none of these conditional types are found, then return a type of `never`. We can now use this distributed conditional type in a function definition, as follows:

```
function compareValues<T extends string | number | Date | boolean>
    (input: T, compareTo : dateOrNumberOrString<T>) {
    // do the comparison
}
```

Here, we have defined a function named `compareValues` that is using a distributed type for the type of `T`, and which allows the type of `T` to be either a `string`, `number`, `Date`, or `boolean` type. The `input` parameter is of type `T`, and the `compareTo` parameter is now using our distributed conditional type `dateOrNumberOrString`. We now have some design time rules in place for code that calls this function. Let's test this design using `Date` types as follows:

```
compareValues(new Date(), new Date());
compareValues(new Date(), 1);
compareValues(new Date(), "1");
```

Here, we call the `compareValues` function with a `Date` type as the first argument. The first call to `compareValues` is legal, as the nature of the second argument is of type `Date`. The second and third calls to `compareValues`, however, will both cause compilation errors as follows:

```
error TS2345: Argument of type '1' is not assignable to parameter of type
'Date'.
error TS2345: Argument of type '"1"' is not assignable to parameter of type
'Date'.
```

Here, we can see that the compiler will not allow the `compareTo` argument to be of type `number` or of type `string` if the `input` argument is of type `Date`. Let's further test our distributed conditional type with numbers, as follows:

```
compareValues(1, 1);
compareValues(1, Date.now());
compareValues(1, "1");
```

Here, the type of the `input` argument is `number`, and we are calling the `compareTo` function with a type of `number`, then `Date`, and then `string`. The first two calls are legal, according to our logic, but the last call will generate an error:

```
error TS2345: Argument of type '"1"' is not assignable to parameter of type
'Date'.
```

Finally, let's break all of the rules, and call our `compareTo` function with a type of `boolean`, as follows:

```
compareValues(true, "test");
```

Here, the type of our `input` argument is `boolean`. Note that our function definition allows this, as the type of `T` can be of type `string`, `number`, `Date` or `boolean`. The distributed conditional type, however, does not, and will therefore generate the following error:

```
error TS2345: Argument of type '"test"' is not assignable to parameter of
type 'never'.
```

So our distributed conditional type is checking the input argument, which is of type `boolean`, not matching any of our conditions, and therefore returning a type of `never`. Our function design has held up, even though we might have made a mistake in allowing the `input` argument to be of type `boolean`.

Conditional type inference

When working with conditional types, we can extract the type of each parameter using the `infer` keyword. This is best explained through some examples, as follows:

```
type extractArrayType<T> = T extends (infer U)[] ? U : never;
let stringType : extractArrayType<["test"]> = "test";
let stringTypeNoArray : extractArrayType<"test"> = "test";
```

Here, we have a conditional type named `extractArrayType` that is using generic syntax, and as such must be used with a type named `T`. Our conditional type then checks whether the type of `T` is an array. If it is an array, we then use the `infer` keyword to infer a type named `U`; otherwise we return the type `never`. Note that inferred type names (`U` in this case) can only be used within a conditional type. We then define a variable named `stringType`, whose type is the result of our `extractArrayType` conditional type. As our type of `T` in this case is an array of `string` types, the type of `U` will be `string`. This means that we have extracted the type out of an array using the `(infer U)` syntax.

The last line of our code snippet, however, will generate the following error:

```
error TS2322: Type '"test"' is not assignable to type 'never'
```

Our conditional type, therefore, determines that the type `"test"` is not an array, and is therefore returning a type of `never`.

Let's take a look at a slightly more complicated case, as follows:

```
type InferredAb<T> = T extends { a: infer U, b: infer U } ? U : T;
type abInferredNumber = InferredAb< { a :number, b: number}>;
let abinf : abInferredNumber = 1;

type abInferredNumberString = InferredAb< { a :number, b: string}>;
let abinfstr : abInferredNumberString = 1;
abinfstr = "test";
```

Here, we have defined a conditional type named `InferredAb`, which checks whether our type has an `a` and a `b` property. If it does, it will infer the type of `U` from the `a` and `b` properties. We then create a second type named `abInferredNumber` that is using our conditional type with an object where `a` and `b` are both numbers. This means that `a: infer U` returns a `number`, and `b: infer U` also returns a number. Therefore, the type of `U` will be a type of number. The variable `abinf` is therefore of type `number`.

We then create a type named `abInferredNumberString`, and use our conditional type with a type where `a` is a `number`, and `b` is a `string`. This means that `a: infer U` will return a `number` type, and `b: infer U` will return a `string` type. So the outcome of our conditional type will be a type union of type `number | string`. This means that when we create a variable named `abinfstr`, and set its type to `abInferredNumberString`, we can assign either a `number` to it, or a `string` to it, since our inferred type is `number | string`.

keyof

TypeScript allows us to iterate through the properties of a type and extract the names of its properties through the `keyof` keyword. `keyof` will therefore return a string literal made up of property names. Let's explore this concept by starting with an interface, as follows:

```
interface IPerson {
    id: number;
    name: string;
    surname: string;
}
```

Here, we have an interface named `IPerson` that has three properties, named `id`, `name`, and `surname`. If we were to write a function that needs its input limited to the string values `"id"`, `"name"` and `"surname"`, we could use a string literal as follows:

```
type PersonPropertyLiteral = "id" | "name" | "surname";

function getKeyOfUsingStringLiteral
    (ppl : PersonPropertyLiteral, value : IPerson) {
    console.log(`${ppl} : ${value[ppl]}`)
}
```

Here, we have defined a string literal named `PersonPropertyLiteral` that limits string values to one of either `"id"`, `"name"`, or `"surname"`. We are then using this string literal in a function named `getKeyOfUsingStringLiteral` to ensure that the first parameter, named `ppl`, fits one of these three values. This is to ensure that when we reference the value parameter using `value[ppl]`, we are correctly using a property name that is part of the `IPerson` interface. Unfortunately, if we ever modify the `IPerson` interface, we will need to also remember to modify the `PersonPropertyLiteral` literal.

The `keyof` keyword, however, will automatically generate a string literal type based on the properties of a given type, so that we do not need to manually create literals in this way. Consider the following function:

```
function getKeyUsingKeyOf(key: keyof IPerson, value: IPerson): void {
    console.log(`${key} :   ${value[key]}`);
}
```

Here, we have a function named `getKeyUsingKeyOf` that uses the `keyof` keyword to accomplish the same result. The type of the parameter `key` is now using the `keyof` keyword to automatically generate a string literal for all of the properties of the interface `IPerson`. We can then use this function as follows:

```
let testPerson : IPerson = { id: 1, name: "test", surname: "true" };

getKeyUsingKeyOf("id", testPerson);
getKeyUsingKeyOf("name", testPerson);
getKeyUsingKeyOf("surname", testPerson);
```

Here, we create a variable named `testPerson` that is of type `IPerson`, and defines the `id`, `name`, and `surname` properties. We are then calling the `getKeyUsingKeyOf` function a few times to log the value of the `id`, `name`, and `surname` properties to the console. Be aware that if we attempt to call this function with a property that does not exist on the `IPerson` interface, as follows:

```
getKeyUsingKeyOf("notaproperty", testPerson);
```

The compiler will generate the following error:

```
error TS2345: Argument of type '"notaproperty"' is not assignable to
parameter of type '"id" | "name" | "surname"'
```

This error is indicating that the interface `IPerson` does not have a property named `notaproperty`, since the result of `keyof IPerson` will only allow a `string` value that is either `"id"`, `"name"`, or `"surname"`.

keyof with number

We can also use the `keyof` keyword when working with numeric properties of an object. Remember that if we define an object with a numeric property, then we need to both define the property and access the property using array syntax as follows:

```
class ClassWithNumericProperty {
    [1] : string = "one";
}
let classWithNumeric = new ClassWithNumericProperty();
console.log(`${classWithNumeric[1]} `);
```

Here, we have defined a class named `ClassWithNumericProperty` that defines a property named 1 to be of type `string`, and a value of `"one"`. Note how we need to define this property using array syntax by defining it as `[1]`, instead of just 1. We then create a class named `classWithNumeric`, and log the value of the property `[1]` to the console. The output of this code is simply:

one

What this shows us is that we are able to use property names that are numeric, if we use array syntax.

With this in mind, let's write some code that will return a `string` value for an `enum` type. Consider the following code:

```
enum Currency {
    AUD = 36,
    PLN = 985,
    USD = 840
}

const CurrencyName = {
    [Currency.AUD]: "Australian Dollar",
    [Currency.PLN]: "Zloty"
}
```

Here, we have defined an enum named Currency, and specified that the value of these enums are their corresponding international currency codes. We then define a constant named CurrencyName that is defining a string value for each of the enum values. We can therefore find a string value for the Australian Dollar enum value in two ways, as follows:

```
console.log(`CurrencyName[Currency.AUD] =
    ${CurrencyName[Currency.AUD]}`);
console.log(`CurrencyName[36] = ${CurrencyName[36]}`);
```

Here, we are finding the string value for the Australian Dollar by referencing the corresponding numeric property, either CurrencyName[Currency.AUD], or simply CurrencyName[36].

We can then use the keyof keyword to generate a numeric literal for the numeric properties of the CurrencyName object, as follows:

```
function getCurrencyName<T, K extends keyof T>
    (key: K, map: T): T[K] {
    return map[key];
}
```

Here, we have defined a function called getCurrencyName, which utilizes generic syntax, and defines a generic type named T, as well as a generic type named K. The key part of this code snippet is the type K extends keyof T. In other words, K must be a numeric literal that is derived from the numeric properties of T. This function has two parameters, named key (for the type of K) and map (for the type of T). Note that it is returning T[K], which means that it is returning a property named K from the type of T. The implementation of this function is really simple in that it is returning map[key], so it is returning the numeric property named [key] from the object named map. The interesting aspect is how we use this function, as follows:

```
let name = getCurrencyName(Currency.AUD, CurrencyName);
console.log(`name = ${name}`);
name = getCurrencyName(Currency.PLN, CurrencyName);
console.log(`name = ${name}`);
```

Here, we are defining a variable named name, which is the result of calling the getCurrencyName function. This call uses two arguments. The first is a value from our CurrencyEnum, and the second is the CurrencyName object itself. The output of this code is as follows:

```
name = Australian Dollar
name = Zloty
```

In the first call to the `getCurrencyName` function, we are specifying the enum value of `Currency.AUD` as our first argument, which is the type `K`. We are then specifying the object `CurrencyName` as our second argument, which is of type `T`. According to the function definition, `K` must `extend keyof T`. As `CurrencyName[36]`, or `CurrencyName[Currency.AUD]` is a property of the object `CurrencyName`, we are satisfying these rules. If, however, we try to reference a numeric property that does not exist on the object `CurrencyName`, as follows:

```
name = getCurrencyName(Currency.USD, CurrencyName);
```

The TypeScript compiler will generate the following message:

```
error TS2345: Argument of type 'Currency.USD' is not assignable to
parameter of type 'Currency.AUD | Currency.PLN'.
```

This error is indicating that there is no property named `Currency.USD` of the object `CurrencyName`, since the `keyof` keyword generates a numeric literal of `Currency.AUD | Currency.PLN` for the type of `T`. So our type `K`, therefore, does not `extend keyof T`, hence the error.

Mapped types

The `keyof` keyword and generic types allow us to do some rather interesting theoretical type mathematics, and map one type to another based on some simple rules. This is best illustrated through a number of code examples, as follows:

```
interface IAbcRequired {
    a: number;
    b: string;
    c: boolean;
}

type PartialProps<T> = {
    [K in keyof T]?: T[K];
}
```

Here, we have defined an interface named `IAbcRequired`, that has three properties, named `a`, `b`, and `c`. We then define a type named `PartialProps`, which is using generic syntax that requires a type named `T`. This `PartialProps` type defines a single property, named `K`, which is of type `keyof T`.

In other words, take all of the properties of type `T`, and include them in this new type named `PartialProps`. The interesting thing about this type definition, is that it is using optional syntax (the `?` symbol) to mark all properties of the type `T` to be optional.

In other words, we have mapped the type of `T` into a new type, and transformed all properties of the type `T` into optional properties.

We can now define a mapped type as follows:

```
type IPartialAbc = PartialProps<IAbcRequired>;
```

Here, we have defined a type name `IPartialAbc` that is using our `PartialProps` mapped type to make all of the properties of the `IAbcRequired` interface optional. We can then use this new mapped type as follows:

```
let abNoCObject: IPartialAbc = { a: 1, b: "test" };
let aNoBcObject: IPartialAbc = { a: 1 };
```

Here, we have defined two variables named `abNoCObject`, and `aNoBcObject`, that are defining the `a` and `b` properties, and then just the `a` property, respectively. So, in effect, we have used the original type of `IAbcRequired`, and mapped it to another type where the properties are optional.

Partial, Readonly, Record, and Pick

Mapped types that transform properties to optional, or transform properties to `readonly`, are seen as so fundamental that they have been included in the standard TypeScript type definitions. In other words, we can use `Partial<T>` to create a type where all properties of `T` are optional, or `ReadOnly<T>` to create a type where all properties of `T` are `readonly`. To create these mapped types for our `IAbcRequired` interface, we can simply write the following:

```
type partialAbc = Partial<IAbcRequired>;
type readonlyAbc = Readonly<IAbcRequired>;
```

Here, the type `partialAbc` is a copy of the `IAbcRequired` type, but with all properties marked as optional. Similarly, the type `readonlyAbc` is a copy of the `IAbcRequired` type, but with all properties marked as `readonly`.

We can also construct a type that is a subset of the properties of another type, using `Pick`. `Pick` is defined, as follows:

```
/**
 * From T pick a set of properties K
 */
type Pick<T, K extends keyof T> = {
    [P in K]: T[P];
};
```

Consider the following code:

```
type pickAb = Pick<IAbcRequired,  "a" | "b">;
let pickAbObject : pickAb = { a: 1, b: "test"};
let pickAcObject : pickAb = { a : 1, c: true};
```

Here, we have defined a type named `pickAb` that is using the generic definition of `Pick` in order to create a new type that only includes the properties `a` and `b` of `IAbcRequired`. We then create an object named `pickAbObject` that is of type `pickAb`, and, as such, needs both an `a` and `b` property. Note that in the last line of this snippet, we are attempting to create an object named `pickAcObject` that is of type `pickAb`, but which has the properties `a` and `c`. This will generate a compiler error, as follows:

error TS2322: Type '{ a: number; c: boolean; }' is not assignable to type 'Pick<IAbcRequired, "a" | "b">'.

The compiler is telling us we cannot assign an object with an `a` and `c` property to an object that has an `a` and `b` property.

The final mapped type that we will explore is `Record`, which is defined, as follows:

```
/**
 * Construct a type with a set of properties K of type T
 */
type Record<K extends keyof any, T> = {
    [P in K]: T;
};
```

With this definition, we can create a completely new type by specifying a list of properties, and their type, as follows:

```
type recordAc = Record< "a" | "c", string>;
let recordAcObject : recordAc = {a : "test", c: "test"};
let recordAcNumbers : recordAc = { a: 1, c: "test"};
```

Here, we have defined a type named `recordAc` that is using the `Record` generic definition to create a type that has the properties `a` and `c` of type `string`. We then create an object named `recordAcObject` that uses this type, and specifies the properties of `a` and `c`. The last line of this code, however, will generate a compiler error, as follows:

```
error TS2322: Type number is not assignable to type string
```

The compiler is telling us that both of the properties of type `recordAc` must be strings.

This concludes our exploration of advanced generics, where we have seen how the many features of TypeScript allow us to mix and match types, and construct them from other types using generic syntax, using a simple syntax that allows us to perform theoretical type mathematics. Just remember that the types that we are creating are just types, and will be compiled away in the resulting JavaScript.

Asynchronous language features

In this section of the chapter, we will discuss some asynchronous language features, and, in particular, promises and the `async` and `await` keywords.

The code samples in this section have been designed to run on Node version 4 and above, which provides an ECMAScript 6 runtime. You can determine which version of Node you are running by executing the following on the command line:

```
node --version
```

You need to ensure that the return value is `v4` or greater to compile and run the code samples in this section. The information returned by the version of Node used in this section is as follows:

```
v11.9.0
```

Promises

Promises are a technique for standardizing asynchronous processing in JavaScript. Remember that there are many occasions where a function is called in JavaScript, but the actual results are only received after a period of time. These occasions typically arise when your code is requesting a resource of some sort, such as posting a request to a web server for some JSON data, or reading a file from disk. The standard JavaScript technique for asynchronous processing is the callback mechanism.

Unfortunately, when working with a lot of callbacks, our code can sometimes become rather complex and repetitive. Promises provide a way of simplifying this callback code. To start off our discussion on promises, let's take a look at some typical callback code, as follows:

```
function delayedResponseWithCallback(callback: Function) {
    function delayedAfterTimeout() {
        console.log(`delayedAfterTimeout`);
        callback();
    }
    setTimeout(delayedAfterTimeout, 1000);
}

function callDelayedAndWait() {
    function afterWait() {
        console.log(`afterWait`);
    }
    console.log(`calling delayedResponseWithCallback`);
    delayedResponseWithCallback(afterWait);
    console.log(`after calling delayedResponseWithCallback`);
}

callDelayedAndWait();
```

We start with a function named `delayedResponseWithCallback` that takes a single argument of type `Function`, named `callback`. If we consider the last line of this function, we see that it is calling `setTimeout` with a 1,000 millisecond or a 1 second delay. This is designed to simulate a delay in processing, that is, an asynchronous function, within our code. The `setTimeout` function takes a function as its first parameter, which will be called after the 1 second delay. In this case, we are passing the function named `delayedAfterTimeout`, which simply logs a message to the console, and then calls our callback function.

The second function in this code snippet is called `callDelayedAndWait`. If we take a look at the last three lines of this function, we see that it is logging a message to the console, and then calling our `delayedResponseWithCallback` function. It is passing in the function `afterWait` as the callback function. The last line of the code executes our `callDelayedAndWait` function. The output of this code is as follows:

```
calling delayedResponseWithCallback
after calling delayedResponseWithCallback
delayedAfterTimeout
afterWait
```

What we can see from the output is the sequence of events that are happening in our code. When we execute the `callDelayedAndWait` function, it sets up a callback function, and then logs the text `calling delayedResponseWithCallback`, to the console. It then invokes the `delayedResponseWithCallback` function, and then continues on to the next line, where it logs the text `after calling delayedResponseWithCallback`. After a 1 second delay, the function `delayedAfterTimeout` is invoked, which then logs the text `delayedAfterTimeout`, to the console, and finally the `afterWait` function is invoked, logging the text `afterWait`, to the console.

While these sorts of callback functions are fairly standard in JavaScript, it can make our code difficult to read, as well as difficult to understand, especially as our code base grows larger and larger. Promises, on the other hand, provide a fluent syntax for handling asynchronous calls.

Promise syntax

A promise is an object that is created by passing in a function that accepts two callbacks. The first callback is used to indicate a successful response, and the second callback is used to indicate an error response. Consider the following function definition:

```
function fnDelayedPromise (
    resolve: () => void,
    reject : () => void)
    {
        function afterTimeout() {
            resolve();
        }
        setTimeout( afterTimeout, 2000);
    }
```

Here, we have defined a function named `fnDelayedPromise` that takes two functions as arguments. These functions are named `resolve` and `reject`, and they both return a `void`. Within the body of the `fnDelayedPromise` function, we are again calling `setTimeout` (on the last line of the function) to wait for 2 seconds before calling the `resolve` callback function.

We can now use this function to construct a `promise` object, as follows:

```
function delayedResponsePromise() : Promise<void> {
    return new Promise<void>(
        fnDelayedPromise
    );
}
```

Here, we have created a function named `delayedResponsePromise` that returns a `new Promise<void>` object. Within the body of the function, we are simply creating and returning a new promise object, and using our earlier function definition named `fnDelayedPromise` as the only argument within its constructor. Note that type `void`, which is used to create a promise, is using generic syntax (`new Promise<void>`) to indicate some information on the return type of the promise. We will discuss the use of the generic `<void>` syntax a little later, when we explore how to return values from promises.

While this syntax may seem a little convoluted, in general practice, these two function definitions are combined in a single code block. The purpose of the previous two snippets has been to highlight two important concepts. Firstly, to use promises, you must return a new promise object. Secondly, a promise object is constructed with a function that takes two callback arguments.

Let's take a look at how these two steps are combined in general practice, as follows:

```
function delayedPromise() : Promise<void> {
    return new Promise<void>
    (
        (   resolve : () => void,
            reject: () => void
        ) => {
            function afterTimeout() {
                resolve();
            }
            setTimeout( afterTimeout, 1000);
        }
    );
}
```

Here, we have a function named `delayedPromise` that returns a new `Promise<void>` object. The first line of this function constructs the `new Promise` object, and passes in an anonymous function definition that takes two callback functions, named `resolve` and `reject`. The body of the code is then defined after the fat arrow `=>`, and is enclosed with matching curly braces `{` and `}`. The body of the code is defining a function named `afterTimeout`, which will be called after a 1 second timeout. Note that the `afterTimeout` function is invoking the `resolve` function callback.

Note that this code snippet has been carefully formatted to clearly show the matching braces (and), and the matching curly braces { and }. Remember that in order to use promises, we must construct and return a `new Promise` object, and the constructor of a `Promise` object takes a function (or anonymous function) with two callback arguments.

Using promises

Promises provide a simple syntax for handling these `resolve` and `reject` functions. Let's take a look at how we would use the promises defined in our previous code snippet, as follows:

```
function callDelayedPromise() {
    console.log(`calling delayedPromise`);
    delayedPromise().then(
        () => { console.log(`delayedPromise.then()`) }
    );
}

callDelayedPromise();
```

Here, we have defined a function named `callDelayedPromise`. This function logs a message to the console, and then calls our `delayedPromise` function. We are using fluent syntax to attach to the `then` function of the promise, and defining an anonymous function that will be called when the promise is resolved. The output of this code is as follows:

```
calling delayedPromise
delayedPromise.then()
```

This promise fluent syntax also defines a `catch` function that is used for error handling. Consider the following promise definition:

```
function errorPromise() : Promise<void> {
    return new Promise<void>
    (
        (    resolve: () => void,
             reject: () => void
        ) => {
          reject();
            }
    );
}
```

Here, we have defined a function named errorPromise using our promise syntax. Note that within the body of the promise function, we are calling the reject callback function instead of the resolve function. This reject function is used to indicate an error. Let's now use the catch function to trap this error, as follows:

```
function callErrorPromise() {
    console.log(`calling errorPromise`);
    errorPromise().then(
        () => { console.log(`no error.`) }
    ).catch(
        () => { console.log(`an error occurred`)}
    );
}

callErrorPromise();
```

Here, we have defined a function named callErrorPromise that is logging a message to the console, and then invoking the errorPromise promise. Using our fluent syntax, we have defined an anonymous function to be called within the then response (that is, on success), and we have also defined an anonymous function to be called within the catch response (that is, on error). The output of this code is as follows:

```
calling errorPromise
an error occurred
```

Callback versus promise syntax

By way of a comparison of the two techniques we have discussed, let's take a look at a simplified version of the callback versus the promise syntax, as follows:

Our standard callback mechanism is as follows:

```
function standardCallback() {
    function afterCallbackSuccess() {
        // execute this code
    }
    function afterCallbackError() {
        // execute on error
    }
    // invoke async function
    invokeAsync(afterCallbackSuccess, afterCallbackError);
}
```

And our promise syntax is as follows:

```
function usingPromises() {
    delayedPromise().then(
        () => {
            // execute on success
        }
    ).catch (
        () => {
            // execute on error
        }
    );
}
```

As we can see, using promises introduces a fluent syntax for handling asynchronous programming.

Returning values from promises

So far, we have defined all of our promise objects as Promise<void>. The void in this case indicates that our promises will not return any values. If we use Promise<string>, this indicates that our promises will return string values. Let's take a look at how to return values from promises, as follows:

```
function delayedPromiseWithParam() : Promise<string> {
    return new Promise<string>(
        (
            resolve: (str: string) => void,
            reject: (str:string ) => void
        ) => {
            function afterWait() {
                resolve("resolved_within_promise");
            }
            setTimeout( afterWait , 2000 );
        }
    );
}
```

Here, we have a function named `delayedPromiseWithParam` that constructs and returns our promise object as usual. Note, however, that the definition of both the `resolve` callback function and the `reject` callback functions now take a single `string` argument. This `string` argument ties into the generic type that has been defined for this promise, that is, `Promise<string>`. If we wanted to use a number type for our `resolve` and `reject` arguments, we would need to define our return type as `Promise<number>`.

The inner workings of the anonymous function are similar to what we have discussed previously, with the exception that the call to `resolve` now includes a `string` as an argument.

Let's take a look at how this return value can be used, as follows:

```
function callPromiseWithParam() {
    console.log(`calling delayedPromiseWithParam`);
    delayedPromiseWithParam().then( (message: string) => {
        console.log(`Promise.then() returned ${message} `);
    } );
}

callPromiseWithParam();
```

Here, we have defined a function named `callPromiseWithParam` that logs a message to the console, and then calls our `delayedPromiseWithParam` function. We then use the fluent syntax to attach an anonymous function to the `then` function of the promise. Note how our anonymous function now takes a single string parameter, named `message`. This corresponds to the promise callback of `resolve : (str: sring )`. The output of this code is as follows:

```
calling delayedPromiseWithParam
Promise.then() returned resolved_within_promise
```

As expected, our promise called the `resolve` callback, that is, `resolve("resolved_within_promise")`, which corresponds to our `then( (message: string) => { ... } )` handler.

Note that promises can only return a single value when calling either the `resolve` or `reject` callback functions. If you need to return a message that contains multiple fields, then you will need to use an interface, as follows:

```
interface IPromiseMessage {
    message: string;
    id: number;
}
```

```
function promiseWithInterface() : Promise<IPromiseMessage> {
    return new Promise<IPromiseMessage> (
        (
            resolve: (message: IPromiseMessage) => void,
            reject: (message: IPromiseMessage) => void
        ) => {
            resolve({message: "test", id: 1});
        }
    );
}
```

Here, we have defined an interface named IPromiseMessage that contains a message of type string, and an id of type number. Our function named promiseWithInterface now returns a Promise<IPromiseMessage>, and the resolve and reject callback functions now use IPromiseMessage as the argument type. Our call to resolve must now construct an object with both a message property and an id property, in order to correctly implement the IPromiseMessage interface. Using interfaces in this way allows our promises to return any type of data.

async and await

As a further language enhancement when working with promises, TypeScript introduces two keywords that work together when using promises. These two keywords are async and await. The usage of async and await can best be described by considering some sample code, as follows:

```
function awaitDelayed() : Promise<void> {
    return new Promise<void> (
        ( resolve: () => void,
          reject: () => void ) =>
        {
            function afterWait() {
                console.log(`calling resolve`);
                resolve();
            }
            setTimeout(afterWait, 1000);
        }
    );
}
```

We start with a fairly standard function named `awaitDelayed` that returns a promise, similar to the examples that we have seen before. Note that in the body of the `afterWait` function, we log a message to the console before calling the `resolve` callback. Let's now take a look at how we can use this promise with the `async` and `await` keywords, as follows:

```
async function callAwaitDelayed() {
    console.log(`call awaitDelayed`);
    await awaitDelayed();
    console.log(`after awaitDelayed`);
}

callAwaitDelayed();
```

We start with a function named `callAwaitDelayed` that is prefixed by the `async` keyword. Within this function, we log a message to the console, and then call the previously defined `awaitDelayed` function. This time, however, we prefix the call to the `awaitDelayed` function with the keyword `await`. We then log another message to the console. The output of this code is as follows:

```
call awaitDelayed
calling resolve
after awaitDelayed
```

What this output is showing is that the `await` keyword is actually waiting for the asynchronous function to be called before continuing on with the program execution. This produces an easy-to-read, and easy-to-follow flow of program logic by automatically pausing execution until the promise is fulfilled.

await errors

Our promise objects generally define both a `success` condition as well as an `error` condition when calling asynchronous functions. In order to trap these error conditions when using `async await` syntax, we can use a `try...catch` block. To illustrate this, let's define a promise that returns an error, as well as an error message, as follows:

```
function awaitError() : Promise<string> {
    return new Promise<string> (
        ( resolve: (message: string) => void,
          reject: (error: string) => void ) =>
        {
            function afterWait() {
                console.log(`calling reject`);
                reject("an error occurred");
```

```
        }
        setTimeout(afterWait, 1000);
    }
  );
}
```

Here, we have a function named `awaitError` that is defining and returning a `Promise<string>`, and is using our standard promise syntax with a 1 second delay. The line to note here is inside the `afterWait` function, where we are calling the `reject` promise callback with an error message. Our corresponding `async await` function will be as follows:

```
async function callAwaitError() {
    console.log(`call awaitError`);
    try {
        await awaitError();
    } catch (error) {
        console.log(`error returned : ${error}`);
    }
    console.log(`after awaitDelayed`);
}

callAwaitError();
```

Here, we have an `async` function named `callAwaitError` that logs a message to the console, and then calls `await awaitError()` within a `try...catch` block. Note again that the program logic will pause when it reaches the `await` keyword for the asynchronous function to return before continuing on with code execution. In this case, however, the call to `await` will result in an error being thrown, which will be trapped by the `catch(error)` block. Within this block, we are logging the error message received to the console. The output of this code is as follows:

```
call awaitError
calling reject
error returned : an error occurred
after awaitDelayed
```

As can be seen by the output, the program execution is pausing on the `await awaitError()` asynchronous function to return. When an error occurs, the `catch` block is activated, and the `catch` argument `error` holds the error message generated within the promise.

Promise versus await syntax

As a refresher of promise versus `async await` syntax, let's compare these two techniques side by side. Firstly, let's examine the `then` and `catch` syntax used by standard promises:

```
function simplePromises() {
    delayedPromise().then(
        () => {
            // execute on success
        }
    ).catch (
        () => {
            // execute on error
        }
    );
    // code here does NOT wait for async call
}
```

Note that in the preceding promise code, we are using .`then` and .`catch` to define anonymous functions to be called depending on whether the asynchronous call was successful or not. Another caveat when using promise syntax is that any code outside of the .`then` or .`catch` block will be executed immediately, and will not wait for the asynchronous call to complete.

Secondly, let's examine the new `async await` syntax :

```
async function usingAsyncSyntax() {
    try {
        await delayedPromise();
        // execute on success
    } catch(error) {
        // execute on error
    }
    // code here waits for async call
}
```

Here, our `async await` syntax allows for a very simple syntax that flows logically. We know that any call to `await` will block code execution until the asynchronous function has returned, including any code defined outside our `try...catch` block.

As can be seen by comparing the two styles side by side, using the `async await` syntax simplifies our code, makes it more human readable, and, as such, less error prone.

await messages

The final topic we will discuss on `async await` is how to process messages that are returned within our promises. Consider the following promise definition:

```
function asyncWithMessage() : Promise<string> {
    return new Promise<string> (
        (
            resolve: (message: string ) => void,
            reject: (message: string) => void
        ) => {
            function afterWait() {
                resolve("resolve_message");
            }
            setTimeout(afterWait, 1000);
        }
    );
}
```

Here, we have defined a standard function returning a promise after a 1 second delay. The code to note here is the call to `resolve` within the `afterWait` function that is sending a message back to the callback. In this case, it is returning a `string` value of `resolve_message`, which matches our `Promise<string>` syntax. Again, we can use interfaces to return multiple values within a promise. Our corresponding `async await` function that uses this promise is as follows:

```
async function awaitMessage() {
    console.log(`calling asyncWithMessage`);
    let message: string = await asyncWithMessage();
    console.log(`message returned: ${message}`);
}

awaitMessage();
```

Here, we have defined an `async` function named `awaitMessage` that is logging a message to the console, and then calling the `asyncWithMessage` function. Note how we retrieved the message returned by the promise by simply defining a variable to hold the return value of the `await` call. We are then logging the received message to the console. The output of this code is as follows:

```
calling asyncWithMessage
message returned: resolve_message
```

As we can see from this code sample, retrieving and processing messages that are returned when using the `await` keyword is very simple. All we need to do is define a variable to hold the return result of the `await` call, and then we have access to our message.

Summary

In this chapter, we have had an in-depth discussion on decorators, generics, advanced generics, and asynchronous programming techniques using promises and `async await`. We have seen how decorators provide a way of injecting code into, or modifying, class definitions. We have also explored the use of experimental metadata information when working with decorators and class definitions. Our discussion then turned to generics, what they are, and how they are used. We worked through generic interfaces, and creating objects within generic functions. We then explored some advanced generic syntax, including conditional types and mapped types. Our final discussion revolved around asynchronous programming techniques using callbacks, promises, and the `async` and `await` keywords.

In the next chapter, we will look at the mechanism that TypeScript uses to integrate with existing JavaScript libraries – declaration files.

5
Declaration Files and Strict Compiler Options

One of the most appealing facets of JavaScript development is the wealth of external JavaScript libraries that have already been published, such as jQuery, Knockout, Underscore, Lodash, or Moment. As we know, TypeScript generates JavaScript, so we can easily use JavaScript libraries in TypeScript. We have already seen how TypeScript uses *syntactic sugar* to enhance our JavaScript development experience by providing a strong typing mechanism. If we are using JavaScript libraries, however, how do we apply this *sugar* to existing JavaScript or JavaScript libraries? The answer is relatively simple—declaration files.

A declaration file is a special type of file used by the TypeScript compiler. It is marked with a `.d.ts` extension, and is then used by the TypeScript compiler within the compilation step. Declaration files are similar to the header files used in C or C++, or interfaces as used in Java. They simply describe the syntax and structure of available functions and properties, but do not provide an implementation. Declaration files, therefore, do not actually generate any JavaScript code. They are there simply to provide TypeScript compatibility with external libraries, or to fill in the gaps for JavaScript code that TypeScript does not know about. In order to use any external JavaScript library within TypeScript, you will need a declaration file.

The TypeScript compiler also has a number of compiler options. These range from options surrounding the setup of a project, such as where to put compiled `.js` files, through to the ability to remove comments from generated JavaScript. In this chapter, we will explore some of these compiler options that focus on the language itself, and how you can harden error-prone TypeScript code by using these compiler options.

This chapter is divided into three main sections. In the first section, we will explore declaration files, show the reasoning behind them, and then build a declaration file of our own, based on some existing JavaScript code. The second section of this chapter is designed to be a quick reference guide to the module definition syntax. In the third section, we will explore some of the TypeScript compiler options.

We will be looking at the following topics in this chapter:

- Global variables
- Using JavaScript code blocks in HTML
- Using structured data
- Writing declaration files
- Writing interfaces for declaration files
- Using union types
- Module merging
- Compiler options

Global variables

Most modern websites use some sort of server engine to generate the HTML for their web pages. If you are familiar with the Microsoft stack of technologies, then you would know that ASP.NET MVC is a very popular server-side engine, used to generate HTML pages based on master pages, partial pages, and MVC views. If you are a Node developer, then you may be using one of the popular Node packages to help you construct web pages through templates, such as Jade, Handlebars, or **Embedded JavaScript** (EJS).

Within these templating engines, you may sometimes need to set JavaScript properties on the HTML page as a result of your server-side logic. As an example, let's assume that you keep a list of contact email addresses on your database, and then surface these to your HTML page through a JavaScript global variable named CONTACT_EMAIL_ARRAY. Your rendered HTML page would then include a <script> tag that contains this global variable and contact email addresses. You may have some JavaScript that reads this array, and then renders the values in a footer. The following HTML sample shows what a generated script would end up looking like this:

```
<body>
    <script type="text/javascript">
        var CONTACT_EMAIL_ARRAY = [
            "help@site.com",
            "contactus@site.com",
```

```
            "webmaster@site.com"
        ];
    </script>
</body>
```

Here, our HTML has a `<script>` block, and within this `<script>` block is some JavaScript. The JavaScript defines a variable named CONTACT_EMAIL_ARRAY that contains some strings. Let's assume that we wanted to write some TypeScript that can read this global variable. Consider the following TypeScript code:

```
class GlobalLogger {
    static logGlobalsToConsole() {
        for(let email of CONTACT_EMAIL_ARRAY) {
            console.log(`found contact : ${email}`);
        }
    }
}

window.onload = () => {
    GlobalLogger.logGlobalsToConsole();
}
```

This code creates a class named GlobalLogger with a single static function named logGlobalsToConsole. The function simply iterates through the CONTACT_EMAIL_ARRAY global variable, and logs the items in the array to the console.

If we compile this TypeScript code, we will generate the following error:

```
error TS2304: Cannot find name 'CONTACT_EMAIL_ARRAY'
```

This error indicates that the TypeScript compiler does not know anything about the variable named CONTACT_EMAIL_ARRAY. It does not even know that it is an array. As this piece of JavaScript is outside any TypeScript code, we will need to treat it in the same way as external JavaScript.

To solve our compilation problem, and make this CONTACT_EMAIL_ARRAY variable visible to TypeScript, we will need to use a declaration file. Let's create a file named globals.d.ts and include the following TypeScript declaration within it:

```
declare var CONTACT_EMAIL_ARRAY: string [];
```

The first thing to notice is that we are using a new TypeScript keyword—declare. The declare keyword tells the TypeScript compiler that we want to define the type of something, but that the implementation of this object (or variable, or function) will be resolved at runtime. We have declared a variable named CONTACT_EMAIL_ARRAY that is of type string []. This declare keyword does two things for us: it allows the use of the CONTACT_EMAIL_ARRAY variable within TypeScript code, and it also strongly types this variable to be an array of strings.

With this globals.d.ts file in place, our code compiles correctly. If we now run this in a browser, the console output of our browser log will look as follows:

So, by using a declaration file named globals.d.ts, we have been able to describe the structure of an external JavaScript variable to the TypeScript compiler. This JavaScript variable is defined outside any of our TypeScript code, yet we are still able to work with the definition of this variable within TypeScript.

This is what declaration files are used for. We are basically telling the TypeScript compiler to use the definitions found within a declaration file within the compilation step, and that the actual variables themselves will only be available at runtime.

 Definition files also bring IntelliSense or code completion functionality to our IDE for external JavaScript libraries and code.

Using JavaScript code blocks in HTML

The samples we have just seen are an example of tight coupling between the generated HTML content (that contains JavaScript code in script blocks) on your web page, and the actual running JavaScript. You may argue, however, that this is a design flaw. If the web page needed an array of contact emails, then the JavaScript application should simply send an AJAX request to the server for the same information in JSON format. While this is a very valid argument, there are cases where including content in the rendered HTML is actually faster.

There used to be a time where the internet seemed to be capable of sending and receiving vast amounts of information in the blink of an eye. Bandwidth and speed on the internet were growing exponentially, and desktops were getting larger amounts of RAM and faster processors. As developers during this stage of the internet highway, we stopped thinking about how much RAM a typical user had on their machine. We also stopped thinking about how much data we were sending across the wire. This was because internet speeds were so fast and browser processing speed was seemingly limitless.

And then came along the mobile phone, and it felt like we were back in the 1990s, with incredibly slow internet connections, tiny screen resolutions, limited processing power, and very little RAM (and popular arcade gaming experiences such as *Elevator Action* – https://archive.org/details/Elevator_Action_1985_Sega_Taito_JP_en). The point of this story is that as modern web developers, we still need to be mindful of browsers that run on mobile phones. These browsers are sometimes running on very limited internet connections, meaning that we must carefully measure the size of our JavaScript libraries, JSON data, and HTML pages to ensure that our applications are fast and usable, even on mobile browsers. For a website to be truly global, it must work in areas of the world where internet connections are slow, or intermittent, and on the lowest possible hardware specifications. Try to remember that a user of your site may be in a small town in the remote Australian outback, where they need to put their internet modem inside a wok and point it at the sky in order to receive a reliable satellite internet connection.

This technique of including JavaScript variables or smaller static JSON data within the rendered HTML page often provides us with the fastest way to render a screen on an older browser, or in the modern age, a mobile phone. Many popular sites use this technique to quickly render the general structure of the page (the header, side panels, and footers) before the main content is delivered through asynchronous JSON requests. This technique works well because it renders the page faster and gives the user faster visual feedback.

Structured data

Let's enhance this simple array of contact emails with a little more relevant data. For each of these email addresses, let's assume that we also want to include some text to render within the footer of our page, along with the email addresses. Consider the following HTML `<script>` tag:

```
<script type="text/javascript">
    var CONTACT_DATA = [
        { DisplayText: 'Help',
        Email: 'help@site.com' } ,
        { DisplayText: 'Contact Us',
        Email: 'contactus@site.com' },
        { DisplayText: 'Webmaster',
        Email: 'webmaster@site.com' }
    ];
</script>
```

Here, we have defined a global variable, named `CONTACT_DATA`, that is an array of objects. Each object has a property named `DisplayText` and a property named `Email`. If we are to use this array within our TypeScript code, we will need to include a definition of this variable in our `globals.d.ts` declaration file, as follows:

```
interface IContactData {
    DisplayText: string;
    Email: string;
}

declare var CONTACT_DATA: IContactData[];
```

Here, we start with an interface definition named `IContactData` to represent the properties of an individual item in the `CONTACT_DATA` array. Each item has a `DisplayText` property that is of the type `string`, as well as an `Email` property, which is also of type `string`. Our `IContactData` interface, therefore, matches the original object properties of a single item in the `CONTACT_DATA` array. We then declare a variable named `CONTACT_DATA` and set its type to be an array of the `IContactData` interfaces.

This allows us to work with the `CONTACT_DATA` variable within TypeScript. Let's now create a class to process this data, as follows:

```
class ContactLogger {
    static logContactData() {
        for (let contact of CONTACT_DATA) {
            console.log(`DisplayText: ${contact.DisplayText},
                Email : ${contact.Email}`);
```

```
        }
    }
}

window.onload = () => {
    ContactLogger.logContactData();
}
```

Here, the `ContactLogger` class has a single static method named `logContactData`. Within this method, we loop through all of the items in the `CONTACT_DATA` array. As we are using the `for...of` syntax, the `contact` variable will be strongly typed to be of type `IContactData`, and therefore will have two properties, `DisplayText` and `Email`. We simply log these values to the console. The output of this code would be as follows:

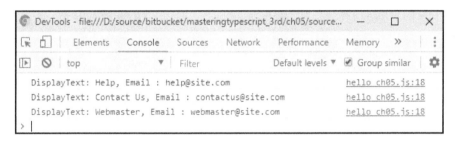

Writing your own declaration file

In any development team, there will come a time when you will need to either bug-fix, or enhance a body of code that has already been written in JavaScript. If you are in this situation, then you would want to try and write new areas of code in TypeScript, and integrate them with your existing body of JavaScript. To do so, however, you will need to write your own declaration files for any existing JavaScript that you need to reuse. This may seem like a daunting and time-consuming task, but when you are faced with this situation, just remember to take small steps, and define small sections of code at a time. You will be surprised at how simple it really is.

In this section, let's assume that you need to integrate an existing helper class—one that is reused across many projects, is well tested, and is a development team standard. This class has been implemented as a JavaScript closure, as follows:

```
ErrorHelper = (function() {
    return {
        containsErrors: function (response) {
            if (!response || !response.responseText)
```

```
                return false;

        var errorValue = response.responseText;

        if (String(errorValue.failure) == "true"
            || Boolean(errorValue.failure)) {
            return true;
        }
        return false;
    },
    trace: function (msg) {
        var traceMessage = msg;
        if (msg.responseText) {
            traceMessage = msg.responseText.errorMessage;
        }
        console.log("[" + new Date().toLocaleDateString()
            + "] " + traceMessage); .
    }
  }
})();
```

This JavaScript code snippet defines a JavaScript object named `ErrorHelper` that has two methods. The `containsErrors` method takes an object named `response` as an argument. This `response` object is then checked for errors. An object does not have an error if the following are true:

- The `response` argument is undefined.
- The `response.responseText` is undefined.

An error condition, however, is returned if the following are true:

- The `response.responseText.failure` property is set to the `string` value of "true".
- The `response.responseText.failure` property is set to the `boolean` value of true.

The `ErrorHelper` closure also has a function called `trace` that can be called with a string, or a `response` object similar to what the `containsErrors` function is expecting.

Unfortunately, this `ErrorHelper` function is missing a key piece of documentation. What is the structure of the object being passed into these two methods, and what properties does it have? Without some form of documentation, we are forced to reverse engineer the code to determine what the structure of the `response` object looks like. If we can find some sample usages of the `ErrorHelper` class, this may help us to guess this structure.

As an example of how this `ErrorHelper` is used, consider the following JavaScript code:

```
var failureMessage = {
    responseText : {
        "failure" :true,
        "errorMessage" : "Message From failureMessage"
    }
}

var failureMessageString = {
    responseText : {
        "failure" : "true",
        "errorMessage" : "Message from failureMessageString"
    }
}

var successMessage = {
    responseText : {
        "failure" : false
    }
}

if (ErrorHelper.containsErrors(failureMessage))
    ErrorHelper.trace(failureMessage);
if (ErrorHelper.containsErrors(failureMessageString))
    ErrorHelper.trace(failureMessageString);
if (!ErrorHelper.containsErrors(successMessage))
    ErrorHelper.trace("success");
```

Here, we start with a variable named `failureMessage` that has a single property, `reponseText`. The `responseText` property in turn has two child properties—`failure` and `errorMessage`. Our next variable, `failureMessageString`, has the same structure, but defines the `responseText.failure` property to be of type `string`, instead of type `boolean`. Finally, our `successMessage` object defines the `responseText.failure` property to be `false`, but it does not have an `errorMessage` property.

In JavaScript JSON format, property names are required to have quotes around them, whereas in JavaScript object format, these are optional. Therefore, the structure `{"failure" : true}` is syntactically equivalent to the structure `{failure : true}`.

The last couple of lines of the preceding code block show how the `ErrorHelper` closure is used. All we need to do is call the `ErrorHelper.containsErrors` method with our variable, and, if the result is `true`, log the message to the console through the `ErrorHelper.trace` function. Our output would be as follows:

The module keyword

To test this JavaScript `ErrorHelper` closure using TypeScript, we will need an HTML page that includes both the `error_helper.js` file, and a TypeScript generated JavaScript file. Assuming that our TypeScript file is called `ErrorHelperTypeScript.ts`, our HTML page would then be as follows:

```
<!DOCTYPE html>
<html>
<head>
    <title></title>
    <script src="error_helper.js"></script>
    <script src="ErrorHelperTypeScript.js"></script>
</head>
<body>

</body>
</html>
```

This HTML is very simple, and includes both the existing `error_helper.js` JavaScript file and the TypeScript-generated `ErrorHelperTypeScript.js` file.

Within the `ErrorHelperTypeScript.ts` file, let's use the `ErrorHelper`, as follows:

```
window.onload = () => {
    var failureMessage = {
        responseText : {
            "failure" : true,
            "errorMessage" : "Error Message from Typescript"
```

```
        }
    }
    if (ErrorHelper.containsErrors(failureMessage))
        ErrorHelper.trace(failureMessage);
}
```

Here, we have a stripped down version of our original JavaScript sample. We first create a `failureMessage` object with the correct properties, and then simply call the `ErrorHelper.containsErrors` method, and the `ErrorHelper.trace` method. If we were to compile our TypeScript file at this stage, we would receive the following error:

error TS2304: Cannot find name 'ErrorHelper'.

This error indicates that there is no valid TypeScript type named `ErrorHelper`, even though we have the full source of `ErrorHelper` in our JavaScript file. TypeScript, by default, will look through all the TypeScript files in our project to find class definitions, but it will not parse JavaScript files. We will need a new TypeScript definition file in order to correctly compile this code.

> This definition file is not included in the HTML file at all; it is only used by the TypeScript compiler and does not generate any JavaScript.

Without a set of helpful documentation on our `ErrorHelper` class, we will need to reverse engineer a TypeScript definition purely by reading the source code. This is obviously not an ideal situation, and is not recommended, but at this stage, it is all we can do. In these situations, the best starting point is simply to look at the usage samples and work our way up from there.

Looking at the usage of the `ErrorHelper` closure in JavaScript, we can see that there are two key pieces that should be included in our declaration file. The first is a set of function definitions for the `containsErrors` and `trace` functions. The second is a set of interfaces to describe the structure of the `response` object that the `ErrorHelper` closure relies upon. Let's start with the function definitions, and create a new TypeScript file named `ErrorHelper.d.ts` with the following code:

```
declare module ErrorHelper {
    function containsErrors(response: any) : boolean;
    function trace(message: any) : void;
}
```

This declaration file starts with the `declare` keyword that we have seen before, but then uses a new TypeScript keyword—`module`. The `module` keyword must be followed by a module name, which in this case is `ErrorHelper`. This module name must match the closure name from the original JavaScript that we are describing. In all of our usages of the `ErrorHelper`, we have always prefixed the functions `containsErrors` and `trace` with the closure name `ErrorHelper` itself. This module name is also known as a namespace. If we had another class named `AjaxHelper` that also included a `containsErrors` function, we would be able to distinguish between the `AjaxHelper.containsErrors` and the `ErrorHelper.containsErrors` functions by using these namespaces, or module names.

The second line of our module declaration indicates that we are defining a function called `containsErrors` that takes one parameter and returns a `boolean`. The third line of this module declaration indicates that we are defining another function named `trace` that also takes a single parameter, but does not return a value. With this definition in place, our TypeScript code sample will compile correctly.

Interfaces

Although we have correctly defined the two functions that are available to users of the `ErrorHelper` closure, we are missing the second piece of information about the functions available on the `ErrorHelper` closure—the structure of the `response` argument. We are not strongly typing the arguments for either of the `containsErrors` or `trace` functions. At this stage, our TypeScript code can pass anything into these two functions because it does not have a definition for the `response` or `message` arguments. We know, however, that both these functions query our parameters for a specific structure. If we pass in an object that does not conform to this structure, then our JavaScript code will cause runtime errors.

To solve this problem and to make our code more stable, let's define an interface for these parameters:

```
interface IResponse {
    responseText: IFailureMessage;
}

interface IFailureMessage {
    failure: boolean;
    errorMessage: string;
}
```

We start with an interface named `IResponse` that has a single property of `responseText`—the same name as the original JavaScript object. This `responseText` property is strongly typed to be of type `IFailureMessage`. The `IFailureMessage` interface is strongly typed to have two properties—`failure`, which is of type `boolean`, and `errorMessage`, which is of type `string`. These interfaces correctly describe the proper structure of the `response` argument for the `containsErrors` and `trace` functions. We can now modify our original declaration for these functions, as follows:

```
declare module ErrorHelper {
    function containsErrors(response: IResponse) : boolean;
    function trace(message: IResponse) : void;
}
```

The function definition for `containsErrors` and `trace` now strongly types the response argument to be of type `IResponse`, which we defined earlier. This modification to the definition file will now force any further usage of the `containsErrors` or `trace` functions to send in a valid argument that conforms to the `IResponse` structure. Let's write some intentionally incorrect TypeScript code and see what happens:

```
var anotherFailure: IResponse = {
        responseText: {
            success: true
        }
    }
```

We start by creating a variable named `anotherFailure` and specify its type to be of type `IResponse`. Unfortunately, the `IResponse` interface does not have a property named `success`, and so we will generate the following TypeScript error:

```
λ tsc
ErrorHelperTypeScript.ts(16,13): error TS2322: Type '{ responseText:
{ success: boolean; }; }' is not assignable to type 'IResponse'.
  Types of property 'responseText' are incompatible.
    Type '{ success: boolean; }' is not assignable to type 'IFailureM
essage'.
      Object literal may only specify known properties, and 'success'
does not exist in type 'IFailureMessage'.
```

As can be seen from this fairly verbose but informative error message, the structure of the `anotherFailure` variable is causing all the errors. Even though we have correctly referenced the `responseText` property of `IResponse`, the `responseText` property is strongly typed to be of type `IFailureMessage`, which requires both a `failure` property and an `errorMessage` property; hence the error.

By creating a strongly-typed declaration file for the existing `ErrorHelper` class, we can ensure that any further TypeScript usage of the existing `ErrorHelper` JavaScript closure will not generate runtime errors.

Union types

We are not quite finished with the declaration file for the `ErrorHelper` class just yet. If we take a look at the original JavaScript usage of the `ErrorHelper` class, we will notice that the `containsErrors` function also allows for the `failure` property of `responseText` to be a string:

```
var failureMessage = {
    responseText : {
        "failure" : "true",
        "errorMessage" : "Error Message from Typescript"
    }
}
```

If we compile this code now, we will get the following compile error:

```
∧ tsc
ErrorHelperTypeScript.ts(11,36): error TS2345: Argument of type '{ re
sponseText: { "failure": string; "errorMessage": string; }; }' is not
 assignable to parameter of type 'IResponse'.
  Types of property 'responseText' are incompatible.
    Type '{ "failure": string; "errorMessage": string; }' is not assi
gnable to type 'IFailureMessage'.
      Types of property 'failure' are incompatible.
        Type 'string' is not assignable to type 'boolean'.
ErrorHelperTypeScript.ts(12,27): error TS2345: Argument of type '{ re
sponseText: { "failure": string; "errorMessage": string; }; }' is not
 assignable to parameter of type 'IResponse'.
```

In the preceding definition of the `failureMessageString` variable, the type of the `"failure"` property is `"true"`, which is of type `string`, and not `true`, which is of type `boolean`. In order to allow for this variant on the original `IFailureMessage` interface, we will need to modify our declaration file. The simplest way to allow for both types would be to use a type union, as follows:

```
interface IFailureMessage {
    failure: boolean | string;
    errorMessage: string;
}
```

Here, we have simply updated the `failure` property on the `IFailureMessage` interface to allow for both `boolean` and `string` types. Our code will now compile correctly.

This completes our definition file for the `ErrorHelper` JavaScript class.

Module merging

As we now know, the TypeScript compiler will automatically search through all the `.d.ts` files in our project to pick up declaration files. If these declaration files contain the same module name, the TypeScript compiler will merge these two declaration files and use a combined version of the module declarations.

Imagine that we have a file named `MergedModule1.d.ts`, containing the following definition:

```
declare module MergedModule {
    function functionA() : void;
}
```

And we also have a second file, named `MergedModule2.d.ts`, that contains the following definition:

```
declare module MergedModule {
    function functionB() : void;
}
```

Now, the TypeScript compiler will merge these two modules as if they were a single definition:

```
declare module MergedModule {
    function functionA() : void;
    function functionB() : void;
}
```

This will allow both `functionA` and `functionB` to be valid functions of the same `MergedModule` namespace and allow the following usage:

```
MergedModule.functionA();
MergedModule.functionB();
```

> Modules can also merge with interfaces and enums. We cannot, however, use this sort of merging syntax with classes.

Declaration syntax reference

When creating declaration files and using the `module` keyword, there are a number of rules that can be used to mix and match definitions. As a TypeScript programmer, you will generally only write module definitions every now and then, and on occasion, you will need to add a new definition to an existing declaration file.

This section, therefore, is designed to be a quick reference guide to this declaration file syntax, or a cheat sheet. Each section contains a description of the module definition rule, a JavaScript syntax snippet, and then the equivalent TypeScript declaration file syntax.

To use this reference section, simply match the JavaScript that you are trying to emulate from the JavaScript syntax section, and then write your declaration file with the equivalent definition syntax. We will start with the function override syntax as an example.

Function overrides

Declaration files can include multiple definitions for the same function. If the same JavaScript function can be called with different types, you will need to declare a function override for each variant of the function.

The JavaScript syntax

```
trace("trace a string");
trace(true);
trace(1);
trace({ id: 1, name: "test" });
```

The declaration file syntax

```
declare function trace(arg: string | number | boolean );
declare function trace(arg: { id: number; name: string });
```

 Each function definition must have a unique function signature.

Nested namespaces

Module definitions can contain nested module definitions, which then translate to nested namespaces. If your JavaScript uses namespaces, then you will need to define nested module declarations to match the JavaScript namespaces.

The JavaScript syntax

```
FirstNamespace.SecondNamespace.ThirdNamespace.log("test");
```

The declaration file syntax

```
declare module FirstNamespace {
    module SecondNamespace {
        module ThirdNamespace {
            function log(msg: string);
        }
    }
}
```

Classes

Class definitions are allowed within module definitions. If your JavaScript uses classes, or the new operator, then *new-able* classes will need to be defined in your declaration file.

The JavaScript syntax

```
var myClass = new MyClass();
```

The declaration file syntax

```
declare class MyClass {
}
```

Class namespaces

Class definitions are allowed within nested module definitions. If your JavaScript classes have a preceding namespace, you will need to declare nested modules to match the namespaces first, and then you can declare classes within the correct namespace.

The JavaScript syntax

```
var myNestedClass = new OuterName.InnerName.NestedClass();
```

The declaration file syntax

```
declare module OuterName {
    module InnerName {
        class NestedClass {}
    }
}
```

Class constructor overloads

Class definitions can contain constructor overloads. If your JavaScript classes can be constructed using different types, or with multiple parameters, you will need to list each of these variants in your declaration file as constructor overloads.

The JavaScript syntax

```
var myClass = new MyClass();
var myClass2 = new MyClass(1, "test");
```

The declaration file syntax

```
declare class MyClass {
    constructor(id: number, name: string);
    constructor();
}
```

Class properties

Classes can contain properties. You will need to list each property of your class within your class declaration.

The JavaScript syntax

```
var classWithProperty = new ClassWithProperty();
classWithProperty.id = 1;
```

The declaration file syntax

```
declare class ClassWithProperty {
    id: number;
}
```

Class functions

Classes can contain functions. You will need to list each function of your JavaScript class within your class declaration in order for the TypeScript compiler to accept calls to these functions.

The JavaScript syntax

```
var classWithFunction = new ClassWithFunction();
classWithFunction.functionToRun();
```

The declaration file syntax

```
declare class ClassWithFunction {
    functionToRun(): void;
}
```

 Functions or properties that are considered as private do not need to be exposed through the declaration file, and can simply be omitted.

Static properties and functions

Class methods and properties can be static. If your JavaScript functions or properties can be called without needing an instance of an object to work with, then these properties or functions will need to be marked as static.

The JavaScript syntax

```
StaticClass.staticId = 1;
StaticClass.staticFunction();
```

The declaration file syntax

```
declare class StaticClass {
    static staticId: number;
    static staticFunction();
}
```

Global functions

Functions that do not have a namespace prefix can be declared in the global namespace. If your JavaScript defines global functions, these will need to be declared without a namespace.

The JavaScript syntax

```
globalLogError("test");
```

The declaration file syntax

```
declare function globalLogError(msg: string);
```

Function signatures

A function can use a function signature as a parameter. JavaScript functions that use callback functions or anonymous functions will need to be declared with the correct function signature.

The JavaScript syntax

```
describe("test", function () {
});
```

The declaration file syntax

```
declare function describe(name: string, functionDef: () => void);
```

Optional properties

Classes or functions can contain optional properties. Where JavaScript object parameters are not mandatory, these will need to be marked as optional properties in the declaration.

The JavaScript syntax

```
var classWithOpt = new ClassWithOptionals();
var classWithOpt1 = new ClassWithOptionals(
    {id: 1});
var classWithOpt2 = new ClassWithOptionals(
    {name: 'test'});
var classWithOpt3 = new ClassWithOptionals(
    {id: 1, name: 'test'});
```

The declaration file syntax

```
interface IOptionalProperties {
    id?: number;
    name?: string;
}

declare class ClassWithOptionals {
    constructor(options?: IOptionalProperties);
}
```

Merging functions and modules

A function definition with a specific name can be merged with a module definition of the same name. This means that if your JavaScript function can be called with parameters and also has properties, then you will need to merge a function with a module.

The JavaScript syntax

```
fnWithProperty(1);
fnWithProperty.name = "name";
```

The declaration file syntax

```
declare function fnWithProperty(id: number);
declare module fnWithProperty {
    var name: string;
}
```

Strict compiler options

The TypeScript compiler allows for the configuration of a number of compiler options. These options can be grouped into five main groups, as follows:

- Basic options
- Strict type-checking options
- Module resolution options
- Source map options
- Experimental options

We have already been exposed to a few of these options, including the use of source maps, and the experimental options related to decorators. In this section, however, we will focus on the strict type-checking options that affect the way that we write our TypeScript code. These options provide us with a compile-time check to ensure that we are not breaking certain basic TypeScript rules, and help us to write more hardened code. Specifically, we will focus on the following options:

- noImplicitAny
- strictNullChecks
- strictPropertyInitialization
- noImplicitThis
- noUnusedLocals
- noUnusedParameters
- noImplicitReturns
- noFallthroughCasesInSwitch
- strictBindCallApply

Each of these compiler options can be found within the tsconfig.json file that is generated when we initialize a TypeScript project through the tsc --init command. We can easily turn these options on or off by simply commenting or un-commenting the appropriate line within the tsconfig.json file.

Note that there is a single compiler option named `strict`, which will turn on all of the `compile` options that we will be discussing. It is recommended to keep this setting to `true` in order to benefit from all of the strict compile options that TypeScript brings to the table. If you are migrating older code to use these new stricter options, then this section of the chapter will explain the effects of each of these strict options on our code.

noImplicitAny

The `noImplicitAny` compiler option is used to check whether function declarations or expressions have not been strictly typed, and will therefore (by default) return an `any` type. This can be explained through a simple code sample, as follows:

```
declare function testImplicitAny();

function testNoType(value) {
}
```

Here, we start with the declaration of a function named `testImplicitAny`. We then create a function named `testNoType` that has a single parameter named `value`. If we compile this code with the `noImplicitAny` compile option set to `true`, the compiler will generate the following errors:

```
error TS7010: 'testImplicitAny', which lacks return-type annotation,
implicitly has an 'any' return type.
error TS7006: Parameter 'value' implicitly has an 'any' type.
```

The first error is telling us that we have declared a function, but have not specified what type this function will return. Even if the function does not return anything, we will need to specify `void` as the return type.

The second error is telling us that the parameter `value` does not have a type specified. We can easily fix these errors by inserting the correct types, as follows:

```
declare function testImplicitAny() : void;

function testNoType(value: string) {
}
```

Here, we have specified that the return type of the `testImplicitAny` function should be of type `void`, and we have specified that the type of the `value` parameter for the `testNoType` function should of type `string`.

strictNullChecks

The `strictNullChecks` compiler option is used to find instances of variables in our code where the value of a variable could be `null` or `undefined`, at the time of usage. This means that when the variable is actually used, if it has not been properly initialized, the compiler will generate an error message. Consider the following code:

```
let a : number;
let b = a;
```

Here, we have defined a variable named `a` that is of type `number`. We then defined a variable named `b`, and assigned the value of `a` to it. With `strictNullChecks` turned on, this code will generate the following error:

error TS2454: Variable 'a' is used before being assigned.

This error is telling us that we are attempting to use the value of `a` before it has been assigned a value of any sort. In other words, at the time we use the variable `a`, it could still be `undefined`.

There are two ways to remove this error message. Firstly, we can ensure that the variable has been assigned before it is used, as follows:

```
let c : number = 2;
let d = c;
```

Here, we have defined a variable named `c` of type `number`, and assigned the value 2 to it. We then create a variable named `d`, and assign the value of `c` to it. This will not generate an error, as the variable `c` has been assigned a value before it is used.

The other way to fix this error message is to let the compiler know that, in this case, we are well aware that the variable could be undefined, as follows:

```
let e : number | undefined;
let f = e;
```

Here, we are defining a variable named `e` of type `number` or `undefined`. We then create a variable named `f`, and assign the value of `e` to it. Note the subtle difference in the types of the variable `e`. By telling the compiler that the variable `e` can be either a `number` or `undefined`, we are explicitly stating that we are aware that `e` could be `undefined`, and will take care to handle this condition correctly.

strictPropertyInitialization

Similar to the `strictNullChecks` compile option, we can also check whether the properties of a class have been initialized correctly using the `strictPropertyInitialization` compiler flag. Consider the following class definition:

```
class WithoutInit {
    a: number;
    b: string;
}
```

Here, we have a standard class definition for a class named `WithoutInit`. This class has two properties, named `a`, of type `number`, and `b`, of type `string`. With the `strictPropertyInitialization` compile option turned on, this code will generate the following errors:

```
error TS2564: Property 'a' has no initializer and is not definitely
assigned in the constructor.
error TS2564: Property 'b' has no initializer and is not definitely
assigned in the constructor.
```

This error indicates that the `a` and `b` properties of the `WithoutInit` class have not been initialized or assigned.

This class can be fixed in one of two ways. Firstly, we can set these values in the constructor, as follows:

```
class WithoutInit {
    a: number;
    b: string;
    constructor(_a: number) {
        this.a = _a;
        this.b = "test";
    }
}
```

Here, we have defined a constructor for our class, which has a single parameter named _a of type `number`. Within our constructor, we are setting the class property named `a` to the incoming value of _a. We are also setting the class property named `b` to the hardcoded value of `"test"`. Now, both of the `a` and `b` properties have been initialized correctly, and the code will not generate any errors.

The second way to fix this code is to explicitly tell the compiler that we are aware that the properties could be uninitialized, as follows:

```
class WithoutInitUndefined {
    a: number | undefined;
    b: string | undefined;
}
```

Here, we have a class named `WithoutInitUndefined`, with two properties named `a` and `b`. Note that the property `a` is defined as either of type `number` or `undefined`, and the property `b` is defined as either `string` or `undefined`. In this way, we are explicitly telling the compiler that we know that `a` and `b` could be `undefined`, and will handle this case ourselves.

noUnusedLocals and noUnusedParameters

With the `noUnusedLocals` and `noUnusedParameters` compiler options set, the TypeScript compiler will generate an error if it finds unused local variables, or unused parameters. Consider the following code:

```
function testFunction(input: string): boolean {
    let test;
    return false;
}
```

Here, we have defined a function, named `testFunction`, that takes a single parameter, named `input`, of type `string`. Within the body of the function, we define a variable named `test`, and then return the `boolean` value of `false`. Compiling this code will generate the following errors:

```
error TS6133: 'input' is declared but its value is never read
error TS6133: 'test' is declared but its value is never read
```

The first error is pointing to the function parameter named `input`. Notice that it is never used in the body of the function, and it is therefore confusing as to why it has been declared in the first place.

The second error indicates that although we have defined a variable named `test` within the body of the function, we have not used it anywhere. So why was it declared in the first place ?

Using these compile parameters will help us to trim out any unused local variables, or unused function parameters.

noImplicitReturns

If a function has declared that it will return a value, then the compiler can ensure that it does, indeed, return a value by using the `noImplicitReturns` option. Often, when we are working with a large function, or if we are re-factoring an existing function, we may inadvertently introduce unwanted logic flaws if we are not careful. Consider the following code:

```
function isLargeNumber(value : number) : boolean | undefined {
    if (value > 1_000_000)
        return true;
}
```

Here, we have defined a function named `isLargeNumber` that can be invoked with a single parameter named `value`. This function can return either a `boolean` or `undefined`. Note that in general, this function should only return a `boolean`, but for the sake of this discussion, we are also allowing `undefined`. This code will generate the following error:

error TS7030: Not all code paths return a value

This error is generated because of the error in our logic within this function. Note that there is only an `if` statement that checks whether the `value` argument is greater than 1 million. There is no `else` statement, or even a default return. So if the `value` argument is anything less than or equal to 1 million, we are simply falling through the `if` statement and doing nothing.

The function definition, however, specifies that we must return either a `boolean` value, or `undefined`, and we have forgotten to return anything in this case. The compiler has, therefore, highlighted a logic error within our function that will need to be fixed.

noFallthroughCasesInSwitch

To further check logic errors in our code, we can use the `noFallthroughCasesInSwitch` compile option to check `Switch` statements. Consider the following code:

```
enum SwitchEnum {
    ONE,
    TWO
}

function testEnumSwitch(value: SwitchEnum) : string {
    let returnValue = "";
    switch(value) {
```

```
        case SwitchEnum.ONE:
            returnValue = "One";
        case SwitchEnum.TWO:
            returnValue = "Two";
    }
    return returnValue;
}
```

Here, we have defined an `enum` named `SwitchEnum` that has two values, `ONE` and `TWO`. We then define a function named `testEnumSwitch` that returns a string value based on the input parameter name `value`, which is of type `SwitchEnum`. Within this function, we define a variable named `returnValue`, and set it to an empty string. We then have a `switch` statement that assigns the value of the `returnValue` variable to either `"One"` or `"Two"`, based on the `enum` passed in. This code will generate the following error:

error TS7029: Fallthrough case in switch.

This error is correctly identifying a logic error within our switch statement. Note that if the input argument value is `SwitchEnum.ONE`, we are assigning the value of the `returnValue` variable to `"One"`. Unfortunately, the logic automatically falls through to the second `case` statement, where the `returnValue` variable is set to `"Two"`. This means that no matter whether the `value` argument that is passed in is `SwitchEnum.ONE`, or `SwitchEnum.TWO`, the return value will always be `"Two"`.

This code needs to be corrected as follows:

```
function testEnumSwitch(value: SwitchEnum) : string {
    let returnValue = "";
    switch(value) {
        case SwitchEnum.ONE:
            returnValue = "One";
            break;
        case SwitchEnum.TWO:
            returnValue = "Two";
    }
    return returnValue;
}
```

Here, the subtle difference that fixes the compile error is the inclusion of the `break` statement in the `case SwitchEnum.ONE` logic. This `break` statement will break the `switch` statement, and avoid the code falling through to the second `case` statement.

So what we have seen then, is the compiler correctly identifying where we have glaring errors in our `switch` statements, and where logic will fall through from one `switch case` to another. While these errors may seem easy to spot in such simple code samples, they can quickly become lost in larger code bases.

strictBindCallApply

JavaScript provides the `bind`, `call`, and `apply` functions that are used when we need to override the value of the `this` variable inside a function. We have already seen the use of the `apply` function in our discussion on decorators in Chapter 4, *Decortators, Generics and Asynchronous Features*. We will discuss the use of the `bind` function in detail in Chapter 7, *TypeScript Compatible Frameworks*. The `strictBindCallApply` compiler option can be used to ensure that the parameters that are used in any of these calls are type safe. To illustrate this concept, consider the following code:

```
class MyBoundClass {
    name: string = "defaultNameValue";

    printName(index: number, description: string) {
        console.log(`this.name : ${this.name}`);
        console.log(`index : ${index}`);
        console.log(`description : ${description}`);
    }
}

let testBoundClass = new MyBoundClass();
testBoundClass.printName(1, 'testDesc');
```

Here, we have defined a class named `MyBoundClass` that has a single property named `name`, which is set to a default value of `"defaultNameValue"`. We have then defined a `printName` function that has two parameters. The first parameter is named `index`, and is of type `number`, and the second parameter is named `description`, which is of type `string`. The `printName` function logs the value of `this.name` to the console, and then also logs the value of the `index` and `description` arguments. We then create an instance of the `MyBoundClass` class, and assign it to the variable named `testBoundClass`. Finally, we call the `printName` function with two arguments. The output of this code snippet is as follows:

```
this.name : defaultNameValue
index : 1
description : testDesc
```

Here, we can see that the values logged to the console are as expected. Note in particular that the value of the `this.name` property is what we set by default for this class. If we now use the JavaScript `call` function, we are able to override the `this.name` property as follows:

```
testBoundClass.printName.call(
    { name: `overridden name property value` },
    1, 'call : whoah !');
```

Here, we are executing the `printName` function of the variable `testBoundClass`, which is an instance of the `MyBoundClass` class. This time, however, we are using the JavaScript `call` function, which uses the the first parameter we supply as the value of `this`. The second and third arguments are then passed through to the `printName` function. The results of this call are as follows:

```
this.name : overridden name property value
index : 1
description : call : whoah !
```

Here, we can see that the `name` property of the `MyBoundClass` class has been overridden from its default value of `"defaultNameValue"` to the value of the `name` property from the object that was passed into the JavaScript `call` function, which was `"overridden name property value"`. In other words, using the `call` function, we are able to override the value of the `this.name` property by specifying a value to be used for the `this` property.

The TypeScript compiler will generate errors if the types of the properties used in the call to the JavaScript `call` function are incorrect. This can be illustrated by the following code:

```
testBoundClass.printName.call(
    { name: `overridden name property value` },
    "string", 12);
```

Here, we are using the JavaScript `call` function to override the value of `this` that is used in the `MyBoundClass` class. Unfortunately, we have provided a `string` value of `"string"` for the first parameter that should have been of type `number`. The TypeScript compiler will generate the following error in this case:

```
error TS2345: Argument of type '"string"' is not assignable to parameter of
type 'number', "string", 12);
```

Here, we can see that the TypeScript compiler does, in fact, generate errors if the parameters supplied to a function are not of the correct types. It enforces these rules even if we use the JavaScript `call` function, as we have specified that the `strictBindCallApply` compiler option is set to `true`.

Note that the format of the `apply` function uses an array to specify the argument list as follows:

```
testBoundClass.printName.apply(
    { name: `overridden by apply` },
    [1, 'apply : whoah !']);
```

Here, we are using the JavaScript `apply` function to override the value of `this` inside the instance of the `MyBoundClass` instance. However, instead of using a parameter list, we are using an array of arguments.

Using the `strictBindCallApply` compiler option will generate errors if any one of the `bind`, `call`, or `apply` functions are used with incorrect parameter types.

Summary

In this chapter, we have outlined what we need to know in order to write and use our own declaration files. We discussed JavaScript global variables in rendered HTML and how to access them in TypeScript. We then moved on to a small JavaScript helper function and wrote our own declaration file for this JavaScript. We then listed a few module definition rules, highlighting the required JavaScript syntax, and showing what the equivalent TypeScript declaration syntax would be.

In the second section of the chapter, we looked at the `strict` options of the TypeScript compiler, and compared the code with and without each of these options.

In the next chapter, we will look at how to use existing third-party JavaScript libraries, and how to import existing declaration files for these libraries into your TypeScript projects.

6
Third-Party Libraries

Our TypeScript development environment would not amount to much if we were not able to reuse the myriad of existing JavaScript libraries, frameworks, and general goodness that makes JavaScript development so popular today. As we have seen, however, in order to use a particular third-party library with TypeScript, we will first need a matching definition file.

Soon after TypeScript was released, Boris Yankov set up a GitHub repository to house TypeScript definition files for third-party JavaScript libraries. This repository, named **DefinitelyTyped** (`https://github.com/borisyankov/DefinitelyTyped`), quickly became very popular, and is currently the place to go for high-quality definition files. DefinitelyTyped currently has over 5,000 definition files, built up over time from hundreds of contributors from all over the world.

If we were to measure the success of TypeScript within the JavaScript community, then the DefinitelyTyped repository would be a good indication of how well TypeScript has been adopted. Before you go ahead and try to write your own definition files, check the DefinitelyTyped repository to see if there is one already available.

In this chapter, we will take a closer look at using these definition files, and cover the following topics:

- Using NuGet within Visual Studio
- Using npm and @types
- Choosing a JavaScript framework
- Using TypeScript with Backbone
- Using TypeScript with Angular 1
- Using TypeScript with ExtJS

Using definition files

There are a number of ways to include definition files within your project. When TypeScript was initially released, the only way to include definition files was to download them manually from DefinitelyTyped, store them into a directory within your project, and then reference them manually. As the popularity of TypeScript started increasing, so did the number of definition files, and thus finding and installing the correct files became more difficult. Several tools then started to emerge to aid with this process. The first of these was a Node-based command-line tool named `tsd`, which allowed for querying the DefinitelyTyped database, and installing the relevant definition files. `tsd` was deprecated in early 2016, in favour of another tool named Typings. Typings also allowed for querying and installing definition files based on the DefinitelyTyped database. One of the major features of Typings was the ability to target a specific version of a definition file, and to store the relevant information in a configuration file named `typings.json`.

With the release of TypeScript 2.0, the ability to install type definition files was folded into the popular `npm` package, and thus didn't require any other tools for managing definition files. If you are using Node, `npm`, and a `package.json` file, then `npm` has all of the features required to include definition files in your project.

If you are working with the Visual Studio or WebMatrix IDEs, then you can use NuGet to accomplish the same thing. In this section of the chapter, we will explore both the NuGet and `npm` methods of managing definition files.

Using NuGet

NuGet is a popular package management platform that will download required external libraries, and automatically include them in within your Visual Studio or WebMatrix project. It can be used for external libraries that are packaged as DLLs, such as StructureMap, or it can be used for JavaScript libraries and declaration files. NuGet is also available as a command-line utility.

Using the NuGet Extension Manager

To use the NuGet package manager dialog within Visual Studio, you will need to open an existing project. Once the project is open, select the **Tools** option on the main toolbar, then select **NuGet Package Manager**, and finally select **Manage NuGet Packages for Solution**. This brings up the NuGet package manager dialog. On the left-hand side of the dialog, click on **Browse**. The NuGet dialog will then query the NuGet website and show a list of available packages. At the top left of the screen is a search box. Click within the **search** box, and type `jquery` to show all packages available within NuGet for jQuery, as shown in the following screenshot:

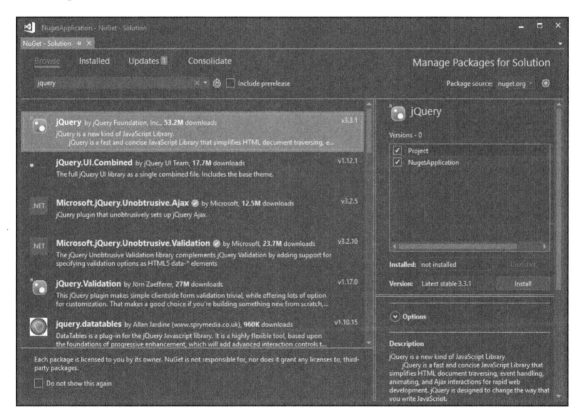

Each package will have an **Install** button highlighted when you select the package in the search results panel. When a package is selected, the right-hand pane will show more details about the NuGet package in question. Note that the project details panel also shows the version of the package that you are about to install. Clicking on the **Install** button will download relevant files, as well as any dependencies, and include them automatically within your project.

The installation directory that NuGet uses for JavaScript files is in fact called `Scripts`, and not the `lib` directory that we created earlier. NuGet uses the `Scripts` directory as a standard, so any packages that contain JavaScript will install the relevant JavaScript files into the `Scripts` directory.

Installing declaration files

You will find that most of the more popular declaration files that are found on the DefinitelyTyped GitHub repository have a corresponding NuGet package. These packages are named `<library>.TypeScript.DefinitelyTyped`, as a standard naming convention. If we type `jquery typescript` into the NuGet search box, we will see a list of these DefinitelyTyped packages returned. The NuGet package we are looking for is named `jquery.TypeScript.DefinitelyTyped`, created by Jason Jarret, and is, at the time of writing, at version 3.1.2, as shown in the following screenshot:

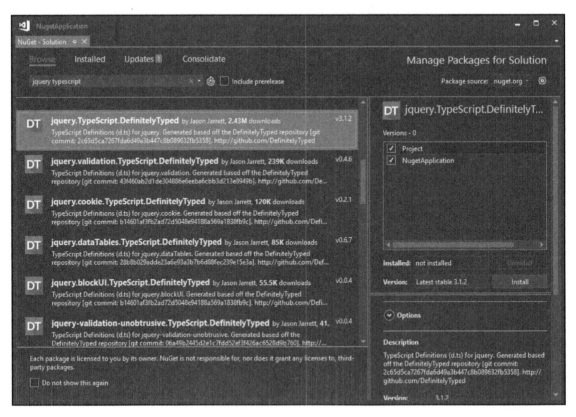

The DefinitelyTyped packages have their own internal version number, and these version numbers do not necessarily match the version of the JavaScript library that you are using.

Installing the `jQuery.TypeScript.DefinitelyTyped` package will create a `typings` directory under the `Scripts` directory, and then include the `jquery.d.ts` definition file. This directory naming standard has been adopted by the various NuGet package authors.

Using the Package Manager Console

Visual Studio also has a command line version of the NuGet package manager available as a console application, and it is also integrated into Visual Studio. Clicking on **Tools**, then **NuGet Package Manager**, and finally on **Package Manager Console**, will bring up a new Visual Studio window, and initialize the NuGet command line interface. The command line version of NuGet has a number of features that are not included in the GUI version. Type `get-help NuGet` to see the list of top-level command line arguments that are available.

Installing packages

To install a NuGet package from the console command line, simply type `install-package <packageName>`. As an example, to install the `jquery.TypeScript.DefinitelyTyped` package, simply type the following:

```
Install-Package jquery.TypeScript.DefinitelyTyped
```

This command will connect to the NuGet server, and download and install the package into your project.

On the toolbar of the **Package Manager Console** window are two drop-down lists, **Package Source** and **Default Project**. If your Visual Studio solution has multiple projects, you will need to select the correct project for NuGet to install the package into from the **Default Project** drop-down list.

Searching for package names

Searching for package names from the command line is accomplished with the `Find-Package` command. As an example, to find available packages that include the `definitelytyped` search string, run the following command:

```
Find-Package definitelytyped
```

This will list packages that match the search criteria as follows:

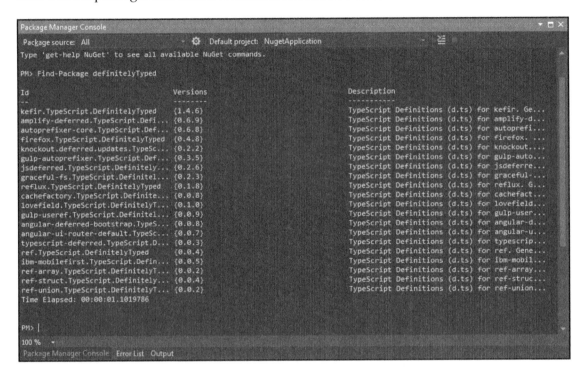

Installing a specific version

There are some JavaScript libraries that are not compatible with jQuery version 2.x, and will require a version of jQuery that is in the 1.x range. To install a specific version of a NuGet package, we will need to specify the `-Version` parameter from the command line. To install the `jquery v1.11.1` package, as an example, run the following from the command line:

```
Install-Package jQuery -Version 1.11.1
```

NuGet will either upgrade or downgrade the version of the package that you're installing if it finds another version already installed within your project. In the preceding example, we had already installed the latest version of jQuery (2.1.1) within our project, so NuGet will first remove `jQuery 2.1.1` before installing `jQuery 1.11.1`.

Using npm and @types

With the release of version 2.0 of the TypeScript compiler, we can now also install declaration files using `npm`. This means that there is no difference in our toolset in order to install project dependencies, as it is to include the declaration files. As an example, to install the Underscore library as a project dependency, we would type the following:

```
npm install underscore
```

And to install the declaration files for Underscore, we can now type the following:

```
npm install @types/underscore
```

Note the `@types` prefix used within the `npm` command. This special syntax instructs `npm` to install the declaration files for Underscore, and is a very subtle but easily remembered syntax.

If we take a look at the `package.json` file within our project directory, we will note that both the Underscore libraries, and the corresponding type libraries are both registered, as follows:

```
{
  "name": "npm_types",
  "version": "1.0.0",
  "description": "",
  "main": "index.js",
  "scripts": {
    "test": "echo \"Error: no test specified\" && exit 1"
  },
  "author": "",
  "license": "ISC",
  "dependencies": {
    "@types/underscore": "^1.8.9",
    "underscore": "^1.9.1"
  }
}
```

Here, we have two entries in the dependencies section of the `package.json` file, one for `underscore` itself, and the other for `@types/underscore`. Note that as with a standard `npm` dependency, we automatically have access to the version of the library that was used.

 This mechanism for including type definitions via `npm` has been adopted as the standard mechanism by TypeScript moving forward.

Using third-party libraries

In this section of the chapter, we will begin to explore some of the older third-party JavaScript libraries, their declaration files, and how to write compatible TypeScript for each of these frameworks. We will compare Backbone, Angular (version 1), and Ext JS, which are all frameworks for building rich client-side JavaScript applications. During our discussion, we will see that some frameworks are highly compliant with the TypeScript language and its features, some are partially compliant, and some have very low compliance.

In the next chapter, we will explore some third-party JavaScript libraries that have been written explicitly with TypeScript in mind, or for which the TypeScript compiler has been modified to work with. In the remainder of this chapter, however, we'll focus on standard third-party libraries that were designed to support JavaScript.

While there are a number of newer frameworks that support TypeScript out of the box, you may find that you need to work with these older frameworks from time to time.

Choosing a JavaScript framework

Choosing a JavaScript framework or library to develop **Single Page Applications (SPAs)** is a difficult and sometimes daunting task. It seems that there is a new framework appearing every other month, promising more and more functionality for less and less code. To help developers compare these frameworks, and make an informed choice, Addy Osmani wrote an excellent article, named *Journey Through the JavaScript MVC Jungle*, available at http://www.smashingmagazine.com/2012/07/27/journey-through-the-javascript-mvc-jungle/.

In essence, his advice is simple—it's a personal choice—so try some frameworks out, and see what best fits your needs, your programming mindset, and your existing skill set. The *TodoMVC* project (`http://todomvc.com`), which Addy started, does an excellent job of implementing the same application in a number of **Model View Something** (**MV***) JavaScript frameworks. This really is a reference site for digging into a fully working application, and comparing for yourself the coding techniques and styles of different frameworks.

Again, depending on the JavaScript library that you are using within TypeScript, you may need to write your TypeScript code in a specific way. Bear this in mind when choosing a framework—if it is difficult to use with TypeScript, then you may be better off looking at another framework with better integration. If it is easy and natural to work with the framework in TypeScript, then your productivity and overall development experience will be much better.

In this section, we will look at some of the older JavaScript libraries, along with their declaration files, and see how to write compatible TypeScript. The key thing to remember is that TypeScript generates JavaScript—so if you are battling to use a third-party library, then crack open the generated JavaScript and see what the JavaScript code looks like that TypeScript is emitting. If the generated JavaScript matches the JavaScript code samples in the library's documentation, then you are on the right track. If not, then you may need to modify your TypeScript until the compiled JavaScript starts matching up with the samples.

When trying to write TypeScript code for a third-party JavaScript framework—particularly if you are working off the JavaScript documentation—our initial foray may just be one of trial and error. The rest of this chapter shows how three different libraries require different ways of writing TypeScript.

Backbone

Backbone is a popular JavaScript library that gives structure to web applications by providing models, collections, and views. Backbone has been around since 2010, and has gained a very large following, with a wealth of commercial websites using the framework. According to an article from October 2013 at infoworld.com (available at `https://www.infoworld.com/article/2612250/application-development/application-development-the-10-hottest-javascript-framework-projects.html?page=2`), Backbone had over 1,600 Backbone-related projects on GitHub at the time that rate over three stars, meaning that it has a vast ecosystem of extensions and related libraries.

Let's take a quick look at Backbone written in TypeScript.

The Backbone environment can be set up with npm, as follows:

```
npm install backbone
npm install @types/backbone
```

Using inheritance with Backbone

From the Backbone documentation, we find an example of creating a Backbone.Model class in JavaScript, as follows:

```
var NoteModel = Backbone.Model.extend ({
    initialize: function() {
        console.log("NoteModel initialized.");
    },
    author: function() {},
    coordinates : function() {},
    allowedToEdit: function(account) {
        return true;
    }
});
```

This code shows typical usage of Backbone in JavaScript. We start by creating a variable named NoteModel that extends (or derives from) Backbone.Model. This can be seen with the Backbone.Model.extend syntax. The Backbone extend function uses JavaScript object notation to define an object within the outer curly braces { ... }. In this example, the NoteModel object has four functions: initialize, author, coordinates, and allowedToEdit.

According to the Backbone documentation, the initialize function will be called once a new instance of this class is created. In our sample, the initialize function simply logs a message to the console to indicate that the function was called. The author and coordinates functions are blank at this stage, with only the allowedToEdit function actually doing something—return true.

If we then right-click on the extend function, and then select the **Goto Definition** option from Visual Studio Code, we will be directed to the definition file for Backbone. Here, we see an interesting piece of documentation for this function, as follows:

```
class Model extends ModelBase {

/**
* Do not use, prefer TypeScript's extend functionality.
**/
public static extend(properties: any, classProperties?: any): any;
```

This declaration file snippet shows some of the definition of the Backbone Model class. Here, we can see that the extend function is defined as public static. Note, however, the comment in the code block—Do not use, prefer TypeScript's extend functionality.

This comment indicates that the declaration file for Backbone is built around TypeScript's extends keyword—thereby allowing us to use natural TypeScript inheritance syntax to create Backbone objects. Let's therefore clean up our code to use the extends TypeScript keyword to derive a class from the base class Backbone.Model, as follows:

```
class NoteModel extends Backbone.Model {
    initialize() {
        console.log(`NoteModel initialized`);
    }
    author() {}
    coordinates() {}
    allowedToEdit(account: any) : boolean {
        return true;
    }
}
```

We are now creating a class definition named NoteModel that uses the TypeScript inheritance syntax to derive a class from the Backbone.Model base class. This class then has the functions initialize, author, coordinates, and allowedToEdit, similar to the previous version of JavaScript.

Let's now create an instance of the NoteModel object by creating an HTML page, as follows:

```
<!DOCTYPE html>
<html>
<head>
    <meta charset="utf-8" />
    <title></title>
    <script src="./node_modules/underscore/underscore.js">
 </script>
    <script src="./node_modules/backbone/backbone.js"></script>
    <script src="./backbone_app.js"></script>
</head>
<body>
    <script >
        window.onload = function() {
            console.log('window.onload called');
            var noteModel = new NoteModel();
        };
    </script>
```

```
    </body>
    </html>
```

Here, we have a standard HTML page that includes both the `backbone.js` file, and the `underscore.js` file (Backbone is dependent on Underscore). We then include our `backbone_app.js` file which contains the definition of the `NoteModel` class. We then have a `<script>` tag that will execute a function when the page loads. Within this function, we are creating an instance of the `NoteModel` class. According to the documentation, the `initialize` function of a Backbone Model will be called by Backbone when an instance of a `Model` class has been created. Checking the console output of this page, we will see the following messages:

```
window.onload called
NoteModel initialized
```

The output to the console shows us that the `window.onload` function was indeed called, and that we have successfully instantiated an instance of a Backbone model.

All of Backbone's core objects are designed with inheritance in mind. This means that creating new Backbone collections, views, and routers will use the same `extends` syntax in TypeScript. Backbone, therefore, is a very good fit for TypeScript, because we can use natural TypeScript syntax for inheritance to create new Backbone objects.

Using interfaces

As Backbone allows us to use TypeScript inheritance to create objects, we can just as easily use TypeScript interfaces with any of our Backbone objects as well. Extracting an interface for the preceding `NoteModel` class would be as follows:

```
interface INoteModel {
    initialize() : void;
    author() : void;
    coordinates() : void;
    allowedToEdit(account: any): boolean;
}
```

We can now update our `NoteModel` class definition to implement this interface as follows:

```
class NoteModel extends Backbone.Model implements INoteModel {
    // existing code
}
```

Our class definition now implements the `INoteModel` TypeScript interface. This simple change protects our code from being modified inadvertently, and also opens up the ability to work with core Backbone objects in standard object-oriented design patterns. We could, if we needed to, apply the *Factory Pattern* described in `Chapter 3`, *Interfaces, Classes and Inheritance*, to return a particular type of Backbone model—or any other Backbone object for that matter.

Using generic syntax

The declaration file for Backbone has also added generic syntax to some class definitions. This brings with it further strong typing benefits when writing TypeScript code for Backbone. Backbone collections (surprise, surprise) house a collection of Backbone models, allowing us to define collections in TypeScript as follows:

```
class NoteCollection extends Backbone.Collection<NoteModel> {
    model = NoteModel;
}
```

Here, we have a `NoteCollection` that derives from or `extends` a `Backbone.Collection`, but also uses generic syntax to constrain the collection to handle only objects of type `NoteModel`. This means that any of the standard collection functions, such as `at()` or `pluck()`, will be strongly typed to return `NoteModel` models, further enhancing our type safety and Intellisense.

Note the syntax used to assign a type to the internal `model` property of the collection class on the second line. We cannot use the standard TypeScript syntax `model: NoteModel`, as this causes a compile time error. We need to assign the `model` property to the class definition, as seen with the `model=NoteModel` syntax.

Using ECMAScript 5

Backbone also allows us to use ECMAScript 5 capabilities to define getters and setters for `Backbone.Model` classes, as follows:

```
interface ISimpleModel {
    name: string;
    id: number;
}
class SimpleModel extends Backbone.Model implements ISimpleModel {
    get name() {
        return this.get('name');
```

```
    }
    set name(value: string) {
        this.set('name', value);
    }
    get id() : number {
        return this.get('id');
    }
    set id(value: number) {
        this.set('id', value);
    }
}
```

Here, we have defined an interface with two properties, named `ISimpleModel`. We then define a `SimpleModel` class that derives from `Backbone.Model`, and also implements the `ISimpleModel` interface. We then have ES5 getters and setters for our `name` and `id` properties. Backbone uses class attributes to store model values, so our getters and setters simply call the underlying `get` and `set` methods of `Backbone.Model`.

Backbone TypeScript compatibility

As we have seen, Backbone allows us to use all of TypeScript's language features within our code. We can use classes, interfaces, inheritance, generics, and even ECMAScript 5 properties. All of our classes also derive from base Backbone objects. This makes Backbone a highly compatible library for building web applications with TypeScript. We will explore more of the Backbone library in later chapters.

Angular 1

AngularJs version 1 (or just Angular 1) is a very popular JavaScript framework, and was built and distributed by Google. It has, however, been superseded by Angular 2, which uses TypeScript as its language of choice, which we will cover in the next chapter. This section of the chapter will discuss writing Angular 1 code with TypeScript, as an example of a semi-compatible third-party library.

Angular 1 takes a completely different approach to building JavaScript SPA's, introducing an HTML syntax that the running Angular 1 application understands. This provides the application with two-way data binding capabilities, which automatically synchronizes models, views, and the HTML page. Angular 1 also provides a mechanism for **dependency injection (DI)**, and uses services to provide data to your views and models.

Let's take a look at a sample from the Angular v1.7 Tutorial (https://docs.angularjs.org/tutorial/step_02), found in step 2, where we start to build a controller named PhoneListController. The example provided in the tutorial shows the following JavaScript:

```
var phonecatApp = angular.module('phonecatApp', []);

phonecatApp.controller('PhoneListController', function ($scope)
{
  $scope.phones = [
    {'name': 'Nexus S',
     'snippet': 'Fast just got faster with Nexus S.'},
    {'name': 'Motorola XOOM with Wi-Fi',
     'snippet': 'The Next, Next Generation tablet.'},
    {'name': 'MOTOROLA XOOM',
     'snippet': 'The Next, Next Generation tablet.'}
  ];
});
```

This code snippet is typical of Angular 1 JavaScript syntax. We start by creating a variable named phonecatApp, and register this as an Angular module by calling the module function on the angular global instance. The first argument to the module function is a global name for the Angular module, and the empty array is a placeholder for other modules that will be injected through Angular 1's dependency injection routines.

We then call the controller function on the newly created phonecatApp variable with two arguments. The first argument is the global name of the controller, and the second argument is a function that accepts a specially named Angular variable, named $scope. Within this function, the code sets the phones object of the $scope variable to be an array of JSON objects, each with a name and snippet property.

If we continue reading through the tutorial, we find a unit test that shows how the PhoneListController controller is used:

```
describe('PhoneListController', function(){
    it('should create "phones" model with 3 phones', function() {
      var scope = {},
          ctrl = new PhoneListController(scope);

      expect(scope.phones.length).toBe(3);
  });

});
```

The first two lines of this code snippet use a global function called describe, and within this function, another function called it. These two functions are part of a unit testing framework named Jasmine. We will cover *unit testing* in Chapter 8, *Test Driven Development*, but for the time being, lets' focus on the rest of the code.

We declare a variable named scope to be an empty JavaScript object, and then a variable named ctrl that uses the new keyword to create an instance of our PhoneListController class. The new PhoneListController(scope) syntax shows that Angular 1 is using the definition of the controller, just like we would use a normal class in TypeScript.

Building the same object in TypeScript would allow us to use TypeScript classes, as follows:

```
var phonecatApp = angular.module('phonecatApp', []);

class PhoneListController  {
    constructor($scope: any) {
        $scope.phones = [
            { 'name': 'Nexus S',
              'snippet': 'Fast just got faster' },
            { 'name': 'Motorola',
              'snippet': 'Next generation tablet' },
            { 'name': 'Motorola Xoom',
              'snippet': 'Next, next generation tablet' }
        ];
    }
};
```

Our first line is the same as in our previous JavaScript sample. We then, however, use the TypeScript class syntax to create a class named PhoneListController. By creating a TypeScript class, we can now use this class as shown in our Jasmine test code—ctrl = new PhoneListController(scope). The constructor function of our PhoneListController class now acts as the anonymous function seen in the original JavaScript sample:

```
phonecatApp.controller('PhoneListController', function ($scope) {
    // this function is replaced by the constructor
}
```

Angular classes and $scope

Let's expand our `PhoneListController` class a little further, and have a look at what it would look like when completed:

```
class PhoneListCtrl {
    myScope: IScope;
    constructor($scope: any, $http: ng.IHttpService, Phone: any) {
        this.myScope = $scope;
        this.myScope.phones = Phone.query();
        $scope.orderProp = 'age';
        _.bindAll(this, 'GetPhonesSuccess');
    }
    GetPhonesSuccess(data: any) {
        this.myScope.phones = data;
    }
};
```

The first thing to note in this class is that we are defining a variable named `myScope`, and storing the `$scope` argument passed in via the constructor into this internal variable. This is again because of JavaScript's lexical scoping rules. Note the call to `_.bindAll` at the end of the constructor—this Underscore utility function will ensure that whenever the `GetPhonesSuccess` function is called, it will use the variable `this` in the context of the class instance, and not in the context of the calling code. We will discuss the usage of `_.bindAll` in detail in a later chapter.

The `GetPhonesSuccess` function uses the `this.myScope` variable within its implementation. This is why we needed to store the initial `$scope` argument in an internal variable.

Another thing we notice from this code is that the `myScope` variable is typed to an interface named `IScope`, which will need to be defined as follows:

```
interface IScope {
    phones : IPhone[];
}
interface IPhone {
    name: string;
    snippet: string;
}
```

This `IScope` interface just contains an array of objects of the type `IPhone` (pardon the unfortunate name of this interface—it can hold Android phones as well).

What this means is that we don't have a standard interface or TypeScript type to use when dealing with $scope objects. By its nature, the $scope argument will change its type depending on when and where the Angular runtime calls it, hence our need to define an IScope interface, and strongly type the myScope variable to this interface.

Another interesting thing to note on the constructor function of the PhoneListController class is the type of the $http argument. It is set to be of type ng.IHttpService. This IHttpService interface is found in the declaration file for Angular 1. In order to use Angular 1 variables, such as $scope or $http, with Typescript, we need to find the matching interface within our declaration file before we can use any of the Angular 1 functions available on these variables.

The last point to note in this constructor code is the last argument, named Phone, which is of type any. Let's take a quick look at the implementation of this Phone service, which is as follows:

```
var phonecatServices =
    angular.module('phonecatServices', ['ngResource']);

phonecatServices.factory('Phone',
    [
        '$resource', ($resource) => {
            return $resource('phones/:phoneId.json', {}, {
                query: {
                    method: 'GET',
                    params: {
                        phoneId: 'phones'
                    },
                    isArray: true
                }
            });
        }
    ]
);
```

The first line of this code snippet again creates a global variable named phonecatServices, using the angular.module global function. We then call the factory function available on the phonecatServices variable, in order to define our Phone resource. This factory function uses a string named 'Phone' to define the Phone resource, and then uses Angular 1's dependency injection syntax to inject a $resource object. Looking through this code, we can see that we cannot easily create standard TypeScript classes for Angular 1 to use here, nor can we use standard TypeScript interfaces or inheritance on these Angular 1 classes.

Angular 1 TypeScript compatibility

When writing Angular 1 code with TypeScript, we are able to use classes in certain instances, but must rely on the underlying Angular 1 functions such as `module` and `factory` to define our objects in other cases. Also, when using standard Angular 1 services, such as `$http` or `$resource`, we will need to specify the matching declaration file interface in order to use these services. We can therefore describe the Angular 1 library as having medium compatibility with TypeScript.

Inheritance – Angular 1 versus Backbone

Inheritance is a very powerful feature of object-oriented programming, and is also a fundamental concept when using JavaScript frameworks. Using a Backbone controller or an Angular 1 controller within the framework relies on certain characteristics or functions being available. We have seen, however, that each framework implements inheritance in a different way.

As JavaScript (prior to EC6) did not have the concept of inheritance, each of these older frameworks needed to find a way to implement it. In Backbone, this inheritance implementation is via the `extend` function of each Backbone object. As we have seen, the TypeScript `extends` keyword follows a similar implementation to Backbone, allowing the framework and language to dovetail each other.

Angular 1, on the other hand, uses its own implementation of inheritance, and defines functions on the Angular 1 global namespace to create classes (that is, `angular.module`). We can also sometimes use the instance of an application (that is, `<appName>.controller`) to create modules or controllers. We have found, though, that Angular 1 uses controllers in a very similar way to TypeScript classes, and we can therefore simply create standard TypeScript classes that will work within an Angular 1 application.

So far, we have only skimmed the surface of both the Angular 1 TypeScript syntax and the Backbone TypeScript syntax. The point of this exercise was to try and understand how TypeScript can be used within each of these two older third-party frameworks.

Be sure to visit `http://todomvc.com`, and have a look at the full source code for the Todo application written in TypeScript for both Angular 1 and Backbone. They can be found on the **Compile-to-JS** tab in the **example** section. These running code samples, combined with the documentation on each of these sites, will prove to be an invaluable resource when trying to write TypeScript syntax with an older external third-party library, such as Angular 1 or Backbone.

ExtJS

ExtJS is a popular JavaScript library that has a wide variety of widgets, grids, graphing components, layout components, and more. With release 4.0, ExtJS incorporated a model, view, controller style of application architecture to their libraries. Although it is free for open source development, ExtJS requires a license for commercial use. It is popular with development teams that are building web-enabled desktop replacements, as its look and feel is comparable to normal desktop applications. ExtJS, by default, ensures that each application or component will look and feel exactly the same, no matter which browser it is run in, and it requires little or no need for CSS or HTML.

The ExtJS team, however, has not released an official TypeScript declaration file for ExtJS, despite much community pressure. Thankfully, the wider TypeScript community has come to the rescue, beginning with *Mike Aubury*. He wrote a small utility program to generate declaration files from the ExtJS documentation (https://github.com/zz9pa/extjsTypescript).

Whether this work influenced the current version of the ExtJS definitions on DefinitelyTyped remains to be seen, but the original definitions from Mike Aubury and the current version from brian428 on DefinitelyTyped are very similar.

Creating classes in Ext JS

ExtJS is a JavaScript library that does things in its own way. If we were to categorize Backbone, Angular 1, and ExtJS, we might say that Backbone is a highly compliant TypeScript library. In other words, the language features of classes and inheritance within TypeScript are highly compliant with Backbone. Angular 1, in this case, would be a partially compliant library, with some elements of Angular 1 objects complying with the TypeScript language features. ExtJS, on the other hand, would be a minimally compliant library, with little or no TypeScript language features applicable to the library.

Let's take a look at a sample ExtJS 4.0 application written in TypeScript. Consider the following code:

```
Ext.application(
    {
        name: 'SampleApp',
        appFolder: '/code/sample',
        controllers: ['SampleController'],
        launch: () => {

            Ext.create('Ext.container.Viewport', {
```

```
            layout: 'fit',
            items: [{
                xtype: 'panel',
                title: 'Sample App',
                html: 'This is a Sample Viewport'
            }]
        });


    }


  }
);
```

We start by creating an ExtJS application by calling the `application` function on the `Ext` global instance. The `application` function then uses a JavaScript object, enclosed within the first and last curly braces `{ }` to define properties and functions. This ExtJS application sets the `name` property to be `SampleApp`, the `appFolder` property to be `/code/sample`, and the `controllers` property to be an array with a single entry—`'SampleController'`.

We then define a `launch` property, which is an anonymous function. This `launch` function then uses the `create` function on the global `Ext` instance to create a class. The `create` function uses the `"Ext.container.Viewport"` name to create an instance of the `Ext.container.Viewport` class, which has the `layout` and `items` properties. The `layout` property can only contain one specific set of values, for example `'fit'`, `'auto'`, or `'table'`. The `items` array contains further Ext JS specific objects, which are created depending on what their `xtype` property suggests.

ExtJS is one of those libraries that isn't intuitive. As a programmer, you will need to have one browser window open with the library documentation at all times, and use it to figure out what each property means for each type of available class. It also has a lot of magic strings - in the preceding sample, the `Ext.create` function would fail if we mistyped the `'Ext.container.Viewport'` string, or simply forgot to capitalize it in the right places. To ExtJS, `'viewport'` is different to `'ViewPort'`. Remember that one of our solutions to magic strings within TypeScript is to use enums. Unfortunately, the current version of the ExtJS declaration file does not have a set of enums for these class types.

Using type casting

We can, however, use the TypeScript language feature of type casting to help with writing ExtJS code. If we know what type of ExtJS object we are trying to create, we can cast the JavaScript object to this type, and then use TypeScript to check whether the properties we are using are correct for that type of ExtJS object. To help with this concept, let's just take the outer definition of the `Ext.application` into account. Stripped of the inner code, the call to the `application` function on the `Ext` global object would be reduced to this:

```
Ext.application(
    {
        // properties of an Ext.application
        // are set within this JavaScript
        // object block
    }
);
```

Using the TypeScript declaration files, type casting, and a healthy dose of ExtJS documentation, we know that the inner JavaScript object should be of the type `Ext.app.IApplication`, and we can therefore cast this object as follows:

```
Ext.application(
    <Ext.app.IApplication> {
        // this JavaScript block is strongly
        // type to be of Ext.app.IApplication
    }
);
```

The second line of this code snippet now uses the TypeScript type casting syntax, to cast the JavaScript object between the curly braces { } to a type of `Ext.app.IApplication`. This gives us strong type checking and Intellisense, as shown in the following screenshot:

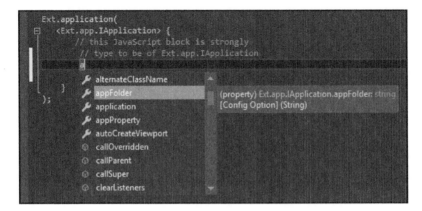

In a similar manner, these explicit type casts can be used on any JavaScript object that is being used to create ExtJS classes. The declaration file for ExtJS currently on Definitely Typed uses the same names for its object definitions as the ExtJS documentation uses, so finding the correct type should be rather simple.

The preceding technique of using explicit type casting is just about the only language feature of TypeScript that we can use with the ExtJS library—but this still highlights how strong typing of objects can assist us in our development experience, making our code more robust and resistant to errors.

An Ext JS-specific TypeScript compiler

If you are using ExtJS on a regular basis, then you may want to take a look at the work done by *Gareth Smith, Fabio Parra dos Santos,* and their team at `https://github.com/fabioparra/TypeScript`. This project is a fork of the TypeScript compiler that will emit ExtJS classes from standard TypeScript classes. Using this version of the compiler turns the tables on normal ExtJS development, allowing for natural TypeScript class syntax, the use of inheritance via the `extends` keyword, as well as natural module naming, without the need for magic strings. The work done by this team shows that because the TypeScript compiler is open source, it can be extended and modified to emit JavaScript in a specific way, or to target a specific library. Hats off to *Gareth, Fabio,* and their team for their ground-breaking work in this area.

Summary

In this chapter, we have had a look at third-party JavaScript libraries and how they can be used within a TypeScript application. We started by looking at the various ways of including community-released versions of TypeScript declaration files within our projects by using package managers such as NuGet and `npm`. We then looked at three types of third-party libraries, and discussed how to integrate these libraries with TypeScript. We explored Backbone, which can be categorized as a highly compliant third-party library; Angular 1, which is a partially compliant library; and ExtJS, which is a minimally compliant library. We saw how various features of the TypeScript language can co-exist with these libraries, and showed what TypeScript equivalent code would look like in each of these cases. In the next chapter, we will look at TypeScript specific third-party libraries, which are either built with TypeScript, or have complete TypeScript integration.

TypeScript Compatible Frameworks
7

One of the watershed moments in the story of the TypeScript language came when it was announced that the Microsoft and Google teams had been working together on Angular 2. Angular 2 was a much anticipated update to the popular Angular (or Angular 1) framework. Unfortunately, this update required a new set of language features in order to make the Angular 2 syntax cleaner and easier to understand. Originally, Google had proposed a new language named AtScript to facilitate these new language features, which were also closely aligned with the ECMAScript 6 and 7 proposals.

After several months of collaboration, it was announced that all of the necessary features of the AtScript language would be absorbed into the TypeScript language, and that Angular 2 would be written in TypeScript. This meant that the providers of new language features (TypeScript and Microsoft) and the consumers of the new language features (Angular 2 and Google) were able to agree on the requirements and immediate future of the language. This collaboration shows that the TypeScript language has had intense scrutiny from a well-renowned JavaScript framework team, and has passed with flying colors.

Angular 2, however, was not the first framework to adopt the TypeScript language, and many third-party JavaScript libraries also offer full support for TypeScript.

In this chapter, we will take a look at some of these more popular JavaScript frameworks that have full TypeScript language integration. We will compare the syntax used in each of these frameworks, by building the same sample MVC application using each framework. In doing so, we will have a side-by-side comparison that will show us how each of these frameworks has tackled the same design problems. Before we begin though, we will start with a general discussion on what an MVC framework is, and how it can help us in our development experience.

We will cover the following topics:

- What is an MVC framework?
- The benefits of using an MVC framework
- An outline of our sample application
- Using Backbone
- Using Aurelia
- Using Angular 2
- Using ReactJs
- Rendering performance analysis

What is MVC?

The acronym MVC stands for Model-View-Controller. It is a programming design pattern that aids in the design and implementation of user interfaces. User interfaces are inherently event driven—in other words, we display something on a screen, and then wait for the user to do something, which will generate some sort of event. This event may be to display a graph, or to hide a panel, or to log out of our application. Unfortunately, the exact sequence of events that a user of our application will follow cannot be completely pre-determined. It is this event-based paradigm that makes user interface design and programming rather more complex than a program that follows a defined sequence of steps.

The other complexity of user interfaces is to try and make components reusable. This means that a single component, such as a menu bar for instance, should be able to be reused across multiple pages. Component reuse offers its own set of challenges, which generally center around which component is responsible for reacting to which events, and how components communicate when many of them are interested in the same event.

The Model-View-Controller design pattern breaks up the responsibilities of a user interface into three main components, as follows:

The Model

The Model in MVC represents data. This is generally a very simple **Plain Old JavaScript Object (POJO)** that has certain properties. As an example of a Model, consider the following TypeScript class:

```
interface IModel {
    DisplayName: string;
    Id: number;
}

class Model implements IModel {
    DisplayName: string;
    Id: number;
    constructor(model : IModel) {
        this.DisplayName = model.DisplayName;
        this.Id = model.Id;
    }
}

let firstModel = new Model({ Id: 1, DisplayName: 'firstModel'});
```

Here, we have defined an interface named `IModel` that has an `Id` and a `DisplayName` property, and a class that implements this interface. We have provided a simple constructor to set these properties. The last line of this snippet creates an instance of this class, with the desired properties.

As can be seen from this snippet, the `Model` class is a very simple POJO that contains some data.

 Models often contain other models, building a nested structure of information. These models often map directly to the structures that are returned in JSON format from REST endpoints.

The View

The View in MVC represents the visual representation of a Model. In web frameworks, this would typically be a snippet of HTML, as follows:

```
<div id="viewTemplate">
    <span><b> {Id} </b></span>
    <span><h1> {DisplayName} </h1></span>
</div>
```

Here, we have an enclosing `div` that contains two spans. The first `span` is rendered in bold, and will display the `Id` property from the model. The second `span` is rendered in `h1` style, and displays the `DisplayName` property from the model.

By separating the view elements of a user interface from the model, we can see that we are free to modify the view as much as we like, without even touching the code for the model. We could apply styles to each element through CSS, or even hide certain properties from the view completely.

This separation gives us the ability to design or modify the display portion independently of the model. This design work can even be handed off to a completely separate and independent team, who have specialist skills in user interface design. As long as the underlying model does not change, both parts of a model and view will work seamlessly together.

As an example of a View, consider the following code:

```
class View {
    template: string;
    constructor(_template: string) {
        this.template = _template;
    }
    render(model: Model) {
        // combine template and view
    }
}
```

Here, we have defined a class named `View` that has a single property, named `template`. When we construct this view, we give it the HTML template that it should use. This `View` class also has a `render` method, which has a single argument named `model`. The `render` method will combine the `template` and the `model`, and return the resulting HTML.

 The preceding examples are pseudo code meant only for illustration purposes, and are not an example of any one such MVC framework.

The Controller

The Controller in an MVC framework does the job of coordinating the interaction between the Model and the View. A Controller will generally accomplish the following steps:

1. Create an instance of a Model
2. Create an instance of the View
3. Pass the instance of the Model to the View
4. Ask the View to render itself (generate the actual HTML based on values in the Model)
5. Attach the resulting HTML to the DOM tree

The Controller in MVC is also responsible for the logic of the application. This means that it can control which views are presented when and what to do when certain events occur.

As an example of what a Controller could look like, consider the following code:

```
class Controller {
    model: Model;
    view : View;
    constructor() {
        this.model = new Model({Id : 1, DisplayName : 'firstModel'});
        this.view = new View($('#viewTemplate').html());
    }
    render() {
        $('#domElement').html(this.view.render(this.model));
    }
}
```

Here, we have defined a `Controller` class that has a `model` property and a `view` property. Our `constructor` function then creates an instance of the `Model` class with specific properties, and an instance of the `View`. The `View` instance is created with the template that is read from a DOM element named `viewTemplate`.

The `Controller` class also defines a `render` function, which sets the actual HTML of a DOM element named `domElement`. This HTML is the result of calling the `render` function on the `View` class, and passing in the `model` to be rendered.

Again, this is pseudo code for describing the responsibilities of a controller in MVC, and is not an actual example of a particular MVC framework.

MVC summary

The following diagram shows the three elements of the MVC design pattern:

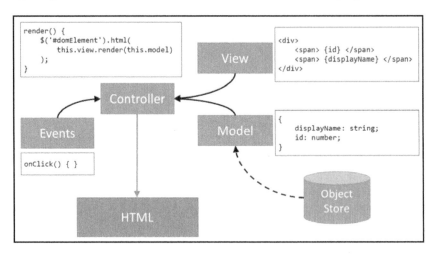

Models are simple objects holding properties, and are typically created from an **Object Store** or a database.

Views are **HTML** visual elements, incorporating model properties within their templates.

Controllers combine models and views, respond to events, and orchestrate generation of the resultant **HTML**.

The Benefits of using MVC

Using an MVC framework brings with it a number of tangible benefits, as follows:

- Decoupling of the various elements used to display information to the user.
- Increased flexibility and reuse.
- A single model may have multiple different views that can be used at different times.
- User interface design activities can be undertaken by a specialist team.
- Changes to the data of a model can trigger events in a completely different controller without each component knowing about the other.

- Views can contain other views in a nested fashion, thereby enhancing reuse.
- Changes in behavior of a component can be made without changing its visual representation (by changing the Controller and not the View).
- Rapid and parallel development.
- Testability of individual components.

Sample application outline

To facilitate a comparison of our various TypeScript frameworks, we will build the same application using each framework, which will accomplish the following:

- Use a view to display a model property
- Construct an array of data, with each array item being a single model instance
- Loop through the array and render each item in a list element
- Respond to a click event on each item rendered
- Display the model properties that were used to render the element
- Construct a form at the bottom of the page
- Set a default value for a form input control
- Interrogate the updated form control value when the user submits the form

We will use the same dataset for our array in each of the four sample applications. This dataset is as follows:

```
interface IClickableItem {
    DisplayName: string;
    Id: number;
}

let ClickableItemCollection : IClickableItem[] = ( [
    { Id: 1, DisplayName : "firstItem"},
    { Id: 2, DisplayName : "secondItem"},
    { Id: 3, DisplayName : "thirdItem"},
]);
```

We start with an interface named `IClickableItem` that has an `Id` property of type `number`, and a `DisplayName` property of type `string`. We then define an array of `IClickableItem` objects, named `ClickableItemCollection`. The reason for using such an array is that it is a very common structure to work with when fetching data from a REST endpoint that returns JSON. If we can interpret a simple array like this, then we can easily substitute this array with JSON data later on.

Our resulting application will appear as follows:

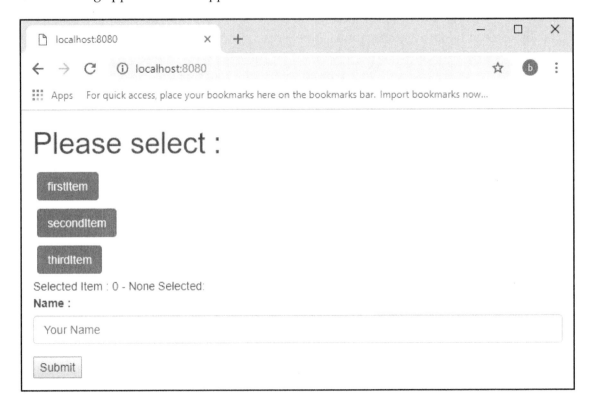

Here, we have rendered a page that has three buttons, generated from our data array. When we click on any one of these buttons, the `Selected Item` text at the bottom of the page will be updated. We also have a simple text input field at the bottom of the page that is labeled `Name`. This input field will have the default value of "`Your Name`" when the page is initially loaded. When the **Submit** button at the bottom of the page is clicked, we will log the value of this input field to the console. Setting data when forms are created, and getting this data after a user has interacted with a form will highlight how each framework handles data binding within a form. While this may seem a very simple form to begin with, it will help to explain the different form handling techniques that each framework uses.

Using Backbone

We will start our exploration of TypeScript frameworks by building the sample application in Backbone. While it can be argued that Backbone is not a TypeScript framework *per se*, we have already seen how it can be used naturally with the TypeScript language syntax. Backbone is also one of the oldest frameworks around, and it is small, light, and extremely fast.

Backbone, however, requires writing a little more code than most frameworks, as it is really the bare-bones of an MVC framework. When working with Backbone, you will need to call rendering functions yourself, and also attach rendered HTML to the DOM tree manually.

To make Backbone development a little easier, the Marionette framework was developed on top of the Backbone framework, in order to simplify and remove a lot of this repetitive code. In fact, there are a number of frameworks that use Backbone as the base framework, and add some additional concepts that are helpful when building web applications. Marionette is also extremely fast, as it adds just a thin layer of functionality across the top of Backbone, while still using the underlying Backbone library.

Rendering performance

If page rendering performance, CPU cycles, and RAM are critical factors in your applications, then you cannot go past Backbone for pure rendering speed.

In a recent project, our team was involved in speed testing both the Marionette and Backbone frameworks in order to determine whether they were suitable for use on embedded devices. These embedded devices had 400-600 MHz CPUs, and 128-256 MB RAM. In comparison to a modern desktop, with a 3.6 GHz CPU and 8 GB of RAM, these are tiny machines indeed. This test application rendered a series of three HTML screens, each with varying complexity. The first page was a very simple page, the second had a variable menu structure, and the third had a rather complex detailed informational view of some data. All code was written in TypeScript.

The processors and RAM available on each device were as follows:

- 400 MHz ARM9 with 128 MB RAM
- 400 MHz PowerPC with 256 MB RAM
- 624 MHz Marvell PXA300 with 256 MB RAM
- 6 GHz Core i7 with 8 GB RAM (desktop)

This test application ran a high-resolution timer, and sent messages through web sockets to the HTML page. The timer started when a message was sent from the timing application to the web page. Once a message was received inside the web application, it decided which page to display. The page display mechanism used the Model View Controller pattern to render HTML to the browser. Once the HTML had been rendered to the screen, a message was sent back to the timing application to stop the clock. In this way, millisecond timing information could be obtained to determine how long it took to render HTML on each of these devices.

This test was repeated a number of times in order to obtain an average rendering time. The results were as follows, with all timings shown in milliseconds:

		400 MHz ARM9 128 MB	400 MHz PowerPC 256 MB	624 MHz Marvel 256 MB	3.6 GHz Core i7 8 GB
Backbone	Simple page	187 ms	131 ms	187 ms	5 ms
	Medium page	241 ms	151 ms	267 ms	11 ms
	Complex page	380 ms	370 ms	379 ms	17 ms
Marionette	Simple page	525 ms	349 ms	501 ms	7 ms
	Medium page	1,043 ms	769 ms	851 ms	19 ms
	Complex page	1,532 ms	847 ms	1,014 ms	32 ms

Looking at the results in this table, we can see that standard Backbone rendering on a slower CPU can take around 130-380 milliseconds on a 400 MHz PowerPC CPU. The same HTML being rendered from Marionette, however, starts at 350 milliseconds, and can go up to 850 milliseconds. This difference can be attributed to the higher CPU cycles that are taken up by the extra processing that Marionette is doing on top of Backbone.

These results tell us, then, that the more logic a framework contains, and therefore the more processing a framework does, the slower it will be on less powerful processors. So when assessing a framework that does a lot of magic behind the scenes, bear in mind that these features will chew up valuable CPU processing time, and may not be suitable for slower devices.

Our decision was to pursue Backbone as an MVC framework for these embedded devices because it offered the fastest speed available. That said, on a modern computer with a fairly decent processor, the difference between 5 milliseconds of rendering time and 32 milliseconds is negligible.

Backbone setup

Setting up a Backbone environment is fairly simple, and can be accomplished through `tsc`, and `npm` as follows:

Initialize the TypeScript environment with `tsc`:

```
tsc --init
```

Initialize `npm`, and install Backbone, Bootstrap, JBone, and the declaration files for Backbone using the `@types` syntax, as follows:

```
npm init
npm install backbone
npm install bootstrap
npm install jbone
npm install @types/backbone
```

 JBone is an implementation of jQuery specifically built for Backbone. It includes all jQuery functionality that Backbone requires, and is significantly lighter and faster than the full jQuery library.

Backbone structure

The first step in building a Backbone application is to identify the elements that we will need in order to build the screen and the desired functionality. In general, one Backbone model will be tied to one Backbone **View**. The interaction between models and views can be seen in the following diagram:

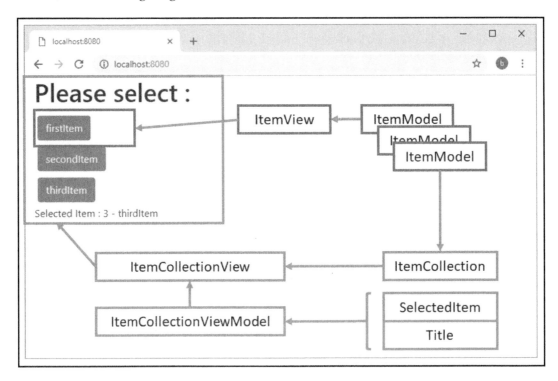

Each one of our selectable buttons will be rendered by a Backbone view named ItemView, which, in turn, uses a single model named ItemModel. These ItemModel models are then housed in a Backbone collection named ItemCollection. The ItemCollectionView view is used to render this collection to the screen. The ItemCollectionView also has an object named ItemCollectionViewModel that exposes two properties named SelectedItem and Title. The Title property will render the text "Please select :" at the top of the screen, and the SelectedItem property will be used to render the "Selected Item : " text at the bottom of the screen, showing which item is currently selected.

Backbone models

For our sample application, we will build three Backbone models. One model will be for each item in our `IClickableItem` array, and will be called the `ItemModel` model. The second model will be for the collection of `ItemModels`, and the third model will be used for the `SelectedItem` and `Title` properties. Let's first take a look at the `ItemModel`, as follows:

```
class ItemModel extends Backbone.Model
    implements IClickableItem {
    get Id() {
        return this.get('Id');
    }
    set Id(value: number) {
        this.set('Id', value);
    }
    get DisplayName() {
        return this.get('DisplayName');
    }
    set DisplayName(value: string) {
        this.set('DisplayName', value);
    }
    constructor(input: IClickableItem) {
        super();
        this.set(input);
    }
}
```

Here, we have a class named `ItemModel` that is derived from `Backbone.Model`, and implements the `IClickableItem` interface. We are using ES5 getter and setter functions for the `Id` and `DisplayName` properties. Within these getter and setter functions, we are calling Backbones, `model.get('<propertyName>')` and `model.set('<propertyName>')` functions. This is because Backbone stores object properties internally as object attributes. Our `constructor` function is simply calling `super`, and then calling the Backbone `set` function to set our internal properties. The `set` function is used to hydrate a Backbone Model from either a standard object, or a JSON structure. This means that we can construct an `ItemModel` instance from a JavaScript object as follows:

```
let itemModelInstance = new ItemModel({Id: 1, DisplayName : 'test'});
```

The ability to construct an internal `ItemModel` in this way means that we can use any element of our `IClickableItem` array, and the resulting Backbone model will hydrate correctly. Backbone models are also designed to accept JSON as an input structure, allowing us to use them when processing the results of a REST endpoint query.

The second Model we will construct is used to house all elements of our `IClickableItem` array, and is therefore a `Collection` of `ItemModel` instances, as follows:

```
class ItemCollection
    extends Backbone.Collection<ItemModel> {
    model = ItemModel;
}
```

This class, named `ItemCollection`, derives from `Backbone.Collection<ItemModel>`, and has a single property named `model`. This `model` property is set to the `ItemModel` class. We can therefore construct an `ItemCollection` as follows:

```
let itemCollection = new ItemCollection(ClickableItemCollection);
```

So, in a single line, we have created a `Backbone.Collection` of `ItemModel` instances from our original array.

The third Backbone Model that we will use is to house the `Title` and `SelectedItem` properties, as follows:

```
interface IItemCollectionViewModel {
    Title: string;
    SelectedItem: IClickableItem;
}

class ItemCollectionViewModel extends Backbone.Model
    implements IItemCollectionViewModel {

    get Title() {
        return this.get('Title');
    }
    set Title(value: string) {
        this.set('Title', value);
    }
    get SelectedItem() {
        return this.get('SelectedItem');
    }
    set SelectedItem(value: IClickableItem) {
        this.set('SelectedItem', value);
    }
```

```
constructor(input?: IItemCollectionViewModel) {
    super();
    this.set(input);
}
```

Here, we have defined an interface named `IItemCollectionViewModel` that has a property named `Title`, of type `string`, and a property named `SelectedItem` of type `IClickableItem`. The `SelectedItem` property will be used to store the item that the user has selected. We then define a class named `ItemCollectionViewModel` that implements this interface, and, as such, must have two properties named `Title` and `SelectedItem`. As we saw with our earlier Backbone models, we are using ES5 getter and setter functions to call the Backbone internal `get` and `set` functions in order to store these properties in Backbone's internal object attributes. Our constructor is used to hydrate the model from a standard object.

Backbone ItemView

As mentioned earlier, we will need to build two views. The first view is named `ItemView`, and will be used to render a single button to the DOM. As such, it is tied to a single `ItemModel` in our collection. Let's take a look at this `ItemView` class, as follows:

```
class ItemView extends Backbone.View<ItemModel> {
    template: (json: any, options?: any) => string;
    constructor(
        options = <Backbone.ViewOptions<ItemModel>>{}
    ) {
        options.events = { 'click': 'onClicked' };
        super(options);

        let templateSnippet = $(`#itemViewTemplate`).html();
            this.template = _.template(templateSnippet);
        _.bindAll(this, 'onClicked');
    }
    render() {
        this.$el.html(
            this.template(this.model.attributes)
        );
        return this;
    }
    onClicked() {
        EventBus.Bus.trigger("item_clicked", this.model.attributes);
    }
}
```

Our `ItemView` class derives from `Backbone.View`, and uses generic syntax to strongly type the Model used by this view to the `ItemModel` class that we built earlier. The constructor function takes an optional argument named `options` that is of type `Backbone.ViewOptions<ItemModel>`, which is also set to an empty object `{}` by default. We can refer to the Backbone definition file to see what options can be sent through in this property.

Note that we have defined a property named `template` for this class, and defined the type of the `template` property to be a function that takes two properties and returns a `string`. This is necessary in order to set the `template` property of the view, as the standard definition file for a `Backbone.View` has the `template` property commented out.

Our `constructor` function starts by setting the `events` property on the `options` object. The `events` property is used by the view to react to certain DOM events, such as `keydown` or `keyup`, or `click`. Each of these events will trigger a function on the view, which, in this case, is the `onClicked` function. Once these options have been configured, our constructor passes this `options` object down to the base `Backbone.View` through the `super` call.

The constructor then sets up the `template` property of the class, which houses the HTML that this class will use to render to the screen. Note that we are using jQuery syntax to extract the HTML of the DOM element with an `id` of `itemViewTemplate` to be used as our HTML template. Our HTML page, therefore, will then need to include the following script in order for Backbone to be able to pick up this template:

```html
<script type="text/template" id="itemViewTemplate">
    <button style="margin: 5px;" class="btn btn-primary" >
        <%= DisplayName %>
    </button>
    <br/>
</script>
```

Here, we have defined a `<script>` tag within our HTML that is of the `"text/template"` type and has an `id` property of `itemViewTemplate`. Within this script, we define a `<button>` element with a `style` property and a `class` property. Note that Backbone uses Underscore's templating engine by default. In order to render a Model's property into the HTML, we use the `<%= PropertyName %>` syntax within the template. This means that `<%= DisplayName %>` will substitute the property named `DisplayName` from our model into the resultant HTML.

Our `ItemView` class then defines a `render` function. This `render` function calls the `html` function of the `$el` internal property, and passes in the result of calling the `template` function with the `attributes` property of the internal model. This `attributes` property is, in fact, a simple object with all of the properties of the internal model. This single call will take the Backbone model, merge it with the HTML template, generate the resultant HTML, and then update the DOM. Note that it also returns `this`, so that any code that uses it can chain commands onto the `render` function.

The final function of our `ItemView` class is the `onClicked` function, which will be invoked when the button that is rendered to the DOM is clicked. Backbone provides us with a very simple message bus that can be used for classes to notify each other when particular events happen. In order to use this event bus, we will create a very simple TypeScript class that has a static function through which we either fire events, or listen to events, as follows:

```
class EventBus {
    static Bus = _.extend({}, Backbone.Events);
}
```

This class, named `EventBus`, has a single static property named `Bus` that uses the underscore `extend` function to combine a blank JavaScript object `{}` with the `Backbone.Events` object. This is all that is required to include a fully-fledged event bus within our Backbone application.

Firing an appropriate event from the `onClicked` function then simply becomes the following:

```
onClicked() {
    EventBus.Bus.trigger("item_clicked", this.model.attributes);
}
```

Here, we are firing an event named `item_clicked`, and attaching the `attributes` property of the model that was used within our `ItemView` as a parameter to the `trigger` function.

Backbone ItemCollectionView

The second view we will build is to render the `Title` property, the `SelectedItem` property, and the collection of `ItemViews`, as follows:

```
class ItemCollectionView extends Backbone.View<ItemCollectionViewModel> {
    template: (json: any, options?: any) => string;
    itemCollection: ItemCollection;
```

```
    constructor(options:
        Backbone.ViewOptions<ItemCollectionViewModel> = {},
        _itemCollection: ItemCollection) {
        super(options);
        this.itemCollection = _itemCollection;

        let templateSnippet =
            $(`#itemCollectionViewtemplate`).html();
        this.template = _.template(templateSnippet);

        this.listenTo(EventBus.Bus, "item_clicked", this.handleEvent);

    }
    render() {
        this.$el.html(this.template(this.model.attributes));
        this.itemCollection.each((item) => {
            var itemView = new ItemView({ model: item });
            this.$el.find('#ulRegions').append(itemView.render().el);
        });

        return this;
    }
    handleEvent(e: ItemModel) {
        this.model.SelectedItem = e;
        this.render();
    }
}
```

Here, we have defined a class named `ItemCollectionView` that is using generic syntax to strongly type the Backbone model to be of type `ItemCollectionViewModel`. We have defined our standard `template` property, and also a property named `itemCollection`, which will be used to store the collection of `IClickableItems`. Our `constructor` function has two parameters, named `options` and `_itemCollection`. The `options` parameter is the standard `Backbone.ViewOptions` type, and the `_itemCollection` parameter is of type `ItemCollection`.

The constructor initializes the base class with a call to `super`, and then sets the internal `itemCollection` property. The template to be used to render this view is then set up by fetching the HTML from a script tag with an `id` of `itemCollectionViewTemplate`. This template is defined in our HTML page as follows:

```
<script type="text/template" id="itemCollectionViewtemplate">
    <h1> <%= Title %> </h1>
    <div id="ulRegions">
    </div>
    <div> Selected Item :
```

```
            <%= SelectedItem.Id %> -
            <%= SelectedItem.DisplayName %>
        <div>
    </script>
```

This template has an <h1> tag, into which the property Title will be injected. It then has a <div> with an id of ulRegions. This <div> is where the buttons will be injected into the DOM when we render this view. More on this a little later. The final part of this template will render the Id and DisplayName attributes of the SelectedItem property so that we can see which button has been selected.

If we now take a look at the render function of this view, we will notice that it is doing slightly more than the previous view was. After calling the html function on the $el property with the template and model, the DOM will effectively have the fully rendered template, complete with model attributes injected. The render function then loops through each of the elements in the itemCollection, and constructs an ItemView for each one. It then appends the result of the render().el on this itemView to the DOM element named ulRegions. So, in essence, the render function of this view is calling the render function on each ItemView, and combining the results.

The only thing left to cover in this view is the last line of the constructor function, where we are calling the listenTo function with three arguments. The first argument is the event bus, as defined earlier, the second is the event to listen to, and the third argument is the function to call when this event is fired. This means that when an individual ItemView is clicked, and the "item_clicked" event is fired, this view will trap that event, and call the handleEvent function.

The handleEvent function is simply setting the internal SelectedItem property of the model to the value of the incoming event named e. Remember that our ItemView will trigger an "item_clicked" event with the attributes of its internal model. This means that the argument e will contain an Id and DisplayName property, and can therefore be strongly typed to ItemModel. Finally, the handleEvent function is calling the render function.

Backbone application

Having created two models, a collection of models, and two views, we will now create a controller to bind these elements together. Backbone, however, does not have a specialist controller class, but we can use a standard TypeScript class to accomplish the work of a controller. This class will be named `ScreenViewApp`, as follows:

```
class ScreenViewApp {
    start() {
        let itemCollection =
            new ItemCollection(ClickableItems);

        let collectionItemViewModel = new ItemCollectionViewModel({
            Title: "Please select :",
            SelectedItem: {
                Id: 0, DisplayName: 'None Selected:'
            }
        });

        let itemCollectionView = new ItemCollectionView(
            {
                model: collectionItemViewModel
            }, itemCollection
        );

        $(`#pageLayoutRegion`).html(
            itemCollectionView.render().el
        );
    }
}
```

Here, we have created a class named `ScreenViewApp` with a single `start` function. The body of the `start` function shows how we create the various elements that are used to render our application to the screen.

The `start` function first creates a new `ItemCollection` model from the `ClickableItems` array. It then sets up a new `ItemCollectionViewModel` with the `Title` and `SelectedItem` properties set to their initial defaults. We then create an instance of the `ItemCollectionView` class, with the required arguments. Note that the first argument is, in fact, an object with a single property named `model`, which is set to the instance of our `collectionViewModel` object. This is a Backbone convention, where we can create a Backbone view with a number of different properties in the constructor, including `events`, `tagNames`, `classNames`, and others. Again, refer to the documentation or the definition file for more options and their uses.

The final line of the start function simply calls the html function on the pageLayoutRegion DOM element to set the rendered HTML. Note that once a Backbone view has been rendered, the final HTML is placed within the el property of the view itself. With this class in place, we can then call the start function from our index.html page, as follows:

```
<script >
    window.onload = function() {
        app = new ScreenViewApp();
        app.start();
    }
</script>

<div id="pageLayoutRegion">
</div>
```

Here, we create an instance of the ScreenViewApp class within the window.onload function, and then call start. Below this <script> tag, we have placed a <div> with the id of pageLayoutRegion, where the resultant HTML will be placed.

Backbone forms

Now that we have the base Backbone application up and running, we can make a few tweaks to include a form at the bottom of the page, and show how to get and set form values within our View. This form will be handled by the ItemCollectionView class and, as such, we will need to update our model with a new property, as follows:

```
class ItemCollectionViewModel extends Backbone.Model
    implements IItemCollectionViewModel {

    ... existing properties

    set Name(value: string) {
        this.set('Name', value);
    }
    get Name() {
        return this.get('name');
    }

    ... existing constructor

}
```

Here, we have simply added a matching pair of ES5 get and set functions to store and retrieve our `Name` property. Once this change is made, we will also need to set this property when we create the `ItemCollectionViewModel` itself. This code is found in the `app.ts` file, in the `start` function, as follows:

```
class ScreenViewApp {
    start() {
    ... existing code

        let collectionItemViewModel = new ItemCollectionViewModel({
            Title: "Please select :",
            SelectedItem: {
                Id: 0, DisplayName: 'None Selected:'
            },
            Name: "Your Name"
        });

        ... existing code
    }
}
```

Here, we have updated the `start` function of the `ScreenViewApp` class to include the `Name` property when we create the `ItemCollectionViewModel`. This property will default to the value `"Your Name"`.

The next modification to our code will be the template itself, within the `index.html` file as follows:

```
<script type="text/template" id="itemCollectionViewtemplate">
    ... existing HTML template

    <div class="form-group">
        <label for="inputName">Name :</label>
        <input type="text" class="form-control input-name"
            id="inputName" value="<%= Name %>" />
    </div>
    <button id="submit-button-button"
    class="submit-button">Submit</button>
</script>
```

Here, we have updated the `itemCollectionViewTemplate` HTML template by including a `<div>` tag with the bootstrap style of `form-group`. Within this `<div>` tag, we have added a `<label>` tag, and an `<input>` tag with a type of `"text"`. Note how we have also added an `id="inputName"` attribute so that we can refer to this input element by `id`. Finally, we have added a `<button>` tag with an `id` of `"submit-button-button"`, and a bootstrap class of `"submit-button"`.

With the template modifications done, we will now need to trap the event where a user clicks on the **submit** button, so that we can interrogate the value that the user has entered into the form. This is very similar to the way that we attached a function to the `click` event on each of our buttons. We will update our `ItemCollectionView` as follows:

```
class ItemCollectionView extends Backbone.View<ItemCollectionViewModel> {
    template: (json: any, options?: any) => string;
    itemCollection: ItemCollection;

    constructor(
        options: Backbone.ViewOptions<ItemCollectionViewModel> = {},
        _itemCollection: ItemCollection)
    {
        options.events = { 'click #submit-button-button': 'submitClick' }
        super(options);
        ... existing code
    }
    submitClick() {
        let name = this.$el.find('#inputName');
        if (name.length > 0) {
            console.log(`name : ${name.val()}`);
        } else {
            console.log(`cannot find #inputName`);
        }
    }
}
```

There are two modifications that we have made to the `ItemCollectionView` class. Firstly, we have added an `events` property to the `options` argument on the first line of the `constructor` function. This is very similar to the way that we trapped the click event on the `ItemView` earlier. Here, however, we have defined that the click event we are interested in is on the element with an `id` of `submit-button-button`. Backbone is using standard JQuery syntax here by using the syntax `#submit-button-button`. When this event fires, we will handle it with the function named `submitClick`.

Our `submitClick` function starts by finding an element that is attached to the view by calling the `this.$el.find` function. Remember that we can reference the DOM within our view by accessing the `$el` property. The `find` function is also using JQuery syntax to locate a DOM element with the `id` of `inputName`, which is, in fact, our input field. If we find an element with this `id` property, then we are extracting the user-entered value of this field by calling the `val()` function.

The following screenshot shows the result of updating the form and clicking the **Submit** button:

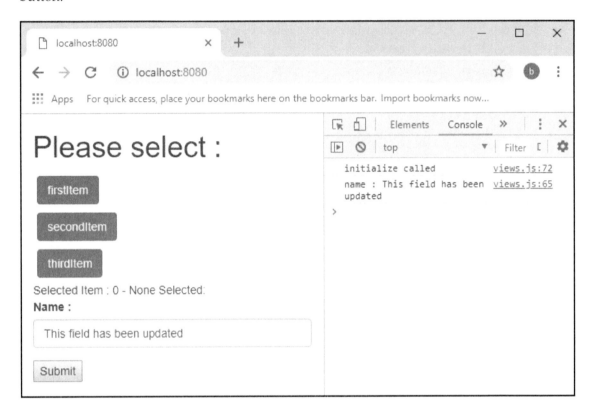

And that is the basics of working with form data in Backbone. As we have seen, we can use the values of a Backbone model in our HTML templates just like any other model property. We can also respond to click events on a particular DOM element by referencing it by its id property. When a form is submitted, we can extract the values of a form element by interrogating its value using JQuery.

Backbone summary

As we noted at the start of this section, Backbone requires us to write a little more code than other frameworks in order to finish off our application. On the flip side of this coin, though, is that the code itself is very readable and logical, and contains no magic whatsoever. It is therefore very simple to pick up and write, and it requires a very small learning curve in order to use. One of the greatest benefits of a no-frills framework such as Backbone is its sheer speed.

Using Aurelia

Aurelia was one of the first SPA frameworks to offer full TypeScript integration. It is a framework that specifically uses ECMAScript 6 features to enhance the development experience. One of the most astounding features of the Aurelia framework is the small amount of code that you need to write in order to get things done. Aurelia understands that if you are writing a standard class, then you probably want to use the class properties to render some HTML. Of all of the frameworks that we will discuss, Aurelia is by far the simplest to use, and the most intuitive. There are no hidden gotchas, or special workarounds to consider. The Aurelia framework has gone to great lengths to make the TypeScript development experience simple.

Aurelia setup

The simplest way to set up a development environment is to use Aurelia's command-line interface, named `aurelia-cli`, which can be installed as follows:

```
npm install aurelia-cli -g
```

Once this has been installed, it can be invoked to create a new project as follows:

```
au new
```

This will take you through a simple set of questions, starting with the name of the base directory that you would like to use. The next question is whether to use ESNext or TypeScript as your development language, and the last question is whether or not to download all project dependencies. Selecting **TypeScript** and then **Yes** to download dependencies will take a few minutes to set up the default project structure. Once this is complete, a new directory will be created based on the project name you selected at the start of the process.

The aurelia-cli program has a number of options. To compile your project, type the following:

```
au build
```

To run your newly created Aurelia application, type the following:

```
au run
```

This will invoke the Aurelia compilation and bundling steps, and then set up an `http` server to serve the application, by default, on port `8080`. Browsing to `http://localhost:8080` will show the default Aurelia screen, as follows:

Aurelia controllers and models

Aurelia combines controllers and models into a single class structure. This means that a standard TypeScript class acts as a controllers, and its properties act as its model. All Aurelia classes are built on the ECMAScript 2016 standard, meaning that there are no getters and setters as we needed in Backbone, nor are there any special constructors required to hydrate the model. Classes can contain other classes, and therefore it is very easy to define complex and nested models. Let's modify the `src/app.ts` file as follows:

```
interface IClickableItem {
    DisplayName: string;
    Id: number;
}

export class App {
    Title = 'Please select :';
    SelectedItem: IClickableItem =
    { Id: 0, DisplayName: "None selected" };

    items: IClickableItem[] = ([
        { Id: 1, DisplayName: "firstItem" },
        { Id: 2, DisplayName: "secondItem" },
        { Id: 3, DisplayName: "thirdItem" },
    ]);

}
```

We start with our standard interface definition for `IClickableItem`. We have then modified the class named `App`, and added three properties. The first is named `Title`, and will hold the text at the top of the screen. The second is named `SelectableItem`, and will hold our currently selected item. The final property is named `items`, and holds our `IClickableItem` array.

And that's all there is to it.

In Aurelia, standard classes are used as a controller, and standard class properties as models.

Aurelia views

Aurelia uses a naming convention to tie classes (or controllers) to their views. Our class is named `App`, and therefore the Aurelia runtime will search within the same directory as the class to find an HTML template with the same name. It will therefore tie `app.ts` to `app.html`, and use `app.html` as a template.

We will modify the existing `app.html` with the following snippet:

```
<template>

  <require from="bootstrap/dist/css/bootstrap.css"></require>

  <h1>${Title}</h1>
  <ul>
    <div repeat.for="item of items" >
      <button style="margin: 5px;" class="btn btn-primary">
         ${item.DisplayName}</button>
    </div>
  </ul>

  <div>
    Selected Item : ${SelectedItem.Id} - ${SelectedItem.DisplayName}
  </div>
</template>
```

Here, we have wrapped an HTML fragment within a `<template>` tag. The first line of this template uses a `<require>` tag with a `from` property that references the `bootstrap.css` file. This is the Aurelia convention for including external dependencies within a template. Note that we will need to install Bootstrap using `npm` as usual before this file becomes available. The template then defines an `<h1>` tag that uses the `${propertyName}` syntax to render the model's property named `Title`. We then have a `<ul>` tag, and within this a `<div>` tag.

The `<div>` tag in this instance is the interesting part of this template. Note how we have injected an attribute named `repeat.for="item of items"`. This syntax is specific to Aurelia, and will loop through the `items` property of the `App` class, and repeat the `<div>` tag for each individual item. This will then be made available to the `<div>` tag via a variable named `item`. We could have called this `arrayItem`, in which case our code would need to be `repeat.for="arrayItem of items"`.

Within the `<div>` tag, we are simply creating a `<button>` tag, and using the data binding syntax of `${item.DisplayName}` to render the `DisplayName` property of each array member.

Aurelia application bootstrap

With our view and models in place, we can turn our attention to the `index.ejs` file at the root of the project directory. This `index.ejs` file is as follows:

```
<!DOCTYPE html>
<html>
  <head>
    <meta charset="utf-8">
    <title><%- htmlWebpackPlugin.options.metadata.title %></title>
    <meta name="viewport" content="width=device-width, initial-scale=1">
    <base href= "<%- htmlWebpackPlugin.options.metadata.baseUrl %>">
    <!-- imported CSS are concatenated and added automatically -->
  </head>
  <body aurelia-app="main">
    <% if (htmlWebpackPlugin.options.metadata.server) { %>
    <!-- Webpack Dev Server reload -->
    <script src="/webpack-dev-server.js"></script>
    <% } %>
  </body>
</html>
```

This is a short, but rather complicated looking HTML file, which is using the EJS templating library to inject values into the HTML file, and to execute `if` statements. We will not modify this file for our sample application, but simply take note of the `<body>` tag.

The `<body>` tag has an extra attribute, named `aurelia-app` that has a value of `main`. This attribute is telling Aurelia that it should look for a `main.js` file in the `src` directory, as the initial starting point for the application. If we now take a look at the `main.ts` file in the `src` directory, we will find an exported function named `configure`, and at the bottom of the function, an interesting line as follows:

```
return aurelia.start().then(
    () => aurelia.setRoot(PLATFORM.moduleName('app'))
);
```

This line of code is calling the `start` function on the `aurelia` object, and once this Promise has completed, it is calling the `setRoot` function with an argument of `PLATFORM.moduleName('app')`. This line is effectively signaling to Aurelia that it should load the module named `app` as the entry point to the application.

With these precious few lines of code in place, we have a running sample application.

Aurelia events

The next requirement for our sample application is to render the currently selected item when a user clicks on one of our buttons. In order to do this, we will need to add a function to our `App` class to act as an event handler, and then bind the `onclick` DOM event to this function. Let's modify our `app.html` template first, as follows:

```
<div repeat.for="item of items"
    click.delegate="onItemClicked(item)">
    <button > ...
</div>
```

Here, we have added a `click.delegate` attribute to the `<div>` tag, and within it, are calling a function named `onItemClicked` with `item` as an argument. Note that this delegate is not defined inside the `<div>` tag, but rather at the `<div>` tag level itself. This means that the `onItemClicked` function needs to be attached to our `App` class, and not our `ClickableItem` class. This is slightly different to our Backbone implementation, where each individual `ItemView` received the `onclick` event.

With this in place, we can modify our App class as follows:

```
export class App {
    Title: string = 'Please select:';
    // existing code

    onItemClicked(event: IClickableItem) {
        this.SelectedItem = event;
    }
}
```

Here, we have added an `onItemClicked` function with a single argument named `event`, which is of type `ClickableItem`. Within this function, we are simply assigning the `event` argument to the `SelectedItem` property. Aurelia will automatically detect that the property named `SelectedItem`, which is used in the `app.html` template, has changed, and will re-render the view.

Aurelia forms

As we have seen with most of the Aurelia code, adding forms to our HTML, and storing form values in our model is very simple. Let's update our Aurelia view to add a `Name` property, which will set the default value of the form control. We will then extract the value of this property on a button click event. Firstly, we will update our App class as follows:

```
export class App {
    ... existing properties
    Name = 'Your Name';

    ... existing code
    onSubmitClicked() {
        console.log(`onSubmitClicked : Name : ${this.Name}`)
    }
}
```

Here, we have simply added a `Name` property to our App class, and set its default value to "`Your Name`". We have also created an `onSubmitClicked` function that is logging the value of this `Name` property to the console.

We can now incorporate the `Name` property into a form by updating the `app.html` template as follows:

```
<template>

    ... existing template

    <div class="form-group">
        <label for="inputName">Name :</label>
        <input type="text" class="form-control input-name"
            id="inputName" value.bind="Name" />
    </div>

    <button id="submit-button-button" class="submit-button"
        click.delegate="onSubmitClicked()">Submit</button>

</template>
```

Here, we have added a `<div>` tag to the template that has the bootstrap class of `form-group`, and created a `<label>` tag and an `<input>` element similar to the changes we made for Backbone. The interesting thing about the `<input>` element is the new attribute named `value.bind`, which is set to the value, `Name`. This is how Aurelia signifies that it should bind the value of the `Name` property to this form control. The act of binding a control with a property means that changes in one will automatically be reflected in the other. So, when we set the value of this property in the class, it will update the form control, and, similarly, when the user updates the form control on the page, the value of the property will be automatically updated.

Aurelia summary

As we have seen, building Model, View, and Controller code within Aurelia is a very simple exercise. Using the power of ECMAScript 2016 classes, and simple HTML templates, we are able to get a lot of work done with very little code. Aurelia also understands that when we create models for rendering information to the user, we may also want to update those models based on user input. The syntax that Aurelia uses to bind models to user input is very simple indeed.

Angular

As mentioned at the start of this chapter, Angular 2 was a complete rewrite of Angular 1, and used TypeScript as its language of choice. The adopted naming convention from the Angular team is that Angular 1 is now called AngularJs, and Angular version 2 and upward is named Angular. Since the release of Angular 2, the Angular team has released several major updates, and the current version of Angular, at the time of writing, stands at Angular 7. The samples in this book are all using Angular 7, so wherever you see the word Angular, remember that it refers to Angular version 7. In this section of the chapter, we will take a look at how the Model View Controller design pattern is used within Angular.

Angular setup

Similar to Aurelia's command-line development environment setup, Angular also has a command-line project setup tool, named the Angular-CLI. This can be installed using npm as follows:

```
npm install -g @angular/cli
```

Once the command-line interface has been installed globally, we can set up an Angular development environment by using the Angular-CLI as follows:

```
ng new my-app
```

The Angular-CLI is named `ng`, and here we have specified that it should create a new project in a new directory named `my-app`. Within this new directory, the Angular-CLI will download and install all necessary components of an Angular application. It will also create a minimal sample project in the `src/app` directory as a head start. To start a development web server, and see this minimal application running, issue the following command:

```
npm start
```

This `start` command will compile all of the sample application source code, and start a web server on port 4200. Browsing to `http://localhost:4200` shows what this sample application contains, as shown in the following diagram:

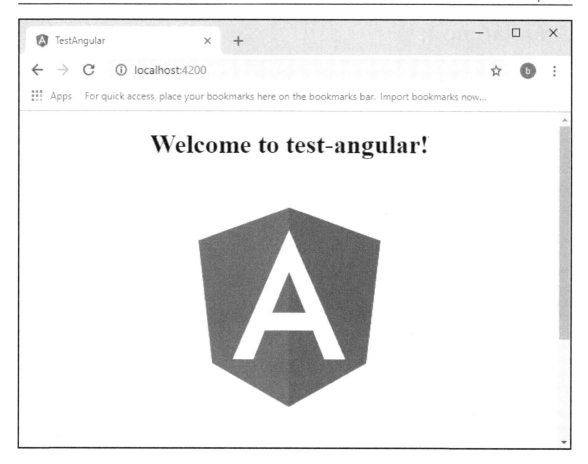

Along with compiling the application, and automatically starting a web server, the npm start command will also watch the source files in the project directory, and automatically recompile the application when files have changed. It will also signal to the web browser to reload the application. This built-in watch, recompile, and reload functionality helps immensely in the development of web applications, allowing immediate feedback when source code changes occur.

 Keep an eye on the console where you are running npm start from. This will show any TypeScript compilation errors that occur when you save your files.

Angular models

Angular models and controllers are built the same way as Aurelia models, in that they are simple classes. Let's start by editing the file named `app/app.component.ts`, and add our Angular models and a single controller as follows:

```
export class ClickableItem {
    displayName: string;
    id: number;
}

let ClickableItemArray : ClickableItem[] = [
    { id: 1, displayName : "firstItem"},
    { id: 2, displayName : "secondItem"},
    { id: 3, displayName : "thirdItem"},
];

// existing @Component code
export class AppComponent {
    Title = 'Please select :';
    items = ClickableItemArray;
    SelectedItem: ClickableItem =
        { Id: 0, DisplayName: "None selected" };
}
```

Here, we have our standard `ClickableItem` class, which has the `DisplayName` and `Id` properties. We are then creating an array named `ClickableItemArray` to hold our array items, as we have seen before. Our final class is called `AppComponent`, and has a `Title` property and an `items` property, similar to our model class for Aurelia. We also have a `SelectedItem` property to hold the value of the currently selected item. Note that we are setting the default value of the `SelectedItem` property to 0, `None Selected`. This will ensure that when the class is created, the `SelectedItem` property will be properly initialized.

Angular views

Angular uses a class decorator named `@Component` to specify that a class can act as an HTML component. Let's take a closer look at this decorator:

```
import { Component } from '@angular/core';

// existing ClickableItem code

@Component({
```

```
        selector: 'app-root',
        templateUrl: './app.component.html',
        styleUrls: ['./app.component.css']
})
export class AppComponent {
        ... existing code

}
```

This code starts with an `import` statement to define the `Component` decorator from a library named `'@angular/core'`. This `import` statement is part of the modular syntax that we will cover in a later chapter, and gives us the ability to easily reference other classes from the Angular framework. The `Component` module that we are importing is, in fact, a class decorator function that will inject Angular properties into our standard TypeScript class.

The `@Component` decorator defines three properties, `selector`, `templateUrl`, and `styleUrls`. The `selector` property is used to reference an HTML DOM element where the View will render into, similar to a standard jQuery selector. The `templateUrl` property specifies where the template HTML file for this component is found, and the `styleUrls` property is used to include CSS files used by the component. Where Aurelia matched the template HTML file by name association, Angular uses the `templateUrl` property of the class.

Let's take a look at this template HTML, in the `app.component.html` file, as follows:

```html
<h1>
    {{Title}}
</h1>

<ul>
    <div *ngFor="let item of items">
        <button class="btn btn-primary">{{item.DisplayName}}</button>
        <br />
    </div>

</ul>

<div *ngIf="SelectedItem">
    <div>Selected : {{SelectedItem.Id}}
        - {{SelectedItem.DisplayName}}</div>
</div>
```

Within this template, we are using the Angular syntax of `{{propertyName}}` to reference properties within our model. This is similar to the `${propertyName}` syntax that Aurelia uses. Our template, again similar to Aurelia, has an `<h1>` element to display the `Title` property, and then has the usual `<ul>` and child `<div>` tags.

Within the `<div>` tag, we are again looping through the `items` property of the `AppComponent` model to render each array item to the DOM. Angular uses the `*ngFor` keyword within its template to indicate a loop construct. The `"let item of items"` is again referencing each array element within the template via the `item` variable name. As we saw with Aurelia, if we changed this to `"let arrayItem of items"`, then we would need to reference each array element through the `arrayItem` variable.

The template that will be used for each array element is to render a `<button>` tag, and display the value of the `item.DisplayName` property.

The final `<div>` tag uses another Angular template keyword, named `*ngIf`. This template keyword will evaluate the `SelectedItem` property of the component, and only render the HTML template if the `SelectedItem` property is a valid object. Within this `<div>`, we are rendering the `Id` and `DisplayName` properties of the `SelectedItem` property. Note that without this `*ngIf` in place, if the class does not have a property named `SelectedItem`, and we attempt to reference a sub-property, as in `SelectedItem.Id`, the Angular runtime will throw reference errors, and fail to render the page. Bear this in mind when you are building more complex Angular pages. Keep an eye on the console of the application when making changes to templates, as it will show any rendering errors, and generally point you to the template involved.

With these changes in place, our Angular application will render the array of `ClickableItem` elements within the HTML page.

Angular events

The next step in this sample application is to wire up our DOM `onclick` events and show which item is currently selected. As with Aurelia, this will require a slight modification to our template, and the addition of a `click` handler on our model. Let's start by updating the template in the `app.component.html` file as follows:

```
<ul>
    <div *ngFor="let item of items"
         (click)="onItemClicked(item)">
         <button class="btn btn-primary">{{item.DisplayName}}</button>
    <br />
```

```
        </div>

    </ul>
```

Here, we have simply added a `(click)="onSelect(item)"` attribute to the `<div>` tag used to render each item to the DOM. Note the slight difference between Aurelia and Angular syntax used here. Where Aurelia uses `click.delegate`, Angular simply uses `(click)`, surrounded by parentheses. We can now define the `onSelect` function within our `AppComponent` class as follows:

```
export class AppComponent {
    ... existing code

    onItemClicked(item: ClickableItem) {
        this.SelectedItem = item;
    }
}
```

Here, we have defined an `onSelect` function that has a `ClickableItem` object as an argument. Within this function, we are simply setting the value of the `SelectedItem` property on our class to the item that was used when raising the event. As we saw with Aurelia, this handler is also at the `AppComponent` level and not at the `ClickableItem`, as it was with Backbone. The reason for this is again that the controlling class, that is, the class that defines the `*ngFor` loop, is the `AppComponent` itself.

With this event handler in place, our sample application is up and running in Angular.

Angular forms

Angular actually provides two different mechanisms to bind component properties to form values. The simpler of these two is called Template-based forms, and the second, slightly more complex way of building forms, is named Reactive forms. For this reason, we will actually create two forms on our application, so that we can explore both of these form-binding methods.

Angular template forms

Angular template forms are very similar to Aurelia form-binding syntax in that we create a property on our component, and bind it automatically to a form input control. Once a property is bound, Angular will ensure that changes made either in the component itself, or by the user entering data into the form, will automatically update the other. To use a template form, we need a property in our component that will be bound to our form control. This is a simple property, as follows:

```
export class AppComponent {
    Title = 'Please select :';
    items = ClickableItemArray;
    Name = 'Your Name';

    ... existing code

    onSubmit() {
        console.log(`onSubmit : Name : ${this.Name}`);
    }
}
```

Here, we have updated our `AppComponent` class to include a property called `Name`, and have set the default value to `'Your Name'`. We have also added a function called `onSubmit` that will log the value of this `Name` property to the console. With this property in place, we can update our HTML template in the `app.component.html` file as follows:

```
<h2>Template Form :</h2>

<div class="form-group">
    <label for="inputName">Name :</label>
    <input type="text" class="form-control input-name"
        id="inputName" [(ngModel)]="Name" />
</div>

<button id="submit-button-button" class="submit-button"
    (click)="onSubmit()">Submit</button>
```

Here, we have added an `<h2>` tag to show the start of the template form. We then create a `<div>` tag with the bootstrap class of `form-group`, similar to both Backbone and Aurelia. We then create a `<label>` tag, and an `<input>` element. Note how we have added an attribute named `[(ngModel)]` with the value `"Name"`. This attribute will be processed by Angular, and indicates that the value of the `<input>` element is bound to the model property called `"Name"`. Again, this is two-way binding, which means that the component property, `Name`, will be kept in sync with the form `<input>` element.

We have also added a `<button>` element, and have specified that the `(click)` handler will call a function named `onSubmit` on the component when the button is clicked. Along with our changes to the `AppComponent` class, this is all that is needed to bind properties of our class to form elements.

Note that we must include the `FormsModule` in our `app.module.ts` file in order to enable the use of forms in our application, as follows:

```
import { FormsModule } from '@angular/forms';
... existing imports

@NgModule({
    ... existing code
    imports: [
        BrowserModule,
        FormsModule
    ]
    ... existing code
})
export class AppModule { }
```

Here, we have imported the `FormsModule` library from `'@angular/forms'`, and have added it to the `imports` array in the `NgModule` decorator for our application.

Template form limitations

While template forms are very simple indeed, and follow a syntax similar to Aurelia forms, it soon becomes difficult to provide advanced functionality on a form using template syntax. As an example, consider the following form control:

```
<input type="text" [(ngModel)]="Name" required minlength="4">
```

Here, we have an input element that is bound to the component property called `Name`. Note that we have two extra attributes, which are actually field validators. One is `required`, which specifies that this input cannot be left blank. The other is `minlength`, which is set to a value of `4`. So using template syntax, this input field will be validated before the form itself becomes valid. It is both `required`, and has a minimum length of `4`.

Unfortunately, when building larger forms, these validators could quite easily change depending on the context of the form, or depending on other input that the user has selected. Because of these limitations in using template syntax, Angular has introduced the concept of Reactive forms.

Angular Reactive forms

Reactive forms have been introduced into the Angular framework to provide the ability to create forms that can change dynamically. In other words, we can modify the validity checks of a particular form control on the fly, or mark some properties as `required` or `disabled` programmatically. As an example of this, some form controls may change the minimum length of input depending on what a user has selected in another control. Or, some form inputs may or may not be required, depending on what the user has selected on another part of a form. By moving the declaration of these forms into the component, we can modify it using standard code, and can exercise greater control over our forms.

In order to use Reactive forms, we will need to import the `ReactiveFormsModule` module in our `app.module.ts` file as follows:

```
import { ReactiveFormsModule } from '@angular/forms';
... existing imports

@NgModule({
    ... existing code
    imports: [
        BrowserModule,
        FormsModule,
        ReactiveFormsModule
    ]
    ... existing code
})
export class AppModule { }
```

Here, similar to the `FormsModule`, we have imported the `ReactiveFormsModule` from `@angular/forms`, and included it in the `imports` array.

Using Reactive forms

In order to use Reactive forms in our `AppComponent`, we will need to set up a new `FormGroup` property, and include the `FormBuilder` class as part of our `constructor` function, as follows:

```
import { FormBuilder, FormGroup, FormControl } from '@angular/forms';
... existing code
export class AppComponent {
    .. existing properties

    reactiveFormGroup: FormGroup;

    constructor(private formBuilder: FormBuilder) {
```

```
    }

    ... existing code
}
```

Here, we have updated our `app.component.ts` file with an `import` of the `FormBuilder`, `FormGroup`, and `FormControl` classes from the Angular framework. We then create a new property on our component class named `reactiveFormGroup`, which is of type `FormGroup`. This property will house the internal structure for our reactive form, and give us access to each of its properties. We have also defined a `constructor` function with a single argument named `formBuilder`, which is of type `FormBuilder`. We will use this `FormBuilder` class to create our internal form.

Angular uses a technique known as **dependency injection** in order to provide components with instances of classes that they need in order to get their work done. We will discuss the concepts of dependency injection at length in a later chapter, but for the time being, just be aware that Angular will create an instance of the `FormBuilder` class and provide it to us via our constructor function.

We are now ready to construct and use our `FormGroup` as follows:

```
export class AppComponent {
    ... existing code
    ngOnInit() {
        this.reactiveFormGroup = this.formBuilder.group({
            nameInput: new FormControl({})
        });

        this.reactiveFormGroup.reset({
            nameInput: 'RF Input'
        });
    }

    ... existing code

    onSubmitRf() {
        console.log(`onSubmitRf : nameInput :
            ${this.reactiveFormGroup.value.nameInput} `);
    }
}
```

Here, we have created a new function named ngOnInit. This is a special Angular function that can be injected into any Angular component, and will be called when the component is initialized. Note that there is an important difference in Angular between the construction of a class, and the initialization of a class. Construction of a class is when Angular creates the class for the first time. As part of this construction process, Angular will figure out what classes are required as defined in the constructor, and provide instances of these classes accordingly, using its internal dependency injection framework.

Initialization of a class, however, occurs just before the class is rendered to the DOM. Angular classes can have properties that are defined in HTML, and it is during the parsing of the HTML elements that initialization occurs, and the ngOnInit function will be called.

Our ngOnInit function is performing two distinct steps in the creation of our Reactive form. The first step is to create the form itself using the group function of the FormBuilder instance. To define a Reactive form property, the property must have a name, and its value must be a FormControl. So, in other words, we are defining a structure that includes the name of each control in our form.

The second step that we need is to define the state of each property, which is done by calling the reset function of our newly created FormGroup. This reset function matches the name of each form control with the value provided. So, looking at the code, we have defined a nameInput form control through the formBuilder instance, and we have set the value of this nameInput form control to 'RF Input' through the reset function. Note that we must match the name of the form control with the name of the default value.

We have also defined a function named onSubmitRf, which will be tied to the **Submit** button for our Reactive form. This function interrogates the form control value by using the reactiveFormGroup property. Each input value can be accessed through the value property of the form, and the name of the form control.
So, reactiveFormGroup.value.nameInput will return the value that the user has set in the form itself.

With the changes to our component in place, we can modify the form template (in app.component.html) as follows:

```
<h2>Reactive Form :</h2>

<form [formGroup]="reactiveFormGroup" (ngSubmit)="onSubmitRf()">
    <div class="form-group">
        <label for="rfInputName">RF Name :</label>
        <input type="text" class="form-control input-name"
            id="rfInputName" formControlName="nameInput" />
    </div>
```

```
    <button type="submit" class="submit-button">Submit Rf</button>

</form>
```

Here, we start with an `<h2>` tag to show the start of the reactive form. We then create a `<form>` tag, and specify two attributes. The first attribute is `[formGroup]`, which uses Angular template syntax to bind the form to a `FormGroup` instance named `"reactiveFormGroup"`. This will bind this form to our component property of the same name. The second attribute is `(ngSubmit)`, which is used to specify the function to be called when the form is submitted. In this case, we are invoking the `onSubmitRf` function in `AppComponent`.

The rest of the template sets up the `<label>` and `<input>` elements, as we have seen before. Note, however a new attribute for the `<input>` element named `formControlName`. This attribute is what Angular uses to bind the value of our form control to the value of the `<input>` element. The value of this attribute must match the name of the form control.

In summary, then, in order to use Reactive forms in Angular, we need three things. Firstly, we need to define the structure and names of the properties of a form and store them in an instance of a `FormGroup` in our component. We then need to call the `reset` function of this `FormGroup` in order to set the default values of each form control. Finally, we need to bind our `FormGroup` to our template using the `[formGroup]` attribute, and bind each HTML element with the respective `FormGroup` property using the `formControlName` attribute.

Angular summary

Angular is quickly becoming a popular framework for large-scale application development. As such, there are many additional libraries that are available to enhance the Angular development experience, including plug-and-play form controls, graphs, data table controls, and the like. The Angular framework provides all of the tools required for a modern application, including lazy loading, route handling, security guards for authorization, and form control validation, among others. With its strong link to TypeScript, it allows the use of object-oriented design patterns, generics, asynchronous programming techniques, and dependency injection right out of the box. The Angular syntax is fairly straightforward, although it requires some knowledge of the overall Angular ecosystem to get right.

Using React

Another TypeScript framework that we will take a look at in this chapter is React. The React framework is open source, and was originally developed by Facebook. React uses a specific inline syntax for combining HTML templates and JavaScript code in the same file, named JSX. There are no string templates to load, like Backbone, or HTML snippets that are in a separate file, like Angular or Aurelia. In React, all templates are mixed in with normal JavaScript code, using an HTML-like syntax. As a simple example of this syntax, consider the following code:

```
render() {
    return <div>Hello <span>React</span></div>;
}
```

Here, we have a standard TypeScript function named `render`. Within this function, we are returning what looks like native HTML, with a `<div>` and a child `<span>`. Note that there are no quotation marks around these HTML elements. They are written inline within our functions with no clear delineation from normal TypeScript code.

TypeScript included support for this unique React/JSX syntax in release 1.6 of the language. To use the new JSX syntax, however, we will need to create our TypeScript files with a `.tsx` extension, instead of the normal `.ts` file extension. When TypeScript encounters files with this `.tsx` extension, it will parse the file as a JSX file, allowing for the inclusion of JSX syntax.

React setup

The process that React uses to generate JavaScript from JSX files creates an extra step in the normal development workflow. Our TypeScript `.tsx` files, once compiled, will generate JavaScript files that convert JSX syntax into a series of calls to the React libraries. As an example, using a `<div>` element in our `.tsx` file will create a call to `React.createElement("div", ...)` in the compiled JavaScript file. These compiled files then need to be combined with the React libraries themselves in order to produce runnable code. For this reason, it is recommended to use a bundling tool such as Webpack to combine the output of the compilation step with the React libraries themselves. Webpack will also create a single output file for loading into a browser, in a process called bundling.

To start a new React project, we will follow a few steps. Firstly, create a directory for your project, and initialize npm, as follows:

```
mkdir react-sample
cd react-sample
npm init
```

Here, we create the directory for our project, change into the directory, and initialize npm in the project directory. This will create a package.json file for us that npm can use. Once initialized, we can install webpack as follows:

```
npm install -g webpack
npm install -g webpack-cli
```

This installs webpack as a global Node module, and the command-line interface for webpack, named webpack-cli. Note that, even though we have webpack installed globally, the webpack command-line tool will still need to find the webpack modules under the node_modules directory. This means that we also need to install webpack as a local module as follows:

```
npm install webpack --save-dev
npm install webpack-cli -save-dev
```

We can now install React, as follows:

```
npm install react react-dom
```

This installs the react and react-dom libraries into the node_modules directory. We will need a number of other utilities, as follows:

```
npm install --save-dev ts-loader source-map-loader
```

This installs the ts-loader and source-map-loader utilities as development dependencies. We will also need to install Boostrap as we did with our previous projects, as follows:

```
npm install bootstrap
```

Once Bootstrap has been installed, we can then install the react declaration files through the @types syntax as follows:

```
npm install @types/react --save-dev
npm install @types/react-dom --save-dev
```

Configuring webpack

As mentioned earlier, webpack is used to bundle TypeScript output with the React libraries and create a single combined JavaScript file that can be used in a browser. In order to do this, however, the compilation options for TypeScript in the `tsconfig.json` file, and the configuration of webpack in the `webpack.config.js` file, must be aligned. The easiest way to get this right is to use one of the handy configuration tools available on the internet. One such tool can be found at `https://webpack.jakoblind.no`, and provides a simple-to-use HTML page to configure some of the options available for webpack, as follows:

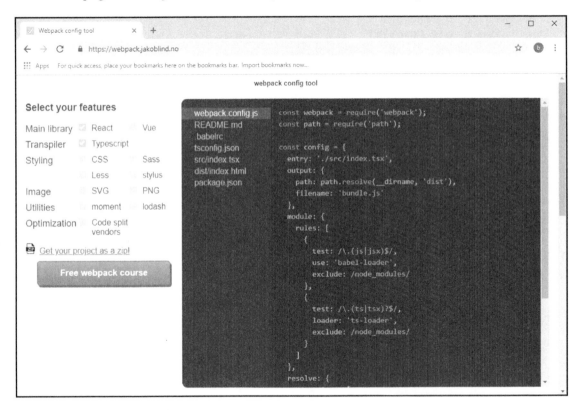

Here, we have specified that we are using React as the Main library, and TypeScript as the transpiler. On the right-hand side of the page, we can see that that this tool generates the correct webpack.config.js file, as well as a corresponding tsconfig.json file. It will also generate a sample index.html file in the dist directory, and an index.tsx file in the src directory. We can either manually create each of these files in our project, or we can download the zip file that is easily extracted. Let's take a look at the tsconfig.json file, as follows:

```
{
    "compilerOptions": {
        "outDir": "./dist/",
        "sourceMap": true,
        "strict": true,
        "noImplicitReturns": true,
        "noImplicitAny": true,
        "module": "es6",
        "moduleResolution": "node",
        "target": "es5",
        "allowJs": true,
        "jsx": "react",
    },
    "include": [
        "./src/**/*"
    ]
}
```

There are three interesting properties that have been set in this file that we have not discussed before. The first is the use of the outDir property to define where our compiled TypeScript files should be written. In this configuration, the outDir property is set to "./dist./", so that all generated .js files will be written to this directory. The second important property is named "jsx", and has a value of "react". This is the compiler option that will tell TypeScript to treat .tsx files as using JSX syntax, and will generate React calls for the JSX that is included in our files. The third important property within this file is the include property, specifying "./src/**/*". This lets webpack know that it should look in the src directory, and any sub-directories, for all input .tsx files.

The final configuration file we need for our development environment is a webpack.config.js file, as follows:

```
const webpack = require('webpack');
const path = require('path');

const config = {
  entry: './src/index.tsx',
  output: {
```

```
        path: path.resolve(__dirname, 'dist'),
        filename: 'bundle.js'
    },
    module: {
      rules: [
        {
          test: /\.(js|jsx)$/,
          exclude: /node_modules/,
          use: 'babel-loader'
        },
        {
          test: /\.(ts|tsx)?$/,
          loader: 'ts-loader',
          exclude: /node_modules/
        }
      ]
    },
    resolve: {
      extensions: [
        '.js',
        '.jsx',
        '.tsx',
        '.ts'
      ]
    }
}

module.exports = config;
```

This file is fairly self-explanatory, so we will not describe each option here. One of the properties to note, however, is the "entry" property at the top of the file, specifying the "./src/index.tsx" file. This index.tsx file will be used as the initial start up file for the React bootstrapping process. The other property to note is the "output" property, specifying that the results of the bundling process should be written to the "./dist/bundle.js" file.

With these files in place, all we need to do is to link our global version of typescript to the local project as follows:

npm link typescript

This will allow webpack to use our global version of the TypeScript compiler in its compilation step.

With our configuration files in place, we can compile and bundle all code simply by typing the following:

webpack

 Running `webpack` at this stage will create an error, as we have not created the `src/index.tsx` file as yet. To resolve this error, simply create a blank `index.tsx` file in the `src` directory.

React ItemView

React models, similar to Aurelia and Angular models, are simple TypeScript classes. As we have covered these models in both of the previous sections, we will jump straight in and take a look at how React composes views.

Firstly, let's create a `src/ReactApp.tsx` source file. Within this file, we will create two views. The first view will be a view for each individual element of the `ClickableItemArray`, and will be named `ItemView`. The second view will be named `ItemCollectionView`, and will render the entire array. This is similar to the two views that we created in Backbone. We will start with the `ItemView` as follows:

```
import * as React from 'react';
import * as _ from 'underscore';


export class ItemModel {
    DisplayName: string = "";
    Id: number = 0;
    onItemClicked(item: ItemModel) { }
}

export class ItemView
    extends React.Component<ItemModel, {}> {
    constructor(input: ItemModel) {
        super(input);
        this.handleClick =
            this.handleClick.bind(this);
    }

    render() {
        return (
            <div>
                    <button className="btn btn-primary"
                        style={{ "marginBottom": "5px" }}
```

```
                    onClick={this.handleClick}>
                    {this.props.DisplayName}
            </button>

        </div>

    );
    }
    handleClick() {
        this.props.onItemClicked(this.props);
    }
}
```

Here, we start with an `import` statement to import all classes from the `'react'` module, and specify a namespace named `React` for these imports. Similarly, we are importing all classes from the `'underscore'` module, and specifying a namespace of _ for these imports. Once again, these `import` statements are part of the modularization syntax that we will cover in `Chapter 10`, *Modularization*. We then define our `ItemModel` model to serve as our data model, as we did in both Aurelia and Angular previously.

Note, however, that the `ItemModel` defines an `Id` property, and a `DisplayName` property, as well as an `onItemClicked` function. This function will be used a little later, and is in fact, a callback function that the parent view will define so that we can fire an event on the parent class when one of the items is clicked.

This code snippet also defines a class named `ItemView`, which is the React view that will be used to render each element of our array. Similar to Backbone, we define a view for each array element, instead of using a looping construct such as `*ngFor`, as we saw in Angular.

In React, all views are referred to as modular, composable components, and so our `ItemView` class derives from, or extends , the `React.Component` base class. This base class uses generic syntax to define two required parameters for the generic type. The first of these parameters is the model to which the view refers, which, in this instance, is the `ItemModel` model. The second object is the default state in which this model will take. As we do not require a default state at this stage, we will leave this as a blank object.

Our `ItemView` has a `constructor` function, a `render` function, and a `handleClick` function. The `constructor` function starts by calling `super` to initiate the base `React.Component` class, and then sets the `handleClick` function to the result of calling the `bind` function on the `handleClick` function with `this` as a parameter. This rather weird looking statement is, in fact, functionally equivalent to calling _.`bindAll(this,` `'handleClick')`, which is the underscore way of ensuring that the instance of the class is used whenever the `handleClick` function is called.

The `render` function is a little more interesting.

All React `render` functions must return a snippet of HTML. However, taking a closer look at this HTML snippet, we notice that it is not being handled as a `string`. In other words, React components can include HTML elements within their `render` function as if they were part of the standard language. This feature is the reason why React files need to be defined with the special `.tsx` extension. By using the `.tsx` extension, we are notifying the TypeScript compiler that we are mixing native HTML and TypeScript code within the same file.

The `render` function returns a `<div>` tag, and, within this, a `<button>` tag. Within the `<button>` tag, we see the React templating syntax that is used to inject the model's `DisplayName` property, through the `{this.props.DisplayName}` syntax. React allows access to the underlying model's properties through the `props` property of the class.

Note that we have also defined a CSS class name for this component, which is `"btn btn-primary"`, but the name of this attribute is `className`, and not simply `class`. This is because React uses HTML attributes as hooks into standard class properties. In other words, in order to use an attribute named `myAttribute` within a React JSX snippet, the class that we are referencing must have a `myAttribute` property defined. For this reason, React has renamed the common HTML attributes, such as `class`, to `className`.

 Note too, that we have defined a `style` attribute using double parentheses, `{{` and `}}`. This style is not using the standard `margin-bottom` CSS property, but is using the renamed `marginBottom` property. This is another instance of React needing to rename slightly some of the most common CSS properties to avoid collision. For a full list of which CSS properties have been renamed, refer to the `StandardLonghandProperties` definition in React's declaration file.

The final function in this view is the `handleClick` function, and it calls the `onItemClicked` function that is part of the original model that was used on construction of this view. It calls this function with the internal model that is referenced through `this.props`. Remember that React stores the values of the model properties internally, and these values can be referenced in the code by using the internal `props` property.

React CollectionView

The second view we will define is the view that will be used to render the entire
ClickableItemArray. As mentioned earlier, React is similar to Backbone, in that we will
define a view for every individual array item (ItemView), and then another view for the
whole collection. This view will be named ItemCollectionView, and will use two
interfaces as follows:

```
export interface IClickableItem {
    Id: number;
    DisplayName: string;
}

export interface IItemCollectionViewProps {
    title: string,
    items: IClickableItem[],
    SelectedItem: IClickableItem;
};
```

Here, we have defined an interface for each of our array items named
IClickableItem that has the Id and DisplayName properties. Our second interface is
named IItemCollectionViewProps, and defines the properties that our collection view
will need. The Title property will contain "Please select", the items property will
contain our array, and the SelectedItem property will contain the currently selected item.
Note that React components are always created by extending React.Component using
generic syntax and passing in a type that defines the properties of the component. This
means that we cannot simply create a property on a React component and expect that it will
be part of the props property. Let's take a look at the definition of this view as follows:

```
export class ItemCollectionView extends
    React.Component<IItemCollectionViewProps, {}> {
    // SelectedItem: IClickableItem;
    // ^^ properties cannot be included like this.
    constructor(input: IItemCollectionViewProps) {
        super(input);
        this.itemSelected = this.itemSelected.bind(this);
        // ^^ this is functionally equivalent to below :
        // _.bindAll(this, 'itemSelected');
    }

    ... other code
}
```

Here, we have defined a class named `ItemCollectionView` that extends
`React.Component`. Again, the generic syntax for React components requires two
arguments, an object describing the properties of the view, and an object describing its
initial state. As we are passing the `IItemCollecitonViewProps` interface in the generic
syntax, we know that this React component will end up having a `Title` property, an `items`
property, and a `SelectedItem` property. The constructor calls `super`, as seen previously,
and then binds the execution context of the `itemSelected` function to the instance of the
class. As noted before, the underscore function `bindAll` is a functional equivalent.

Let's now take a look at the render function, as follows:

```
render() {
    let _this = this;

    let buttonNodes =
        this.props.items.map(function (item) {
            return (
                <ItemView
                    onItemClicked={_this.itemSelected}
                    DisplayName={item.DisplayName}
                    Id={item.Id}
                />
            );
        });

    return <div>
        <h1>{this.props.title}</h1>
        <ul>
            {buttonNodes}
        </ul>
        <div>Selected Item :
            {this.props.SelectedItem.Id} -
            {this.props.SelectedItem.DisplayName}</div>
    </div>;
}
```

Here, we start our `render` function with the age-old JavaScript trick of defining a local
variable named `_this`, which is set to `this`. The reason that we are doing this, is so that we
can refer to the instance of the `ItemCollectionView` class a little later. The `render`
function is divided into two sections.

The first section is the definition of a variable name, `buttonNodes`, which calls the `map` function on the `items` property, as seen in the call to `this.props.items.map`. This `map` function will loop through each item in the `items` array, and return an HTML snippet. The snippet returned is an HTML element named `ItemView`. This element name is the same as the class name of the `ItemView` class that we defined earlier. This element has an HTML attribute named `onItemClicked`, and then the `DisplayName` and `Id` attributes that the `ItemView` needs. The `onItemClicked` property is using the local variable, `_this`, to pass the `itemSelected` function as a callback function to `ItemView`. The `itemSelected` function of `ItemCollectionView` will therefore be invoked (through the callback) when an `ItemView` is clicked.

The second section of the `render` function returns the HTML snippet for the entire `ItemCollectionView`. This consists of an `<h1>` tag, which renders the `title` property via the `{this.props.title}` syntax. The next tag is a `<ul>` tag, and, within this, the `{buttonNodes}` variable. This HTML snippet, therefore, will include the results of our `map` function as defined by the `buttonNodes` variable. In this way, React allows us to use any TypesScript variable or function within our HTML templates in a simple and intuitive manner. The final part of this HTML snippet will render the currently selected item inside a `<div>` tag.

There is one more function that we need to define in this `ItemCollectionView` class, as follows:

```
itemSelected(item: IClickableItem) {
    this.props.SelectedItem.Id = item.Id;
    this.props.SelectedItem.DisplayName = item.DisplayName;

    this.setState({});
}
```

Here, we have defined the `itemSelected` function, which will be used as the callback when an `ItemView` is clicked. This function has a single parameter named `item`, of type `IClickableItem`. The function signature, therefore, matches the definition of the `onItemClicked` function of the `ItemModel` that we used to render each element of the collection. This function sets the value of the `Id` and `DisplayName` properties of the internal property named `SelectedItem` to match the incoming values. Again, to reference an internal property of a particular view, we must use the `props` property. Finally, this function calls the react function named `setState` with an empty object. This call to `setState` will rerender the entire view to the DOM.

React bootstrapping

In order to see the results of our view definitions rendered in our sample application, we will need to bootstrap our React code, similar to what we did for Aurelia and Angular. To do this, we will modify the `app/index.tsx` file as follows:

```tsx
import * as React from "react";
import * as ReactDOM from "react-dom";


import { ItemCollectionView, IClickableItem }
    from "./ReactApp";


let ClickableItemArray: IClickableItem[] = [
    { Id: 1, DisplayName: "firstItem" },
    { Id: 2, DisplayName: "secondItem" },
    { Id: 3, DisplayName: "thirdItem" },
];

ReactDOM.render(
    <ItemCollectionView items={ClickableItemArray}
        title="Please select:"
        SelectedItem={
            { Id: 0, DisplayName: "None Selected " }
        } />,
    document.getElementById("app")
);
```

Here, we start with the standard `import` statements at the start of the file. The first two import statements make all classes from the `"react"` library and `"react-dom"` library available under the `React` and `ReactDOM` namespaces, respectively. The third `import` statement makes the `ItemCollectionView` class and the `IClickableItem` interface available from the `ReactApp.tsx` file that we created earlier.

We then create a variable named `ClickableItemArray`, which is our array of `ClickableItem` objects. Finally, we call the `ReactDOM.render` function, to render an element to the DOM of the `ItemCollectionView` type. Note how we have specified three attributes for this `ItemCollectionView` element.

The first attribute is named items, and the value of this item is the instance of the array we created named ClickableItemArray. Again, React is allowing us to use the {variableName} syntax to inject the value of the ClickableItemArray variable into the DOM. The second attribute in this snippet is named title, and is set to the string value of "Please select: ". The third attribute is named SelectedItem, and represents the initial state of the SelectedItem property on initial startup, hence, "None Selected". After we have defined these DOM elements, note how we include a comma, and then a call to document.getElementById.

This syntax is React's way of selecting a DOM element within the HTML page, and injecting the generated HTML. The id of the element is "app", and, as such, will match a <div id="app"> element within our HTML.

We will now need to create an index.html file in order to bootstrap and render our React application. This index.html file (at the root directory of our project) is as follows:

```
<!DOCTYPE html>
<html>

<head>
    <title>React starter app</title>
    <link rel="stylesheet" type="text/css"
        href="./node_modules/bootstrap/dist/css/bootstrap.css" />
    <script src="./node_modules/underscore/underscore.js"></script>
</head>

<body>
    <div id="app"></div>
    <script src="./dist/bundle.js"></script>
</body>

</html>
```

This HTML file includes a <link> tag to load the bootstrap.css file, as well as a <script> tag for loading the underscore library. The <body> element defines a <div> tag named "app", where React will render the ItemCollectionView into. Lastly, we include a <script> tag to download the bundle.js file in the dist directory. Note that, because webpack is combining the React libraries with our compiled TypeScript classes into the bundle.js file, this HTML file becomes very simple. We do not need to load any special libraries, as everything has been combined into a single bundle.js file for us.

Our React application is now ready to run. Simply fire up a browser, and open the `index.html` file in your source directory. Note that where Aurelia and Angular require a web server to be running within your development environment, React and Backbone do not.

React forms

React forms are built around the concept of a form state. Where we can bind properties of a React component using the `props` property of the component, when we deal with forms, we need to work with the `state` property. This `state` property will hold a set of sub-properties that will be bound to our form controls. As an example of this, consider the following code:

```
export class ItemCollectionView
    ... existing class code
{

    constructor(input: IItemCollectionViewProps) {
        super(input);

        this.state = { inputName: 'Your Name' };

        ... existing contructor code
    }
```

Here, we have added a single line to the constructor function of our `ItemCollectionView` component, which is assigning an object to the `state` property of the React component. The contents of this object are simply a property named `inputName`, which has a value of `'Your Name'`. This technique is how we create form controls in React, and set their default values. We can bind this value to our React template, as follows:

```
render() {

... existing code
return <div>
    <h1>{this.props.title}</h1>
    ... existing code
    <form>
        <div className="form-group">
            <label>Name :</label>
            <input type="text"
        className="form-control"
        value={this.state.inputName}
            />
```

```
            </div>
            <button className="submit-button"
                type="submit" value="Submit">Submit</button>
        </form>
    </div>;
    }
```

Here, we have modified the `render` function on the `ItemCollectionView` component. We have added a `<form>` tag, with a `<label>` tag, and an `<input>` tag, as we have done with the other frameworks. Note how the `<input>` tag has a `value` attribute. This `value` attribute is directly referencing the `inputName` property of the `state` variable in our component. Remember that we set the value of this property in our constructor, so if we fire up our page now, we will see the value of the input control set to `'Your Name'`. So far, so good.

Unfortunately, if we attempt to modify the value of this input control on the page, we will see that it appears to be read-only. While the default value has been set correctly, there is no way for our user to modify it. What we need to do now is to attach to React's state change life cycle.

React state change

To detect a change in the state of a control in React, we will need to create a function that can be called whenever a change occurs, as follows:

```
onChange(event: React.ChangeEvent<HTMLInputElement>) {
    let valueName = event.target.name;
    this.setState({ [valueName]: event.target.value });
    console.log(`onChange : ${event.target.name} : ${event.target.value}`);
}
```

Here, we have created a function named `onChange` that has a single argument named `event`, of type `React.ChangeEvent`. Within this function, we are finding the `name` of the HTML element through `event.target.name`, and then calling the `setState` function with the updated value (found through `event.target.value`). This function will therefore update the `state` property on our component. Note that we are also logging a message to the console to show what the `event.target.name` and `event.target.value` values were.

There are two problems with this code. Firstly, how do we know that the `name` property on `event.target.name` will match the internal property of our `state` object? The answer is to update the template, and specify the `name` HTML attribute for our control, as follows:

```
<div className="form-group">
    <label>Name :</label>
    <input type="text"
        className="form-control"
        name="inputName"
        value={this.state.inputName}
        onChange={this.onChange}
    />
</div>
```

Here, we have updated the `<input>` control with two extra attributes. The first is the `name` attribute, which is set to `inputName`. This will ensure that the `onChange` function receives the string `"inputName"` in the `event.target.name` property. The second attribute that we have included is the `onChange` handler, which will call the `onChange` function in our component when the value changes. The input control is now wired up to send the correct information to the `onChange` handler.

React state properties

If we attempt to compile our code at this stage, however, we will generate a compile error as follows:

```
TS2345: Argument of type '{ [x: string]: string; }' is not assignable to
parameter of type '{ inputName: string; }
```

This error highlights the second problem in the `onChange` function, which is caused by the following line of code:

```
this.setState({ [valueName]: event.target.value });
```

Here, we are calling the `setState` function with an object that is using an index property: `[valueName]`. At runtime, this will equate to `[inputName]` : `event.target.value`. While this is valid TypeScript, and we can use this technique to assign the value of a property, remember that a React component uses generic syntax to define both the internal properties of a component, and the `state` properties of a component. The cause of this error is, in fact, the definition of the React component, as follows:

```
export class ItemCollectionView extends
    React.Component<
        IItemCollectionViewProps, // props properties
        { inputName: string } // state properties
    > {

    ... existing code

}
```

Here, we can see that we are creating the `ItemCollectionView` component, and deriving (or extending) it from `React.Component`. `React.Component` uses two generic properties in its definition. The first property defines the internal `props` structure, and is set to `IItemCollectionViewProps`. The second property defines the structure of the `state` property, and is set to `{ inputName: string }`. This is the definition that is causing the compilation error.

To fix this, we could update the definition to the following:

```
{ inputName: string, [key: string] : any }
```

This definition now includes an index property of the string type: `[key:string]`. As we do not know what type this index property will return, we can leave the type as `any`. While this is one solution to our problem, we can also use a mapped type to accomplish the same thing, as follows:

```
type StringProps<T> = {
    [key: string]: any;
}

export class ItemCollectionView extends
    React.Component<
        IItemCollectionViewProps, // internal properties
        StringProps<{ inputName: string }> // state properties
    > {

    ... existing code

}
```

Here, we have defined a mapped type named StringProps that uses generic syntax for the type of T. This mapped type simply defines an index property of the string type for our type. The updated version of the definition for the ItemCollectionView class now uses StringProps< { inputName: string }>. This has the same affect as our earlier solution. The benefit of this mapped type, however, is that we can reuse it for any React component, and it makes our code a little cleaner.

We can now attach a handler to the form itself, as follows:

```
render() {
... existing code
    return <div>
    ... existing template
        <form onSubmit={this.onSubmit} >
        ... existing template
        </form>
    </div>;
}
onSubmit(e: React.FormEvent) {
    console.log(`onSubmit : state :
        ${this.state.inputName}`);
    e.preventDefault();
}
```

Here, we have updated the render function, and added an onSubmit handler to the form itself. This handler will call the onSubmit function, which will simply log the value of the inputName property of the state object to the console. Note that we are calling e.preventDefault() to ensure that the HTML page is not submitted itself, which would cause a full-page refresh.

With these changes in place, our React form is complete. We have seen how to use the state object to store form variables, and how to attach these state variables to our input controls. We have also discussed React's change detection life cycle, and made some changes to our React component definition to use these events correctly. If we fire up our application now, and start to type some text into the form control, note what happens in the console:

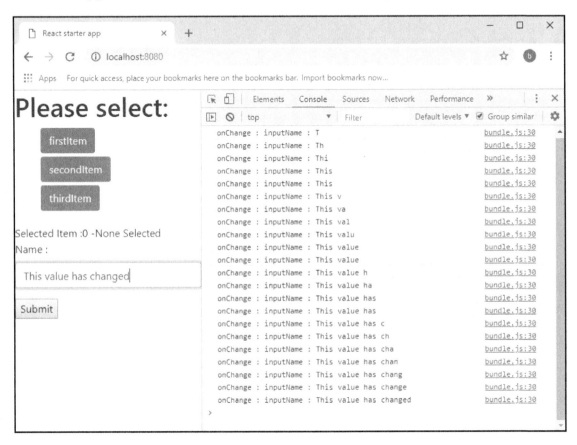

Here, we can see that the `onChange` event is firing for every keystroke that the user enters. This is slightly different to the other frameworks we have worked with, where these changes are essentially hidden until the value of the input control is needed.

React TypeScript features

TypeScript has supported the JSX syntax that React uses for some time. Over the past few releases, the team has also included some extra JSX features to make React programming a little easier. The updates to the TypeScript language for React include rest syntax for template properties, and support for default properties.

JSX template rest syntax

When we have a number of properties that are included in a component, we need to name each property as part of our template, as follows:

```
return (
    <ItemView
        onItemClicked={_this.itemSelected}
        DisplayName={item.DisplayName}
        Id={item.Id}
    />
);
```

Here, we are constructing an `ItemView` component in our `render` function. The `ItemView` component needs three properties, named `onItemClicked`, `DisplayName`, and `Id`. When the list of properties for a component becomes large, it becomes very tedious and error prone to have to name each property in our template.

TypeScript now supports using rest syntax in these cases, as follows:

```
return (
    <ItemView
        onItemClicked={_this.itemSelected}
        {...item}
    />
);
```

Here, we are constructing an `ItemView` component in our template as normal, and specifying the `onItemClicked` property. We are then using rest syntax, `{...item}`, to automatically assign each property for us.

Default properties

Another feature that the TypeScript team has incorporated for React and JSX is support for default properties. If we take a look at how we construct our `ItemCollectionView`, we can see how this can be of use:

```
ReactDOM.render(
    <ItemCollectionView items={ClickableItemArray}
        title="Please Select:"
        SelectedItem={
            { Id: 0, DisplayName: "None Selected" }
        }
    />,
    document.getElementById("app")
);
```

Here, we are creating an instance of our `ItemCollectionView` component. As the component has three properties, that is the `items`, `title`, and `SelectedItem` properties, we need to define these values when we create the component. While this works, it would be handy to be able to set the default values of these properties in the component itself. In other words, why would the user of a component need to set the default values of a component? Surely the component itself should make these decisions.

To cater for this scenario, TypeScript has included support for the `defaultProps` property as follows:

```
export class ItemCollectionView extends
    React.Component {
    ... existing code

    static defaultProps = {
        title: "Please select:",
        SelectedItem: { Id: 0, DisplayName: "None Selected" }
    };

    ... existing code
}
```

Here, we can see that the `ItemCollectionView` class now has a `static` property named `defaultProps`. This property contains a `title` and a `SelectedItem` property, and is setting these to their default values. Hence, the component itself is now defining these default properties. We can now remove them from the creation of the component as follows:

```
ReactDOM.render(
    <ItemCollectionView items={ClickableItemArray}
```

```
        />,
        document.getElementById("app")
    );
```

Here, we have no mention of the `title` or `SelectedItem` properties on the creation of the component, and leave the default values of these to the component itself.

React summary

In this section of the chapter, we have explored how to build our sample application using React. As we have seen, React uses JSX syntax, which combines HTML-style declarations right inside our TypeScript classes. For this reason, we need to use a `.tsx` extension for our TypeScript files instead of the standard `.ts` extension. We have seen how to create child components, and how a React component can make use of these child components in its own rendering function. We have built our sample application and seen how to use arrays of components, how to handle DOM events such as `onClick`, and how React uses callback functions to pass messages from a child component to a parent component.

We have also explored form processing, and seen how to set the default value of a form component in our code, and how to process the `state` variable to trap changes to our form values. Finally, we saw some improvements to the support for JSX within the TypeScript compiler, using rest syntax for component properties, and how to use default properties.

React is a very popular framework, and is different to other frameworks in the use of the JSX syntax. React components should be designed to handle a single small element of an overall screen, such that these components can be reused anywhere. React development is therefore about defining these components, and building your application up from the components that you have at hand.

Performance comparison

Now that we have built the same application using a couple of different TypeScript compatible libraries, we can compare apples with apples in terms of performance. Each framework is loading an HTML page, which will load the required libraries, along with the `bootstrap.css` files, and any dependent packages. Each sample application is doing exactly the same things, which include the following:

- Loading an array of objects to use as the default collection
- Rendering a single view for each of the objects in the collection

- Combining each single view into a view for the entire collection
- Rendering a title element, and a selected item element to show which item is currently selected
- Attaching the generated HTML to the DOM

If we run each version of this application in the same browser, and open up our handy developer tools, we can start to compare how long each of these frameworks takes in order to render our application to the browser, as shown in the following screenshot:

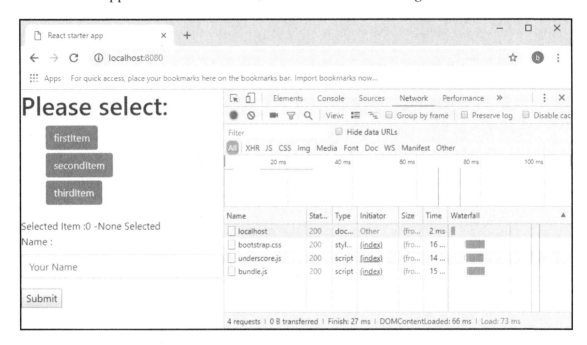

On the bottom-right of this screenshot, we can see three numbers represented in milliseconds. The important one is the Load number, which is the amount of time that the entire page took to load and render to the DOM. As we can see from this screenshot, the page took 73 milliseconds to render completely. This is the React version of our application.

Next up is Backbone, which loads in approximately 36 milliseconds:

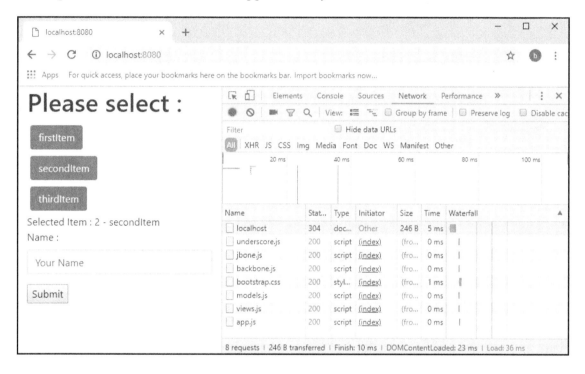

Backbone is rendering the page in less than half of the time taken for React.

So how does Angular fare, then?

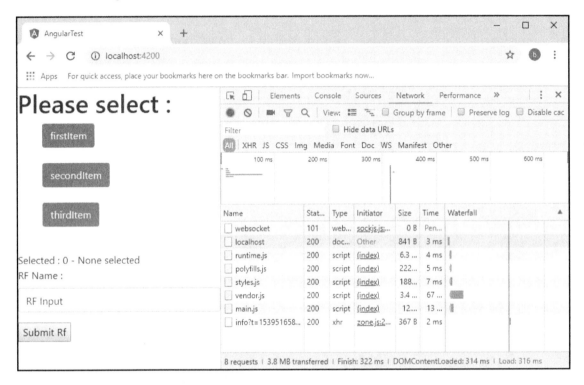

Here, we can see that Angular is rendering the page in approximately 316 milliseconds, which is 10 times slower than Backbone, and five times slower than React.

Last up is Aurelia, as follows:

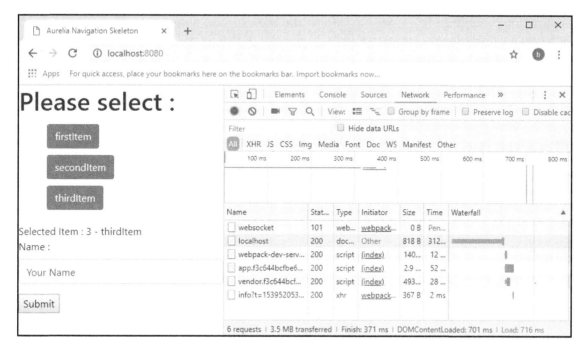

Aurelia is taking a whopping 716 milliseconds to load and render the page. In terms of performance, then, in first place is Backbone, which loads and renders the page in 36 milliseconds. In second place is React, which loads and renders in 73 milliseconds, which is double the amount of time that Backbone took. In third place is Angular, which is taking 316 milliseconds, and in last place is Aurelia, at 716 milliseconds.

What we can see from these results, then, is that the more that a framework does the heavy lifting for you, the more processing it will be doing in the background, and the slower the page loading times will be. Comparing the amount of code we needed to write for Backbone, and the amount we needed to write for Aurelia, it is obvious that Aurelia is doing a lot of background work, identifying when we need to re-render an element, and automatically updating the DOM. While this sort of functionality is excellent from a development point of view, it can affect rendering performance.

As mentioned earlier in this chapter, when targeting older CPUs, and slower network connections, you may need to ensure that your application renders as fast as possible. This is particularly relevant if you are targeting older browsers on older phones in areas where network coverage is slow or intermittent. In the end, however, it is a matter of personal choice. If the Aurelia framework helps your team to build and deliver applications at a very high speed due to the small amount of code required, then the speed of rendering the application may not be of such importance.

Summary

In this chapter, we took a deep dive look into what an MVC framework is, and discussed each of its elements. We discussed the role and responsibilities of the Model, the View, and the Controller in MVC, and how they interact together to create user interfaces. We also had a brief discussion on the benefits of using MVC frameworks. We then took a look at four MVC frameworks that either have very tight integration with TypeScript, or have been written with TypeScript in mind. We implemented the same basic application in each of these frameworks, and compared the differences in concepts and syntax between Backbone, Aurelia, Angular, and React. We also discussed some performance implications to think about when working with each of these frameworks.

In our next chapter, we will take a look at automated testing—unit testing, integration testing, and acceptance testing for our TypeScript applications.

8
Test-Driven Development

In our last chapter, we took an in-depth look at the MVC design pattern and built a sample application using four different frameworks that all use that pattern. We saw that each framework does things slightly differently in terms of models and views, and that each framework had the notion of a controller component, or an application component. The basic principles of the MVC design pattern have given rise to other similar patterns, for instance **Model View Presenter (MVP)** and **Model View View Model (MVVM)**. When discussing this group of patterns together, they are described by some as **Model View Whatever (MVW)**, or MV*.

Some of the benefits of this MV* style of writing applications include modularity and separation of concerns, which we will cover in later chapters. But this MV* style of building applications also brings with it a huge advantage—the ability to write testable JavaScript. Using MV* allows us to unit test, integration test, and acceptance test almost all of our beautifully hand-crafted JavaScript. We can write tests for individual classes, and then extend these tests to cover groups of classes. We can test our models, but we can also test our views, along with our rendering functions—to ensure that DOM elements are correctly shown on the page. We can also simulate button clicks, drop-down selects and animations. These tests can then be extended into page transitions, including login pages and home pages. By building a large set of tests for our application, we will gain confidence that our code works as expected, and allow us to refactor our code at any time.

Refactoring refers to the ability to modify our code without fear that the overall functionality will change. This means that if we have a set of tests, then we are free to rewrite any part of the underlying code, so long as the tests pass. There is an old saying that without tests, you are not refactoring, you are just randomly changing things. In a large body of code, even a one-line change could have unwanted side-effects that are not easily found unless you have tests in place.

In this chapter, we will look at test-driven development in relation to TypeScript. We will discuss some of the more popular testing frameworks, write some unit tests using these frameworks, and then discuss test runners and continuous integration techniques.

The topics that we will be looking at in this chapter are as follows:

- Test-driven development
- Unit, integration and acceptance tests
- Jasmine
- Jasmine runners
- Browser automation
- Continuous integration

Test-driven development

Test-driven development (TDD) is really a way of thinking about our code that should be part of a standard development process. It is a development paradigm that starts with tests, and drives the momentum of a piece of production code through these tests. TDD means asking the question *how do I know that I have solved the problem?* instead of just *how do I solve the problem?* This is an important idea to grasp. We write code in order to solve a problem, but we should be able to prove that we have solved the problem through the use of automated tests.

The basic steps of a test-driven approach are the following:

- Write a test that fails
- Run the test to ensure that it fails
- Write code to make the test pass
- Run the test so see that it passes
- Run all tests to see that the new code does not break any other
- Repeat

Using TDD practices is really a mindset. Some developers follow this approach and write tests first, while others write their code first and their tests afterward. Then, there are some that don't write tests at all. If you fall into the last category, then hopefully, the techniques you will learn in this chapter will help you to get started in the right direction.

There are so many excuses out there for not writing unit tests. Things such as *the test framework was not in our original quote*, or *it will add 20% to the development time*, or *the tests are outdated so we don't run them anymore*. The truth is, though, that in this day and age, we cannot afford not to write tests. Applications grow in size and complexity, and requirements change over time. An application that has a good suite of tests can be modified far more quickly, and will be much more resilient to future requirement changes than one that does not have tests. This is when the real cost savings of unit testing becomes apparent. By writing unit tests for your application, you are future-proofing it, and ensuring that any change to the code base does not break existing functionality.

We also want to write our applications to stand the test of time. The code we write now could be in a production environment for years, which means that sometimes, you will need to make enhancements or bug fixes to code that was written years ago. If an application has a full suite of tests surrounding it, then making modifications can be done with confidence that the changes made will not break existing functionality.

TDD in the JavaScript space also adds another layer to our code coverage. Quite often, development teams will write tests that target only the server-side logic of an application. As an example, in the Visual Studio space, these tests are often written to only target the MVC framework of controllers, views, and underlying business logic. It has always been fairly difficult to test the client-side logic of an application—in other words, the actual rendered HTML and user-based interactions.

JavaScript testing frameworks provide us with tools to fill this gap. We can now start to unit-test our rendered HTML, as well as to simulate user interactions such as filling in forms and clicking on buttons. This extra layer of testing, combined with server-side testing, means that we have a way of unit testing each layer of our application—from server-side business logic, through server-side page rendering, right through to user interactions. This ability to unit test frontend user interactions is one of the greatest strengths of any JavaScript MV* framework. In fact, it could even influence the architectural decisions you make when choosing a technology stack.

Unit, integration, and acceptance tests

Automated tests can be broken up into three general areas, or types of tests—unit tests, integration tests, and acceptance tests. We can also describe these tests as either black-box or white-box tests. White-box tests are tests where the internal logic or structure of the code under test is known to the tester. Black-box tests, on the other hand, are tests where the internal design and or logic are not known to the tester.

Unit tests

A unit test is typically a white-box test where all of the external interfaces to a block of code are mocked or stubbed out. If we are testing some code that does an asynchronous call to load a block of JSON, for example, unit testing this code would require mocking out the returned JSON. This technique ensures that the object under test is always given a known set of data. When new requirements come along, this known set of data can grow and expand, of course. Objects under test should be designed to interact with interfaces, so that those interfaces can be easily mocked or stubbed in a unit test scenario.

Integration tests

Integration tests are another form of white-box tests that allow the object under test to run in an environment close to how it would in real code. In our preceding example, where some code does an asynchronous call to load a block of JSON, an integration test would need to actually call the REST services that generate the JSON. If this REST service relied upon data from a database, then the integration test would need data in the database that matched the integration test scenario. If we were to describe a unit test as having a boundary around the object under test, then an integration test is simply an expansion of this boundary to include dependent objects or services.

Building automated integration tests for your applications will improve the quality of your product immensely. Consider the case of the scenario that we have been using—where a block of code calls a REST service for some JSON data. Someone could easily change the structure of the JSON data that the REST service returns. Our unit tests will still pass, as they are not actually calling the REST server-side code, but our application will be broken because the returned JSON is not what we are expecting.

Without integration tests, these types of errors will only be picked up in the later stages of manual testing. Thinking about integration tests, implementing specific datasets for integration tests, and building them into your test suite will eliminate these sorts of bugs early.

Acceptance tests

Acceptance tests are black-box tests, and are generally scenario-based. They may incorporate multiple user screens or user interactions in order to pass. These tests are also generally carried out by the testing team, as they may require logging in to the application, searching for a particular set of data, updating the data, and so on. With some planning, and a wealth of tools already available, we can also automate these acceptance tests, so that they are run as part of an automated test suite. The more acceptance tests a project has, the more robust it will be.

 Note that in the test-driven development methodology, every bug that is picked up by a manual testing team must result in the creation of new unit, integration, or acceptance tests. This methodology will help to ensure that once a bug is found and fixed, it never reappears again.

Unit testing frameworks

There are many JavaScript unit testing frameworks available, and also a few that have been written in TypeScript. Two of the most popular JavaScript frameworks are Jasmine (http://jasmine.github.io/) and QUnit (http://qunitjs.com/). If you are writing node-based TypeScript code, then you might want to have a look at Mocha (https://github.com/mochajs/mocha/wiki).

Although there have been attempts at writing unit testing frameworks in TypeScript and for TypeScript, such as MaxUnit by KnowledgeLake, or tsUnit by Steve-Fenton, these frameworks never really took off. Their limited set of features compared to the battle-hardened, tried-and-tested frameworks meant that they had a lot of catching up to do, and were eventually abandoned.

The ease with which TypeScript can integrate with JavaScript libraries means that developers looking for a fully featured set of unit testing tools can reuse the JavaScript test libraries as if they were written in TypeScript.

For the rest of this chapter, we will be using Jasmine 3.2 as our testing framework.

Jasmine

Jasmine is a behavior-driven JavaScript testing framework that has been around longer than some of the oldest JavaScript frameworks themselves. Backbone was originally released in October 2010, but Jasmine was actually released one month earlier, in September 2010. Jasmine was originally a port of the popular Java testing framework named jUnit, and was called jsUnit. The age of this framework shows that it has stood the test of time, and has been constantly updated with new features to allow even the most modern frameworks to use it.

Jasmine has a very simple syntax, and is designed so that it can be read and understood easily. It can also be extended easily, and is the recommended framework for Aurelia as well as Angular unit and integration testing. Installation of Jasmine using npm is as follows:

```
npm install jasmine --save
```

The relevant declaration files for Jasmine can be installed by using @types as follows:

```
npm install @types/jasmine -save-dev
```

We can run Jasmine directly from the command line in Node by installing Jasmine as a global module, as follows:

```
npm install -g jasmine
```

Once installed, we will need to initialize our project directory for Jasmine to use, as follows:

```
jasmine init
```

This will create a spec directory, where our tests should reside, and a spec/support/jasmine.json file, as follows:

```
{
  "spec_dir": "spec",
  "spec_files": [
    "**/*[sS]pec.js"
  ],
  "helpers": [
    "helpers/**/*.js"
  ],
  "stopSpecOnExpectationFailure": false,
  "random": true
}
```

Here, Jasmine has set up a sample `jasmine.json` file that has a few standard properties. The `spec_dir` property tells Jasmine that it should look in the `/spec` directory to find runnable tests. The `spec_files` property specifies that any file that ends with `.spec.js` or `.Spec.js` will be considered to be a Jasmine test specification. We will not use the `helpers` directory just yet, although it is there to load files that our tests may need. The `stopSpecOnExpectationFailure` property set to `false` means that Jasmine will continue to run all tests in the suite, regardless of failure. The `random` property is used to randomly select a test to run from the entire suite.

Our full suite of tests (which do not actually have any tests yet), can be run as follows:

```
jasmine
```

As there are no tests in the specs folder as yet, Jasmine will report as such:

```
Finished in 0.001 seconds
Incomplete: No specs found
```

A simple Jasmine test

Jasmine uses a simple format for writing tests. Let's create a `spec/SimpleJasmine.spec.ts` file with the following TypeScript code:

```
describe('spec/SimpleJasmine.spec.ts', () => {
    it('should fail', () => {
        let undefinedValue;
        expect(undefinedValue).toBeDefined('should be defined');
    })
});
```

This snippet starts by calling the Jasmine `describe` function, which takes two arguments. The first argument is the name of the test suite, and the second is an anonymous function that contains each test in our test suite. Within this anonymous function, we are calling the Jasmine function named `it` to describe an actual test, which also takes two arguments. The first argument is the test name, and the second argument is an anonymous function that contains our actual test.

This test starts by defining a variable, named `undefinedValue`, but it does not actually set its value. Next, we use the Jasmine `expect` function. Just by reading the code of this `expect` statement, we can quickly understand what the unit test is doing. It is expecting that the `undefinedValue` value should be defined, that is, not equal to `undefined`.

The Jasmine `expect` function takes a single argument, and returns a value that can be used in fluent syntax to be assessed by what is known as a **matcher**. The matcher in this case is `toBeDefined`. So the `expect` function passes the value it has been given to the matcher, which will either pass or fail. Most matchers can be called with a single string as an argument, which will simply log the message given to the console. The `expect` keyword is similar to the `Assert` keyword in other testing libraries.

In this case, our matcher is expecting that the value of the `undefinedValue` variable should be defined, so this test should immediately fail.

We can run our simple test from the command line, which will fail with the following message:

```
λ Cmder                                                          —  □  ✕

E:\temp\jasmine_tests  (jasmine_tests@1.0.0)
λ jasmine
Randomized with seed 98927
Started


Failures:
1) spec/SimpleJasmine.spec.ts a value should be defined
   Message:
     Expected undefined to be defined 'should be defined'.

   Stack:
     Error: Expected undefined to be defined 'should be defined'.
         at <Jasmine>
         at UserContext.<anonymous> (E:\temp\jasmine_tests\spec\SimpleJasmine.spec.js:8:32)
         at <Jasmine>

1 spec, 1 failure
Finished in 0 seconds
Randomized with seed 98927 (jasmine --random=true --seed=98927)

E:\temp\jasmine_tests  (jasmine_tests@1.0.0)
λ



λ cmd.exe                                    Search      🔍 ⊞ ▾ ▣ ▾ 🔒 ▢ ≡
```

Here, we can see that our test has failed with the `'should be defined'` message. Jasmine is also telling us exactly where in our JavaScript file the test failed, which will help immensely when debugging.

Note carefully the name that we are giving this test suite. Our describe function is being called with the name of the actual TypeScript file on disk, `'spec/SimpleJasmine.spec.ts'`. While the name of the test suite can actually be anything, it helps when running hundreds of tests to know exactly which file was responsible for the failing test. When a test fails, Jasmine will log a full-stack trace for the failure, which can easily be 20 plus lines of stack trace in production systems. Making the cause of the failure immediately traceable to a particular test file helps immensely when trying to find the cause of a test failure.

Now that we have a test that is failing, we can make the test pass. This is as simple as assigning a value as follows:

```
let undefinedValue = "test";
expect(undefinedValue).toBeDefined('should be defined');
```

Here, we have assigned the value of `"test"` to the `undefinedValue` variable . This test will now pass as follows:

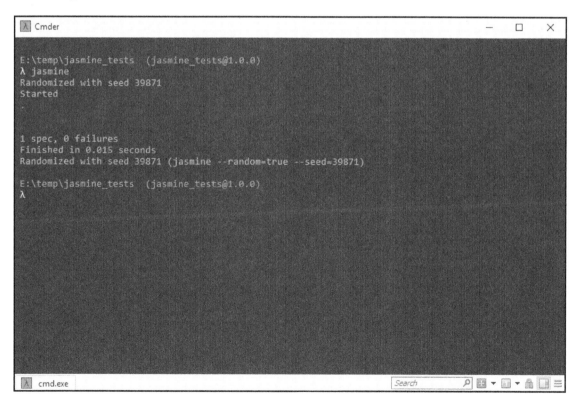

Excellent. We are following the TDD mantra by firstly writing a failing test, running the test to see that it fails, and then writing the code to make the test pass.

Test reporters

If we look at the console output of the Jasmine test runner, we see that it is showing a green dot for each test that we have run, and then a count of how many tests were run, and how many failures we encountered. But what if we would like to see the name of each test that we have run on the console? This is where Jasmine reporters come in. Jasmine reporters allow us to modify the output of each test suite, and the output of each test itself to give a more detailed description. We can configure a test reporter by injecting some code into a file in the `helpers` directory, which Jasmine will load and run before each test run.

A number of Jasmine reporters have already been written, and are included in the `npm` package named `jasmine-reporters`. We will need to install this package as follows:

```
npm install jasmine-reporters --save-dev
```

Let's create a JavaScript configuration file in the `spec/helpers` directory named `attachTapReporter.js`, as follows:

```
var reporters = require('jasmine-reporters');

var tapReporter = new reporters.TapReporter();
jasmine.getEnv().addReporter(tapReporter)
```

Here, we are simply loading the package named `jasmine-reporters` through a call to a function named `require`. This is part of the module-loading capability of JavaScript, which we will explore in a later chapter.

One of the objects that we can create from the `jasmine-reporters` package is named `TapReporter`. We create a new instance of this class and then get a handle to the Jasmine environment through a call to `jasmine.getEnv()`. Once we have a handle, we can call the `addReporter` function, and pass in the instance of our `TapReporter` class.

If we now run our tests from the command line, we will see a more verbose description of each of our tests being logged to the console, as follows:

```
λ Cmder                                                          —    □    ×

E:\temp\jasmine_tests   (jasmine_tests@1.0.0)
λ jasmine
Randomized with seed 04583
Started
TAP version 13
.ok 1 - spec/SimpleJasmine.spec.ts : expect false not to be truthy
.ok 2 - spec/SimpleJasmine.spec.ts : a value should be defined
.ok 3 - spec/SimpleJasmine.spec.ts : expect value toBe(2)
.ok 4 - spec/SimpleJasmine.spec.ts : expect string toContain value
.ok 5 - spec/SimpleJasmine.spec.ts : expect true to be truthy
.ok 6 - spec/SimpleJasmine.spec.ts : expect value not to be null
.ok 7 - spec/SimpleJasmine.spec.ts : expect objects to be equal


7 specs, 0 failures
Finished in 0.046 seconds
Randomized with seed 04583 (jasmine --random=true --seed=04583)
1..7
# 7 specs, 0 failures, 0 skipped, 0 disabled in 0.046s.
# NOTE: disabled specs are usually a result of xdescribe.

E:\temp\jasmine_tests   (jasmine_tests@1.0.0)
λ

λ cmd.exe                                          Search
```

Note that the output that we are seeing is the result of running seven tests, each with the name of the test suite, and the name of the test itself. This screenshot actually includes all of the tests that we will write in the next section.

Matchers

As seen in our first simple test, Jasmine uses a fluent syntax to allow us to attach Jasmine matchers after the expect(...) statement. In our first test, we used the .toBeDefined matcher. Jasmine, however, has a wide range of matchers that can be used within tests, and also allows us to write and include custom matchers. Let's take a quick look at some of these matchers:

```
it("expect value toBe(2)", () => {
    let twoValue = 2;
    expect(twoValue).toBe(2);
})
```

Here, we are using the `.toBe` matcher to test that the value of the `twoValue` variable is indeed 2.

```
it("expect string toContain value ", () => {
    let testString = "12345a";
    expect(testString).toContain("a");
});
```

In this test, we are using the `toContain` matcher to test that the "12345a" string contains the value "a".

```
it("expect true to be truthy", () => {
    let trueValue = true;
    expect(trueValue).toBeTruthy();
});
```

In this test, we are using the `toBeTruthy` matcher to test that the `trueValue` variable is set to the Boolean value of `true`.

We can also reverse the value of any expectation by using the `.not` matcher as follows:

```
it("expect false not to be truthy", () => {
    let falseValue = false;
    expect(falseValue).not.toBeTruthy();
});
```

Here, we are using the `.not.` matcher, and then the `toBeTruthy` matcher to test that the `falseValue` variable is indeed `false`. We can also use the `.not` matcher on other combinations of matchers, as follows:

```
it("expect value not to be null", () => {
    let definedValue = 2;
    expect(definedValue).not.toBeNull();
});
```

This test is checking that the value of the `definedValue` variable is not `null`, using the `toBeNull` matcher.

We can also check that two JavaScript objects are equal as follows:

```
it("expect objects to be equal", () => {
    let obj1 = {a : 1, b : 2};
    let obj2 = {b : 2, a : 1};

    expect(obj1).toEqual(obj2);
});
```

In this test, we have defined two objects, named `obj1` and `obj2` that have the same properties. The `toEqual` matcher will correctly identify that these two objects have the same properties and values, and are therefore considered equal.

Be sure to head over to the Jasmine website for a full list of matchers, as well as details on writing custom matchers.

Test start-up and tear-down

As in other testing frameworks, Jasmine provides a mechanism to define functions that will run before and after each test, or as a test start-up and tear-down mechanism. In Jasmine, the `beforeEach` and `afterEach` functions act in this way, as can be seen from the following test:

```
describe("beforeEach and afterEach tests", () => {
    let myString : string | undefined;

    beforeEach(() => {
        myString = "this is a string";
    });
    afterEach(() => {
        expect(myString).toBeUndefined();
    });

    it("should find then clear the myString variable", () => {
        expect(myString).toEqual("this is a string");
        myString = undefined;
    });

});
```

In this test, we define a variable named `myString` at the start of the test. As we know from JavaScript lexical scoping rules, this `myString` variable will then be available for use within the scope of the enclosing function, which is the `describe` function. This means that the `myString` variable will be available within each of the following `beforeEach`, `afterEach` and `it` functions. In our `beforeEach` function, this variable is set to a string value of `"this is a string"`. Within the `afterEach` function, the variable is tested to see that it has been reset to `undefined`. The expectation within our test checks is that this variable has been set through the `beforeEach` function. At the end of our test, we then reset the variable to `undefined`. Note that the `afterEach` function is also calling an `expect`—in this case to ensure that the test has reset the variable back to `undefined`.

In a very similar vein, Jasmine provides the `beforeAll` and `afterAll` functions that will be called before the full test suite runs, and after the full test suite runs. These functions are generally used to set up class instances or variables that each test would need. A typical example of this would be to set up a database connection, for instance. The initial creation of a database connection is typically a time-consuming task, so these could be set up in the `beforeAll` function, and then closed in the `afterAll` function.

Forcing tests

As your test suite starts to grow, it becomes necessary at development time to limit the run of an entire test suite down to one specific test, or to one specific suite of tests. This is generally to find the cause of a specific failure, or to focus on a single suite of tests during the development of the code. Jasmine provides the `fdescribe` and `fit` functions to *force* the execution of tests as follows:

```
fdescribe("This is a forced suite", () => {
    it("This is not a forced test", () => {
        expect(true).toBeFalsy('true should be false');
    });
    fit("This is a forced test", () => {
        expect(false).toBeFalsy();
    })
});
```

Here, we have replaced the `describe` function with an `fdescribe` function. Or, more simply, we have inserted an `f` before the `describe`. This will cause Jasmine to *force* this test to run, at the expense of any other tests. In other words, Jasmine will not run any other test suite except this one. This is very handy during development time, as we can limit the test run to a specific suite as we are developing the tests.

Note, too, how we have replaced the `it` function with a `fit` function in the second test in this suite. By inserting an `f` before the `it` function, we can force only a specific test to run. In this example, the first test will fail, as it is expecting `true toBeFalsy`. The second test, however, will pass. If we were to run our test suite at this stage, we would find one spec has run, with zero failures.

The `fdescribe` and `fit` functions work from the most restrictive to the least restrictive. In other words, if no tests have been marked with `fit`, then all tests in an `fdescribe` suite will be run. If multiple tests in an `fdescribe` suite have been marked with `fit`, then only those marked with `fit` will be run. If a suite has not been marked with `fdescribe`, but a single test has been marked with `fit`, then only that test will run.

Note that, under no circumstances, should you check in tests marked as `fdescribe` or `fit`. This will mean that your build servers will only run a tiny portion of your tests, instead of the entire suite. Jasmine will, in fact, warn you if it finds any tests that were forced, and log this to the console, as can be seen in the following screenshot:

Here, we can see that **1 spec** out of **10 specs** were run, and that Jasmine has marked the test run as **Incomplete**.

Skipping tests

In a similar fashion to forcing tests, tests can be skipped using `xit` instead of `it`, and `xdescribe` instead of `describe`. This means that the tests will not be run as part of your suite. While there are legitimate reasons to skip tests in a production system, these reasons should always be an extreme circumstance, and should always be very short-lived.

We can skip a test in two ways. The first is by marking the test with an x, so instead of using `it`, use `xit`. The second way of skipping a test is by calling the `pending` function, as follows:

```
describe("skipped test examples", () => {
    xit("skipped test with no reason", () => {
        expect(false).toBeTruthy();
    });
    it("", () => {
        expect(false).toBeTruthy();
        pending("this test should be implemented correctly");
    })
});
```

Here, we have two tests. The first test is skipped by using `xit`, and the second test is skipped due to a call to the `pending` function. Note that the call to the `pending` function is actually after the expectation. If we look closely at the expectation, we can see that this test should fail, as we are expecting `false toBeTruthy`. What this means is that the call to the `pending` function can occur anywhere within the test itself, and when Jasmine finds a call to `pending`, it will skip the entire test.

There is a subtle and important difference between the use of `xit` and the use of the `pending` function. The `pending` function allows us to give a reason for the skipping of the test. If we run this test, we will see the output as follows:

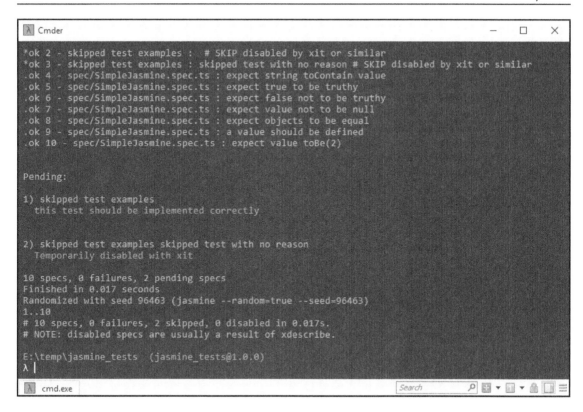

```
λ Cmder                                                      —   □   ×

*ok 2 - skipped test examples :  # SKIP disabled by xit or similar
*ok 3 - skipped test examples : skipped test with no reason # SKIP disabled by xit or similar
.ok 4 - spec/SimpleJasmine.spec.ts : expect string toContain value
.ok 5 - spec/SimpleJasmine.spec.ts : expect true to be truthy
.ok 6 - spec/SimpleJasmine.spec.ts : expect false not to be truthy
.ok 7 - spec/SimpleJasmine.spec.ts : expect value not to be null
.ok 8 - spec/SimpleJasmine.spec.ts : expect objects to be equal
.ok 9 - spec/SimpleJasmine.spec.ts : a value should be defined
.ok 10 - spec/SimpleJasmine.spec.ts : expect value toBe(2)


Pending:

1) skipped test examples
   this test should be implemented correctly


2) skipped test examples skipped test with no reason
   Temporarily disabled with xit

10 specs, 0 failures, 2 pending specs
Finished in 0.017 seconds
Randomized with seed 96463 (jasmine --random=true --seed=96463)
1..10
# 10 specs, 0 failures, 2 skipped, 0 disabled in 0.017s.
# NOTE: disabled specs are usually a result of xdescribe.

E:\temp\jasmine_tests  (jasmine_tests@1.0.0)
λ |

λ  cmd.exe                                    Search
```

Here, we can see that two tests were skipped. The first test shows the "Temporarily
disabled with xit" message, where the second test shows the message that we
specified in the call to the pending function, which was "this test should be
implemented correctly". This makes it very clear to anyone in our team why this test
was skipped. It acts as a signal that the test should be re-enabled when the reason for
skipping it is no longer valid.

Data-driven tests

There are times where a set of tests for the same piece of code needs to be repeated over
and over with slightly different inputs. If you were testing the ability of a function to
recognize the occurrence of a string, for example, you would want to hit that test with
multiple different strings. These sorts of tests are called data-driven tests. The outcome of
each test would be the same, but we need to make sure that we are testing our code under
multiple different circumstances.

To show how extensible the Jasmine testing library is, *J P Castro* wrote a very short, but powerful utility to provide data-driven tests within Jasmine. His blog on this topic can be found at `http://blog.jphpsf.com/2012/08/30/drying-up-your-javascript-jasmine-tests/`, and the GitHub repository can be found at `https://github.com/jphpsf/jasmine-data-provider`. This simple extension allows us to write intuitive Jasmine tests that take a parameter as part of each test, as follows:

```
describe("data driven tests", () => {
    using("valid values", [
        "first string",
        "second_string",
        "!!string!!"
    ], (value) => {
        it(`${value} should contain 'string'`, () => {
            expect(value).toContain("string");
        });
    });
});
```

Note here the use of the `using` function within a `describe`. This `using` function is what allows us to call our test multiple times, with each invocation of the test using the next value of our array. The `using` function takes three parameters—a string description of the value set, an array of values, and a function definition—which is then calling our test itself.

So, our test in this example will be invoked three times, the first time with the `"first string"` value, the second time with the `"second_string"` value, and the third time with the `"!!string!!"` value. Note also in the call to `it`, that we are also changing the test name on the fly, to include the `value` parameter that is passed in. This is necessary in order for each test to have a unique test name.

The implementation of this using the function in JP Castro's blog was written in JavaScript, but we can easily replicate this simple function in TypeScript as follows:

```
export function using<T>
    (name: string, values: T[], func: Function) {
    for (var i = 0, count = values.length; i < count; i++) {
        func.apply(Object, [values[i]]);
    }
}
```

Here, we are using generic syntax to define a function named `using` that is declared with a type of `T`. It has three parameters. The first parameter is a `string`, which is the `name` of the dataset. The second parameter is an array of `values` of type `T`. Using generic syntax for this parameter means that we have restricted all elements in the array to be of the same type. This means that we cannot mix numbers and strings in our array, for example. The third parameter is a `Function`, which will contain the test itself.

Within this function, we are simply looping through all of the items in the array and calling the `apply` function on the callback that was passed in as the `func` argument. The `apply` function will call a function with a given `this` value, and the arguments for the function specified as an array. Note that we are using `Object` as the first argument to the `apply` function. This means that the original value of `this` will be used when calling the function itself. In effect, this will call whatever function we passed in (which happens to be our test) repeatedly, once for each value in the array, and with the correct `this` value.

So, with a little creative code, we have implemented the ability for Jasmine to call tests with a data-driven array of values. The output of this test is as follows:

```
λ Cmder                                                    —   □   ×

E:\temp\jasmine_tests  (jasmine_tests@1.0.0)
λ jasmine
Randomized with seed 77927
Started
TAP version 13
.ok 1 - data driven tests : !!string!! should contain 'string'
.ok 2 - data driven tests : second_string should contain 'string'
.ok 3 - data driven tests : first string should contain 'string'


3 specs, 0 failures
Finished in 0.018 seconds
Randomized with seed 77927 (jasmine --random=true --seed=77927)
1..3
# 3 specs, 0 failures, 0 skipped, 0 disabled in 0.018s.
# NOTE: disabled specs are usually a result of xdescribe.

E:\temp\jasmine_tests  (jasmine_tests@1.0.0)
λ

λ cmd.exe                              Search  🔍 ⊞ ▾ ▢ ▾ 🔒 ▢ ≡
```

Here, we can see that our test was run three times, once for each of the values that we used in our array.

Using spies

Jasmine also has a very powerful feature that allows your tests to see whether a particular function was called, and also to determine the actual parameters it was called with. This is known as **spying** on a function. When we create a spy, we are temporarily hijacking the function call, and overriding it with a Jasmine `spy` function. Let's take a look at a `simple` spy, as follows:

```
class MySpiedClass {
    testFunction(arg1: string) {
        console.log(arg1);
    }
}
describe("simple spy", () => {
    it("should spyOn a function call", () => {
        let classInstance = new MySpiedClass();
        let testFunctionSpy
            = spyOn(classInstance, 'testFunction');

        classInstance.testFunction("test");
        expect(testFunctionSpy).toHaveBeenCalled();
    });
});
```

We start with a class named `MySpiedClass`, which has a single function named `testFunction`. This function takes a single argument and logs the argument to the console.

Our test starts by creating a new instance of `MySpiedClass`, which is assigned to a variable named `classInstance`. We then create a Jasmine spy named `testFunctionSpy`, by calling the Jasmine `spyOn` function. This `spyOn` function takes two arguments—the class instance itself, and the name of the function to spy on. In this test, the class instance is named `classInstance`, and the function we wish to spy on is named `testFunction`. Once we have a spy created, we can call the function and set an expectation on whether the function was called. This is the essence of a spy. Jasmine will watch the `testFunction` function of the instance of `MySpiedClass` to see whether or not it was called.

Jasmine spies, by default, block the call to the underlying function. In other words, they replace the function you are trying to call with a Jasmine delegate. This is part of the hijacking process we mentioned earlier. If you need to spy on a function, but also need the body of the function to still execute, you must specify this behavior using the `.and.callThrough()` fluent syntax.

While this is a very trivial example, spies become very powerful in a number of different testing scenarios. We can call the method of a class and test that each function call that that class makes is executed correctly. Spies can also be used to return data, which is very handy when using classes that make calls to REST endpoints. When we run a unit test, we can mock up the actual call to the REST endpoint, so that it never gets called during test execution.

Spying on callback functions

Let's see how we can use a spy to test whether a callback function was invoked correctly. Consider the following TypeScript code:

```
class CallbackClass {
    doCallback(id: number, callback: (result: string) => void ) {
        let callbackValue = "id:" + id.toString();
        callback(callbackValue);
    }
}

class DoCallback {
    logValue(value: string) {
        console.log(value);
    }
}
```

Firstly, we define a class named `CallbackClass` that has a single function, `doCallback`. This `doCallback` function takes an `id` argument, of type `number`, and also a `callback` function. The `callback` function must take a `string` as an argument and return `void`.

The second class that we have defined, named `DoCallBack`, has a single function, named `logValue`. This function signature matches the callback function signature required on the `doCallback` function we defined earlier. Using Jasmine spies, we are now able to test the logic of the `doCallback` function of the `CallbackClass`.

This function must create a string based on the `id` argument that was passed in and then invoke the `callback` function. Our tests must therefore accomplish two things. Firstly, we need to ensure that the string generated within the `doCallback` function is formatted correctly, and secondly, we need to ensure that our callback function was indeed invoked with the correct parameters. Our Jasmine test for this functionality is as follows:

```
describe("using callback spies", () => {
    it("should execute callback with the correct string value",
        () => {
        let doCallback = new DoCallBack();
        let classUnderTest = new CallbackClass();

        let callbackSpy = spyOn(doCallback, 'logValue');
        classUnderTest.doCallBack(1, doCallback.logValue);

        expect(callbackSpy).toHaveBeenCalled();
        expect(callbackSpy).toHaveBeenCalledWith("id:1");

    });
});
```

This test code firstly creates an instance of the `CallbackClass` class, and also an instance of the `DoCallback` class. We then create a spy on the `logValue` function of the `DoCallback` class. Remember that the `logValue` function is passed into the `doCallBack` function as the callback function parameter, and will be invoked with the formatted string.

Our `expect` statements on the last two lines verify that this callback chain has indeed been executed correctly. The first `expect` statement simply checks that the `logValue` function was invoked, and the second `expect` statement checks that it was called with the correct parameters. So, we have tested the internal implementation of the `CallbackClass` and the `doCallback` function, checking that it formats the string properly, and also checking that the callback function itself was invoked.

Using spies as fakes

Another benefit of Jasmine spies is that they can act as fakes. In other words, instead of calling a real function, the call is temporarily overridden to call a fake function. These fake functions can also return values—which can be very useful for generating small mocking frameworks. Consider the following test:

```
class ClassToFake {
    getValue() : number {
        return 2;
```

```
        }
    }
describe("using fakes", () => {
    it("calls fake instead of real function", () => {
        let classToFake = new ClassToFake();
        spyOn(classToFake, 'getValue').and.callFake ( () => {
            return 5;
        });
        expect(classToFake.getValue()).toBe(5);
    });
});
```

We start with a class named `ClassToFake`, which has a single function, `getValue`, which returns 2. Our test then creates an instance of this class. We then call the Jasmine `spyOn` function to create a spy on the `getValue` function, and then use the `.and.callFake` syntax to attach an anonymous function as a fake function. This fake function will return 5 instead of the original `getValue` function that would have returned 2. The test then checks to see whether the call to the `getValue` function on the `ClassToFake` instance will return 5. In this test, Jasmine will substitute our new fake function for the original `getValue` function, and therefore return 5 instead of 2.

There are a number of variants of the Jasmine fake syntax, including methods to throw errors, or return values—again, consult the Jasmine documentation for a full list of its faking capabilities.

Asynchronous tests

The asynchronous nature of JavaScript—made popular by AJAX and jQuery—has always been one of the draw-cards of the language, and is the principal architecture behind Node-based applications. Let's take a quick look at an asynchronous class, and then describe how we should go about testing it. Consider the following TypeScript code:

```
class MockAsyncClass {
    executeSlowFunction(success: (value: string) => void) {
        setTimeout(() => {
            success("success");
        }, 1000);
    }
}
```

This `MockAsyncClass` has a single function, named `executeSlowFunction`, which takes a function callback named `success`. Within the `executeSlowFunction` code, we are simulating an asynchronous call with the `setTimeout` function, and only calling the success callback after `1000` milliseconds (1 second). This function is therefore simulating an asynchronous function, as it will only execute the callback after a full second.

Our test for this `executeSlowFunction` may appear as follows:

```
describe("asynchronous tests", () => {
    it("failing test", () => {

        let mockAsync = new MockAsyncClass();
        let returnedValue!: string;
        console.log(`1. calling executeSlowFunction`);
        mockAsync.executeSlowFunction((value: string) => {
            console.log(`2. executeSlowFunction returned`);
            returnedValue = value;
        });
        console.log(`3. checking returnedValue`);
        expect(returnedValue).toEqual("success");
    });

});
```

Firstly, we instantiate an instance of the `MockAsyncClass`, as well as a variable named `returnedValue`. Note how we need to use the definite assignment operator here (`!`) to allow the code to compile correctly. We then call `executeSlowFunction` with an anonymous function for the `success` parameter. This anonymous function sets the value of `returnedValue` to whatever was passed in from the `MockAsyncClass`. Our expectation is that the `returnedValue` should equal `"success"`, but, if we run this test now, our test will fail with the following error message:

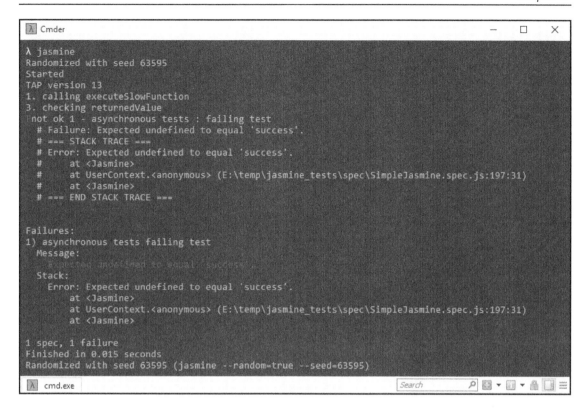

What is happening here, is that because `executeSlowFunction` is asynchronous, JavaScript will not wait until the callback function is called before executing the next line of code. This can be verified through the use of our console logging statements. Our test execution flow is expected to follow 1, then 2, then 3. If we check the console output of this test, we can see the following:

1. **`calling executeSlowFunction`**
3. **`checking returnedValue`**

This means that the expectation (at 3) is being called before `executeSlowFunction` has had a chance to call our anonymous callback function (setting the value of `returnedValue`). In fact, the entire test has completed before the `executeSlowFunction` has even had a chance to log anything to the console.

Using done()

Jasmine uses a function named done to help us with these sorts of asynchronous tests. In any beforeEach, afterEach, or it function, we pass an argument named done (which is a function), and then invoke it at the end of our asynchronous code. Let's rewrite our previous test for executeSlowFunction, as follows:

```
describe("asynch tests with done", () => {
    let returnedValue!: string;

    beforeEach((done) => {
        returnedValue = "no_return_value";
        let mockAsync = new MockAsyncClass();
        console.log(`1. calling executeSlowFunction`);
        mockAsync.executeSlowFunction((value: string) => {
            console.log(`2. executeSlowFunction returned`);
            returnedValue = value;
            done();
        });
    });

    it("should return success after 1 second", (done) => {
        console.log(`3. checking returnedValue`);
        expect(returnedValue).toEqual("success");
        done();
    });
});
```

In this version of our asynchronous test, we have moved the returnedValue variable outside of our test, and have included a beforeEach function to run before our actual test. This beforeEach function firstly resets the value of returnValue, and then sets up the MockAsyncClass instance. Finally, it calls the executeSlowFunction on this instance.

Note how the beforeEach function takes a parameter named done, and then calls done() after the returnedValue = value line has been called. Notice too, that the second parameter to the it function also now takes a done parameter, and calls done() when the test is finished.

If we execute this test now, we will see the following:

Here, we can see that the order of the console logs is, indeed, in the correct order, as follows:

1. `calling executeSlowFunction`
2. `executeSlowFunction returned`
3. `checking returnedValue`

So, what have we accomplished here? We have modified our original test and split it into two halves. The first half is the `beforeEach` function, which invokes our `executeSlowFunction`, storing the return value in the `returnValue` variable. Our actual test, therefore, is waiting for the `done()` function to execute, and then runs the remainder of the test. This test structure means that we are invoking our asynchronous function, and only executing our test and expectations once the asynchronous function has been executed.

From the Jasmine documentation:

"The spec will not start until the done *function is called in the call to* beforeEach, *and this spec will not complete until its* done *function is called. By default, Jasmine will wait for five seconds before causing a timeout failure. This can be overridden using the* jasmine.DEFAULT_TIMEOUT_INTERVAL *variable."*

Using async await

If the asynchronous function that we are testing is using promises, then we can easily include the async await syntax to run asynchronous tests. As an example, let's build a class that uses a promise to return a value, as follows:

```
class MockAsyncWithPromiseClass {
    delayedPromise(): Promise<string> {
        return new Promise<string>
            ((resolve: (str: string) => void,
                reject: (str: string) => void
            ) => {
                function afterTimeout() {
                    console.log(`2. resolving promise`);
                    resolve('success');
                }
                setTimeout(afterTimeout, 1000);
            });
    }
}
```

Here, we have a class named MockAsyncWithPromiseClass that has a single function named delayedPromise, which returns a promise of type string. Within this function, we set up an anonymous function named afterTimeout, which will resolve the promise with the 'success' value. We then call this internal anonymous function after 1 second. As with our earlier asynchronous functions, this means that the promise will only be fulfilled after 1 second. Our unit test can now use the async, await keywords as follows:

```
describe("async test with async keyword", () => {
    it("should wait for async to return with value ", async () => {
        let mockAsyncWithPromise = new MockAsyncWithPromiseClass();
        let returnedValue!: string;
        console.log(`1. calling delayedPromise`);
        returnedValue = await mockAsyncWithPromise.delayedPromise();
        console.log(`3. checking returnedValue`);
        expect(returnedValue).toEqual("success");
    });
```

```
    });
```

Here, we have a test named `"it should wait for async to return"`. Note how we have included the `async` keyword after the test description. This allows us to use the `await` keyword within this test function.

Our test starts by creating an instance of `MockAsyncWithPromiseClass`. We then call the `delayedPromise` function using the `await` keyword, and assign the result to the variable named `returnedValue`. Note that we have a couple of console logs to show the order of execution of the functions within this test. Running this test will show that using the `await` keyword with a function that returns a promise behaves as expected:

1. **calling delayedPromise**
2. **resolving promise**
3. **checking returnedValue**

HTML-based tests

The tests we have been running up until this stage have all been rather simple, and do not need to have an HTML page, or an active DOM. As soon as we start to run tests that require a DOM, we will need to inject our tests into a running browser in order for them to run correctly. Jasmine can easily be run in a browser by setting up an HTML page for running tests. Typically, this file will be named `SpecRunner.html`, as follows:

```html
<html>
<head>
    <link rel="stylesheet" type="text/css"
        href="node_modules/jasmine-core/lib/jasmine-core/jasmine.css">
    <script type="text/javascript"
        src="node_modules/jquery/dist/jquery.js"></script>
    <script type="text/javascript"
        src="node_modules/jasmine-core/lib/jasmine-core/jasmine.js">
    </script>
    <script type="text/javascript"
        src="node_modules/jasmine-core/lib/jasmine-core/jasmine-html.js">
    </script>
    <script type="text/javascript"
        src="node_modules/jasmine-core/lib/jasmine-core/boot.js">
    </script>
    <script type="text/javascript"
        src="node_modules/jasmine-jquery/lib/jasmine-jquery.js">
    </script>
    <script type="text/javascript"
        src="html_spec/HtmlTests.spec.js"></script>
```

```
</head>
<body>
</body>
</html>
```

This is a simple HTML page that includes a number of JavaScript source files. Jasmine exposes three of these files upon installation, which are `jasmine.js`, `jasmine-html.js`, and `boot.js`. Note that these files must be included in this exact order, otherwise the page will fail to load correctly. The other files that are included are `jquery.js` and `jasmine-jquery.js`. These files are not part of the standard Jasmine install, and will therefore need to be installed through `npm` as follows:

```
npm install jquery jasmine-jquery --save-dev
```

The final file that we are including is `html_spec/HtmlTests.spec.js`, which is the result of the compilation of our `.ts` file, and contains our tests themselves. We can create this file and insert a simple test just to see that things are working correctly, as follows:

```
describe("simple HTML test", () => {
    it("should pass", () => {
        expect(true).toBeTruthy();
    });
});
```

With this test in place, we can open up our `SpecRunner.html` file, and see that Jasmine is running our tests in the browser as follows:

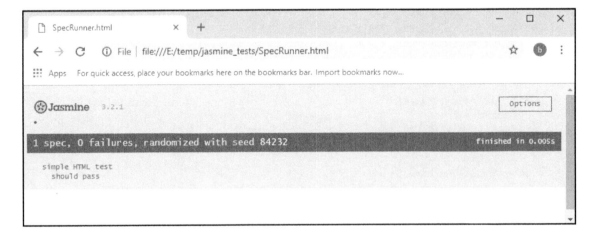

Jasmine fixtures

On many occasions, our code is responsible for either reading in, or, in most cases, manipulating DOM elements from JavaScript. This means that any running code that relies on a DOM element could fail if the underlying HTML does not contain the correct element, or group of elements. In order to test functions that modify the DOM in any way, we will need to provide either a copy of, or the real DOM elements in order for our tests to pass.

One of the extension libraries for Jasmine, named jasmine-jquery, allows us to do exactly this. The jasmine-jquery library lets us inject HTML elements into the DOM before our tests execute, and will then automatically remove them from the DOM after the test is run. This is why we included this library within our SpecRunner.html file.

Let's take a look at an example of a class that modifies a DOM element, as follows:

```
class ModifyDomElement {
    setHtml() {
        let elem = $('#my_div');
        elem.html('<p>Hello World</p>');
    }
}
```

This ModifyDomElement class has a single function, named setHtml, that is using jQuery to find a DOM element with the ID of my_div. The HTML of this div is then set to a simple "Hello World" paragraph. Obviously, this class requires the existence of a DOM element named my_div in order to function correctly. Let's now take a look at how we can use the setFixtures function from the jasmine-jquery library within a test to set up this DOM element, as follows:

```
describe("fixture tests", () => {
    it("should modify a dom element", () => {
        setFixtures('<div id="my_div"></div>');
        let modifyDom = new ModifyDomElement();
        modifyDom.setHtml();
        var modifiedDomElement = $('#my_div');
        expect(modifiedDomElement.length).toBeGreaterThan(0);
        expect(modifiedDomElement.html()).toContain("Hello");
    });
});
```

The test starts by calling the jasmine-jquery function, setFixtures. This function will inject the HTML provided as a string parameter directly into the DOM for the duration of the test. The test then creates an instance of the ModifyDomElement class, and calls the setHtml function, which will modify the my_div element.

The remainder of the test uses the jQuery $ function to find a DOM element with an ID of my_div, and stores this in the variable named modifiedElement. The modifiedElement variable is then passed onto our two expectations. Note that the first expect statement tests to see if the length property of the modifiedDomElement variable is > 0. This is the easiest way of figuring out whether the element was in fact found in the DOM. If it was found, we then check the internal HTML of the element, to ensure that it contains the string "Hello".

The fixture methods provided by jasmine-jquery also allow for loading raw HTML files off disk, instead of having to write out lengthy string representations of HTML. This is also particularly useful if your MV* framework uses HTML file snippets. In addition, jasmine-jquery also has utilities for loading JSON from disk and purpose-built matchers that work with jQuery. Be sure to check out the documentation at https://github.com/velesin/jasmine-jquery.

DOM events

There will be times when the code you are writing must respond to DOM events, such as onclick or onselect. Luckily, writing tests that need these DOM events can also be simulated by using jQuery, jasmine-jquery, and spies as follows:

```
describe("click event tests", () => {
    it("should trigger an onclick DOM event", () =>{
        setFixtures(`
            <script>
            function handle_my_click_div_clicked() {
                // do nothing at this time
            }
            </script>
            <div id='my_click_div'
            onclick='handle_my_click_div_clicked()'>Click Here</div>`);
        var clickEventSpy = spyOnEvent('#my_click_div', 'click');
        $('#my_click_div').click();
        expect(clickEventSpy).toHaveBeenTriggered();
    });
});
```

This test is again calling the `setFixtures` function from the `jasmine-jquery` library. This `setFixtures` function is doing two things. Firstly, it is defining a function within a `<script>` tag named `handle_my_click_div_clicked`. Secondly, it is defining a `<div>` with an ID of `my_click_div`, and then attaching the DOM event of `onclick` to call the `handle_my_click_div_clicked()` function. This single function call is therefore setting up all of the required HTML for the `onclick` event. Without this `<script>` tag, running our tests will produce an error:

```
ReferenceError: handle_my_click_div_clicked is not defined
```

Our test then sets up a Jasmine spy named `clickEventSpy`. This spy uses the `jasmine-jquery` function named `spyOnEvent`, which takes two parameters—a jQuery selector for the element to spy on, and a DOM event name.

We then use jQuery to trigger the event by calling `$('#my_click_div').click()`. Remember that the default behavior of a spy is to hijack the function definition and call our spy instead. The last line of this test is our expectation, where we are expecting the spy to have been triggered. The `toHaveBeenTriggered` function is a Jasmine matcher that is provided by the `jasmine-jquery` library.

 jQuery and DOM manipulation provide us with a way of filling in forms, clicking on the **submit**, **cancel**, and **ok** buttons, and generally simulating user interaction with our application. We can easily write full acceptance or user acceptance tests within Jasmine using these techniques—further solidifying our application against errors and change.

Jasmine runners

Firing up a web page in order to run our tests every time we make a change to one of our tests can quickly become labor-intensive and error-prone. We have already explored the use of Grunt in our build tools in order to detect file changes and automatically recompile our TypeScript files when a file is saved. In this section, we will explore a few test runners that will detect changes to our test suite and automatically rerun our tests without intervention. Using test runners gives us instant feedback on the status of all tests as we are writing our code and saving changes.

Testem

Testem is a Node-based test runner. It is run from the command line and opens up a simple interface to view test results. Testem will automatically detect changes to JavaScript files and execute tests on the fly, providing instant feedback during the unit testing phase. Testem also has a very handy feature that allows multiple browsers to connect to the same testem instance. This allows us to connect an instance of Chrome, Firefox, IE, Opera, Safari, QupZilla, or pretty much any type of browser to the same testem runner. Testem will rerun our tests in each and every browser and present a summary view as follows:

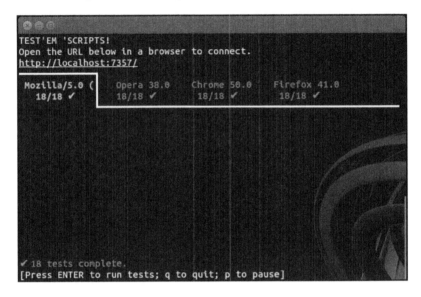

Testem also has a continuous integration setting that can be used on build servers. More info can be found at the GitHub repository (`https://github.com/airportyh/testem`).

Testem can be installed through Node with the following command (Note that you may need to prefix it with `sudo` on a Linux-based system.):

```
npm install -g testem
```

Testem, by default, will try to load any JavaScript files in the current directory, parse them for any tests, and then run them when a browser is connected. Testem therefore creates a simple HTML page in memory, and serves this page to our browsers. We will need to configure testem by creating a simple `testem.json` file in our `test` directory as follows:

```
{
    "framework": "jasmine2",
    "src_files": [
```

```
        "node_modules/jquery/dist/jquery.js",
        "node_modules/jasmine-jquery/lib/jasmine-jquery.js",
        "html_spec/HtmlTests.spec.js"
    ]
}
```

This file is a simple JSON format file that specifies two properties, `framework` and `src_files`. The `framework` property indicates that we are using `"jasmine2"` as our test framework, and the `source_files` property includes some extra JavaScript files that are needed for our tests, along with the `html_spec/HtmlTests.spec.js` file itself. With this `testem.json` file in place, we are able to run our test suite. Note that even though we are specifying `jasmine2` as our framework, we are able to use Jasmine 3.0 and higher.

Testem has a number of powerful configuration options that can be specified in the configuration file. Be sure to head over to the GitHub repository for more information.

Note that testem is a good choice for unit testing, but is not a good choice for integration or acceptance testing. The nature of the framework means that Testem builds an HTML page on the fly based on our configuration file. During integration testing, we generally want HTML pages to be created by a web server.

Karma

Karma is a test runner built by the AngularJs team, and features heavily in the Angular tutorials. It is a unit-testing framework only, and the AngularJs team recommends end-to-end or integration tests to be built and run through Protractor. Karma, like Testem, runs its own instance of a web server in order to serve pages and artifacts required by the test suite, and it has a large set of configuration options. It can also be used for unit tests that do not target Angular. To install Karma to work with Jasmine, we will need to install a few packages using `npm`:

```
npm install -g karma-cli
npm install karma --save-dev
npm install karma-jasmine --save-dev
npm install karma-chrome-launcher --save-dev
npm install karma-jasmine-jquery --save-dev
npm install karma-jquery --save-dev
```

To run Karma, we will need a configuration file. We can generate a standard `karma.conf.js` file by running the following on the command line:

```
karma init
```

This will ask a few questions about the frameworks that we are using. Go ahead and accept the defaults at this stage. Once a default `karma.conf.js` file has been created, we can modify it slightly so that it will run our existing tests.

Firstly, we will need to modify the `frameworks` option, as follows:

```
frameworks: ['jquery-3.3.1', 'jasmine-jquery', 'jasmine'],
```

Here, we have included `jquery-3.3.1` and `jasmine-jquery` in the frameworks option, so that we can use `jasmine-jquery` within Karma. We will also need to add a `plugins` option as follows:

```
plugins: [
    require('karma-jasmine'),
    require('karma-chrome-launcher'),
    require('karma-jasmine-jquery'),
    require('karma-jquery'),
    require('karma-spec-reporter')
],
```

Here, we have told Karma that it needs to load a set of modules that we will need in our tests. The `karma-jasmine`, `karma-jasmine-jquery`, and `karma-jquery` modules will set up our environment to be able to use jQuery and `jasmine-jquery`. The `karma-chrome-launcher` module is used to launch an instance of Chrome when running our tests. Note that we have also included a `karma-spec-reporter`, which is a Jasmine reporter to give us better information on the command line.

The final change we need to make is to tell Karma where to find our test files, as follows:

```
files: [
    'html_spec/**/*spec.js'
],
```

Here, we have specified that Karma should look in the `html_spec` directory, and include any file that ends with `spec.js`.

With these modifications to the configuration file, we can start Karma by simply typing:

```
karma start <path to karma.config.js>
```

This will start Karma, which will automatically start an instance of Chrome for us, and run all of our tests. Note that Karma will continue running in the background, and as soon as modifications are found in any of the test files, it will rerun all of our tests, as shown in the following image:

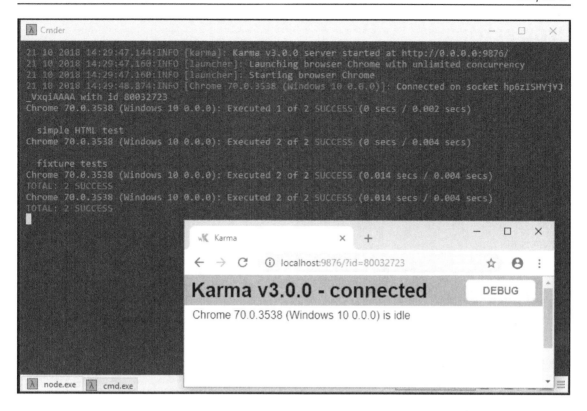

Headless testing

When running unit tests in a continuous integration environment, we may need to run our tests with a headless browser. A headless browser does not open up a new window that we can interact with, and in fact, does not have a GUI at all. This makes it a good choice for build servers that do not have a UI installed. The browser of choice for headless testing used to be PhantomJs, which offered an ES5-compatible browser. Unfortunately, the PhantomJs project has been suspended, due to lack of active contribution. Chrome, however, has an option to run headless, which therefore gives us a full working version of Chrome that we can run on build servers. To run a Karma suite with Chrome in headless mode, simply modify the `browsers` property of the `karma.config.js` file, as follows:

```
browsers: ['ChromeHeadless'],
```

This simple setting is all that we need to run Chrome in a headless configuration.

Protractor

Protractor is a node-based test runner that tackles end-to-end, or automated acceptance testing. Unlike Testem and Karma, which create a web page for unit testing purposes, Protractor is used to programmatically control a web browser. Just like manual testing, Protractor has the ability to browse to a specific page, and then interact with the page from JavaScript. As a simple example, suppose that your website has a login page, and all further functionality requires a valid login. Using Protractor, we can start each test by browsing to the login page, entering valid credentials, and then continue to browse to each page that is part of our test suite.

Using Protractor, we can also check metadata properties within the HTML page—such as the page title—or we can fill in forms and click on buttons. Protractor can be installed with npm as follows:

```
npm install -g protractor
```

We will get to running Protractor a little later, but first, let's discuss the engine that Protractor uses under the hood to drive the browser.

Using Selenium

Selenium is a driver for web browsers. It allows the programmatic remote control of web browsers, and can be used to create automated tests in Java, C#, Python, Ruby, PHP, Perl, and even JavaScript. Protractor uses selenium under the covers to control web browser instances. To install the Selenium Server for use with Protractor, run the following command:

```
webdriver-manager update
```

To start the Selenium Server, run the following command:

```
webdriver-manager start
```

If all goes well, Selenium will report that the server has started, and will detail the address of the Selenium Server. Check your output for a line similar to the following:

```
RemoteWebDriver instances should connect to: http://127.0.0.1:4444/wd/hub
```

Note that you will need Java to be installed on your machine, as the web driver-manager uses Java to start the Selenium Server.

Once the server is running, we will need a configuration file for Protractor (similar to Karma), that, by convention, is named `protractor.conf.js`. The contents of this file are as follows:

```
exports.config = {
    seleniumAddress: 'http://localhost:4444/wd/hub',
    specs: ['protractor_tests/*.js']
}
```

Here, we are simply assigning some properties to the `exports.config` object. The first property that we are setting is `seleniumAddress`, which is the instance of the Selenium Server, as we saw earlier. The second property, named `specs`, is the list of tests to run. This `specs` property therefore looks for any `.js` files in the `protractor_tests` directory.

Now for the simplest of tests:

```
describe("simple protractor test", () => {
    it("should navigate to google and find a title", () => {
        browser.driver.get('http://www.google.com');
        expect(browser.driver.getTitle()).toContain("Google");
    });
});
```

Our test starts by opening the page at `'http://www.google.com'`. It then expects to see that the title of the page is set to `'Google'`. We can now run Protractor to execute this test, as follows:

```
protractor
```

If you keep an eye on your screen, you will see Protractor starting a new instance of a Chrome browser session, and then navigate to the Google home page.

It will then execute the expectation. Our command-line output is as follows:

Finding page elements

Selenium has a number of functions that we can use in order to find HTML elements on a page during testing. We can search for an element using its `id` property, or we can use a CSS selector, or `xpath`. As an example of this, consider the following test:

```
it('should search for the term TypeScript', async () => {
    browser.driver.get("https://www.google.com");

    await browser.driver.findElement(
        By.id("lst-ib")).sendKeys("TypeScript");
    await browser.driver.findElement(
        By.xpath('//*[@id="lst-ib"]')).sendKeys(Key.ENTER);

    browser.sleep(5000);

});
```

Here, we have written a test that browses to `www.google.com`, and then using the Selenium function named `findElement`. The first call to `findElement` uses the Selenium static function named `By.id`, which takes a single string argument. This will query the DOM and find an element with a matching `id` attribute. Once we have found this element, we can simulate entering data by using the `sendKeys` function, which has the effect of typing the word `"TypeScript"` into the search box on the Google home page.

We can also query DOM elements using `xpath`. The second call to `findElement` in our test uses the `By.xpath` function to query using an `xpath` matcher. Note that in this test, the `By.id` query and the `By.xpath` query will find the same element, which is the search input box. We can also simulate hitting the *Enter* key, or the *Tab* key by using the in-built enums for special keys, which in this case is `Key.ENTER`.

The final call in our test is for the browser to sleep for 5 seconds. There are a number of functions that we can use with Selenium, including moving the mouse, clicking on **Elements**, or pausing the browser for debugging purposes.

We can easily use the Chrome developer tools to find the correct elements to use in our Selenium tests, either by ID, by css or by `xpath`. If we open the developer tools using *F12*, and then right-click on the particular element we are interested in, we can select the **Inspect** menu option to open the developer tools and show the DOM tree. If we then right-click on a particular element in the DOM tree, we can use the **Copy** menu item, and then the **Copy selector** menu item to copy the css selector to the clipboard.

In a similar fashion, we can also copy the `xpath` selector to the clipboard, as shown in the following screenshot:

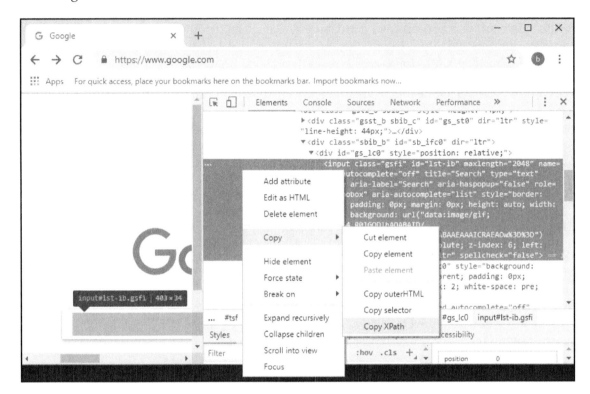

Chrome even allows us to search the DOM tree using an `xpath` or css selector. If we navigate to the **Console** tab, we can search through an `xpath` selector by typing in the following:

```
$x(" ... xpath selector goes here")
```

Or, we can search by css selector by typing:

```
$(" ... css selector goes here")
```

These tools are invaluable when it comes to finding elements on our pages when we are building Selenium test suites.

Using continuous integration

When writing unit tests for any application, it quickly becomes important to set up a build server and run your tests as part of each source control check in. When your development team grows beyond a single developer, using a continuous integration build server becomes imperative. This build server will ensure that any code committed to the source control server passes all known unit tests, integration tests, and automated acceptance tests. The build server is also responsible for labeling a build, and generating any deployment artifacts that need to be used during deployment. The basic steps of a build server are as follows:

- Check out the latest version of the source code, and increase the build number
- Compile the application on the build server
- Run any server-side unit tests
- Package the application for deployment
- Deploy the package to a build environment
- Run any server-side integration tests
- Run any JavaScript unit, integration, or acceptance tests
- Mark the change set and build number as passed or failed
- If the build failed, notify those responsible for breaking it

 The build server should fail if any one of the preceding steps fails.

Benefits of CI

Using a build server to run through the preceding steps brings huge benefits to any development team. Firstly, the application is compiled on the build server—which means that any tools or external libraries will need to be installed on the build server. This gives your development team the opportunity to document exactly what software needs to be installed on a new machine in order to compile or run your application.

Secondly, a standard set of server-side unit tests can be run before the packaging step is attempted. In a Visual Studio project, these would be C# unit tests built with any of the popular .NET testing frameworks—MsTest, nUnit, or xUnit.

Next, the entire application's packaging step is run. Let's assume for a moment that a developer has included a new JavaScript library within the project, but forgotten to add it to source control. In this case, all of the tests will run on their local computer, but will break the build because of a missing library file. If we were to deploy the site at this stage, running the application would result in **404 errors – file not found**. By running a packaging step, these sorts of errors are quickly found.

Once a successful packaging step has been completed, the build server should deploy the site to a specially marked build environment. This build environment is only used for CI builds, and must therefore have its own database instances, web service references, and so on, set up specifically for CI builds. Again, actually doing a deployment to a target environment tests the deployment artifacts, as well as the deployment process. By setting up a build environment for automated package deployment, your team is again able to document the requirements and process for deployment.

At this stage, we have a full instance of our website up and running on an isolated build environment. We can then easily target specific web pages that will run our JavaScript tests, and also run integration or automated acceptance tests—directly on the full version of the website. In this way, we can write tests that target the real life website REST services, without having to mock up these integration points. So, in effect, we are testing the application from the ground up. Obviously, we may need to ensure that our build environment has a specific set of data that can be used for integration testing, or a way of generating the required datasets that our integration tests will need.

Selecting a build server

There are a number of continuous integration build servers out there, including TeamCity, Jenkins, and **Team Foundation Server (TFS)**.

Team Foundation Server

TFS is a Microsoft product that will require a license for the server component, as well as a per-developer license. TFS needs a specific configuration on its build agents to be able to run instances of a web browser, as this is disabled by default. It also uses Windows Workflow Foundation to configure build steps, which takes a fair amount of experience and knowledge to modify.

Jenkins

Jenkins is an open-source, free to use CI build server. It has wide community usage and many plugins. Installation and configuration of Jenkins is fairly straightforward, and Jenkins allows processes to run browser instances, making it compatible with browser-based JavaScript unit tests. Jenkins build steps are command line-based, and it sometimes takes a little nous to configure build steps correctly.

TeamCity

A very popular and very powerful build server that is free to set up is TeamCity. TeamCity allows for free installation if you have a small number of developers (< 20), and a small number of projects (< 20). A full commercial license is only around $1,500.00, which makes it affordable for most organizations. Configuring build steps in TeamCity is much easier than in Jenkins or TFS, as it uses a Wizard-style of configuration depending on the type of build step you are creating. TeamCity also has a rich set of functionality around unit tests, with the ability to show graphs per unit test, and is therefore considered best of breed for build servers.

Integration test reporting

We have seen how to create and run tests using Jasmine, Testem, Karma, and Protractor. Each of our samples have successfully reported the number of tests executed, and the success or failure of the test suite. We have used simple configuration files and simple HTML files to set up and execute our tests.

In a real-world application, however, it is often necessary to run server-side logic or use server-side HTML rendering. For instance, most applications will require some sort of authentication, or login, before allowing calls to custom REST endpoints through JavaScript. Unfortunately, calling any of these REST endpoints from a normal HTML page will return **401** (unauthorized) errors. For cases like these, we should run our tests against the full website.

Each of the CI servers that we have mentioned so far have their own way of capturing and reporting the results of an automated test run. For TeamCity environments, for example, the output of a test run needs to follow the TeamCity requirements for test reporting. Luckily, the jasmine-reporters package that we discussed earlier already has support for most CI build servers.

We can set up our Protractor configuration file to use a Jasmine reporter, as follows:

```
exports.config = {
    seleniumAddress: 'http://localhost:4444/wd/hub',
    specs: ['protractor_tests/*.js'],
    onPrepare: function() {
        var jasmineReporters = require('jasmine-reporters');
        jasmine.getEnv().addReporter(
            new jasmineReporters.TeamCityReporter());
    }
}
```

Here, we have included an `onPrepare` property in our configuration settings, in order to run an anonymous function. This function simply creates a variable named `jasmineReporters` through a call to `require`, and then adds a new `TeamCityReporter` to the Jasmine runtime environment. The `require` function call is part of a module-loading mechanism that we will cover in a later chapter.

Running our tests with Protractor will now output messages to the command line that TeamCity understands, as follows:

Summary

In this chapter, we have explored test-driven development from the ground up. We have discussed the theory of TDD, explored the differences between unit, integration, and acceptance tests, and had a look at what a continuous integration build server process looks like. We then explored Jasmine as a testing framework, learned how to write tests, used expectations and matchers, and also explored Jasmine extensions to help with data-driven tests and DOM tests through fixtures. Finally, we had a look at test runners, discussed where and when they are best used, and used Protractor to drive web pages through Selenium and report the results back to a build server.

In the next chapter, we will explore how to create tests for our TypeScript compatible frameworks: Backbone, Aurelia, Angular, and React.

Testing Typescript Compatible Frameworks

9

In Chapter 7, *TypeScript Compatible Frameworks*, we discussed TypeScript compatible frameworks, and explored how Backbone, Aurelia, Angular, and React use the MVC or the MV* design patterns to write models, views, and controllers. We implemented the same sample application in each of these frameworks, in order to be able to compare the similarities between them, and note the subtle differences. Then, in our last chapter, we started exploring test-driven development, and discussed the use of Jasmine as a test framework. We also explored using various test runners, including Testem and Karma, and finally explored Protractor for running integration, or end-to-end, tests.

In this chapter, we will essentially be combining our work from the previous two chapters, and will be discussing how to unit and integration test each of our TypeScript compatible frameworks. For each of these frameworks, then, we will cover the following topics:

- The setup of a unit-testing framework
- Writing basic unit tests
- Checking the DOM for rendered elements
- Checking initial form values
- Modifying form values
- Submitting forms

Testing our sample application

You will recall that our sample application had the following features:

- Use a view to display a model property.
- Construct an array of data, with each array item being a single model instance.
- Loop through the array and render a `<button>` element for each item.
- Respond to a click event on each button element.
- Display the currently selected item.
- Display a form with an input field, preset to a value.
- Respond to a form submit event.

If we were to outline some of the tests that we could write, we would ideally like our tests to cover the following scenarios:

- **Model tests**: These tests cover the creation and use of models within our application
- **Application state tests**: These tests cover the default values or state of elements that are created
- **Rendering tests**: These tests would interrogate the DOM elements that are rendered for each application element, and ensure that they are attached to the DOM correctly
- **DOM event tests**: These tests ensure that the application reacts correctly to DOM events, such as the clicking of an element
- **Form tests**: These tests ensure that form elements are created with the correct default values, and that form values are read correctly following user input
- **Form submission tests**: These tests ensure that the correct functions are called when a form is submitted

Backbone testing

In this section, we will take a look at the tests we will need to write to cover the required functionality of our Backbone sample application.

Test setup

One of the benefits of writing applications in Backbone is that the framework itself does not have many dependencies. To run a Backbone application, we need to have loaded the Underscore library, the jQuery library (or equivalent), and the Backbone framework itself. Once these libraries have been loaded into our browser, we just need to include all of the files that we have written for the application. By way of an example of this, let's take a look at the <head> tag in our index.html file as follows:

```html
<head>
    <link rel="stylesheet"
        type="text/css"
        href="./node_modules/bootstrap/dist/css/bootstrap.css">
    <script
        src="./node_modules/underscore/underscore.js"></script>
    <script
        src="./node_modules/jbone/dist/jbone.js"></script>
    <script
        src="./node_modules/backbone/backbone.js"></script>
    <script src="./models.js"></script>
    <script src="./views.js"></script>
    <script src="./app.js"></script>
</head>
```

Here, we have included the bootstrap.css, underscore.js, jbone.js, and the backbone.js files, as mentioned earlier. We then included the models.js, views.js and app.js files in order for the browser to have loaded all of the source files required to run the application. As there are so few files involved, we can easily set up a testing environment using Testem by creating a testem.json file in the project root directory as follows:

```json
{
    "framework": "jasmine2",
    "src_files": [
        "node_modules/jquery/dist/jquery.js",
        "node_modules/jasmine-jquery/lib/jasmine-jquery.js",
        "node_modules/underscore/underscore.js",
        "node_modules/backbone/backbone.js",
        "models.js",
        "views.js",
        "app.js",
        "models.spec.js"
    ]
}
```

Here, we have a simple configuration file for Testem that specifies each of the files that the application needs using the `src_files` property. The files listed in this configuration match the files that we saw in the `index.html` earlier, with the addition of the `jasmine-jquery.js` file that will be used to set up fixture code. The only other file we have listed here is a test file itself, named `models.spec.js`, which will contain our test code. We can run our tests by running `testem` on the command line, and then connecting a browser instance to `localhost:7357`, as we did in the previous chapter.

Model tests

Backbone models represent the core method of storing states within our application. When we create a view, we base it on the data contained in the underlying models. When we respond to user interaction, we store the results of this interaction in a model, and so correctly setting and getting values from our models is a fundamental feature of our application. In production applications, these models are generally created, or hydrated from JSON data that is retrieved from a REST endpoint. It is therefore important to test that our models can be created correctly, and that getting or setting values on our model works as intended.

When we construct a Backbone model, we use a POJO within the constructor to assign values to each of the models properties. Hence, when faced with the following interface:

```
interface IClickableItem {
    DisplayName: string;
    Id: number;
}
```

We construct a new instance of our `ItemModel` class, as follows:

```
itemModel = new ItemModel({Id : 1, DisplayName : 'testDisplay'});
```

Remember that internally, Backbone stores these POJO values as attributes on the class instance itself, which leads us to some boilerplate code when writing a TypeScript version of a `Backbone.Model`, as follows:

```
class ItemModel extends Backbone.Model implements IClickableItem {
    get DisplayName(): string
        { return this.get('DisplayName'); }
    set DisplayName(value: string)
        { this.set('DisplayName', value); }
    get Id(): number { return this.get('Id'); }
    set Id(value: number) { this.set('Id', value); }
    constructor(input: IClickableItem) {
```

```
            super();
        this.set(input);
        }
    }
```

Each property in our interface (in this case, `IClickableItem`) must define a pair of `get` and `set` functions, and use Backbone's `this.get` or `this.set` functions to store these properties correctly. As we are writing code to get this done, we need to write unit tests to ensure that this works correctly.

Our initial set of unit tests are as follows:

```
describe('ItemModel tests', () => {
    let itemModel : ItemModel;
    beforeEach( () => {
        itemModel = new ItemModel(
            {Id : 10, DisplayName : 'testDisplayName'}
        );
    });
    it('should assign an Id property', () => {
        expect(itemModel.Id).toBe(10);
    });
    it('should assign a DisplayName property', () => {
        expect(itemModel.DisplayName).toBe('testDisplayName');
    });
});
```

Here, we are defining a variable to hold an instance of our `ItemModel`, named `itemModel`. Note that its definition is outside of the `beforeAll` function, and so it is available to each of our unit tests. Our `beforeEach` function initializes an instance of the `ItemModel` class, with default values, for each of our tests to reuse.

The first test, named `'should assign an Id property'`, is checking that the `Id` property returns the same value as was used in the constructor, which in this case is `10`. Likewise, we have another test for the `DisplayName` property, and can check that its value is, in fact, `'testDisplayName'`.

We can now extend these tests to verify that the set functions work correctly, as follows:

```
it('should set an Id property', () => {
    itemModel.Id = -10;
    expect(itemModel.Id).toBe(-10);
});
it('should set a DisplayName property', () => {
    itemModel.DisplayName = 'updatedDisplayName';
    expect(itemModel.DisplayName).toBe('updatedDisplayName');
});
```

As an added set of tests, we can even bypass the set and get functions, and verify that the underlying Backbone functions also set the properties correctly, as follows:

```
it('should update the Id property when calling calling set', () => {
    itemModel.set('Id', 99);
    expect(itemModel.Id).toBe(99);
});
it('should update the DisplayName property when calling set', () => {
    itemModel.set('DisplayName', 'setDisplayName');
    expect(itemModel.DisplayName).toBe('setDisplayName');
});
```

Here, we are testing that the internal set and get Backbone functions accomplish exactly the same thing as using the TypeScript property getter and setter syntax.

Complex model tests

We can use the same techniques to test that complex models are instantiated correctly. Consider the following test suite:

```
describe("model.spec.ts : ItemCollectionViewModel tests", () => {
    let itemCollectionViewModel: ItemCollectionViewModel;
    beforeEach(() => {
        itemCollectionViewModel = new ItemCollectionViewModel({
            Title: "testTitle",
            SelectedItem: {
                Id: 10,
                DisplayName: "testDisplayName"
            },
            Name: "testName"
        });
    });
```

Here, we are creating an instance of our complex model, named `itemCollectionViewModel`. The interesting bit is the construction of this complex model with a POJO. We are calling the constructor in our `beforeEach` function, and simply nesting POJOs within each other. We are setting the `Title` property, and then setting the `SelectedItem` property to another POJO that has the `Id` and `DisplayName` properties. Finally, we set the `Name` property.

> These POJOs are using the same structure as what we expect to be returned in JSON format from backend REST endpoints. Defining object tests like these can therefore easily extend into integration tests that will call an actual web service, and rehydrate our models from POJOs.

Our unit tests for this complex model can then simply traverse the available properties to ensure that everything is set correctly, as follows:

```
it("should set the Title property", () => {
    expect(itemCollectionViewModel.Title).toBe("testTitle");
});
it("should set the SelectedItem.Id property", () => {
    expect(itemCollectionViewModel.SelectedItem.Id).toBe(10);
});
it("should set the SelectedItem.DisplayName property", () => {
    expect(itemCollectionViewModel.SelectedItem.DisplayName)
        .toBe("testDisplayName");
});
it("should set the Name property", () => {
    expect(itemCollectionViewModel.Name).toBe("testName");
});
```

Our first test checks the value of the `Title` property, and then the following tests check the value of the `SelectedItem` property (which is a child Backbone model), and the `Name` property.

> Using simple tests like these can also help to test scenarios where some of the properties are not set. In other words, where complex models are being hydrated from a REST endpoint, there may be cases where some of the properties are simply omitted. This scenario is fairly common in REST endpoints where the returned JSON structure may change depending on the use case. Our tests can therefore cater for these variations, and ensure that all functionality works as expected, for a variety of combinations of properties.

Rendering tests

Once we are happy that our Backbone models are hydrating correctly, we can turn our attention to their views, and write some tests to ensure that they render these model properties correctly to the DOM. We will use Jasmine's `setFixtures` function to set up our Backbone templates, as follows:

```
describe("views.spec.ts : ItemView tests", () => {
    let itemModel: ItemModel;

    beforeEach(() => {
        jasmine.getFixtures().fixturesPath = "./";
        loadFixtures("views.spec.html");
        itemModel = new ItemModel({
            Id: 10,
            DisplayName: "testDisplayName"
        });
    });
```

Here, we have created and instantiated an `ItemModel` instance named `itemModel` for reuse within each test. We are also calling the Jasmine function `loadFixtures` in order to inject the HTML `<script>` tags that we will require into the DOM. Note that we are using the Jasmine `loadFixtures` function, instead of the `setFixtures` function that we used earlier, which allows us to load the fixture HTML from a file on disk. In order to use this `loadFixtures` function, however, we need to tell Jasmine where the file is and, as such need to set the `fixturesPath` property correctly, using the `jasmine.getFixtures()` function. The `views.spec.html` file contains the same HTML templates that we used in our `index.html` file.

The `<script>` tag that our `ItemView` will use is the `itemViewTemplate` script, which defines the following HTML:

```
<button style="margin: 5px;" class="btn btn-primary" >
    <%= DisplayName %>
</button>
```

This template uses the `DisplayName` property of the `ItemModel` instance inside a `<button>` tag.

Our test, therefore, will be looking for these HTML elements once the `ItemView` has been rendered, as follows:

```
it("should render an ItemView correctly", () => {
    let itemView = new ItemView({ model: itemModel });
    let renderedHtml = itemView.render().el;
    expect(renderedHtml.innerHTML).toContain(
        `<button style="margin: 5px;" class="btn btn-primary">`);
    expect(renderedHtml.innerHTML).toContain(
        `testDisplayName`);
    expect(renderedHtml.innerHTML).toContain(
        `</button>`);
});
```

In this test, we are creating an instance of the `ItemView` class, and instantiating it with our model. We then call the `render` function on the `itemView` instance, and store the value of the `el` property into a variable named `renderedHtml`. This `el` property is what will be attached to the DOM, and contains the HTML that has been generated as a result of the `render` function.

Our test then checks for the existence of a `<button>` element, and that the `<%= DisplayName %>` substitution has occurred correctly.

Our view tests, therefore, have accomplished the following:

- Created an instance of an `ItemModel`
- Created an instance of an `ItemView`, using `ItemModel`
- Called the `render` function on the `ItemView`
- Verified that the rendered HTML contains the correct elements

DOM event tests

The next set of functionality within our application that we will need to test are our DOM events. The basic flow of these tests is as follows:

- Construct an instance of an `ItemView`, with its corresponding `ItemModel`
- Render the HTML
- Find the `<button>` element, and simulate a DOM `click` event
- Ensure that the `onClicked` function of the `ItemView` is called
- Ensure that the `onClicked` function triggers an event bus message

Our first test will simulate a click event, and use a Jasmine spy on the `onClicked` function of the `ItemView`, as follows:

```
it("should trigger onClicked event", () => {
    let clickSpy = spyOn(ItemView.prototype, 'onClicked');
    let itemView = new ItemView({ model: itemModel });
    itemView.render();
    let itemButton = itemView.$el.find(`button`).trigger('click');
    expect(clickSpy).toHaveBeenCalled();
});
```

The first line of this test uses the `spyOn` function from Jasmine to attach a spy to the `onClicked` function of our `ItemView`. Note, however, that we are specifying `ItemView.prototype` as the input to our `spyOn` function. Remember that when our Backbone view is constructed, we specified via the `options.events` property what functions to bind to DOM events. By the time we have completed running the constructor, we cannot then attach a spy to this function (as it is already bound to the DOM event). The solution, therefore, is to bind to the `prototype` view before the actual view is constructed.

Once we have a spy in place, we can construct the view, and call the `render` function. Once the `render` function has been called, we can use standard jQuery DOM searches on the view, and trigger a click, as seen in the following line:

```
let itemButton = itemView.$el.find(`button`).trigger('click');
```

Here, we are using fluent syntax and jQuery $ functions to find a `button` element and `trigger` a DOM click event.

Our test passes, since the DOM click event calls our `onClicked` function of `ItemView`.

The final test we need to build is one to ensure that the use of the message bus is working correctly. Remember that when an `ItemView` element is clicked, it will trigger an event on the message bus, and include its model properties as part of this message. On the other side of the message bus, the `ItemCollectionView` is listening for this event, and it will update the DOM to show our currently selected item.

Our test, therefore, is as follows:

```
it("should trigger an event bus event", () => {

    let eventTriggered = false;
    EventBus.Bus.on("item_clicked", () => {
        eventTriggered = true;
    });
    let itemView = new ItemView({ model: itemModel });
    itemView.render();
    let itemButton = itemView.$el.find(`button`).trigger('click');

    expect(eventTriggered).toBeTruthy();
});
```

In this test, we start by setting up a flag named `eventTriggered`, which is set to `false`. We then call the `on` function of the `Event.Bus` object to register an event bus listener. This listener will listen for messages of the type `"item_clicked"`, and when received, will update the `eventTriggered` flag to indicate that this message was received. We then construct an `ItemView` as we have done previously, and trigger the button click through the DOM. Our test is expecting that the `eventTriggered` flag will be switched from `false` to `true`. With this test in place, we know that the `ItemView` is rendering elements correctly to the DOM, and that these elements are responding to click events as designed, and pushing messages onto the event bus.

Collection view tests

Our testing thus far has focused on the models that we will be using in our application, and the `ItemView` view, which is responsible for rendering a single button. We now need to extend our tests to the `ItemCollectionView` class, to ensure that this class renders elements correctly to the DOM, and that it can work with our form correctly. Let's start by setting up our test suite as follows:

```
describe("views.spec.ts : ItemCollectionView tests", () => {
    let renderedHtml: JQuery<HTMLElement>;
    let submitSpy: jasmine.Spy;
    let itemCollectionView: ItemCollectionView;
    beforeEach(() => {

        jasmine.getFixtures().fixturesPath = "./";
        loadFixtures("views.spec.html");

        let itemCollection = new ItemCollection(ClickableItems);
```

```
let collectionViewModel = new ItemCollectionViewModel({
    Title: "testItemCollection Title",
    SelectedItem: {
        Id: 10, DisplayName: "testSelectedItemDisplayName"
    },
    Name: "testName"
});

submitSpy = spyOn(ItemCollectionView.prototype
    , 'submitClick').and.callThrough();
itemCollectionView = new ItemCollectionView({
    model: collectionViewModel
}, itemCollection);

renderedHtml = itemCollectionView.render().$el;

});
```

There is a fair amount of code to get through here, but nothing that we have not seen before. We start the test suite by declaring three variables to hold information that each test will need. These are `renderedHtml`, which will hold the HTML that is rendered by the `ItemCollectionView`. If we are looking for DOM elements, we will use this variable as our starting point. The `submitSpy` variable is used to store our Jasmine spy for the `submitClick` function that is called when the form is submitted. Note that it is using the `.and.callThrough` function to allow the underlying code to be executed. The `itemCollectionView` variable holds the instance of the `ItemCollectionView` itself, so that we can interrogate its properties.

The `beforeEach` function sets up the prerequisites for the test. Firstly, it loads the required DOM elements through a call to `loadFixtures`, and then creates an instance of the `ItemCollection` class, and an instance of the `ItemCollectionViewModel` class. Following this, the test setup creates our Jasmine spy on the `submitClick` function, creates an instance of the `ItemCollectionView` class, and finally calls the `render` function on `itemCollectionView` to store the rendered HTML. With the test setup in place, we can test the various DOM elements as follows:

```
it("should render <h1> tag correctly", () => {
    let h1Tag = renderedHtml.find('h1');
    expect(h1Tag.html()).toContain('testItemCollection Title');
});
```

Here, we have a test that is checking to see whether the `Title` property of the `ItemCollectionView` is correctly rendered within an `<h1>` tag. Our next test is as follows:

```
it("should render id=ulRegions correctly", () => {
    let ulRegions = renderedHtml.find('#ulRegions');
    let buttons = ulRegions.find('button');

    expect(buttons.length).toBe(3, 'should find 3 buttons');
    let firstButton = buttons[0].innerHTML;

    expect(firstButton).toContain('firstItem');
});
```

Here, we have a test the checks that three buttons have been rendered into the `<div>` element with an `id` of `'ulRegions'`. We are also then picking off the first button in this array to check that it has rendered the `DisplayName` property correctly.

We can continue to write tests that verify that the `selectedItem` element contains the default `DisplayName` property, and that the form group is rendered to the DOM correctly. We will not discuss these tests here, but be sure to check the sample code for examples of these tests. The final set of tests we will discuss is for our form.

Form tests

When working with forms in our applications, there are generally two things that we need to test. The first is the population of values in a form, and the second is retrieving these values once the user has submitted the form. Remember that in large applications, a user will generally either enter new data into a form (to create something), or the user might be modifying existing data through a form (to update something). This is why we need to test setting the initial values of a form. Our test is as follows:

```
it("should find form-group input with value", () => {
    let formGroup = renderedHtml.find('.form-group');
    let input = formGroup.find('input');
    expect(input.length).toBeGreaterThan(0,
        'could not find form-group label');
    expect(input.attr('value')).toContain('testName');
});
```

Here, we have a simple test that is finding the `form-group` element in the DOM using a CSS selector, and storing the HTML into a variable named `formGroup`. We are then finding the `input` element within this form, and checking the attribute named `value` to ensure that it has been created with the correct default value. Once we are satisfied that the form input has been populated correctly, we can write a test that enters something into the input field, and submits the form as follows:

```
it("should enter text into input and submit the form", () => {
    let formGroup = renderedHtml.find('.form-group');
    let input = formGroup.find('input');
    expect(input.length).toBeGreaterThan(0,
        'could not find form-group label');
    // simulate input into the control
    input.val('test');
    // find and click on the submit button
    let submit = renderedHtml.find('#submit-button-button');
    expect(submit.length).toBe(1, 'could not find submit button');
    submit.click();
    // check that the submitClicked function was called
    expect(submitSpy).toHaveBeenCalled();
    // check that the property was updated.
    expect(itemCollectionView.inputNameValue).toBe('test');
});
```

Here, our test starts by finding the `form-group` element using a CSS selector as we have done before. We then find the `input` element within this HTML, and call the `val` function to set the value of the input element. This call, that is `input.val('test')`, is what is simulating user input into the form element. Once we have set the value of the input element successfully, we then search for the **Submit** button by `id`, and click it. The act of clicking on the **Submit** button will call the `submitClicked` function of our `ItemCollectionView` class, which will then be able to interrogate each form field and extract the values that the user has entered. Note that we are then checking the value of the `inputNameValue` property of our view to ensure that it has been updated correctly. We will need a slight modification to our `ItemCollectionView` class to set this property as follows:

```
inputNameValue: string | undefined;

submitClick() {
    let name = this.$el.find('#inputName');
    if (name.length > 0) {
        this.inputNameValue = <string | undefined>name.val();
    } else {
        this.inputNameValue = undefined;
    }
```

```
}
```

Here, we have added an internal property named `inputNameValue` to our `ItemCollectionView` class that will store the value that is entered by our user. Note that we have defined this field as being of type `string` or `undefined`. The `submitClick` function has also been updated slightly in order to store the value of the input element into this variable.

Our Backbone test suite is now complete.

Backbone testing summary

As we have seen, when testing Backbone applications, we are able to perform a wide range of unit tests using Jasmine and Jasmine-jQuery alone. We are able to create model tests, view-rendering tests, and even DOM event tests without leaving the Jasmine environment. We have created and tested the functionality of each of our classes to ensure that they render the correct elements to the DOM, and that we can interact with a form by simulating user input, submitting the form, and then interrogating the form values for use within our view.

Aurelia testing

In this section, we will explore the unit-testing capabilities of the Aurelia framework. We will write some unit tests for the application that we have written, in order to ensure that the initial state of the application is correct, as well as to ensure that the rendered HTML is correct. These tests will follow the general scenarios that we outlined at the beginning of the chapter.

Aurelia test setup

One of the questions that the Aurelia command-line interface asks when setting up a new Aurelia application (`au new`) is whether or not to configure unit-testing. If we answer `yes` to this question, then all of the testing configuration files and dependencies are installed automatically. In the interests of time, we will not investigate how to retrospectively add unit-testing capabilities to an existing Aurelia application, but will instead assume that this has already been configured.

To run Aurelia unit tests, simply type the following:

```
au karma
```

This will invoke the built-in Karma test runner, and execute any tests found in the /test/unit directory that match the filename convention of *spec.js.

The au build command must be executed before any tests are compiled and included in a new test run. Aurelia provides the --watch command-line argument that will automatically re-execute the current command if modifications to files on disk are detected. This means that running au karma --watch will compile and rerun any Karma unit tests automatically when our TypeScript source files are modified. This is a very useful feature that provides instant feedback when writing unit tests.

Aurelia unit tests

Our first set of unit tests will need to verify that the App class (our entry point) has been constructed correctly. When the application is first loaded, it will render a title, three buttons, and also indicate that no item has been selected. These HTML elements are bound to the Title, SelectedItem and items properties of the App class itself. Let's create an app.spec.ts file in the /test/unit directory, and write a test to verify that these properties have been set correctly, as follows:

```
describe('/test/unit/app.spec.ts : App tests', () => {
    let app: App;

    beforeAll(() => {
        app = new App();
    });

    it('should set Title property ', () => {
        expect(app.Title).toBe('Please select :');
    });
});
```

The first line of this test uses the import statement to import the App class from the '../../src/app' file. Note that the ../../ reference is necessary because any import statement that uses a path must set the path relevant to the file that is doing the import.

We then use the standard Jasmine `describe` syntax to set up a test suite, and configure a variable named `app` to hold an instance of the `App` class. Our first test verifies that the `Title` property of the `App` class (on construction) contains the phrase `"Please select"`. This test is therefore checking the initial state of the `Title` property of the `App` class when first constructed. We can then check each of the other internal variables as follows:

```
it('has a property named items', function () {
    expect(application.items).toBeDefined();
});
it('has an array of clickable items', function () {
    expect(application.items.length).toBe(3);
});
it('sets currentElement property in constructor', function () {
    expect(application.currentElement).toBeDefined();
});
it('sets currentElement.idValue to 0', function () {
    expect(application.currentElement.idValue).toBe(0);
});
it('sets currentElement.displayName to none', function () {
    expect(application.currentElement.displayName).toBe('none');
});
```

Here, we have a few tests for the `items` variable—which is an array of length 3, and a few tests for the `SelectedItem` variable, which should be set to `Id = 0` and `DisplayName = 'None selected'`. These tests are verifying that when an `App` instance is created, the initial state of the class is set correctly.

Rendering tests

Our next round of tests will cover rendering elements to the DOM. Aurelia provides a set of helper classes, similar to Jamine's `setFixture` functionality, in order to attach HTML to the DOM, and render views using these temporary DOM elements. Our test suite, therefore, needs to include the following two import statements at the top of the file:

```
import {StageComponent} from 'aurelia-testing';
import {bootstrap} from 'aurelia-bootstrapper';
```

These import statements include a class named `StageComponent`, and a function named `bootstrap`. The `StageComponent` class is the helper utility that Aurelia provides in order to house an instance of our item under test, which in our case is an instance of the `App` class. The `bootstrap` function is the standard method of creating and bootstrapping an Aurelia application.

Our test setup, then, is as follows:

```
var app: any;

beforeEach(() => {
    app = StageComponent.withResources('app')
        .inView(`
        <h1>` + '${Title}' + `</h1>`)
        .boundTo(new App());
});

afterEach(() => {
    app.dispose();
});
```

Here, we have defined a variable named `app` to house an instance of our `StageComponent` class. Even though this `app` variable will house an instance of our `App` class, we cannot set its type to anything other than `any`. Unfortunately, attempting to use the correct type for the `app` variable will cause compilation errors. The creation of the `StageComponent` class uses a fluent style to effectively chain together three commands—`withResources`, `inView`, and `boundTo`. The `withResources` function call registers our `app` code with the `StageComponent`, and the `inView` function defines the HTML DOM that we need for our tests. This `inView` function is very similar to the `setFixtures` function that we used with Jasmine, but has one significant difference. Generally, when we need to include large portions of HTML within our code, we can simply wrap it all within two backticks, that is, ` and `. Unfortunately, Aurelia uses the syntax of `${<propertyName>}` within HTML templates to signify parameter substitution. This clashes with the standard TypeScript string literal syntax. Therefore, whenever we need a `${<propertyName>}` Aurelia tag, we will need to close the backtick, and manually add the Aurelia tag in a single quote, as follows:

```
`<h1>` + '${Title}' + `</h1>`
```

The final `boundTo` function call creates a new instance of the `App` class, and binds this new instance to the `StageComponent`.

Note that we have also defined an `afterEach` function that calls the `dispose` method of the `app` variable. This is to ensure that the DOM elements that were created by the `StageComponent` are cleaned up correctly after each test.

Our first test must verify that the `Title` property of the `App` class is rendered correctly to the DOM, as follows:

```
it('should render Title property', (done) => {
    app.create(bootstrap).then(() => {
        const titleElement = document.querySelector("h1");
        expect(titleElement).toBeDefined();
        expect(titleElement.innerHTML).toContain('Please select :');
        done();
    }).catch(e => { // note this gives better error messages.
        console.log(`error : ${e}`);
    });
});
```

The first thing to note about this test is the use of the `(done)` parameter on the `it` function. Aurelia uses Jasmine's asynchronous testing features whenever we use the `StageComponent`. We must therefore remember to pass in the `done` parameter as part of our test function, and also to call the `done` function once our test has completed.

The test itself starts by calling the `create` function on the instance of the `StageComponent` (which houses our `App` test instance), passing in the `bootstrap` function. This `create` function returns a promise, to which we can add a fluent style `then` function where we can define the actual content of our test. Once we are inside the promise, all of Aurelia's bootstrapping and binding has already taken place. We are then able to query the DOM through the `document.querySelector` function. In this test, we are finding the first `<h1>` element, and checking that the HTML rendered contains the string `'Please select :'`.

Note that we have also created a `catch` function for the promise that was returned by Aureila on the call to `create(bootstrap)`. This `catch` function simply logs the error message to the console. While this is not strictly necessary, it does help to improve the error logging when tests fail.

Before we embark on writing any further tests, we will need to update the template that Aurelia is using in the `inView` function call as follows:

```
.inView(`
<h1>` + '${Title}' + `</h1>
<ul>
<div repeat.for="item of items" click.delegate="onItemClicked(item)">
<button style="margin: 5px;" class="btn btn-primary">`
    + '${item.DisplayName}' + `</button>
</div>
</ul>

<div>
```

```
Selected Item : ` + '${SelectedItem.Id} - ${SelectedItem.DisplayName}' + `
</div>

<div class="form-group">
<label for="inputName">Name :</label>
<input type="text" class="form-control \
    input-name" id="inputName" value.bind="Name" />
</div>

<button id="submit-button-button" class="submit-button"
    click.delegate="onSubmitClicked()">Submit</button>
`)
```

Here, we have simply copied the full `app.html` file, and included it within the `inView` function call. As noted earlier, any time that we have used Aurelia's `${<propertyName>}` parameter substitution, we will need to switch to a normal JavaScript single-quote syntax.

Our next test will verify that the array of buttons has been rendered to the DOM as follows:

```
it('should render buttons', function (done) {
    app.create(bootstrap).then(function () {
        var ulItemList = document.querySelectorAll(
            'ul > div > button');
        expect(ulItemList).toBeDefined();
        expect(ulItemList.length).toBe(3);
        for (var i = 0; i < ulItemList.length; i++) {
            var itemElement = ulItemList[i];
            expect(itemElement.innerHTML).toContain('Item');
        }
        done();
    }).catch(e => {
        console.log(`error : ${e}`);
    });
});
```

In this test, we are using the `document.querySelectorAll` function to return an array of button elements. Note the CSS selector syntax that we have used: `ul > div > button`. This CSS selector will return each `button` element within a `div` element that are children of the `ul` element. We are then looping through each element returned, and checking that the `innerHTML` property contains the word `'Item'`. Remember that the button text displayed on the page was `firstItem`, `secondItem`, and `thirdItem`, so each of these buttons will contain the word `'Item'`. While this may not be a definitive test, it shows how we are able to use standard CSS selectors to return more than one child item.

We can now test that the form itself has been rendered correctly, as follows:

```
it('should render form with input element', function (done) {
    app.create(bootstrap).then(function () {
        let formGroup = document.querySelector(
            '.form-group');
        let inputElement = formGroup.querySelector('input')
        expect(inputElement.value).toBe('Your Name');
        let submitButton = document.querySelector('#submit-button-button');
        expect(submitButton.innerHTML).toBe('Submit');
        done();
    }).catch(e => {
        console.log(`error : ${e}`);
    });
});
```

In this test, we are searching the DOM for an element with the CSS class of `form-group`, which is used to identify the enclosing `<div>` for our form. We then store this element in the variable `formGroup`, and then use this `formGroup` variable as a base to find a child input element. Our test checks that the `value` of the input element is `'Your Name'`, which is the default value that we have set for the form. The last element we will search for is the **Input** button, which has an `id` attribute of `'submit-button-button'`. If the inner HTML property contains the text `'Submit'`, then our test will pass. Note that we could check for a few more CSS classes, or elements of our form, but for the sake of brevity, we have tested for the most important form elements.

Aurelia DOM events

Unfortunately, Aurelia does not provide a testing mechanism to test DOM events. This means that we cannot easily create a test that enters data into an input field, and then clicks on the **Form submit** button, as we did with Backbone. Consider the following HTML snippet:

```
<button id="submit-button-button"
    class="submit-button"
    click.delegate="nSubmitClicked()">Submit
</button>
```

Here, we have the HTML snippet that renders our **Submit** button. We have already seen tests that make sure that this button is rendered onto the screen, and that the name of the button is, in fact, **Submit**. But take a closer look at the function name for the `click.delegate` attribute. It contains a very subtle misspelling of the `onSubmitClicked` function in our View, and is missing the starting "`o`". If we compile this version of our code, Aurelia will not indicate this error in the build step. It is only at runtime, when we physically click on the button itself that we get a runtime error as follows:

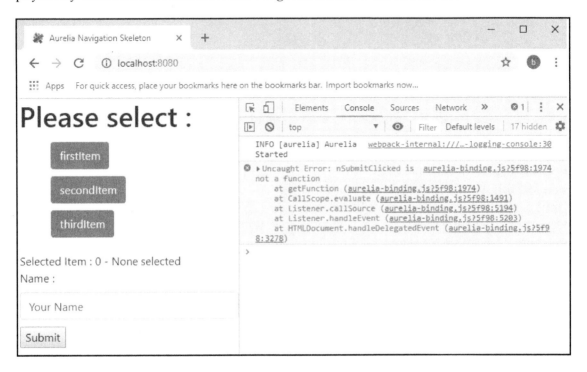

The error that we are seeing is a very simple one to recreate. What this means is that we are not able to unit test the resultant DOM interactions between our rendered HTML, and our Aurelia classes. This lack of unit-testing means that we will need to utilize end-to-end testing using tools such as Protractor to find these sorts of errors within our application, which is a far more expensive exercise than simply writing a unit test.

Aurelia test summary

This concludes our section on Aurelia unit and integration testing. We have seen that Aurelia provides an `au karma` option to run Karma for unit-testing purposes, and that all configuration and dependencies are automatically installed for us by the Aurelia command-line setup. We explored how to create a component, how to test initial application state, and how to test the rendering of elements to the DOM. Unfortunately, we were not able to test the DOM events themselves, and will need to perform integration testing through Protractor in order to test the application as a whole.

Angular testing

In this section, we will take a look at unit tests for our existing Angular application, similar to what we have done with Backbone and Aurelia.

Angular test setup

When creating a project using the Angular-CLI (by issuing an `ng new` command), the default project setup already includes all of the boilerplate code to run unit tests using Karma, and end-to-end tests using Protractor. This default setup is a very handy feature of Angular, shortening the development effort of configuring a test environment, and giving us the ability to dive right in and write tests from the beginning of a project.

To run unit tests using Karma, we can type the following from the command line:

```
ng test
```

This command-line option will compile and package our application, and run any tests that it finds within the `src` directory. Any TypeScript file where the name matches `*.spec.ts` will be designated as a test file, and any tests within this file will be executed. In addition, running Karma in this way will also automatically watch our files for changes, and recompile and rerun our tests since changes have been detected.

The Angular default project creates `.spec.ts` files within the source directory, right alongside the components under test. This means that within the `src/app` directory, we will find both `app.component.ts`, and `app.component.spec.ts`. While this is the default setting, there is no reason why we cannot split the `.spec.ts` files into their own directory, if need be. Having the tests within the same directory as the component under test, however, allows us to quickly open up and modify tests if the component itself changes. It also helps to identify which components do not have unit tests.

Running `ng test` on our Angular sample project at this stage, however, will generate a few compile time errors, as follows:

```
Can't bind to 'formGroup' since it isn't a known property of 'form'. ("
    <h2>Reactive Form :</h2>
    <form [ERROR ->][formGroup]="reactiveFormGroup"
(ngSubmit)="onSubmitRf()">
        <div class="form-group">
            <labe"): ng:///DynamicTestModule/AppComponent.html@28:6
    No provider for ControlContainer ("
```

Let's take a look at the existing `app.component.spec.ts` file to find the cause of the error, which is as follows:

```
describe('/src/app/app.component.spec.ts : AppComponent ', () => {
    beforeEach(async(() => {
        TestBed.configureTestingModule({
            declarations: [
                AppComponent
            ]
        }).compileComponents();
    }));
```

Here, we have a `describe` function that marks that start of our test suite, and a `beforeEach` function that is setting up the test environment for our component. Note that this function is marked as `async`, which allows us to use `async await`-style syntax within this `beforeEach` function.

The first thing that this Angular test does is to call the `TestBed.configureTestingModule` function with an object as its single argument. This object has a single property named `declarations`, which is an array of components. As the only component under test at this stage is the `AppComponent`, this is the only one listed here. The `configureTestingModule` function returns a promise, so we can then use fluent syntax to call the `compileComponents` function once this call has completed.

The `configureTestingModule` function is used to set up any dependencies that our component may need. This function is, in essence, providing our component with a mini Angular environment in which to run. This means that any `import` statements used within our component will need to have a corresponding entry in the `configureTestingModule` function.

If we take a look at the `app.component.ts` file, we will see at the top of the file that we are importing three classes as follows:

```
import { FormBuilder, FormGroup, FormControl } from '@angular/forms';
```

Here, we have imported the `FormBuilder`, `FormGroup` and `FormControl` classes from the module named `'@angular/forms'`. This `import` statement is the cause of the compilation errors. As our test is completely independent of the running application, it must provide an enclosed environment for the component to run within. The trick to fixing this error is to import the modules that these classes are a part of, as follows:

```
import { FormsModule, ReactiveFormsModule } from '@angular/forms';
describe('/src/app/app.component.spec.ts : AppComponent ', () => {
    beforeEach(async(() => {
        TestBed.configureTestingModule({
            declarations: [
                AppComponent
            ],
            imports: [
                FormsModule,
                ReactiveFormsModule
            ]
        }).compileComponents();
    }));
```

Here, we have added an `import` statement at the top of the file to import the `FormsModule` and the `ReactiveFormsModule` from the `'@angular/forms'` library. We have also added an `imports` property to the object passed to the `configureTestingModule` function, and listed both the `FormsModule` and the `ReactiveFormsModule` within it.

Note that in Angular, groups of classes, interfaces and functions can be included within what is known as a module. In our example, our `AppComponent` needs the `ngModel` function, which is part of the `FormsModule`, and it needs the `FormBuilder`, `FormGroup`, and `FormControl` classes, which are part of `ReactiveFormsModule`. This means that by importing the `FormsModule` and `ReactiveFormsModule` at the start of our test, all of the classes, interfaces and functions that those modules provide are available to our test environment.

Making this slight change to our test specification will allow us to compile our tests. Next, we will look at building some tests for our Angular component.

Angular model tests

To start off with, we will create a series of tests that will check the internal state of the
`AppComponent` class once instantiated, in a file named
`src/app/app.component.spec.ts` as follows:

```
describe('/src/app/app.component.spec.ts : AppComponent ', () => {
    let fixture: ComponentFixture<AppComponent>;
    let app: AppComponent;
    beforeEach(async(() => {
        TestBed.configureTestingModule({
            declarations: [
                AppComponent
            ],
            imports: [
                FormsModule,
                ReactiveFormsModule
            ]
        }).compileComponents();
        fixture = TestBed.createComponent(AppComponent);
        app = fixture.debugElement.componentInstance;

    }));

});
```

Here, we have defined our test suite with a `beforeEach` function. We start our test suite by
defining two variables named `fixture` and `app`. The `fixture` variable is of
type `ComponentFixture<AppComponent>`, and is the result of the call to
`TestBed.createComponent(AppComponent)`. This `fixture` variable houses the
representation of the `AppComponent` in the DOM, and it can be used to query the DOM or
manipulate the DOM elements directly. We will use this `fixture` property later when we
start to interact with DOM elements.

The `app` variable is the instance of the `AppComponent` class itself, and is accessed through
the `debugElement.componentInstance` property of the `fixture` variable. Once we have
a handle to the `AppComponent` class instance, we can start to test that each of its properties
has been initialized correctly as follows:

```
it('should create the app', () => {
    expect(app).toBeTruthy();
});

it('should set the Title property', () => {
    expect(app.Title).toBe('Please select :');
```

```
    });

    it('should set the SelectedItem property', () => {
        expect(app.SelectedItem.Id).toBe(0);
        expect(app.SelectedItem.DisplayName).toBe('None selected');
    });

    it("should set the items property to an array", () => {
        expect(app.items.length).toBe(3);
        for (let item of app.items) {
            expect(item.DisplayName).toContain("Item");
        }
    });
```

Here, we have four tests. The first test just ensures that the `app` variable has been created correctly. While this may seem a trivial test, it really should be the first test for any new Angular component, and is, in fact, the first test that the Angular CLI creates. This test is very helpful when starting to test components, as it will force the test framework to ensure that all of the components dependencies have been imported correctly. Remember how we needed to modify the `beforeEach` function and ensure that the `FormsModule` and `ReactiveFormsModule` were imported correctly before the tests would compile? Well, this simple test is really there to ensure that tests for a component can compile, and that the dependencies that the component needs have been initialized correctly.

The next three tests ensure that the `Title`, `SelectedItem` and `items` properties of the `AppComponent` class were instantiated correctly. These tests ensure that the internal state of the class is correct at the time of creation.

Angular rendering tests

We can now turn our attention to the generated HTML that our app produces, and test whether our component has rendered elements to the DOM correctly, as follows:

```
    it("should render 0 - none selected to the DOM", () => {
        fixture.detectChanges();
        fixture.whenStable().then(() => {
            const domElement = fixture.debugElement.nativeElement;

            let selectedItemDiv =
                domElement.querySelector("#selectedItemText");
            expect(selectedItemDiv).toBeTruthy();
            expect(selectedItemDiv.innerHTML).toContain('0 - None selected');
        });
    });
```

Here, we have defined a test that will check that the text, `0 - none selected`, has been rendered to the DOM. Our test starts with a call to the `fixture.detectChanges` function. This function is provided by the Angular test framework, and will trigger a change detection cycle for the component. In essence, the `detectChanges` function will create the component within the DOM. We then attach to the `fixture.whenStable` promise using a `then` function, which will wait for the component to finish rendering to the DOM before calling our promise. These two calls to `detectChanges` and `whenStable` are always used as a pair in Angular tests.

Note that the `detectChanges` function will create an instance of our component. This means that if we need to create spies on any of the functions within our component, these spies will need to be created before the `detectChanges` function is called.

Our test then creates a variable named `domElement` to reference the `debugElement.nativeElement` of the fixture itself. This is the native DOM element of the component, and is used for DOM searches. We are then creating a variable named `selectedItemDiv`, which is the result of using the `querySelector` function on the `domElement` reference. This `querySelector` function uses standard jQuery search patterns to find elements, and in this instance is searching for the DOM element that has an `id` attribute of `selectedItemText`. Our first `expect` is checking whether the element was in fact found, and the final `expect` is checking the `innerHTML` property of our DOM element to see whether it contains the text `'0 - None selected'`.

Hence, our basic test cycle for Angular is as follows:

- Use the `TestBed.configureTestingModule` function to set any dependencies for our component under test
- Compile the component using the `compileComponents` function
- Call the `TestBed.createComponent` function to set up a unit-testing environment for our component
- Call the `detectChanges` function to trigger an Angular change detection cycle
- Attach to the `whenStable` promise to wait for our component to be rendered into the DOM
- Use the `debugElement.nativeElement` property of the fixture to obtain a handle to the rendered DOM
- Use the `querySelector` function to query the DOM using jQuery syntax

Using this testing template, we can now check for the remainder of our DOM elements as follows:

```
it("should render 3 buttons to the DOM", () => {
    fixture.detectChanges();
    fixture.whenStable().then(() => {
        const domElement = fixture.debugElement.nativeElement;

        let selectedItemDiv = domElement.querySelector("ul");

        let buttons = selectedItemDiv.querySelectorAll('div > button');
        expect(buttons.length).toBe(3);

        for (let button of buttons) {
            expect(button.innerHTML).toContain('Item');
        }

    });
});
```

Here, we have written a test that is checking for the existence of the three buttons from our collection. Our test starts by finding the first `<ul>` element in the DOM, and then uses the `querySelectorAll` function to find all `<button>` elements within this `<ul>` element. The `querySelectorAll` function will return an array of elements, where the `querySelector` function will only return the first matched element. Our test is then looping through each of these buttons, and checking that each button contains the text `'Item'`.

Our next test will check that our first form has been rendered correctly as follows:

```
it("should render a boostrap form-group to the DOM", () => {
    fixture.detectChanges();
    fixture.whenStable().then(() => {
        const domElement = fixture.debugElement.nativeElement;

        let selectedItemDiv = domElement.querySelector(".form-group");
        let formGroup = domElement.querySelector(".form-group input");

        expect(formGroup.value).toBe(`Your Name`);
    });
});
```

Here, we are finding the DOM element that has a class of `form-group` by using the `".form-group"` query selector, and within this element, the first `input` element. We expect that the `value` of the `input` element will be set correctly when the form is initialized.

The final rendering test is for the second reactive form as follows:

```
it("should render an Angular formGroup to the DOM", () => {
    fixture.detectChanges();
    fixture.whenStable().then(() => {
        const domElement = fixture.debugElement.nativeElement;

        let formGroup = domElement.querySelector("form input");

        expect(formGroup.value).toBe(`RF Input`);
    });
});
```

Here, we are finding a `form` DOM element, and within it, the first `input` element. We expect that the `value` of the input element will be set correctly when the form is initialized.

That completes our DOM rendering tests in Angular.

Angular form tests

The final set of tests that we will build will target our two forms, and simulate a user entering values into the form fields, as well as clicking on the submit button. The first test is for our standard form, as follows:

```
it("should set a value on the form, and click submit", () => {
    let submitSpy = spyOn(app, 'onSubmit');
    fixture.detectChanges();
    fixture.whenStable().then(() => {
        const domElement = fixture.debugElement.nativeElement;

        let formInput = domElement.querySelector(".form-group input");

        expect(formInput.value).toBe(`Your Name`);
        formInput.value = 'Updated Value';

        let submitButton =
            domElement.querySelector('#submit-button-button');
        expect(submitButton).toBeTruthy();
        submitButton.click();

        expect(submitSpy).toHaveBeenCalled();
    });
});
```

Here, we have a test that starts by creating a spy named `submitSpy` on the `onSubmit` function of our component. Remember that the call to `detectChanges` will actually create our component and attach it to the DOM, so any spy we create must be before the `detectChanges` call. Our test starts off with the same code that we used in the previous DOM rendering test, as we are finding the `input` element and expecting that its initial `value` property is set correctly. We then set the `value` property of the `formInput` variable. This call is simulating a user entering a value into the `input` element. We then find the `Submit` button using the `querySelector` function as usual, and then call the `click` function on the button. Again, this will simulate a user clicking on the **Submit** button. The test then expects that our `submitSpy` was called.

So using these sorts of form tests, we are able to interact with our HTML form, and simulate user actions within a unit test.

We will also need to create some tests for our reactive form as follows:

```
it("should set a value on the reactive form, and click submit", () => {
    let submitSpy = spyOn(app, 'onSubmitRf');
    fixture.detectChanges();
    fixture.whenStable().then(() => {
        const formGroup = app.reactiveFormGroup;
        expect(formGroup).toBeTruthy();
        expect(formGroup.value.nameInput).toBe('RF Input');

        formGroup.controls['nameInput'].setValue('Updated RF Value');

        const domElement = fixture.debugElement.nativeElement;

        let submitButton =
            domElement.querySelector('#rf-submit-button');
        expect(submitButton).toBeTruthy();
        submitButton.click();

        expect(submitSpy).toHaveBeenCalled();
    });
});
```

This test has a few interesting tweaks in order to work with Angular's reactive forms. In order to get or set values from a reactive form, we will need to reference the `FormGroup` within the component directly. In our test, we create a variable named `formGroup` in order to reference the `reactiveFormGroup` property on our `app` instance directly. It is always a good idea to check that the `FormGroup` instance has been created correctly, as this may occur later in the page life cycle than we expect. For this reason we test that the `formGroup` variable itself returns a true value. Once we have a reference to the `FormGroup` instance, we can check that the `nameInput` value was set correctly using the `formGroup.value.nameInput` property.

Remember that when we set the initial value of a `FormGroup`, we used the `reset` function as follows:

```
this.reactiveFormGroup.reset({
    nameInput: 'RF Input'
});
```

What this does to the `FormGroup` internally is to create a POJO with the single property named `nameInput`. Any one of these property names can be accessed through the `value` property on the `FormGroup`, thereby giving us access to this property by checking `formGroup.value.nameInput`, or for the fully qualified name of `app.reactiveFormGroup.value.nameInput`.

The next line of our test sets the value of this form control as follows:

```
formGroup.controls['nameInput'].setValue('Updated RF Value');
```

Again, when we construct a reactive form, the `FormGroup` element itself is created as follows:

```
this.reactiveFormGroup = this.formBuilder.group({
    nameInput: new FormControl({})
});
```

So, the `FormGroup` itself is created with an object that has a set of properties, and each of these properties is an instance of a `FormControl`. The `FormGroup` object therefore allows access to each of these controls through the `controls` property. We can then reference an individual control by name. Once we have a handle to the `FormControl` we need, we can call the `setValue` function to simulate the user updating the value on our form. Once our form value has been set, we can query the DOM for the correct **Submit** button and click it to trigger the form submission. We then `expect` that the `onSubmitRf` function will be called through the use of our spy.

Angular testing summary

Angular includes all of the necessary libraries and configuration to enable both unit-testing with Karma, and acceptance testing through Protractor out of the box with a new project. The framework has been built with testing firmly in mind, and therefore has a full component life cycle that we can tap into in our testing code. We are able to test every element of our code, including DOM rendering tests, and form interactions. While the setup of a test through the `ComponentFixture` classes may take a little while to understand and configure, it is an excellent framework that provides everything a component will need to run in an isolated environment.

React testing

In the final section of this chapter, we build a set of unit tests for our React sample application. Similar to what we have done with the other frameworks, we will verify that our initial application state is correct on startup, and then work through DOM rendering tests. Finally, we will build a set of tests that will fill in form values, and then submit the form.

Multiple entry points

Our React sample application uses Webpack as a compilation and bundling tool in order to convert our TypeScript files into usable React components. During Webpack's bundling process, we need to specify the entry point of our application, and also specify the output filename. Therefore, given an entry point of `/app/index.tsx`, and an output filename of `/dist/bundle.js`, all of our TypeScript code files will end up in the `bundle.js` file.

This is all well and good, but when creating tests, our entry point is not the application itself, but instead the test specification. This means that we need to configure Webpack to generate different bundles, based on different entry points. This can be accomplished fairly simply, with an update to the `webpack.conf.js` file, as follows:

```
const config = {
    entry: {
        app: './src/index.tsx',
        test: './test/react.app.tests.tsx'
    },
    output: {
        path: path.resolve(__dirname, 'dist'),
        filename: '[name].js'
    },
```

Here, we have modified our entry property from a single file (entry :
"./app/index.tsx") to include a second entry file named test. This allows our browser application to use one .tsx file as an entry point, and our test application to use another .tsx file as an entry point.

The second modification we have made is to use the [name] of the entry point as the output of the Webpack bundling process. This means that we will end up with two bundled packages, app.js, with an entry point of /app/index.tsx, and test.js, with an entry point of /tests/react.app.tests.tsx. Webpack will compile the application, and generate these bundles for us in the dist directory.

Using Jest

React suggests using Jest as its default test runner. All of our previous samples have been using Karma as a test runner, but the integration between React and Jest means that it is very simple to set up, and we can get our tests up and running very quickly. We will use Jest for our React tests in this section. To install Jest, simply type the following:

```
npm install jest -save-dev
```

Along with Jest, we will need Jasmine and its types as follows:

```
npm install jasmine @types/jasmine --save-dev
```

Once installed, we need to make a small change to our package.json file in order to fire up Jest and run our tests, as follows:

```
{
    "name": "react-sample",
    "version": "1.0.0",
    "description": "",
    "main": "index.js",
    "scripts": {
        "test": "jest"
    },
    ... existing properties
```

Here, we have modified the scripts property, and replaced the existing test property with the word "jest". What this means is that we can run npm from the command line, and use the test argument to start an npm process that will run jest. Remember that Jest is installed as a project dependency, and is not installed globally, so simply running jest from the command line will not work.

By creating an npm script entry named test, we can use the npm environment that is installed locally, and npm will be able to find the jest executable in the node_modules directory.

We can therefore run Jest from the command line as follows:

```
npm test
```

Unfortunately, we have not written any tests as yet, so Jest will respond with a test failure, as follows:

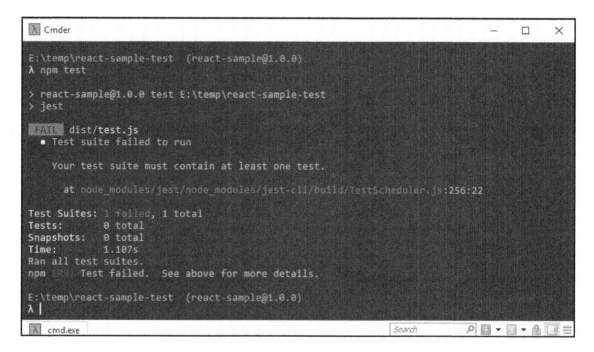

Basic React Test format

Let's start by writing a set of tests that check the internal state of the application on startup. Remember that there are two properties of our React app that are set as default properties. These are the title property, and the SelectedItem property. Our test for the title property will be as follows:

```
import * as React from "react";
import * as ReactDOM from "react-dom";
import * as ReactTestUtils from "react-dom/test-utils";
```

```
import { ItemCollectionView, ClickableItemArray } from '../src/ReactApp';

describe('/test/react.app.tests.tsx : ArrayView tests', () => {

    let renderer: any;

    beforeEach(() => {
        renderer = ReactTestUtils.renderIntoDocument(
            <ItemCollectionView items={ClickableItemArray} />
        );
    });

    it('should render Title property', () => {
        let domNode = ReactDOM.findDOMNode(renderer) as Element;
        let title = domNode.querySelector("h1") as Element;
        expect(title.textContent).toBe('Please select:');
    });
});
```

The structure of this test file should be fairly familiar by now. We start with some `import` statements, for loading the `React`, `ReactDOM` and `ReactTestUtils` libraries. We then load our `ItemCollectionView` React component, as well as the `ClickableItem` array from the `src/ReactApp.tsx` file. Our test is using Jasmine, and so has the familiar `describe`, `beforeEach` and `it` functions.

Our test sets up a variable named `renderer`, which is assigned within the `beforeEach` function. We are using a function named `renderIntoDocument` of the `ReactTestUtils` static instance in order to create a test instance of our `ItemCollectionView` component. Note that the `renderIntoDocument` function takes a React-style HTML snippet that is very similar to the one found in `index.tsx`. It is using React syntax to set up a test environment for the `ItemCollectionView` component. This is very similar to the other frameworks that create a specific test environment for the object under test. `ReactTestUtils` has a number of functions available for creating and manipulating the environment for our object under test.

Our test starts by creating a variable named `domNode`, which will hold the topmost DOM element for our component. We then use the `ReactDom.findDOMNode` function, and pass in the `renderer` variable as an argument. This function will return a handle to the topmost DOM element that is created for our component. Once we have this handle, we can use it to call a standard `querySelector` or `querySelectorAll` function to find elements within the DOM. Our test is using the `querySelector` function to find the first `<h1>` element, and then checking that the `textContent` of this element has been set to `'Please select:'`.

This is the process that we will follow for most of our React tests. We use the instance returned by the `renderIntoDocument` function call to find the topmost DOM node for our component, and then use this DOM node to query for each element we are looking for. Running `npm test` now will execute this test, and report one passing test, as follows:

Initial state tests

As mentioned earlier, our React application starts with an initial state. The `title` property is set, the `SelectedItem` property is set, and the application should render three buttons to the screen. Let's now extend our test suite to check for these elements. Firstly, we will test that the `SelectedItem` property has been rendered to the DOM correctly, as follows:

```
it('should render SelectedItem property', () => {
    let domNode = ReactDOM.findDOMNode(renderer) as Element;
    let selectedItem = domNode.querySelector("#selectedItem") as Element;
    expect(selectedItem.innerHTML).toContain("0 -None Selected");
});
```

Here, we have used the same pattern as our earlier test to find a DOM element with the id of selectedItem. We are then checking that the innerHTML element is rendered correctly. There is nothing really special about this test, other than the fact that we are using the innerHTML property of the DOM node instead of the textContent property as used earlier. Let's now check that the buttons have been rendered correctly, as follows:

```
it('should find three buttons', () => {
    let domNode = ReactDOM.findDOMNode(renderer) as Element;
    let ulElement = domNode.querySelector("ul") as Element;
    let buttons = ulElement.querySelectorAll("button")
        as NodeListOf<HTMLButtonElement>;

    expect(buttons.length).toBe(3);
    for (let i = 0; i < buttons.length; i++) {
        expect(buttons[i].textContent).toContain("Item");
    }

});
```

There are a few things that are of interest in this test. We start by obtaining a handle to the DOM node through the call to ReactDOM.findDOMNode as usual. We then use this handle to find the first <ul> element, which we store in the variable named ulElement. Note how we then use this ulElement handle to again call querySelectorAll in order to find all of the child button elements. This means that we are able to target our DOM searches by finding a top-level element, and then using this element in further queries to refine our searches.

Our search for the buttons within the top-level <ul> element is using the querySelectorAll function, as we are expecting an array of button elements to be found. The second interesting thing about this DOM search for buttons is the type that the querySelectorAll function returns. We are casting the return type to be of type NodeListOf<HTMLButtonElement>. This means that we expect the call to the querySelectorAll function to return a list of DOM nodes of type HTMLButtonElement. The TypeScript definition files for React have an exhaustive list of what elements can be returned from the call to the querySelector and querySelectorAll functions.

If we right-click on the `querySelector` function, and select **Go to Definition**, we will see the definition of this function as follows:

```
querySelector<K extends keyof HTMLElementTagNameMap>
    (selectors: K): HTMLElementTagNameMap[K] | null;
```

This function definition tells us the following information:

The generic parameter that is passed in named K, is using the `keyof` keyword to constrain the type of K to only allow values that are properties of the `HTMLElementTagNameMap` type. If we again right-click on the `HTMLElementTagNameMap` type, we will see that it is an interface that defines all of the possible combinations of the type K, and their return types, as follows:

```
interface HTMLElementTagNameMap {
    "a": HTMLAnchorElement;
    "abbr": HTMLElement;
    "address": HTMLElement;
    "applet": HTMLAppletElement;
    "area": HTMLAreaElement;
    . . .
}
```

The `keyof` operator, when applied to this interface, will return a string literal that must equal either "a", or "abbr", or "address", or "applet" and so forth. This means that we are only able to invoke the `querySelector` function with a defined set of strings, where each string maps to the defined set of HTML types that we can use. Each of these string values, which are generated by the use of the `keyof` keyword, will return an element of a certain type. In our case, the string literal "button" will return a type of HTMLButton element. This is an example of a very good and practical use of the `keyof` keyword that allows the arguments of a function call to be restricted to a certain set of strings, and where each string value will return a different type.

Once we have a list of our buttons, we are able to check that their `textContent` fields have been set correctly.

React form input

Let's now write a set of tests for our React form. The first test that we will write will be to check that the input element has been set to the correct initial value. Again, this test is important in the life cycle of forms, since in a real-world application, we could be setting these initial values from an existing database record. Our test is as follows:

```
it('should render a form with default value ', () => {
    let domNode = ReactDOM.findDOMNode(renderer) as Element;
    let form = domNode.querySelector("form") as Element;
    expect(form).toBeTruthy();

    let label = form.querySelector("label")!;
    expect(label.innerHTML).toContain("Name :");

    let input = form.querySelector("input")!;
    expect(input.value).toBe('Your Name');
});
```

Here, our test starts by searching for a `form` element within the rendered DOM, and then it checks that the `form` element has indeed been found. The test then finds the `label` for our input element, and ensures that it has been set to `"Name :"`. Take another look, however, at the `querySelector` function for the label element. Note that we are using TypeScript's non-null assertion operator here (`!`) to mark the type that the `querySelector` returns. This is done to tell the compiler that we are sure that the value returned will not be `null` or `undefined`. Without this non-null assertion operator, TypeScript will generate numerous compile errors stating that the variable could possibly be null.

In an earlier chapter, when discussing the non-null assertion operator, the author argued that there should not be any cases in standard code where this operator should be used. This seems to be a good case for it, however. Let's take a look at why. Our test has an assertion directly after attempting to find the DOM element. In this case, we do not need to program defensively in order to deal with the variable if it could be `null`. Our test will fail if the element cannot be found, or if the element does not have the correct text in the `innerHTML` property. We can, therefore, indicate to the TypeScript compiler that we are OK with the element being `null`, since our test will fail if it is anyway. In this case, the non-null assertion operator saves us from making our tests overly complex.

Our test continues by finding the `input` element within the DOM, and then checks the `value` attribute of the `input` element to ensure that it is set to the value `"Your Name"`. Remember that the HTML syntax to set an initial input element's value is as follows:

```
<input type="text" value="Your Name"/>
```

So `value` is an attribute of the input element, and must be set when rendering the form to prepopulate the input element.

Let's now take a look at how to update a form value, as shown in the following test:

```
it('should update form value', () => {

    let domNode = ReactDOM.findDOMNode(renderer) as Element;
    let form = domNode.querySelector("form") as Element;
    expect(form).toBeTruthy();

    let input = form.querySelector("input")!;
    input.value = 'updatedInputValue';

    ReactTestUtils.Simulate.change(input);

    expect(renderer.state.inputName).toBe('updatedInputValue');

});
```

Here, we have a test that finds the `form` element, and then finds the child `input` element. We then set the value of the input element to `'updatedInputValue'` by simply setting the `value` property. We then call the `ReactTestUtils.Simulate.change` function, passing in the element that we want to update. The `Simulate` function will dispatch a DOM event with optional data to the control. This is how we update the DOM element, similar to Angular's `detectChanges` function. Once this is done, we can check the `state` property of our `renderer` variable to ensure that the `inputName` property has been updated correctly.

Remember that React uses the `state` property to both get and set values that our component is working with. Once a user has changed a value on a form, because this value is bound to a property on a React component, the `state` property will contain the updated value.

React form submission

Our final set of tests for React forms will be to submit the form itself. Remember that we have declared a function that will be called when the form is submitted, as follows:

```
<form onSubmit={this.onSubmit} >
```

Here, our React component has specified that the onSubmit function should be called when the form itself is submitted. This function can then be used to convert the form's values into a JSON structure for submitting to a REST endpoint. While we will not show how to interact with a REST endpoint here, the important step for our tests is to ensure that the onSubmit function is called.

Using the React testing framework, there are actually two ways that we can simulate a form submission event. Let's take a look at the first, as follows:

```
it('should trigger onSubmit when form is submitted', () => {

    let spy = spyOn(ItemCollectionView.prototype, 'onSubmit');

    let testRenderer = ReactTestUtils.renderIntoDocument(
        <ItemCollectionView items={ClickableItemArray} />
    ) as any;

    let formForSubmit =
        ReactTestUtils.findRenderedDOMComponentWithTag
            (testRenderer, 'form');
    ReactTestUtils.Simulate.submit(formForSubmit);

    expect(spy).toHaveBeenCalled();
});
```

Here, we have a test that starts by creating a spy for the onSubmit function of our React component. Again, we need to create this spy before the component is rendered to the DOM, so we attach the spy to the definition of the ItemCollectionView class by using the ItemCollectionView.prototype property. We then create a testRenderer variable, and call the ReactTestUtils.renderIntoDocument function to create the ItemCollectionView component, and render it into the DOM.

We then use the ReactTestUtils.findRenderedDOMComponentWithTag function to find the instance of our form. This function is similar to our previous DOM search functions. Once we have a handle to the form, we can call the ReactTestUtils.Simulate.submit function to submit the form. Our test then checks that the spy has been called, or, in other words, that the onSubmit function has been called on our component.

Note that while the `ReactTestUtils.Simulate.submit` function will submit the form for us, there is another way to trigger the form submission. Our form also has a button named `"Submit"`, which has been rendered as follows:

```
<button className="submit-button" type="submit"
    value="Submit">Submit</button>
```

This button is of the `"submit"` type, and clicking on it will therefore trigger the form submission. This means that a more accurate test for form submission would be to trigger a click event on this button, and ensure that the form is submitted correctly. Our test for this is as follows:

```
it('should trigger onSubmit when button is clicked', () => {
    let spy = spyOn(ItemCollectionView.prototype, 'onSubmit');

    let testRenderer = ReactTestUtils.renderIntoDocument(
        <ItemCollectionView items={ClickableItemArray} />
    ) as any;

    let button =
        ReactTestUtils.scryRenderedDOMComponentsWithTag
            (testRenderer, 'button');
    ReactTestUtils.Simulate.submit(button[3]);

    console.log(`after calling submit form`);
    expect(spy).toHaveBeenCalled();

});
```

Our test starts by creating a spy and rendering the React component to the DOM as usual. Note, however, that we are using another React testing function named `scryRenderedDOMComponentsWithTag`. This function will return all elements that it finds within the DOM that match the tag name. We are searching for elements of the `button` type, and therefore will actually find four elements within our component. The first three buttons are rendered as selectable items, and the fourth button is our form **Submit** button. Our test, therefore, calls the `ReactTestUtils.Simulate.submit` function with the fourth button in order to submit the form. We then expect that the spy has been called, which means that the `onSubmit` function on our component has been triggered on form submission.

React testing summary

React has a similar testing range to the other frameworks that we have covered, and allows for the creation of a component into a DOM specifically set up for the component under test. We can query this DOM to find each of the elements we are looking for, and ensure that they are displayed correctly. We then explored the techniques that React uses in order to set form values when a form is created, and to extract these values when they have been updated. Similar to Jasmine's `setFixtures` and Angular's `TestBed`, React provides a library named `ReactTestUtils` to aid with rendering components into the DOM, and simulating events. React uses Jest as a test runner instead of Karma.

Summary

In this chapter, we covered a fair bit of ground. We took an in-depth look at how to unit test each of our TypeScript compatible frameworks. All of the test frameworks we used allowed us to create components within a test DOM designed for the component under test. We were able to query DOM elements, ensure that they were initialized correctly, and simulated a user entering values into a form, and clicking on the **Submit** button. All of our frameworks provided a similar set of functionality, except for Aurelia, which did not allow us to test DOM events, such as button clicks.

unit-testing is really a mindset. Some developers, and indeed some development teams, are able to think about components from a testability point of view, writing unit tests as they are developing components. Some developers prefer to build an entire component first, and then build a set of unit tests to cover the functionality. Whichever path your team chooses, remember that without unit tests, we are really just randomly changing stuff every time we modify some code. Unit tests give our code the ability to change completely internally, without the risk of breaking any functionality. Unit tests give our applications a quality seal of approval to ensure that they work correctly at all times.

In our next chapter, we will take an in-depth look at modularization, using both CommonJs (using Node) and AMD-style module loading (using Require). We will also explore the SystemJs method of module loading, which combines both CommonJs and AMD in a single format.

10
Modularization

Modularization is a popular technique used in modern programming languages that allows programs to be built from a series of smaller libraries, or modules. Writing programs that use modules encourages programmers to write code that conforms to the design principle called **Separation of Concerns**. The basic principle of Separation of Concerns is that we should program against a defined interface. This means that, the code that is implementing this interface can be refactored, improved, enhanced, or even completely replaced without the rest of the program being affected. This also helps when testing our code, since the code that is providing the implementation of an interface can easily be stubbed, or mocked out in a test scenario.

JavaScript, prior to ECMAScript 6, did not have a concept of modules. Popular frameworks and libraries, such as **Node** and **Require**, implemented their own module loading syntax libraries to fill this gap. Unfortunately, two different approaches to module loading, and in particular the module loading syntax, were adopted by the JavaScript community. These two syntax styles were known as **CommonJS** (used in Node), and AMD, or **Asynchronous Module Definition** (used in Require). Fortunately, TypeScript has always supported both CommonJS and AMD module syntax.

Now that the ECMAScript 6 module syntax has been published, TypeScript has adopted and implemented it, and will automatically generate the correct module syntax for either CommonJS or AMD, based on a single compiler option.

In this chapter, we will explore what modules are, take a look at the ECMAScript 6 syntax for modules, and highlight the differences between CommonJS and AMD module syntax. We will then take a closer look at how Require uses AMD module syntax, and how SystemJS allows for using CommonJS module syntax in a browser. We will then explore CommonJS modules with regard to Node, and build a simple Node application using the Express framework. Following on from building a Node application, we will explore the world of cloud providers, and show how to build and deploy an application that does not need a server in order to run.

We will be covering the following topics in this chapter:

- Module basics
- AMD module loading
- SystemJS module loading
- Using Express with Node
- Amazon Web Services Lambda functions

Module basics

So what is a module? Essentially, a **module** is a separate TypeScript file that exposes classes, interfaces, or functions for reuse in other parts of the project. Creating modules helps to structure your code files into logical groups. As your application becomes larger and larger, it makes sense to have each of your Models, Views, Controllers, helper functions, and so on, in separate source files, so that they can be easily found.

Consider the following directory tree:

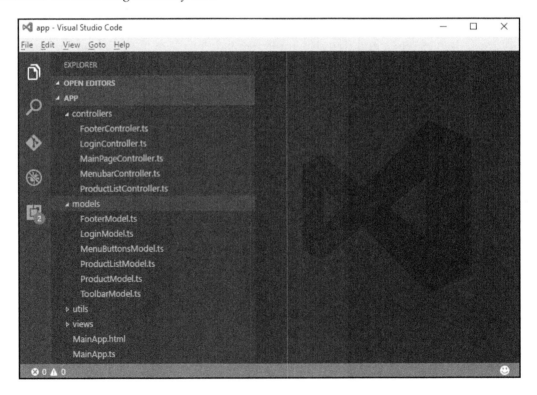

In this project structure, we have a separate directory for controllers, models, utils, and views. Within each of these directories, we have several files. Each filename is a clear indication of what we expect the file to contain. A FooterControler.ts file, for example, is expected to contain a controller class that handles the footer of our application. This structure makes our programming lives much simpler.

The problem with so many source files is that each file needs to be referenced by our HTML page in order for the application to work. Given the preceding directory structure, our HTML page would need to name each file as a source script, as follows:

```
<html>
    <head>
        <script src="./Main.js"></script>
        <script src="./controllers/FooterController.js"></script>
        <script src="./controllers/LoginController.js"></script>
        <script src="./controllers/MainPageController.js">
            </script>
        <script src="./controllers/MenuBarController.js"></script>
        <script src="./controllers/ProductListController.js">
            </script>
        <!--all other files here ..-->

        <script src="./views/ToolbarView.js"></script>

    </head>
    <body>
    </body>
</html>
```

Including each JavaScript file in the HTML page is both time-consuming and error-prone. To overcome this issue, there are two options available—either use a bundling process, or use a module loader. Bundling essentially means that we run a post-compile step to copy (or bundle) all of the source files into a single file, so that we only need to include a single file in our HTML page. While this is a valid solution to our problem, it means that the HTML page must load this bundled file all in one go before the web page is ready to render. If this bundled file is large, it means that our browser will need to wait until the file is loaded, which could impact on our overall page loading time.

Module loaders, on the other hand, allow the browser to load all files simultaneously in separate threads, meaning that our page loading time is significantly reduced. Module loaders also allow for each of our individual JavaScript source files to define which files they have a dependency on. In other words, if our HTML page loads the Main.js file, and the Main.js file specifies that it needs the FooterController.js file as well as the MainPageController.js file, the module loader will ensure that these two files are loaded before executing the logic in the Main.js file. This technique essentially allows us to define a dependency tree per source file.

Once a source file has been loaded by a module loader, any file that has a dependency on this file will not need the browser to reload the file from the website. This keeps the number of requests to the web server down to a minimum, and speeds up our page loading time.

Exporting modules

There are two things we need in order to write and use modules. Firstly, a module needs to be exposed to the outside world in order to be consumed. This is called **exporting**, and uses the TypeScript keyword export. This means that, within a particular source file, you may have functions and classes that are considered internal, and should not be made available to the outside world. Only components that are designed to be used outside of the source file should be exported. As an example of this, consider a module written in a file named lib/Module1.ts:

```
export class Module1 {
    print() {
        print(`Module1.print()`);
    }
}

function print(functionName: string) {
    console.log(`print() called with ${functionName}`);
}
```

Here, we have a class named Module1, and a function named print within the same source file. The Module1 class, however, has added the export keyword to its class definition, and as such, the Module1 class will be available to be used by the outside world.

The print function, however, does not use the export keyword. This means that the print function is only available for use within the Module1.ts source file, and is not available for use by the outside world. This function is therefore private in scope. The Module1 class is very simple, and defines a print function. Within this Module1.print function, a call is made to the private print function defined at the end of the file.

The export keyword, therefore, is exposing the entire Module1 class for use to the outside world.

Importing modules

In order to consume a module that has been exported, any source file that needs this module must import the module using the TypeScript import keyword. In our preceding sample, if we wish to consume the Module1 class, we would need to import it as follows:

```
import {Module1} from './lib/Module1';

let mod1 = new Module1();
mod1.print();
```

Here, we are in a file named main.ts, which sits at the root of the project. The first line of this file uses the import statement to import the definition of the Module1 class from the lib/Module1 file. Note the syntax of this import statement. Following the import keyword is a name in braces {Module1}, and then a from keyword, followed by the filename of the module itself. The module name {Module1} matches the name of the exported class in the './lib/Module1' file. Note too, that we do not specify a .ts or a .js extension when importing modules. The module loader will take care of mapping our import statement to the correct module filename on disk.

Once the module has been imported, we can use the class definition of Module1 as normal. In the last two lines of the preceding code snippet, we are simply creating an instance of the Module1 class, and calling the print function. The output of this code is as follows:

```
print() called with Module1.print()
```

 As we are running in a default Node environment, we will need to invoke our compiled main.js file by running node main from the command line.

Module renaming

When importing a module, we can rename the exported module as follows:

```
import {Module1 as m1} from './lib/Module1';
let m1mod1 = new m1();
mod1.print();
```

Here, we have imported the same module from `'./lib/Module1'`, but have used the `as` keyword when specifying the module name, that is, `{Module1 as m1}`. This means that we can now refer to the class named `Module1` (as according to our `export` definition) as simply `m1`. The last two lines of this code sample show how we can now create a class (of type `Module1`) by using the new `m1` name. The output of this code sample is exactly the same as the previous code:

print() called with Module1.print()

We can also have multiple names for an exported module, but these names need to be specified within the module itself. Consider the following module definition:

```
export class Module1 {
    print() {
        print(`Module1.print()`);
    }
}

export {Module1 as NewModule};
```

Here, on the last line of this code snippet, the `Module1` class has also been exported with the name `NewModule`. This allows a consumer to use either the name `Module1` or `NewModule` when importing the module, as follows:

```
import {NewModule} from './lib/Module1';
let nm = new NewModule();
nm.print();
```

Here, we are importing the `Module1` class using the name `NewModule`, and then using the `NewModule` class name to create an instance of the `Module1` class. The output of this code is exactly the same as we have seen previously:

print() called with Module1.print()

Default exports

When a module file only exports a single item, we can mark this item as a default export. This is accomplished with the `default` keyword. Consider a module file named `lib/Module2.ts`, as follows:

```
export default class Module2Default {
    print() {
        console.log(`Module2Default.print()`);
    }
}
export class Module2NonDefault {
    print() {
        console.log(`Module2NonDefault.print()`);
    }
}
```

Here, we have marked the `Module2Default` class as the default export for this module. Note that we can only have a single default export per module, but we are able to export other items within the file using standard export syntax. This can be seen in the second export of the `Module2NonDefault` class.

If a module has a default export, we can use a simpler syntax for importing it, as follows:

```
import Module2Default from './lib/Module2';

let m2default = new Module2Default();
m2default.print();
```

Here, we have removed the { . . . } braces, and are importing the default export as `Module2Default`. The name that we use in the import statement can be anything, and it can be renamed in our import statement as follows:

```
import m2rn from './lib/Module2';

let m2renamed = new m2rn();
m2renamed.print();
```

Here, we are importing the default export from the `'./lib/Module2'` file, as seen previously, but we are renaming it to `m2rn`. Note that, just as we used renamed module names earlier, we will need to refer to the module by the new name, as seen in the usage of this module, that is, `new m2rn()`.

While it may serve a purpose in some cases, renaming modules on import can make our code more difficult to read. As a habit, try to keep the module names on import the same as the module names that have been exported. This helps when reading our code, knowing exactly which module we are referring to in the original file.

Exporting variables

As we have with other exported elements, we are also able to export variables that have been defined within a module. Consider the following export in `lib/Module1.ts`:

```
var myVariable = "This is a variable.";
export { myVariable }
```

Here, we are defining a variable named `myVariable`, and setting the value within the `Module1.ts` file. We are then exporting the variable itself, by wrapping the variable name in braces, that is, `{ myVariable }`. We can then import and use this variable as follows:

```
import { myVariable } from './lib/Module1';
console.log(myVariable);
```

While this may seem a little strange, and at first sight is breaking object-oriented coding principles, this technique is used by numerous frameworks to inject functionality into existing singleton instances. We will explore this technique later in this chapter, when we discuss setting up routes with the Express engine.

Along with variables and functions, interfaces can also be exported using the `exports` keyword. In large projects, where REST endpoints are used, there are a number of tools that can automatically generate interfaces that describe the inputs and outputs of a REST endpoint. Using these tools will create a large number of interface definitions that can be imported into our code.

Import types

There are times where we need to write a global script that does not use modules. This means that we do not have the ability to use the `import` keyword in our code. Note that the `import` keyword does two things for us. Firstly, it imports the declaration file for a module, so that we have access to the type signatures of exported variables and functions through our development environment. Secondly, at runtime, it will load the JavaScript file for us to use. When we are not using modules, we need to specify each of the JavaScript files within our HTML file, as seen earlier in the chapter.

Unfortunately, when we attempt to write code without modules, we lose the ability for the development environment to use the declaration files. This means that we are not able to see what properties, functions or variables have been exported during development. If we have access to the declaration files, however, we can import just these types using what is called import types.

As an example, let's create a declaration file for a module name Module3. This will be created in a file named Module3.d.ts as follows:

```
export declare class Module3 {
    print(): void;
    add(): void;
    remove(): void;
    id: number;
    name: string;
}
```

Here, we have declared a class named Module3 that has three functions, named print, add and remove, and an id and name property. Let's now create a function that uses this class in a non-module file named import_types.ts, as follows:

```
function printWithoutModule( mod3 : any) {
    mod3.print();
}
```

Here, we have a function named printWithoutModule that has a single argument named mod3. We need to specify the type of this class as any in order to use it. Unfortunately, using the any type means that we lose all type safety.

We can, however, use the import keyword to import the declaration file for this class as follows:

```
function printModule3(mod3: import("./Module3").Module3) {
    mod3.print();
}
```

Here, we have used the import keyword to import our Module3.d.ts file, and cast the type of mod3 to the Module3 definition correctly. This means that our editor will automatically pick up the correct functions and properties of our Module3 class.

What we have done here is to import only the types that were found in the declaration file for use in our code.

AMD module loading

The module exporting and importing syntax that we have used thus far uses what is known as the CommonJS syntax, and is the default mechanism for module loading when using Node. Traditionally, this module loading syntax was not available for use within a browser, and as such, an alternative to CommonJS became popular, named Asynchronous Module Definition, or AMD. One of the most prevalent libraries to use AMD is RequireJS, or simply Require. In this section, we will reuse the source code for the modules we created in Node, and recompile them for use with AMD. We will then show how to use Require to load these modules in the browser.

AMD compilation

In order to compile our code to use the AMD module syntax, we will need to change the module setting in our `tsconfig.json` file, as follows:

```
{
    "compilerOptions": {
        "module": "amd",
        "target": "es5",
        "noImplicitAny": false,
        "sourceMap": false
    },
    "exclude": [
        "node_modules"
    ]
}
```

Here, we have specified the `"module"` parameter to be `"amd"`, instead of `"commonjs"`. This change specifies to the TypeScript compiler that the output of the compilation step must generate JavaScript code that uses the AMD module syntax. Let's take a look at what this means in terms of our module files.

Consider the following TypeScript module definition, as found in our `lib/Module3.ts` file:

```
export class Module3 {
    print() {
        console.log(`Module3.print()`);
    }
}
```

Here, we are exporting a class named `Module3`. When we compile this class with the CommonJS module option, TypeScript generates the following JavaScript file:

```
"use strict";
var Module3 = /** @class */ (function () {
    function Module3() {
    }
    Module3.prototype.print = function () {
        console.log("Module3.print()");
    };
    return Module3;
}());
exports.Module3 = Module3;
```

In this generated JavaScript file, we have the standard closure pattern being used to define a JavaScript class named `Module3`. Note the last line of the file, however. TypeScript has generated an `exports.Module3 = Module3;` line, which will attach our `Module3` class to the `exports` variable. This is the standard way to create modules when using JavaScript.

If we modify our compile options to "`amd`", instead of "`commonjs`", TypeScript will generate the following JavaScript for the same `lib/Module3.ts` file:

```
define(["require", "exports"], function (require, exports) {
    "use strict";
    var Module3 = /** @class */ (function () {
        function Module3() {
        }
        Module3.prototype.print = function () {
            console.log("Module3.print()");
        };
        return Module3;
    }());
    exports.Module3 = Module3;
});
```

Looking closely at this file, the inner class definition for the `Module3` closure, and the `exports.Module3 = Module3;` line are exactly the same as we saw earlier. The entire class definition has, however, been wrapped in a function named `define`. This is the difference between CommonJS and AMD modules. AMD uses a `define` function that takes two parameters: an array of strings, and a function definition.

The array of strings, that is, `["require", "exports"]`, is in fact a dependency array that specifies which libraries must be loaded before attempting to load this module. The function definition is called once the dependent libraries have been loaded. In addition, each of the items specified in the dependency array then become parameters that are available within the callback function. Hence `function(require, exports)` allows access to the `require` and `exports` arguments within the callback function. By having access to the `exports` global variable, we can now attach our `Module3` class definition to the `exports` variable that has been passed in as an argument.

 We have not changed our `Module3.ts` TypeScript file in any way in order to support both CommonJs and AMD module loading syntax. The TypeScript compiler has taken care of the module definitions automatically for us.

AMD module setup

Now that we have our modules compiling in AMD syntax, we can focus our attention on loading and using them in a browser. In order to load and use AMD modules in a browser, we will make use of the Require module loader. Require is a standard JavaScript framework, and as such can be installed via npm. Once installed within our project, we will also need the relevant declaration files. We can install Require using npm as follows:

```
npm install requirejs --save
```

And then install the declaration files, as follows:

```
npm install @types/requirejs --saveDev
```

With the Require framework and our declaration file in place, we can now configure Require to load our AMD modules.

Require configuration

Require uses a global configuration file, typically called `RequireConfig.js`, that serves as the entry point to our browser application. Let's go ahead and create a TypeScript file, named `RequreConfig.ts`, as follows:

```
require.config( {
}) ;

require(['main'], (main: any) => {
```

```
    console.log(`inside main`);

});
```

Here, we start with a call to the `require.config` function, passing in a configuration object that sets some default values. At this stage, we are calling the `require.config` function with a blank object. We will delve a little deeper into the available configuration parameters a little later in this chapter.

Following our call to `require.config`, we are then calling the `require` function with two arguments. The `require` function is very similar to the `define` function that we saw earlier. The first parameter to `require` is an array of strings, which lists the files to be loaded, and the second parameter is a callback function. As with the `define` function, each dependency listed in the first array of strings will be available within the callback function as a parameter.

In our code sample, then, the only dependency listed is `main`, which translates to our `main.js` file. Note that Require will automatically append the `.js` extension when attempting to load JavaScript files. Once the `main.js` file has been loaded, it will be available within the function definition as the argument `main`.

AMD browser configuration

The only remaining task, then, is to incorporate this `RequireConfig.js` file into our browser HTML, as follows:

```html
<html>
<head>
<script
    type="text/javascript"
    src="./node_modules/requirejs/require.js"
    data-main="./RequireConfig" >
</script>
</head>
<body>
</body>
</html>
```

This is a very simple HTML file that has only a single `<script>` tag to load the
`"./node_modules/requirejs/require.js"` file. This will cause the browser to load the
`require.js` module loader. Note, however, that this script tag has an attribute named
`data-main`. This `data-main` attribute is used by Require to load the initial configuration
file, which in our case is `RequireConfig.js`. Again, Require will automatically append
the `.js` extension for files, so this attribute is simply specified as `data-`
`main="./RequireConfig"`.

Once the `require.js` file has been loaded, the `RequireConfig.js` file will be loaded and
executed, and this will begin the module loading process.

If we use the **Network** tab on our **Developer Tools** within the browser, we will see how
Require is loading and parsing each of our module files, and automatically downloading
them for use, as follows:

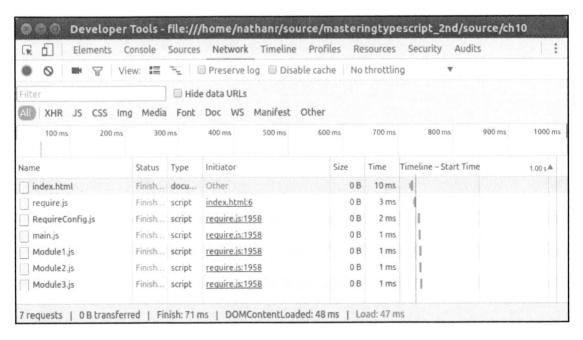

The browser starts by loading the `index.html` file, the `require.js` file, and then we see
that it is loading our `RequireConfig.js` file. Within our `RequireConfig.js` file, we
specified that we needed to load `main.js`, so this is the next file that Require will load. This
`main.js` file then used the `import` module syntax to import the files, `lib/Module1` and
`lib/Module2`. We can see then that these two files are being loaded next by Require.
Interestingly, our `lib/Module1` file also imports the `lib/Module3` file, so Require also
loads this file.

As can be seen by the network diagnostics, Require is recursively parsing each of our module files, starting with `RequireConfig.js`, and dynamically loading all modules that it finds. In this way, we are free to define modules as and when we please, all by simply using the `export` and `import` module syntax. As long as we import our dependencies within a module, the module loader will automatically load these files on our behalf.

AMD module dependencies

When working with modules, it is often the case that one module must be loaded before another. When module B needs to have module A loaded already, we can say that module B has a dependency on module A. When building a standard HTML page, this dependency is fairly easy to get right. All we need to do is ensure that the `<script>` tag for module A is included in the web page above the `<script>` tag for module B. Unfortunately, this is slightly more difficult when using AMD module loading.

With AMD module loading, each module is loaded independently and asynchronously. This means that the order by which we specify our modules is not enough. What we need in this case is to be able to describe the dependencies between modules, so that the AMD module loader can coordinate these module requests.

The Require AMD module loader uses settings in the call to `require.config` to specify dependencies, along with other module characteristics. As an example of needing to load files in a very specific order, let's set up a Jasmine testing environment using AMD module loading.

If you recall in the previous chapter, we set up a `SpecRunner.html` file for unit testing of Backbone samples. This `SpecRunner.html` file loaded three base files, as follows:

```
<script type="text/javascript"
    src="./<path_to_jasmine>/jasmine.js" >
</script>
<script type="text/javascript"
    src="./<path_to_jasmine>/jasmine-html.js" />
</script>
<script type="text/javascript"
    src="./<path_to_jasmine>/boot.js" >
</script>
```

The Jasmine framework has three component files that need to be loaded in the correct order: `jasmine.js` first, then `jasmine-html.js`, and finally `boot.js`. Loading `boot.js` before `jasmine.js` will generate runtime errors, and therefore `boot.js` has a dependency on `jasmine.js`. Let's take a look at the `RequireConfigSpecRunner.ts` file, which shows what the `require.config` file looks like for a Jasmine environment:

```
require.config( {
    baseUrl: ".",
    paths: {
        'jasmine' :
                './node_modules/jasmine-core/lib/jasmine-core/jasmine',
        'jasmine-html' :
                './node_modules/jasmine-core/lib/jasmine-core/jasmine-html',
        'jasmine-boot' :
                './node_modules/jasmine-core/lib/jasmine-core/boot'
    },
    shim : {
        'jasmine': {
            exports: 'window.jasmineRequire'
        },
        'jasmine-html' : {
            deps: ['jasmine'],
            exports: 'window.jasmineRequire'
        },
        'jasmine-boot' : {
            deps: ['jasmine-html'],
            exports: 'window.jasmineRequire'
        }
    }
});
```

Here, we have included two new properties in our call to `require.config`, namely `paths` and `shim`. We will discuss the `shim` property in a moment, but for the time being let's focus on the `paths` property. The `paths` property contains a property entry for each of our Jasmine files. The important thing to note here, though, is that these are named entries, and that the name of the entry must be used throughout the rest of the Require configuration. If we take a look at the first entry, which is named `'jasmine'`, and points to `'./node_modules/jasmine-core/lib/jasmine-core/jasmine'`, the name of this entry is therefore `'jasmine'`, and all references to this file must use the `'jasmine'` name from here on out. We could easily have named this `'jasminejs'`, or `'jjs'`, as long as the name of the entry is used consistently throughout the Require configuration. The `'jasmine-boot'` entry is a perfect example of this naming scheme, as the actual file is simply named `boot.js`, and not `jasmine-boot.js`, but the named entry is `'jasmine-boot'`.

Also note that Require will append the `.js` file extension to each of these entries when it loads the file from disk.

The next configuration block is the `shim` property. This `shim` property contains an entry for each of our named libraries. The `shim` entry for each of these libraries may contain an `exports` and/or a `deps` entry. The `exports` entry is used to specify the JavaScript global namespace that this library will attach to. As a simple example of what this `exports` property should contain, consider the following `shim` entries for jQuery, Underscore, and Backbone (Note that these are not included in our current `require.config`, but are shown here for illustration purposes):

```
'jquery' : {
    exports: '$'
},
'underscore' : {
    exports: '_'
},
'backbone' : {
    exports: 'Backbone'
}
```

The jQuery library's `exports` property is simply `'$'`. This means that the jQuery library is being attached to the `$` namespace by Require, which allows us to use any jQuery function by prefixing it with `$`, as in `$('#elementId')`. Likewise, the Underscore library uses the `_` character as its namespace, and it is used by simply calling `_.bind( ... )`. As a final example, the Backbone library uses the `Backbone` namespace, and is used by calling `new Backbone.Model`, for example. Each of these libraries therefore defines the global namespace in the `exports` property.

Along with the `exports` property in our `shim` configuration, each of our modules can also specify a `deps` entry, which is an array of strings. The `deps` entry is used to describe module dependencies. If we start at the bottom of the `shim` entries, we will see that the `'jasmine-boot'` entry specifies the `'jasmine-html'` entry as a dependency. Likewise, the `'jasmine-html'` entry specifies `'jasmine'` as a dependency. Require will therefore take note of these dependencies, and load our modules in order.

> The `deps` property is an array of strings, which means that a single entry can specify multiple dependencies.

Bootstrapping Require

As we saw with our minimal implementation earlier, the module loading process is kicked off with an initial call to the `require` function. Assuming that we have a very simple Jasmine test in the `test/SimpleTest.ts` file, we can bootstrap our test environment at the bottom of the `RequireConfigSpecRunner.js` file as follows:

```
var specs = [
    'test/SimpleTest'
];

require(['jasmine-boot'], (jasmineBoot) => {
    require(specs, () => {
        (<any>window).onload();
    });
});
```

This setup is interesting for a variety of reasons. Firstly, we have defined a variable named `specs` that is a simple string array. It contains a single entry, namely `'test/SimpleTest'`, which is a reference to our Jasmine test suite. Note, then, where this `specs` variable is used. It is used in a call to `require`, which is nested inside an outer call to `require`. This outer call is telling `require` that it must load the `'jasmine-boot'` module before executing the callback function. As the `'jasmine-boot'` module's `shim` entry specifies a dependency path, this callback function will only execute once all dependencies have been met.

Once the outer callback function is executed, the body of this function is again calling the `require` function, but this time with an array that lists all Jasmine files within our suite. This inner call to Require will already have the dependent modules loaded (that is, the Jasmine files) before it is executed. Once all modules in the `specs` array have been loaded, the callback function then simply calls `window.onload()`, which will kick off the Jasmine test run.

Also note that the `window` global variable needs to be cast to a type of `<any>` in order to allow TypeScript compilation.

With this Require configuration and bootstrapping code in place, we can fire up our browser and run the SpecRunner.html file to execute all tests. Again, firing up our developer network tools, we can see the order in which each of our modules are loaded:

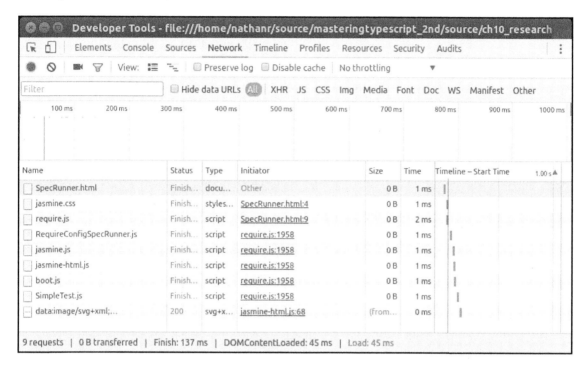

This module loading order matches what is defined in our require.config file, and is using the deps property of each of the entries to determine the order of files to load. The SpecRunner.html file is loaded first, along with jasmine.css and, finally, the require.js file itself. We specified that Require should load the RequireConfigSpecRunner file by using the data-main attribute in our HTML file. Require therefore loads this file, and starts to interpret the entries within it. Note that it loads jasmine.js first, which has no dependencies, and then loads jasmine-html, which has a dependency on jasmine. It then loads boot.js. Once all the dependencies within the require.config file have been loaded, it will run the inner require code that loads SimpleTest.js.

Fixing Require config errors

Quite often, when developing AMD applications with Require, we can start to get unexpected behavior, strange error messages, or simply blank pages. These strange results are generally caused by the configuration for Require, either in the `paths`, `shim` or `deps` properties. Fixing these AMD errors can be quite frustrating at first, but generally, they are caused by one of two things – incorrect dependencies or `file-not-found` errors.

To fix these errors, we will need to open the debugging tools within the browser that we are using, which for most browsers is achieved by simply hitting *F12*.

Incorrect dependencies

Some AMD errors are caused by incorrect dependencies in our `require.config`. These errors can be found by checking the console output in the browser. Dependency errors would generate browser errors similar to the following:

```
ReferenceError: jasmineRequire is not defined
ReferenceError: Backbone is not defined
```

This type of error might mean that the AMD loader has loaded Backbone, for example, before loading Underscore. So, whenever Backbone tries to use an Underscore function, we get a `not defined` error, as shown in the preceding output. The fix for this type of error is to update the `deps` property of the library that is causing the error. Make sure that all prerequisite libraries have been named in the `deps` property, and the errors should go away. If they do not, then the error may be caused by the next type of AMD error, a `file-not-found` error.

404 errors

File not found, or 404 errors are generally indicated by console output similar to the following:

```
Error: Script error for: jquery
http://requirejs.org/docs/errors.html#scripterror
Error: Load timeout for modules: jasmine-boot
http://requires.org/docs/errors.html#timeout
```

To find out which file is causing the preceding error, switch to the **Network** tab in your debugger tools and refresh the page. Look for 404 (file not found) errors, as shown in the following screenshot:

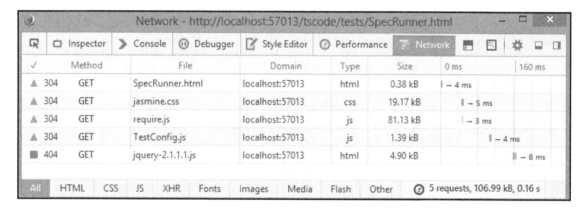

In this screenshot, we can see that the call to `jquery.js` is generating a `404` error, as our file is actually named `/Scripts/jquery-2.1.1.js`. These sorts of errors can be fixed by adding an entry to the `paths` parameter in `require.config`, so that any call to `jquery.js` is replaced by a call to `jquery-2.1.1.js`.

Require has a good set of documentation for common AMD errors (`http://requirejs.org/docs/errors.html`) as well as advanced API usages, including circular references (`http://requirejs.org/docs/api.html#circular`), so be sure to check the site for more information on possible AMD errors.

SystemJS module loading

SystemJS is a module loader that understands both CommonJS module format, AMD module format, and even the new ES6 module format. It works in both Node and the browser, and as such, describes itself as a universal module loader. Before SystemJS came along, Node-based solutions used CommonJS format, and browser-based solutions used AMD format. Now we can use CommonJS format in the browser, and even mix and match module syntax. In this section, we will take a look at how to configure SystemJS for loading CommonJS modules in the browser.

SystemJS installation

SystemJS can be installed using npm as follows:

```
npm install systemjs --save
```

The relevant declaration files can be installed using @types as follows:

```
npm install @types/systemjs --saveDev
```

SystemJS browser configuration

In order to use SystemJS within our browser, we will need to include the `system.js` source file, and then run a configuration script for SystemJS, similar to our `RequireConfig.js` file. Our HTML page is as follows:

```html
<html>
<head>
</head>
<body>
    <script
        src="./node_modules/systemjs/dist/system.js">
    </script>
    <script src="./SystemConfig.js"></script>
</body>
</html>
```

Here, we have included two script files. One for the `system.js` framework itself, and one for a file named `SystemConfig.js`. This `SystemConfig.js` file is generated from the following `SystemConfig.ts` file:

```
SystemJS.config({
    packages : {
        'lib' : { defaultExtension: 'js' }
    }
});
SystemJS.import('app.js');
```

Our SystemJS configuration file starts with a call to the `SystemJS.config` function, and includes a configuration object. Within this object, we have only specified one property, named `packages`. This `packages` property specifies a `lib` property and, within this, a single property named `defaultExtension : 'js'`. SystemJS uses the `packages` property to specify options for each of our source directories, or packages. The `lib` property therefore relates to all files contained within the `./lib` directory. The `defaultExtension` property tells SystemJS that all modules within the `./lib` sub-directory have a default extension of `.js`.

This means that when SystemJS encounters a module import, such as `import {Module1} from './lib/module1'`, it will append the default extension of `'.js'` to the module filename, and therefore load a file named `'./lib/module1.js'`.

The second part of our SystemJS configuration file is a call to the `SystemJS.import` function, specifying the `app.js` file as the starting point for our application. Once SystemJS has loaded the `app.js` file, it will begin to parse our code for all other imported modules, and then load them for use. If we view the **Network** tab in our browser **Developer Tools**, we will see the following files loading:

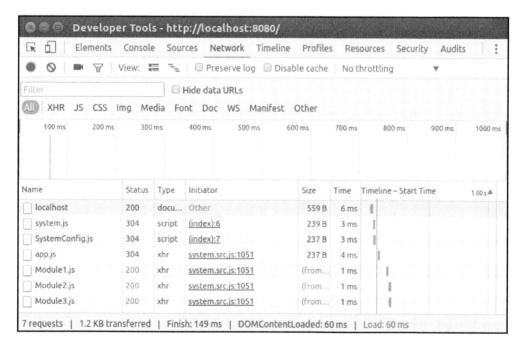

Note that with both AMD modules, and SystemJS modules, the Chrome browser assumes that these are being served from a running web server. If you attempt to load a page from disk, that is, hit *Ctrl+O* from Chrome, and navigate to your file on disk, you will receive a number of errors, as shown in the following screenshot:

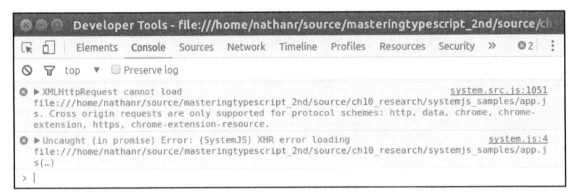

Other browsers, such as Firefox, do not show these errors. Chrome does, however, supply a command-line option that allows this behavior, `--allow-file-access-from-files`. Alternatively, in order to load a page that uses SystemJS, simply run `http-server` from the root directory of your project, and then browse to the URL shown on the console. When `http-server` starts, it will show the IP address and port you should point your browser to, as follows:

```
Starting up http-server, serving ./
Available on:
  http://127.0.0.1:8080
  http://192.168.1.101:8080
```

SystemJS module dependencies

So far, we have shown how to configure SystemJS to load modules as dependencies, when they are imported using `import` statements within our code. Let's finish this discussion on SystemJS by showing how to treat module dependencies, as we did with AMD. As with our AMD module dependency sample, we will build a unit testing framework with Jasmine and SystemJS. Remember that Jasmine has a specific module loading order. This means that the core `jasmine.js` file must be loaded before `jasmine-html.js`, and then, when that is done, we can load the `boot.js` module and run our tests.

Let's assume that we have two very simple test suites in the `test` directory, named `SimpleTest.ts`, and `SimpleTest2.ts`. These two files are just executing a sanity test. `SimpleTest.ts` is as follows:

```
describe('SimpleTest.ts : sanity test', () => {
    it('should pass', () => {
        expect(true).toBeTruthy();
    });

});
```

And `SimpleTest2.ts` is as follows:

```
describe('SimpleTest2.ts : sanity test 2', () => {
    it('should pass', () => {
        expect(true).toBeTruthy();
    });

});
```

In order to run these tests, we will also need a `SpecRunner.html` file, as follows:

```
<html>
<head>
    <link rel="stylesheet"
      type="text/css"
      href="./node_modules/jasmine-core/lib
          /jasmine-core/jasmine.css" />
</head>
<body>
    <script src="./node_modules/system.js/dist/system.js">
        </script>
    <script src="./SystemConfigSpecRunner.js"></script>
</body>
</html>
```

Here, we have a standard HTML file that loads the `jasmine.css` file and `system.js` itself. Note that we are then loading the `SystemConfigSpecRunner.js` file that holds our configuration. This `SystemConfigSpecRunner.ts` file is as follows:

```
SystemJS.config({
    baseUrl : '.',
    packages : {
        'lib' : { defaultExtension: 'js' }
        ,'test' : { defaultExtension: 'js' }
    },
     paths: {
```

```
            'jasmine' :
                './node_modules/jasmine-core/lib/
                jasmine-core/jasmine.js',
            'jasmine-html' :
                './node_modules/jasmine-core/lib/
                jasmine-core/jasmine-html.js',
            'jasmine-boot' :
                './node_modules/jasmine-core/lib/
                jasmine-core/boot.js'
        },
        meta : {
            'jasmine-boot' : {
                deps : ['jasmine-html']
                ,exports: 'window.jasmineRequire'
            },
            'jasmine-html' : {
                deps : ['jasmine']
                ,exports: 'window.jasmineRequire'
            },
            'jasmine' : {
                exports: 'window.jasmineRequire'
            }
        }
    });

    SystemJS.import('jasmine-boot').then( () => {
        Promise.all([
            SystemJS.import('test/SimpleTest'),
            SystemJS.import('test/SimpleTest2')
        ])
        .then(() => {
            (<any>window).onload();
        })
        .catch(console.error.bind(console));

    });
```

There are two parts to this configuration file. Firstly, we call the `SystemJS.config` function with a configuration block, and then, near the bottom of the file, we call the `SystemJS.import` function to load and boot our Jasmine test environment. Let's focus on the configuration block to start off with.

Our configuration blocks start by specifying the `baseUrl` property as `'.'`. This tells SystemJS that all module requests are relative to the current directory. The next property is `packages`, and as we have seen before with SystemJS, this sets the default extension to `js` for the `'lib'` and `'test'` sub-directories.

The third property in our configuration block is the `paths` property. This property is very similar to the AMD version of the `paths` property, with one notable exception—the inclusion of the `.js` file extension on each of the path properties. As we saw with the Require version of the `paths` property, these paths are **named properties**, and as such the name given in the `paths` property (for example, `'jasmine'`) must be used consistently throughout the configuration block.

The next property that we need is the `meta` property. The format and usage of the `meta` property is exactly the same as the `shim` property used in Require, and accomplishes the same thing. The `meta` property is where our dependencies are set for each of the Jasmine libraries. As with the Require version, we specify both the `deps` property (for dependencies), and the `exports` property (for our global namespace).

Bootstrapping Jasmine

Let's now take a closer look at the call to `SystemJS.import` at the bottom of the `SystemConfigSpecRunner.ts` file:

```
SystemJS.import('jasmine-boot').then( () => {
    Promise.all([
        SystemJS.import('test/SimpleTest'),
        SystemJS.import('test/SimpleTest2')
    ])
    .then(() => {
        (<any>window).onload();
    })
    .catch(console.error.bind(console));

});
```

Here, we are bootstrapping the Jasmine environment by loading the Jasmine module named `'jasmine-boot'`. As with Require, SystemJS will find and load all dependencies that have been specified in our dependency tree for `'jasmine-boot'`, which in this instance, includes both `'jasmine-html'` and `'jasmine'` itself. We then attach a fluent style `.then` function to execute once Jasmine has been loaded. Within this function, we are then loading our two test suites with a call to `Promise.all`. This technique is similar to the one we used with Require, where we split the loading of test specs outside of our `SystemJs config` block, so that it is easier to add multiple tests without major modifications to the SystemJS configuration. The `Promise.all` function loads all spec files, and again uses a fluent syntax to attach a `then` function that will be executed when all files have been loaded. The function simply calls `window.onload()`, and as we saw with Require, will force Jasmine to execute all tests. The final call is to `catch`, where we log any errors to the console.

Our SystemJS configuration is complete. With this in place, we can load our `SpecRunner.html` file to execute our Jasmine tests. We now know how to specify and use module dependencies with SystemJS.

Using Express with Node

In this section of the chapter, we will continue our exploration of modules by showing how to build a simple Node web server application. In order to accomplish this, we will make use of the ExpressJS (or simply Express) web framework for Node. Express provides us with a library of reusable Node modules to handle the basic functionality required for building a web server. This includes routing, a template engine for generating web pages, libraries for handling sessions and cookies, authentication, and error messages (think 404 errors), to name a few. Express provides a rich set of modules and APIs to cover everything you would need for a production web server application.

Express setup

In order to build an Express application, we will need to install Express in our development environment, as well as include the various declaration files that are needed for TypeScript compilation. Express can be installed using npm as follows:

```
npm init
npm install express --save
```

Once Express has been installed, we will need the corresponding declaration files, as follows:

```
npm install @types/express --saveDev
```

Express uses a series of other npm libraries whose declaration files are not included in the core `express.d.ts` declaration file. In order to allow for TypeScript compilation, we will need to install a few other declaration files as follows:

```
npm install @types/express-serve-static-core --saveDev
npm install @types/serve-static --saveDev
npm install @types/mime --saveDev
npm install @types/node --saveDev
```

We can now write the simplest of web applications for Express, in a file named `simple_app.ts`, as follows:

```
import express from 'express';

let app = express();

app.get('/', (req: express.Request, res: express.Response) => {
    res.send('Hello World');
});

app.listen(3000, () => {
    console.log(`listening on port 3000`);
});
```

We start by importing the Express module, `from 'express'`, and attaching it to a namespace named `express`. Note how we are using the default export named express from the express library.

We then create a local variable named `app`, and assign a new instance of `express()` to it. The express module that we imported has a default constructor function that we are using to create our Express application.

We then call the `get` function on our `app` instance. This will set up what is known as a route handler in Express. The first argument is the string `'/'`, which tells Express that any HTTP request to `'/'` should be handled by our handler function, which is the second argument to the `get` function. Within this function, we are simply calling the `res.send` function to send the `'Hello World'` string to the HTTP request. Note how we are strongly typing the `req` parameter to be of type `express.Request`, and the `res` parameter to be of type `express.Response`.

Express allows us to set up multiple route handlers, such that '/login' can be handled by a particular handler function, or '/users' by another. If no other handlers are specified, Express will route the request to the closest matching handler. This means that if a handler for '/login' is defined, it will handle all requests that start with '/login'. In our sample application, we have only specified a handler for '/', so all requests will be routed to this handler.

The final part of our application calls the listen function on the app instance, and essentially sets up the listening loop. The first argument is the port number to listen on, and the second is a function that is called on initial application startup. Here, we are simply logging a message to the console.

We can compile and then run this Node Express application by typing the following:

```
tsc
node simple_app.js
```

Our Express application will start up on port 3000, and wait for HTTP requests. Firing up a browser, and pointing it to http://locahost:3000 will trigger the request handler, rendering **Hello World** to the browser, as follows:

Using modules with Express

If we wrote all handlers for our application in a single file, with an app.get function for each application route, this would become a maintenance headache very quickly. What we really need to do is create a separate module for each of our request handlers, and then reference them from our main application. Luckily, this is very simple using the standard module syntax.

As an example of how to do this, let's create a handler function in a new module file. This file will be named SimpleModuleHandler.ts, as follows:

```
export function processRequest(
    req : express.Request, res: express.Response) {
    console.log(`SimpleModuleHandler.processRequest`);
```

```
        res.send('Hello World');
    };
```

Here, we are exporting a function named `processRequest`, which is a request handler function. As such, it has two parameters named `req` and `res`, which hold the HTTP request and response objects. This new handler function simply logs a message to the console, and then calls the `res.send` function to write a string to the response stream as we did earlier. Our `simple_app.ts` file can then be modified to use this module as follows:

```
import express from 'express';
import { processRequest } from './SimpleModuleHandler';

let app = express();

app.get('/', processRequest );

app.listen(3000, () => {
    console.log(`listening on port 3000`);
});
```

We have made two changes to our Express application. Firstly, we imported the `processRequest` function from the module file named `'./SimpleModuleHandler'`. Secondly, we modified the `app.get` function call. The `app.get` function call now references the `processRequest` function from the imported module. This means that when an HTTP request is received by our application, it will be processed by the `processRequest` function from the `SimpleModuleHandler` module. Running this application will now log a message to the console whenever a request is processed, as seen in the following console output:

```
> node simple_module_app.js
listening on port 3000
SimpleModuleHandler.processRequest
```

Express routing

So far, we have learned that we can register a request handler against a particular HTTP request. In a more complex application, however, we like to be able to register different request handlers in different modules in order to structure our code in a better way. Express provides what is known as a route handler for just this purpose. We can create many different request handlers and register them with the global instance of the express route handler.

Express provides a global Router object to handle registration of new route handlers, as well as to manage application routing as a whole. Let's create two new modules in a directory named routes, named Login.ts and Index.ts. We will use the Index.ts module to handle requests to '/', and the Login.ts module to handle requests to '/login'. This structure helps us to segregate application functionality into separate modules, and helps us to manage our code. In a production application, we may have a large number of distinct routes, each written within their own separate modules, and each handling GET or POST or PUT requests.

Our Index.ts file, in the routes directory will be as follows:

```
import express from 'express';
var router = express.Router();

router.get('/', (req : express.Request, res: express.Response) => {
    res.send(`Index module processed ${req.url}`);
});

export { router } ;
```

Here, we start by importing the express module, as we have done previously. We then call the Router function on the express module, and assign this to a local variable named router. This Router function acts as a kind of singleton instance, meaning that the call to express.Router returns the same router instance no matter where it was called from. In this way, we can attach new routes to the same global Express router handler, and specify both the path ('/') and the route handler function ((req, res) => {}) for each route. In the preceding sample, our Index route handler function simply logs a message to the browser.

Note the last line of this module. We are exporting the variable named router, using the variable export syntax (export { router }). Remember that this router variable was set using the express.Router() function at the beginning of the module, and then used to attach a new route handler, in the call to router.get. As we have modified this global router instance, we need to re-export it for use by our application. This means that we are essentially attaching a new route handler to the Express router singleton instance.

Let's now take a look at the `Login.ts` module, which is almost identical:

```
import * as express from 'express';
var router = express.Router();

router.get('/login', (req: express.Request, res: express.Response) => {
    res.send(`Login module processed ${req.url}`);

});

export { router } ;
```

Here, the `Login.ts` module also modifies the global `express.Router` instance, and this time attaches a route handler for the `'/login'` path. Again, this handler simply logs a message to the browser. The final line in this module is again exporting the `router` variable via the `export { router }` statement. Express, then, is giving us the ability to chain multiple route handlers to the same `express.Router` instance by importing and then re-exporting the same `router` variable.

Let's now update our application to use these two route handlers, as follows:

```
import express from 'express';
let app = express();

import * as Index from './routes/Index';
import * as Login from './routes/Login';

app.use('/', Index.router);
app.use('/', Login.router);

app.listen(3000, () => {
    console.log(`listening on port 3000`);
});
```

Our application is now simply importing the `Index` and `Login` modules from their respective files, and then calling the `app.use` function to register our route handlers. Note how we are referencing the exported `router` local variable from each module, as seen in the call to `Index.router` and `Login.router`. These two lines, therefore, are registering our route handlers for our application to use.

With these routing modules in place, any web browser request to `'/'` will be handled by the `Index.ts` module, and any request to `'/login'` will be handled by the `Login.ts` module. In this way, we are starting to organize our code into logical modules, each responsible for a distinct area of application functionality.

Express templating

Each of our route handlers are currently logging very simple messages to the browser. In a real-world application, however, we will need to render complete HTML pages. These pages would have a standard HTML structure, use CSS style sheets, and depending on the creativity of the design team, could easily become very complex. To support the complexity of generating HTML pages, most frameworks provide a templating engine.

Express also provides a complete template framework, which can use a choice of different template engines, including Pug, Mustache, Jade, Dust, and **Embedded JavaScript templates** (**EJS**) to name a few. Introducing a template engine within our Express application is as simple as installing the template engine of choice, and configuring Express to use it.

In this sample application, we will use the Handlebars engine. Handlebars uses standard HTML snippets, and introduces variables within the HTML templates using a simple double brace {{ and }} syntax. Template engines, such as Pug or Jade use their own custom formats to represent HTML elements, which are a mix of HTML keywords, class names, and variable substitution. As a quick comparison, consider a Handlebars template as follows:

```
<!DOCTYPE html>
<html>
  <head>
    <title>{{title}}</title>
    <link rel='stylesheet' href='/stylesheets/style.css' />
  </head>
  <body>
    {{{body}}}
  </body>
</html>
```

This template looks very much like standard HTML, with a few elements that will be substituted, such as {{title}} and {{{body}}}. A similar Jade template would be as follows:

```
doctype
html
  head title #{title}
  link(rel='stylesheet', href='/stylesheets/style.css'
    body
```

While this Jade template saves us a lot of typing, it does mean that we will need to learn and understand the various keywords and subtle syntax used in Jade in order to render valid HTML. Note how there are no recognizable HTML elements, which have instead been replaced by a custom Jade syntax. For the sake of simplicity, then, and to avoid learning a completely new syntax for HTML templates, we will use Handlebars as our template engine, as it uses recognizable HTML syntax, interspersed with substitution variables.

Using Handlebars

Handlebars can be installed via npm as follows:

```
npm install hbs --save
```

Once Handlebars has been installed, all we need to do is add three lines to our application source file (app.ts), as follows:

```
import express from 'express';
let app = express();

import * as Index from './routes/Index';
import * as Login from './routes/Login';

import * as path from 'path';
app.set('views', path.join(__dirname, 'views'));
app.set('view engine', 'hbs');

app.use('/', Index.router);
app.use('/', Login.router);
```

Here, we have added an import for the module named 'path'. The path module allows us to use several handy functions when working with directory pathnames. One of the variables exposed by the path module is the __dirname variable, which holds the full pathname of the current directory. We are using this __dirname variable in a call to the path.join function, which will return the full pathname to the local views directory. We are then setting the 'views' global Express parameter to this directory. Handlebars will, by default, use this global parameter to find the path where template files are stored.

Our last change to our app.ts file is to call app.set with the argument 'view engine', and the value 'hbs'. This function call indicates to Express that it should use Handlebars as the template engine. These are the only changes we need to make to our Express application.

Now that we have registered a template library, we can update our `routes/Index.ts` router to use a Handlebars template, as follows:

```
import express from 'express';
var router = express.Router();

router.get('/', (req: express.Request, res: express.Response) => {

    res.render('index',
        {
          title: 'Express'
        }
    );
});

export { router };
```

Here, we have updated the route handler function to call `res.render` instead of `res.send`, as was used previously. This `res.render` function takes the name of the template as its first parameter, and then uses a POJO to use as input to the template engine.

If we run our web application at this stage, we will generate an error indicating that Handlebars cannot find the view named `"index"`, as follows:

```
Error: Failed to lookup view "index" in views directory
"/express_samples/views" at EventEmitter.render
(//express_samples/node_modules/express/lib/application.js:579:17)
at ServerResponse.render
(//express_samples/node_modules/express/lib/response.js:960:7)
at //express_samples/routes/Index.js:7:9
at Layer.handle [as handle_request]
```

We will now need to create an `index` view template. This template must exist in the `views` sub directory, and as such will be named `views/index.hbs`. Handlebars uses the `.hbs` extension to specify Handlebars template files. This file is as simple as the following:

```
<h1>{{title}}</h1>
<p>Welcome to {{title}}</p>
```

Our `index.hbs` template file contains an `<h1>` element and a `<p>` element. Both of these elements use the `{{title}}` argument passed into the view template for parameter substitution.

Our rendered HTML page is now starting to look like the real thing. However, we still need the `<doctype>`, `<head>`, and `<body>` tags to be rendered in order for this to be valid HTML. Handlebars, similar to other rendering engines, allows us to specify a base layout template that will be used as the base layout for all pages. This is by default named `layout.hbs`, as follows:

```
<!DOCTYPE html>
<html>
  <head>
    <title>{{title}}</title>
    <link rel='stylesheet' href='/stylesheets/style.css' />
  </head>
  <body>
    {{{body}}}
  </body>
</html>
```

Here, we have defined the basic layout template to be used for each view. Handlebars will create HTML pages starting with this template, and then substitute any specific view template within the `{{{body}}}` tag. This base template has included a style sheet in the `<link>` tag in our `<head>` element, as we would expect in a standard HTML page. Note how the `<title>` element uses the `{{title}}` substitution parameter. Our login request handler renders this page with an object that includes a `title` property. Handlebars will therefore use this object to replace the `{{title}}` parameter with the passed-in object value. Our resulting page is as follows:

And our source HTML for this page is as follows:

Express POST events

Our Express application currently only renders an index page using the Handlebars template engine. Let's now extend our application to render a login form, and then process the results when a user completes this form, and posts it back to our application.

In order to do this, we will need a login route handler that will accept both HTML GET actions, as well as HTML POST actions. Our application will need to be modified in a few places. Firstly, we will need a handler for a GET request that will use an associated login.hbs view template to render the login form. Secondly, we will need another handler to process the POST request once the user has filled in the form and hit the submit button. This POST handler will need to parse the POST data.

Let's start with the login.hbs view in the views directory, which contains a simple HTML form, as follows:

```
<h1>Login</h1>
<p>
<form method="post">
    <p>{{ErrorMessage}}</p>
    <p>Username : <input name="username"></input></p>
    <p>Password : <input name="password"></input></p>
    <button type="submit">Login</button>
</form>
</p>
```

Here, we have created an HTML form that contains a few standard form elements. To start with, we have a `<p>` element to display the view property named `{{ErrorMessage}}`, which will be used to display any submission errors to the user. Following this, we have two input fields, named `username` and `password`, and a button named Login to `submit` the form.

Now that we have this view in place, we can update our `routes/Login.ts` file to render this view on a GET request, as follows:

```
import express from 'express';
var router = express.Router();

router.get('/login', (req: express.Request, res: express.Response) => {
    res.render('login',
        {
            title: 'Express Login'
        }
    );
});

export { router };
```

Here, we have modified our route handler to simply render the `'login'` view, and set the `title` property to a string containing the value `'Express Login'`. Running our application now and navigating to `http://localhost:3000/login` will invoke our login request handler, and display our simple login form as follows:

Now that our login form has been rendered, we can focus on processing the form values when they have been submitted. Clicking on the Login button will cause the HTML page to generate a POST message to the login request handler. We therefore need to specify a handler that will pick up this POST message. In order to do this, we need to modify our Login.ts handler, and included a new POST handler, as follows:

```
router.post('/login', (req, res, next) => {
    if (req.body.name.length > 0) {
        req.session!['username'] = req.body.username;
        res.redirect('/');
    } else {
        res.render('login', {
            title: 'Express',
            ErrorMessage: 'Please enter a user name'
            });
    }
});
```

Here, we are calling the post method of the router module. As we saw with the get function, Express uses the post function to set up a POST event handler within our module.

This post handler is checking the request.body.username property to read the form data out of the posted form request. If the username property is valid (which in this case is just that it has been entered), we store the value in the session property named req.session['username'], and redirect the browser to the default page. If the username property has not been entered, we simply re-render the login view, and display an error message.

Before we test this new login page, however, we will need to install and configure a few node modules, as follows:

```
npm install body-parser --save
npm install cookie-parser --save
npm install express-session --save
```

The body-parser module is used to parse form data as a result of a POST event, and attach this form data to the request object itself. This means that we can simply use req.body to dereference the form's data.

The `cookie-parser` and `express-session` modules are used for session handling. In our login `POST` handler, we are setting a session variable to the `username` property of the form data. This will not work without these two modules.

The final change we need to make is to import these modules into our application, and run through any configuration that they need. We will therefore need to update our `app.ts` application file as follows:

```
// existing code
app.set('view engine', 'hbs');

import bodyParser from 'body-parser';
import cookieParser from 'cookie-parser';
import expressSession from 'express-session';

app.use(bodyParser.json());
app.use(bodyParser.urlencoded({ extended: false }));
app.use(cookieParser());
app.use(expressSession({ secret : 'asdf' }));

// existing code
app.use('/', Index.router);
```

Here, we are importing the new modules using our standard `import` module syntax. We are then running through four `app.use` function calls, in order to configure each of our modules. The `body-parser` module uses the `json()` function call to return middleware that Express will use to convert incoming requests into objects attached to `req.body`. The `body-parser` also needs to set the `urlencoded` property in order to allow for JSON-like objects to be exposed. These two settings will create a POJO available via the `req.body` property when receiving `POST` requests.

The `cookie-parser` module is configured by simply using the exported constructor function, and the `express-session` module is also configured in the same way. Note that both the `cookie-parser` and `express-session` modules are needed in order to store variables in the `req.session` object.

With these modules in place, our `POST` request handler will be able to query `req.body.username` to find the username that was entered, and `req.body.password` to find the corresponding password. It will also be able to store values in the session.

HTTP Request redirection

Now that we have a working login module to handle a simple login request, we can redirect the browser session back to our home page, and the `Index.ts` request handler via the call to `res.redirect('/')`. Let's update our `Index.ts` request handler to work with the `username` value that we have stored in the session, as follows:

```
router.get('/', (req, res, next) => {
    res.render('index',
        {   title: 'Express'
            ,username : req.session!['username']
        }
    );
});
```

Here, we have simply added a new property to the object that is passed to our `index.hbs` template named `username`. The value of this property is retrieved from our session. We can now update our `index.hbs` view template as follows:

```
<h1>{{title}}</h1>
<p>Welcome to {{title}}</p>

{{#if username}}
    <p>User : {{username}} logged in.
{{else}}
    <p>Click <a href="/login">here to login</a></p>
{{/if}}
```

Here, we have added a code block within our Handlebars template that uses some JavaScript logic to render different HTML based on the `username` property. If the `username` property has a value, then we show that the user has logged in. If not, we render a link to the `'/login'` request handler to allow the user to log in. Our changes could not have been simpler.

Firing up our application now, we will see the home page, with a link to log in, as follows:

Following the link to log in, we will then be presented with the **Login** screen, as follows:

Once we have filled in the form, and clicked on **Login**, the login request handler will process our request, and then redirect our browser to the home page, as follows:

Note how the **Click here to login** link has disappeared, according to our logic, and the value of the username (from the session) is displayed, as the user is now logged in.

In this section of the chapter, we explored modularization as it applies to Node and the Express engine. We started with a simple Express application, and built a simple request handler as a Node module. We then explored the routing capability of Express, and built two distinct modules, one to handle requests to our main page, and the other to handle login functionality. We then introduced Handlebars as a rendering engine, and built three views: a `layout.hbs` view that held the overall page structure, a view for the main page, and a view for the login page. We then worked with a `POST` request handler and showed how to parse form values, and store a property in the user's session. Finally, we showed how redirection works, and tied these two pages together to implement login functionality in our application.

AWS Lambda functions

Node has been rather a game changer in the web application world. One of the reasons for this is the lightweight hardware specifications that are needed to run a Node web server. Node applications can be run on pretty much any hardware, starting from something as small as a Rasberry Pi. This means that the cost of setting up a Node web server is dramatically reduced compared to the cost of a server that runs a .NET or Java web application. In the modern age of cloud computing, this means that a small, low-cost cloud server can easily be used to host a Node application.

Most cloud services, including Azure, Amazon and Google, have taken this concept a step further, and now offer the ability to run code without the need for a server at all. This means that we are provided with a runtime environment that has all of the dependencies we need in order to respond to a web request. If we take Node as an example, as long as we have the basic Node modules available to us at runtime, setting up a handler to respond to a single web request requires just a few lines of code. Cloud service providers have been able to bundle all of the dependencies into a miniature runtime environment for exactly this purpose. All we need to do is to upload the few lines of code to handle a web request, and the cloud service provider will ensure that the environment required is available to handle this request.

Microsoft Azure provides what are called Azure functions for this purpose, and **Amazon Web Services** (**AWS**) provides what are called Lambda functions. AWS Lambda functions can be written in .NET, Go, Java, Node, Python or even Ruby. In this section of the chapter, we will take a look at setting up a simple AWS Lambda function to show how to create and use a Node module in one of these preconfigured runtime environments.

Lambda function architecture

Before we go ahead and build a Lambda function, let's first explore the three pieces of the AWS architecture that work together to respond to a web request. The first thing that we need to define is an API endpoint, or in AWS terms, an API resource. An API resource has a path, which will correspond to a URL, and an action, which can be GET, POST, PUT, or any of the other standard REST actions. As an example, a single GET request for the /test/hello URL is a single API resource, as can be seen in the following screenshot:

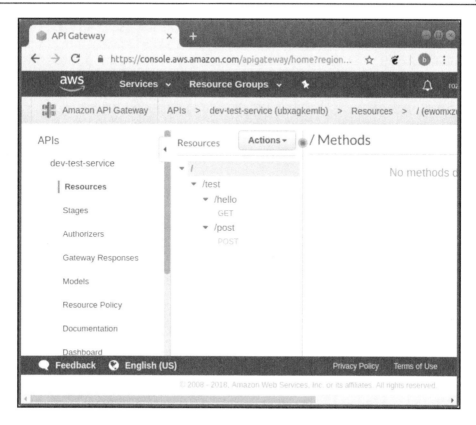

Here, we can see two API resources. The first is a `GET` request to
the `/test/hello` URL, and the second is a `POST` request to the `/test/post` URL.

Secondly, each API resource has what is known as a stage. A stage is an area where this
API will be deployed, and allows for further configuration of an API depending on its
intended purpose. As an example, you may set up a stage named `dev`, another named
`test`, and a final stage named `prod`. This allows for deployment to the `dev` or `test` stage
without impacting anything in the `prod` stage. The stage name makes up the first part of
the URL for any particular API endpoint. As an example, for a stage named `dev`, the full
path to a `GET` request for the API resource named `/test/hello` is `/dev/test/hello`.

The final architectural component is the AWS Lambda function itself. An API resource can be configured to execute an AWS Lambda function. This AWS Lambda function will execute within the context of the API resource, and is given information about this context on execution.

Using AWS resources and AWS Lambda functions is very similar to using a Node Express handler. Both have a path that specifies which handler will respond to the request, and both have some code that will execute when the endpoint is requested. AWS resources, however, introduce a stage, which is similar to setting up an entirely new Node Express instance on another server.

AWS setup

In order to use AWS, we will need to set up an AWS account. We will not cover the creation of an account here, but it is a relatively simple registration process. AWS provides a range of account and billing options, as well as a free tier that will not incur any costs. This free tier does have limitations, which are very generous, so be sure to read the terms and conditions to ensure that your usage of the free tier does exceed these usage limits.

Once we have an account set up, we will need to create a user that has programmatic access to the AWS API. The AWS API allows us to use external tools to create and manipulate any of the services available through AWS, including the creation of virtual machines, setting up security groups, and generally anything that the GUI interface can do. To create a user, open up the identity and access management section, select **Users**, and then **Add user**.

Add a name for your user, and ensure that the **Programmatic access** checkbox is selected, as shown in the following screenshot:

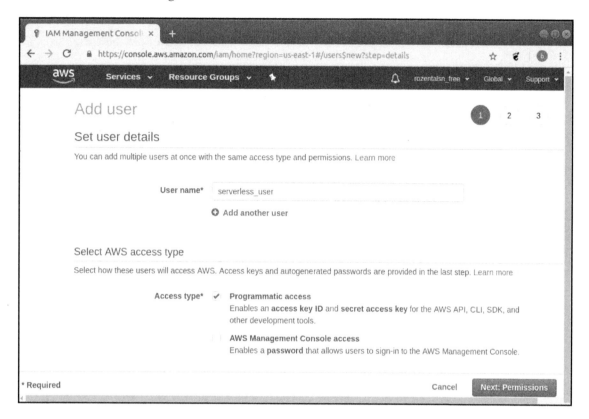

Click on the **Next: Permissions** button, and then select the **Attach existing policies directly** tab to show the list of policies that are available. Select the **AdministratorAccess** policy, and then click on **Next: Tags**:

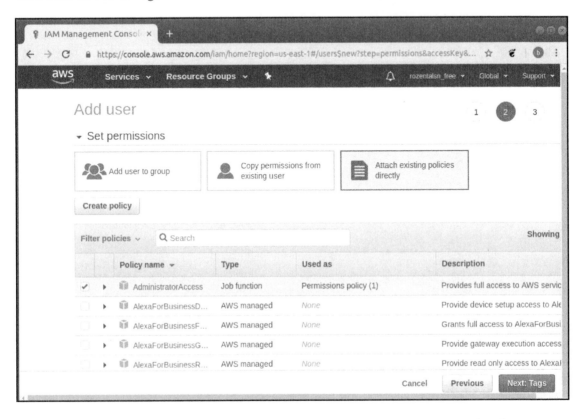

We will not create any tags for this user, so go ahead and click the **Next: Review** button, and then **Create User**. This will create the user for us, and then present the **Add user** success screen, as shown in the following screenshot:

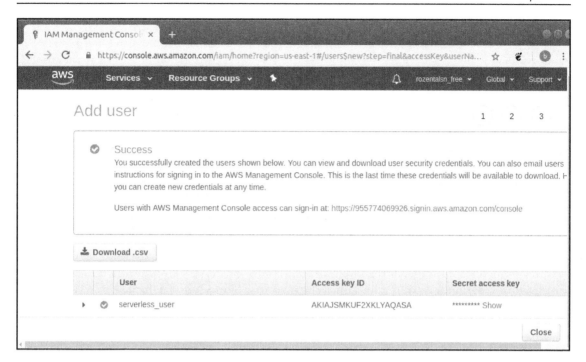

Here, we can see that a new user named **serverless_user** has been created successfully, and that it has been assigned an **Access key ID**, as well as a **Secret access key**. We will need both of these keys to be able to do anything using the AWS API, so make sure to store these values somewhere safe. There is also a **Download .csv** button that will allow us to download a csv file with these keys in it.

Now that we have a user configured that can use the AWS API, we can create an API resource, and attach a Lambda function to it.

Serverless

All of the AWS services that are available for use have a GUI portal that allows us to create, remove, configure and manage anything AWS-related. While this does allow us to explore the many options and configurations available, it is very easy to forget exactly what steps were required to configure a particular resource. When we have a large system to deploy into a particular AWS account, it makes sense to script these configuration and setup options so that we can easily repeat the steps time and time again. This process is called automated deployment.

Serverless is an open source automated deployment package that can target multiple cloud platforms. It can be used to deploy to multiple vendors, including AWS, Azure, Google Cloud, or even a local development environment. It is very flexible and extendable, and hides much of the low-level API function calls that are required by each vendor. In this section of the chapter, we will configure Serverless to deploy an Amazon Web Services API resource, attach it to a stage, and upload the source for an AWS Lambda function, all with simple configuration files. We will then write a simple Node-based sample program to access these newly created REST endpoints.

Serverless, being a Node module, is easily installed by simply running the following command on the command line:

```
npm install -g serverless
```

This will install Serverless as a global node module, and make it available for use from the command line. Once installed, we can check the version currently installed by executing the following:

```
serverless -v
```

At the time of writing, Serverless is at version 1.34.1, and as such shows the version as follows:

```
1.34.1
```

Serverless configuration

In order to use Serverless with our AWS Account, we will need to set up our credentials on the command line. This step will require the information that we downloaded when we created our AWS user with programmatic access, in particular the API **Access key ID**, and the **Secret access key**.

To set up Serverless with our AWS credentials, execute the following on the command line:

```
serverless config credentials --provider aws --key <insert access key> --
secret <insert secret key>
```

Here, we have specified configuration options for the credentials that Serverless will use to access the AWS API. The options that we have specified include aws as the API provider, as well as the API **Access Key ID** and **Secret access key**.

Once this step is complete, Serverless will store these credentials for subsequent use.

We can now create a standard Serverless template for an AWS Lambda function by executing the following on the command line:

```
serverless create --template aws-nodejs --path serverless-sample
```

This will create a new directory named serverless-sample, and within it, a serverless.yml file and a hander.js file. Let's first take a look at the generated handler.js file, as follows:

```
'use strict';

module.exports.hello = async (event, context) => {
  return {
    statusCode: 200,
    body: JSON.stringify({
      message: 'Go Serverless v1.0! Your function executed
        successfully!',
      input: event,
    }),
  };

};
```

Here, we have a JavaScript file that uses the module.exports property to expose a function named hello, as seen in the use of module.exports.hello =. This function is the AWS Lambda function itself, and is defined as an async function that has two parameters, named event and context. The event and context parameters are filled in by AWS in order to pass information from the API resource to the Lambda function. The body of the function returns a JavaScript object that has a statusCode and a body property. This object represents a standard HTTP response, and the statusCode property is the HTTP return code. In this example our HTTP request will return a 200, OK response. The body property contains a message property, as well as an input property.

Note how closely this code resembles an Express handler. Aside from the `event` and `context` parameters, both the Express handlers and our AWS Lambda handlers both attach a function to `module.exports`, and both return HTTP responses.

Serverless deployment

Now that we have an AWS Lambda function, we will need to attach it to an AWS resource, for which we need to specify the `stage`, and `path` properties. Serverless has created a `serverless.yml` file that contains this required information. Let's take a look at this file, as follows:

```
service: serverless-sample

provider:
  name: aws
  runtime: nodejs8.10

functions:
  hello:
    handler: handler.hello
```

Here, our `.yml`, or YAML file, has a number of properties. Note that YAML uses indentation to arrange properties, so that the top-level properties are all at the same indentation, and child properties are indented. This means that the `service`, `provider`, and `functions` properties are all at the same level, and that the `provider` property has two child properties named `name` and `runtime`. Following this indentation pattern, the `functions` property has a child property named `hello`, which in turn has a child property named `handler`.

The properties in this file specify that the service name will be `serverless-sample`, and that the service provider will be AWS. Also, the runtime engine that will be used for the AWS Lambda function will be NodeJs version 8.10. The `functions` property provides a name for the Lambda, and finally the `handler` property specifies the JavaScript file to use, which in this case is named `handler`, followed by a dot, and then the name of the function that is exported, which is `hello`.

There are a number of things that seem to be missing from this YAML file, however. We still need to specify the REST endpoint path, as well as the HTML method, which should be GET. We also need to specify the stage and AWS region that this Lambda should be placed in. The documentation for Serverless explains where these properties should be placed, and is well described at docs.serverless.com. Let's go ahead and modify this file as follows:

```
service: serverless-sample

provider:
  name: aws
  runtime: nodejs8.10
  stage: dev
  region: us-east-1

functions:
  hello:
    handler: handler.hello
    events:
      - http:
          path: test/hello
          method: get
```

Here, we have made two modifications. Firstly, we have added the stage and region properties that will deploy our Lambda function to the dev stage, and the us-east-1 region. We have also added an events property at the same level as the existing handler property, and added an http property with a path property of test/hello, and a method property specifying get. Note how the http property has a leading dash (-).

Once these minor changes have been made, we can deploy our Lambda function by executing the following on the command line:

```
serverless deploy
```

Serverless will then package our Lambda function, and deploy it to our AWS account using the user that we configured earlier. If all goes well, Serverless will log to the console the full URL for our newly created Lambda function, as shown in the following screenshot:

Our Lambda function has been deployed successfully, and Serverless has reported the full URL in the console. If we copy and paste this URL value into a browser, we will see that our AWS Lambda function has responded to our GET request, and returned a rather large JSON object, as shown in the following screenshot:

```
{
    "message": "Go Serverless v1.0! Your function executed successfully!",
    "input": {
        "resource": "/test/hello",
        "path": "/test/hello",
        "httpMethod": "GET",
        "headers": {
            "Accept":
"text/html,application/xhtml+xml,application/xml;q=0.9,image/webp,image/apng,*/*;q=0.8",
            "Accept-Encoding": "gzip, deflate, br",
            "Accept-Language": "en-GB,en-US;q=0.9,en;q=0.8",
            "cache-control": "max-age=0",
            "CloudFront-Forwarded-Proto": "https",
            "CloudFront-Is-Desktop-Viewer": "true",
            "CloudFront-Is-Mobile-Viewer": "false",
            "CloudFront-Is-SmartTV-Viewer": "false",
            "CloudFront-Is-Tablet-Viewer": "false",
            "CloudFront-Viewer-Country": "AU",
            "Host": "dso2yf67fd.execute-api.us-east-1.amazonaws.com",
            "upgrade-insecure-requests": "1",
            "User-Agent": "Mozilla/5.0 (X11; Linux x86_64) AppleWebKit/537.36 (KHTML, like Gecko)
Chrome/70.0.3538.77 Safari/537.36",
            "Via": "2.0 d8af458c1f500953a862b2a5e3684979.cloudfront.net (CloudFront)",
            "X-Amz-Cf-Id": "TpnSM3ddFhFDVdRBQ6QR0YgGBjD6WZLv3tMkmD9lvWsPVxbdsWysFg==",
            "X-Amzn-Trace-Id": "Root=1-5c0fb175-651421000612e500decc3400",
            "X-Forwarded-For": "203.164.30.25, 52.46.58.170",
            "X-Forwarded-Port": "443",
            "X-Forwarded-Proto": "https"
        },
```

TypeScript Lambda functions

The sample Lambda function that Serverless has created for us is in a standard JavaScript file named `handler.js`. Let's now look at how we can use TypeScript to generate a compatible JavaScript file that can be used as a Lambda function. To start off with, let's first initialize npm within this directory as follows:

```
npm init
```

This command will create a `packages.json` file within the `serverless-sample` directory, so that we can use it to install any node modules that we may need. We can then initialize TypeScript within this directory as per usual:

```
tsc --init
```

This will create a `tsconfig.json` file, which is ready for TypeScript compilation. To use Lambda functions within TypeScript, we will need to install two packages, as follows:

```
npm install aws-lambda --save
npm install @types/aws-lambda --saveDev
```

Before we create a TypeScript Lambda function, we will need to update the `tsconfig.json` file to include the `es2015` and `dom` standard libraries, as follows:

```
"module": "commonjs",
"lib": [
    "es2015",
    "dom"
],
```

These `lib` entries will allow us to use promises within our code.

Let's now create a file named `tshandler.ts` with the following content:

```
import { APIGatewayProxyEvent,
   APIGatewayProxyResult,
   Handler,
   Context } from 'aws-lambda';

export const handler: Handler =
   (event: APIGatewayProxyEvent, context: Context):
    Promise<APIGatewayProxyResult> => {
      return new Promise<APIGatewayProxyResult>((resolve, reject) => {
        console.log(`event : ${JSON.stringify(event, null, 4)}`);
        resolve({
           statusCode: 200,
           body: JSON.stringify({
           message: 'TypeScript Serverless v1.0!',
           input: event,
        }, null, 4)
      });
    })
   }
```

Here, we start by importing a few types from the `aws-lambda` module. We then `export` a constant function named `handler`, which is of type `Handler`. This `Handler` type ensures that we define a function with the `event` and `context` parameters and that the function returns a Promise of type `APIGateWayProxyResult`.

As we can see, just by converting our code from JavaScript to TypeScript, we are able to make use of strong typing, and understand the inputs and outputs of each of our functions, as defined in the declaration file. Our `handler` function simply returns a new Promise, and duplicates the `200` HTTP response as it did in the JavaScript version.

Let's now update our `serverless.yml` file to deploy this Lambda function to a new endpoint, as follows:

```
functions:
  hello:
    (... existing )
  tslambda:
    handler: tshandler.handler
    events:
      - http:
          path: tshandler/test
          method: get
```

Here, we have created a new property under the `functions` property that is at the same level as the existing `hello` property, named `tslambda`. The `handler` property is made up of the JavaScript file name, without the `.js` extension, and the name of the function that has been exported, hence, `tshandler.handler`. The `events` property now specifies that the URL path to our new TypeScript Lambda function is `tshandler/test`, and that this is for a `GET` request. Once we deploy this using `serverless deploy`, the new REST endpoint will be shown in the console, as follows:

https://dso2yf67fd.execute-api.us-east-1.amazonaws.com/dev/tshandler/test

As we can see, the URL includes the stage property, `dev`, as well as the URL path of `tshandler/test` that we have specified. If we fire up a browser, and copy this URL, we will see that our new TypeScript Lambda function returns a similar JSON packet to the Serverless sample, as follows:

We have just successfully compiled a TypeScript Lambda function, and deployed it to our AWS account.

Lambda node modules

In any normal Node-based development, we are able to make use of the myriad of node modules that have been written and made available as open source projects. So far in this chapter, we have used modules such as `Express`, `cookie-parser`, `lodash`, and even `jasmine` and `SystemJs`.

When developing Lambda functions, we are also able to use any node module that we need, as long as it is included during our deployment. In much the same way that we must issue an `npm install <module_name>` command in order to download the module to our `node_modules` directory, we need to be able to include these node modules in the runtime of an AWS Lambda function. Fortunately, the process of including node modules is very simple, and builds upon the standard `npm` mechanism that we have become accustomed to.

As an example of how to include external node modules in an AWS Lambda function, let's create a `POST` event handler that will accept some data within the Lambda function. This `POST` handler will include a node module named `http-status-codes` that includes human-readable definitions for all of the HTTP status codes that a Lambda function may need to return. Installation is via `npm` as follows:

```
npm install http-status-codes
```

Note that the `http-status-codes` npm module follows the modern trend of including a TypeScript definition file as part of the module itself, which means that we do not have to install a separate `@types` package just to allow TypeScript integration. With this package installed, we can create a new file named `posthandler.ts`, as follows:

```
import { APIGatewayProxyEvent,
         APIGatewayProxyResult,
         Handler,
         Context } from 'aws-lambda';
import * as HttpStatusCodes from 'http-status-codes';

export const postHandler: Handler =
    (event: APIGatewayProxyEvent, context: Context):
        Promise<APIGatewayProxyResult> => {
        return new Promise<APIGatewayProxyResult>(
          (resolve, reject) => {
            console.log(`event.body :
              ${JSON.stringify(event.body)}`);
            resolve({
                statusCode: HttpStatusCodes.OK,
                body: JSON.stringify({
                    message: 'TypeScript Serverless POST
                      executed successfully!',
                    bodyReceived: event.body
                }, null, 4)
            });
        })
    }
```

Here, we have imported the necessary modules from `aws-lambda`, and have also imported a static class named `HttpStatusCodes` from the `http-status-codes` module. Our exported function is named `postHandler`, and returns a Promise as we have seen previously. There are two notable changes to this Lambda function. The first is that we are logging a message to the console that contains the properties of the `event.body` object. This is similar to how we used the Express `body-parser` module to automatically parse the body of an HTTP `POST` request, and give us access to the underlying object. Our code can therefore reference any one of the `POST` parameters in this way.

The second notable change is in the use of the `HttpStatusCodes.OK` static `enum` in our `resolve` function. This `enum` is part of the `http-status-codes` module, and allows our code to use human-readable and understandable values for standard HTTP response codes. The `body` property of this Lambda function simply returns a JSON object that echoes the `event.body` arguments received, so that we can check that what we sent has been received correctly.

With the Lambda function in place, we can now update our `serverless.yml` file as follows:

```
provider:
  (... existing)

package:
 include:
   - ../node_modules/http-status-codes/**

functions:
  hello:
    (... existing)
  tsLambda:
    (... existing)
  posthandler:
    handler: posthandler.postHandler
    events:
      - http:
          path: posthandler/post
          method: post
```

Here, we have include a new top-level property named `package`, and underneath this a property named `include` that references the `node_modules/http-status-codes` directory. This is how we are able to include an external node module as a dependency for our Lambda function.

We have also added a `posthandler` property underneath the `functions` property that specifies all of the parameters that we need to deploy our `postHandler` AWS Lambda function. Deploying this to our AWS account will create a REST endpoint that will handle a `POST` event at the URL `/dev/posthandler/post`.

Lambda logging

Our code for the `postHandler` Lambda function includes a call to the `console.log` function to log the value of the `event.body` parameter. If this were a standard Node console application, we would be able to simply monitor the command line to see the results of this call to `console.log`. Unfortunately, as this code is an AWS Lambda function, we will need to find another way to access the logs that are produced when we execute this function. As always, the AWS web-based GUI provides a mechanism to view these logs, but it is fairly time-consuming to find and constantly refresh the web-page to see the latest results. Fortunately, Serverless provides a simple command-line interface that uses the AWS API to monitor the console logs on the AWS cloud instance, and report them on the command line. We can monitor any Lambda event logs by simply executing the following:

```
serverless logs -f <lambda_name> -t
```

As an example of this, let's monitor the logs of our GET handler as follows:

```
serverless logs -f tslambda -t
```

The output of this command can be seen in the following screenshot:

```
                    nathanr@nero260: /tmp/serverless-sample

 File  Edit  View  Search  Terminal  Help
 nathanr@nero260:/tmp/serverless-sample$ serverless logs -f tslambda -t
 START RequestId: 172d3e3d-fe06-11e8-a583-317f60e5e1e7 Version: $LATEST
 2018-12-12 20:04:34.737 (+08:00)        172d3e3d-fe06-11e8-a583-317f60e5e1e7      event : {
     "resource": "/tshandler/test",
     "path": "/tshandler/test",
     "httpMethod": "GET",
     "headers": {
         "Accept": "text/html,application/xhtml+xml,application/xml;q=0.9,image/webp,image/ap
 ng,*/*;q=0.8",
         "Accept-Encoding": "gzip, deflate, br",
         "Accept-Language": "en-GB,en-US;q=0.9,en;q=0.8",
         "cache-control": "max-age=0",
         "CloudFront-Forwarded-Proto": "https",
         "CloudFront-Is-Desktop-Viewer": "true",
         "CloudFront-Is-Mobile-Viewer": "false",
         "CloudFront-Is-SmartTV-Viewer": "false",
         "CloudFront-Is-Tablet-Viewer": "false",
         "CloudFront-Viewer-Country": "AU",
         "Host": "dso2yf67fd.execute-api.us-east-1.amazonaws.com",
         "upgrade-insecure-requests": "1",
         "User-Agent": "Mozilla/5.0 (X11; Linux x86_64) AppleWebKit/537.36 (KHTML, like Gecko
 ) Chrome/70.0.3538.77 Safari/537.36",
         "Via": "2.0 41a05bbd6a4b41079be7716f6db52c5f.cloudfront.net (CloudFront)",
         "X-Amz-Cf-Id": "kuuUSTWFbLT-75IpOFcZNBIcYzuUWH2mpUs1ov3nOTSp0Ep8My3ySQ==",
         "X-Amzn-Trace-Id": "Root=1-5c10f952-173ec9b001d74e58f971a0b8",
         "X-Forwarded-For": "203.164.30.25, 52.46.58.81",
         "X-Forwarded-Port": "443",
```

Node REST testing

So far, we have created a GET AWS Lambda request handler, and a POST AWS Lambda handler. The GET requests are fairly simple to test, as we can simply copy and paste the URL into a web browser to execute a GET request. POST handlers, however, need a tool such as Postman in order to construct the correct data packet to send to the server. For the purposes of this exercise, let's use a very simple Node-based program that will issue a GET request to our TypeScript handler, and then issue a POST request.

When developing large-scale applications that use REST endpoints, we often need to use the results of a REST request as input into another REST request. As an example of this, consider an authentication REST endpoint that accepts a username and password combination, and returns an encrypted token. This token is then sent with every subsequent REST request so that the server can verify the identity of the user.

In order to chain REST requests, we can easily use the `async await` capabilities of TypeScript. In addition to this, we can also use any number of node modules that provide a promise-like interface for REST requests. One such library is named Axios, and can be installed as per usual through `npm`:

```
npm install axios
```

Our test program, named `test_rest.ts`, is as follows:

```typescript
import axios, { AxiosResponse } from 'axios';

async function run() {

    console.log(`get request`);

    let getResult = <AxiosResponse>await axios({
        method: 'GET',
        url: `https://2yf35yfd.execute-api.us-east-1.amazonaws.com
            /dev/tshandler/test`
    }).catch((err) => {
        console.log(`err : ${err}`);
    });

    console.log(`getResult : ${JSON.stringify(getResult.data, null, 4)}`);

}

run();
```

Here, we start by importing the global function name `axios`, as well as the `AxiosResponse` type from the `axios` module. We then define an `async` function named `run`. This `run` function is executed right at the bottom of the code sample. Our `run` function logs a message to the console and then calls the `axios` function with an object that has a `method` property and a `url` property. This function is marked as `async`, so that the code execution will wait for the result of this request before continuing. The result is assigned to an internal variable named `getResult`. The `method` property specifies that this is a GET request, and the `url` property is the full URL of our Lambda function. We have a `catch` handler just in case an error occurs. The code then logs the result of the GET request to the console.

We can now run this test program (after compiling it with `tsc`) by executing it on the command line, as follows:

```
node test_rest
```

The output of this will match what we have seen when testing this GET request in the browser, as follows:

```
get request
getResult : {
    "message": "TypeScript Serverless v1.0!",
    "input": {
        "resource": "/tshandler/test",
        "path": "/tshandler/test",
        "httpMethod": "GET",
    . . .
```

We can now update our test code to issue a POST request as follows:

```
... existing code
console.log(`posting`);

let postResult = <AxiosResponse>await axios.post(
`https://2yf35yfd.execute-api.us-east-1.amazonaws.com/dev/posthandler/post`
,
    { testValue: 1, testStringValue: "testString" })
    .catch((err) => {
        console.log(`err : ${err}`);
    });

console.log(`postResult : ${JSON.stringify(postResult.data, null, 4)}`);
```

Here, we have created a variable named `postResult`, which will hold the result of the POST request. Notice that we are using one of the utility functions from `axios` named `post`. This `post` function is a simplified version of the call to the `axios` function that we used earlier, and attaches all of the correct properties that a POST needs. As an example of this, we no longer need to specify the `method` property of POST when using this function.

The `post` function can be called with a string as the first argument, and an object as the second argument. These arguments correspond to a `url` property and a `data` property, which can be seen clearly if we navigate to the definition of this function. In our test code, we specify the full URL to our POST Lambda function, and attach an object with a `testValue` and `testStringValue` property. As usual, we have a `catch` handler just in case something goes wrong, and we log the returned result to the console.

Executing this code against our POST Lambda function will show the following results:

```
posting
postResult : {
    "message": "TypeScript Serverless POST executed successfully!",
    "bodyReceived": "{\"testValue\":1,\"testStringValue\":\"testString\"}"
}
```

As we can see from this result, our Lambda function is operating correctly, and successfully parsing the POSTed data through the event.body property.

Summary

In this chapter, we have had a look at using modules, both CommonJS and AMD. We explored the syntax used for modularization, and showed how to both export and import modules. We then explored the use of AMD module syntax using the Require library, and discussed how to take care of module dependencies. We then explored the use of CommonJS module syntax, and showed the equivalent structure for module dependencies using SystemJS. Our journey continued with an in-depth discussion on Node and Express modules, where we put together a sample application to render both an index and a login page, and handle logins through session information. We then discussed how to set up and use a cloud-based execution environment for our code without the need for a server at all, as well as covering Amazon Web Services and AWS Lambda functions.

In the next chapter, we will tackle object-oriented programming principles, and take a look at some useful design patterns.

11

Object-Oriented Programming

In 1995, the **Gang of Four (GoF)** published a book named *Design Patterns: Elements of Reusable Object-Oriented Software*. In it, the authors, Erich Gamma, Richard Helm, Ralph Johnson, and John Vlissides, describe a number of classic software design patterns, which present simple and elegant solutions to common software problems. If you have never heard of design patterns, such as a Factory pattern, Composite pattern, Observer pattern, or Singleton pattern, then reading through this GoF book is highly recommended.

The design patterns presented by the GoF have been reproduced in many different programming languages, including Java and C#. Vilic Vane has authored a book named *TypeScript Design Patterns*, in which each of these GoF patterns is implemented and discussed from a TypeScript perspective.

In `Chapter 3`, *Interfaces, Classes, and Inheritance,* of our book, we took some time to build a classic Factory pattern implementation, which is one of the more popular design patterns described by the GoF. TypeScript, with its ES6 and ES7 language-compatible constructs, is a perfect example of an object-oriented language. With classes, abstract classes, interfaces, inheritance, and generics, TypeScript applications can now take full advantage of any of the GoF design patterns.

Describing the implementation of each of these GoF patterns in the TypeScript language is a subject that cannot be covered in a single chapter, and would do injustice to the excellent coverage of the GoF patterns covered by Vilic Vane.

In this chapter, therefore, we will focus on the process of writing object-oriented code, and work through an example of two of the GoF design patterns that work very well together when dealing with complicated UI layouts. These are the **State** and **Mediator** design patterns, which focus on application state, and how objects interact with each other. We will build an Angular 2 application that uses a rather complex UI design, and which includes a number of sophisticated CSS animated transitions. We will then start the process of reworking our original application to apply object-oriented design principles, and discuss how objects in our application interact. We will then implement the State and Mediator design patterns in order to encapsulate the logic that is used to determine what UI elements are shown depending on the state of the application.

In this chapter, we will be covering the following topics:

- Object-oriented principles
- Using interfaces
- SOLID principles
- User interface design
- The State pattern
- The Mediator pattern
- Modular code

Object-oriented principles

Any application that we build should be assessed in terms of object-oriented best practices. Robert Martin published what is known as the SOLID design principles, which is an acronym for five different object-oriented best practices. Following these practices will help to ensure that the code we write is easy to maintain, easy to understand, easy to extend, and resilient to change. In our current fast-paced world, we generally don't have the luxury of taking extraordinary amounts of time to modify our applications in order to keep up with ever-changing requirements. The faster we can deliver updates to satisfy our business needs, the better chance we have of keeping ahead of our competition. Sticking to the SOLID design principles gives us a good foundation that will easily enable modifications to existing code in order to satisfy these rapidly changing demands on our code base.

Programming to an interface

One of the primary notions that the GoF adhere to, is the idea that programmers should *program to an interface, not an implementation.* This means that programs are built using interfaces as the defined interaction between objects. By programming to an interface, client objects are unaware of the internal logic of their dependent objects, and are therefore much more resilient to change. By defining an interface, we are starting to cement an API that describes what functionality an object provides, how it should be used, and also how multiple objects interact with each other.

SOLID principles

An extension of the program to an interface principle is what has been coined as the SOLID design principles, which are based on the ideas of Robert Martin. This is an acronym for five different principles, as detailed in the following:

- Single responsibility
- Open-closed
- Liskov substitution
- Interface segregation
- Dependency inversion

The SOLID design principles deserve a mention whenever object-oriented programming is discussed. Let's review each one briefly.

Single responsibility

The idea behind the single responsibility principle is that an object should have just a single responsibility. *Do one thing, and do it well.* We have seen examples of this principle in the various TypeScript compatible frameworks that we have worked with. As an example, a Model class is used to represent a single model. A Collection class is used to represent a collection of these models, and a View class is used to render models or collections.

If any one of our classes starts to become a super class—in other words, it is doing many different types of things—then this is an indication that we are breaking this principle. As a simple example, if your source code file for a particular class starts to get very long, then this class is possibly doing too much. Think about what this class' primary responsibility is, and then break out the functionality of the class into smaller classes.

Open-closed

The open-closed principle states that an object should be open to extension, but closed for modification. In other words, once an interface has been designed for a class, changes over time to this interface should be achieved through inheritance, and not by modifying the interface directly.

Note that if you are writing libraries that are consumed by third-parties through an API, then this principle is essential for API design. An API should always try to ensure backward compatibility, and as such, changes should only be made through a new, versioned release.

Liskov substitution

The **Liskov Substitution Principle (LSP)** says that if one object is derived from another, then these objects can be substituted for each other without breaking functionality. While this principle seems fairly easy to implement, it can get pretty hairy when dealing with typing rules related to advanced class hierarchies, such as lists of objects, or actions on objects, which are commonly found in code that uses generics. In these instances, the concept of variance is introduced, and objects can be either covariant, contra-variant, or invariant. We will not discuss the finer points of variance here, but keep this principle in mind when writing libraries or code using generics.

Interface segregation

The idea here is that many interfaces are better than one general-purpose interface. If we tie this principle with the single responsibility principle, we will start to look at our interfaces in terms of smaller pieces of the puzzle working together, rather than interfaces encompassing large portions of functionality.

Dependency inversion

This idea states that we should depend on abstractions (or interfaces), rather than instances of concrete objects. Again, this is the same principle as programming to an interface, and not an implementation.

User interface design

As an example of the use of the SOLID design principles, let's build an application that uses a complex UI design, and see how these principles can help us break up our code into smaller, manageable modules, separated by interfaces.

In this section, we will build an Angular application that will provide a left-to-right panel style page layout. We will use Bootstrap to provide a little styling, and some CSS-based transitions to slide panels in from the left or right. This will provide the user with a slightly different browsing experience to the common up-down scrolling design that most websites utilize.

Conceptual design

Let's take a look at what this left-to-right design will look like conceptually as follows:

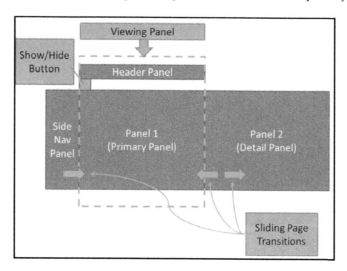

The **Viewing Panel** will be our main page, with a **Header Panel** and a **Button** to control showing or hiding the side navigation pane on the left-hand side. When the left-hand side pane is opened, it will use a CSS animation in order to slide in from the left.

When it is closed, it will again use an animation to slide back to the left. Likewise, when a button is clicked to show the second panel (**Panel 2**), this detail panel will slide in from the right, using a CSS animation, and will end up occupying the entire **Viewing Panel**. The following screenshot shows the **Viewing Panel** with the **Header Panel** and left-hand side panel visible:

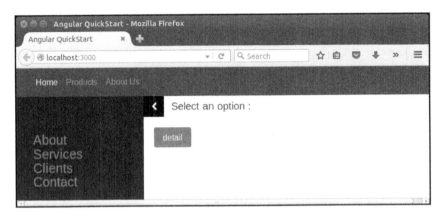

Here, we can clearly see the header panel at the top, the left-hand side menu panel, and two buttons. The first button is to the left of the **Select an option:** text, and it is simply a < arrow that will hide the left-hand side panel. Clicking on this button uses a CSS animation to slide the left-hand side panel to the left so that it is out of the way. This can be seen in the animated transition for the left-hand side panel, as follows:

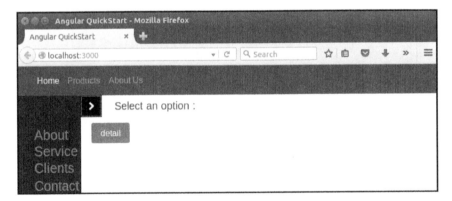

Here, we have paused the CSS animation to show that the left-hand side panel is in the process of collapsing, and the main panel is being expanded to fill the entire view panel. Note that the show/hide button has changed from a < arrow to a > arrow. This subtle change indicates to the user that the side panel can be expanded by clicking on the > button.

If the **detail** button is clicked, this will cause the left-hand side panel and the main page to slide to the left, revealing the second page through another CSS animation, as can be seen in the animated page transition for the right-hand detail panel, as follows:

Here, the second page is transitioning from the right-hand side, and both the left-hand side panel and the main page are sliding to the left.

Angular setup

Now that we have a conceptual view of what our application will look like, we can start implementing this layout by setting up an Angular application. As we have seen in earlier Angular projects, we start by issuing an `ng new` command to use the Angular command line interface. This process will set up all of the required dependencies that Angular needs, and create an initial `app.component.ts` and `app.component.html` file for us.

Our `app/app.component.ts` file could not be simpler:

```
import { Component } from '@angular/core';

@Component( {
    selector : 'app-root',
    templateUrl : 'app/app.component.html',
    styleUrls: ['app/app.component.css']
})
export class AppComponent
{
    title = "angular-sample";
}
```

Here, we import the `Component` module as we have seen before, and then define three properties to pass to the `@Component` decorator. However, note that instead of specifying a `template` property, which normally contains HTML, we have specified a `templateUrl` property. This instructs Angular to load the named file from disk, and use it as the component template. Similarly, we have specified a CSS file to be used by our component through the `styleUrls` property. Our `AppComponent` class, then, just has a single property named `title`.

Using the `templateUrl` property to load a separate file containing our HTML template is an example of the dependency inversion principle. Our `AppComponent` class is dependent on an HTML template in order to render the component to the browser. When using the `template` property, we have a tight coupling between the HTML template, and the class itself. This means that any modification to the template requires recompilation of the module. By splitting the template out into a separate, loadable file, we have broken this tight coupling, and the module class can be modified independently from its HTML template.

Our `app.component.html` file is currently very simple, as follows:

```
<div>
    {{title}}
</div>

<div>
    <button>detail</button>
</div>
```

Here, we have two `<div>` elements. The first contains our title, and the second contains a button.

Using Bootstrap and Font-Awesome

Now that we have the basics of our Angular application, we can flesh out the HTML that it will contain. In order to do this, we will use the Bootstrap framework, and icons from Font-Awesome. Bootstrap is an HTML-based, CSS driven method of building common web components that provide much of the functionality and styling needed in modern websites. From buttons to icons, to tabs or alerts, and almost everything in-between, Bootstrap provides a simple syntax to add professional looking styling to our site. It has also been built as a responsive framework, meaning that it will automatically adjust to render optimally for mobile, tablet, or desktop devices.

Font-awesome is an open source set of icons that is free to use for commercial projects, with a very wide range of available icons. To include Bootstrap and Font-awesome styling in our web page, we first need to install them through npm, as follows:

```
npm install bootstrap --save
npm install font-awesome --save
```

To include the boostrap.css and font-awesome.css files into our application, we can simply edit the angular.json file in the base directory, and add two entries to the styles property, as follows:

```
"styles": [
  "styles.css",
  "./node_modules/bootstrap/dist/css/bootstrap.min.css",
  "./node_modules/font-awesome/css/font-awesome.css"
],
```

We can now start to flesh out the page design in our app.component.html page, starting with the navigation bar at the top of the screen, as follows:

```
<nav class="navbar navbar-expand-lg navbar-dark bg-dark ">
  <a class="navbar-brand"> </a>
  <ul class="navbar-nav mr-auto">
    <li class="nav-item nav-link active">Home</li>
    <li class="nav-item nav-link">Products</li>
    <li class="nav-item nav-link">About Us</li>
  </ul>
</nav>
```

Here, we have created a top navigation bar, by specifying a <nav> link, and have set some Bootstrap-specific CSS classes to create a dark navbar that occupies a band across the top of the page. Within this <nav> link, we have an <a> tag, which is just a blank element, and then we define a child <ul>, with three <li> links within it. These links are named Home, Products, and About Us, and they will be rendered as navigation links.

Note that the samples in this chapter use Bootstrap version 4.1.3, which has some differences to earlier versions. If the preceding HTML navigation bar does not render correctly, then check your package.json file, and ensure that the Bootstrap version is correct, as follows:

```
"dependencies": {
  .. other npm libraries ...
  "bootstrap": "^4.1.3",
  ... other npm libraries ...
}
```

Creating a side panel

We can now take a look at creating our left-hand side panel. A great resource for HTML elements, CSS styling, and animations is the W3Schools website (https://www.w3schools.com/). The how-to section of the documentation provides a huge library of samples, including slideshows, modal boxes, progress bars, and responsive tables to name just a few. We will use a sample from the side navigation section, called `Sidenav Push Content`. This example shows how to create a side navigation screen that pushes the main content of the page over as it expands, instead of creating an overlay. We will start with some HTML added to our `app.component.html` file, as follows:

```
<div id="mySidenav" class="sidenav">
  <a href="#">About</a>
  <a href="#">Services</a>
  <a href="#">Clients</a>
  <a href="#">Contact</a>
</div>
```

Here, we have described a `<div>` element with an `id` of `mySideNav`, and a CSS class of `sidenav`. This `<div>` element contains four sub-links. To turn this into an attractive side navigation bar, we will now need to edit our `app.component.css` file to add a few styles, as follows:

```
/* The side navigation menu */
.sidenav {
    height: 100%; /* 100% Full-height */
    width: 250px; /* 0 width - change this with JavaScript */
    position: fixed; /* Stay in place */
    z-index: 1; /* Stay on top */
    top: 55px;
    left: 0;
    background-color: #111; /* Black*/
    overflow-x: hidden; /* Disable horizontal scroll */
    padding-top: 60px; /* Place content 60px from the top */
    transition: 0.3s;
}

/* The navigation menu links */
.sidenav a {
    padding: 8px 8px 8px 32px;
    text-decoration: none;
    font-size: 25px;
    color: #818181;
    display: block;
    transition: 0.3s
}
```

```
/* When you mouse over the navigation links, change their color */
.sidenav a:hover, .offcanvas a:focus{
    color: #f1f1f1;
}
```

With these few CSS styles in place, our side navigation panel starts to take shape, as can be seen in the following screenshot:

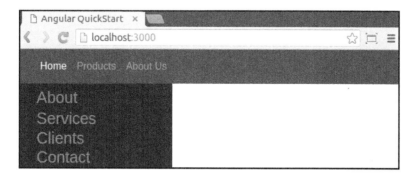

Here, we have a nicely styled side navigation bar. Unfortunately, our main page content has disappeared behind this side navigation bar, meaning that we will need to apply a surrounding `<div>` element and some styles to ensure that the left-hand panel pushes our main panel content over to the right. Our main panel content then becomes:

```
<div id="main" class="main-content-panel">
    <div class="row">
        <div class="col-sm-1">
            <button>
                <span class="fa fa-chevron-left"> </span>
            </button>
        </div>
        <div class="col-sm-11">
            <div class="row-content-header">{{title}}</div>
        </div>
    </div>
    <div class="main-content">
        <button class="btn btn-primary">
            detail
        </button>
    </div>
</div>
```

Here, we have wrapped our main content in a `<div>` element with an `id` of `"main"`, and a class of `"main-content-panel"`. This `<div>` element is then broken down into a row that consists of two columns, of sizes 1 and 11. This row houses our show/hide side panel button, and the `{{title}}` element. Beneath this header row is our main content, which simply includes a single button named `detail`. Our corresponding CSS for this section of HTML is as follows:

```
#main {
    margin-left: 250px;
    transition: .3s;
}

#main-body {
    transition: .3s;
}

.main-content {
    padding: 20px;
}

.row-content-header {
    padding: 5px;
    font-size: 20px;
}
```

There are two key styles here that affect our page content. The first is the `margin-left: 250px` element of the `#main` style. This `margin-left` value is the CSS property that pushes our main content over to the right when the left-hand panel is visible. This property matches the corresponding side panel value of `.sidenav { width: 250px; }`. In other words, the side panel has a width of 250px, and the main panel has a left margin of 250px. These two values combined show the left-hand panel, and also push the main panel over to the right. We will adjust these two values from 250px to 0px in order to show or hide the left-hand panel.

The second key style is the `transition: .3s;` property, which defines how long it takes to animate both the side panel collapsing and expanding, and the main panel being pushed to the right, or expanding to fill the screen. With these styles in place, we can now attach some code to kick off an animated page transition. To get this to work, we need to register a click handler in the HTML, and then implement the click handler in our `app.component.ts` file.

Firstly, let's examine the button click Document Object Model (DOM) event in the `app.component.html` file:

```
<button (click)="showHideSideClicked()">
    <span class="fa fa-chevron-left"> </span>
</button>
```

Here, we have defined a function named `showHideSideClicked`, which will be called whenever we click on the **show/hide** button. Our changes to the `app.component.ts` file are as follows:

```
export class AppComponent
{
    title = "Select an option :";
    isSideNavVisible = true;
    showHideSideClicked() {
        if (this.isSideNavVisible) {
            document.getElementById('main')
                .style.marginLeft = "0px";
            document.getElementById('mySidenav')
                .style.width = "0px";
            this.isSideNavVisible = false;
        } else {
            document.getElementById('main')
                .style.marginLeft = "250px";
            document.getElementById('mySidenav')
                .style.width = "250px";
            this.isSideNavVisible = true;
        }
    }
}
```

Here, we have added a property to the `AppComponent` class, named `isSideNavVisible`, and set it to `true` by default. This property is keeping track of whether the side navigation bar is visible or not. We have then implemented the `showHideSideClicked` function. If the side navigation bar is visible, we set the `marginLeft` style of the main panel to `0px`, and also set the `width` of the `mySideNav` element to `0px`. This essentially collapses the side panel, and makes the main panel fill the whole screen. If the side navigation bar is collapsed, we do the opposite, and also set the `isSideNavVisible` property at the same time. Running our application at this stage shows and hides the left-hand panel quite nicely, using the `transition: .3s` property to apply a visually appealing animation.

Creating an overlay

We can now turn our attention to the second page, which will slide in from the right, when we click on the **Detail** button. Our HTML snippet is as follows:

```
<div id="mySidenav" class="sidenav">
... existing sidebar ...
</div>

<div id="myRightScreen" class="overlay">
    <button class="btn button-no-borders"
    (click)="closeClicked()">
        <span class="fa fa-chevron-left"></span>
    </button>
    <div class="overlay-content">
        <h1>page 2</h1>
    </div>
</div>
... existing main panel ...
<div id="main" class="main-content-panel">
```

Here, we have inserted a `<div>` element with an `id` of `myRightScreen`, and specified the CSS class of `overlay`. This is a simple `<div>` element that contains a button at the top, with a click handler of `closeClicked`, and an `<h1>` element to show `page 2`. As with the side navigation bar, we will need some CSS styling to accomplish two things. Firstly, we need to set the second page over to the right, and then we need a way to slide it in from the right when the detail button is clicked. Our CSS is as follows:

```
/* The Overlay (background) */
.overlay {
    height: 100%;
    width: 100%;
    position: fixed; /* Stay in place */
    z-index: 1; /* Sit on top */
    left: 0;
    top: 54px;
    overflow-x: hidden; /* Disable horizontal scroll */
    transition: 0.3s;
    transform: translateX(100%);
    border-left: 1px solid;
}
```

Here, there are two styles that are controlling how the second page is revealed. The first is the transform: translateX(100%) style, and the second is the transition: 0.3s style. The transform style in this case is essentially moving the X starting position of the <div> element to 100%. This means that by default, it is offset on the X axis 100% of the page width, and therefore is not visible. The transition: 0.3s style is again just animating the show or hide of the panel.

Let's implement some of the click handlers on our page to see this in action. Firstly, we need to handle the click event of the detail button, as follows:

```
buttonClickedDetail() {
    document.getElementById('myRightScreen')
        .style.transform = "translateX(0%)";
    document.getElementById('main')
        .style.transform = "translateX(-100%)";
}
```

Here, we are doing two things. Firstly, we are setting the transform property of the second page to a value of translateX(0%). This is doing the opposite of the translateX(100%), and is setting the X starting position of the <div> element to 0%. With the translate CSS property in place, this gives us the sliding in from the right effect that we are after. The second thing that we are doing in this function is to set the transform property of our main <div> element to translateX(-100%). Again, this has the effect of sliding the main panel over to the right. Before we test this transition, let's implement the closeClicked function that will close the right panel, as follows:

```
closeClicked() {
    document.getElementById('myRightScreen')
        .style.transform = "translateX(100%)";
    document.getElementById('main')
        .style.transform = "translateX(0%)";
}
```

Here, we are doing the opposite action to the buttonClickedDetail function, in order to slide the second page panel over to the right, and also reveal our main panel. These two functions are working in conjunction to set the translateX properties of both the myRightScreen<div> element, and the main <div> element.

If we fire up our page now, we will be able to click on the **Detail** button, and see the second page slide in from the right.

Coordinating transitions

So far, we have created a simple web application that has a main panel, a left-hand side panel and a second page panel, and added some CSS styles and transitions to create a visually pleasing page structure. Unfortunately, there are some issues with our current implementation. If we are on the main page, and our left-hand side panel is visible, then clicking on the **Detail** button does not close the left-hand panel before sliding in the right panel. This causes the second page to show on top of the left-hand panel, as follows:

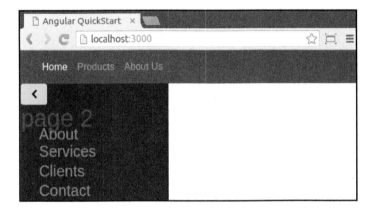

Here, we can see that the second page, which has slid in from the right is displaying on-top of the navigation panel. To fix this, we could call the `showHideSideClicked` function that we already have, in order to hide the side panel first. This seems to fix the issue, but introduces another bug. If we have the side panel visible, and then show and hide the **Detail** panel, the side panel remains closed. To fix this bug, we could call the `showHideSideClicked` function again when we close the right hand panel, but this solution unfortunately presents its own quirky bugs.

While we could rework the logic of our application to iron out all of these bugs, we are quickly falling into a frustrating cycle of trying to fix one thing, only to find it has another undesired side effect. What we really need is a mechanism to keep track of all of these visual elements, and control how the application reacts to the user input. This is where the **State** and **Mediator** design patterns come to the rescue.

The State pattern

The GoF describe two design patterns named the State pattern, and the Mediator pattern. The State pattern uses a set of concrete classes that are derived from a base class to describe a particular state. As an example, consider creating an `enum` to describe the states that a door can be in. At first glance, a door could be either `Open` or `Closed`. In this case, a simple `if...else` control flow will likely take care of any logic we wish to apply.

Consider, however, what happens to our control flow and logic if we needed a `Locked` and `Unlocked` state, or if it were a sliding door for a `SlightlyAjar`, `HalfOpen`, `AlmostFullyOpen`, and `FullyOpen` state. The State design pattern allows us to easily define these states, and adjust our logic based on the current state of an object.

If we think about our application a little, we know that our screens will be in one or another particular state at any point in time. We are either on the main screen panel or on the second page panel. Also, the left-hand side panel is either visible or hidden. This combination gives us three states, as follows:

- The main panel only
- The main panel with side navigation
- The detail panel

State interface

The State pattern helps us to define these states in code. The basic principle of the State design pattern is that we create an interface or an abstract base class that defines the properties of each state, and we then create concrete classes for each specialization. In our application, then, we have two main questions that we need to ask each state:

- Is the side panel visible?
- Are we on the main panel or the detail panel?

Additionally, if we are on the main panel, then we also need to know whether to show the > arrow on the top left of the main panel, or the < arrow. This is tied to whether the side panel is visible or not. Let's create a file named `StateMediator.ts` to hold our interfaces, as follows:

```
export enum StateType {
    MainPanelOnly,
    MainPanelWithSideNav,
    DetailPanel
```

```
    }

export enum PanelType {
    Primary,
    Detail
}

export interface IState {
    getPanelType() : PanelType;
    getStateType() : StateType;
    isSideNavVisible() : boolean;
    getPanelButtonClass() : string;
}
```

Here, we start with an enum for StateType, which lets us know which of the three states we are in. We then define the PanelType enum for whether we are on the Primary or Detail panels. Our interface, IState, has four functions. The getPanelType returns a PanelType enum value, and the getStateType function returns the StateType enum value. The isSideNavVisible function simply returns a boolean value indicating if the side navigation panel is visible or not. The final function, getPanelButtonClass, will return a class name for switching the show/hide button from a chevron left icon (<) to a chevron right icon (>), depending on the state of the side panel.

With this interface in place, we have defined what questions we can ask each of our concrete state classes. Depending on whether we are on the main panel or the detail panel, the answer to this question will change slightly. This is the essence of the State design pattern. Define an interface that gives you the answers you need for all states, and then program to that interface. This shields any logic we build to consume these states from the definition of the states themselves. In other words, adding or removing a new state class will not affect any code we have written against the IState interface.

Concrete states

Now, let's examine the three concrete state classes, as follows:

```
export class MainPanelOnly
    implements IState {
    getPanelType() : PanelType { return PanelType.Primary; }
    getStateType() : StateType { return StateType.MainPanelOnly; }
    getPanelButtonClass() : string { return 'fa-chevron-right';}
    isSideNavVisible() : boolean { return false; }
}
```

We start with a state class named `MainPanelOnly`, which is used to describe the state when the side navigation bar is not visible, and we are on the main viewing panel. This is a very simple class that implements the `IState` interface and as such, simply returns the correct values for each of the four functions. As we can see by the return values, we are on `PanelType.Primary`, the `isSideNavVisible` function returns `false`, and we need an `'fa-chevron-right'` class to display on our show/hide button. Our other two concrete states are very similar, as follows:

```
export class MainPanelWithSideNav
    implements IState {
    getPanelType() : PanelType { return PanelType.Primary; }
    getStateType() : StateType { return StateType.MainPanelWithSideNav; }
    getPanelButtonClass() : string { return 'fa-chevron-left';}
    isSideNavVisible() : boolean { return true; }
}

export class DetailPanel
    implements IState {
    getPanelType() : PanelType { return PanelType.Detail; }
    getStateType() : StateType { return StateType.DetailPanel; }
    getPanelButtonClass() : string { return '';}
    isSideNavVisible() : boolean { return false; }
}
```

Here, the `MainPaleWithSideNav` state class is the same as the `MainPanel` class, except that it returns true for the `isSideNavVisible` function, and `'fa-chevron-left'` for the panel button class. The `DetailPanel` state class returns `PanelType.Detail, false` for the `isSideNavVisible` function, and a blank class name for the panel button.

These three classes are very simple, and they describe the state that the UI elements should be in when they are in the current state. These classes help us to encapsulate the logic that is used in our application to manage the various UI elements on our screen.

The Mediator pattern

Now that we can describe the various states that our UI is in, we can begin to apply the logic that is required to move between these states. We will use the Mediator pattern to accomplish this. The purpose of the Mediator pattern is to define how a set of objects interact with each other, and it does this by injecting an object in-between the ones that affect each other. This means that the objects in question do not actually communicate with each other, they work against an interface. This promotes loose coupling between objects.

There are essentially two parts to the Mediator pattern. The first part is to define an interface that the Mediator can call in order to apply the changes that it needs. The Mediator, in this case, is communicating with our UI classes. In our application, we will need the Mediator to be able to signal the UI to either show or hide the side navigation panel, and show or hide the detail panel. The Mediator also needs to switch the show/hide button from a < chevron to a > chevron, depending on the current application state.

The second part of the Mediator pattern is the logic of how to move from one state to another. The Mediator itself will keep track of what state the application is in, and then coordinate UI actions in order to move from one state to another.

By defining an interface for these interactions, we are following object-oriented best practices, and shielding the Mediator code from the actual implementation of the UI changing logic. We can also code and test this Mediator logic without an actual UI in place.

Therefore, our interface for the Mediator class is as follows:

```
export interface IMediatorImpl {
    showNavPanel();
    hideNavPanel();
    showDetailPanel();
    hideDetailPanel();
    changeShowHideSideButton(fromClass: string, toClass: string);
}
```

Here, we have distilled all of the UI changes required by our application into five functions. We can either show or hide the side navigation panel, show or hide the detail panel, or update the CSS class button.

Looking back at our work so far, we have simplified our business logic into two parts. First, we have defined the states that our UI will be in at any point in time, and second, we have defined the functions required to update our UI. We are already on the way to building a modular, object-oriented, easy-to-understand, and easy-to-maintain application. We will tackle the implementation of the Mediator logic a little later, after we have performed some housekeeping on our existing code.

Modular code

So far, our application has all of its HTML, CSS, and business logic as part of the `AppComponent` class. Although we have already broken this class down into separate `app.component.html` and `app.component.css` files, it really contains a number of separate components all in one. Let's take this opportunity to modularize our code, and create three separate classes. These three separate classes will be, as follows:

- A `NavbarComponent` class to render and handle the navigation bar at the top of the screen.
- A `SideNavComponent` class to render the left-hand side navigation panel.
- A `RightScreenComponent` to handle the detail panel that slides in from the right.

This means that the `AppComponent` class becomes the central application class, and it will be responsible for coordinating each of these components.

Navbar component

Our first task is to create a `NavbarComponent` class that will have the sole responsibility of rendering the navigation bar at the top of the screen. To do this, we will create a `navbar.component.ts` file and a `navbar.component.html` file in our `app` directory. This can easily be accomplished using the Angular-CLI, by executing the following on the command line:

```
ng generate component navbar
```

This command will create a new directory in the `src/app` folder, and generate the necessary files for our new component, including the main `.ts` file, a `.css` file, an `.html` file, as well as a `.spec.ts` file for testing. It will also generate standard code for creating the component, as well as modifying the `app.module.ts` file to automatically make this component available for use.

The contents of the `navbar.component.html` file can be simply copied from our existing `app.component.html` file, as follows:

```
<nav class=" navbar navbar-inverse bg-inverse
navbar-toggleable-sm">
    <a class="navbar-brand"> </a>
    <div class="nav navbar-nav">
        <a class="nav-item nav-link active">Home</a>
        <a class="nav-item nav-link">Products</a>
```

```
            <a class="nav-item nav-link">About Us</a>
        </div>
    </nav>
```

The Angular-CLI will have created the `NavbarComponent` class for us, as follows:

```
import { Component, OnInit } from '@angular/core';

@Component({
  selector: 'app-navbar',
  templateUrl: './navbar.component.html',
  styleUrls: ['./navbar.component.css']
})
export class NavbarComponent implements OnInit {

  constructor() { }

  ngOnInit() {
  }

}
```

This is a very basic Angular class that references our HTML file, and specifies a selector property in the `@Component` decorator. To use this new component in our application, we will simply drop in a `<app-navbar>` tag in our current `app.component.html` file.

Note that the Angular-CLI has modified the `app.module.ts` file to register the component for us, as follows:

```
import { AppComponent } from './app.component';
import { NavbarComponent } from './navbar/navbar.component';

@NgModule({
  declarations: [
    AppComponent,
    NavbarComponent
  ],
  imports: [
    BrowserModule
  ],
  providers: [],
  bootstrap: [AppComponent]})
```

Note the module import statement that references our `navbar.component` module, and the updated `declarations` array of the `@NgModule` decorator. By updating the `declarations` array, the `<app-navbar>` tag will be made available for use within any HTML template.

SideNav component

In a similar manner, let's now create a component for the left-hand side navigation panel, as follows:

```
ng generate component sidenav
```

This will create three source files in the app/sidenav directory as we have seen before, and register our component by modifying the app.module.ts file. The sidenav.component.html file is again a simple cut and paste from our existing HTML file, as follows:

```html
<div id="mySidenav" class="sidenav">
  <a href="#">About</a>
  <a href="#">Services</a>
  <a href="#">Clients</a>
  <a href="#">Contact</a>
</div>
```

The auto-generated SideNavComponent class needs to be updated with two new functions, as follows:

```typescript
import { Component } from '@angular/core';

@Component( {
    selector: 'app-sidenav',
    templateUrl: './sidenav.component.html',
    styleUrls: ['./sidenav.component.css']
})

export class SideNavComponent {

    closeNav() {
        document.getElementById('mySidenav')
            .style.width = "0px";
    }
    showNav() {
        document.getElementById('mySidenav')
            .style.width = "250px";
    }

}
```

Here, we have created two functions in this class, named `closeNav` and `showNav`. These two functions set the `style.width` CSS property to `0px` and `250px`, respectively. What we have done here is to essentially encapsulate all of the functionality surrounding the side navigation bar into the `SideNavComponent` class. This is the single responsibility design principle – that states a class should just have a single responsibility.

We will also need to remove the `css` from the `app.component.css` file that applies to this `sidenav` bar, and drop it into the `sidenav.component.css` file. This is an example of encapsulation. The `sidenav` component has everything that it needs, including styles, HTML templates, tests and code encapsulated into a single element.

We can now drop in the `<app-sidenav>` tag into our `app.component.html` file.

RightScreen component

Let's now go ahead and create the last component in our application, which covers the right hand or detail screen, named `RightScreenComponent`. Again, this is generated as follows:

```
ng generate component rightscreen
```

This will create a `rightscreen.component.ts` file, an HTML file, and a CSS file for this component. We will not focus on the HTML and CSS files for this component yet, as they are a simple cut and paste from the existing HTML and CSS from our `app.component` files. Let's instead take a look at the updates to the Angular class for this component, as follows:

```
import { Component, EventEmitter, Output } from '@angular/core';

@Component( {
    selector: 'rightscreen-component',
    templateUrl: './rightscreen.component.html',
    styleUrls: ['./rightscreen.component.css']
})

export class RightScreenComponent
{
    @Output() notify: EventEmitter<string>
        = new EventEmitter<string>();

    closeClicked() {
        this.notify.emit('Click from nested component');
    }

    closeRightWindow() {
```

```
        document.getElementById('myRightScreen')
            .style.transform = "translateX(100%)";
    }

    openRightWindow() {
        document.getElementById('myRightScreen')
            .style.transform = "translateX(0%)";
    }
}
```

Here, we have defined three functions: `closeClicked`, `closeRightWindow`, and `openRightWindow`. The `closeRightWindow` and `openRightWindow` functions set the `style.transform` values for this component, as we have discussed earlier.

The really interesting part of this class is the `closedClicked` function, and the use of something called an `EventEmitter` class. Note how we have imported both the `EventEmitter` class and the `Output` decorator in our `import` statement at the top of the file. Angular uses the `@Output` property decorator and the `EventEmitter` generic class to enable components to notify other components when events occur.

Remember that this panel has a button on the top left-hand side, which is used to close the panel and return to the main screen. The HTML for this button is as follows:

```
<button class="btn btn-default" (click)="closeClicked()">
    <span class="fa fa-chevron-left"></span>
</button>
```

We know that the Angular syntax for handling a DOM click event is to specify `(click)="<handlerFunction>"`. In our preceding HTML, this `<handlerFunction>` is called `closeClicked`, and therefore must be defined in our component class itself.

However, this `RightScreenComponent` class is only in control of its own HTML area, and cannot therefore include any functionality that is for the application itself. In this case, then, all we need to do is to raise an event stating that the **Close** button has been clicked, and leave it up to another part of the application to react to this event and do something. Again, this ties into our design principle of single responsibility.

Let's take a closer look at this EventEmitter syntax:

```
@Output() notify: EventEmitter<string>
    = new EventEmitter<string>();

closeClicked() {
    this.notify.emit('Click from nested component');
}
```

We set up our event emitter by decorating the notify property with the @Output decorator. We then specify that the type of this property is EventEmitter<string>, and then immediately create an instance of the EventEmitter class. The EventEmitter class is a generic class, meaning that we can substitute a <number> value, or <boolean> value, or even a complex class in this declaration.

As the notify property is an instance of an EventEmitter class of type string, we can call this.notify.emit with a string argument in our closeClicked function. This takes care of emitting an event when a user clicks on this button within our RightScreenComponent class.

We now need to define an event handler for this event. As the AppComponent class is responsible for both creating and controlling this RightScreenComponent class, we make a change to our app.component.html file to register for this notification event. The inclusion of the <app-rightscreen> tag now becomes the following:

```
<app-rightscreen (notify)='onNotifyRightWindow($event)'>
</app-rightscreen>
```

Here, we have added an attribute to our <app-rightscreen> tag to register for a (notify) event, and then called the onNotifyRightWindow function within our AppComponent class. The implementation of this function for the time being can just pop up an alert so that we can test whether the firing and registering for this event is working correctly:

```
onNotifyRightWindow(message:string):void {
    alert('clicked');
}
```

We will hook up this event handler a little later to our Mediator class in order to trigger the switch to move to a different state.

Child components

Our `AppComponent` class is the owner of our entire application. It renders the HTML used for the entire page, which includes the `navbar`, `sidenav`, `rightscreen`, and main panel components. As such, it is also the parent of these sub-components. In other words, all of these components are children of the `AppComponent` class, and are referred to as child components. What we need now is find a way for the `AppComponent` class to reference the `SideNavComponent` and `RightScreenComponent` classes within the class itself. This is to tie in the instances of these classes that are created through the HTML tags, `<app-sidenav>` and `<app-rightscreen>`.

Angular provides the `@ViewChild` property decorator for this purpose. To use this decorator, our `AppComponent` class needs to be updated, as follows:

```
import { Component, ViewChild } from '@angular/core';
import { SideNavComponent } from './sidenav.component';
import { RightScreenComponent } from './rightscreen.component'
.. @Component ...
export class AppComponent
{
    @ViewChild(SideNavComponent)
    private sideNav : SideNavComponent;
    @ViewChild(RightScreenComponent)
    private rightScreen: RightScreenComponent;
    .. the rest of the class ...
```

There a few changes that we need to make. Firstly, we need to import the `ViewChild` decorator from the `@angular/core` module, and then import the `SidenavComponent` and `RightScreenComponent` modules. Secondly, we need to create two private properties, named `sideNav` and `rightScreen`, to hold the instances of our child components.

We then use Angular's `@ViewChild` decorator with the class name that we wish to reference. This means that the `@ViewChild(SidenavComponent)` function will connect the `private sideNav` property to the correct instance of the `SidenavComponent` class.

Similarly, we are asking Angular to connect the instance of the `RightscreenComponent` class used in our HTML to the `private rightScreen` variable. In this way, our `AppComponent` class now has programmatic access to these two classes that were referenced in the HTML.

Mediator interface implementation

Now that the `AppComponent` class has references to its child components, we can focus on the implementation of the `IMediatorImpl` interface in this class, as follows:

```
export class AppComponent implements IMediatorImpl {

    ... existing code ...

    showNavPanel() {
        this.sideNav.showNav();
        document.getElementById('main').style.marginLeft
            = "250px";
    }
    hideNavPanel() {
        this.sideNav.closeNav();
        document.getElementById('main').style.marginLeft = "0px";
    }
    showDetailPanel() {
        this.rightScreen.openRightWindow();
        document.getElementById('main').style.transform =
            "translateX(-100%)";
    }
    hideDetailPanel() {
        this.rightScreen.closeRightWindow();
        document.getElementById('main').style.transform =
            "translateX(0%)";
    }
    changeShowHideSideButton(fromClass: string, toClass: string) {
        if (fromClass.length > 0 && toClass.length > 0) {
            document.getElementById('show-hide-side-button')
                .classList.remove(fromClass);
            document.getElementById('show-hide-side-button')
                .classList.add(toClass);
        }
    }
}
```

We start with the `showNavPanel` function, which calls the implementation of the `showNav` function on the `sideNav` child component, and then sets the `marginLeft` style on the main DOM element. Likewise, the `hideNavPanel` function does the opposite. The `showDetailPanel` function calls the implementation of the `openRightWindow` function on the `rightScreen` child component, and then sets the `transform` property on the main DOM element.

With this implementation in place, we can now focus on the Mediator class itself.

The Mediator class

The `Mediator` class is responsible for coordinating the overall application state, and the interactions between our various UI classes. As such, it really needs to have three key ingredients. Firstly, it needs to have the concrete implementation of the `IMediatorImpl` interface, so that it can call the various functions it needs to when the UI needs updating. We have just implemented the `IMediatorImpl` interface in our `AppComponent` class, so we will need to pass a reference to the `AppComponent` instance to the Mediator class.

Secondly, the `Mediator` class needs a concrete instance of each of our State classes, so that it can recreate both the current state of the application, as well as the desired next state. It can then compare the current state and the desired next state to figure out what changes will need to occur to move from state to state.

Thirdly, the `Mediator` class needs to store the current state of the application. As it is responsible for moving from state to state, it makes sense for the Mediator to be the single source of truth for anything state-related. Also, where UI functionality is dependent on the current state of the application, we can forward any queries about what to do through to the Mediator class to make a decision for us.

Bearing these elements in mind, let's take a look at the properties and constructor of our `Mediator` class, as follows:

```
export class Mediator {
    private _mainPanelState = new MainPanelOnly();
    private _detailPanelState = new DetailPanel();
    private _sideNavState = new MainPanelWithSideNav();

    private _currentState: IState;
    private _currentMainPanelState: IState;
    private _mediatorImpl: IMediatorImpl;

    constructor(mediatorImpl: IMediatorImpl) {
        this._mediatorImpl = mediatorImpl;
        this._currentState = this._currentMainPanelState =
            this._sideNavState;
    }
}
```

We start with the three concrete instances of our three State classes, named _mainPanelState, _detailPanelState, and _sideNavState. Following this, we have two properties, named _currentState and _currentMainPanelState, which are both of type IState. These properties will be used to store the current state of the application itself, and the main panel. Remember that if we switch from the main panel to the detail panel and then back again, the side navigation panel should reappear in the same state as we left it. This is what the _currentMainPanel state variable will be used for.

The next function we will implement within the Mediator class is a simple factory function to retrieve the concrete instance of a State object given the StateType enum value as an input, as follows:

```
getStateImpl(stateType: StateType) : IState {
    var stateImpl : IState;
    switch(stateType) {
        case StateType.DetailPanel:
            stateImpl = this._detailPanelState;
            break;
        case StateType.MainPanelOnly:
            stateImpl = this._mainPanelState;
            break;
        case StateType.MainPanelWithSideNav:
            stateImpl = this._sideNavState;
            break;
    }
    return stateImpl;
}
```

This is a simple helper function that returns the correct implementation of a State object given a StateType enum value.

We can now focus on the heart of the Mediator class – managing the changes to the UI when we move from state to state, as follows:

```
moveToState(stateType: StateType) {
    var previousState = this._currentState;
    var nextState = this.getStateImpl(stateType);

    if (previousState.getPanelType() == PanelType.Primary &&
        nextState.getPanelType() == PanelType.Detail ) {
            this._mediatorImpl.showDetailPanel();
    }
    if (previousState.getPanelType() == PanelType.Detail &&
        nextState.getPanelType() == PanelType.Primary) {
            this._mediatorImpl.hideDetailPanel();
    }
```

```
if (nextState.isSideNavVisible())
    this._mediatorImpl.showNavPanel();
else
    this._mediatorImpl.hideNavPanel();

this._mediatorImpl.changeShowHideSideButton(
    previousState.getPanelButtonClass(),
    nextState.getPanelButtonClass() );

this._currentState = nextState;
if (this._currentState.getPanelType() == PanelType.Primary ) {
        this._currentMainPanelState = this._currentState;
}
}
```

This function, named `moveToState`, contains all of the UI logic to handle our three application states. We start by declaring two variables, named `previousState` and `nextState`. The `previousState` variable is where we are now, and the `nextState` variable is where we want to be, as passed in through the `stateType` argument. Once we have these two State objects, we can start to compare their properties, and then call the `IMediatorImpl` interface functions accordingly.

Consider the first `if` statement. The logic here simply states the following:

- If we were on the primary panel, and we wish to move to the detail panel, then tell the UI to show the detail panel.

The second `if` statement states the following:

- If we are on the detail panel, and wish to move to the primary panel, then tell the UI to hide the detail panel.

Our third `if` statement states the following:

- If our State tells us that the side navigation panel should be visible, then show it, otherwise hide it.

We then make a call to the UI to switch the **show/hide** button from our current state icon to our future state icon. This will have the effect of switching the button from < to > , or vice versa, based on the properties of our two states.

Once we have finished updating the UI, we need to store our current state.

Finally, our last `if` statement states that if we are on the main panel, update the internal value of the `_currentMainPanelState` property. We need to store this value so that when we switch to the detail panel and back again, we restore our side navigation bar correctly.

This function contains, in simple, human-readable statements, how to move from state to state. Our logic has boiled down into asking a few simple questions, and responding accordingly.

Using the Mediator

The last step in the implementation of the State and Mediator design pattern is to trigger the change of the state. This trigger could be purely within our code, or it could be as a result of actions on our UI. To begin with, we will need to create a new instance of the `Mediator` class, and register our `AppComponent` class as the implementation for the `IMediatorImpl` interface, as follows:

```
export class AppComponent
    implements IMediatorImpl
{
    ... existing code ...
    mediator: Mediator = new Mediator(this);
```

Here, we are specifying that the `AppComponent` class implements the `IMediatorImpl` interface, and are then defining a local variable named `mediator`. This local variable calls the `Mediator` constructor, passing in `this` (our `AppComponent` class instance). This call essentially registers our `AppComponent` class as the implementation of the `IMediatorImpl` interface that the `Mediator` uses to make changes to the UI.

Once we have registered our `AppComponent` class with the Mediator, we can use the Mediator to trigger a state change. As an example of this, let's ensure that when the application first starts up, we only show the main panel – or in other words, move to the `StateType.MainPanelOnly` state. To do this, we will need to tap into Angular's component-rendering life cycle, and implement a function named `ngAfterViewInit`, as follows:

```
export class AppComponent
    implements IMediatorImpl, AfterViewInit
{
    ... existing code ...

    ngAfterViewInit() {
        this.mediator.moveToState(StateType.MainPanelOnly);
    }
```

Here, we have indicated that the `AppComponent` class implements the `AfterViewInit` interface. This interface defines a single function, named `ngAfterViewInit`, which we are using to move to the `MainPanelOnly` state. The `ngAfterViewInit` function is automatically called by the Angular framework after the initial view of the component has been initialized. This means that Angular has already parsed our component's HTML, created all child views, and has rendered the HTML to the browser. Only at this stage do we have a reference to our `SideNavComponent` child view, and our `RightScreenComponent` view, which are needed by the Mediator.

Our application now loads up, and is in the correct starting state.

Reacting to DOM events

We are almost there in our implementation of the State and Mediator pattern. The final piece of the puzzle is hooking up our DOM click events to trigger a state change. Let's modify the `buttonClickedDetail` function as follows:

```
buttonClickedDetail() {
    this.mediator.moveToState(StateType.DetailPanel);
}
```

The `buttonClickedDetail` function is invoked when a user clicks on the **Detail** button on our main panel. All that this event handler now needs to do is to call the `moveToState` function on the Mediator to move to the `DetailPanel` state. Very simple indeed.

We also need to modify the event handler function that is called when a user is on the detail panel, and click on the < button to return to the main panel. Remember that we hooked up an `EventEmitter` class in the `RightScreenComponent` file to an event handler in our `AppComponent` class, named `onNotifyRightWindow`. We can now modify this handler as follows:

```
onNotifyRightWindow(message:string):void {
    this.mediator.moveToState(
        this.mediator.getCurrentMainPanelState());
}
```

Here, we are simply moving to the previous main panel state. Again, very simple indeed.

The last user interaction that we need to handle is when the user clicks on the **show/hide** side navigation bar button. This button will either show or hide the side navigation bar. Remember that the effect of clicking on this button will be slightly different, depending on whether the side navigation bar is currently open or closed. The AppComponent class, therefore, should not be making this decision – as it is based on the current state.

It makes sense, then, to simply trap this event from our AppComponent class, and then forward the decision making to our Mediator class, as the Mediator class holds all of the information needed about our current state.

Our event handler in our AppComponent class is as follows:

```
showHideSideClicked() {
    this.mediator.showHideSideNavClicked();
}
```

Here, we are simply calling the showHideSideNavClicked function on the Mediator class, which is implemented as follows:

```
showHideSideNavClicked() {
    switch (this._currentState.getStateType()) {
        case StateType.MainPanelWithSideNav:
            this.moveToState(StateType.MainPanelOnly);
            break;
        case StateType.MainPanelOnly:
            this.moveToState(StateType.MainPanelWithSideNav);
            break;
    }
}
```

This function simply queries the _currentState object, and switches to the MainPanelOnly state, or the MainPanelWithSideNav state accordingly.

There is one final thing we need to do to complete our implementation of the State and Mediator pattern, which is to set the initial state of the application. This can be done by calling the Mediator moveToState function when the AppComponent class has been created and rendered itself to the DOM. To trap this event, Angular provides the AfterViewInit interface, which is implemented by the ngAfterViewInit function. We will need to update the definition of the AppComponent class to implement the interface, as well as to provide the implementation, as follows:

```
export class AppComponent implements IMediatorImpl, AfterViewInit {

    .. existing code ...
```

```
ngAfterViewInit() {
    this.mediator.moveToState(StateType.MainPanelWithSideNav);
}
```

Here, we have added the `AfterViewInit` interface to the list of interfaces that the `AppComponent` class implements. We have also provided an implementation of the `ngAfterViewInit` function, which simply calls the `moveToState` function with the desired initial state, which in this case is `StateType.MainPanelWithSideNav`.

Our implementation of the State and Mediator pattern is now complete.

Summary

In this chapter, we took an in-depth look at building an Angular application from the ground up. We experimented with a left-to-right page transition design and learned how to manipulate CSS styles and CSS transitions to create a visually appealing application. Unfortunately, our initial attempts in creating this application ended up with a lot of confusing and hard-to-fix local variables, as we attempted to keep all of the page elements under control.

We then took a step back, and discussed how the State and Mediator design patterns could help us to manage page transitions. We then re-built our application into meaningful components, and took a detailed look into how to apply the State and Mediator patterns to manage our application state, and complex page transitions.

In the next chapter, we will take a look at the concept of dependency injection, and how we can use the new language features of TypeScript to implement this powerful and simple object-oriented design paradigm.

12
Dependency Injection

In our last chapter, we explored the concepts of object-oriented programming, and worked through the process of building an application that conformed to object-oriented design principles. The **Gang of Four** (**GoF**) design patterns can be broken down into three main groups. The first of these groups is named **Creational patterns**, and covers numerous ways of creating objects. The second of these groups is named **Structural patterns**, and describe methods of designing object hierarchies that work together to achieve encapsulation and loose coupling. The third of these groups is named **Behavioral patterns**, and are designed to cover the behavior of a group of objects together in order to achieve certain goals. Over time, these patterns have sparked a wider interest in finding the simplest and best solutions for a wide range of programming problems.

As systems have become larger and more complex, a number of design patterns have emerged on top of the original set from the GoF. These patterns include the **Domain Model** pattern, **Domain Events** pattern, **Service Location** pattern, and **Dependency Injection** (**DI**) patterns, to name a few. In this chapter, we will discuss both the Service Location and DI design patterns, and build a simple dependency injector. To begin our discussion, let's first identify what a service is.

A service focuses on one thing, and one thing only, and is based on the single responsibility design principle. As an example, consider the case of loading and hydrating an object from a data store. This object may be the information related to a single customer, or an array of customers that have been retrieved based on a search pattern. We would design a service for loading a single customer record into a customer object, and we would also design a service to search for customer records based on a set of search criteria. Each of these services would require another service that is solely responsible for returning a database connection. A database connection service may rely on another service that reads a system configuration file to load configuration options for many parts of the system. These services therefore have a dependency tree, which means the system must load and initiate some services before it can load and initiate others. Services, therefore, enable us to write loosely coupled systems.

With this in mind, there are two design patterns that can help us deal with locating and using services in a large application. The first of these is named Service Location, where we build a central **registry** of available services, and then request these services as needed. The second of these is an extension of the Service Location pattern, and is named DI. With DI, instead of asking for available services, these services are automatically injected into our code before we need them, and are therefore ready for us to use.

In this chapter, we will start by working through an example of how the Service Location pattern helps us to find information that we need as and when we need it. We will build a service locator, and show how this pattern is used in order to make our code more modular and loosely coupled. We will then discuss the drawbacks of the service locator pattern, and discuss how DI is a better pattern to use for our use cases. Finally, we will build a DI framework of our own, using TypeScript decorators.

This chapter is an in-depth discussion on the concepts of DI, how it originated out of the Service Location pattern, and how a DI framework can be built using TypeScript. If you are using a framework, such as Angular, you will find that it already has a sophisticated DI framework already built-in, and as such, you will be able to use it as a natural extension of your code. By building a DI framework from scratch, we will stretch our knowledge on how TypeScript and object-oriented concepts can be used to solve some rather complicated objectives.

In this chapter, we will explore the following topics:

- Object dependency
- Service Location
- Interface Resolution
- Constructor Injection
- Decorator Injection
- Dependency Injection

Sending mail

To begin our discussion on DI, let's create a simple Node application that sends an email. Sending mail is a common requirement of most systems, and is generally one of the first use cases that need to be built in order to allow users to register with a website. Even before a user has logged into your site, their registration details need to be captured, and part of this process usually includes an email address verification. So, let's explore how to send an email using Node.

Using nodemailer

There are a variety of Node-based packages that we can import to give us email capability. In this chapter, we will use the `nodemailer` package, which can be installed as follows:

```
npm install --save nodemailer
```

Once installed, we will need a few declaration files using `@types`, as follows:

```
npm install @types/node --saveDev
npm install @types/nodemailer --saveDev
npm install @types/nodemailer-direct-transport --save
npm install @types/nodemailer-smtp-transport --save
npm install @types/nodemailer-bluebird --save
```

With the `nodemailer` package installed, and the relevant TypeScript declaration files in place, we can follow the examples on the Nodemailer website, and send an email in three simple steps. Let's create a `NodeMailer.ts` file, as follows:

```
import * as nodemailer from 'nodemailer';

var transporter = nodemailer.createTransport(
    `smtp://localhost:1025`
);

var mailOptions : nodemailer.SendMailOptions = {
    from : 'from_test@gmail.com',
    to : 'to_test@gmail.com',
    subject : 'Hello',
    text: 'Hello from node.js'
};

transporter.sendMail( mailOptions, (error, info) => {
    if (error) {
        return console.log(`error: ${error}`);
    }
    console.log(`Message Sent ${info.response}`);
});
```

Here, we have imported the `nodemailer` module, and then set up a `transporter` variable that uses the SMTP server found at localhost port `1025`. Once we have a connection to the SMTP server, we set up a `mailOptions` variable that contains the details of our email, such as the sender, recipient, subject, and email body. These properties are named `from`, `to`, `subject`, and `text`, respectively. Finally, the call to the `sendMail` function on the `transporter` variable will send the actual email.

Running the code at this stage will generate an error, as the SMTP server will not be found.

Using a local SMTP server

There are a number of local SMTP server implementations that we can use for development purposes. If you are working in a Windows environment, then take a look at **Papercut**. Papercut is a simple standalone executable that can be fired up to act as a local SMTP server. If you prefer Node-based solutions, then smtp-sink is a simple package that also provides a local SMTP server. The installation of smtp-sink is as simple as executing the following:

```
npm install -g smtp-sink
```

Once installed, it can be started by simply typing:

```
smtp-sink
```

The default options for smtp-sink will start an SMTP server on port 1025, and a web server on port 1080, where emails can be viewed by pointing a browser to http://localhost:1080/emails.

With smtp-sink running, our sample application will be able to send an email to the local SMTP server.

A service class

The code that we have built to send an email, can be refactored into a single class, which encapsulates all of the setup code for us. The MailService.ts file is as follows:

```
import * as nodemailer from 'nodemailer';

export class MailService {
    private _transporter: nodemailer.Transporter;
    constructor() {
        this._transporter = nodemailer.createTransport(
            `smtp://localhost:1025`
        );
    }
    sendMail(to: string, subject: string, content: string) {
        let options = {
            from: 'from_test@gmail.com',
            to: to,
            subject: subject,
```

```
            text: content
        }

    this._transporter.sendMail(
        options, (error, info) => {
            if (error) {
                return console.log(`error: ${error}`);
            }
            console.log(`Message Sent ${info.response}`);
        });
    }
}
```

Here, we have built a class named `MailService` that encapsulates the internal workings of the `nodemailer` package, and only exposes a simple function, named `sendMail`. The `sendMail` function has also reduced the number of parameters that we need in order to send an email. Note that we have removed the `from` parameter, in favor of hardcoding this sender mail address within the class. This will ensure that all emails sent from our application will come from the same email address. We will tackle the issue of hardcoding the sender's email a little later, but at least this piece of information is now centralized into a single place.

We can use this class, as follows:

```
import MailService from './app/MailService';

let gmailService = new MailService();

gmailService.sendMail(
    '<test_user>@gmail.com',
    'Hello',
    'Hello from gmailService');
```

Here, we have simply created an instance of the `MailService` class, and called the `sendMail` function to send a simple email.

At this point, our `MailService` class is working as expected, and is sending emails correctly. Unfortunately, the call to the `sendMail` function does not currently provide any feedback to the calling code. It would be far better if the `sendMail` function provided a mechanism to let us know whether the mail was sent correctly or not. We should, therefore, refactor our `sendMail` function to expose the results of the actual call to send the email, as follows:

```
sendMail(to: string, subject: string, content: string)
    : Promise<void>
    {
```

```
            let options = {
                from: '<fromaddress>@gmail.com',
                to: to,
                subject: subject,
                text: content
            }

        return new Promise<void> (
                (resolve: (msg: any) => void,
                    reject: (err: Error) => void) => {
                this._transporter.sendMail(
                    options, (error, info) => {
                        if (error) {
                            console.log(`error: ${error}`);
                            reject(error);
                        } else {
                            console.log(`Message Sent ${info.response}`);
                            resolve(`Message Sent
                                ${info.response}`);
                        }
                    })
            }
        );
    }
```

Here, we have modified the signature of the `sendMail` function to return a `Promise` object. The implementation of this `Promise` object essentially wraps the call to `this._transporter.sendMail` in a new `Promise` object, and calls either the `reject` callback if there is an error, or the `resolve` callback if the email was sent correctly.

By returning a `Promise` object, we can now detect the result of the email as follows:

```
gmailService.sendMail(
    "test2@test.com",
    "subject",
    "content").then( (msg) => {
        console.log(`sendMail result :(${msg})`);
} );
```

Here, we have simply used fluent syntax and called `then` on the `Promise` object to execute a function after the `sendMail` function completes.

Configuration settings

When writing code that is sending emails, it makes sense to use different settings for your email services depending on the deployment environment. When developers are working with email code, they should be able to use a local SMTP server, so that they can quickly verify emails that are sent to and from different email accounts, without actually sending out emails. In a testing environment, testers should be able to specify which accounts they wish to use as the sending account, and what SMTP server to use. In a **Factory Acceptance Testing (FAT)** environment, these email settings may change once more, so that emails from any of the test environments don't affect the FAT environment. The final settings would, of course, be set for a production environment.

Changing settings depending on where the code is deployed is a common problem that is generally solved through a configuration file of some sort. Configuration values are read in from a file on disk, and these are used throughout the system. Different environments use different configuration files, and the system code does not need to be changed simply to change these settings.

In our code samples, there are currently two values that are good candidates for configuration settings. These are the SMTP server connection string, and the from email address that all emails are sent from.

These settings can easily be expressed as an interface, as follows:

```
export interface ISystemSettings {
    SmtpServerConnectionString: string;
    SmtpFromAddress: string;
}
```

Here, the `ISystemSettings` interface defines the two properties that will need to change when changing environments. The `SmtpServerConnectionString` property will be used to connect to the SMTP server, and the `SmtpFromAddress` property will be used to specify the originating address for all emails.

We can now modify our `MailService` class to use this interface, as follows:

```
import * as nodemailer from 'nodemailer';
import { ISystemSettings } from './ISystemSettings';

export class MailService {
    private _transporter: nodemailer.Transporter;
    private _settings: ISystemSettings;
    constructor(settings: ISystemSettings) {
        this._settings = settings;
        this._transporter = nodemailer.createTransport(
```

```
                this._settings.SmtpServerConnectionString
        );
    }

    sendMail(to: string, subject: string, content: string):
      Promise<void> {
        let options: nodemailer.SendMailOptions = {
            from: this._settings.SmtpFromAddress,
            to: to,
            subject: subject,
            text: content
        }
    ... existing code ...
```

Here, we have imported the ISystemSettings interface, created a local variable named _settings to hold this information, and have modified our constructor function to accept an instance of an object that implements the ISystemSettings interface.

This ISystemSettings interface is used in two places. Firstly, when we call the nodemailer.createTransport function, we use the SmtpServerConnectionString property. Secondly, when we construct the options object, we use the SmtpFromAddress property.

Using the MailService class now means that we must provide both of these parameters when constructing the object, as follows:

```
let mailService = new MailService({
    SmtpServerConnectionString : 'smtp://localhost:1025',
    SmtpFromAddress : 'smtp_from@test.com'
});

mailService.sendMail(
    "test2@test.com",
    "subject",
    "content").then( (msg) => {
        console.log(`sendMail result :(${msg})`);
} );
```

Here, we have constructed an object that conforms to the ISystemSettings interface, that is, it has both an SmtpServerConnectionString property and an SmtpFromAddress property. This object is then passed into the GMailService constructor.

Object dependency

Our changes to the `MailService` class have introduced an object dependency. In order for the `MailService` class to function, it is now dependent on an instance of a class that provides the implementation of the `ISystemSettings` interface. `mailService` is therefore dependent on a class that implements the `ISystemSettings` interface.

This dependency is actually a good thing. It means that we can provide different versions of classes that implement the `ISystemSettings` interface, without making any changes to our `MailService` code. This allows us to configure the environment that the `MailService` class runs within, whether in development, testing, FAT, or production.

It also allows us to test some boundary conditions. In other words, what happens if the SMTP server is not running, or not configured correctly ? Does the `MailService` class correctly report that an error has occurred? What actions does our code need to take when the service cannot send an email correctly?

Service Location

Our current implementation of the `MailService` class relies on the calling code to create an instance of the `ISystemSettings` interface, and pass this through in the constructor. When we write code that creates an instance of the `MailService` class, we are therefore forced to provide the `ISystemSettings` interface at the time of construction. This is a compile-time dependency. In other words, changing the instance of `ISystemSettings` requires changes to the source code, and then recompilation. It would be far better, however, if we set these options at runtime.

In order to accomplish this, the `MailService` class needs to request an instance of the class that is implementing the `ISystemSettings` interface at runtime, not at compile time.

If a class itself requests the concrete object that is currently implementing an interface, then this process is called **Service Location**. In other words, the class itself is attempting to locate the service that is providing the implementation of an interface.

In order for this to work, however, we need a central registry that can answer the following question: give me the concrete class that is currently implementing this interface. This is the essence of the Service Location design pattern.

Let's create a simple class that implements the Service Location design pattern. To do this, we will need a service locator class that will need to do two things. Firstly, it needs to provide a mechanism to register implementations of a class against an interface. Secondly, it needs to provide a mechanism for a class to resolve the current implementation of an interface.

We can implement a simple service locator, as follows:

```typescript
import { ISystemSettings } from './SystemSettings';

export type IRegisteredClasses = ISystemSettings | undefined;

export class ServiceLocator {
    static registeredClasses: Map<string, IRegisteredClasses>;
    static initialised: boolean = false;

    static init() {
        this.registeredClasses =
            new Map<string, IRegisteredClasses>();
        this.initialised = true;
    }

    public static register(
        interfaceName: string, instance: IRegisteredClasses)
        : void {
        if (!this.initialised) {
            this.init();
        }

        this.registeredClasses.set(interfaceName, instance);
    }
    public static resolve(interfaceName: string):
        IRegisteredClasses {
            return this.registeredClasses.get(interfaceName);
    }
}
```

Here, we start with the definition of a type alias named `IRegisteredClasses`, which will allow us to describe which interfaces are able to be registered with the service locator. We then define a class, which is the service locator itself, and as such, is named `ServiceLocator`. It has two internal properties named `registeredClasses`, and `initialised`. The `registeredClasses` property is used to store instances of each registered class within a `Map`. The `initialised` property is just used to ensure that the `Map` property is created correctly before first use, within the `init` function.

The `register` function takes two parameters – an `interfaceName` of type `string`, and a class instance of type `IRegisteredClasses`. The `register` function adds the class instance to the `registeredClasses` internal `Map`, using the `interfaceName` parameter as a key. The `resolve` function returns the instance of the class based on the `interfaceName` parameter that is passed in as a key.

This very simple `ServiceLocator` class can then be used as follows:

```
import { ServiceLocator, IRegisteredClasses } from
    './ServiceLocator';
import { ISystemSettings } from './SystemSettings';

let settings: ISystemSettings = {
    SmtpServerConnectionString: ``,
    SmtpFromAddress: `from_test@test.com`
}

ServiceLocator.register('ISystemSettings', settings);

let currentSettings: IRegisteredClasses =
ServiceLocator.resolve(`ISystemSettings`);

if (currentSettings) {
    console.log(`SmtpFromAddress :
        ${currentSettings.SmtpFromAddress}`);
} else {
    console.log(`currentSetting is undefined.`);
}
```

Here, we have constructed an instance of an object to provide the two properties required by the `ISystemSettings` interface, and named it `settings`. We then call the `register` function to register this object with the `'ISystemSettings'` key. Once an object has been registered, we can then call the `resolve` function of the `ServiceLocator` class to retrieve the currently registered object for this key. We then print the results to the console.

We can now update our `MailService` class to use the `ServiceLocator` class as follows:

```
export class MailService {
    private _transporter: nodemailer.Transporter | undefined;
    private _settings: ISystemSettings | undefined;
    constructor() {
        this._settings =
            ServiceLocator.resolve(`ISystemSettings`);
        if (this._settings) {
            this._transporter = nodemailer.createTransport(
                this._settings.SmtpServerConnectionString);
```

```
        }
    }
    ... existing code ...
```

Here, we have updated the `constructor` function of the `MailService` class to use the service locator pattern. Our internal `_settings` property still holds the instance of the `ISystemSettings` object, but the `MailService` class itself is requesting the instance of the `ISystemSettings` interface itself, from the `ServiceLocator` class.

We can now construct an instance of the `MailService` class, as follows:

```
    let gmailService = new MailService();
```

Note how we have hidden the internal dependencies of the `MailService` class away from the user of the class by using the service locator pattern. The class itself requests the resources that it needs in order to perform its functions.

Service Location anti-pattern

The ideas behind the service locator pattern were first introduced by Martin Fowler around 2004, in a blog titled *Inversion of Control Containers and the Dependency Injection pattern* (`http://martinfowler.com/articles/injection.html`). Since then, this pattern has been built and field-tested in a number of different languages and environments. In his book, *Dependency Injection in .NET*, Mark Seeman argues that the Service Location pattern is in fact an anti-pattern.

Mark's reasoning is that it is too easy to misunderstand the usage of a particular class when Service Location is used. In the extreme case, each function of a class may use different services, which means that the user of the class needs to read through the entire code base to understand what dependencies a class has.

Dependency Injection

Mark Seeman argues that a better way of using Service Location is to list all of the dependencies of a class in the class constructor, and then hand over the process of constructing a class to something that understands how to resolve all of these dependencies. The process of constructing a class can be thought of as assembling a class instance, and filling in the available services.

In this way, when a class instance is requested, the dependencies of the class are resolved for us, and the assembler process simply gives us an instance of the class that works correctly. In other words, all of the dependencies that a class has are injected into the class by the assembler before the class is given to us.

This is the essence of the DI design pattern.

Building a dependency injector

In this section of the chapter, we will use the knowledge we have gained in writing a service locator, and combine this with TypeScript decorators in order to create a simple DI framework. Before we do, however, let's discuss the problem of interface resolution.

Interface resolution

As we know, the `interface` keyword is a TypeScript language construct that we use to define the shape of classes or objects. Wherever we need to define a custom type, and need the TypeScript compiler to ensure that properties and functions are available on an object, we use an interface. Interfaces are particularly handy when describing services, where any number of services could provide the same functionality to our code. In order to create a usable dependency injector, we need to be able to answer the following question: given an interface, how do we obtain the service that is currently implementing it?

In our current Service Location implementation, we are simply using `string` values to both `register` and `resolve` an interface, as shown in the two calls to the `ServiceLocator` class. `register` is shown as follows:

```
ServiceLocator.register('ISystemSettings', smtpSinkSettings);
```

`resolve` is shown as follows:

```
this._settings = ServiceLocator.resolve('ISystemSettings');
```

Unfortunately, using strings in these cases is something to be avoided. It is too easy to mistype the string itself, and to introduce runtime errors as a result. Again, we cannot use the interface name itself in this case, as interfaces are compiled away in the resulting JavaScript.

Enum resolution

As we have seen in previous chapters, magic strings are a prime example where we can refactor our code to use an `enum` resolution. As an example of this, let's consider a `ServiceLocator` class built around an `enum` resolution, as follows:

```
interface ISystemSettings {
}

interface IMailService {
}

enum Interfaces {
    ISystemSettings,
    IMailService
}

class ServiceLocatorTypes {
    public static register(
        interfaceName: Interfaces, instance: any) {}
    public static resolve(
        interfaceName: Interfaces) {}
}

ServiceLocatorTypes.register(Interfaces.ISystemSettings, {});

ServiceLocatorTypes.resolve(Interfaces.ISystemSettings);
```

Here, we start with two interfaces that we wish to use with our service locator, named `ISystemSettings` and `IMailService`. Note that, we have excluded the internal properties of these interfaces to simplify the code under discussion.

Next, we have defined an `enum` named `Interfaces`, which contains an entry for each of the interfaces that we wish to use. Our class definition (again without function implementations) for the `ServiceLocatorTypes` class simply shows the change to the `register` and `resolve` function signatures to use the `enum` named `Interfaces`.

The last two lines of this code snippet show how the `Interfaces` enum would be used when calling the `register` and `resolve` functions. By using an `enum` to store our interface names, we have eliminated the use of magic strings, and now have a central `enum` to describe all interfaces that will be used by the system.

Class resolution

As an alternative to the `enum` implementation, we could also use special purpose classes. This is best illustrated by looking at a code sample, as follows:

```
interface ISystemSettings { }
class IISystemSettings { }

interface IMailService { }
class IIMailService { }

class ServiceLocatorGeneric {
    public static register<T>(
        interfaceName: {new(): T;}, instance: any) {}
    public static resolve<T>(
        interfaceName: {new() : T}) {}
}

ServiceLocatorGeneric.register(IISystemSettings, {});

ServiceLocatorGeneric.resolve(IISystemSettings);
```

Here, we start with an interface named `ISystemSettings`, which is the interface that we wish to use with our service locator. We then define a class named `IISystemSettings` that has no functions or properties, but is only used for interface resolution. The naming of this class is important. By convention, we have named this class to be the same as the interface that we are describing, but have added an extra `'I'` to the start of the name. This means that an interface named `ITest` would have a corresponding class named `IITest`, whose sole purpose is to provide a unique name (in place of an `enum`) when used with a DI framework.

Our `ServiceLocatorGeneric` class has also modified the `register` and `resolve` function signatures to accommodate the use of a class name instead of an `enum`. We are now using generic syntax, and requiring that the `interfaceName` argument is of type `{ new() : T; }`. Remember, from our discussion on generics that when using a function that needs to call the `new()` function to create an instance of a class when given a class name, it needs to be referenced by the class constructor.

Let's look at the implementation of the `register` function, as follows:

```
public static register<T>(
    t: { new(): T },
    instance: IRegisteredClassesGeneric) : void
{
    if (!this.initialised) {
```

```
            this.init();
    }
    let interfaceInstance = new t();
    let interfaceName = interfaceInstance.constructor.name;
    console.log(`ServiceLocator registering : ${interfaceName}`);

    this.registeredClasses.set(interfaceName, instance);
}
```

Here, we have updated our `register` function to use generic syntax, with the type of T. The first parameter of the register function is named `t`, and uses the `t: { new() : T }` syntax to allow us to create an object of type T in our code. After checking whether the `init` function has been called, we then create an instance of this generic class. Once created, we are able to find out the `name` of this class by querying the `constructor.name` property. This property will be used instead of our magic-string or `enum` implementation that we used earlier.

This generic syntax then allows us to call the `register` and `resolve` functions by simply providing a class name, as seen in the last two lines of the previous code snippet. If we compare the `enum` style resolution to the class name resolution style, we end up with the following code snippets. An `enum` style resolution is shown as follows:

```
ServiceLocatorTypes.register(Interfaces.ISystemSettings, {});
```

A class name resolution is demonstrated as follows:

```
ServiceLocatorGeneric.register(IISystemSettings, {});
```

In the rest of this chapter, we will use class name resolution for a number of reasons:

The definition of an interface and the class name used for interface resolution are defined in the same source file. With an `enum` style resolution, interface definitions are scattered across the code base, but the `enum` instance is in a single file. This gives us two places to modify code when a new interface to be used in Service Location is needed.

Using class definitions means there is less code to type. While this may seem like a trivial reason, it also means that there is less code to read. As developers, we spend all day reading and writing code, and the less we need to read to get the message across, the better.

The double I I interface naming standard is a visual trigger that indicates that this code is using Service Location. Whenever we read code, and see this double I I prefix, we immediately know that Service Location is in play. This helps us distinguish between standard interfaces and Service Location based interfaces fairly quickly.

Let's now take a quick look at the `resolve` function of our `ServiceLocatorGeneric` class, as follows:

```
public static resolve<T>(t: { new(): T }): IRegisteredClassesGeneric {
    let interfaceInstance = new t();
    let interfaceName = interfaceInstance.constructor.name;
    console.log(`ServiceLocator resolving : ${interfaceName}`);
    return this.registeredClasses.get(interfaceName);
}
```

Here, we have added the generic type of `T` to the `resolve` function, and again create a new instance of the class of type `T` in order to find out the `constructor.name` property. We then use this property to find the class that is registered against the interface.

Constructor injection

Earlier, we discussed the benefits and anti-patterns at play when using a service locator pattern, and picked up on Mark Seeman's ideas that DI should only occur on class constructors. We have been using Service Location in our `MailService` class within the `constructor` function, as follows:

```
export default class MailService {
    private _transporter: nodemailer.Transporter;
    private _settings: ISystemSettings;

    constructor() {
        this._settings =
            ServiceLocator.resolve('ISystemSettings');
        this._transporter = nodemailer.createTransport(
            this._settings.SmtpServerConnectionString
        );
    }
}
```

Here, we have specified a local _settings property of type ISystemSettings, and are using the `ServiceLocator` to resolve this internal property. The switch to a DI pattern using a constructor injection would be as follows:

```
export default class MailServiceDi {
    private _transporter: nodemailer.Transporter;
```

```
    private _settings: ISystemSettings;

    constructor(_settings?: IISystemSettings) {
        this._transporter = nodemailer.createTransport(
            this._settings.SmtpServerConnectionString
        );
    }
```

There are a few points to note about this code. Firstly, we still have the private _settings property, which is typed to the ISystemSettings interface. This means that we can still refer to this._settings within the body of the code. Secondly, we have now included a parameter in our constructor: _settings?: IISystemSettings. We are therefore expecting the dependency injector to find the implementation of the ISystemSettings interface, or more correctly, the class that is registered against the IISystemSettings key, and inject this into our class, so that the private _settings property contains this implementation.

For our dependency injector to work, the name of the constructor parameter and the name of the private property must both be the same.

Let's take a look at what the result of the constructor injection would look like, after the class itself has been processed by the dependency injector framework, as follows:

```
export default class MailServiceDi {
    private _transporter: nodemailer.Transporter;
    // private _settings: ISystemSettings;
    get _settings() : ISystemSettings {
        return ServiceLocatorGeneric.resolve(IISystemSettings);
    }

    constructor(_settings?: IISystemSettings) {
        this._transporter = nodemailer.createTransport(
            this._settings.SmtpServerConnectionString
        );
    } }
```

Here, we have an example of what the class should look like after injection. The private _settings property has been replaced by a get function of the same name, that is, get _settings(). This function internally calls our ServiceLocator class to resolve the interface. By creating a simple get function, we have essentially injected our dependency. This raises another question, however. How do we modify a class at run-time in order to inject the dependencies that it needs, and create get functions? The answer is by using Decorators.

Decorator injection

At the beginning of Chapter 4, *Decorators, Generics, and Asynchronous Features*, we discussed the use of decorators, and how they are invoked when a class is defined. Decorators are not invoked when a class is instantiated, so their usage is limited to interrogating and manipulating class definitions. Decorators, as we know, can be applied to classes, properties, functions, and parameters. Let's build a simple class decorator, and see what information it gives us about a class.

Remember that there are three things about a class that we are interested in during this exercise. Firstly, we need to find the definition of the class constructor. Once we know what the constructor looks like, we need to find the list of parameters that the constructor uses. Each of these parameters will then become getters that use our service locator to resolve dependencies. The last piece of information we will need is to find the type that each constructor parameter is expecting. Once we have this information, we can build a simple getter function to return the correct type within our decorator.

Using a class definition

Before we begin, bear in mind that in order to use decorators, our `tsconfig.json` file must be configured correctly, as follows:

```
{
    "compilerOptions": {
        "target": "es6",
        "module": "commonjs",
        "lib": [
            "es6"
        ],
        "strict": true,
        "esModuleInterop": true,
        "experimentalDecorators": true,
        "emitDecoratorMetadata": true,
    }
}
```

Here, we have included the `"experimentalDecorators" : true` option, as well as the `"emitDecoratorMetadata" : true` option in order for our code to use decorators, as we did in Chapter 4, *Decorators, Generics and Asynchronous Features*. We have also defined that we wish to use ES6 as our compile target, and have included the `es6` library in our `lib` definition. We will also need to install the reflect-metadata package, as follows:

```
npm install reflect-metadata
```

Let's put together a simple class decorator, and see what information we can deduce from the class. Our decorator, in the `Decorator.ts` file is as follows:

```
import 'reflect-metadata';
export function ConstructorInject(classDefinition: Function) {
    console.log(`classDefinition:`);
    console.log(`================`);
    console.log(`${classDefinition}`);
    console.log(`================`);
}
```

Here, we are importing the `reflect-metadata` module, and have then created a decorator that is simply logging the value of the `classDefinition` argument to the console.

We can now decorate our `MailServiceDi` class with this decorator, and see what happens:

```
import { ConstructorInject } from './ConstructorInject';

@ConstructorInject
export default class MailServiceDi {
    private _transporter: nodemailer.Transporter;
    private _settings: ISystemSettings;
    constructor(_settings?: IISystemSettings) {
    }
}
```

Here, we have imported our `ConstructorInject` decorator, and applied it to our `MailServiceDi` class. Note that for the sake of brevity, we have removed the body of the constructor code that configures the `_transporter` property. If we now create an instance of this class, it will be as follows:

```
import MailServiceDi from './MailServiceDi';
var gmailDi = new MailServiceDi();
```

We will generate the following console output from our `ConstructorInject` decorator, as follows:

```
classDefinition:
================
class MailServiceDi {
    constructor(_settings) {
    }
}
================
```

As we can see, the `classDefinition` parameter is populated with the full class definition for the `MailServiceDi` class. This definition, however, is not the TypeScript definition of our class, but it is the JavaScript definition of our class. This means that we have lost the type information on each of our constructor parameters, as this information is compiled away. What we do have, however, is the name of the properties that this class uses in its constructor.

 The generated JavaScript will always include the constructor as the first function. If we were to add any other function at the top of the class definition, and write the constructor at the bottom of the class definition, TypeScript will always move the constructor function to the top of the class definition.

Parsing constructor parameters

By having access to the full class definition, we can use simple string searching to find the properties of the class constructor. If we find the first open bracket ' (' character, and the next close bracket ') ' character, we can extract a string that contains all of our constructor parameter names. Let's update our `ConstructorDecorator` code, as follows:

```
let firstIdx = classDefinition.toString().indexOf('(') + 1;
let lastIdx = classDefinition.toString().indexOf(')');
let arr = classDefinition.toString().substr(
firstIdx, lastIdx - firstIdx);

console.log(`class parameters :`);
console.log(`${arr}`);
console.log(`===================`);
```

The output of this code is as follows:

```
=================
class parameters :
_settings
===================
```

We can test this code by inserting another parameter in our constructor, and checking the output. So, if the `MailServiceDi` class has two arguments, the respective code snippet will be as follows:

```
constructor(_settings?: IISystemSettings, testParameter?: string) {
}
```

Then, the parsing of the constructor will produce the following code snippet:

```
class parameters :
_settings, testParameter
===================
```

So, by some simple string extrapolation, we are able to find out what property names are required by this class. We can then easily parse this array within our `ConstructorInject` function, as follows:

```
let splitArr = arr.split(', ');

for (let paramName of splitArr) {
    console.log(`found parameter named : ${paramName}`);
}
```

Here, we are creating an array named `splitArray` from the string containing our parameter names, and logging each entry to the console. The output of this would be as follows:

```
found parameter named : _settings
found parameter named : testParameter
```

So we now have an array that specifies what the parameter names are for our `constructor` function.

Finding parameter types

Now that we know what each of our constructor parameter names are, we need to match these with a parameter type. In order to do this, we will need to make use of the reflect-metadata package in our `ConstructorInject` decorator, as follows:

```
let parameterTypeArray =
    Reflect.getMetadata("design:paramtypes", classDefinition);
console.log(`parameterTypeArray:`);
console.log(`===================`);
console.log(`${parameterTypeArray}`);
console.log(`===================`);

for (let type of parameterTypeArray) {
    console.log(`found type : ${type.name}`);
}
```

Here, we are calling the `Reflect.getMetadata` function, and using the
`"design:paramtypes"` argument to extract an array from the class definition. We then
print this array to the console, and then loop through the array to print the `name` property
of each element in the `"design:paramtypes"` array. The output of this code is as follows:

```
parameterTypeArray:
====================
class IISystemSettings {
},function String() { [native code] }
====================
found type : IISystemSettings
found type : String
```

This type of information is exactly what we need to build a constructor injector. Note that
the first parameter, which we know has the name `_settings`, is of type
`IISystemSettings`. The second parameter, which is named `testParameter`, is of type
`String`.

Injecting properties

We can now combine the results of both arrays to match the parameter name with the type
name in our decorator code, as follows:

```
for (let i = 0; i < splitArr.length; i++) {
    let propertyName = splitArr[i];
    let typeName = parameterTypeArray[i];

    console.log(`
        parameterName : ${propertyName}
        is of type    : ${typeName.name}`);
}
```

Here, we are looping through the `splitArr` array (which contains our parameter names),
and using the same index on the `parameterTypeArray` property to match property names
with type names. The result is as follows:

```
parameterName : _settings
is of type    : IISystemSettings

parameterName : testParameter
is of type    : String
```

With this information at hand, we can now use JavaScript to inject the property that we require, as follows:

```
Object.defineProperty(classDefinition.prototype, propertyName, {
    get : function() {
        return ServiceLocatorGeneric.resolve(
            eval(typeName)
        );
    }
});
```

Here, we are using the `Object.defineProperty` function that JavaScript provides to create a property at runtime and attach it to the definition of our class. The `defineProperty` function takes three parameters. The first parameter is the prototype of the class to be modified. The second parameter is the `propertyName` itself, and the third parameter is the definition of the property. Our property definition is a simple getter function, that then calls the `ServiceLocatorGeneric.resolve` function, passing in the `typeName` function. Note how we have called the `eval` function, passing it the `typeName` function that we retrieved from our `parameterTypeArray`. This step is necessary in order to send the class definition to the service locator instead of a simple string.

Using dependency injection

Now that we are injecting property functions through our `ConstructorInjector` decorator, we can use our dependency injector framework as follows:

```
import GMailServiceDi from './app/GMailServiceDi';
import { ServiceLocatorGeneric } from './app/ServiceLocator';
import { IISystemSettings } from './app/ISystemSettings';

ServiceLocatorGeneric.register(IISystemSettings, {
    SmtpServerConnectionString : 'smtp://localhost:1025',
    SmtpFromAddress : 'smtp_from@test.com'
});

var gmailDi = new GMailServiceDi();

gmailDi.sendMail("test@test.com", "testsubject", "testContent"
).then( (msg) => {
    console.log(`sendMail returned : ${msg}`);
} ).catch( (err) => {
    console.log(`sendMail returned : ${err}`);
});
```

After importing the various modules into our sample, we call
`ServiceLocatorGeneric.register` to register the object that is providing the
`IISystemSettings` interface. We then simply create an instance of the `MailServiceDi`
class, with no parameters. At this stage, our dependency injector has done all of the work
for us, and has injected the correct properties for immediate use.

Note how simple this object constructor is, that is, `new MailServiceDi()`. It looks just like
any other normal instantiation of an object. Once the class has been instantiated, we can call
the `sendMail` function as we have done before.

Recursive injection

As a final test of our DI framework, let's now inject the `MailServiceDi` class into another
class. This means that our new class will be dependent on the `IMailServiceDi` interface,
which is itself dependent on the `ISystemSettings` interface. This is an example of a
recursive dependency tree.

We start by defining an interface for the `MailServiceDi` class itself, as follows:

```
export interface IMailServiceDi {
    sendMail(to: string, subject: string, content: string)
    : Promise<void>;
}

export class IIMailServiceDi { }
```

Here, we have taken the definition of the `sendMail` function, which returns a `Promise`,
and created an interface named `IMailServiceDi`. We have also created the class that will
be used as a type lookup by our DI framework, named `IIMailServiceDi`.

With these interfaces in place, we can create a class that is dependent on the
`IMailServiceDi` interface, as follows:

```
import { IMailServiceDi, IIMailServiceDi } from "./MailServiceDi";
import { ConstructorInject } from "./Decorators";

@ConstructorInject
export class MailSender {
    private mailService: IMailServiceDi | undefined;

    constructor(mailService?: IIMailServiceDi) { }

    async sendWelcomeMail(to: string) {
        if (this.mailService) {
```

```
            let response = await this.mailService
         .sendMail(to, "Welcome", "Welcome from MailSender");
         console.log(`MailSender.sendMail returned :
            ${response}`);
      }
   }
}
```

Here, we have created a class named `MailSender`, and used the `ConstructorInject` decorator to decorate the class. Our class has a private property named `mailService`, which is of type `IMailServiceDi`. This is the property that will be created by our DI framework. The `constructor` function simply uses the `IIMailService` class to indicate that the private `mailService` property should be injected. The `MailSender` class has a `sendWelcomeMail` function that uses an `async await` pattern to call the `MailServiceDi sendMail` function.

To test this class, we need to register the `MailServiceDi` class with our DI framework, and then create a new instance of the `MailSender` class, and call the `sendWelcomeMail` function as follows:

```
let mailServiceDi = new MailServiceDi();
ServiceLocatorGeneric.register(IIMailServiceDi, mailServiceDi);

let mailSender = new MailSender();
mailSender.sendWelcomeMail("test@test.com");
```

The output of this code is as follows:

```
ServiceLocator resolving : IIMailServiceDi
ServiceLocator resolving : IISystemSettings
Message Sent 250
MailSender.sendMail returned : Message Sent : 250
```

Here, we can see that the DI framework is calling the `ServiceLocator` class to resolve `IIMailServiceDi`. This is during the constructor of the `MailSender` class. As the `MailServiceDi` class is dependent on the `ISystemSettings` interface, a second call is made to resolve `IISystemSettings`.

Summary

In this chapter, we discussed the service locators and DI design patterns. We started by creating a class to send emails, and then created our own simple service locator that could resolve instances of classes given a string name. We then moved to a more resolute Service Location pattern that used class names instead of magic strings as the key to both registering and resolving instances of classes. We then discussed the pitfalls of the Service Location pattern, and implemented a DI framework using decorators.

In our next chapter, we will take a look at what it takes to build applications that combine a web server, such as Node and Express, with a TypeScript-friendly framework, such as Angular.

13
Building Applications

Thus far, we have explored the various tools and techniques that we need to use in order to build an application using some of the most popular TypeScript frameworks. We have focused on building an Angular site with a rather complex screen flow, and learned how we can use the State and Mediator design patterns to handle this complexity in a modular way. We have also explored the use of Node and Express that allow us to build a server-side application to handle page generation, and route handling. In the first section of this chapter, we combine the two, and explore how to serve an Angular website from a Node Express server. We will build upon the Angular application that we built in `Chapter 11`, *Object-Oriented Programming*, and use it as the basis for further development.

Once we have Express serving our Angular application, we can then explore a number of other requirements that our web server will need to fulfill. How do we log in to the application? How do we manage security access rights on the server, and avoid storing cookies in the browser? How do we configure our Express server so that it can be deployed into a number of different testing environments? In the second section of this chapter, we will explore tools and techniques for building a full-blown Express server that will fulfill these requirements. We will then update our Angular application to integrate with this Express web server. Some of the topics that we will cover include ensuring that our application can serve unauthenticated users just the Login page, and, once logged in, open up the full set of functionality.

In the final section of this chapter, we will explore the integration of external authentication providers such as Google to provide a single sign-on experience. We will cover the following topics:

- Node and Angular integration
- Express server configuration and server logging
- Using Brackets to design UI screens
- Angular routing and Auth Guards
- POSTing data to an Express endpoint in Angular

- Using Observables
- Using JWT tokens
- Integration with Google authentication

Node and Angular integration

The default setup for an Angular application configured using the Angular CLI already contains a number of options that can be used in a production setting. One of these options is the outputPath property, which specifies where compiled JavaScript files are written to. By using a separate path for output files, we know that we can distribute the contents of this directory as a fully working version of our site.

The outputPath option can be found in the angular.json file, under the **Projects** | **Angular-sample** | **Architect** | **Build** | **Options** configuration section. This property is, by default, set to "dist/angular-sample", and therefore, when we issue an ng build command, we will notice that the Angular CLI will generate a number of files in this directory. These include main.js, polyfill.js, runtime.js, styles.js, and vendor.js. These JavaScript files are the output of the Angular compilation step. Along with these JavaScript files, there is also an index.html file within this directory, whose contents are as follows:

```html
<!doctype html>
<html lang="en">

<head>
    <meta charset="utf-8">
    <title>AngularSample</title>
    <base href="/">

    <meta name="viewport" content="width=device-width, initial-scale=1">
    <link rel="icon" type="image/x-icon" href="favicon.ico">
</head>

<body>
    <app-root></app-root>
    <script type="text/javascript" src="runtime.js"></script>
    <script type="text/javascript" src="polyfills.js"></script>
    <script type="text/javascript" src="styles.js"></script>
    <script type="text/javascript" src="vendor.js"></script>
    <script type="text/javascript" src="main.js"></script>
</body>

</html>-
```

This HTML file is automatically generated by the Angular compiler step, and essentially contains an `<app-root>` tag and a `<script>` tag for each of the generated JavaScript files. The `<app-root>` tag is used as the base DOM element where our application's elements will be rendered into.

Let's now generate a production build for our application using the Angular CLI as follows:

```
ng build --prod
```

Here, we have specified the `--prod` option when using `ng build`, which will perform some extra compilation steps to generate a production-ready version of our Angular application. If we then check the generated `index.html` file in the `dist` directory, we will notice a few minor changes, as follows:

```
<!doctype html>
<html lang="en">

<head>
  ... existing html ...
    <link rel="stylesheet" href="styles.06e5b622c6ba37e242d1.css">
</head>

<body>
    <app-root></app-root>
    <script type="text/javascript"
        src="runtime.06daa30a2963fa413676.js"></script>
    <script type="text/javascript"
        src="polyfills.a5acfd4a5754e593d36f.js"></script>
    <script type="text/javascript"
        src="main.85661e3d3f241cd36aa4.js"></script>
</body>

</html>
```

Here, we can see that a new `<link>` element has been generated that references a CSS file, and how the list of `<script>` tags has been reduced down from five files to three. Note, too, that the Angular compiler has added a long random string into the filenames for the CSS file and the JavaScript files. This string is part of the versioning mechanism that Angular uses to ensure that when an application is modified, the corresponding JavaScript file name is automatically changed, so that any browser will be forced to re-request the file.

The interesting thing to note is that Angular can change the contents of the `index.html` file that is generated based on a number of factors. It is therefore important that we serve this `index.html` file from the `dist` directory, to ensure that the HTML used and the files that are referenced match one another.

The generated JavaScript files are also optimized for production use and are minified and uglified during the compilation step.

Angular Express server

In a nutshell, then, to serve an Angular application from an `http` server, we really just need to serve up the `index.html` file that is in the `dist` directory. Ideally, this `index.html` file will be in the base directory of the `http` server, so that it will be the default file if none is specified. Let's set up an Express server to accomplish this.

Firstly, we will create an `express` directory, and a `main.ts` file within this directory that will contain our Express server code. The `express/main.ts` file is as follows:

```
import express from 'express';
import path from 'path';

let app = express();

app.use(`/`, express.static(__dirname + '/angular-sample'));

app.get(`*`, (req: any, res: any) => {
    res.status(200).sendFile(
        path.join(__dirname + '/angular-sample/index.html'));
});

app.listen(9000, () => {
    console.log(`Express server listening on PORT: 9000`);
});
```

Here, we start with the usual `import` statements for the `express` and `path` modules, and then create the `app` variable, which is an instance of `express`. We then configure express to set the default directory to be `angular-sample` through the use of the `express.static` function. We will run the express server from the `dist` directory, so this statement is specifying that the server should look in the `angular-sample` sub-directory for all static files. This means that any HTML file or CSS file will, by default, be served from the `angular-sample` sub-directory.

We then have a single handler, which states that any GET request will return the angular-sample/index.html file. In essence, this single handler will redirect all GET requests to our Angular application. What this means is that a call to localhost:9000/test/test, for example, will, in fact, return the index.html file. Angular then gets a chance to interpret the /test/test URL, and can initiate behavior based on its own internal routes. We can still specify routes in our Express server, but any URL that Express does not match will automatically be passed through to Angular. We will explore routes within Angular a little later, but just bear in mind that Express gets the first chance of matching a route, and, if it is not matched, then it is passed through to Angular using this directive.

Our Express application then starts up and listens on port 9000.

Before we are able to run our Express server, however, we will need to configure TypeScript to compile this Express main.ts file, and output the results to the dist directory. In order to do this, we will need to create a tsconfig.json file within the express directory as follows:

```
{
    "compilerOptions": {
        "target": "es5",
        "module": "commonjs",
        "lib": [
            "es2016",
            "dom"
        ],
        "outDir": "../dist",
        "strict": true,
        "moduleResolution": "node",
        "esModuleInterop": true
    }
}
```

This is a standard tsconfig.json file as we have used with Node before. The only discernible change is the outDir property, which will place any generated JavaScript files in the ../dist directory. This is the same directory that Angular uses for its output. We can compile our Express server (from the root project directory) as follows:

```
tsc -p express
```

The -p compile option allows us to specify a sub-directory to compile, which, in this case, is the sub-directory named express. Hence, all files within the express directory will be compiled using the tsconfig.json file found within this directory.

Note that we now have two TypeScript projects within the same root project directory. We have the Angular project, whose source is under the `src` directory, and we have the Express project, whose source is under the `express` directory. This means that they will share the same `node_modules` directory when compiling. So we will need to install the relevant Express node modules from the base project directory as follows:

```
npm install express
npm install @types/node --saveDev
```

Our compilation command for the Express sub-directory will now generate a `main.js` file in the `dist` directory. We can start our Express server as follows:

```
node dist/main
```

Express server configuration

Now that we have an Express server running, let's refactor the code to allow for some simple configuration. As mentioned earlier, the configuration of an Express server can easily change depending on where it is deployed. On a local development environment, we may want to use a local SMTP server, for example, but in a testing and production environment, we would want to use the real thing. Having a set of `config` files to drive these settings means that we can deploy the same code to multiple environments without having to recompile the code.

To easily parse configuration files, we will use a Node package named `config`, which can be installed as follows:

```
npm install config
npm install @types/config --saveDev
```

We can now update our `main.ts` file as follows:

```
import config from 'config';

... existing code ...

enum ConfigOptions {
    PORT = 'port'
}

let port = 9000;

if (config.has(ConfigOptions.PORT)) {
    port = config.get(ConfigOptions.PORT);
```

```
    } else {
        console.log(`no port configuration found, using default : ${port}`);
    }

    app.listen(port, () => {
        console.log(`Express server listening on PORT: ${port}`);
    });
```

Here, we have imported the `config` module, as usual. We then define a string `enum` named `ConfigOptions`, which will hold the string constants that will be used as keys for our configuration options. At this stage, we only have a single option, named `PORT`, which corresponds to the `port` key.

We then define a local variable named `port`, and set it to the default value of `9000`. The next line queries our configuration options to see whether a value named `port` has been defined, using the `config.has` function. If our configuration option has a key named `port`, we override the local `port` variable with this value. Otherwise, we log a message to the console to indicate that there was no configuration option named `port` found, and we are reverting to the default value of `9000`.

We then start the Express server on the configured port by specifying the local variable, `port`, in our call to `app.listen`.

With this configuration code in place, we can now create a directory named `config`, and within this a file named `default.json`, as follows:

```
{
    "port": "9999"
}
```

The `config` package will attempt to find a file named `config/default.json` to use as the initial configuration file. With this file in place, when we start our Express server, it will modify the port number to be `9999`, as found in the configuration file.

The advantage of using a package such as `config` to configure our Express server is that we can also use environment variables or command-line overrides to set each of our `config` settings. This means that we can run our `main.js` program as follows:

```
node dist/main --NODE_CONFIG='{"port": "8888"}'
```

Here, we have used the command line to override our `port` configuration option from the command line. Please refer to the documentation on the node `config` package for further information.

Server logging

In any production system, server logs are an integral part of monitoring and troubleshooting a live running system. For Node applications, this is no different. There are a couple of handy modules that we will take a quick look at to enhance our server logging so that it can be more useful in a production setting.

The first module is named `rotating-file-stream`, and will rotate logs on the server according to a configurable set of rules. When logging in a production environment, we need to take care that server logs do not get too large, otherwise we could run the risk of running out of disk space. With a rotating log, a new file will be created after a period of time, with a new name, and the maximum size of log files can be configured. This ensures that we can limit the amount of files that are generated, and do not run the risk of overloading the server.

The second utility is named `moment-timezone`, and is used to manipulate dates and times by taking into consideration the configured time zone. We can therefore represent the same date and time in multiple time zones. It also has a full range of utilities that can handle any input date format, which is incredibly useful when working with dates and times. REST endpoints generally use ISO string format for representing dates, and these are generally in UTC. JavaScript, however, uses a native `Date` object, which represents the number of milliseconds since an epoch. Correctly converting between these date representations can become highly confusing, frustrating, and time-consuming. Throw in multiple time zones, and it can quickly become a nightmare. The `moment-timezone` library, however, makes working with dates and times within a time zone very simple.

We will update our server code in three ways. Firstly, we will add a `timezone` configuration parameter, as we have done for the server `port` earlier. Secondly, we will configure a rotating file stream for our server logs. Finally, we will write a simple logging function that will use the rotating file stream and our configured time zone to log messages to the console in both UTC and local time.

First up is the configuration of our time zone, which is accomplished as follows:

```
enum ConfigOptions {
    PORT = 'port',
    TIMEZONE = 'timezone'
}

let timezone = "Australia/Perth";

if (config.has(ConfigOptions.TIMEZONE)) {
    timezone = config.get(ConfigOptions.TIMEZONE);
} else {
```

```
        serverLog(`no timezone specified, using ${timezone}`)
    }
```

Here, we have added a `TIMEZONE` enum value to our `ConfigOptions`, and set the internal string value to `'timezone'`. We then create a local variable named `timezone`, and set it to the default of `'Australia/Perth'`. We then check through the `config.has` function if our current runtime configuration has an override value for `timezone`, and use it if it has. This is no different to the logic that we used to set the default `port` property. We will discuss the `serverLog` function a little later.

Next up, we will install the `rotating-file-stream` module as follows:

```
npm install rotating-file-stream
```

We can create a rotating log as follows:

```
var logDirectory = path.join(__dirname, 'log')

// ensure log directory exists
fs.existsSync(logDirectory) || fs.mkdirSync(logDirectory)

// create a rotating write stream
var accessLogStream = rfs('main.log', {
    interval: '10s', // rotate every 10 seconds
    path: logDirectory,
    maxFiles: 7
});
```

Here, we start by figuring out the directory name for `log` files based on the current working directory of the Express server by using the `path.join` function and the `__dirname` variable. We then ensure that the directory exists, by using a Boolean or comparison. If `fx.existsSync` returns `true`, we will not execute the `fs.mkdirSync` function. If it returns `false`, because the directory does not exist, then the `fs.mkdirSync` function will execute, and create the directory.

We then create a rotating file stream named `accessLogStream` by calling the `rfs` function with a few parameters. The first is the name of the log file, and the second parameter is a set of configuration parameters for this file stream. We have set the rotation interval to `10` seconds, just for testing, and set the `path` for log files to our newly created `log` directory. We are then specifying that the maximum number of files we want in this directory is `7`. These parameters can easily be tuned for production use, and it also makes sense to retrieve these values from a configuration setting.

Once we have a rotating file stream, we can create a function for our server to use for logging messages, as follows:

```
function serverLog(message: string) {
    let now = moment.tz(timezone);
    let nowISOFormat = now.toISOString();
    let nowLocalFormat = now.format('YYYY-MM-DD HH:mm:ss.SSS');
    let logMessage = `UTC : ${nowISOFormat} :
        local : ${nowLocalFormat} : ${message}`;
    accessLogStream.write(`${logMessage}\n`);
    console.log(logMessage);
}
```

Here, we have defined a simple function named `serverLog` that accepts a parameter named `message`, which is of type `string`. The first thing we do in this function is to create an instance of a moment date time in the currently configured time zone, by calling the `moment.tz` function and passing in our time zone string, which is currently set to `'Australia/Perth'`. We then create a variable named `nowISOFormat` by calling the `toISOString` function of the moment date time object. Remember that moment time zone stores all dates in UTC format, and so this string will represent the UTC date time in ISO format. We then create another variable named `nowLocalFormat` by calling the `format` function on the `now` variable, and pass in the date format. This call will take into account our currently configured time zone, as the underlying moment object has been created with a time zone setting.

Once we have our time strings, we log a message to the console, showing both the UTC date time, and the local date time. Note that we are writing a message to our rotating file stream by using the `accessLogStream` variable that we created earlier. We are also logging a message to the standard console.

To test that the rotating file stream is working correctly, let's log a message using our `serverLog` function every 500 milliseconds, as follows:

```
setInterval(() => {
    serverLog(`timeout reached`);
}, 500);
```

With our test function in place, we can run our Express server as usual:

node dist/main

The console output will now log messages every 500 milliseconds, and we will write to our rotating file stream at the same time. The output is now as follows:

```
                        nathanr@nero260: /tmp/server_logging
File  Edit  View  Search  Terminal  Help
UTC : 2019-01-12T04:03:04.759Z : local : 2019-01-12 12:03:04.759 : Express server lis
tening on PORT: 9000
UTC : 2019-01-12T04:03:05.259Z : local : 2019-01-12 12:03:05.259 : timeout reached
UTC : 2019-01-12T04:03:05.761Z : local : 2019-01-12 12:03:05.761 : timeout reached
UTC : 2019-01-12T04:03:06.262Z : local : 2019-01-12 12:03:06.262 : timeout reached
UTC : 2019-01-12T04:03:06.764Z : local : 2019-01-12 12:03:06.764 : timeout reached
UTC : 2019-01-12T04:03:07.265Z : local : 2019-01-12 12:03:07.265 : timeout reached
UTC : 2019-01-12T04:03:07.767Z : local : 2019-01-12 12:03:07.767 : timeout reached
UTC : 2019-01-12T04:03:08.267Z : local : 2019-01-12 12:03:08.267 : timeout reached
UTC : 2019-01-12T04:03:08.768Z : local : 2019-01-12 12:03:08.768 : timeout reached
UTC : 2019-01-12T04:03:09.270Z : local : 2019-01-12 12:03:09.270 : timeout reached
UTC : 2019-01-12T04:03:09.771Z : local : 2019-01-12 12:03:09.771 : timeout reached
UTC : 2019-01-12T04:03:10.272Z : local : 2019-01-12 12:03:10.272 : timeout reached
UTC : 2019-01-12T04:03:10.773Z : local : 2019-01-12 12:03:10.773 : timeout reached
UTC : 2019-01-12T04:03:11.275Z : local : 2019-01-12 12:03:11.275 : timeout reached
UTC : 2019-01-12T04:03:11.776Z : local : 2019-01-12 12:03:11.776 : timeout reached
UTC : 2019-01-12T04:03:12.277Z : local : 2019-01-12 12:03:12.277 : timeout reached
UTC : 2019-01-12T04:03:12.778Z : local : 2019-01-12 12:03:12.778 : timeout reached
UTC : 2019-01-12T04:03:13.279Z : local : 2019-01-12 12:03:13.279 : timeout reached
UTC : 2019-01-12T04:03:13.780Z : local : 2019-01-12 12:03:13.780 : timeout reached
UTC : 2019-01-12T04:03:14.281Z : local : 2019-01-12 12:03:14.281 : timeout reached
UTC : 2019-01-12T04:03:14.782Z : local : 2019-01-12 12:03:14.782 : timeout reached
UTC : 2019-01-12T04:03:15.283Z : local : 2019-01-12 12:03:15.283 : timeout reached
UTC : 2019-01-12T04:03:15.785Z : local : 2019-01-12 12:03:15.785 : timeout reached
UTC : 2019-01-12T04:03:16.286Z : local : 2019-01-12 12:03:16.286 : timeout reached
```

Here, we can see that our `serverLog` function is logging UTC time, as well as the local time and the message to the console.

We have seen then, that we can configure our Express server quite easily using the `config` package, and can log messages to a rotating file stream on our server. We have also seen how the `moment-timezone` package helps us by providing simple utility functions to handle date and time objects in multiple time zones.

The UI experience

At the start of every web-based project, the requirements around the **User Interface** (**UI**) start to be discussed. What will the application look like, what CSS styles will it use, and how will our user interact with the system? The UI experience is all about ease of use, intuition, and simple workflow. As such, it can either make or break an otherwise good website. The focus on a good **user interface experience** (**UX**) means that many companies employ specialist teams to either design the UI for *look and feel*, or to design the UI experience, including workflow. Depending on the skills of the UX team, their output may be a set of images that show what the user experience should look like, or it may, in fact, be a set of HTML pages and CSS files.

There will come a time, however, where every developer needs to put together a UI, so understanding the process and working with tools that are designed for design is a necessary step of building applications. In this section of the chapter, we will work with Bootstrap as a base for CSS styling of our website, and also look at an editor named Brackets that is great for rapid HTML prototyping.

Using Brackets

When working with HTML and CSS during the design phase, we are constantly editing and tweaking both: the HTML files and the CSS stylesheet, to get our pages to look good. One of the best tools for this job is an editor named **Brackets**. Brackets is an open source editor that is specifically targeted to web designers and frontend developers. It has many features that are geared around quick editing of HTML and CSS elements, including live preview, right-click to edit CSS, color pickers, and more. One of the handiest features, however, is live preview.

In live preview mode, a separate browser window is opened, and any changes made to your HTML or CSS files will be automatically refreshed within the browser. Having instant feedback when applying CSS styles, or editing HTML, is an incredible time-saver. Brackets with a live preview window is shown in the following screenshot:

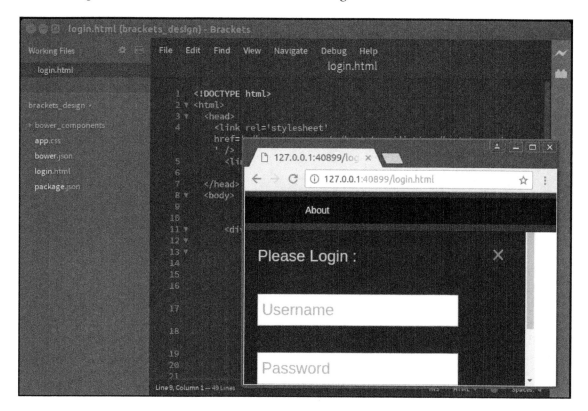

Installing Brackets is as simple as downloading the installer from their website, `brackets.io`, and executing it. Once installed, we can enhance the default functionality through the use of Brackets extensions. Brackets has a really slick and simple extension manager, which helps to find and install available extensions. Brackets will also automatically notify us when updates to these extensions are available.

To install an extension, click on **File | Extension Manager**, or click on the lego-block icon on the right-hand side vertical sidebar. We will be using a single extension named Emmet, but there are literally hundreds of Brackets extensions available. In the search bar, type Emmet, and then click on the **Install** button for the Emmet extension (authored by *Sergey Chikuyonok*):

Brackets does not have the concept of a project *per se*, but instead just works off a root folder. Let's create a new folder on our filesystem, and then open this folder in Brackets using **File | Open Folder**.

Using Emmet

Let's now create a simple HTML page by using **File** | **New**, or simply pressing *Ctrl+N*. Instead of writing our HTML file by hand, we will use Emmet to generate our HTML. Type in the following Emmet string:

```
html>head+body>h3{index.html}+div#content
```

Now, hit *Ctrl+Alt+Enter*, or, from the **File** menu, select **Emmet** | **Expand Abbreviation**.

Voilà! Emmet has generated the following HTML in a millisecond, not bad for one line of code:

```
<html>
<head></head>
<body>
    <h3>index.html</h3>
    <div id="content"></div>
</body>
</html>
```

Hit *Ctrl+S* to save the file, and enter index.html as the filename.

Only when we have saved the file will Brackets start to do syntax highlighting based on the file extension.

Let's take a closer look at the Emmet abbreviation string that we entered earlier. Emmet uses the > character to create a child, and the + character to denote a sibling. If we use { } next to an element, then this means that the element's content will be set to the value provided inside the braces. So the Emmet string that we entered previously said: Create an html tag with a child head tag, and then create another child tag of html named body. Within this body tag, create an h3 tag with the content index.html, and then create a sibling div tag with the id of content. Head over to the Emmet website (emmet.io) for further information, and remember to keep a cheat-sheet handy (docs.emmet.io.cheat-sheet) when you are learning and working with Emmet string shortcuts.

Let's now add a script tag to our index.html file. Move your cursor in-between the <head></head> tags, and type the following Emmet string:

```
link
```

Now, hit *Ctrl+Alt+Enter* to have Emmet generate a full `<link>` tag, and conveniently place our cursor between the quotes ready for the filename. The filename that we are looking for is `bootstrap-min.css`. Go ahead and start by typing `./`. Note how Brackets understands that you are looking for a CSS file, and will automatically start providing Intellisense, or code-completion options to help you find the file, as follows:

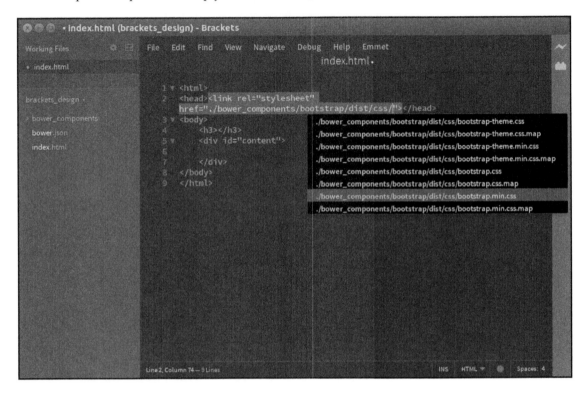

With our `bootstrap.min.css` file included, we can start to flesh out the content of our HMTL page. Before we continue editing this HTML file, go ahead and bring up the live preview browser window by hitting the *lightning-bolt* icon on the right-hand side of the window. As we make changes to the HTML file, these will automatically be reflected in the preview browser window.

At the beginning of the `<body>` tag, we can create a Bootstrap container with the following Emmet string:

```
div.container.h-100>div.row>div.col
```

This will generate the following HTML:

```
<div class="container h-100">
    <div class="row">
        <div class="col"></div>
    </div>
</div>
```

This Emmet string is stating the following: Create a `div` element with the class of `container` and `h-100`. Within this `div`, element, create a child `div` element with the class of `row`, and, within this `div` element, create another `div` element with the class of `col`. The results of processing this Emmet string is the HTML, as seen in the preceding code block.

We can now place our cursor within the innermost `<div>` tag, and create a Bootstrap `jumbotron` with the following Emmet string:

```
div.jumbotron>img+h2{Jumbotron}+div.form-group
```

This Emmet string will create a `div` element with the `jumbotron` CSS class, and then a child `img` element, an `h2` element, and a `div` element, as follows:

```
<div class="jumbotron">
    <img src="" alt="">
    <h2>Jumbotron</h2>
    <div class="form-group"></div>
</div>
```

Creating a login panel

The HTML that we have generated forms the basis of a centered panel that we can use as a login panel. We would like the `jumbotron` to be centered within the page, both horizontally and vertically. Let's apply some Bootstrap styles and CSS to accomplish this. So far, we have an outer element with a CSS class of `'container'`, and an inner element with the class of `'jumbotron'`. Let's update the outer element as follows:

```
<div class="container h-100">
    <div class="row align-items-center h-100">
        <div class="col-6 mx-auto">
            <div class="jumbotron">
            ... jumbotron body ...
            </div>
        </div>
    </div>
</div>
```

Here, we are showing the outer element with the CSS class of 'container', which also has a class of 'h-100'. This means that it will occupy 100% of the screen height. We then have a <div> element with the classes of 'row align-items-center h-100'. These styles mean that the entire row will be centered, with a height of 100%. Within this row element, we create a <div> element with the style of 'col-6 mx-auto'. Essentially, this is creating a single column of size 6, which means that it will occupy half of the screen. As the row itself is centered, this column will be centered within the row as well. We can now update the <div> element with the class of 'jumbotron', as follows:

```
<div class="jumbotron text-center shadow-lg p-3 mb-5 bg-white rounded">
    <img src="logo.jpg" class="img-fluid">
    <h2>Please Login</h2>
    <div class="form-group">
        <input class="form-control" type="text" placeholder="Username">
    </div>
    <div class="form-group">
        <input class="form-control" type="password"
            placeholder="Password">
    </div>
    <div class="form-group">
        <button class="btn btn-primary" type="submit" >Login
        </button>
        <button class="btn btn-primary">Login with Google</button>
    </div>
    <div *ngIf="error">
        <div class="alert alert-danger">
        {{error}}
        </div>
    </div>
</div>
```

Here, we have defined the full HTML for the inner 'jumbotron' element. This jumbotron has a number of elements, as follows:

- A logo
- An <input> element for the username
- An <input> element for the password
- A <button> with the text Login
- A <button> with the text Login with Google
- An error message element

Along with this HTML, we only need a single CSS style (defined in `app.css`) as follows:

```
body,html {
    height:100%;
}
```

This HTML, combined with the CSS, results in the following screen:

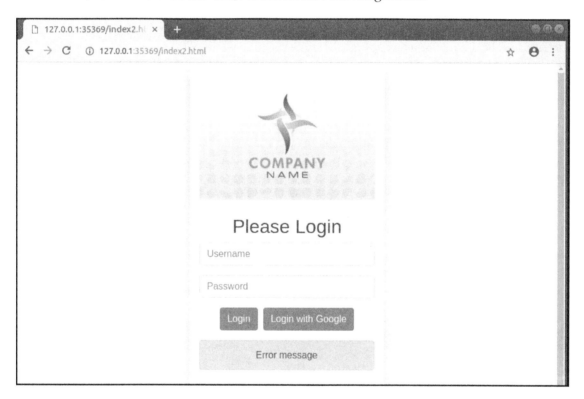

Here, we can see that we have a centered `jumbotron` that contains a login form. This form has two input elements, which are **Username** and **Password**, as well as a **Login** button, and a **Login with Google** button. Underneath these buttons is an area for error messages.

With this HTML and CSS in place, we can use Brackets to quickly and easily create new styles, or tweak this layout to our heart's content. We have not invested a great deal of time or effort in creating these layouts either; we have simply been tweaking HTML and CSS. This design phase of a project can therefore be accomplished very quickly—and only relies on minimal HTML and CSS knowledge. With template screens like these, we can also start conversations with customers to determine whether the look and feel of the site is as expected, without having to build an entire application.

Now that we have an initial design in place, we can start to implement these screens in our Angular application.

Authentication

Almost every website we visit nowadays requires a registration and login process. Even though browsing through a site may not require a login, as soon as we start to interact with the site, and add items to a shopping cart, for example, we need to create some sort of profile and perform a login. Corporate-based websites generally ask for a login before we can even start to interact with the site, as permissions for what you can do on the website vary depending on what your role is.

Luckily, we are able to log in to a wide range of websites using an external authentication process, such as Facebook or Google. This means that we are able to reuse a Google or Facebook login, and do not need to remember a separate username and password combination for every site.

In this section of the chapter, we will update our application to show how authentication works within Angular, and implement both a username/password login process, as well as an external authentication process. Along the way, we will explore routing within Angular, using guards to block access to certain areas of the site, and then use JWT tokens instead of browser cookies for holding user information. Finally, we will show how to integrate with Google authentication as an example of integrating external authentication into our site.

Angular routing

In `Chapter 10`, *Modularization*, under the *Using Express with Node* section, we explored how an Express server uses routing in order to generate different pages based on the URL that was entered into the browser. We also showed how we can get Express to redirect the browser to a different page based on whether a user was logged in or not. Our Angular application, however, is a **Single Page Application (SPA)**, so we need to implement any page navigation based on a URL within Angular itself. In order to do this, we will use Angular routing.

Angular routing is similar to Express routing, where we define what routes we need, and then attach a class to handle this route. To set up routing within Angular, let's create a file named `app.routing.module.ts` in the `app` directory as follows:

```
import { NgModule } from "@angular/core";
import { RouterModule, Routes } from '@angular/router';

export const routes: Routes = [
    { path: 'login', component: LoginPanelComponent },
    { path: '', component: SecureComponent },
];

@NgModule({
    imports: [RouterModule.forRoot(routes)],
    exports: [RouterModule]
})

export class AppRoutingModule { }
```

Here, we have imported the `NgModule` from `@angular/core`, as usual, and then have imported the `RouterModule` and `Routes` from `@angular/router`. We then create a `const` variable named `routes` that is an array. The first element of this array contains a `path` property of `'login'` and a component property of `LoginPanelComponent`. The second element of this array contains a `path` property that is empty, and a component property of `SecureComponent`. This is the essence of Angular routing.

The `routes` variable declares that if we append the `'login'` value to our URL, then the component that will handle this route is `LoginPanelComponent`. So, in our development environment, the `http://localhost:4200/login` URL will resolve to the `LoginPanelComponent`. Any other URL will resolve to the `SecureComponent`.

The final part of this file is to create a class named `AppRoutingModule`, and decorate it with the `@NgModule` decorator, which has an `imports` and `exports` property. The `imports` property is used to register the defined routes variable with the `RouterModule`, and the `exports` property exports the `RouterModule`. This is similar to how we registered routes in Express, where we need to re-export the modified route once we had made configuration changes.

If we attempt to compile at this stage, we will generate errors because neither of these components exist as yet. Let's create these two components using the Angular CLI as follows:

```
ng generate component login-panel --skip-import
```

This command will generate a directory named `login-panel` under the `src` directory, and create the required CSS, HTML, and `.ts` files for the new component. We use `--skip-import` to skip the step that attempts to include this component in the closest module. We will therefore need to manually include this component in our `app.module.ts` file ourselves. We can create the `SecureComponent` in a similar fashion as follows:

```
ng generate component layout/secure --skip-import
```

This will generate a component named `secure.component.ts` in the `src/app/layout/secure` directory. We will leave the generated HTML as default for the moment, just to ensure that our Angular routing works correctly. With these components in place, we can get our `app.routing.module.ts` file to compile correctly by importing the components as follows:

```
import { LoginPanelComponent } from "./login-panel/login-panel.component";
import { SecureComponent } from "./layout/secure/secure.component";
```

Once our `AppRoutingModule` class is compiling correctly, we can include these components in our `app.module.ts` file as follows:

```
@NgModule({
  declarations: [
    .. existing components ...
    SecureComponent,
    LoginPanelComponent
  ],
  imports: [
    BrowserModule,
    AppRoutingModule
  ],
  providers: [],
  bootstrap: [AppComponent]
})
export class AppModule { }
```

The final step in setting up routing is to instantiate and activate the router when an HTML file is rendered for the first time. This is accomplished by replacing our HTML in the `app.component.html` file with the following:

```
<router-outlet></router-outlet>
```

If we compile and run our application now, we will be automatically directed to the
SecureComponent HTML file, as this is registered to render when no child URL is
provided, as follows:

If we now modify the URL to be localhost:4200/login, the Angular router will redirect
our request to be handled by LoginPanelComponent, and therefore render the following
screen:

We therefore have Angular routing in place, and can render two different components
based on the URL of the browser.

What this means, however, is that we will need to move the existing HTML, CSS, and .ts
code that we used in AppComponent into the new SecureComponent. For the sake of
brevity, we will not discuss the details of how this is done, but it should be a fairly simple
exercise to copy the HTML, CSS, and functions implemented for the AppComponent into
the new SecureComponent, and get it compiled correctly.

Using UI-designed HTML

In *The UI Experience* section of this chapter, we showed how to use Brackets to quickly modify HTML and CSS in order to achieve our desired page design in a very short period of time. Fortunately, integrating this HTML into our Angular application is a piece of cake. If we simply copy and paste the contents of the `<body>` tag into our `login-panel.component.html` file, we are almost there:

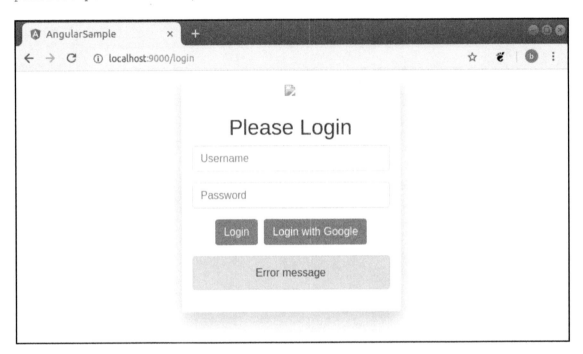

As we can see, the `LoginPanelComponent` is rendering our HTML as designed in Brackets, with the exception of the logo. To fix the logo, we need to be able to include images as part of our Angular compilation step, such that they are included in the output `dist` directory. A clue to the mechanism that Angular uses can be found in the `angular.json` file under the `projects` | `angular-sample` | `architect` | `build` | `options` property tree, and is named `"assets"`, as follows:

```
"assets": [
    "src/favicon.ico",
    "src/assets"
],
```

Here, we can see that Angular has the concept of "assets" that will be included in the build, and consists of the `src/favicon.ico`, and anything under the directory named `src/assets`. This means that we can create an `assets` directory under the `src` directory, and copy our logo image into this directory. This will result in the `assets` directory being included under our `dist` directory, under the `angular-sample/assets` folder. Remember that our Express application serves any static files that it finds within the `angular-sample` directory through the following configuration setting:

```
app.use(`/`, express.static(__dirname + '/angular-sample'));
```

Up until this point, we have used this configuration setting to serve the base Angular `index.html` file, but it will also work for any sub-directory found under the `angular-sample` directory. This means that we can copy any images we need for our application into the `assets` folder, and we can change the `src` property of the `<img>` tag as follows:

```
<img src="/assets/logo.jpg" class="img-fluid">
```

Here, our generated `LoginPanelComponent` is referencing the logo image in the static directory named `assets`, as seen in the `src` property, which is now `assets/logo.jpg`. The generated HTML, therefore, will render the logo correctly.

Auth Guards

Our application can now render the `SecureComponent` or the `LoginPanelComponent`, depending on the URL that is provided by the browser. Currently, if no URL is provided, the application will render the `SecureComponent`, which is the main screen for our site. But what if we need to make sure that the `SecureComponent` is only rendered if the user has already logged into the website. In other words, how do we protect users from accessing areas of our site if they have not logged in? Angular uses what are known as authentication guards, or Auth Guards, to accomplish this.

The basic premise of an Auth Guard is to allow our code to check whether a user has the correct authorization to access a particular route. This is done by creating a function that returns `true` if the user is allowed access, or `false` if they are not. We can configure an Auth Guard in our Angular routing configuration as follows:

```
export const routes: Routes = [
    { path: 'login', component: LoginPanelComponent },
    { path: '', component: SecureComponent, canActivate: [AuthGuard] },
];
```

Here, we have updated the `app.routing.module.ts` file and modified the routing configuration for the `SecureComponent` by adding another property named `canActivate`, which references a class named `AuthGuard`. This `AuthGuard` class needs to implement a single function, named `canActivate`, which must return a `boolean` value of either `true` or `false`. Let's create a new directory named `src/guards`, and within it, create a new file named `auth.guard.ts`, as follows:

```
import { Injectable } from '@angular/core';
import { CanActivate, ActivatedRouteSnapshot, RouterStateSnapshot,
    Router } from '@angular/router';

@Injectable({
    providedIn: 'root'
})
export class AuthGuard implements CanActivate {

    constructor() { }

    canActivate(route: ActivatedRouteSnapshot, state: RouterStateSnapshot):
     boolean {
        return false;
    }

}
```

Here, we have created a class named `AuthGuard` that implements the `CanActivate` interface, and therefore must define the `canActivate` function. We will not use the `route` or `state` arguments within this function, we will just return `false`. This indicates that no one will be able to access our `SecureComponent` just yet. If we fire up our application now, however, we will get a single blank screen.

What is happening here is that the `AuthGuard` is blocking access to the `SecureComponent`, so it renders a blank screen, as expected, but the application has not been configured to do anything else. What we need to do here is to redirect the browser to the login screen if access to the `SecureComponent` has been blocked. We can do this very easily by Angular's internal routing capabilities. We will need to modify the `AuthGuard` in two places, as follows:

```
export class AuthGuard implements CanActivate {

    constructor(private router: Router) { }

    canActivate(
        route: ActivatedRouteSnapshot,
        state: RouterStateSnapshot): boolean
```

```
        {
            this.router.navigate([`/login`]);
            return false;
        }
    }
```

Here, we have updated the `contructor` function to use Angular's dependency injection framework to access the `Router` instance. In our `canActivate` function, we have used the private `router` variable to redirect the browser to the login URL by calling the `navigate` function. This ensures that anyone browsing to our application that is not authenticated will be redirected to the `LoginPanelComponent`.

Login form binding

Now that we have an Auth Guard and routing working within our application, let's update the `LoginPanelComponent` to capture the username and password that is entered on the form, and post this back to our Express server. For simplicity, we will use standard form-based data binding. Our updated HTML is as follows:

```html
<div class="form-group">
    <input class="form-control" type="text"
    placeholder="Username" name="username" [(ngModel)]="username">

</div>
<div class="form-group">
    <input class="form-control" type="password"
    placeholder="Password" name="password" [(ngModel)]="password">
</div>

<div class="form-group">
    <button class="btn btn-primary" type="submit"
    (click)="onLoginClicked()">Login</button>
    <button class="btn btn-primary" >Login with Google</button>
</div>

<div *ngIf="error">
    <div class="alert alert-danger">
        {{error}}
    </div>
</div>
```

Here, we have used the `[(ngModel)]` syntax to bind the username input control to a `username` property on the component. We have also bound the password input control to a `password` property. We have then set a `(click)` action on the Login button to call a function named `onLoginClicked` when the user clicks on the Login button. Finally, we have bound a property named `error` to the error panel at the bottom of the screen. We are using an `*ngIf` directive to ensure that this panel only displays if there is an actual error.

Our modifications to the `login-panel.component.ts` file are as follows:

```
export class LoginPanelComponent implements OnInit {
    username: string;
    password: string;
    error: string;

    constructor(private router: Router) { }

    ngOnInit() {
    }

    onLoginClicked() {
        console.log(`LoginPanelComponent :
            this.username : ${this.username}`);
        this.error = "login not implemented yet.";
    }
}
```

Here, we have added a `username`, `password`, and `error` property to our component so that we can bind these variables to our form. We have updated our constructor function to request the `Router` object, so that we can redirect the user to our `SecureComponent` upon successful login. Our `onLoginClicked` function simply logs a message to the console to ensure that our data binding is working correctly. Finally, we set the `error` property to a message stating that this functionality is not implemented yet.

Before we fire up the application, we will need to remember to include the `FormsModule` in our `app.module.ts` file, otherwise we will get some strange errors. The `imports` property of the `AppModule` should now read as follows:

```
imports: [
    BrowserModule,
    AppRoutingModule,
    FormsModule
],
```

With these modifications in place, we have a functional Login page that accepts user input in the username and password input elements, ready for usage in the `onLoginClicked` function. We are now ready to POST our username and password combination to a backend server to request authentication.

Using HttpClient

In order for our Express server to receive a POST, we will need to create a route handler, and register it with our server. Let's create a file named `express/routes/userRoutes.ts` as follows:

```
import * as express from 'express';
import { serverLog } from '../main';

var router = express.Router();

router.post(`/login`, (req: any, res: any, next: any) => {
    serverLog(`POST /login`);

    if (req.body.username && req.body.username.length > 0
        && req.body.password && req.body.password.length > 0) {

        res.json({ success: true });

    } else {
        serverLog(`/login - Error : Invalid username or password`);
        res.status(401).send('Invalid username or password');
    }

});

export { router };
```

Here, we have created a route handler to handle a POST event to the `/login` URL. Within this handler, we log a message to the console using our `serverLog` function, and then check that we have received both a `username` and `password` as part of the request body. We also check that the `username` and `password` strings have a length of > 0. If they are both valid, we then simply return a JSON string with a single property named `success`, which is set to `true`. If we encounter an invalid username and password combination, we return a **401 HTTP** status with a message.

This route handler can easily be registered with our Express server as follows:

```
app.use('/', userRoutes.router);
```

Our Express server can now handle a POST event to the login endpoint, and will just ensure that both the username and password are not blank, and return success. With this route handler in place, we can now turn our attention to updating our Angular application to use this endpoint.

When integrating with REST endpoints, it is recommended that we do not interact with these endpoints directly from our forms, but rather go through an Angular service. By creating services, we are conforming to the Single Responsibility design principle, and also designing our code to be more modular. Our Angular form is simply responsible for interacting with a user, validating input and updating the UI accordingly. We will use an Angular service to POST data to our Express server.

Let's create a service through the Angular CLI as follows:

```
ng generate service services/user
```

This command will create a generic service in a file named src/app/services/user.service.ts. We will update this file as follows:

```
import { Injectable } from '@angular/core';
import { HttpClient, HttpHeaders } from '@angular/common/http';

@Injectable({
    providedIn: 'root'
})
export class UserService {

    constructor(private httpClient: HttpClient) { }

    authenticateUser(username: string, password: string)
        : Observable<Object> {
        const headers = new HttpHeaders();
        headers.append('Content-Type', 'application/json');
        const user = {
            username: username,
            password: password
        };
        return this.httpClient.post(
            '/login', user,
            { 'headers': headers });
    }
}
```

Here, we have a simple service class named `UserService`. Within the constructor, we are requesting an instance of an `HttpClient` class through Angular's dependency injection framework. We then have a single function named `authenticateUser` that accepts two parameters, named `username` and `password`. Within this function, we set up an instance of the `HttpHeaders` class, and use this to set the `Content-Type` to `application/json`. We then create a simple JavaScript object containing the `username` and `password`, and then call the `post` method of the `httpClient` instance. This `post` method is invoked with three arguments. The first argument is the URL of the endpoint to which we are posting, which, in this case, is `/login`. The second is our JavaScript object, and the third argument are our HTTP headers.

As we can see from this code, the use of the `HttpClient` object is very simple. We can use any one of the available `get`, `post`, `put`, or `delete` functions that it exposes for simple REST integration.

The interesting thing about our `UserService` class is the type that is returned from the `authenticateUser` function. Note that we are returning the result of the call to `httpClient.post`, which is, in fact, an Observable.

Using Observables

Angular's `HttpClient` class uses Observables as the mechanism to handle asynchronous calls to REST endpoints. Observables are an implementation of the Observable design pattern, and are provided by the JavaScript library named *Reactive Extensions for JavaScript*, or simply RxJS. The Observable design pattern uses two concepts named registration and notification. An object that is interested in an event will register with an Observable object. When this event occurs, the Observable object will notify all objects that have registered for this event through a notification step. The RxJS library has extended the basic Observable design pattern to allow for a more fine-grained control over when and where these events are raised. The advantage of using Observables, however, is that the RxJS library allows for working with what are called Observable sequences.

As an example of what an Observable sequence is, and what it can do, let's assume that we are reading values from an event stream, which will send a new random number every second, for a period of 10 seconds. This is our Observable sequence. We will receive an event once every 10 seconds with the new value of the random number.

The RxJS library allows us to configure Observables to work with this data sequence in many different ways. As an example, we can register an Observable that will wait until a specific number of events have occurred before doing something. Or, we can wait until all data is returned before doing something else. We can also mix and match Observables to do things such as calculate the average of the last three numbers, or trigger a new event if the number is over a certain threshold. So the advantage of using Observables is that we are not only able to react to events, we are also able to react to event sequences.

Observables are therefore a perfect fit for asynchronous programming, and allow us to use a very simple syntax to register for an event, and then execute some code once that event has been raised. The Angular team has incorporated RxJS into the core Angular library, and uses it extensively for HTTP requests. We will discuss some of the interesting ways in which Observables can be used and combined in a later section.

Observables in RxJS use the `subscribe` function to perform registration for an event. The syntax of this `subscribe` function is as follows:

```
let testObservable: Observable<object>;
testObservable.subscribe(
    (success: Object) => {
        // successful call
    },
    (error: any) => {
        // error condition
    },
    () => {
        // complete, or finally()
    }
)
```

Here, we call the `subscribe` method an Observable with three functions as arguments. The first function will be called when the Observable returns successfully. The second function will be called if any error occurred, and the third function will be called when the Observable is complete. Note that the complete function will be called after either the success or the error functions, whichever occurs. This is the basic syntax of working with Observables.

Note that the error and complete functions are optional, so these can be excluded from the function signature. In production systems, however, it is good practice to always include at least the error handler.

Let's now integrate our `UserService` with our `LoginPanelComponent` so that we can post a `username` and `password` to the login Express endpoint. Our updates to the `LoginPanelComponent` are as follows:

```
constructor(private userService: UserService,
private router: Router) { }

onLoginClicked() {
    console.log(`LoginPanelComponent : this.username : ${this.username}`);

    this.userService.authenticateUser(this.username, this.password)
        .subscribe((response: Object) =>
    {
        console.log(`LoginPanelCompenent : response :
            ${JSON.stringify(response)}`);
        localStorage.setItem('token', response);
        this.router.navigate([``]);
    }, (err) => {
        console.log(`onLoginClicked() : error :
            ${JSON.stringify(err, null, 4)}`);
        this.error = `${err.message}`;
    }, () => {
        // finally
        console.log(`finally.`);
    });
}
```

Here, we have updated our constructor function to request an instance of the `UserService` class, along with the `Router` class. We have then updated our `onLoginClicked` function to call the `authenticateUser` function on the `userService`, and `subscribe` to the results of this Observable. We have also defined all three of our success, error, and complete functions for this Observable. The success function has a single parameter, which will include the `response` received from the Express server. We log this `response` object to the console, and then create an item in `localStorage` named `'token'` to hold this `response` object. We then use the `navigate` function on our router object to redirect the browser to the main page.

Our error handler will log the error message to the console, as well as updating the error message shown to the user. The complete function simply logs a message to the console.

Note that we are using Local Storage as a mechanism to store the authentication state. We could have used a cookie for this purpose, but HTML5 allows us to use Local Storage, which has many advantages over simple cookies. As an example, cookies are sent and received on every request, meaning that HTTP traffic can be affected. Also, Local Storage allows for 5 MB of information to be stored locally, instead of the minimal 4 KB that cookies allow.

Now that we know whether the user has logged in correctly, we can update our AuthGuard class to check whether a user has an item in localStorage named 'token' as follows:

```
export class AuthGuard implements CanActivate {

    constructor(private router: Router) { }

    canActivate(
        route: ActivatedRouteSnapshot,
        state: RouterStateSnapshot): boolean
    {
        let token = <Object>localStorage.getItem('token');
        console.log(`Authguard : token : ${token}`);

        if (token) {
            return true;
        }

        return false;
    }

}
```

Here, we have updated the canActivate function of our AuthGuard class to check for the existence of an item in localStorage named 'token'. If it exists, we log the contents of the token to the console, and then allow access to this route by returning true. If there is nothing in localStorage, we return false.

With these changes in place, we can now log in to the application. The flow of events for this sequence is as follows:

1. Enter username and password on the login screen.
2. Click on the **Login** button.
3. The onLoginClicked handler will use the UserService to post to the Express login handler.
4. The Express handler returns a successful response.

5. The `LoginPanelComponent` stores this response in Local Storage.
6. The `LoginPanelComponent` then redirects the browser to the `SecureComponent` page.
7. The `AuthGuard` that is protecting access to the `SecureComponent` checks to see that it can find an item in Local Storage.
8. The `AuthGuard` therefore allows access to the `SecureComponent`.

Note that we currently do not have a mechanism to log out once we have logged in. Local Storage is also persisted across browser shutdown, which means that even restarting the browser will not allow us to log out. For the time being, we can hit *F12* to go to our handy Developer tools, and manually remove the token from Local Storage, as shown in the following screenshot:

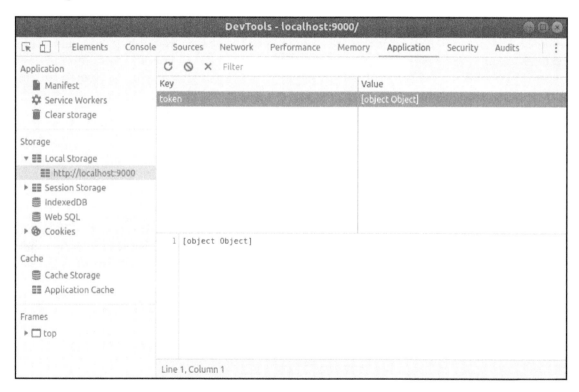

Using JWT tokens

The mechanism of securely authenticating whether a request comes from an authorized source has been simplified greatly with the introduction of the **JSON Web Token (JWT)** standard, which is described in the open standard RFC 7519. The idea behind JWT is that a standard JSON object is encrypted using a *secret* key. This encryption process is known as *signing* a token. Only a holder of the *secret* key can verify that this token is valid. In other words, a server creates a token using its secret key, and then any request that comes into the server can verify that the token was signed correctly. JWT tokens are therefore stateless, and can be used quite easily in a load-balanced environment. As long as all servers that are within the load balanced cluster know what the secret key is, they can all validate an incoming token, irrespective of which server generated it. JWT tokens can also be configured to have an expiration time, and can, therefore, be valid for a short period of time.

In the stateless world of REST endpoints, we will need to ensure that only valid users of our systems are able to access certain endpoints. We can easily configure our endpoints to require a JWT token, and then validate that it was issued using the correct key before taking action.

In this section of the chapter, we will show how to issue and validate JWT tokens. One of the popular libraries that are available for working with JWT tokes is called `jsonwebtoken`. We can install the `jsonwebtoken` library for working with JWTs from `npm` as follows:

```
npm install jsonwebtoken
```

The first part of working with JWT tokens is to actually create one. Remember that in order to create a token, we need to have a secret. This secret should not be visible to anyone other than the server that is creating tokens, so it is best that we create our tokens in our Express server.

Let's update our Express login router to create and sign a JWT token as follows:

```
import * as jwt from "jsonwebtoken";
const jwtSecret = '0e4253ef-5e4f-4d62-8eeb-c80e36a68c8a';

router.post(`/login`, (req: any, res: any, next: any) => {
    serverLog(`POST /login`);

    if (req.body.username && req.body.username.length > 0
        && req.body.password && req.body.password.length > 0) {

        let user_context = {
            username: req.body.username,
```

```
        token: ''
    }

    var token = jwt.sign(user_context, jwtSecret);
    user_context.token = token;
    res.json(user_context);

} else {
    serverLog(`/login - Error : Invalid username or password`);
    res.status(401).send('Invalid username or password');
}

});
```

Here, we have imported the jsonwebtoken library and named it jwt. We then create a variable named jwtSecret, and assign a GUID string to it. This is the secret that the server will use to sign the JWT token.

In our post handler, we create a JavaScript object that has a username property. This will be the contents of our token. We then use the sign function from the jwt library, passing in the JavaScript object as the first argument, and the secret as the second object. Once the object is signed, we simply return it. That is all there is to creating a JWT token. We simply create a standard JavaScript object, and then use the library to encrypt and sign the object.

Let's log in to our application now, and take a look at this token. If we navigate to our Developer tools, and open the **Application** tab, we can see the token that is stored in Local Storage. It is simply a string as follows:

```
eyJhbGciOiJIUzI1NiIsInR5cCI6IkpXVCJ9.eyJ1c2VybmFtZSI6ImF1c2VybmFtZSIsImlhdC
I6MTU0NzcwOTg2NX0.ciS4MqQxxx8eCf2zXoAqGPlf6DS_Jo8JuEpB11qLPuA
```

The interesting thing about JWT tokens is that anyone can decode them, but only the server with the secret that was used to sign it can verify the token. As an example of how to decode this token, let's head over to the website at jwt.io, and simply paste this string into the Encoded text box as follows:

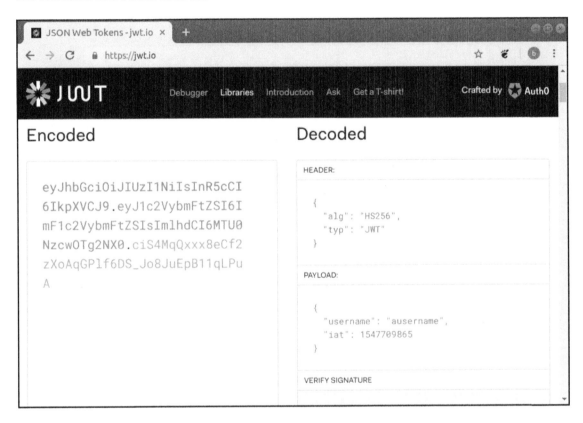

Here, we can see that the JWT token has been decoded, and shows us the actual payload on the right-hand side. This payload includes our username property, as well as the iat property, which indicates when the token will expire. Note that we did not need to let the website know what the secret was in order for it to decode the token. This is what is meant by anyone can decode a token, but only the server with the secret key can verify it.

The open nature of JWT tokens means that we cannot store any sensitive information within a JWT token. If we were to store our password, for instance, then anyone could gain access to the token and decode it to figure out our password.

Verifying JWT tokens

Again, when a token is being used, it is up to the server that generated the token to verify that it is valid before use. Let's create a POST handler in our Express server that will verify the token as follows:

```
router.post(`/validate-user`, (req: any, res: any, next: any) => {
    serverLog(`POST /validate-user`);

    console.log(`req.body : ${JSON.stringify(req.body)}`);

    if (req.body.token && req.body.token.length > 0) {

        try {
            let verifiedJwt = jwt.verify(req.body.token, jwtSecret);
            return res.json(verifiedJwt);
        } catch (err) {
            serverLog(`/validate-user : token error`);
            res.status(401).send('invalid auth token');
        }
    } else {
        serverLog(`/validate-user : token not found error`);
        res.status(401).send('Invalid auth token');
    }

});
```

Here, we have defined a route handler for a POST to the endpoint named validate-user. This handler checks for the existence of a token payload, and then calls the verify function on the jwt library. The verify function takes the token itself as input, as well as the secret that we used to sign the token in the first place. Note that we have wrapped this call in a try catch block, as the jwt library will throw an exception if the token cannot be verified correctly. If the token is valid, we simply return its contents as a JSON structure. If the token cannot be verified, we return a **401 HTTP** status code with an error message.

Our two Express endpoints, then, have successfully created, or signed a JWT token, as well as verified this token. Both parts of this have used the same secret key.

Note the importance of this verification step. The token is a simple string, and can be decoded fairly easily. This means that it can also be modified very easily. Even the website at jwt.io can modify the contents of the token and generate a new encrypted string. Once a JWT token has been modified, however, it will fail verification. This means that it is impossible to regenerate a modified token without the secret key. So each time a server needs to do something on behalf of a user, it must verify that the token provided has not been tampered with in any way.

Using Observables in anger – of, pipe, and map

We now have a REST endpoint that can verify our JWT token. What we need to do, then, is to call this endpoint from our Angular application to ensure that the user that is logged in has a valid JWT token. Remember that when we log in, we store this token in Local Storage, and redirect to our SecureComponent. The SecureComponent is protected by our AuthGuard, which checks for the existence of this token. We therefore need to contact our Express server, which generated this token, in order to verify it.

The most obvious place to put this code is in the AuthGuard itself, so that any attempt to access the SecureComponent will need to verify the JWT token by POSTing to our Express server before continuing. Again, we should not be accessing REST endpoints from our code directly, so we will need a service that can contact the server on our behalf. As we already have a UserService for this purpose, we can simply create another function in this service to do the actual call to the Express server, as follows:

```
validateUser(token: Object): Observable<Object> {
    const headers = new HttpHeaders();
    headers.append('Content-Type', 'application/json');
    const payload = {
        token: token
    };
    return this.httpClient.post(
        '/validate-user', payload,
        { 'headers': headers });
}
```

Here, we have created a function named validateUser that takes a single parameter named token of type Object, and returns an Observable of type Object. Within this function, we are simply constructing a POST request to the validate-user endpoint, with the token as the content. This is simple enough, and mirrors what we did for the login endpoint.

Our changes to the AuthGuard are where things start to get a little tricky. We will update our canActivate function as follows:

```
canActivate(route: ActivatedRouteSnapshot,
state: RouterStateSnapshot):
    Observable<boolean>
{
    let token = <Object>localStorage.getItem('token');
    console.log(`Authguard : token : ${token}`);
    return this.userService.validateUser(token).pipe(
        map( (e: Object) : boolean => {
            console.log(`Authguard : e ; ${JSON.stringify(e)}`)
```

```
            return true;
        } ),
    catchError((err) => {
        // 401 unauth errors will be caught here.
        this.router.navigate(['/login']);
        return of(false);
    })
  );
}
```

Here, there are a number of modifications to the `canActivate` function. Firstly, we are not simply returning a `boolean` value, but we are returning an `Observable` of `boolean`. Secondly, we have updated this function to call the `validateUser` function of the `UserService` in order to POST to the REST endpoint and validate our token. The third modification to note is that we are using the `pipe` method instead of the `subscribe` method. We will discuss the `pipe` method in detail a little later. Within this `pipe` method, we have a call to a `map` method, as well as a `catchError` method. Again, we will discuss these methods in detail next.

In terms of logical flow, then, what we are doing within this function is as follows:

1. Retrieving the JWT token from Local Storage
2. Calling the `validateUser` function on the `UserService` and passing in the token
3. This will issue a POST to our endpoint, and either return a valid response, or an error
4. If a valid response is returned, return `true` so that the `AuthGuard` succeeds
5. If an error occurs, navigate to the `/login` URL, and return `false` so that the `AuthGuard` fails

The syntax of this function looks pretty hairy, and can get pretty confusing, so let's break it down into smaller pieces, and discuss each piece individually.

Our `canActivate` function now returns a type of `Observable<boolean>`, instead of a plain old `boolean`. Let's see how we can convert a `boolean` value into an Observable of `boolean`.

To wrap a `boolean` value, or any other value for that matter, within an Observable, we can use the `of` function. As an example of this, consider the following code:

```
function usingObservableOf(value: number) : Observable<boolean> {
    if (value > 10) {
        return of(true);
```

```
        } else {
            return of(false);
        }
    }
```

Here, we have defined a function named `usingObservableOf` that takes a `number` as a single parameter. It is returning the `Observable<boolean>` type, which means that it must return an Observable. The body of the function checks to see whether the `value` argument passed in is greater than 10. If it is, we return `of(true)`, which, in effect, turns our Boolean `true` value into an `Observable<boolean>`. We can see the use of this `of` function in our `canActivate` function, within the `catchError` section.

The body of our `canActivate` function is retrieving the token that is stored in Local Storage, and then calling the `validateUser` function of our `UserService`. The problem that we have, however, is that the `validateUser` function returns a type of `Observable<Object>`, which will contain the JSON returned by the `/validate-user` endpoint. Unfortunately, we cannot simply return this result from our `canActivate` function, as we need to return a type of `Observable<boolean>`. To overcome this, we use the `pipe` function and the `map` and `catchError` operators from RxJS.

The `pipe` function is used to combine two functions into one, and will execute each of these functions in sequence. It returns a single function. So instead of using `subscribe` on the `validateUser` function, we create a new function using `pipe` that combines the `map()` and `catchError()` functions. A stripped-down version of how this is put together is as follows:

```
function usingPipe( subject: Observable<Object>) {
    subject.pipe(
        map(() => {}),
        catchError((err) => {
            return of(false);
        })
    );
}
```

Here, we have a function named `usingPipe` that takes a single parameter named `subject` of type `Observable<Object>`. We then use the `pipe` function on the `subject` argument, and chain together two functions.

The first function is created from the `map` function, and the second function is created from the `catchError` function. Note that both the `map` and the `catchError` functions use a function as an input argument. Where the map function will automatically return an `Observable`, the `catchError` function does not. This is why we need to use the `of` function to create an Observable from the `boolean` value of `false`.

The `map` function, or, more correctly, the `map` operator from the RxJS library is used to transform each of the items in an Observable using a function. As a simple example of this, consider the following code:

```
function usingMap(subject: Observable<Object>): Observable<boolean> {
    return subject.pipe(
        map((object: Object): boolean => {
            return false;
        }));
}
```

Here, we have a function named `usingMap` that has a single parameter named `subject` which is of type `Observable<Object>`. This function, however, returns a type of `Observable<boolean>`. This means that each of the items in the input Observable stream need to be converted from an `Object` to a `boolean`. We are using the `pipe` function directly on the `subject` argument, and providing a simple function for `map` to use. Note the signature of this anonymous function. It accepts an input type of `Object`, and returns a `boolean`. This is how we can use `pipe` and `map` to transform an Observable stream from one type to another.

Our `canActivate` function is combining the `pipe`, `map`, and `catchError` functions into a single workflow in order to convert the result of the `validateUser` REST call from an `Observable<Object>` into an `Observable<boolean>`.

Our new version of the `AuthGuard`, therefore, is calling the REST endpoint at `/validate-user`, and sending in the token it has retrieved from Local Storage. If the endpoint returns success, then the `AuthGuard` knows that the token it used was successfully validated, and will allow access to the `SecureComponent`.

So we have seen how to create a JWT token, how to decode it, and how to verify it. We have also seen how we can use the power of Observables to transform data from one type to another.

External authentication

As we mentioned at the start of the chapter, most modern websites allow registration through external authentication services, such as Facebook, Google, or LinkedIn. What this means is that these external authentication services validate a user's credentials, and then forward our application some details about the user. These details generally include the username, email address, and possibly even a link to a picture that we can use on our site. This is a fairly easy replacement for the standard registration process, where we gather and store information about a user and their password. The use of external authentication services also makes our sites more appealing and accessible to a broader range of users.

In this section of the chapter, we will integrate with Google to allow anyone who has a valid Google account to access our site. The libraries and process used for external authentication are very similar between the major authentication service providers, so we will focus on Google authentication.

Obtaining a Google API key

To help with easy integration of authentication providers, we can turn to the open source world, and use the Angular library named `angular-6-social-login-v2`. This can be installed easily through `npm` as usual:

```
npm install angular-6-social-login-v2
```

Once this is installed, we will need to register our application with Google, and generate a Google API key. The documentation for the angular social login package contains a link to the following page that we can use to generate a key: `https://developers.google.com/identity/sign-in/web/sign-in#before_you_begin`.

In order to generate a key, we will need a valid Google account, and then it is just a matter of following the prompts on this page, which will walk us through key generation.

Click on the **Configure a Project** button, and type in a name for your project, as follows:

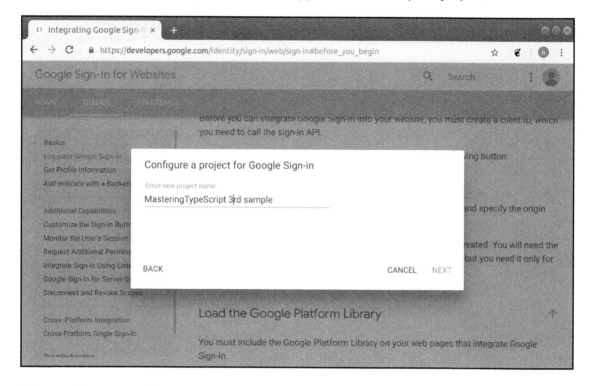

Here, we have entered a project name of **MasteringTypeScript 3rd sample**. This name can be anything. Once entered, click on the **NEXT** button to move to the next step. The next step asks for a name with which to configure your Oauth client, and will appear on the user consent screen. Once this is complete, the final piece of information that is required is to configure the Oauth client.

Select the web browser as the source by selecting it from the dropdown, and then enter the URL that will be used by the web server. For the purposes of development, we can enter `http://localhost:9000` here, which is the base URL of our sample application, as shown in the following screenshot:

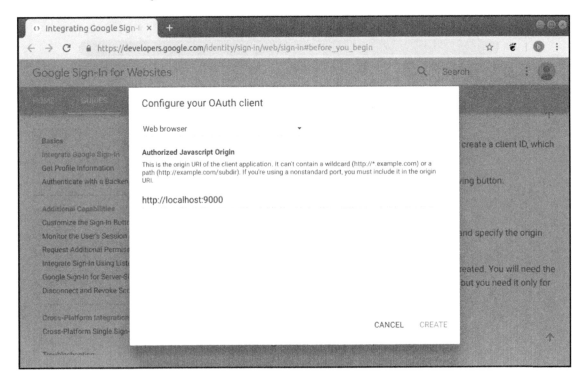

Once configured, we will be given a Client ID, and a client secret. Copy these values to a safe place, as we will be using these later.

Configuring social login

The process of integrating the Angular social login library is not a difficult one, and is broken down into two parts. Firstly, we will need to configure a provider, and secondly, we will need to use this provider to obtain a user token. The various social providers are all configured as services, and, as such, require modifications to the `app.module.ts` file as follows:

```
import {
    SocialLoginModule,
    AuthServiceConfig,
```

```
        GoogleLoginProvider
    } from 'angular-6-social-login-v2';

    export function getAuthServiceConfig(): AuthServiceConfig {
        let config = new AuthServiceConfig([{
            id: GoogleLoginProvider.PROVIDER_ID,
            provider: new GoogleLoginProvider(`<your client id goes here>`)
        }]);
        return config;
    }

    @NgModule({
        declarations: [
            ... existing declarations ...
        ],
        imports: [
            SocialLoginModule,
            ... existing modules ...
        ],
        providers: [
            {
                provide: AuthServiceConfig,
                useFactory: getAuthServiceConfig
            }
        ],
        bootstrap: [AppComponent]
    })
    export class AppModule { }
```

Here, we import the `SocialLoginModule`, `AuthServiceConfig`, and
`GoogleLoginProvider` classes from the `angular-6-social-login-v2` module. We then
create a function named `getAuthServiceConfig` that returns an instance of a new
`AuthServiceConfig` class with an array of service provider configurations. Each
configuration array element needs an `id` and a `provider` property. The `id` properties
simply uses one of the included provider values that are included in the library, which, in
this case, is `GoogleLoginProvider.PROVIDER_ID`. For Facebook, we would use
`FacebookLoginProvider.PROVIDER_ID`. The `provider` property creates an instance of a
provider by initializing it with the Client ID that we obtained when registering our
application with Google. Make sure to replace the `<your client id goes here>` string
with the Client ID that we obtained from Google.

We then need to update the `imports` property of our module, to include the `SocialLoginModule`, as well as create a `providers` property entry to reference our `getAuthServiceConfig` factory function. The `providers` entry has two properties, named `provide`, and `useFactory`. These properties are used to configure the `AuthService` that we will use to connect to the Google Authentication service.

This completes the configuration of our external authentication providers. We have simply set up a factory method in order to correctly set the Client ID that Google will need to verify that we have registered for API access.

Using Google user data

We can now focus on incorporating a Google login in our `LoginPanelComponent`. First up, we need to set a click handler for the **Login with Google** button as follows:

```
<button class="btn btn-primary"
    (click)="onLoginGoogleClicked()">Login with Google</button>
```

Here, we have updated our `login-panel.component.html` file and linked the function named `onLoginGoogleClicked` to the click `event` on our form. We can then update our component itself as follows:

```
constructor(
    private userService: UserService,
    private router: Router,
    private socialAuthService: AuthService) { }
onLoginGoogleClicked() {
    this.socialAuthService.signIn(GoogleLoginProvider.PROVIDER_ID)
        .then((userdata) => {
        this.userService.authenticateGoogleUser(userdata)
            .subscribe((response: any) => {
            localStorage.setItem('token', response);
            this.router.navigate([``]);
        }, (err) => {
            console.log(`onLoginClicked() : error :
                ${JSON.stringify(err, null, 4)}`);
            this.error = `${err.message}`;
        });
    }).catch((error) => {
        console.log(`error : ${error}`);
    });
}
```

Here, we have included a private constructor variable named `socialAuthService` that will be set to the instance of the `AuthService` by Angular's dependency injection framework. We then define the `onLoginGoogleClicked` function that uses this `AuthService` to call the `signIn` function with the correct `PROVIDER_ID` for Google. Note that this call returns a Promise, so we have defined both a `.then` handler for a successful response, and a `.catch` handler in case of an error.

When the Google authentication service returns with a success response, it will provide us with a JSON structure that includes information related to the logged-in user. We then pass this user data into a new function on our `UserService` that will POST to a new endpoint in order to generate a locally signed JWT token. Once we have a signed token, we can store it in Local Storage, and redirect the user to the `SecureComponent`.

The implementation of the `authenticateGoogleUser` is a simple `HttpClient` POST method in the `UserService` in order to send the user data to our Express server as follows:

```
authenticateGoogleUser(data: any) {
    const headers = new HttpHeaders();
    headers.append('Content-Type', 'application/json');

    return this.httpClient.post(
        '/login-google', data,
        { 'headers': headers });
}
```

This function simply constructs a POST to the Express endpoint named `/login-google`, and sends the user data as the JSON body. We can implement the route handler in the Express server `userRoutes.ts` file as follows:

```
router.post(`/login-google`, (req: any, res: any, next: any) => {
    serverLog(`POST /login-google`);
    if (req.body.name & req.body.name.length > 0) {

        let user_context = {
            username: req.body.name
        }

        var token = jwt.sign(user_context, jwtSecret);
        res.json(token);

    } else {
        serverLog(`/login-google - Error : Invalid google token`);
        res.status(401).send('Invalid google token');}

});
```

Here, we have defined a POST handler for the endpoint named /login-google. This handler just checks that the name property of the JSON data that was posted is valid. If so, it constructs an Object named user_context that contains a single property named username, and sets its value to the value of the name property. As we did with the /login route handler, we create a JWT token, and sign it using the sign function of the jwt library, passing in our server secret. We then return this token to the caller of the REST endpoint.

So what have we accomplished in relation to an external authentication service such as Google? The steps that we have worked through are as follows:

1. Install the angular-6-social-login-v2 library.
2. Register our application with Google and obtain a Client ID and Client Secret.
3. Update the app.module.ts file to configure and register the AuthServiceConfig provider.
4. Create a click handler event for when a user clicks on the **Login with Google** button.
5. Call the signIn function of the AuthService instance in order to authenticate our user with Google, and return a JSON user data structure.
6. POST this user data structure to our Express server using an Angular service.
7. Generate a JWT token that is signed by our Express server.
8. Store this JWT token in Local Storage so that the AuthGuard can allow the user to navigate to the SecureComponent.

Summary

In this chapter, we have explored some of the fundamental building blocks in application development. We started out by building an Express server that was capable of serving our Angular application, and then explored how we can set and use configuration variables and server logging to build a production-ready Express server. We then explored the use of Brackets and Emmet to help in the rapid design of mockup web pages.

The bulk of this chapter, however, has focused on authentication. We explored the use of Angular routing and Auth Guards to define a secure section of the application that is only available to logged-in users of the system. We then worked through how to send POST and GET requests to a REST endpoint through the use of the HttpClient and Express routing. To secure our application correctly, we then implemented the generation and verification of JWT tokens. Finally, we explored the use of an external authentication provider to enable our site users to log in with Google.

In our next chapter, we will combine all of our acquired knowledge and build a complete Angular application that incorporates all of the building blocks that we have been working with throughout this book. We will even find time to introduce some new design patterns that help when building a complete application. We will work with JSON data, write unit and acceptance tests to cover as much functionality as possible, and explore some more Observable capabilities.

14
Let's Get Our Hands Dirty

In this, our final chapter, we will use the techniques and principles that we have learned up to this point to build a sample web application. This application will use the left-to-right panel design that we explored in `Chapter 11`, *Object-Oriented Programming*, which uses the State and Mediator design pattern to control screen state. We will continue to interact with REST endpoints, as we discussed in `Chapter 13`, *Building Applications*. We will implement a fully working REST API using Express, that will read data from a backend database. We will then look at some new techniques for working with Observables that will allow us to combine data, filter data, and coordinate asynchronous requests to a REST API. We will also discuss and implement the Domain Events design pattern to help with communication between independent application components.

We already have all of the building blocks and the in-depth knowledge required to put together a sample application at our fingertips, so this chapter is all about reuse and component integration. For the purposes of this chapter, we will extend the Angular sample application that we have been working on, which we last updated in the previous chapter, `Chapter 13`, *Building Applications*.

This chapter will cover the following topics:

- Overview of the application
- Database structure
- Building database-driven endpoints with Express
- Design principles of REST API endpoints
- Working with REST API endpoints in Angular
- Using the Observable `concatMap` function
- Using the Observable `forkJoin` function
- The Domain Events design pattern
- Raising and consuming Domain Events
- Using the Observable `filter` function

Board Sales application

Our application will be a simple one, called **Board Sales**, which will list a range of windsurfing boards on the main page, and then allow the user to view details of any one of the boards on sale by clicking on it. Clicking on a particular board will slide the board detail panel in from the right-hand side. We will also use the left-hand side navigation panel to provide the user with options to filter the **Board List**. If a user clicks on a particular filter, then the range of boards shown will be filtered to match this selection. The main page will be as follows:

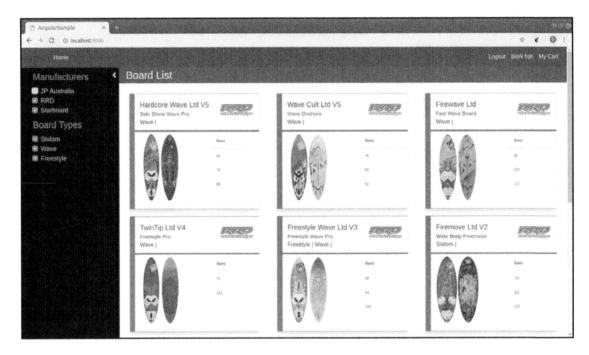

Here, we can see that we have a top navigation bar, a side-navigation panel on the left-hand side showing filter options, and a main panel with a series of boards displayed.

Modern windsurfing boards come in a range of sizes, and are measured by volume. As we can see in the board list view, each board is shown with a table of available sizes next to it. Smaller volume boards are generally used for wave sailing, and larger volume boards are using for racing, or slalom. Those boards that sit in-between can be categorized as freestyle boards, and are used for performing acrobatic tricks on flat water. Each board has a manufacturer, which corresponds to the logo shown next to each board. Our filter panel on the left-hand side allows the user to select either the manufacturer, or a board type as a filter. So to view only boards made by **RRD**, the user can click on the **RRD** filter under **Manufacturers**. Likewise, to filter the board list by **Slalom** boards, the user can click on the **Slalom** filter on the left-hand panel.

Clicking on any particular board will show the board detail screen, as follows:

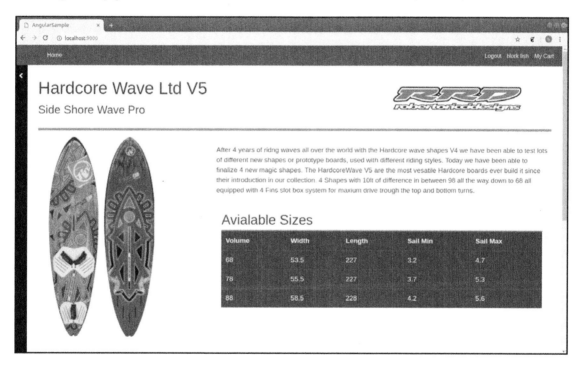

Here, we have a detailed view of a board, with a larger image, and a more comprehensive description of the board itself, along with an expanded table of available sizes.

One important aspect of choosing a windsurfing board is the range of sail sizes that it supports. In very strong winds, smaller sails are used to allow the windsurfer to control the power generated by the wind. Likewise, in lighter winds, larger sails are used to generate more power. The combination of board size, board type, and available sail sizes are all used to select the correct board for the sailor and sailing conditions. The detail view therefore lists the minimum and maximum sail sizes that the board can support.

Database-driven APIs

In order to provide the data that is needed for this application, we will store and retrieve data from a traditional database. We will provide a REST endpoint for each of our database tables that we will need. Node supports a wide variety of databases, including traditional relational databases such as Oracle or SQL Server, or object databases such as MongoDB or CouchDB. For the sake of this exercise, we will use Sqlite3 as a backing database.

Sqlite3 is a very small, fast, and self-contained database engine. It supports SQL language queries and standard table structures, and is contained within a single file on disk, or even as an in-memory temporary database. It can be installed on Windows, Linux, and macOS, and has a very small footprint. Sqlite3 also has some very simple, yet powerful, GUI tools to help with database design and data input, such as DB Browser for SQLite (http://sqlitebrowser.org/).

Database structure

The main tables that we will need for our sample application include the `Board` table, the `Manufacturer` table, and the `BoardType` table. The `Board` table is as follows:

```
CREATE TABLE `Board` (
    `id`   INTEGER NOT NULL DEFAULT 1 PRIMARY KEY
          AUTOINCREMENT UNIQUE,
    `name`       TEXT NOT NULL,
    `short_description`    TEXT,
    `long_description`    TEXT,
    `img` TEXT
);
```

Here, we can see the CREATE command for our Board table. It has an id property that will automatically increment, and also serves as the primary key. Along with the id property, each board has a name property, a short_description, long_description, and an img property. The img property will be used to load the relevant image for display.

The Manufacturer table is as follows:

```
CREATE TABLE `Manufacturer` (
    `id`   INTEGER NOT NULL DEFAULT 1 PRIMARY KEY
          AUTOINCREMENT UNIQUE,
    `name`       TEXT NOT NULL,
    `logo`       TEXT NOT NULL
);
```

Here, we can see that each entry in the Manufacturer table will have an id property, a name property, and a logo property. To link a row in the Board table with the Manufacturer table, we will need a mapping table named BoardManufacturer, as follows:

```
CREATE TABLE `BoardManufacturer` (
    `id`   INTEGER NOT NULL DEFAULT 1 PRIMARY KEY
          AUTOINCREMENT UNIQUE,
    `board_id`   INTEGER NOT NULL,
    `manufacturer_id` INTEGER NOT NULL
);
```

Here, we can see that each row in the BoardManufacturer table will have a board_id property and a manufacturer_id property. We will use this table to link a particular board with its manufacturer.

The BoardType table is very similar to the Manufacturer table, as follows:

```
CREATE TABLE `BoardType` (
    `id`   INTEGER NOT NULL DEFAULT 1 PRIMARY KEY
          AUTOINCREMENT UNIQUE,
    `name`       TEXT NOT NULL
);
```

Here, we will store the `id` and `name` properties of the board types that we will need, as shown in the following screenshot:

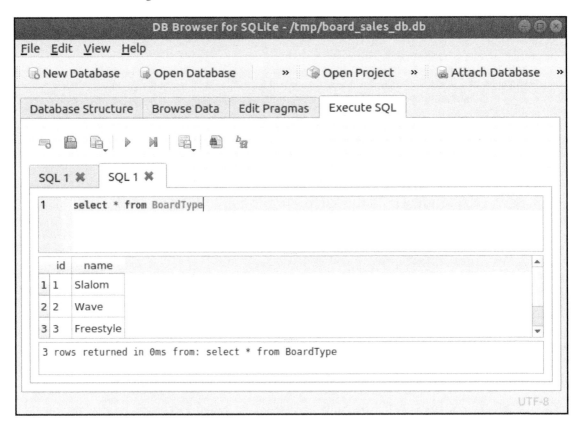

Here, we can see that the `BoardType` table contains three entries for our board types, which are `Slalom`, `Wave`, and `Freestyle`.

In order to link a board with its board type, we will again create a mapping table as follows:

```
CREATE TABLE `BoardBoardType` (
    `id`   INTEGER NOT NULL DEFAULT 1 PRIMARY KEY
          AUTOINCREMENT UNIQUE,
    `board_id`   INTEGER NOT NULL,
    `board_type_id`   INTEGER NOT NULL
);
```

Here, we have created a table named `BoardBoardType`, which will contain entries for each board we have in our database, and its list of board types. Note that some boards can be categorized as more than one type, so they may be both wave boards and freestyle boards. In this case, the `BoardBoardType` table will contain two entries for the same `board_id`.

Note that in traditional databases, foreign keys and unique indexes are used in order to maintain referential integrity of the data within a database. For the sake of brevity, we have not included any of these safeguards, but these should really be put in place for any production database. Please refer to the sample code that accompanies this chapter for the full Sqlite3 database.

Express API endpoints

In order to provide the data that we have stored in our database to our application, we will create a set of REST endpoints in our Express server that will connect to our database, execute a SQL query, and return data as JSON objects. In order to work with an Sqlite3 database, we will use the `sqlite3` node library, which can be installed as follows:

```
npm install sqlite3
npm install @types/sqlite3 --saveDev
```

In order to serve data to our application, we will create a new Express handler in the `express/routes` directory named `dataRoutes.ts` as follows:

```
import * as express from 'express';
import { serverLog } from '../main';

var router = express.Router();

router.get(`/boards`, async (req: any, res: any, next: any) => {
    serverLog(`GET /boards`);
    res.json({ result: 'success' })
});

export { router };
```

Here, we have a standard Express handler that is serving GET requests from the path named `/boards`. For the time being, this handler is simply logging a message using our `serverLog` function, and returning a JSON payload with a single property named `result`. As we have seen before, we must re-export the router from this file as seen on the last line of the preceding code snippet. We can then register this handler with our Express server in our `express/main.ts` file as follows:

```
... existing code

app.use('/', userRoutes.router);
app.use('/api', dataRoutes.router);

... existing code
```

Here, we have added a new `app.use` function call to register all routes from the `dataRoutes.ts` file with the Express server, under a base URL path named `/api`. This means that in order to access any of our REST endpoints, we will need to add the `/api` path to the beginning of the URL. Using a base URL in this way allows us to differentiate standard Express handlers from REST handlers. Let's now connect to our database within the `/boards` handler and return all the rows found as follows:

```
router.get(`/boards`, async (req: any, res: any, next: any) => {

    serverLog(`GET /boards`);
    let db = new Database('./database/board_sales_db.db');

    let boardsArray: any[] = [];

    db.each(`select
        b.id, b.name, b.short_description,
        b.long_description, b.img
        from Board b
    `, (err: Error, row: any) => {
            let board = {
                id: row.id, name: row.name,
                short_description: row.short_description,
                long_description: row.long_description,
                img: row.img
            };
            boardsArray.push(board);

        }, (err: Error, count: number) => {
            // complete

            if (err) {
                serverLog(`err : ${err}`);
```

```
            res.status(503).send(err);
        } else {
            console.log(` => returning array`);
            res.json(boardsArray);
        }
    });

});
```

Here, we have started to use the Sqlite3 API in order to connect to a database and return results. Our handler has been updated to create a local variable named db that is a new instance of the Database class. This db variable represents a connection to the Sqlite3 database, and has a single constructor argument. This argument is the path to the Sqlite3 database file itself. Our handler then creates a new array named boardsArray, which is set to an empty array.

We then use the each function of the Database class to execute a SQL query. The each function has three parameters. The first parameter is of type string, and is the SQL command to execute. The second parameter is a function that will be executed for each result that is returned by the database, and the third parameter is a function that will be executed once all results are returned. The API for Sqlite3 that we are working with is using a standard callback mechanism. In other words, the second parameter that we have defined in our call to db.each is a callback function that will be invoked for each record returned by the database. The third parameter is a further callback function that will be invoked once all records have been read.

This double callback design is actually quite handy. Within the first callback, we know that we are dealing with only a single database record. We are therefore able to construct a JavaScript object that represents this single record, and add it to our array of records to return. Within the second callback, we know that all records have been processed from the database. If there was some sort of error, we return a response with a status of 503, and include an error message. If all goes well, we return the entire contents of the boardsArray local variable as a JSON structure.

Browsing to the URL of `localhost:9000/api/boards` will now return a JSON structure with the data from our database, as seen in the following screenshot:

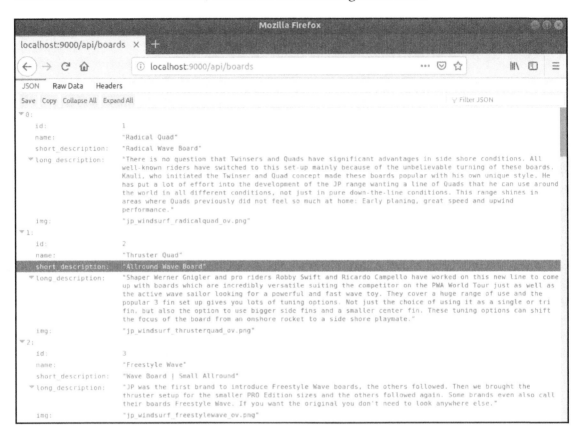

There are a number of endpoints that we will need in order to provide the necessary data for our application. We will not discuss each of these in detail, as the implementation of each route handler is the same. In other words, connect to the database, execute a SQL query, and return the results. The only difference between each of these handlers is the handler route, the SQL query that is executed, and the corresponding JSON data structure that is returned. For the sake of brevity, we will only list each of the endpoint routes, and the SQL query that is used. Please refer to the sample code of this chapter for full implementations.

Our list of manufacturers will be served by the endpoint named `/api/manufacturers`, and consists of the following SQL query:

```
select id, name, logo from Manufacturer
```

Our list of board types will be served by the endpoint named `/api/board-types`, and will run the following SQL query:

```
select id, name from BoardType
```

Linking a particular board to a manufacturer is resolved by the `/board-manufacturers` endpoint, which will run the following query:

```
select id, board_id, manufacturer_id from BoardManufacturer
```

Again, please refer to the sample code for the full implementations.

Parameterized API endpoints

When designing REST endpoints, the general rule of thumb is to provide an endpoint for each of the logical groups of data that will be queried. The name of this endpoint should be a plural, indicating that it will return an array of results. So the `/api/boards` endpoint will return a list of data relating to all the boards within the database. Search criteria can then be implemented on this endpoint to filter results. As an example, the `/api/boards?type=1&manufacturer=2` URL should apply the type and manufacturer values as a filter in order to limit the search of all boards in the system.

When we need to work with a single instance of an item, we append the `id` of the item we wish to query to the plural endpoint name. In other words, to retrieve information about a board with the `id` of 3, we will use the `/api/boards/3` URL. This conforms to our paradigm where all information relating to boards in the system are retrieved from the `/api/boards` endpoint. By providing an `id`, we are limiting the boards returned by this endpoint to a single board.

Bear in mind that we may provide multiple endpoints that will retrieve the same data. Consider an endpoint that is accessed through the `/api/board-types/2/boards` URL. This endpoint will return a single board type with an `id` of 2, and then return all of the boards that are related to this board type. Likewise, we may have an endpoint named `/api/boards/1/board-types` that returns the board types related to a board that has an `id` of 1. It is always prudent to design API endpoints with an idea of how users will be interacting with our data, and help them to work with data in an intuitive manner.

In order to allow an Express endpoint to use a parameter within an endpoint name, we use a colon and provide a name for this parameter, as follows:

```
router.get(`/boards/:boardId`, (req: any, res: any, next: any) => {
    let boardId = req.params.boardId;
    serverLog(`GET /boards/${boardId}/sizes`);
    let db = new Database(databaseName);

    let board: any = {};

    let sqlString = `select b.id, b.name, b.short_description,
        b.long_description, b.img
        from Board b
        where b.id=${boardId}`;

    ... db.each code ...
```

Here, we have defined a handler with the route of /boards/:boardId. Express will therefore match this handler with any request that starts with /boards/ and appends a parameter. This means that this handler will be invoked if the incoming URL matches either the /boards/1, or /boards/2, or even /boards/abcd-efg URLs. The boardId parameter is then accessible through the req.params property, by using the name of the parameter itself. In this instance, we have named the parameter :boardId, and it is therefore accessible through the req.params.boardId property. Note how the SQL statement that we are executing has been updated to use a where clause that includes this boardId parameter.

We are not limited to a single parameter within a route handler, and this parameter can also appear anywhere within our URL. As an example of this, consider the following handler:

```
router.get(`/boards/:boardId/sizes`,
    (req: any, res: any, next: any) => {

    let boardId = req.params.boardId;
    serverLog(`GET /boards/${boardId}/sizes`);
    let db = new Database(databaseName);

    let boardSizeArray: any[] = [];

    let sqlString = `select board_id, volume, length, width,
        sail_min, sail_max
        from BoardSize where board_id=${boardId}`;

    ... db.each code ...
```

Here, we have a handler that is defined as `/boards/:boardId/sizes`. This handler will be invoked by a URL such as `/boards/1/sizes`, or `/board/3/sizes`. Note that no matter where the `boardId` parameter is specified within the URL, it is still accessible from the `req.params.boardId` property. In the preceding sample, we are using the `boardId` parameter to filter records from the `BoardSize` table based on a `boardId`.

In a similar vein, we can request a list of types that a specific board has with the following handler:

```
router.get(`/boards/:boardId/types`,
    (req: any, res: any, next: any) => {
    let boardId = req.params.boardId;
    serverLog(`GET /boards/${boardId}/types`);
    let db = new Database(databaseName);

    let boardSizeArray: any[] = [];

    let sqlString = `select b.id, bbt.board_type_id,
    bt.name from Board b
    INNER JOIN BoardBoardType bbt ON b.id = bbt.board_id
    INNER JOIN BoardType bt ON bbt.board_type_id = bt.id
    where b.id = ${boardId}`;

    ... db.each code ...
```

Here, we have defined a handler that will be invoked by the `/boards/:boardId/types` URL. This handler will return all of the board types that are associated with a particular board. Note that this handler uses two `INNER JOIN` statements in order to retrieve data from the `BoardBoardType` table, as well as the `BoardType` table. The returned JSON structure is as follows:

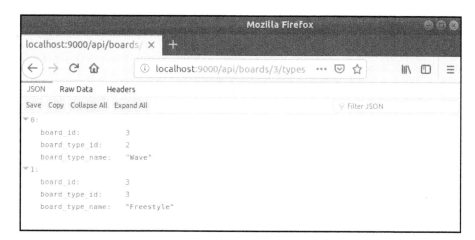

Here, we can see the results of the REST API query to the
`/api/boards/3/types` endpoint. Our `INNER JOIN` statements have matched and
returned values from the `BoardBoardType` table (which associates a board with a board
type), as well as the names from the `BoardTable` that will be used for display purposes.

Let's recap then on the API endpoints that we have built thus far:

- `/api/boards` will return an array of all boards that are in the system.
- `/api/manufacturers` will return an array of all manufacturers in the system.
- `/api/board-manufacturers` will return an array of all boards and their manufacturers.
- `/api/boards/:boardId` will return the information related to a single board in the system, identified by a particular `boardId`.
- `/api/boards/:boardId/sizes` will return an array of the available sizes for a particular board.
- `/api/boards/:boardId/types` will return an array of associated types for a particular board.

Note that a particular board only has a single manufacturer, and we will need the
information related to a manufacturer (such as their name and logo) when we display a
board. For this reason, we will update the SQL query for `/api/boards` and
`/api/boards/:boardId` as follows:

```
select b.id, b.name, b.short_description,
    b.long_description, b.img,
    bm.manufacturer_id as mfid,
    mf.name as mfname,
    mf.logo as mflogo
    from Board b
    INNER JOIN BoardManufacturer bm
    ON b.id = bm.board_id
    INNER JOIN Manufacturer mf
    ON bm.manufacturer_id = mf.id
```

Here, we are selecting records from the `Board` table, and then joining this data with the
`BoardManufacturer` table, and then with the `Manufacturer` table. The
`BoardManufacturer` table associates a particular board with a manufacturer, and the
`Manufacturer` table contains the name and logo to be used. We may as well return all of
this data in one hit.

Angular REST services

In order to interact with our newly created REST endpoints, we will follow the Single Responsibility design paradigm, and create an Angular service. This service will be marked with the @Injectable decorator, which allows us to use Angular's DI framework to inject an instance of this service when and where it is needed. Let's create a new file in the /app/services directory named board.service.ts as follows:

```typescript
import { Injectable } from "@angular/core";
import { HttpClient } from "@angular/common/http";
import { Observable } from "rxjs";
@Injectable({
    providedIn: 'root'
})
export class BoardService {
    constructor(private httpClient: HttpClient) { }

    getManufacturerList(): Observable<Object> {
        return this.httpClient.get('/api/manufacturers');
    }

    getBoardTypesList(): Observable<Object> {
        return this.httpClient.get('/api/board-types');
    }

    getBoardsList(): Observable<Object> {
        return this.httpClient.get('/api/boards');
    }

    getBoardManufacturers(): Observable<Object> {
        return this.httpClient.get('/api/board-manufacturers');
    }

    getBoardDetails(boardId: number): Observable<Object> {
        return this.httpClient.get(`/api/boards/${boardId}`);
    }

    getBoardSizes(boardId: number): Observable<Object> {
        return
        this.httpClient.get(`/api/boards/${boardId}/sizes`);
    }

    getBoardTypes(boardId: number): Observable<Object> {
        return
        this.httpClient.get(`/api/boards/${boardId}/types`);
    }
}
```

Here, we start by importing the `Injectable` decorator and the `HttpClient` class that we will use for asynchronous queries to our REST endpoint. Each call using the `HttpClient` will return an Observable, so we need to import this as well.

Our `BoardService` class has a constructor that uses Angular's DI framework to declare a private variable named `httpClient` through which we can call our API. The class then has a number of functions, each of which relates to our REST endpoints as discussed earlier. Note that the last three functions, named `getBoardDetails`, `getBoardSizes`, and `getBoardTypes`, all require a single parameter named `boardId` of the `number` type. This parameter is then injected into the URL such that we are calling the correct parameterized REST endpoint.

Creating a service in this way, and providing functions on this service to call our endpoints, means that we are hiding the intricacies of URL construction from our calling code. In order to get the available types for a board, we just call `getBoardTypes`, and provide the `id` of the board as a single argument. This is far simpler than having to remember that the URL is `/api/boards/:boardId/types`. It also makes our code more reusable, and ensures that the only place where we need to understand how to construct the correct URL is within the `BoardService` class itself.

Note that in this version, each function call returns a type of `Observable<Object>`. While this is syntactically correct, and we are, in fact, returning a JSON structure that maps to an Object type, it would be far better for our code to define the interfaces that each call returns. In this way, any user of the service will understand immediately what information is available for each function call.

Let's update our `getManufacturersList` function to use an interface as follows:

```
export interface INameId {
    id: number;
    name: string;
}

export interface IManufacturer extends INameId {
    logo: string;
}

... existing code

getManufacturerList(): Observable<IManufacturer[]> {
    return this.httpClient.get('/api/manufacturers')
        as Observable<IManufacturer[]>;
}
```

Here, we have defined three interfaces. The INameId interface consists of an id of type number, and a name of type string. The IManufacturer interface adds a logo property to this INameId interface. We have also updated the getManufacturerList function to return an Observable of type IManufacturer[]. This interface matches the JSON data structure that is returned from our REST endpoint.

We can then define three additional interfaces to round out our service as follows:

```
export interface IBoardSize {
    board_id: number;
    volume: number;
    width: number;
    length: number;
    sail_min: string;
    sail_max: string;
}

export interface IBoardType {
    board_id: number;
    board_type_id: number;
    board_type_name: string;
}

export interface IBoard extends INameId {
    short_description: string;
    long_description: string;
    img: string;
    manufacturer_logo: string;
    mfid: number;
    mfname: string;
    mflogo: string;
}
```

Here, we have defined the IBoardSize interface, as well as the IBoardType interface, and the IBoard interface. Each of the properties of these interfaces match the JSON structure that we are returning from our REST endpoints.

The OpenAPI specification

In large-scale systems, the definition of a REST API, and what data is returned by each endpoint, needs to be used in various ways. Take documentation for example. A public REST API needs to have each of its endpoints listed in a formal document, and this document also needs to define the type of each property, as well as the constraints of each property. As an example of these constraints, consider a POST call to an endpoint. If our endpoint defines a property of type `number`, then how does the user of this endpoint know what the upper and lower limits of this number are? Is it a 32-bit number, or a 64-bit number? Is it signed or unsigned? If the endpoint defines a `string` property, then how many characters are allowed?

The OpenAPI specification is a standardized way of describing the nature of a REST API. Along with describing what endpoints are available, the standard also allows describing what operations are allowed on each endpoint. Does an endpoint allow POST and PUT, or is it simply GET requests only. If it is a GET request, then what query parameters are allowed? The OpenAPI specification allows the producer of a REST API to make all of the nuances of a particular system available in a standard format.

With the OpenAPI specification available for a REST API, we can use a number of tools to help with the consumption of this API, including documentation, client code generators, and even automatic server stub generation. We will not discuss the generation of an OpenAPI specification here, but bear in mind that it is a standard, and generating a specification for your API will help those that consume it immensely.

One of the benefits of an OpenAPI specification is that we can generate client libraries based on the API definitions. This means that the interfaces that we have just built by hand can be automatically generated by tools. If we include these tools into our build steps, we can be certain that any changes to the API will automatically be reflected in our code. Also, if the API has breaking changes, then our build will fail if it is relying on a property that has suddenly disappeared. Finding bugs like these early on in the development process is far less expensive to fix than finding the same bugs in a test or production environment.

The BoardSales application

Our sample application will need a few updates in order to use the REST API that we have defined, and generate the pages that we require. The steps that we will need to accomplish are broadly as follows:

- Create a board list component to list all boards as retrieved from the /api/boards endpoint.
- Integrate this board list component into our main page.
- Load and display the Manufacturer list and Board type list in our sidenav component from the /api/manufacturers and /api/board-types endpoints.
- Respond to a click event on a board in the board list and display the board details in our rightscreen component.
- Respond to filter events when a user filters the list of boards based on either manufacturer or board type.

As we make changes to the application, we will discuss the use of the Domain Events design pattern, as well as take a deep dive into the various ways of using Observables to work with and manipulate data.

The BoardList component

Let's start our application updates by creating and integrating a board-list component that will display the list of all boards that are available. This component will query the /api/boards endpoint for data, and will serve as the main page for our site. This BoardListComponent can be created by using the Angular CLI as follows:

```
ng generate component board-list --skip-import
```

This command will generate a /src/app/board-list directory, and also create the .ts, .html, .css, and .spec.ts files for our component. We will need to register this BoardListComponent as a module in the app.module.ts file as follows:

```
@NgModule({
    declarations: [
        ... existing components ...
        BoardListComponent
    ],
    imports: [
    ... existing code ...
```

Here, we have simply added the `BoardListComponent` class to the list of components in the `declarations` array. Remember that adding an entry here will allow us to include the `<app-board-list>` element within an HTML file in our application. We can now update the `SecureComponent` HTML file as follows:

```
<app-navbar></app-navbar>

<app-sidenav></app-sidenav>

<div id="sidenav_expand_panel" class="sidenav_expand"
    (click)="showHideSideClicked()">
    <span id="show-hide-side-button" class="filter-button fa ">
    </span>
</div>

<app-rightscreen (notify)='onNotifyRightWindow($event)'>
</app-rightscreen>

<div id="main" class="main-content-panel">
    <div> ... page title ... </div>
    <div class="main-content">
        <app-board-list></app-board-list>
    </div>
</div>
```

Here, we have the four main components that make up our main page, each referenced by their element names. The `<app-navbar>` element will render the navigation panel at the top of the screen, and the `<app-sidenav>` element will render the left-hand side panel that we will use for filtering. The `<app-rightscreen>` element will render the detail panel when a board is selected. We then have a `<div>` element that represents the main content panel of our page, and within this, the `<app-board-list>` element that will render the full list of boards.

Note that the previous HTML code sample is a stripped-down version of the full file, in order to show the placement of the main elements. The `... page title ...` elements are not shown here. Accompanying these HTML files are the relevant CSS styles that are used for each element, as stored in the `.css` files for each component. Again, for the sake of brevity, we will not discuss these styles, or list them here, so please refer to the sample code for the full implementation.

We have also introduced a <div> element with an id of sidenav_expand_panel, in-between the <app-sidenav> and <app-rightscreen> elements. This is an upgraded version of the button we used earlier for expanding and collapsing the <app-sidenav> element, and is actually a panel that is 30px wide and fills the page from top to bottom. In order to animate this panel, and to compensate for the extra width, we will need to update the SecureComponent as follows:

```
showNavPanel() {
    this.sideNav.showNav();
    document.getElementById('main').style.marginLeft = "280px";
    document.getElementById('sidenav_expand_panel')
        .style.left = "250px";
}
hideNavPanel() {
    this.sideNav.closeNav();
    document.getElementById('main').style.marginLeft = "30px";
    document.getElementById('sidenav_expand_panel')
        .style.left = "0px";
}
showDetailPanel() {
    this.rightScreen.openRightWindow();
    document.getElementById('main').style.transform =
        "translateX(-100%)";
    document.getElementById('sidenav_expand_panel').style.transform =
        "translateX(-100%)";
}
hideDetailPanel() {
    this.rightScreen.closeRightWindow();
    document.getElementById('main').style.transform =
        "translateX(0%)";
    document.getElementById('sidenav_expand_panel').style.transform =
        "translateX(0%)";
}
```

Here, we have updated the showNavPanel function to include setting the style.left property of the element with an id of sidenave_expand_panel to 250px. This is very similar to our existing code that sets the style.marginLeft property for the main element. Likewise, within the hideNavPanel function, we are setting the style.left property for the sidenav_expand_panel to 0px. The showDetailPanel and hideDetailPanels have also been updated to include a style.transform property for the sidenav_expand_panel. Again, this code is similar to how we are animating the main element.

Our main page should now show the `board-list` component as follows:

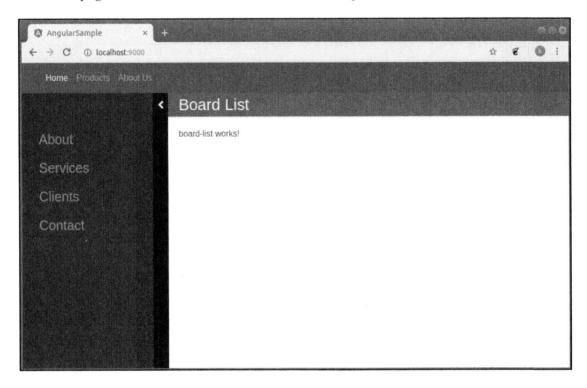

Rendering REST data

Now that we have the skeleton `BoardListComponent` in place, we can integrate with our `BoardService`, and query our `/api/boards` REST endpoint in order to fetch a list of boards to display. Our updates are as follows:

```
export class BoardListComponent implements OnInit {
    boardList: IBoard[] = [];
    constructor(private boardService: BoardService) { }
    ngOnInit() {
        this.boardService.getBoardsList()
            .subscribe((result: IBoard[]) => {
            this.boardList = result;
        });
    }
}
```

Here, we have a property named `boardList` that holds an array of elements of type `IBoard`. We have then updated our `constructor` function to inject an instance of the `BoardService` service, and store it in a private variable named `boardService`. Our `ngOnInit` function then calls the `getBoardList` function on the `boardService` instance, and defines a `subscribe` function. Within the `subscribe` function, we are simply setting the local variable `boardList` to the results of the call to the REST endpoint. We can make a simple update to our HTML file as follows:

```
<div *ngFor="let board of boardList;">
    <p>{{board.name}}</p>
</div>
```

Here, we have updated the HTML template and added a `<div>` element that is using the `*ngFor` syntax to iterate through all the items in the `boardList` array. Each array element will then generate a `<p>` element, and render the `name` property to the DOM. At this stage, after a few lines of code, we can see the results of querying our REST endpoint as follows:

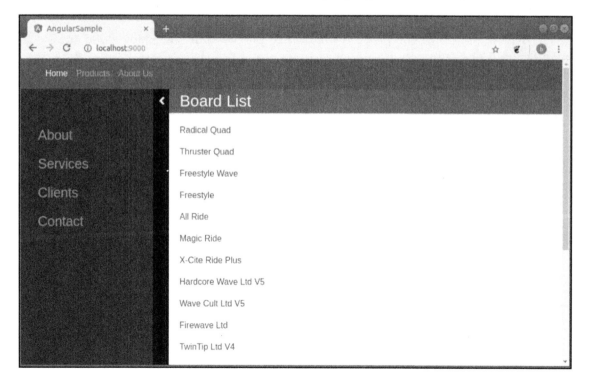

Now that we have the basics of the page in place, we can update our HTML in order generate a more visually appealing list, which will include an image of the board, the manufacturers' logo, and a brief description. The HTML for each board will have two rows, with the top row showing the board name and brief description, and the bottom row showing the board image and sizes. Our top row is as follows:

```
<div class="row">
    <div class="col-sm-8 board-name-panel">
        <div class="board-name">{{board.name}}</div>
        <div class="board-desc">{{board.short_description}}</div>
    </div>
    <div class="col-sm-4 float-right board-name-panel">
        <img src="/assets/images/{{board.mflogo}}"
          class="img manufacturer-logo" />
    </div>
</div>
```

Here, we have defined a Bootstrap row, and within this, two columns of size `col-sm-8` and `col-sm-4`. The first column is used to render the `board.name` and `board.short_description` property, and the second column is used to display the manufacturers' logo through the `board.mflogo` property.

The second row in our HTML for each board is as follows:

```
<div class="row">
    <div class="col-sm-7">
        <div class="board-name">
            <img src="/assets/images/{{board.img}}"
                class="img board-image" />
        </div>
    </div>
    <div class="col-sm-5 size-table">
        <table class="table">
            <thead>
                <tr> <th scope="col">Sizes</th> </tr>
            </thead>
            <tbody>
                <div *ngFor="let size of board.sizes">
                    <tr>
                        <td>{{size.volume}}</td>
                    </tr>
                </div>
            </tbody>
        </table>
    </div>
```

Here, we have a Bootstrap row element that has two columns of size `col-sm-7` and `col-sm-5`. The first column is used to render an image of the board, and the second column includes a table with a header of `Sizes`. This table element then uses a `*ngFor` to loop through the `sizes` property of the current board, in order to render the available sizes for each board. We will discuss how to populate the sizes property of each board a little later, but with this HTML in place, and a healthy dose of CSS, our list of boards becomes more visually appealing, as follows:

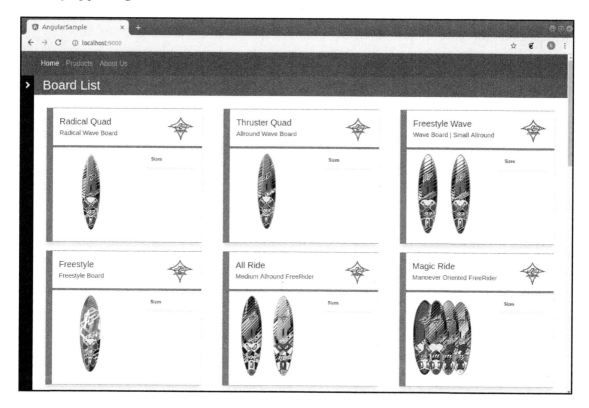

Observables – concatMap

Our list of boards is currently using data from the `/api/boards` REST endpoint, and therefore has access to the general information relating to a board, such as its `name`, `short_description`, and manufacturer logo. Remember that most windsurfing boards come in a range of sizes, with each size having a slightly different volume, width, and length, in order to support different sail sizes. What we have here, then, is a one-to-many relationship between a board and its sizes, as a single board may have many sizes.

Our REST endpoints, however, do not return the sizes of a board within the JSON structure for a single board. This means that for each board in our list, we will need to make a secondary call to the REST endpoints in order to retrieve its sizes. The argument could easily be made that the REST endpoint that retrieves details about a board should include an array including its sizes. This would arguably be the most natural way for the endpoint to behave.

There are, however, cases where a secondary REST call needs to be made for each item in a collection, so we will use this example to discuss a technique using Observables that accomplishes this exact requirement: the `concatMap` operator.

The `concatMap` operator will emit one value of an Observable at a time in order, and allow the value of that Observable to be subscribed to. It will not emit another Observable item until the previous `subscribe` completes. This means that we are able to process Observable items one by one, and execute another action on the Observable item before processing another one. We can therefore use the `concatMap` operator to make a secondary call to our REST endpoint for each element in the Observable. Remember that the `/api/boards` endpoint returns an array of boards. We will need to execute a call to the `/api/boards/:boardId/sizes` endpoint for each element of the array, and then update the original board that we were working with the returned sizes.

There are five steps that we will need to work through in order to use the `concatMap` operator correctly, so let's make some incremental changes to our code, and introduce these steps one by one.

The first step is to import the correct operators from the RxJS library as follows:

```
import { from } from 'rxjs';
import { concatMap } from 'rxjs/operators';

interface IBoardExtended extends IBoard {
    sizes: IBoardSize[];
}

... class definition ...

ngOnInit() {
    this.boardService.getBoardsList()
        .subscribe((result: IBoardExtended[]) => {
        // this.boardList = result;
        // use concatMap here
    });
}
```

Here, we start by importing the `from` function from the `'rxjs'` library, as well as the `concatMap` function from the `'rxjs/operators'` library. We then define an interface named `IBoardExtended`, which adds the `sizes` property to the existing `IBoard` interface definition. This `sizes` property is an array of type `IBoardSize`, and will house the results of the individual calls to the `/api/board/:boardId/sizes` endpoint.

We have then updated our `ngOnInit` function, and, in particular, have commented out the line that sets the internal `boardList` property to the result of the call to the `getBoardList` function. We will use this `result` variable with the `concatMap` operator. Before we use the `concatMap` operator, however, we will need to create an Observable from the `IBoardExtended` array, as follows:

```
let boardSizes = from(<IBoard[]>result).pipe(
    ... pipe each element of the array here
);
```

Here, we are creating a local variable named `boardSizes`, which will hold the results of the `pipe` function call. We are using the `from` function to create an Observable from the array of boards that were retrieved as a result of querying the REST endpoint at `/api/boards`. We then call the `pipe` function on this Observable. What this code is saying is that we are creating an Observable from the `IBoard` array, and then piping these results into another `function`.

Within the `pipe` function, we can then use the `concatMap` function as follows:

```
let boardSizes = from(<IBoard[]>result).pipe(
    concatMap(
        // first function
        (board: IBoardExtended) => {
         // this is called for each board in the array
         // returns an Observable
        },
        // second function
        (board: IBoardExtended, sizes: IBoardSize[]) => {
         // board is the original array element
         // sizes is the result of the Observable
        }
    ) // end concatMap
);
```

Here, we call the `concatMap` function within the `pipe` function. We are therefore piping our Observable into the `concatMap` function.

The `concatMap` function receives a single Observable item, and can then call another function before the next Observable item is received. The `concatMap` function can be used with either one parameter, or two. The first parameter, which must be a function is the function that will be called for each item in the Observable. The second parameter, which is also a function, is called once the first function has completed, and provides two arguments. The first argument is the value of the original Observable that was used, and the second argument is the result of the first function. In other words, the first function is used to operate on the Observable item, and the second function is the result of this operation. This is a little bit easier to understand with a code sample, as follows:

```
concatMap(
    // first function
    (board: IBoardExtended) => {
        console.log(`concatmap 1 : ${board.name}`);
        return this.boardService.getBoardSizes(board.id);
    },
    // second function
    (board: IBoardExtended, sizes: IBoardSize[]) => {
        console.log(`concatmap 1 : board.id : ${board.id}`);
        console.log(`concatmap 1 : sizes.length :
            ${sizes.length}`);
        board.sizes = sizes;
        return result;
    })
```

Here, we have defined both functions as parameters to the `concatMap` function itself. The first function logs the `name` property of the array element that was passed in through the `board` argument. It then calls the `getBoardSizes` function using the `id` of the incoming `board` element. This function will be called for every element of the array. The `getBoardSizes` function will execute a REST call, and return an Observable, which will contain the result of the REST API call.

The second function logs two messages to the console, which show us the `id` of the board we are currently dealing with, and the `length` of the `sizes` array that was retrieved from the `/api/boards/:boardId/sizes` REST endpoint. It then assigns the `sizes` array to the `sizes` property of the original `board` array element, and returns the value of the original `result` argument.

The only thing left to do is to subscribe to the `concatMap` Observable, and set the internal `boardList` property as follows:

```
this.boardService.getBoardsList().subscribe((result: IBoardExtended[]) => {
    // this.boardList = result;
    let boardSizes = from(<IBoard[]>result).pipe(
        ... concatMap functions
    );

    boardSizes.subscribe((boardList: IBoardExtended[]) => {
        this.boardList = boardList;
    });
});
```

Here, we are calling the `subscribe` function on the `boardSizes` variable, and within this anonymous function, we are setting the internal `boardList` property to the result of the Observable.

So what have we accomplished? The steps that have been executed in this body of code are as follows:

1. Subscribe to a call to the `/api/boards` endpoint.
2. Create an Observable out of the array that is returned, from the `result` variable.
3. Pipe this Observable to the `concatMap` function.
4. Define the first function that will be called for each element of the array.
5. Within this function, call the `/api/boards/:boardId/sizes` endpoint.
6. When this REST call completes, execute the second function provided to `concatMap`.
7. Assign the returned array from this second REST call to the `sizes` property of the original array element.
8. Subscribe to the Observable created using the `from` and `pipe` calls.
9. Assign the updated array to the internal `boardList` property.

If we take a look at the console logs that are produced within this body of the code, we will see the following:

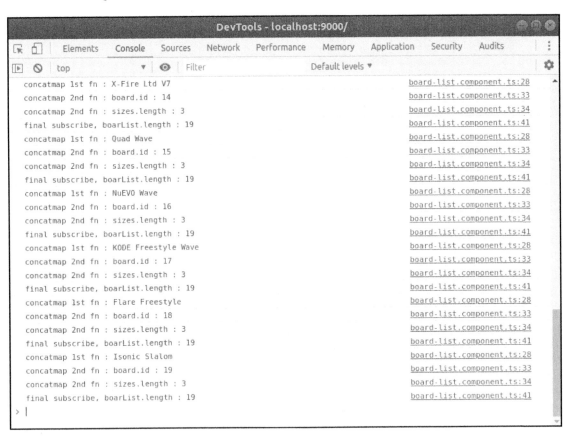

Here, our logs are showing that the `concatMap` function is indeed processing each element of the array one after the other, as expected.

With the `concatMap` code in place, each board will now have a `sizes` property, and our HTML will be able to render these sizes within the Sizes table as follows:

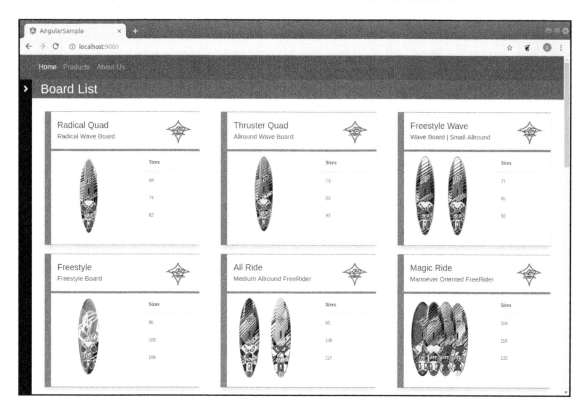

Observables – forkJoin

Our work with the Board List screen is not quite complete. Along with a set of sizes that are related to a board, each board also has a set of board types. Remember that a board can be classified as either a Wave board, a Freestyle board, or a Slalom board, or a combination of all three. This introduces another one-to-many relationship between a board and its types, along with the existing one-to-many board to board sizes relationship. We already have a REST endpoint that will return the types for each board, and can therefore replicate our `concatMap` functionality to retrieve the list of board types in a similar manner, as follows:

```
this.boardService.getBoardsList().subscribe((result: IBoardExtended[]) => {
    let boardSizes = from(<IBoard[]>result).pipe(
        ... existing concatMap code ...
    );
```

```
    let boardListTypes = from(<IBoard[]>result).pipe(
        concatMap((board: IBoardExtended) => {
            return this.boardService.getBoardTypes(board.id);
        }, (board: IBoardExtended, types: IBoardType[]) => {
            board.types = types;
            return result;
        })
    );
```

Here, we are using the same basic code to define a variable named `boardListTypes` that will hold the result of the call to the `concatMap` function. This variation, however, calls the `getBoardTypes` function of the `listService`, and assigns the result to the `types` property of each board. We will need to update the definition of the `IBoardExtended` interface as follows:

```
interface IBoardExtended extends IBoard {
    sizes: IBoardSize[];
    types: IBoardType[];
}
```

Here, we have simply added a `types` property to the `IBoardExtended` interface that will hold an array of `IBoardType` elements. The second anonymous function that was passed into the `concatMap` function will set this property when the REST endpoint returns a result.

If we continue in the same vein as our previous `concatMap` code, we would need to subscribe to the `boardListTypes` Observable as well, as follows:

```
boardSizes.subscribe((boardList: IBoardExtended[]) => {
    this.boardList = boardList;
});

boardListTypes.subscribe((boardList: IBoardExtended[]) => {
    this.boardList = boardList;
});
```

Here, we are subscribing to both the `boardSizes` Observable, as well as the `boardListTypes` Observable, and setting the internal `boardList` property to the array returned.

We do have a potential problem here, however.

Due to the asynchronous nature of calling REST endpoints, and the asynchronous nature of working with Observables, we are not sure in which order the final subscribe functions will be executed. It could be that the boardSizes Observable completes first, and then the boardListTypes Observable completes a few milliseconds later. Or it could be the other way around. If we have code that needs both Observables to complete before proceeding, we have no way of determining that they have both completed. Fortunately, the RxJS library provides a mechanism to wait for multiple Observables to complete, a function named forkJoin.

The RxJS forkJoin function allows us to subscribe to an array of Observables, and will only execute once all Observables are complete, as follows:

```
forkJoin([boardSizes, boardListTypes]).subscribe((result) => {
    console.log(`forkJoin : result.length : ${result.length}`);
    console.log(`forkJoin : result[0].length :
        ${result[0].length}`);
    console.log(`forkJoin : result[1].length :
        ${result[1].length}`);
    this.boardList = result[1];
});
```

Here, we are calling the RxJS forkJoin function, which is using a single parameter. This parameter is an array of all of the Observables that we need to wait for. As usual, the forkJoin function emits a new Observable, so we need to subscribe to this, and then process the result. The result argument within the subscribe function is, in fact, an array of all of the results from each of our original Observables. This means that the length of the result array will match the number of Observables that we have provided to the forkJoin function. Each array element, in turn, will contain the results of the individual Observable that we are waiting for results from. So in our previous code snippet, result[0] will hold the results of the boardSizes Observable, and result[1] will contain the results of the boardListTypes Observable.

The forkJoin function is very handy when we have a number of REST calls that need to be completed before we can render a page. Each call can be added to the array of Observables for the forkJoin function, and the results of each call can be referenced through the array returned.

Note that we are setting the local this.boardList property to the result of the boardListTypes Observable by using result[1]. We are not using the result of the boardSizes Observable at all. If we fire up our page, however, we will see that for each board in our list, both the board.sizes array and the board.types array have successfully been populated.

The key to this quirk in our code is that both the `boardSizes` and the `boardListTypes` Observables are operating off the result of the initial `getBoardsList` Observable. This can be seen if we condense our code to the relevant lines, as follows:

```
this.boardService.getBoardsList().subscribe(
    (result: IBoardExtended[]) => {
    let boardSizes = from(<IBoard[]>result).pipe(
    ... existing code ...
    let boardListTypes = from(<IBoard[]>result).pipe(
    ... existing code ...
```

Here, we have the original Observable from the `boardService.getBoardsList` function call, which is accessed through the `result` argument. It is providing an array of `IBoardExtended` objects into the `subscribe` function. Note, however, that both the `boardSizes` and the `boardListTypes` Observables are working off the same array, which is named `result`, as both are using `from(<IBoard[]>)result).pipe`. This means that both Observables are actually reading and modifying the same array in memory.

Unit-testing Observables

Before we continue with our application, let's take a quick look at how we can unit-test our `BoardListComponent`, and, in particular, its use of Observables. The `BoardListComponent` class uses the `BoardService` in order to load information from three different REST Endpoints. It calls the `getBoardList`, `getBoardSizes`, and `getBoardTypes` functions of the `BoardService`. It also coordinates these calls using `concatMap` and `forkJoin`. Each of the calls to the `BoardService` return Observables. Fortunately, mocking Observables within a unit test is relatively simple. Let's update the `board-list.component.spec.ts` file that was automatically generated using the Angular CLI, as follows:

```
describe('/src/app/board-list/board-list.component.spec.ts', () => {
    let component: BoardListComponent;
    let fixture: ComponentFixture<BoardListComponent>;
    let mockBoardService : BoardService;
    beforeEach(async(() => {
        TestBed.configureTestingModule({
          declarations: [ BoardListComponent ],
          providers: [BoardService, BroadcastService],
          imports: [HttpClientModule]
        })
        .compileComponents();

        fixture = TestBed.createComponent(BoardListComponent);
```

```
    component = fixture.componentInstance;
    mockBoardService = TestBed.get(BoardService);

}));
```

Here, we have defined a `describe` function that will execute our test suite. The name of the test suite matches the full name of the path to the test file itself, which is a suggested best practice from a previous chapter: `Chapter 8`, *Test-Driven Development*. We then have a `component` variable and a `fixture` variable, as discussed in `Chapter 9`, *Testing TypeScript Compatible Frameworks*. We then define a variable named `mockBoardService`, which has a type of `BoardService`. We will set the value of this variable to the instance of the `BoardService` that the Angular testing framework injects.

We then have a `beforeEach` function that calls the `configureTestingModule` function of the `TestBed` class, and defines three properties. These properties are `declarations`, `providers`, and `imports`. We are already familiar with the `declarations` property, which lists the Angular components that need to be defined for this particular test. The `providers` property lists all of the classes that are used within Angular's DI framework. As our `BoardlistComponent` needs both the `BoardService` and the `BroadcastService`, these services are listed here. The final property used in the `configureTestingModule` function is the `imports` property, which lists which modules must be imported. The only dependency here is on the `HttpClientModule`. Once we have called the `compileComponents` function, we set up the `fixture` and `component` variables as usual.

The last line of this code snipped sets the variable named `mockBoardService` to the result of the call to the `TestBed.get` function, and provides the `BoardService` class name as a single argument. This gives us access to the `BoardService` that has been injected into the test framework. Our unit test is as follows:

```
it('should load boards, sizes and types', () => {
    spyOn(mockBoardService, 'getBoardsList').and
    .returnValue( of([
        { id : 1}, {id: 2}
    ]) );
    spyOn(mockBoardService, 'getBoardSizes').and
    .returnValue( of([
        {board_id: 1, volume : 800}, {board_id: 2, volume : 600}
    ]))
    spyOn(mockBoardService, 'getBoardTypes').and
    .returnValue( of([
        {board_id: 1, board_type_id: 1},
        {board_id: 2, board_type_id : 2}
    ]))
```

```
    fixture.detectChanges();

    fixture.whenStable().then ( () => {
      expect(component).toBeTruthy();
      expect(component.boardList.length)
        .toBe(2, 'boardList.length should be 2');
      expect(component.boardList[0].sizes.length)
        .toBe(2, 'sizes.length should be 2');
      expect(component.boardList[0].types.length)
        .toBe(2, 'types.length should be 2');
    });
  });
```

Here, we have defined a test named `'should load boards, sizes and types'`. The purpose of this test is to ensure that when our `BoardlistComponent` loads, it calls the `loadAndFilterBoardList` function, which, in turn, calls the `getBoardList`, `getBoardSizes`, and `getBoardTypes` functions. The first line of this test creates a Jasmine spy by calling the `spyOn` function, with two parameters. The first parameter is the `mockBoardService` variable, which is the test instance of the `BoardService` class. The second parameter is the name of the function that we wish to spy on, which, in this case, is the `getBoardsList` function.

Note how we are using this spy. We call the `and.returnValue` function in order to override the default behavior of the `getBoardList` function. We then use the `of` function Observable to create an Observable out of an inline array that has two array elements. This is how simple it is to create an Observable within a unit test. We have simply created a spy on the function that our code will call, and returned an Observable out of an inline array. We then repeat this pattern for the `getBoardSizes` and `getBoardTypes` calls to the `mockBoardService`.

Using spies and inline Observables in this way allows us to control the exact JSON structure of data that is returned from a service, and gives us an opportunity to create test cases with different array sizes, different array element properties, and even empty arrays.

Once we have set up each of our spies, we call the `detectChanges` function on the `fixture` variable, which will trigger the change detection routines within Angular, and invoke the `ngOnInit` function. We then use the `whenStable` promise to wait for the component to complete rendering, and can then run a series of expect statements.

Our first expect statement just checks that the `component` variable itself has been initialized. This tests that the `BoardListComponent` class has been created successfully. We then have another `expect` statement to check that the total number of records in the `boardList` property is correctly set to 2. In other words, there were 2 records that were returned from the `getBoardList` function. We then have two `expect` statements that check that the `sizes` property of the first element in the `boardList` array has been set correctly, and that the `types` property has been set correctly.

Our test is therefore accomplishing the following:

- Create an instance of the `BoardListComponent`.
- Find the injected `BoardService` instance, and store a reference to it.
- Use this reference to override the `getBoardsList` function and return an inline Observable, whose data is strictly controlled within the test.
- Repeat this technique for the `getBoardSizes` and `getBoardTypes` function calls.
- Load and render the component.
- Ensure that the `boardList` property of the `BoardListComponent` contains two array elements.
- Ensure that the `sizes` property and `types` property of this array element has been set correctly.

Our unit test using Observables is complete.

A large-scale Angular application will typically have many different components that are combined in various ways to form user screens. Each of these components will generally load data from REST API endpoints, and could use a variety of endpoints in order to load all of the data required to render the component. When we start to write custom code that depends on multiple data sources, as we have in this example, it is prudent to write unit tests to ensure that the logic of our application works as expected. Using Observables within our components allows us to quickly and simply mock out the data that would have been returned from an endpoint within a unit test.

As we have seen, the process of setting up and using Observables in a unit test environment is both simple and intuitive. By creating tests that have fine-grained control over the data and the data structure that are returned by services gives our application much better stability, by being able to test edge cases that we may not have originally designed for.

The Domain Events design pattern

Now that we have a list of boards on the main page of the site, let's take a look at what happens when a particular board is clicked. We will need to identify which board has been clicked on, and then show the details of this board on the right-hand side screen. This right-hand side screen will be animated, and will slide in from the right to occupy the whole screen. The animation and transition of screens is already in place, so what we need to do is to somehow get a message from the `board-list` component through to the `rightscreen` component to tell it what board to display. We also need to get a message through to our `Mediator` to tell it to move to the correct state of `StateType.DetailPanel`.

The Domain Events design pattern allows us to generate events in one part of our application, and have other areas of our application respond to these events. When a domain event occurs, the parts of our application that are interested in these events can react to the event happening. This pattern enables us to decouple areas of our application from each other, and design our solution accordingly. The Domain Event design pattern was first discussed by *Martin Fowler* in a blog post named *Domain Event* (`https://martinfowler.com/eaaDev/DomainEvent.html`). His description of this pattern is that it captures the memory of something interesting that affects the domain.

In modern GUI frameworks, our User Interface is made up of many different components, each of which will render a specific area of the screen. In our current application, these components include the `board-list` component, the `rightscreen` component, the `navbar` component, and the `sidenav` component. We also have a `login-panel` component and a `secure` component. In a larger application, there may be many, many more. What we need is a mechanism to exchange messages between these components. If an interesting event happens in the `board-list` component, then we should be able to react to this event in the `rightscreen` component, or the `secure` component.

The implementation of a Domain Events design pattern can be easily achieved by creating an Event Bus. This is essentially a central place where any component can broadcast an event, and any other component can listen to these broadcast events. In Chapter 7, *TypeScript Compatible Frameworks*, we compared the event-passing mechanisms that are available in each of the frameworks that we discussed, and used an Event Bus mechanism in our Backbone application. We will implement a similar concept in our Angular application.

The Angular framework uses the concept of services that can be injected into a component using dependency injection. To implement our Event Bus, we can simply create a service that allows for components to both broadcast an event, or subscribe to an event. Any component, therefore, that needs to send an event, or act on an event, can simply use the same service.

Let's create a new file in the `services` directory named `broadcast.service.ts` as follows:

```
import { Subject, Observable } from "rxjs";
import { filter, map } from "rxjs/operators";
import { Injectable } from "@angular/core";

export interface IBroadcastEvent {
    key: string;
    data?: any;
}

@Injectable({
    providedIn: 'root'
})
export class BroadcastService {
    private _eventBus: Subject<IBroadcastEvent>;

    constructor() {
        this._eventBus = new Subject<IBroadcastEvent>();
    }

    broadcast(key: any, data?: any) {
        this._eventBus.next({ key, data });
    }

    on(key: any): Observable<IBroadcastEvent> {
        return this._eventBus.asObservable()
            .pipe(filter(event =>
                event.key === key
            ));
    }
}
```

Here, we start by importing the `Subject` and `Observable` classes from the RxJS library, as well as the `filter` and `map` operators. In order to make this class compatible with Angular's DI framework, we import the `Injectable` decorator as well. We then define an interface named `IBroadcastEvent` that has a property named `key` of type `string`, and an optional `data` property of type `any`. Note that we could strongly type the data property to be a type union instead of `any`, but for the purposes of this sample, we will allow the `data` property to carry any type of data.

We then define a service named `BroadcastService` that has a single property named `_eventBus`. This `_eventBus` property is of type `Subject<IBroadcastEvent>`. The RxJS documentation states that an RxJS `Subject` is a special type of Observable that allows values to be multicast to many Observers. This means that we can have many different Observers, which are objects that are interested in events, and that the Subject Observable will send a message to each and every one of them. Observables are, by nature, unicast, which means that every Observer gets their own Observable, where Subjects are multicast. This provides the perfect mechanism for the Domain Events pattern.

Our `constructor` function is simply creating an instance of the `Subject` class, and then we define two functions, named `broadcast` and `on`.

The `broadcast` function is used by a component to signal an event to any interested party. This function has two parameters, named `key` of type `string`, and `data` of type `any`. The implementation of this function simply calls the `next` function of the `_eventBus` property with an object that contains both the `key` and `data` contents.

The `on` function is used by a listening component to register its interest in a specific event. This function has a single parameter named `key`, which matches the name of the event that it is interested in, and returns an Observable. The implementation of the `on` function uses the RxJS `filter` function to only return an Observable where the incoming `key` string matches the `key` of the event that was raised. This means that if an event was raised with the key of `'my-event-key'`, then only the listeners that specified the same `'my-event-key'` will receive data.

The Observable `filter` operator is the crux of this implementation. Suppose that we have two listeners that have registered with the `BroadcastService`. Both are connected to an Observable and are waiting for data to be made available. When the `key` matches both the broadcaster and the listener, the listener is sent some data. If the `key` does not match the listener, then no data is sent.

To see this in practice, let's use `BroadcastService` to raise an event when a board is selected, and then listen to this event to show the detail screen related to the same board.

Raising and consuming Domain Events

When a user clicks on a particular board in the board-list component, we can trap this event by adding a click handler in our board-list.component.html file as follows:

```
<div *ngFor="let board of boardList;"
    class="col-sm-4 board-detail-clickable"
    (click)="buttonClickedDetail(board)">
```

Here, we have added a (click) event handler on the outer <div> element that is generated for each of the boards in our board list. The click handler is named buttonClickedDetail, and has a single argument that is set to the current array element of the boardList array. The corresponding function in our board-list.component.ts file is as follows:

```
... existing imports ...
import { BroadcastService } from '../services/broadcast.service';

... existing code ...
export class BoardListComponent implements OnInit {

    boardList: IBoard[] = [];

    constructor(private boardService: BoardService,
        private broadcastService: BroadcastService) { }

    buttonClickedDetail(board: IBoard) {
        this.broadcastService.broadcast(
            'board-detail-clicked', board);
    }
}
```

Here, we have imported the BroadcastService as part of our existing import statements, and have also updated the constructor function to include a private variable named broadcastService that will hold the instance of the BroadcastService that is injected into this class instance. We have then defined a buttonClickedDetail function that will be invoked when the user clicks on the <div> element of the HTML. This function simply calls the broadcast function of the broadcastService instance with two arguments. The first argument corresponds to the key property that we have discussed previously, and is a simple string value of 'board-detail-clicked'. The second argument is the full board class that is the array element.

Our `board-list` component is now raising a Domain Event to indicate that a board has been clicked by the user, and that the application should show the details of this board.

We will implement the "listener" part of the Domain Event pattern in our `secure` component as follows:

```
export class SecureComponent implements IMediatorImpl, AfterViewInit {

    constructor(private broadcastService: BroadcastService) {
        _.bindAll(this, [`boardDetailClicked`]);
        this.broadcastService.on(
            'board-detail-clicked')
        .subscribe(this.boardDetailClicked);
    }

    boardDetailClicked(value: IBroadcastEvent) {
        console.log(`SecureComponent :
            boardDetailClicked: ${JSON.stringify(value)}`);
        this.rightScreen.setBoard(value.data);
        this.mediator.moveToState(StateType.DetailPanel);
    }
}
```

Here, we have updated our `constructor` function to include a private variable named `broadcastService`, as we have seen previously. Within the `constructor` function, we make a call to the `bindAll` function of the underscore library, to bind the `boardDetailClicked` function to the correct instance of the `this` variable. Remember that when an event occurs on an HTML page, the context of this event is related to the page itself, and is not automatically related to the instance of the `SecureComponent` class that generated the page. The `bindAll` function corrects this context such that the instance of the `SecureComponent` that receives the event is retained when the event occurs.

Within our `constructor` function, we then call the `on` function of the `BroacastService` to register a function that will act as an event handler when the event occurs. The `on` function requires a single parameter, which is the name of the event itself, which, in this case, is set to `'board-detail-clicked'`. As the `on` function of the `BroadcastService` returns an Observable, we must call the `subscribe` function to react to changes in the Observable. Instead of defining an anonymous function to be used with `subscribe`, we have used a class function instead, which is named `boardDetailClicked`.

The `boardDetailClicked` function receives a single parameter named `value`, which is of type `IBroadcastEvent`. Within this function, we are logging the contents of `IBroadcastEvent` to the console for debugging purposes, and then call a new function named `setBoard` on the `rightscreen` component. Remember that the `rightscreen` component is a `ViewChild` component, and, as such, allows us to directly call functions on the `RightscreenComponent` class itself. The function that we are calling is named `setBoard`, and will pass the `data` property of the Domain Event that we received. This `data` property is, in fact, an object that contains all of the data related to a single board.

Once we have called the `setBoard` function of the `rightscreen` component, we invoke the `moveToState` function of the `Mediator` class to transition our screen state from the `MainPanel` state to the `DetailPanel` state. This will initiate the screen animation, and display the detail panel. We will need to implement the `setBoard` function in the `rightscreen` component as follows:

```
export class RightscreenComponent implements OnInit {

    board: IBoardExtended;

    setBoard(value: IBoardExtended) {
        console.log(`Rightscreen : setBoard received :
            ${JSON.stringify(value, null, 4)}`);
        this.board = value;
    }
}
```

Here, we have updated the `RightscreenComponent` class to include a local property named `board`, which is of type `IBoardExtended`. We have then defined the `setBoard` function, which accepts a `value` parameter of type `IBoardExtended`, and simply logs a message to the console before setting the internal `board` property to the incoming `value`.

If we run our application now, and click on a board, we will see this `console.log` message showing up in our Developer tools as follows:

Here, we can see that the `RightscreenComponent` has received a message using the `BroadcastService` that contains all of the information we need to render the detail panel for a particular board. It already includes both the `sizes` array and the `types` array that were loaded initially on the `board-list` component screen. With this information available, we can update the HTML file to render this information to our user.

Note that for the sake of brevity, we will not discuss the full HTML file here, as there are various elements and CSS classes at play in order to generate an aesthetically pleasing screen. Please refer to the sample code that is available for this chapter to view the related HTML and CSS files.

Once our HTML and CSS files are in place, our detail screen is as follows:

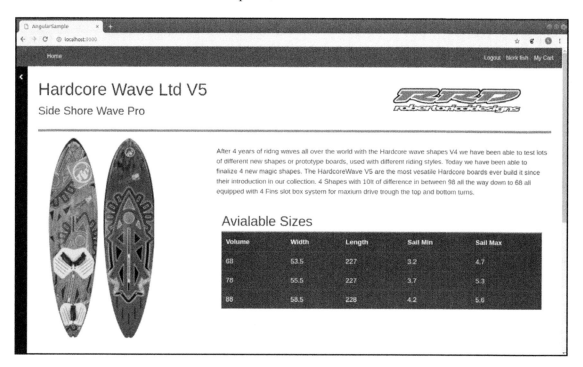

Here, the `rightscreen` component has been updated to show the full details of the selected board, with more information on the available sizes. With our board list and board detail screens completed, we can now look at filtering the board list from the `sidenav` component.

Observables – data filtering

The board list on the main page shows all boards that are currently available. When purchasing a windsurfing board, however, sailors generally purchase a board depending on the type of windsurfing that they will be doing. Wave sailors will purchase a Wave board, and sailors who race each other will purchase a Slalom board.

Let's use our `sidenav` component to allow a user to filter the list of boards that are displayed based on either the board type, or the board manufacturer. Our `sidenav` component will have two groups of checkboxes as follows:

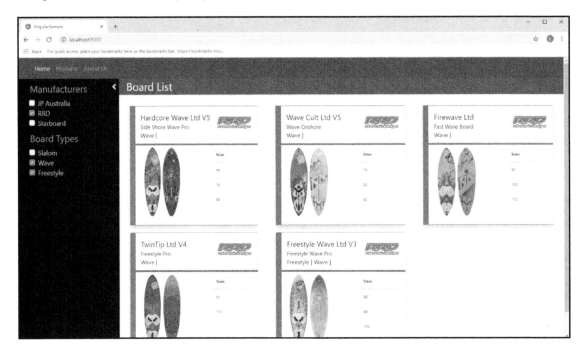

Here, we can see that the user has selected to only view boards that are manufactured by RRD, and that are of the Wave or Freestyle type.

We will need two properties within our `SidenavComponent` class to house this data, as follows:

```
export interface IManufacturerCheck extends IManufacturer {
    checked: boolean;
}

export interface IBoardTypeCheck extends IBoardType {
    checked: boolean;
}

... existing component definition ...
export class SidenavComponent implements OnInit {

    manufacturerCheckList: IManufacturerCheck[] = [];
    boardTypeCheckList: IBoardTypeCheck[] = [];
```

```
constructor(private boardService: BoardService,
    private broadcastService: BroadcastService) { }
```

Here, we have added an interface named IManufacturerCheck that extends the existing IManufacturer interface, and adds a checked property of type boolean. In a similar fashion, we have also created an interface named IBoardTypeCheck that extends the existing IBoardType interface. We will need to toggle this checked property when a user selects or deselects a checkbox on our page. We have also updated the SidenavComponent class, and included two arrays named manufacturerCheckList and boardTypeCheckList to store this information.

Our constructor function has been updated to use Angular's DI framework to inject an instance of both the BoardService class, as well as the BroadcastService class. We will use the BoardService class to query our REST endpoints, and we will use the BroadcastService a little later to send a Domain Event indicating that the user has changed their selection options. We will need to update our ngOnInit function to call our REST services, and load these two arrays as follows:

```
ngOnInit() {
    let manufacturerListObservable =
        this.boardService.getManufacturerList();
    let boardTypesListObservable = this.boardService.getBoardTypesList();

    forkJoin([manufacturerListObservable,
        boardTypesListObservable]).subscribe((results) => {
        for (let manufacturer of <any>results[0]) {
            manufacturer.checked = true;
        }
        this.manufacturerCheckList = <any>results[0];

        for (let boardType of <any>results[1]) {
            boardType.checked = true;
        }
        this.boardTypeCheckList = <any>results[1];

    }, (err: Error) => {
        console.log(`error : ${JSON.stringify(err)}`);
    });
}
```

Here, we are defining two Observable variables. The first is named
`manufacturerListObservable` and is the result of the call to the `getManufacturerList`
function of the `BoardService`. The second is named `boardTypesListObservable`, and is
set to the result of the call to the `getBoardTypesList` function.

We then use the `forkJoin` function in order to execute both of these Observables, and
subscribe to the results. As we discussed earlier in the chapter, the `forkJoin` function will
return the results of each Observable in an array. This means that we can access the results
of the `manufacturerListObservable` call by referencing the first array element returned,
as seen by the use of `results[0]`. Likewise, we can access the results of the
`boardTypesListObservable` call by referencing the second array element, which is
`results[1]`.

Each of these Observables will return an array, so we then loop through the elements of
each array, and set the `checked` property to `true`. This `checked` property is then bound to
the `checkbox` element in our HTML as follows:

```
<div *ngFor="let manufacturer of manufacturerCheckList;
        let i_manuf = index "
    class="custom-control custom-checkbox">
    <input type="checkbox" class="custom-control-input"
        id="manufacturer_{{i_manuf}}_check"
        [(ngModel)]="manufacturer.checked"
        (change)="onManufacturerChanged()">
    <label class="custom-control-label"
        for="manufacturer_{{i_manuf}}_check">
        {{manufacturer.name}}
    </label>
</div>
```

Here, we have the HTML snippet that is used to loop through each element of the
`manufacturerCheckList` array, and generate an `<input>` element and a `<label>`
element. Note how we have two statements within the `*ngFor` directive. The first
statement is `let manufacturer of manufacturerList;`, which will allow us to
reference each array element through a local variable named `manufacturer`. The second
statement in this `*ngFor` directive is `let i_manuf = index`. This statement is giving us
access to the index within the array for each element, and making it available through the
`i_manuf` variable.

We are then creating an <input> element of the checkbox type, and assigning an id to this element. Note how we are using the i_manuf local variable within the generation of this id. The id attribute is defined as manufacturer_{{i_manuf}}_check, which will use the i_manuf variable as a substitution parameter to generate an id such as "manufacturer_0_check", or "manufacturer_1_check", depending on the value of the array index. We are then binding the value of this checkbox through the [(ngModel)] directive to the value of the checked property in the manufacturerCheckList array. Note that we have also defined a (change) event handler that is bound to the function named onManufacturerChanged. Our <label> element is using the same index substitution technique in order to bind the label to the correct <input> element.

Let's now take a look at the implementation of the onManufacturerChanged function as follows:

```
onManufacturerChanged() {
    let checkedItems = _.where(this.manufacturerCheckList,
        { checked: true });

    let manufIds = _.map(
        checkedItems, (manufacturer) => { return manufacturer.id });

    this.broadcastService.broadcast('manufacturer-changed', manufIds);
}
```

Here, we are creating a variable named checkedItems that uses the Underscore libraries' where function to only return elements in the manufacturerCheckList array where the checked property is set to true. Remember that each checkbox <input> element on the screen is bound to the corresponding array element within the manufacturerCheckList array by Angular, so clicking on the checkbox will automatically update the components internal memory. We can therefore query the internal array to find out which items are currently checked or not.

We then create a new local variable named manufIds that uses the Underscore libraries' map function to create an array with only the manufacturer.id property and nothing else. This means that if our array has values such as 1 – JP Australia, and 2 – RRD, then this map function will only return the id properties, in order to create an array of [1,2]. We then use the boardcastService to broadcast a Domain Event named 'manufacturer-changed' with the array of manufacturer ids.

Note that the implementation of the checkbox array for the `boardTypeCheckList` follows the same pattern, so we will not discuss it here. The only principal difference is that it will raise a broadcast event named `board-types-change` with the array of board types that are checked. Again, please refer to the sample code that accompanies this chapter for the full source.

We can now turn our attention to filtering the list of boards that are displayed on the main page depending on what checkboxes the user has selected. We will need to register a listener for each of these events in our `board-list` component as follows:

```
export class BoardListComponent implements OnInit {

    boardList: IBoard[] = [];
    selectedManufacturerList: number[] = [];
    selectedBoardTypeList: number[] = [];

    constructor(private boardService: BoardService,
        private broadcastService: BroadcastService) {
        _.bindAll(this, [`onManufacturerSelectedEvent`,
            `onBoardTypeSelectedEvent`]);
        this.broadcastService.on('manufacturer-changed')
            .subscribe(this.onManufacturerSelectedEvent);
        this.broadcastService.on('board-types-changed')
            .subscribe(this.onBoardTypeSelectedEvent);
    }

    onManufacturerSelectedEvent(event: IBroadcastEvent) {
        this.selectedManufacturerList = event.data;
        this.loadAndFilterBoardList();
    }

    onBoardTypeSelectedEvent(event: IBroadcastEvent) {
        this.selectedBoardTypeList = event.data;
        this.loadAndFilterBoardList();
    }
    ngOnInit() {
        this.loadAndFilterBoardList();
    }
```

Here, we have updated our `BoardListComponent` class, and introduced two new local variables named `selectedManufacturerList`, and `selectedBoardTypeList`. Both of these variables are arrays of type `number`. Remember that when we modify a checkbox for the list of manufacturers, we send an event named `manufacturer-changed`, which includes the list of manufacturers that are currently selected. Likewise, we send an event when the list of currently selected board types is changed.

These events, however, are independent of each other. A change in the selected manufacturer list does not affect the currently selected board type list, and vice versa. This means that we need to store the current state of both lists in our BoardListComponent so as to be able to use both filters on the list of boards that are displayed.

Our constructor function is simply setting up the event handler for the BroadcastService events, which will trigger the onManufacturerSelectedEvent, or the onBoardTypeSelectedEvent. Within these event handlers, we are simply setting the values of either the selectedManufacturerList array, or the selectedBoardList array, and calling the loadAndFilterBoardList function.

Note that we have moved the body of the code that used to be in the ngOnInit function into a new function named loadAndFilterBoardList, so that we can call the same load routine when the page is initially loaded, as well as when we receive any of the Domain Events.

The loadAndFilterBoardList function is as follows:

```
loadAndFilterBoardList() {
    this.boardService.getBoardsList()
        .subscribe((result: IBoardExtended[]) => {

    ... existing concatMap functions ...

        forkJoin([boardSizes, boardListTypes])
            .subscribe((result) => {
                // this.boardList = result[1];
                this.boardList = [];

            from(result[0]).pipe(filter(
                (board: IBoardExtended) => {

                let boardTypeIds = _.map(board.types,
                    (type: IBoardType)
                    => { return type.board_type_id });

                let boardTypeFound = true;
                if (this.selectedBoardTypeList.length > 0) {
                    boardTypeFound = false;
                    for (let type of boardTypeIds) {
                        if (_.contains
                            (this.selectedBoardTypeList, type)) {
                            boardTypeFound = true;
                            break;
                        }
                    }
                }
```

```
            }

            if (this.selectedManufacturerList.length > 0) {
                return (_.contains
                    (this.selectedManufacturerList, board.mfid)
                    && boardTypeFound);
            } else {
                return boardTypeFound;
            }
        })).subscribe((board: IBoard) => {
            this.boardList.push(board);
        });
    });
});
}
```

Here, we have copied the existing ngOnInit implementation into a new function named loadAndFilterBoardList. As we discussed earlier, we are subscribing to the getBoardsList function, and, within this, defining two Observables that are the result of our concatMap functions that will load the sizes and type arrays for each board. We then have a forkJoin, so that we can wait for both of these Observables to complete before we attempt to filter the results. The filtering mechanism occurs inside the subscribe function of the forkJoin.

Instead of simply assigning all of the records that were retrieved from the REST server to the internal boardList variable, as we had done before, we start by clearing this boardList array. We then use the from, pipe, and filter functions of the RxJS library to create an anonymous function that will be used to filter the results.

This filtering mechanism does three things. Firstly, it creates an array of board type IDs from the board item itself, and assigns this to a variable named boardTypeIds. It then loops through the array of selected board types, and compares this list to the type list of the board that it is comparing to. If a match is found, the boardTypeFound flag is set, and the loop is broken. Bear in mind that we are matching a many-to-many relationship here. A board can have many board types, for example, Wave and Freestyle. If the user has indicated that they wish to see all Wave boards, then a board with the types of Wave and Freestyle will still constitute a match.

The filtering code will then finally check the board manufacturer against the list of currently selected manufacturers. If a match is found, and the board type matches, the filter function will return `true`, and the current board will be added to the board list that is used for display. We can see the results of this filtering mechanism in the following screenshot:

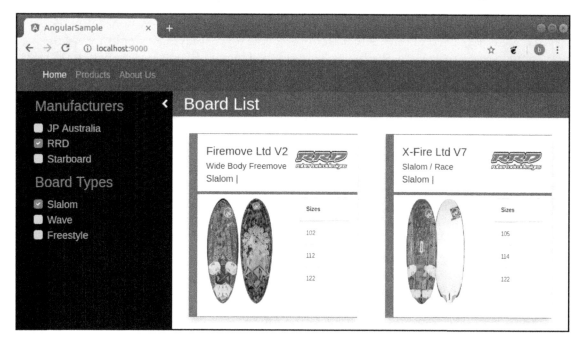

Here, we have selected only the manufacturer named **RRD**, and the board type, **Slalom**. Our board list, therefore, is only showing **Slalom** boards that are manufactured by **RRD**.

Our sample BoardSales application is now complete.

Summary

If we look back at the work we have done in this chapter on the sample application, we will notice that the architecture used is of sound quality. Our application is made up of a number of independent components. Each of these components conform to the Single Responsibility design principle and are dedicated to only one area of responsibility. We have created display components that are responsible for displaying a single area of the application screen real estate. We have also used the Domain Events design pattern to react to events within our application. One component may raise an event, but another component may be interested in this event. We are also using the State and Mediator design pattern to control the animation and display of the various elements of our screen real estate.

We have also discussed the use of various Observable techniques to help with the asynchronous nature of REST calls, and to respond to the series of events when we need to combine data from various sources. We have seen how to use the `concatMap` function to process an Observable stream one element at a time, and have also created Observable streams using the `from` and `pipe` functions. We have seen how to wait for multiple Observables to complete using the `forkJoin` function, how to notify multiple observers using `Subject`, along with using the `filter` function to filter Observable elements. We have built Angular unit tests to ensure that the code we have written to use Observable data streams is of the highest quality.

Hopefully, you have enjoyed the journey of building this sample application, and seeing the various techniques that we have discussed in earlier chapters, put into practice. We have finally arrived at an industrial strength, enterprise-ready, TypeScript built, single-page Angular, and Node application.

Other Books You May Enjoy

If you enjoyed this book, you may be interested in these other books by Packt:

Hands-On Functional Programming with TypeScript
Remo H. Jansen

ISBN: 978-1-78883-143-7

- Understand the pros and cons of functional programming
- Delve into the principles, patterns, and best practices of functional and reactive programming
- Use lazy evaluation to improve the performance of applications
- Explore functional optics with Ramda
- Gain insights into category theory functional data structures such as Functors and Monads
- Use functions as values, so that they can be passed as arguments to other functions

TypeScript 3.0 Quick Start Guide
Patrick Desjardins

ISBN: 978-1-78934-557-5

- Set up the environment quickly to get started with TypeScript
- Configure TypeScript with essential configurations that run along your code
- Structure the code using Types and Interfaces to create objects
- Demonstrate how to create object-oriented code with TypeScript
- Abstract code with generics to make the code more reusable
- Transform the actual JavaScript code to be compatible with TypeScript

Leave a review - let other readers know what you think

Please share your thoughts on this book with others by leaving a review on the site that you bought it from. If you purchased the book from Amazon, please leave us an honest review on this book's Amazon page. This is vital so that other potential readers can see and use your unbiased opinion to make purchasing decisions, we can understand what our customers think about our products, and our authors can see your feedback on the title that they have worked with Packt to create. It will only take a few minutes of your time, but is valuable to other potential customers, our authors, and Packt. Thank you!

Index

null 92, 93
null operands 94
object rest and spread 97
tuples 100
type aliases 91
type guards 89
undefined 92, 93
union types 88
TypeScript
  about 11
  benefits 13

U

UI-designed HTML
  using 580
undefined 92, 93
union types 88
unit testing frameworks 339
unit tests 337, 338
unit-testing Observables 642
User Interface (UI) 568
user interface design
  about 497
  angular setup 499
  Bootstrap, used 500
  conceptual design 497, 498
  Font-Awesome, used 500
  overlay, creating 506
  side panel, creating 502, 504
  transitions, coordinating 508
user interface experience (UX)

about 568
Brackets, used 568
Emmet, used 571
login panel, creating 573, 575

V

View 267, 268
Viewing Panel 498
Visual Studio Code
  about 25
  breakpoints, setting up 28
  debugging 31
  exploring 25
  installing 25
  launch.json file, creating 28
  project, building 28
  tasks.json file, creating 25, 27
  web pages, debugging 29

W

W3Schools
  URL 502
weak type 113
WebStorm
  about 40
  files 41
  HTML application, building 43
  project, creating 40
  reference link 40
  web page, running in Chrome 44, 46

Printed in Great Britain
by Amazon